secrets of the DIGITAL DARKROOM

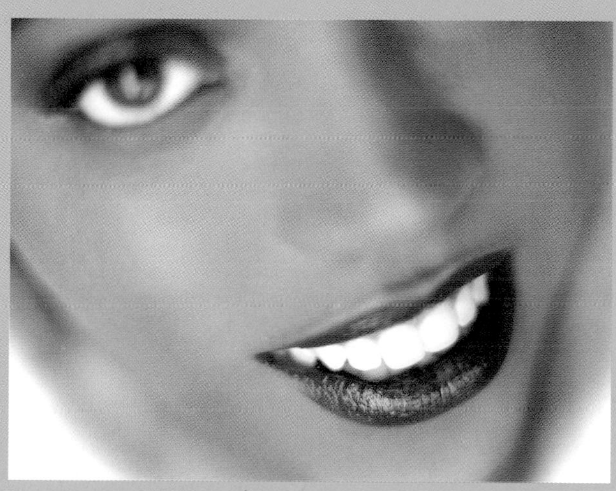

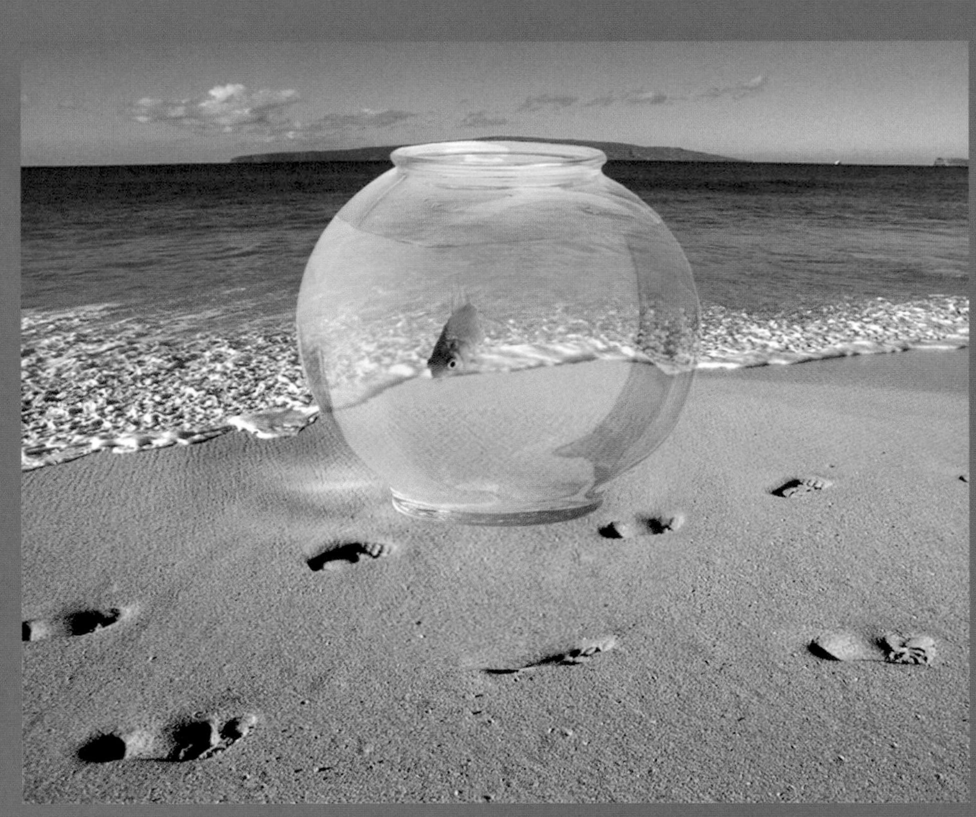

secrets of the digital darkroom

Peter Cope

& Simon Joinson

ILEX

CONTENTS

First published in the United Kingdom in 2003 by
ILEX
The Old Candlemakers
West Street
Lewes
East Sussex BN7 2NZ
www.ilex-press.com.

Copyright © 2003 by The Ilex Press Limited

This book was conceived by
ILEX
Cambridge
England

Publisher: Alastair Campbell
Executive Publisher: Sophie Collins
Creative Director: Peter Bridgewater
Editorial Director: Steve Luck
Design Manager: Tony Seddon
Editor: Stuart Andrews
Designer: Ginny Zeal
Development Art Director: Graham Davis

Any copy of this book issued by the publisher as a paperback is sold subject to the condition that it shall not by way of trade or otherwise be lent, resold, hired out, or otherwise circulated without the publisher's prior consent in any form of binding or cover other than that in which it is published and without a similar condition including these words being imposed on a subsequent purchaser.

British Library Cataloguing-in-Publication Data
A catalogue record for this book is available from the British Library

ISBN 1-904705-07-3

All rights reserved. No part of this publication may be reproduced or used in any form, or by any means —graphic, electronic, or mechanical, including photocopying, recording, or information storage-and-retrieval systems—without the prior permission of the publisher.

Printed and bound in China

For further information on this book please visit:
www.digitaldarkroomsecrets.com

INTRODUCTION

For many decades, the photographic darkroom has not merely been the place where photographic emulsions were processed to deliver – ultimately – prints, but also a gloomy domain in which a darkroom wizard, through processes that seemed akin to alchemy, could transform the mundane into something extraordinary. Along the way, some tremendous works of art have appeared from behind those closed, light-tight doors.

By design and by nature, some of those processes have remained a mystery to the world outside. In fact, the most advanced techniques aren't always clear even to those who know them, while some of the most astonishing effects prove difficult to repeat consistently, even under the most controlled conditions.

But times are changing. The techniques of digital imaging are bringing the world of the creative darkroom worker to us all. We can take any image and make it better. We can take that same image and manipulate it into something bizarre or wacky. And we can do any of this – and a whole lot more – with a level of ease and consistency that would make the darkroom expert seethe with envy.

And that is not all. Digital imaging and the possibilities offered by the digital darkroom have opened up great new creative opportunities beyond anything possible using traditional means. Some darkroom professionals treat the new ways with mistrust. Indeed a number of them regard the use of digital methods as cheating.

With options to 'layer' images on top of each other, blend those layers together and use transparency, digital methods of photomontage offer supreme flexibility.

The versatility and precision of our digital tools make it simple to correct, adjust or manipulate the whole or any part of an image.

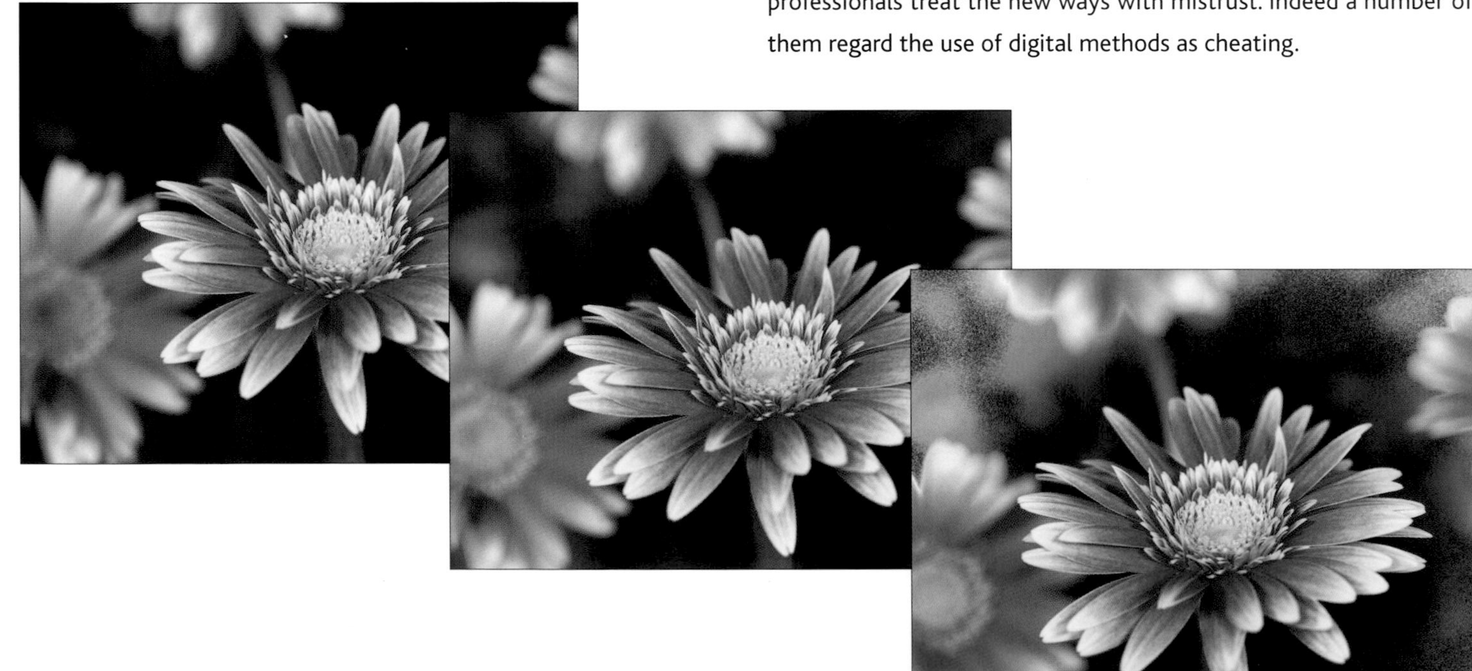

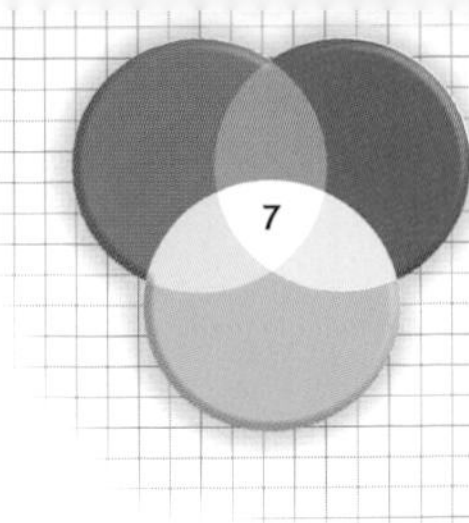

I'm confident that, after reading this book, you will not agree. If something complex can be made simple, why not make it so? If you can make a bad image look better, then who cares about the means employed? In this book, you will discover some of the secrets that the experts have jealously guarded for so long. You will see how easy it is to transform your images into real works of art. If you know your way around the traditional, chemical darkroom, you will also find out how to recreate some of the oldest techniques with a computer, monitor and mouse. What's more, you will also discover many of the techniques, tricks and manoeuvres that have previously been the preserve of the skilled professional.

You won't need to be a computer expert, either. We will introduce the concepts and tools used in digital imaging as we go, and if you need equipment you will find advice in Section Five, towards the back of the book. The digital darkroom really is open to everyone, so get to work!

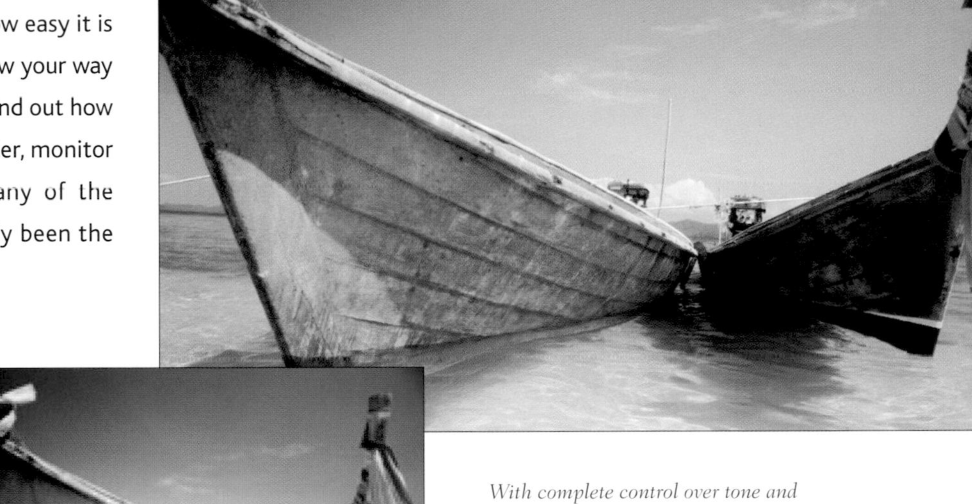

With complete control over tone and colour, it's up to you whether you opt for bright and colourful pictures, or the rich subtleties of monochrome.

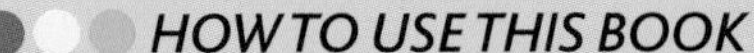

HOW TO USE THIS BOOK

This book has been designed for anyone who wants to set up a digital darkroom, needs to sharpen their image manipulation skills or simply have fun with digital photography.

While we use Photoshop – the world's leading photo-editing application – for many of the examples, that does not mean that this is another Photoshop manual. While you will need a basic working knowledge to use these techniques, we are not going to bombard you with irrelevant information or a mass of technical jargon. If you don't use Photoshop or Photoshop Elements, don't worry. These techniques can easily be replicated in other image-editing packages.

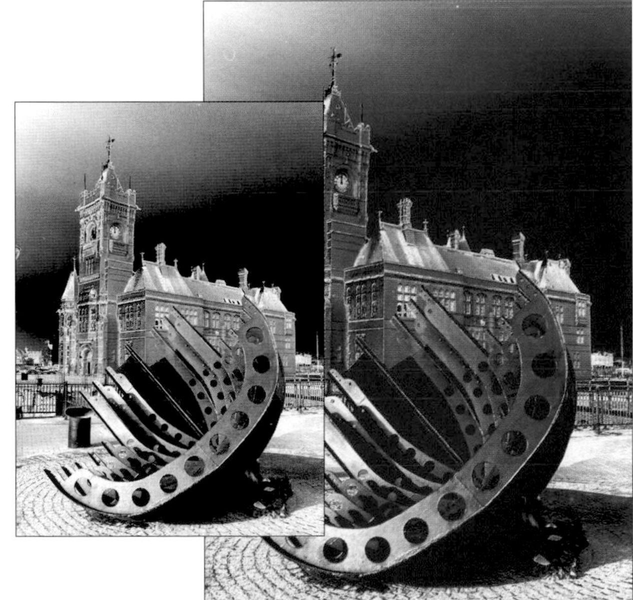

Digital techniques can also bring the mehods of the past back to life. Duotones, sepia tones, cyanotypes and solarization can transform a strong photo into an image that's guaranteed to turn heads.

SECTION ONE

the digital world

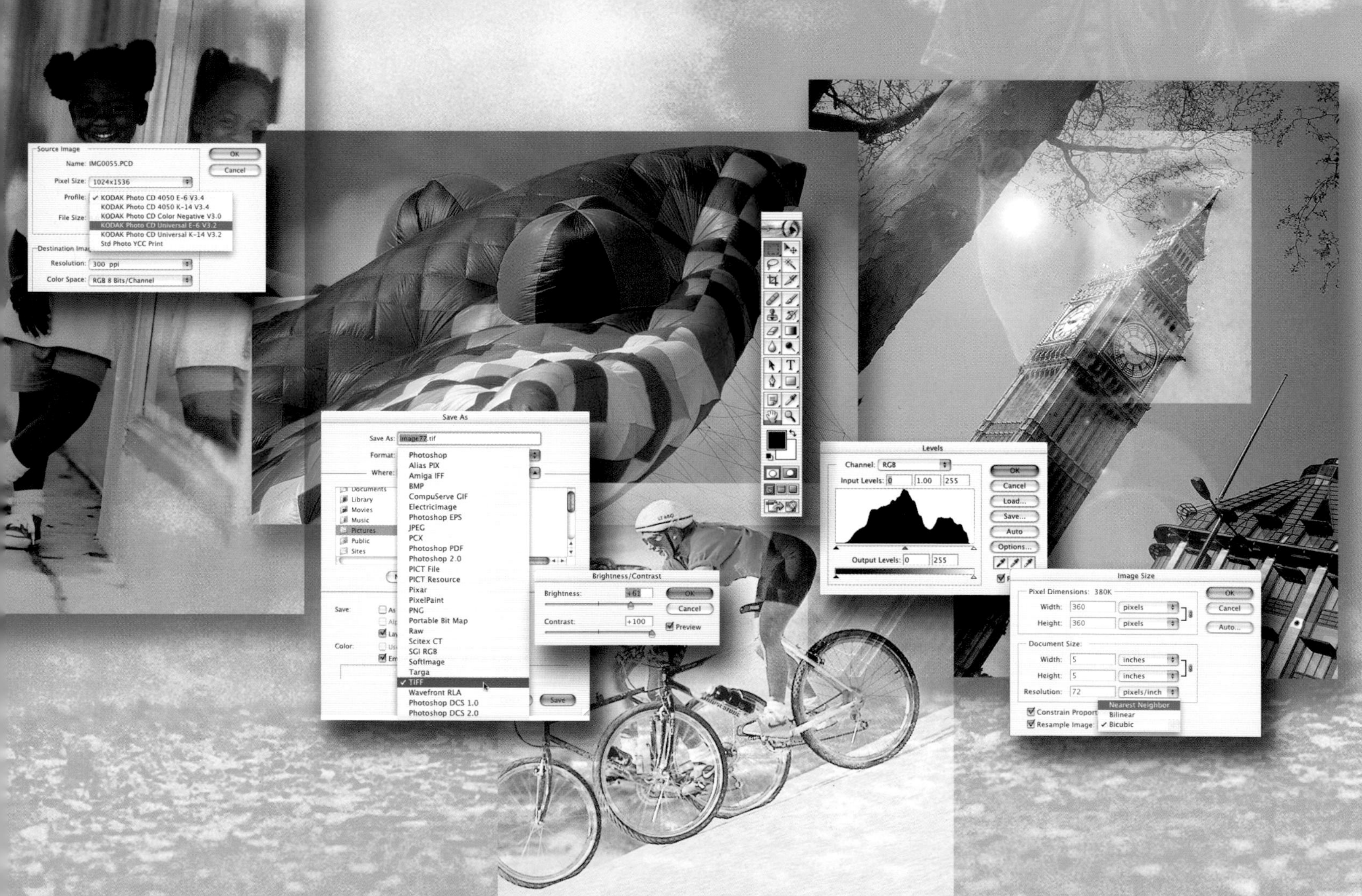

Some of us have spent a lifetime developing our skills in the darkroom. We've worked hard to master photographic technique, we've learned about lenses, f-stops and exposure, and then we've discovered how to develop, enlarge and print. Along the way, we have also probably swallowed a whole dictionary of jargon.

And now many of us are making the move into the digital world. Even though we can see good reasons for adopting new techniques, it's understandable that those of us with a conventional photographic background could be wary of the tasks ahead. There's no need to worry. Though digital imaging is comparatively new and uses some novel hardware, it represents evolution rather than revolution. All that experience we have gained at the viewfinder, or while breathing unpleasant chemical fumes over the enlarger, still has a place.

This section aims to give you a feel for what digital imaging makes possible, as well as a basic understanding of its fundamental concepts. Pixels, bit depth, bitmaps and vectors might seem like gibberish to you now, but you'll soon understand what they are and the part they have to play in the digital image. Think of the next few pages as a guide, taking you through the doorway into a brave new world.

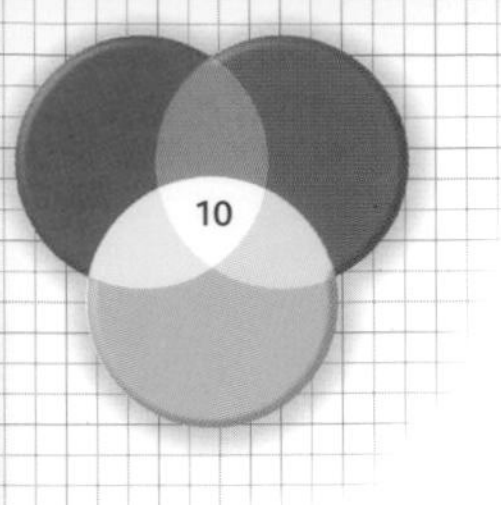

THE DIGITAL WORLD
Understanding the digital process

The step from the world of chemical processing to the digital darkroom can be intimidating. Even the most fundamental aspects of the image are subject to change. The familiar 'grain' of the traditional photograph is replaced by the 'pixel' of the digital image, and new issues of resolution and colour depth come into play. Luckily, the basic concepts are easy to grasp. In many important respects the actual process of acquiring and working with a digital image bears a close resemblance to the process of taking, developing and printing a photograph via traditional means. If you are new to computers, just remember one thing: all the time you spend learning new ideas and methods will be repaid by the speed, flexibility and power that the digital darkroom provides. Trust me, you'll never look back.

The digital process begins just as it does in old-fashioned chemical photography – with acquisition. You may have 35mm prints or negatives, or you may have images stored on a digital camera, but the first thing that you will need to do is to get them onto your computer.

ACQUISITION

Acquisition may require the use of a film or flatbed scanner, or it may just be a case of connecting your digital camera to your computer. Either way, this part of the process is now quite painless and getting better all the time. With an eye on the consumer market, the companies behind the hardware are working hard with the likes of Microsoft and Apple to make acquisition as automatic a process as possible.

That's good news for beginners, but as experienced photographers we're always wary of too much automation. We know that even at this stage, we can start to manipulate our images and improve their quality. By careful hardware and software configuration, we can ensure that the pictures which arrive on our computer's hard disk contain as much information as possible. Shadow and highlight detail, for example, are notoriously difficult to preserve under automatic control.With some deft work on our part, we can ensure that both extremes are captured.

If you have ever processed film in the darkroom, you will know that by careful modulation of the processing chemicals and times, you can work on the contrast, grain and detail of your photos. We can achieve an equivalent – or superior – level of control by careful use of the digital image acquisition tools used with our camera or scanner.

MANIPULATION

From acquisition we go on to manipulation. Here, by virtue of our image-editing software, we can take a good image and transform it into an excellent one. Indeed, while it might horrify the purists, we can also take an average image – even a mediocre one – and make it into something just as special. There really is no limit to what we can achieve.

The simplest enhancements, such as improving colour rendition or contrast, can be achieved in a couple of mouse clicks, once you know how. Fine-tuning just takes a working knowledge of the most basic image-editing tools. More complex (and even startling) effects take only a few clicks more. To achieve the same results using traditional methods would take great expertise and many hours of toil, and that's assuming that it's possible at all.

OUTPUT

Whatever our editing comprises – from simple adjustments to something more complex – the fact that the resulting artwork exists in a digital format means that we can output it in a variety of ways. Printing onto paper is still a very popular choice, and we can do so using inexpensive Inkjet printers, or by using resources in local stores or on the Web. But we also have other options: we can post our pictures onto a website; e-mail them across the world; or copy them onto CD or DVD. There's nothing to stop us from sharing our photos with a worldwide audience, if we want.

DIGITAL CONVERGENCE

We live in a world where everything is rapidly going digital. We've already spent two decades listening to digital music, but now we can watch digital television, see digital films on DVD, take digital photos on a digital camera and shoot digital video on a DV camcorder. The downside of the digital revolution is that buying into it requires a little investment. Still, there are benefits. Apart from obvious improvements in terms of quality, the move from analog to digital media has made it much, much easier to capture, use and share still and moving images or sound.

The payoff for the photographer is the freedom digital media gives us to explore new creative opportunities. We can find and download images from the Internet, take a still frame from a digital video that we shot with a DV camcorder and use it as part of a photomontage, or combine sounds and shots into a knockout slideshow. That sort of project is not within the scope of this book, but if you want to experiment, go ahead. Make the most of the digital revolution!

FAREWELL TO FILM?

This revolution isn't a rejection of the old, however. One of the great things about the digital process is that it enables us to give our old photographs a new lease on life. If you have boxes of old prints or negatives rotting in the attic, you can scan them and repair them, and even produce entirely new pictures from the old. The images we thought lost to poor exposure or bad printing practices can be reworked into new forms and preserved for posterity. In the digital darkroom, it seems that anything is possible.

A simple photograph of a London landmark, made special by a quick rotation and the application of basic colour and lighting effects. It takes only minutes in the digital darkroom.

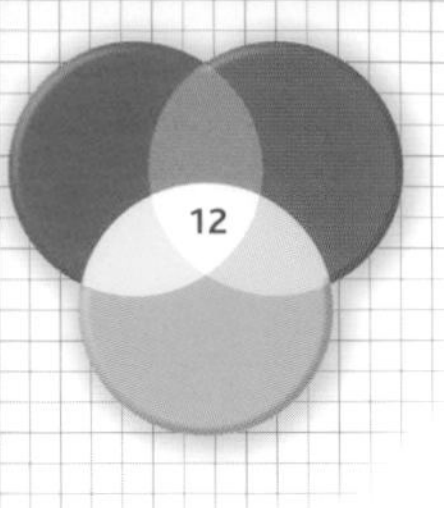

Understanding the digital image

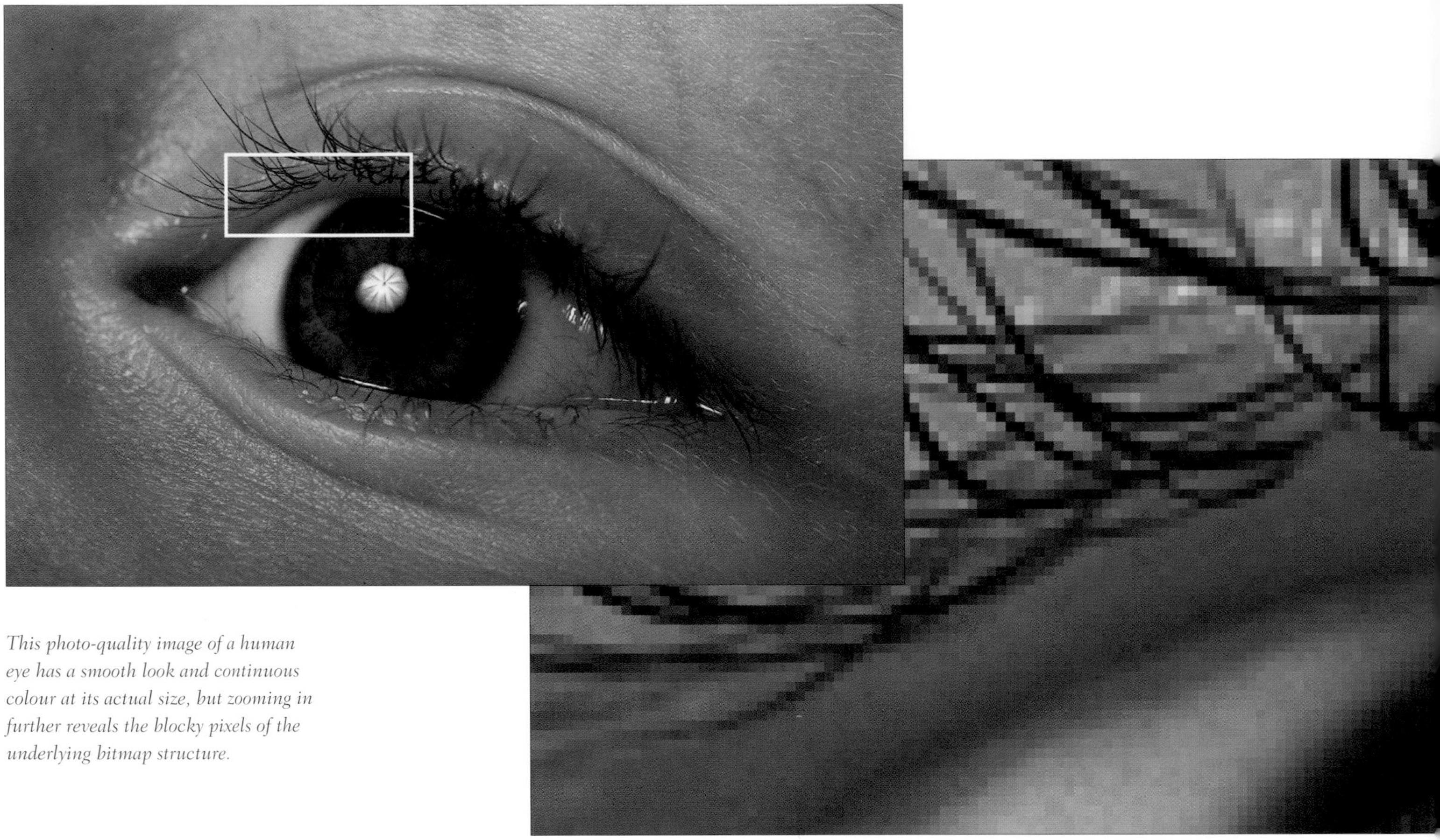

This photo-quality image of a human eye has a smooth look and continuous colour at its actual size, but zooming in further reveals the blocky pixels of the underlying bitmap structure.

In recent years, we have finally reached a point where it is becoming impossible to distinguish a print produced by conventional means from one with digital origins, at least as far as quality is concerned. Indeed, the two worlds successfully meet in many photo-finishing labs where conventional film stock is printed digitally and digital image files are output to traditional photographic paper.

But this confluence tends to mask the fundamental aspects of the digital image. It is produced and exists in a totally different way from a conventional photograph, and while there are similarities in the terminology we use, the interpretations are often quite different. So, how do we define the digital image?

BITMAP IMAGES

There are, in fact, two kinds of digital image. As photographers, the one that we are usually concerned with is the bitmap. The other, the vector graphic, is more important in the fields of illustration, 3D graphics and technical drawing.

In basic terms, a bitmapped image comprises a large matrix of small points that we describe as pixels. In an image, each pixel adopts a particular colour, brightness and contrast level appropriate to its position in the overall picture. On its own, the pixel is just a block. It's the way that the pixels are arranged within the grid that fools the eye into seeing areas of continuous tone.

As a result, if you look at a bitmap image in extreme close-up, all you will see is the pixels in

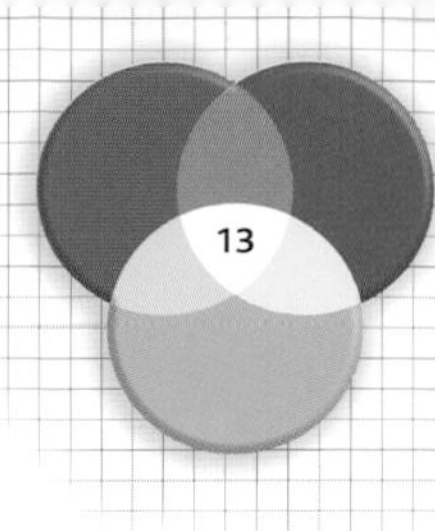

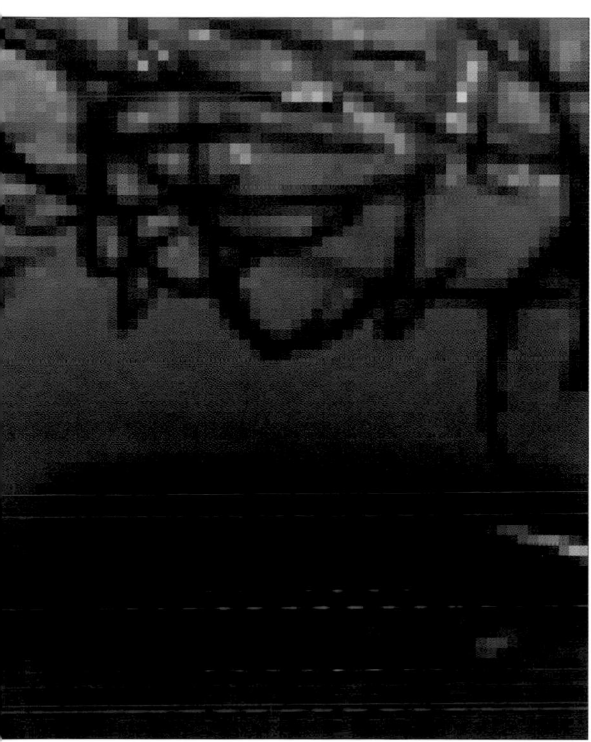

their grid. Think of them as the digital equivalent of grain, which acts in a similar way to limit how far you can enlarge a photo or a portion of an image. It's only when you pull away from the bitmap image – and you can't see the pixel structure – that it resolves as a full-colour, high-definition photographic image.

Bitmap images are produced by digital cameras and scanners, operated on in our image-editing software, and output when we have finished our manipulations. They are at the centre of everything we do in the digital darkroom. To further understand how they work, and how to use them, we need to understand the two defining characteristics of the bitmap image: resolution and colour-depth.

Vector graphics

Bitmaps are not the only type of digital image. Illustrators and graphic designers use a number of applications that produce vector graphics. The shapes and forms created using vector graphics are described not by a pixel matrix, but as formulae. Rather than needing to define every point, a vector graphic will be determined in size, shape, colour and position by a mathematical expression. Not only is this a more efficient way of defining an object, it also means that to transform the object we need only to apply transformations to that expression. We can resize or alter the object's shape merely by running calculations on the defining data, not the pixels themselves. This avoids the most common pitfall of bitmap images – as the image gets larger, the pixels themselves become more visible. Theoretically, a vector graphic can be drawn at any size without losing anything in quality.

Even if you never touch any application except Photoshop, you will still come into contact with vector graphics. In Photoshop, for example, a range of vector graphic shapes can be generated (from the humble line to more complex forms) and will retain their vector characteristics while you edit your image. Text is also treated as a vector graphic, enabling it to be resized and rescaled as required until you have saved the final image. Vectors are used at times to select elements of an image, although these 'clipping paths' will usually come into play only when we transfer images between Photoshop and an illustration application. They enable, for example, text to flow smoothly around an outline of any shape that you care to define.

Conversely, bitmap images can be used in environments – including illustration applications – that are really designed for handling vector graphics. While we won't be doing so in this book, combining bitmaps and vectors in this way can be another powerful way of squeezing something extra from your photos.

We can create this twin circle image in both bitmap and vector form. By magnifying the bitmap (bottom), it's easy to see its pixel nature in the blocky edge. In contrast, the vector graphic (top) maintains its clean lines, even with heavier magnification.

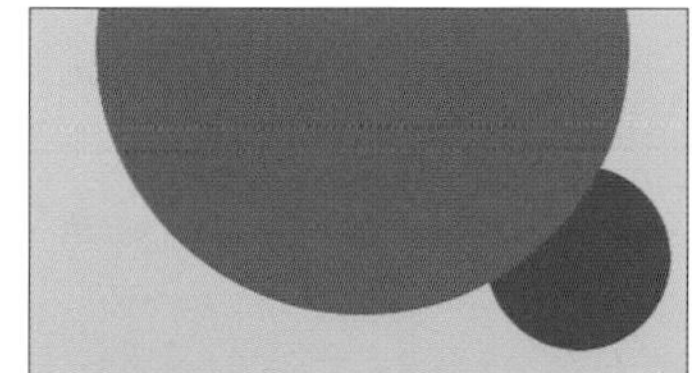

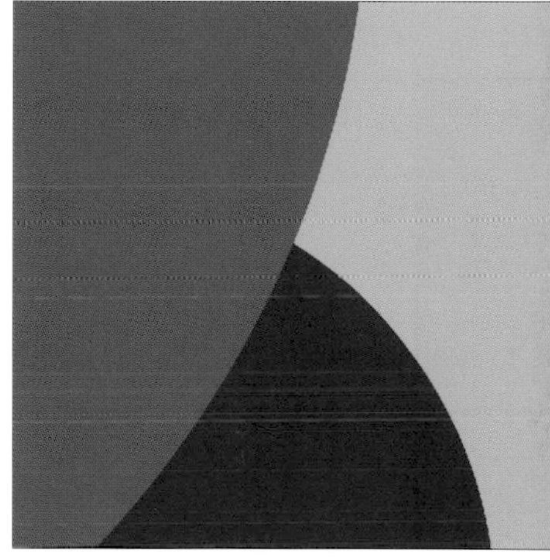

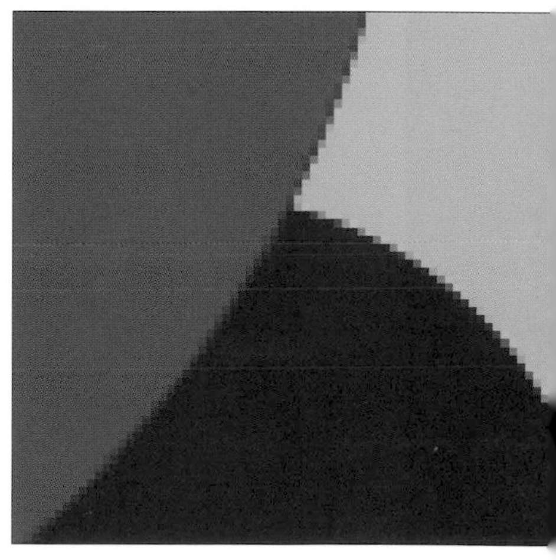

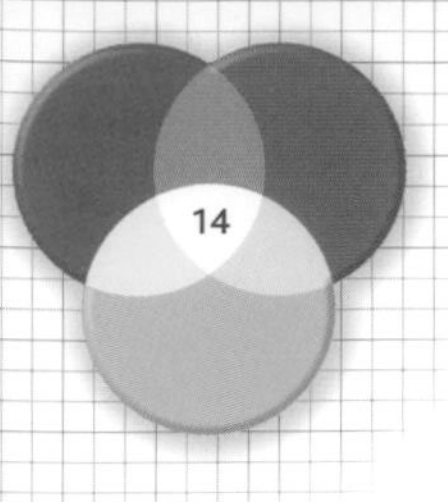

Resolution

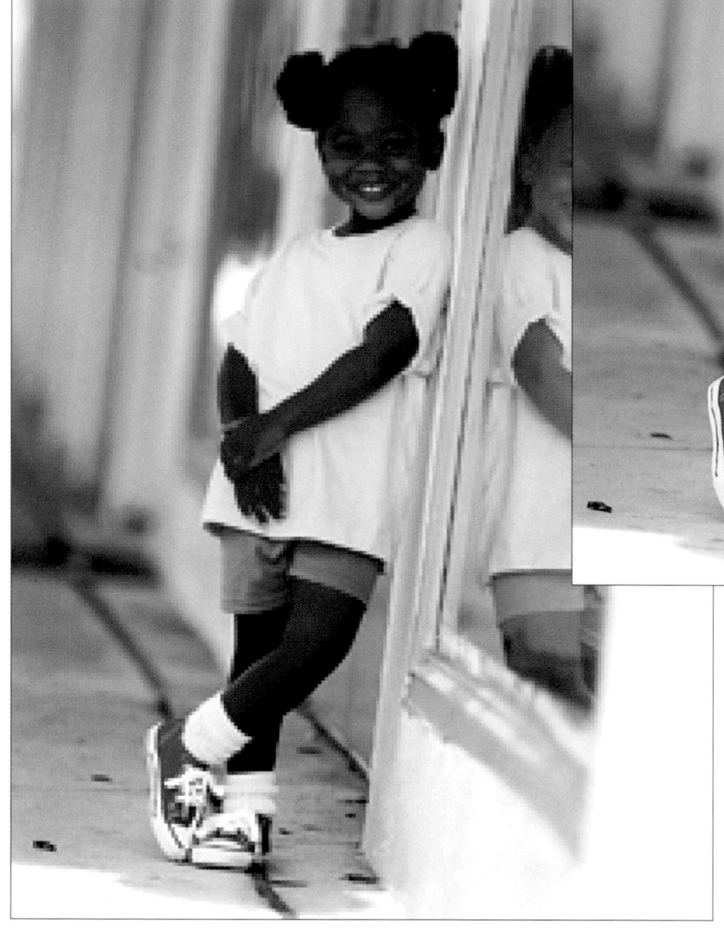

The same image shown with a resolution of 100 ppi (left) and 300 ppi (right). When a section is displayed to the same size, as here, the image at 100 ppi exhibits pixelation that indicates it has been enlarged beyond the limit of its resolution limit. For the printed page (this book for example), illustrative material is typically produced to 300 ppi.

As soon as we start to talk about digital images, the word 'resolution' is guaranteed to crop up. Confusingly, it isn't always used in the same way. You will see resolutions described for screens (1024 x 768), digital cameras (5 megapixel) and printers (1,440 dpi).

For our purposes, resolution refers to the number of pixels that make up a digital image. In effect, we use it as a measure of detail, and we quote it in terms of the number of pixels found in a particular area of an image – in general practice, pixels per inch (ppi). The same unit is often used to describe scanner resolutions and digital camera resolution and, unusually, is also used in territories where metric measurements are the norm.

But that's still only half the story. To be fully meaningful, the resolution of an image needs to be specified in terms of the image size. For instance, the images printed here have a nominal resolution of 300 ppi. If we take a 300 ppi image of 2 x 4 inches (5 x 10 cm), containing around 1.8 million pixels, and expand it to 6 x 12 inches (15 x 30 cm) without adding any new pixels, the resolution would drop to 100 ppi.

We can also consider resolutions in terms of file size. Two versions of the same image saved at different resolutions might be described as 350K and 10MB. To the seasoned professional, these would equate to a quarter-screen image and printed image measuring 148 x 210 mm, but for the sake of clarity it's better to work in ppi and exact dimensions.

THE IMPORTANCE OF RESOLUTION

When we talk about resolution, then, we should really be talking about the amount of pixel information contained within an image of a certain size. This becomes particularly important when we want to use an image on screen or in print. If we try to use a small, 300 ppi image to fill

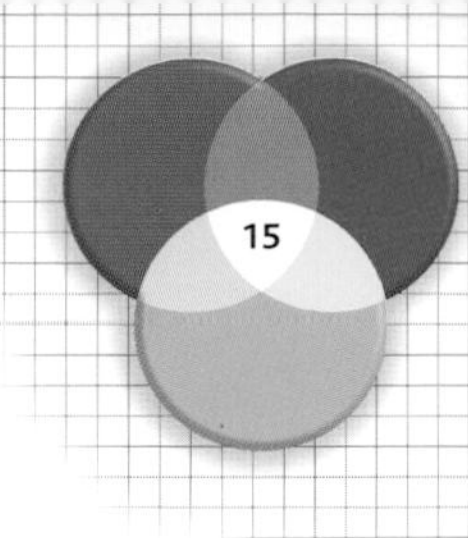

DIGITAL CAMERA RESOLUTION

When using – or even choosing – a digital camera, it pays to consider the resolution in terms of the print size that can ultimately be produced. A typical 3-megapixel camera will produce images of around 2000 x 1500 pixels. If we take an optimum printing resolution of 300 pixels per inch, this will produce prints of around 7 x 5 inches (18 x 12.5 cm), and in fact we could produce satisfactory images in the order of 8 x 6 inches (20 x 15 cm). As a general rule, however, these are the file sizes required to produce corresponding prints:

3 x 5 inches (7.5 x 12.5 cm)	*1.9 MB*
4 x 6 inches (10 x 15 cm)	*2.75 MB*
8 x 10 inches (20 x 25.5 cm)	*5 MB*
8 x 12 inches (20 x 30 cm)	*7 MB*
12 x 16 inches (30 x 40 cm)	*12.8 MB*

A Web image requires lower resolution and therefore a smaller file size. A screen filling 800 x 600 pixel image would be only 1.5 MB.

an A4 print, the bitmap structure will become visible, and the final print is not going to show your work at its best. Large, high-resolution images, however, take up more hard-disk space and are also much slower to work with. The trick is to maintain a balance.

As a general rule, if you are going to print out an image, it needs to fill the area you have in mind at a resolution of 300 ppi. Even if your printer boasts a super 1200 dpi resolution (we describe print resolutions in terms of dots per inch, rather than pixels), a 300 ppi image will still contain all the detail that your printer needs. If you are preparing an image for use on screen – to put on the Web, for example – you can go much lower. In fact, a resolution of 72 ppi will do.

Changing the Resolution

Photoshop, like most other image editors, allows you to change the resolution in two ways: through rescaling or resampling. Either way, you need to choose *Image* > ***Image Size*** from the menu. When rescaling, you simply change the physical dimensions (*Pixel Dimensions* or *Document Size*) and leave the resolution alone, but because the total number of pixels remains the same, an enlarged image will reveal the ugly pixel structure.

In resampling, the software adds new pixels when enlarging, or discards pixels when reducing. However, resampling to enlarge an image (upsampling) is rarely recommended. Although the resolution increases, no more information is being added. The enlargement just smooths over the jagged pixel structure, while averaging the tonal and contrast levels.

Downsampling is much more effective, and a very common professional practice. To downsample, we specify the new image size in pixels and select a method of resampling those pixels to generate the new image. Of the three – Nearest Neighbor, Bilinear and Bicubic – the last usually provides the best results.

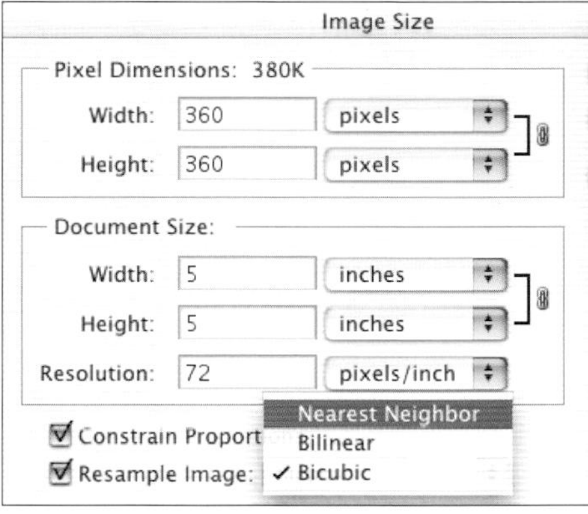

The dialog where physical and pixel size changes are enacted. Checking the Constrain Proportions *box preserves the original aspect ratio. Checking the* Resample Image *box permits the selection of an interpolation regime.*

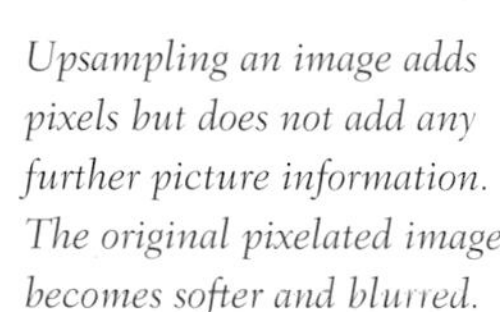

Upsampling an image adds pixels but does not add any further picture information. The original pixelated image becomes softer and blurred.

Although downsampling the same image gives a more heavily pixelated result, it is used when images are reduced in size, so this does not affect the perceived image quality.

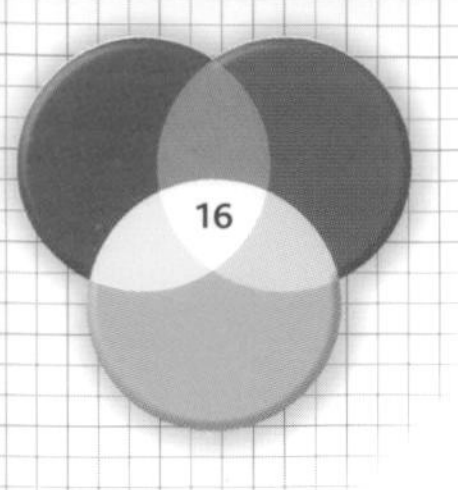

Colour

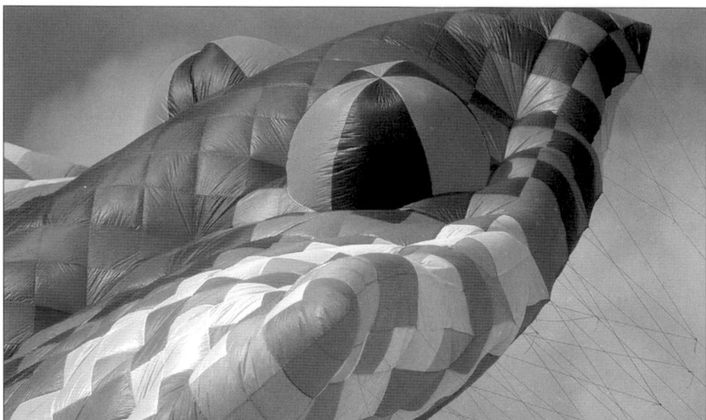

8-BIT

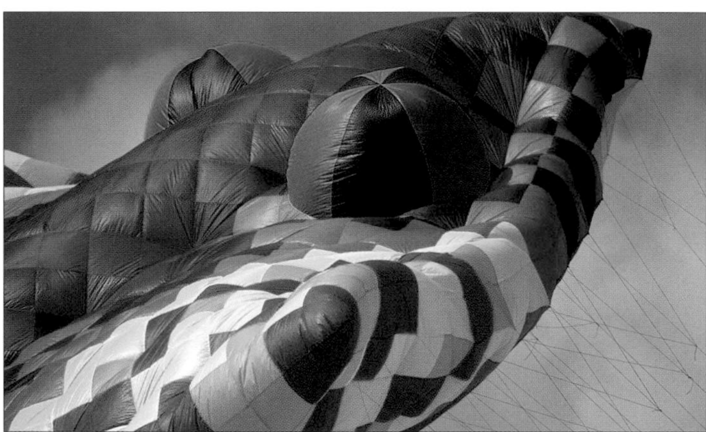

24-BIT

1-BIT (BITMAP MODE):: *When each pixel is represented by only 1 binary bit, the result is a harsh black-and-white image.*
2-BIT: *A second bit permits additional greys but still results in a heavily posterized monochrome image.*
8-BIT: *When 8 bits are used for each pixel, a full range of 256 greyscale tones can be shown.*
24-BIT: *With 8 bits used in each of the three colour channels, we get a full-colour (16.7 million colour) image.*

MORE BITS?

Many scanners (and other image-capture devices) capture images with bit depths of 16 bits or 48 bits per colour channel. This yields a colour palette of billions of colours, beyond the range our eyes can discriminate and adding to the file size. Is there any benefit in recording images to this bit depth when we can't ever print at this quality? Yes. Having excess information means that when we start editing (which always affects the tonal range) we don't create images that look tonally compressed.

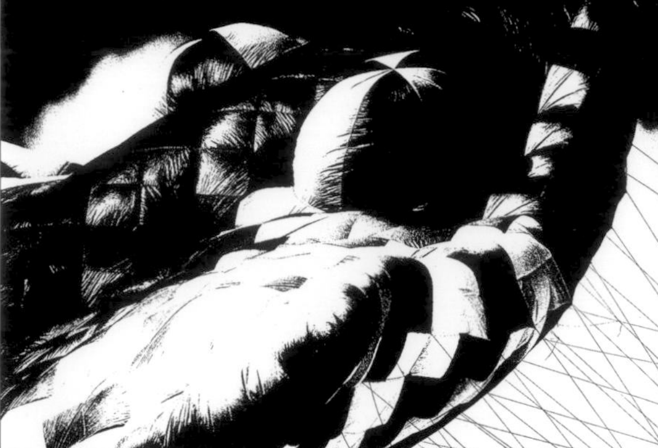

1-BIT

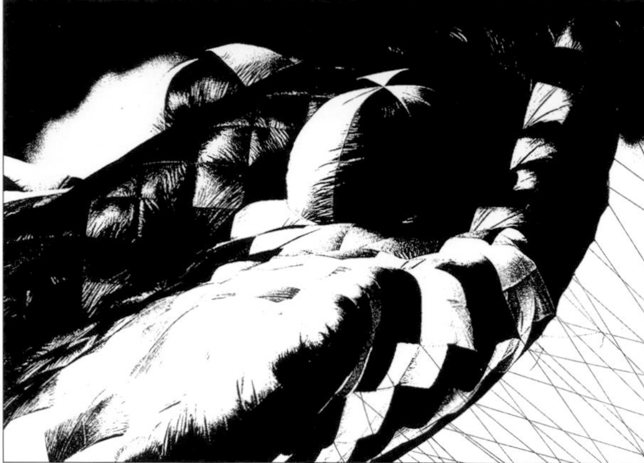

2-BIT

Resolution determines the quality of a digital image in terms of physical size and the amount of detail captured in it, but when we look at the overall quality of that image, there are other factors at play. The most important one, by far, is colour, and the fundamental concept to grasp is that of bit depth. If resolution describes the linear quality of an image in terms of detail, it is the bit depth that describes the quality in tonal terms.

BIT DEPTH

If we were to take a simple bitmap image, where every pixel on the screen was either pure black or pure white, then the information for each pixel would consist of a single piece of data, or bit – 1 or 0, corresponding to black or white. To get even the most basic grey tones, we need to add more information to the pixel, in the form of a second bit. With two bits, we would have four combinations: 00, 01, 10 and 11, with 00 and 11 representing black and white, and 01 and 10 delivering two intermediate grey tones. In practice, this 2-bit image would be very posterized, so for photographic images we need to add more information for each pixel. For a monchrome image, this works out to 8 bits per pixel, for 256 shades between black and white. Of course, a colour image is more demanding.

To work with images at true photographic quality, we need to work with 8 bits for each of the red, green and blue colours that make up a pixel, for an overall bit depth of 24 (3 x 8) and the ability to represent more than 16 million colours.

COLOUR MODES

As image-editing applications are designed for both screen and print use, they offer a range of colour systems to use when manipulating images. Typically these include *Bitmap*, *Grayscale* and *RGB Color*, plus *CMYK Color*, *Lab Color*, *Indexed Color* and *Duotone*. Though most of us work in the default *RGB* mode, it is helpful to know a few of the alternatives.

Bitmap: Based on a 1-bit bit depth, images in *Bitmap* mode are composed of pixels that are either black or white. This often results in harsh, heavily posterized images (see left).

Grayscale: Uses 8-bits to represent an image with a full 255 tonal gradations from black to white. Any colour information is discarded.

RGB Color: The default mode in most applications, *RGB* assigns a tonal intensity value (again in the 0–255 range) to every pixel for each of the colours red, green and blue, giving an overall bit depth of 24.

CMYK Color: Similar to the *RGB Color* mode, but with a tonal intensity value assigned for each of the colours used in commercial print: cyan, magenta, yellow and black (K), giving images with a 32-bit colour depth.

Indexed Color: A mode where the total number of colours is limited to 256 in order to keep final file sizes low. Additional colours are replaced by those in the working palette.

Duotone: A mode used to increase the tonal range of a greyscale image by introducing additional colours (*see page 120*).

In Photoshop, colour modes can be changed by selecting *Image* > ***Mode***. It is not possible to convert directly between all modes. To convert an *RGB Color* image to a *Duotone*, for instance, you first need to convert it to a *Grayscale*.

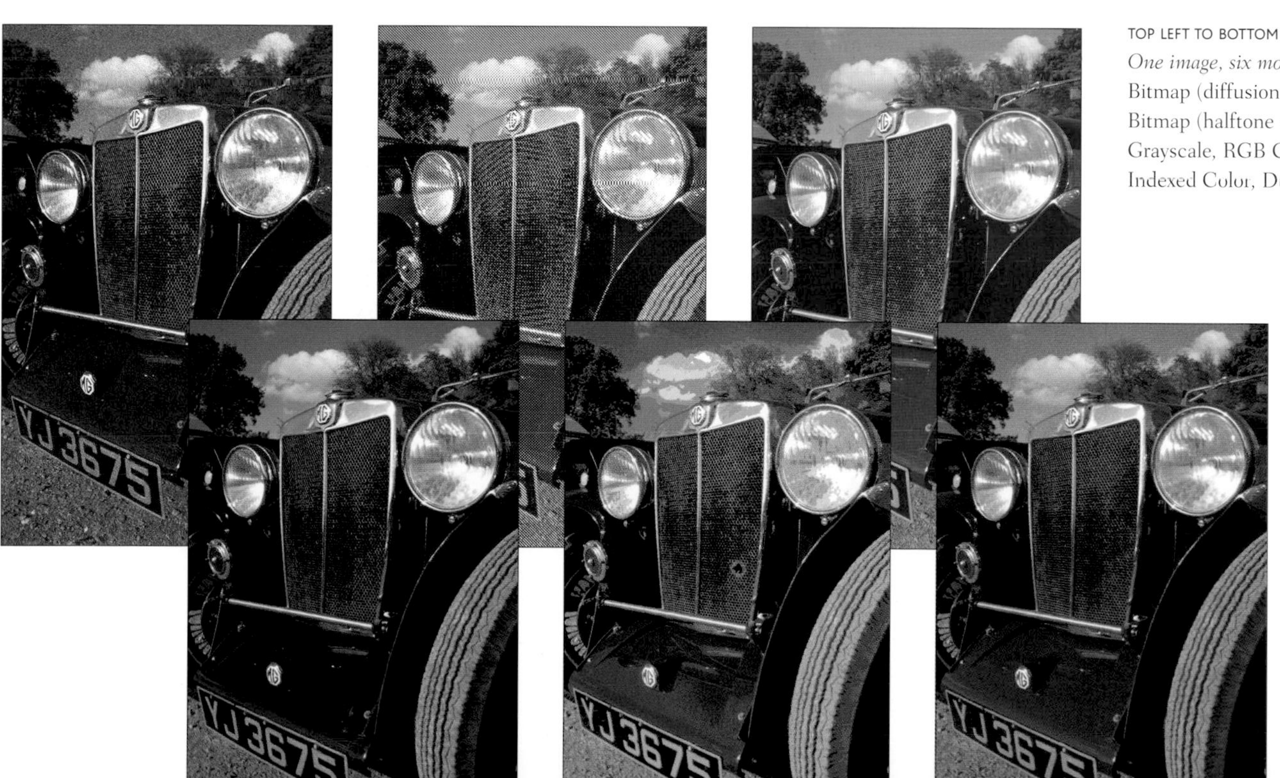

TOP LEFT TO BOTTOM RIGHT
One image, six modes: Bitmap (diffusion dithering), Bitmap (halftone screen), Grayscale, RGB Color, Indexed Color, Duotone.

SECTION TWO
basic techniques

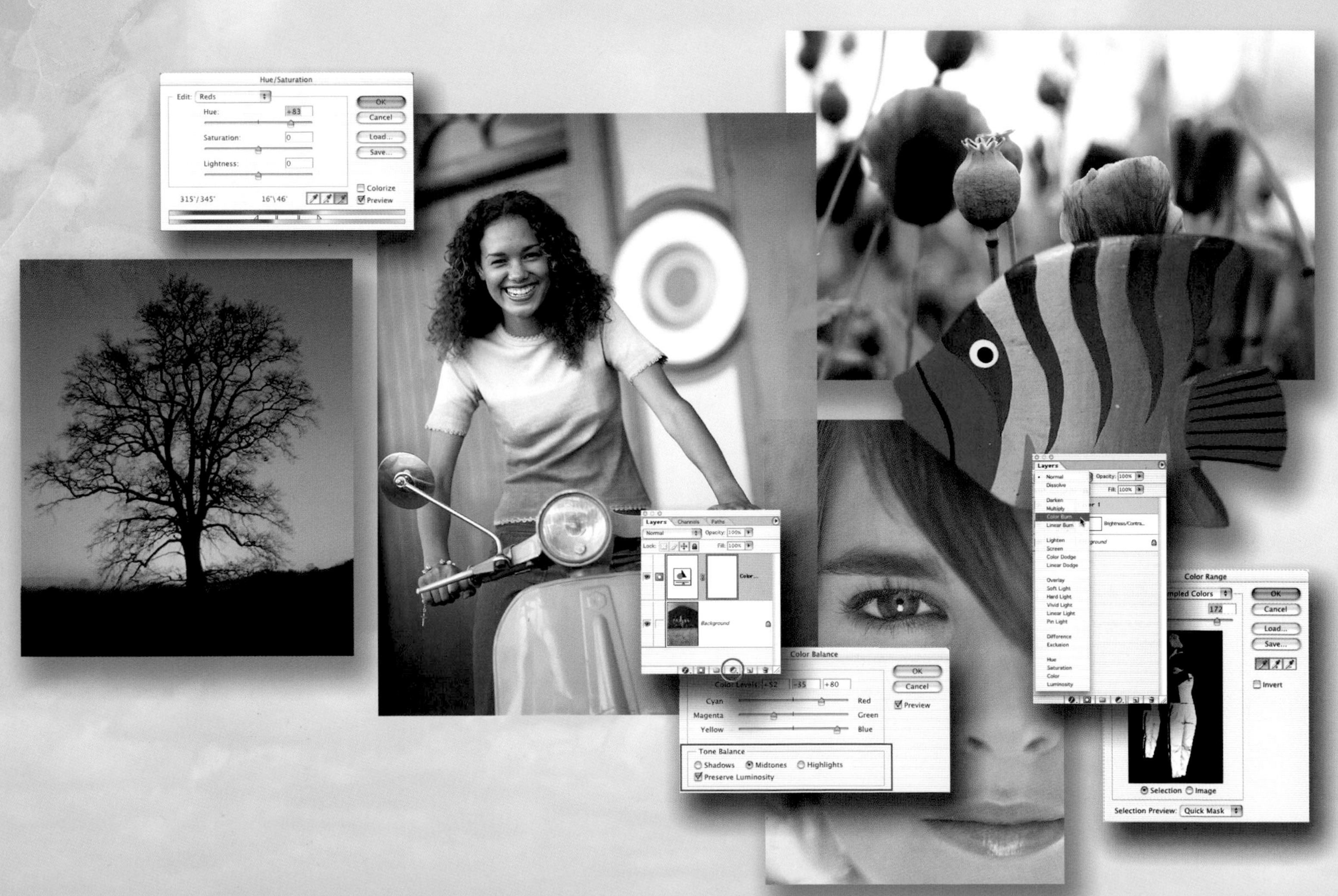

Now that we understand the concepts, it's time to start weaving some darkroom magic of our own.

If you are new to digital image editing, your first experiences can be daunting. With this in mind, it's a good idea to follow a structured approach in your first forays, and break down the process into logical and manageable steps. Following the lead set by the darkroom worker, we can divide our work into several neat stages. These don't all apply to every image; they just give us a framework within which to work:

First of all, we make simple corrections – minor adjustments to the image that can sort out the problems of poor photography or bad scanning. This process might start with cropping or resizing, before moving into simple brightness, contrast and colour corrections. Until we get past this stage, we can't move on to more constructive image editing. This chapter will show you how to do all of this, with broad alterations to sort out colour casts and exposure problems, and tweaks to fine-tune your images and bring the best out of them. If an image is lacking focus, we can even sharpen it in our software.

The next step is retouching and repair. We all have old images that haven't quite stood the test of time. With our digital darkroom tools we can repair the destructive effects of age upon our photos. More impressively, we can do the same to the human subjects of our photos, where that's needed.

Enhancement is where we begin to use our own creative powers to improve on nature. We can move (or remove) a part of the scene, delete the street furniture that compromises our view of an historic building, or add elements to a photo that were never there in the first place. In order to do so, we need to learn a little more about our digital tools. This chapter will give you the low-down on selections, channels and filters, giving you the skills to move beyond the realms of the traditional darkroom, and give your imagination free rein.

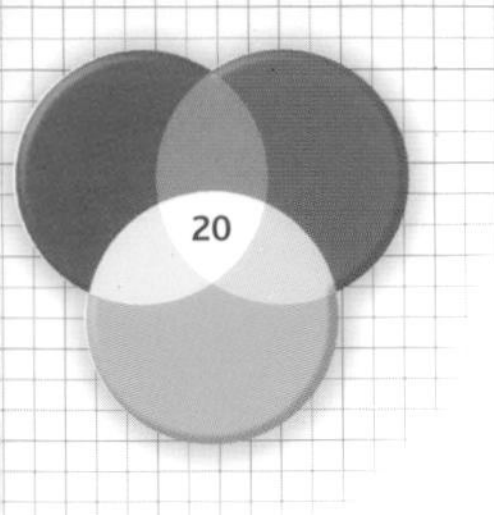

BASIC TECHNIQUES

Composition and cropping

With its potential for special effects and elaborate photomontage, the digital darkroom does have its glamorous side, but in many cases we need to use it for something altogether more prosaic: correction. Using the tools at our disposal, we can bring out the best from our images, ensuring we have captured the full range of tones, adjusting the colours, brightness and contrast, and making sure that our photo has the right emphasis and framing. Once we have developed these skills, it is time to learn some of the fundamentals of image-editing, and how these techniques can be applied for quick, creative results. Understand these basics to really get to grips with the digital darkroom.

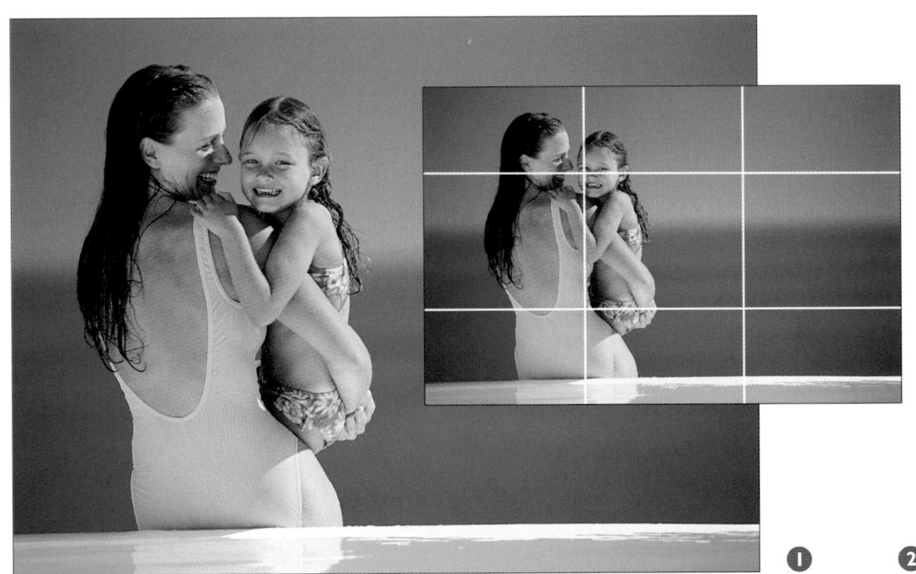

1

2

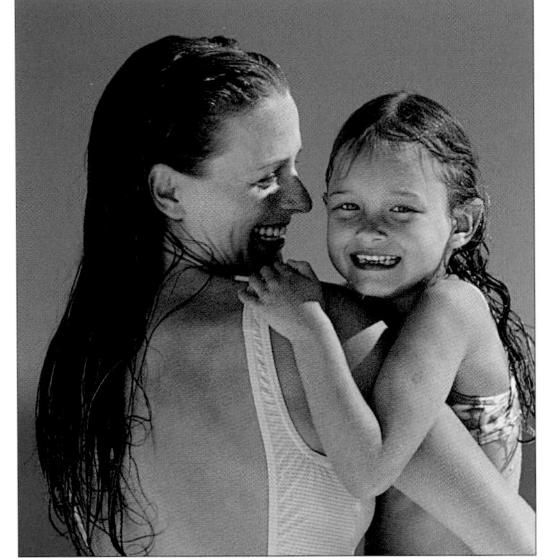

As any photography manual will tell you, composition is the key to taking a successful picture. A skilled photographer will assess the scene in camera, make decisions on angles, perspective, balance and depth of field, then aim for a strong composition that makes the basic image a powerful one. On occasion, however, we either don't have the time or we make the wrong choices. All is not lost. Using the tools in our digital darkroom, we can take that weak or off-balance composition and turn it into the raw material of a successful image. In these situations, the *Crop* tool is our friend, enabling us to define the region of the print that we want to use and discard or hide the rest.

USING THE CROP TOOL

1 *This photograph is a good example of one that can benefit from some judicious cropping. A well-exposed charming grouping of mother and child, it is already a strong composition in that it takes advantage of the 'rule of thirds'. This is one of the basic rules of visual composition and states that, if we divide an image into approximately equal thirds both horizontally and vertically, the principle subjects of that image should fall on the intersection points. In this case, the faces of the mother and child fall on one intersection point in the upper left corner, while their bodies are aligned along the first vertical third-line. The sea and sky on the right of the image adds to its attractions.*

2 While this image might be appropriate for an advertising shot, the subjects occupy only part of the frame. If we crop away much of the surroundings and concentrate on the subjects, we get another strong image with a very different emphasis. Note how once again the rule of thirds adds compositional strength, with both heads placed along the top horizontal third-line.

3 But we need not stop there. By cropping even closer, we get a very effective portrait. As long as our image has sufficient resolution, we can even go for an ultra close-up that is more a character study of two people enjoying themselves. This is a good example of how taking high-resolution images offers us extra creative choices.

The only serious drawback with the *Crop* tool is that, by default, it deletes the cropped parts of the image. When experimenting with different crops, it is a good idea to work on a copy of the image if you don't wish to lose parts of the image once you save. In Photoshop, however, there is another option: you can choose to *Hide* or *Delete* cropped areas. The *Delete* option dumps excess portions, while *Hide* merely conceals them. This is useful if you want to retain the whole image, but it also results in larger file sizes.

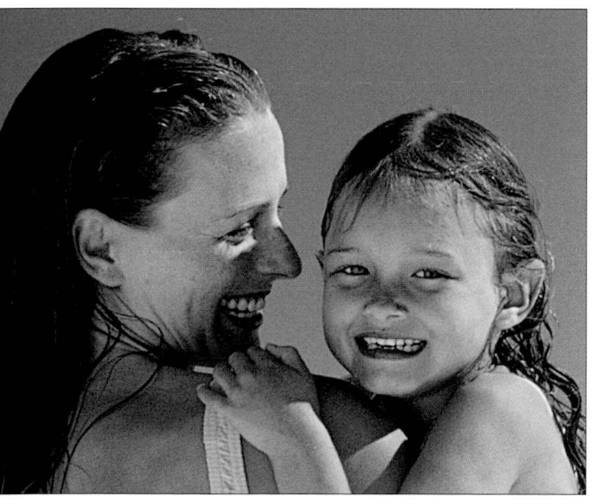

3

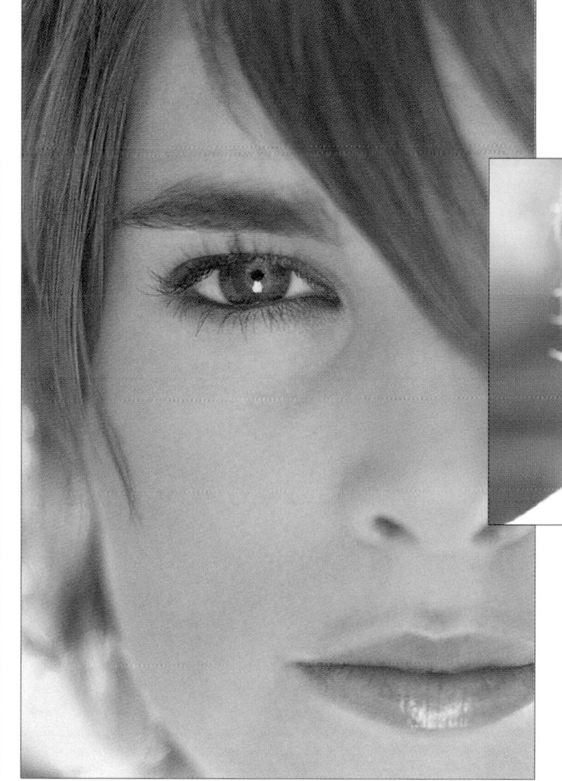

Secrets of successful cropping

The cropping process can be used to achieve different end results. As a compositional tool, it can be used to change the position of key elements relative to the frame. It can also be used to produce a portrait format image from one that was originally landscape. We can also identify and isolate a small detail in an image. If our photo lacks a strong focal point, intelligent cropping can often produce one.

Many images have distracting details – for example, a patch of bright sky or perhaps a passer-by – that serve as distractions from the principal subject matter. With slight but judicious cropping, these elements can be removed and a more effectively balanced and focused image – in compositional terms – can result.

In the example above, tight cropping on a portrait has produced an image with more impact. By selecting only a partial face, the strong coloration and geometry of the hair becomes a striking feature by itself.

DARKROOM SECRETS 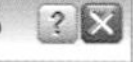

LEAD IN WITH THE MOTION

For great compositions involving moving objects, borrow a tip from the film world and lead in with the motion. Rather than follow the logical rules of static photography, place moving subjects so that they appear to be moving towards the centre of the frame. Placed centrally, they make a composition which suggests that the subjects are leaving the picture. Subconsciously, this lessens our interest in the image. Experiment with your compositions to imply movement within the frame.

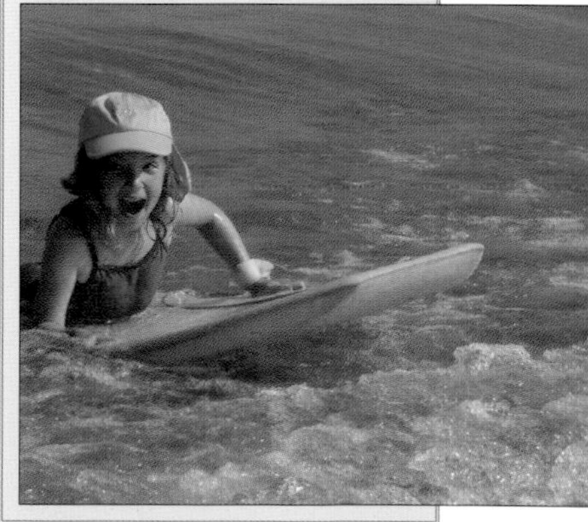

Basic image corrections

DARKROOM SECRETS 

ROTATE CANVAS

You can, in many cases, use the *Image* > ***Rotate Canvas*** command to rotate the whole image to correct alignment problems. Select *Arbitrary* and then set the angle (clockwise or anticlockwise) through which the image should be rotated. This can be a little hit and miss, and you may have to undo your rotation and enter a new modified value until you get absolute precision.

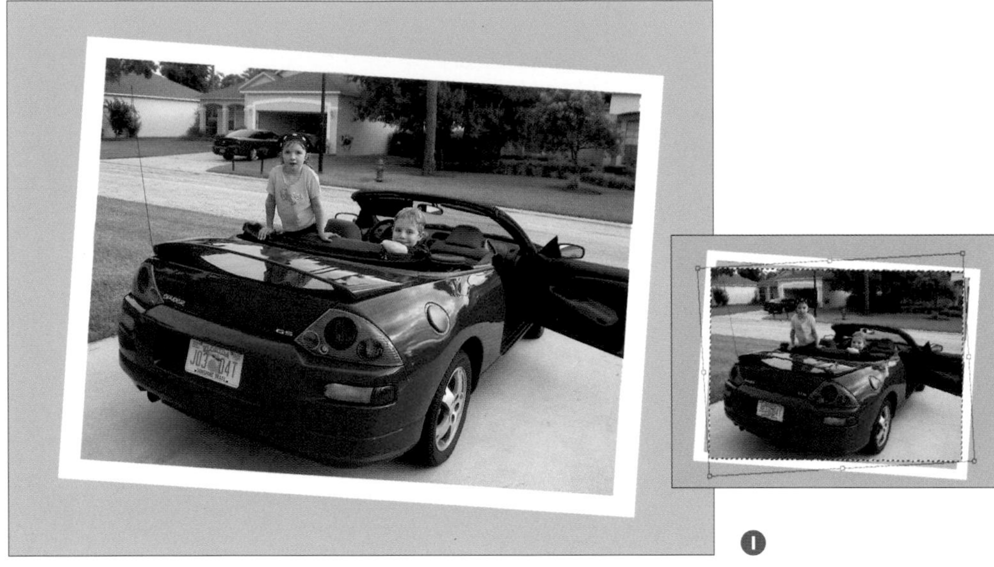

1

2

The *Crop* tool can be used to dramatic effect, but image-editing applications have other tools that can sort out fundamental problems with an image. For example, we don't always take photographs straight if we are shooting without a tripod, and if you use a scanner to import 35mm photos, there will be occasions when the print is not quite square. When using a transparency adaptor or slide scanner, there is also a possibility that the slide or negative will end up reversed.

No need to worry: the *Rotate*, *Skew* and *Flip* tools are ideal for correcting these basic image linearity problems.

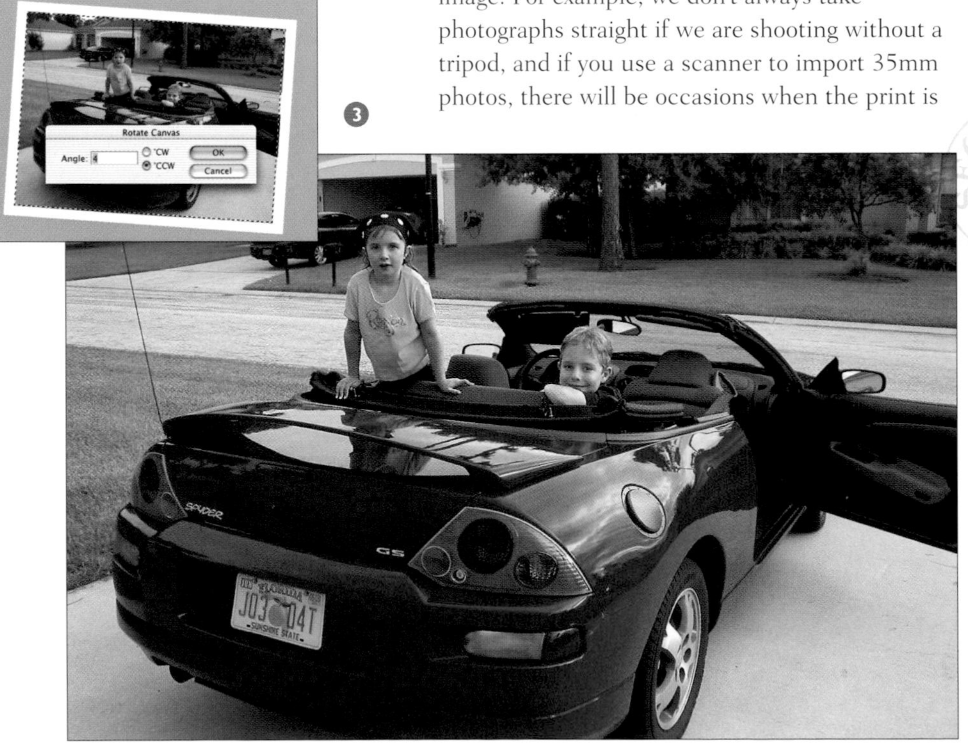

3

STRAIGHTENING A SCAN

1 *Here is a typical skewed scan (for the sake of clarity, we have exaggerated the angle slightly). Straightening it is relatively easy.*

2 *Use the* Polygonal Lasso *(see page 48) to select the image area. Now select* Edit > Transform > **Rotate** *from the menu bar, and use the handles to rotate the image until all edges are either perfectly horizontal or vertical. Select* View > **Show Grid** *or pull down a guide (*View > **Show Guides***) if you need something to work from.*

3 *Double-click within the image to apply the rotate, then invert the selection (*Select > **Inverse***) and press Delete to trim the image. In some cases, this rotation can soften the image. See* Sharpening an Image *(page 34) to find out how to correct this problem.*

USING ROTATE AND FLIP FOR CREATIVE EFFECTS

The Rotate *and* Flip *commands are mainly used as corrective tools to straighten out images or reverse and invert incorrectly placed ones. We can also use them, however, to produce striking novel imagery and even kaleidoscopic effects.*

Combining an image with its vertical or horizontal mirror image can create a very powerful sense of symmetry. This image of the Taj Mahal has been combined with a flipped copy of itself and the two joined seamlessly to create a powerful reflection effect.

You can do more than just flip or rotate a whole image. Strong elements within an image can be identified, then cropped and used as the basis for a new composition. From this image of a Japanese kite, a small section from the head has been selected and then used four times to produce a symmetrical pattern.

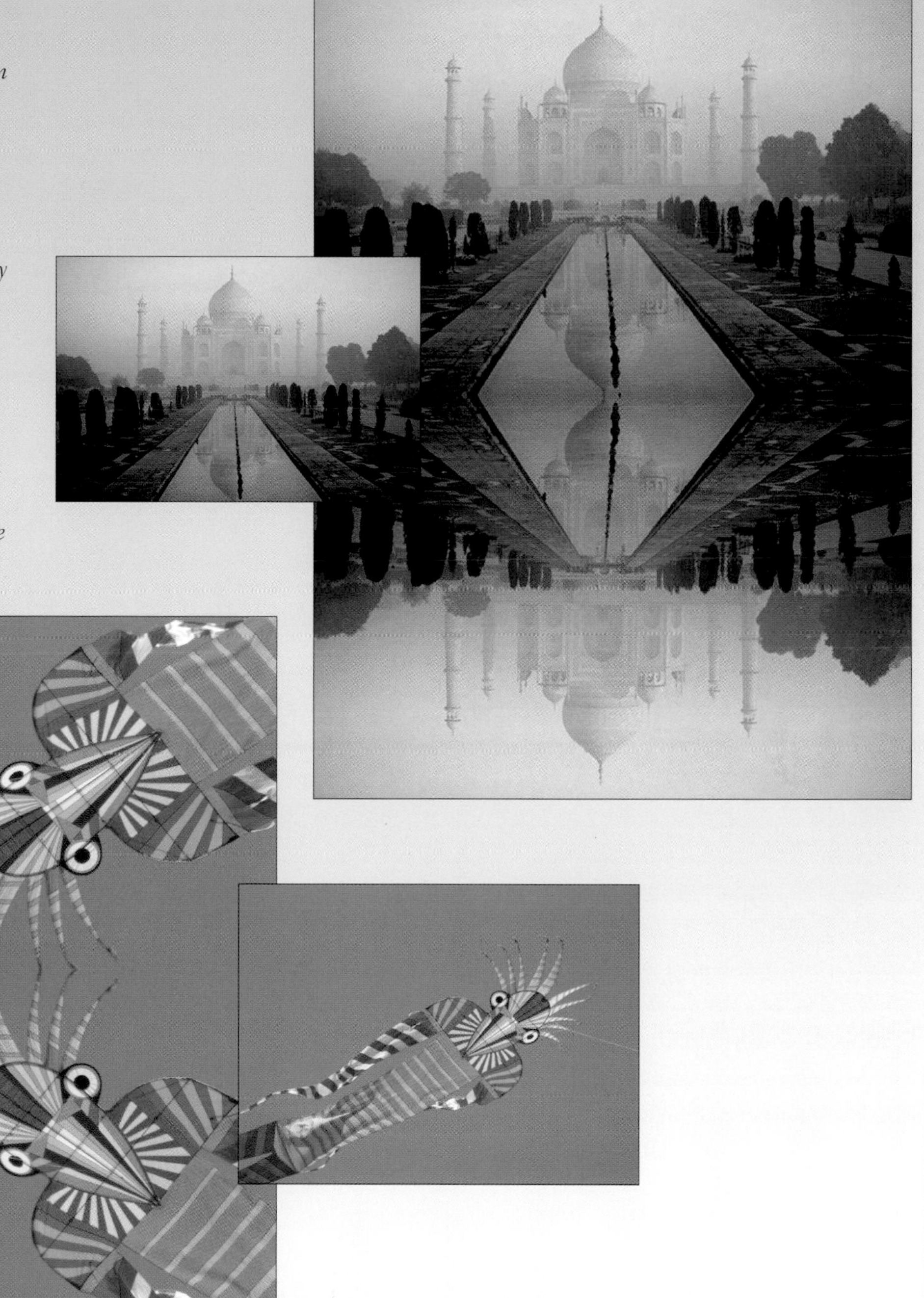

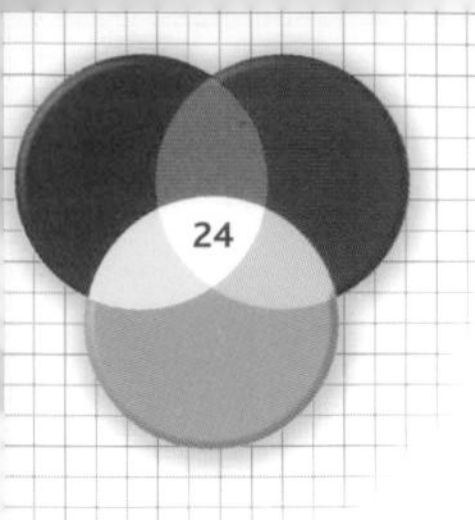

Controlling brightness and contrast

DARKROOM SECRETS 

WHICH FILE FORMAT?

Most digital cameras output in a JPEG format, and it is a good format to use for e-mailing images or putting them on the Web. However, you should avoid using JPEGs while you're editing an image. As it is a lossy format – image information is discarded each time the image is saved – multiple saves will compromise overall quality. The TIFF format does not discard data during compression, which makes it a safe bet, but if you are doing something complex, with multiple layers or special effects, stick to the application's native format. These formats, such as Photoshop's .PSD, retain layers and other information and offer you more flexibility later on.

There are many reasons why digital images have incorrect brightness and contrast characteristics. The problems could have begun with the camera that took the photos in the first place. Complex lighting could have fooled the rudimentary metering system or an inappropriate manual setting may have been used. Or perhaps the transfer to the digital domain was not achieved with the accuracy required. Whatever the reason, we can still make good on these shortcomings. In place of revised enlarger exposure times and graded printing paper, we can change the tone levels recorded in the digital image through a combination of automated and manual controls.

Whenever we start work in an image, one of our primary aims is to get the broadest range of tones in an image and so to reproduce the greatest amount of detail. As long as the image features a good distribution of tones, we want to brighten the lightest areas of the image so that they can be printed as the lightest white possible, and deepen the darkest areas to the darkest printable black. This in turn gives us the greatest range of intermediate steps over which the remaining tones can be spread.

COLOR CAST IN AUTO LEVELS

Auto Levels *is a remarkably effective feature, but sometimes it can get things wrong. Often it improves the contrast but, depending on the colour of the subject matter, it can introduce an inaccurate colour cast. If this is the case, adjust the contrast but not the colour by applying* Auto Levels *to a* Levels *adjustment layer. Go to* Layer> New Adjustment Layer> **Levels**, *then click on the* Auto *button. Having done that, set the blend mode between the adjustment layer and the background to* Luminosity (see page 62 for more details). *Note that, from version 7 onwards, Photoshop features* Auto Color *controls as well as* Auto Levels *and* Auto Contrast. *However, using the adjustment layer method still seems to give better contrast results.*

USING AUTO LEVELS

In Photoshop, the most expedient way to distribute the range of tones is to click on the Auto Levels option (*Image > Adjustments >* ***Auto Levels***). You can also achieve the same result by clicking on the *Auto* button in the *Levels* dialog box. Photoshop will automatically make the darkest pixels in the image black and the lightest white – regardless of whether they should actually be defined as black or white – and distribute the intermediates accordingly. Be careful, however. This adjustment will be made for each of the colour channels in the image (red, green and blue for an RGB image), and this can sometimes result in an alteration of the overall colour balance. Use the Undo function (*Edit>* ***Undo***) if this happens.

If using *Auto Levels* results in an unpleasant colour shift, you do have an alternative. You can use the *Auto Contrast* control instead. This attends only to the contrast, leaving colour balance unchanged. Conversely, the *Auto Color* tool addresses the colour elements without affecting the contrast levels.

WHY NOT USE THE BRIGHTNESS/ CONTRAST COMMAND?

If you know that contrast is a problem, it can be tempting to head straight for the standard *Brightness/Contrast* commands. Don't. These are good for making quick, rough adjustments to an image, but their crude nature can adversely affect the coloration and tonal range in an image. The Contrast control, in particular, can cause as many problems as it solves, reducing image detail as soon as it is moved in either direction.

As a result, you should feel free to use the *Brightness/Contrast* controls for quick, provisional changes, but not for your 'final' image. Why? These controls use a linear transformation, a process that throws out picture information in an

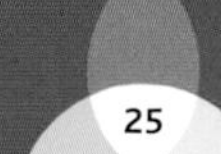

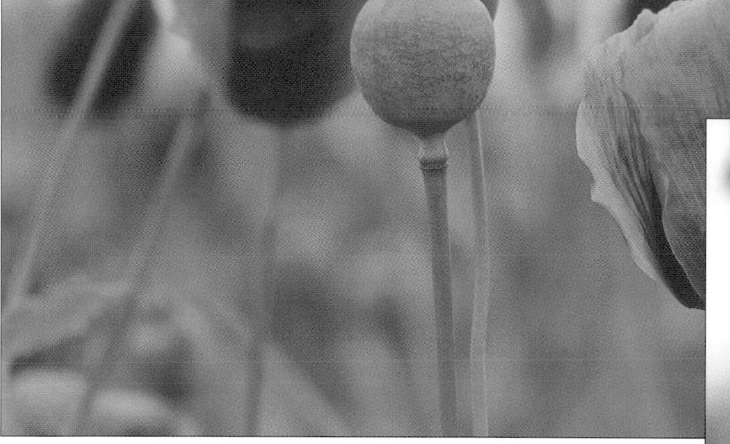

ORIGINAL

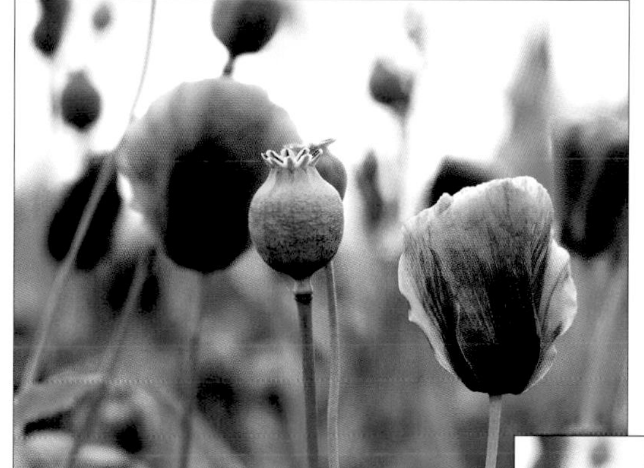

AUTO CONTRAST

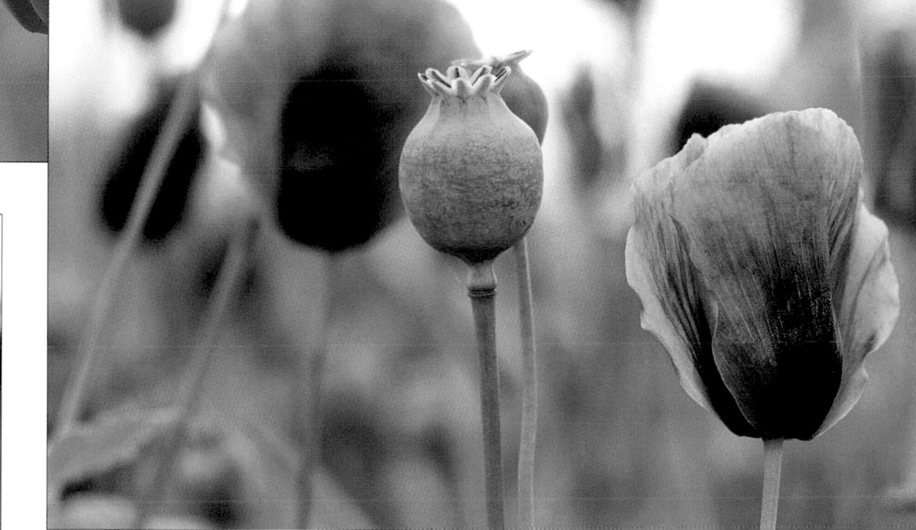

AUTO COLOR

indiscriminate way, applying transformations equally to all pixels. When you increase the brightness in an image using the Brightness slider, the tone of each pixel is increased by an identical amount. Highlights become clipped because their value cannot be increased any further. At the other end of the range, all your shadows become a murky grey because you lose true black.

The strength of the *Auto Levels* command is that it is nonlinear, and while it also discards some visual information, it doesn't do so to anywhere near the same degree. It uses a much more intelligent method of determining what changes need to be made to the image in order to achieve the corrections. You will retain your true blacks, avoid unnecessary white clipping in the highlighted areas, and you will get a more effectively brightened result.

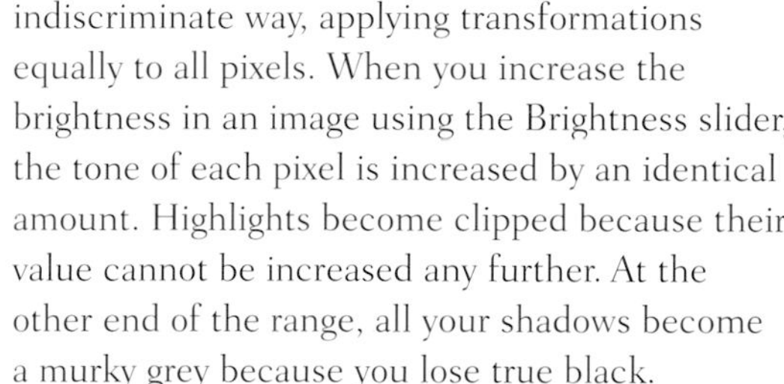

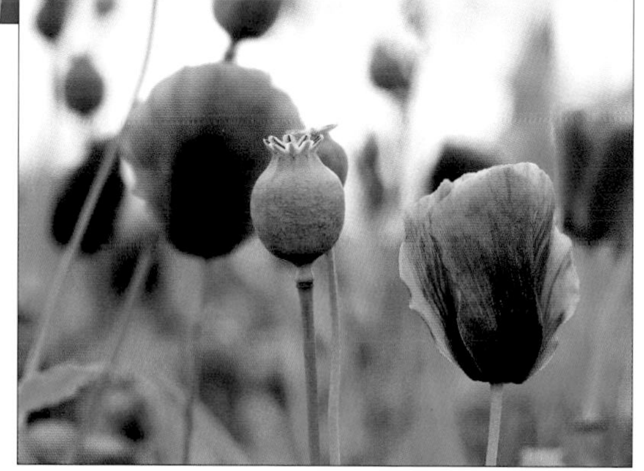

AUTO LEVELS

This image has been corrected using each of the Auto correction features. Applying Auto Levels *has boosted the contrast but overbrightened the colours.* Auto Contrast *leaves the original pallid coloration but does enhance the contrast.* Auto Color *gives the most satisfactory result, with improved contrast and tone, but no unnatural colour cast.*

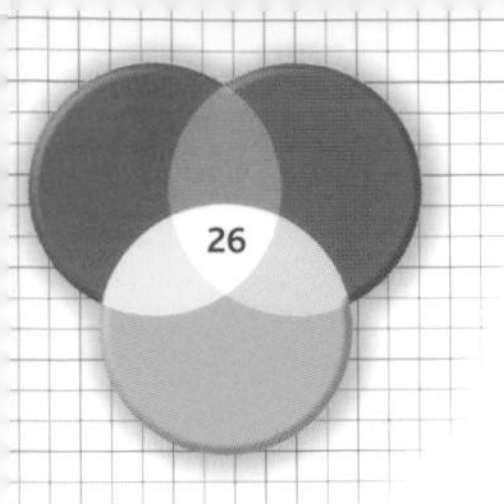

Brightness and contrast: fine-tuning

1

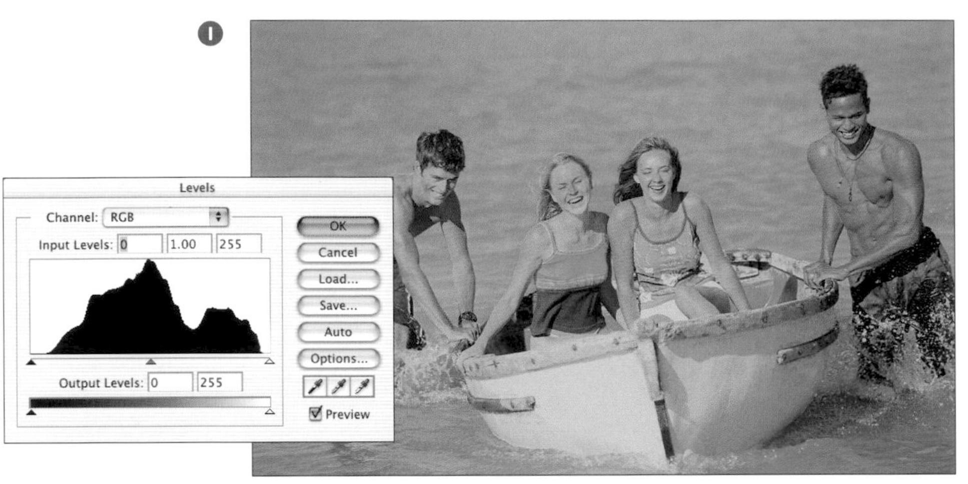

2

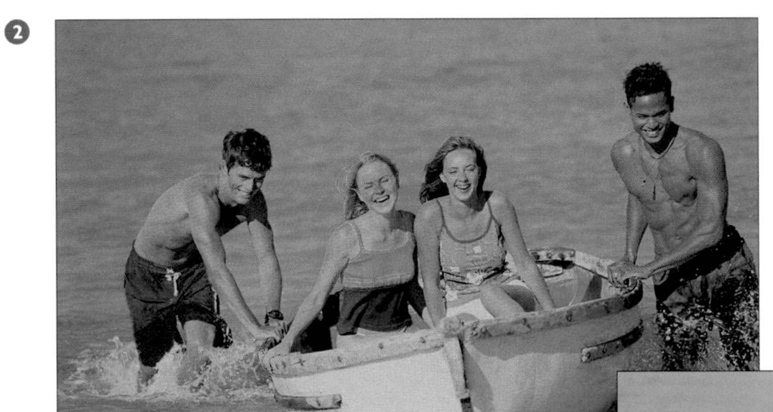

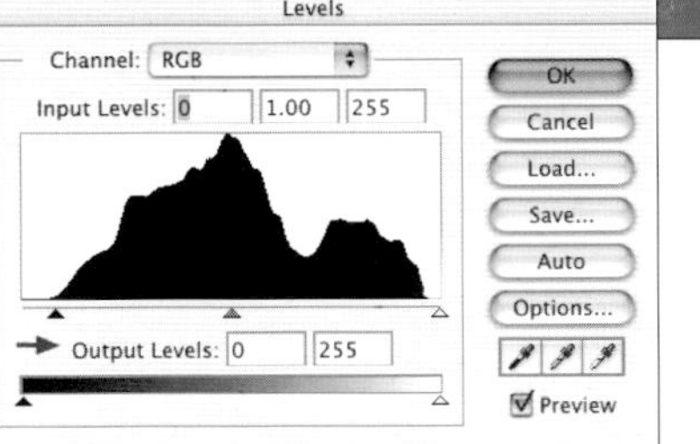

3

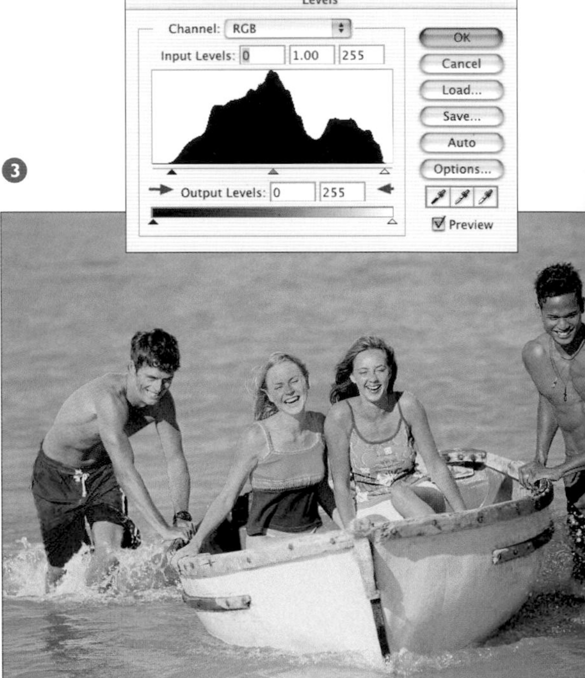

4

While they usually provide a neat, one-click answer, *Auto Levels, Auto Contrast* and *Auto Color* can't cope with every brightness or contrast correction. For fine control, we have to turn to the *Levels* dialog (*Image > Adjustments >* ***Levels***). This provides excellent correction control – as long as you know how to use it!

Take a look at the *Levels* palette for an image with weak colours or contrast, and you should see these problems reflected in the central histogram. If the tonal values at the extreme right and left of the histogram are empty, then the black and white levels are not being filled, throwing the whole balance out of skew.

TUNING LEVELS

1 *With a nasty green tinge and an overall lack of contrast, this image needs correction. Look at the left and right of the histogram and you can see that the black and white tonal values are missing. Our adjustments – which will restore these tones – begin by moving the black point slider (the small triangle beneath the left-hand corner of the histogram) to the first significant group of pixels in the histogram curve, ignoring any individual or small pixel groups. In many images, this will be at the start of the main upward slope.*

2 *Now repeat the process with the white point slider (to the bottom right of the histogram), drawing this in to touch the last group of pixels.*

3 *The image already shows signs of improvement, but we can attend to any exposure problems by adjusting the midpoint slider (between the black and white point sliders) to the right or the left. As a rule, 'average' exposure is achieved when the slider point sits midway in the area beneath the graph.*

4 *The final image benefits from an overall improvement in definition, brightness and contrast, while the green cast has disappeared.*

THE LEVELS PALETTE

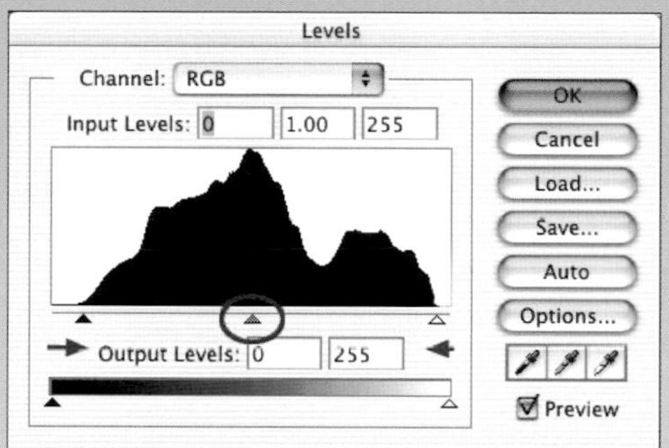

The Levels palette contains the histogram, output level (with controls), and the black, white and grey point buttons.

The histogram is a graphic way of representing all the tones that appear in an image. With just a little practice, you will be able to see, at a glance, all the tones in a image and identify shortcomings that are detrimental to image quality. Each of the 255 tones that comprise an image will be ranged along the histogram's x axis from 1 (black) at the left through to 255 (white) at the right. The amount of each tone is indicated by the height of the corresponding histogram bar. Missing tones will be indicated by a blank space. We can move the black, white and midpoint sliders under the histogram (as in the example) to expand the tonal range in an image, should any tones be missing at the extremes.

We can also use the Output sliders to trim the tonal range by moving these in slightly.

If we have a precise black or white in the image, we can click on the corresponding eye dropper button and use the dropper that appears to identify those points and make precise tonal range settings. The grey point button (circled) can be used to identify a neutral grey in the image, and selecting this will adjust for any colour casts in the image.

DARKROOM SECRETS 

THRESHOLD MODE

In much of our discussion, we have made the assumption that an image contains true whites and blacks, so that remaining tones can be distributed between these extremes. Though most images will contain a near black and a near total white, it can sometimes be important to identify these areas, in order to assess whether or not they are significant.

You can see which parts of the image are being 'forced' to be black or white by holding down the Option key (Mac) or Alt key (Windows) when using the input level sliders. Clicking with the mouse button will highlight the pixels being used to determine the selected level.

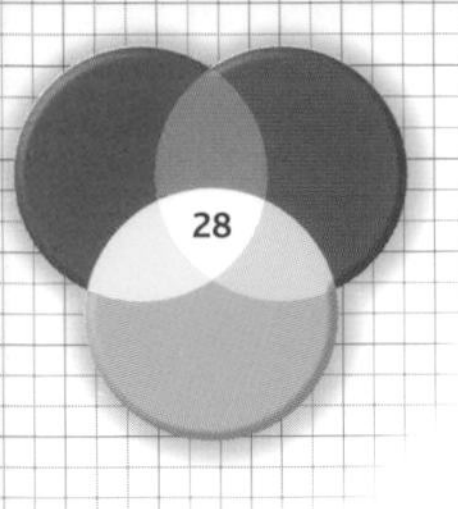

Colour correction

The original portrait has been almost ruined by a strong green colour cast. Photoshop's Variations tool makes it easy to eliminate. Just by choosing the variation that comes nearest to your ideal, you can move step by step towards the perfect picture.

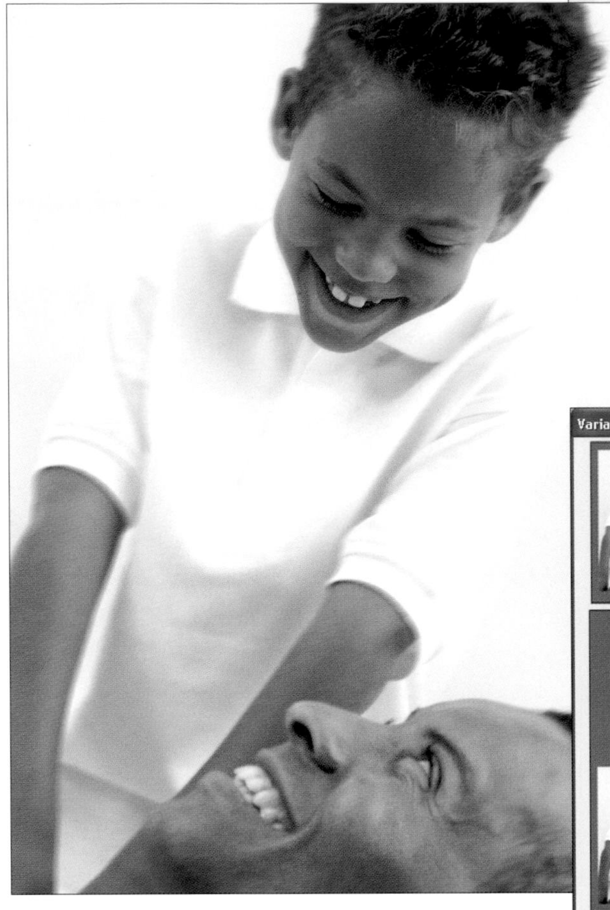

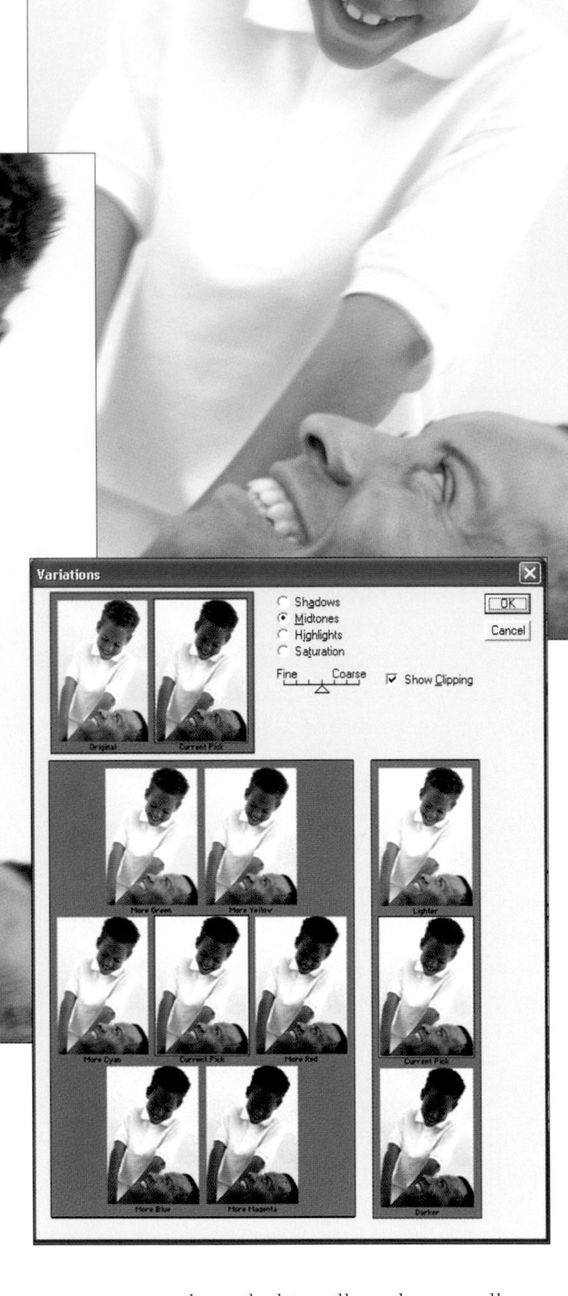

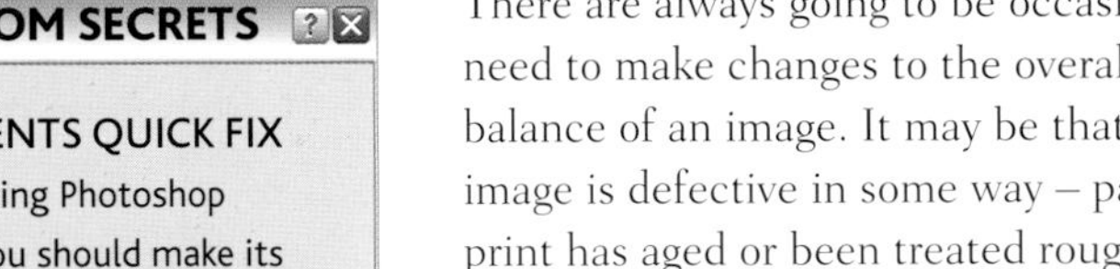

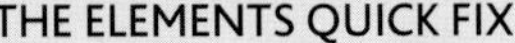

DARKROOM SECRETS

THE ELEMENTS QUICK FIX

If you are using Photoshop Elements, you should make its *Color Cast* quick-fix tool (*Enhance> Color> Color Cast*) your first resort for any colour problems. It can handle the corrections for most kinds of colour cast, but it is particularly adept with shots that have been taken in shadow areas or where the only illumination comes from a blue sky.

There are always going to be occasions when we need to make changes to the overall colour balance of an image. It may be that our original image is defective in some way – particularly if a print has aged or been treated roughly – or it may be that it has been balanced for lighting different than that used to illuminate the subject. Whatever the reason, we need the ability to change colours in the image, either overall or selectively.

USING VARIATIONS

In the traditional darkroom, there is a useful tool that makes colour corrections fairly simple. It comprises a hexagonal grid of windows, each with a different filter combination. Rather like a test strip, printing through this will produce small image segments, each made under slightly different filtration. It is then easy to assess which filter combination is ideal and apply that to the image as a whole.

Photoshop features a similar tool, which compares the original image as a thumbnail with a series of surrogates, each with a different colour bias. You can then select the surrogate with a more natural bias. In fact, this feature, called

FAST FIXES

Fast fixes for colour cast problems are provided in many applications. Photoshop Elements has its own Color Cast *command (see* Darkroom Secrets *on the opposite page). In Photoshop itself, a similar feature is offered (in a somewhat obscure position) as the* Set Gray Point *button in the* Levels *dialog box.*

Using either of these controls involves identifying an area within the image that is white, black or a neutral grey (or, rather, should be white, black or neutral). Clicking on this will cause all colour within the image to be adjusted so that there is no cast in the neutral area. A little care needs to be exercised to ensure that the pixels selected really should be neutral. If not, strange and sometimes extreme colour casts can be applied. It is easy to select some anomalous colour pixels, particularly if the image has been stored as a compressed JPEG file.

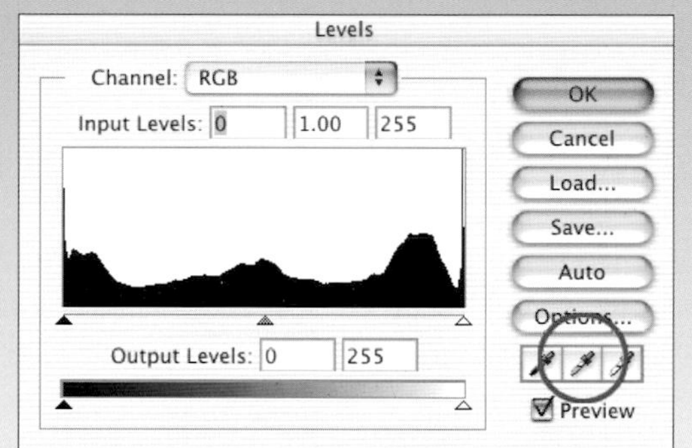

This image of a blackbird, taken with a digital camera, suffers from over-dark shadow areas with a slight colour cast.

This time, we make the corrections to the brightness first and then adjust the slight green cast in the shadows. This limits the colour correction to those areas, as there is no obvious colour cast in the remainder of the image.

As a side effect, the image also benefits from an improved tonal range.

Variations, offers more control than the darkroom test panel, enabling changes to be made to shadows, midtones or highlights, or even different corrections to each. You can also vary the adjustment between fine and coarse and alter image brightness in similar increments.

Open your image and then the *Variations* panel by selecting *Image > Adjustments >* ***Variations*** (choose *Enhancements >* ***Variations*** in Photoshop Elements).

Variations was used on the image of the boy and father (left) to eradicate the unsightly green cast by selecting *More Magenta* twice. To avoid a mauve bias, it was also necessary to select more yellow once. The final image has good skin tone and no overall cast in any of the areas that can be described as 'neutral'.

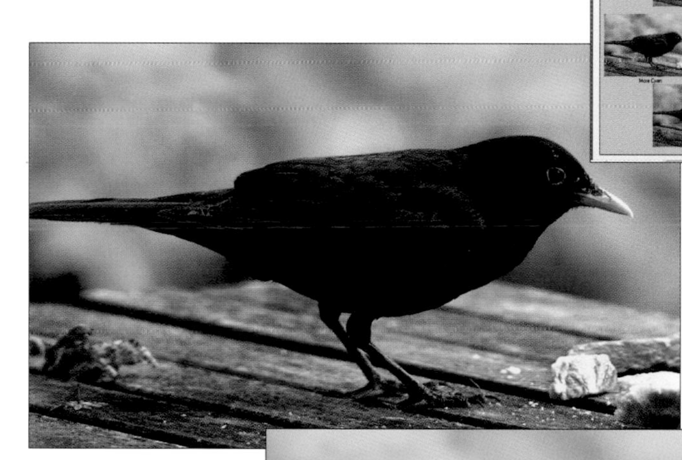

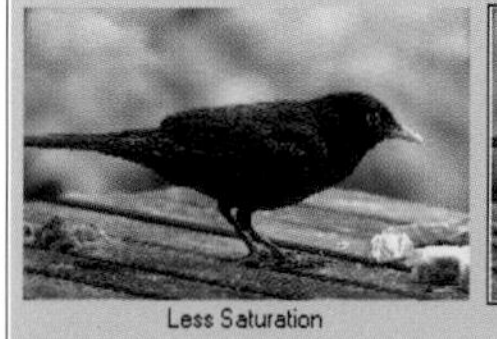

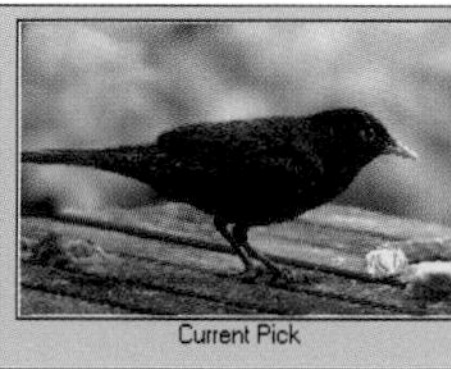

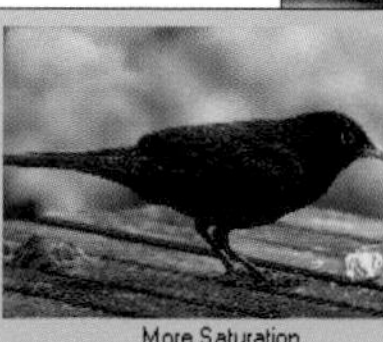

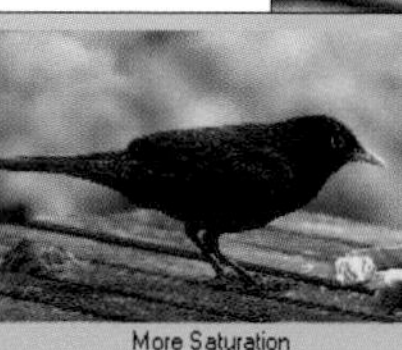

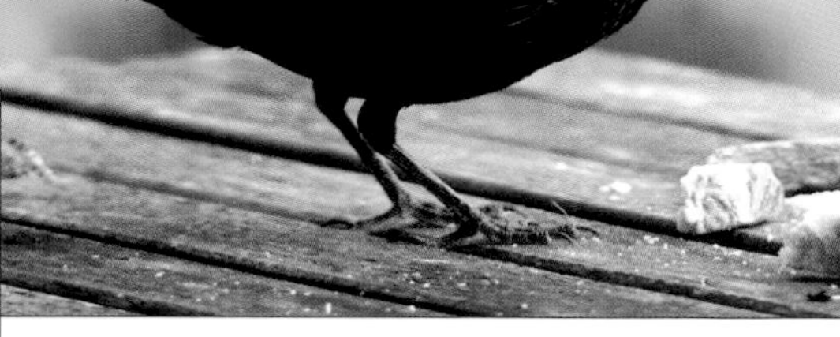

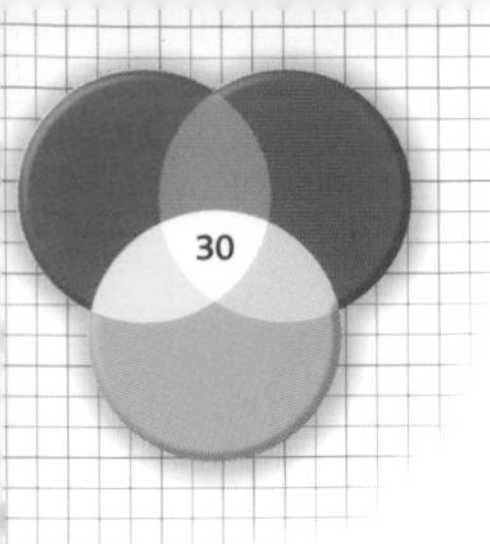

Colour correction: fine-tuning

DARKROOM SECRETS

SLIGHT CHANGE OF HUE

The *Hue/Saturation* tool provides an excellent means of adjusting the colour balance and making very subtle colour corrections. However, the effect of changing the hue by just a couple of degrees can be very subtle indeed. To see exactly which pixels are being affected, move the slider all the way to the left or right. Then you'll get an obvious – if absurd – interpretation. On the basis of these changes, you will be able to interpret smaller alterations more effectively and, where necessary, change the parameters.

While very useful, there are times when it is best to abandon the incremental *Variations* command in favour of a more continuous adjustment that leaves room for tighter control.

Traditional darkroom workers will be familiar with colour enlargers, where colour dials let a precise colour combination be entered. Photoshop has a very similar feature: the *Color Balance* control (*Image* > *Adjust* > ***Color Balance***). This permits (using sliders rather than dials) changes in the cyan and red, magenta and green, and yellow and blue levels. Changes here can alter both the dominant colour of the image (including any colour casts) and also the cast of the highlights, shadows or midtones.

Once again, it might be better to alter the colour balance using an adjustment layer. By doing so, it is possible to apply changes to the colour in an image without affecting the image itself. This is very useful if you think that you may need to return to the original coloration in the future, and it also enables you to fine-tune the changes made at a later point.

It is also possible to apply the corrections to only part of the image by using a layer mask (*see page 60*), and the adjustment layer includes a built-in layer mask for this purpose. Being layer-based also means that you can apply the corrections either to all those image layers below the adjustment layer or only to those selected.

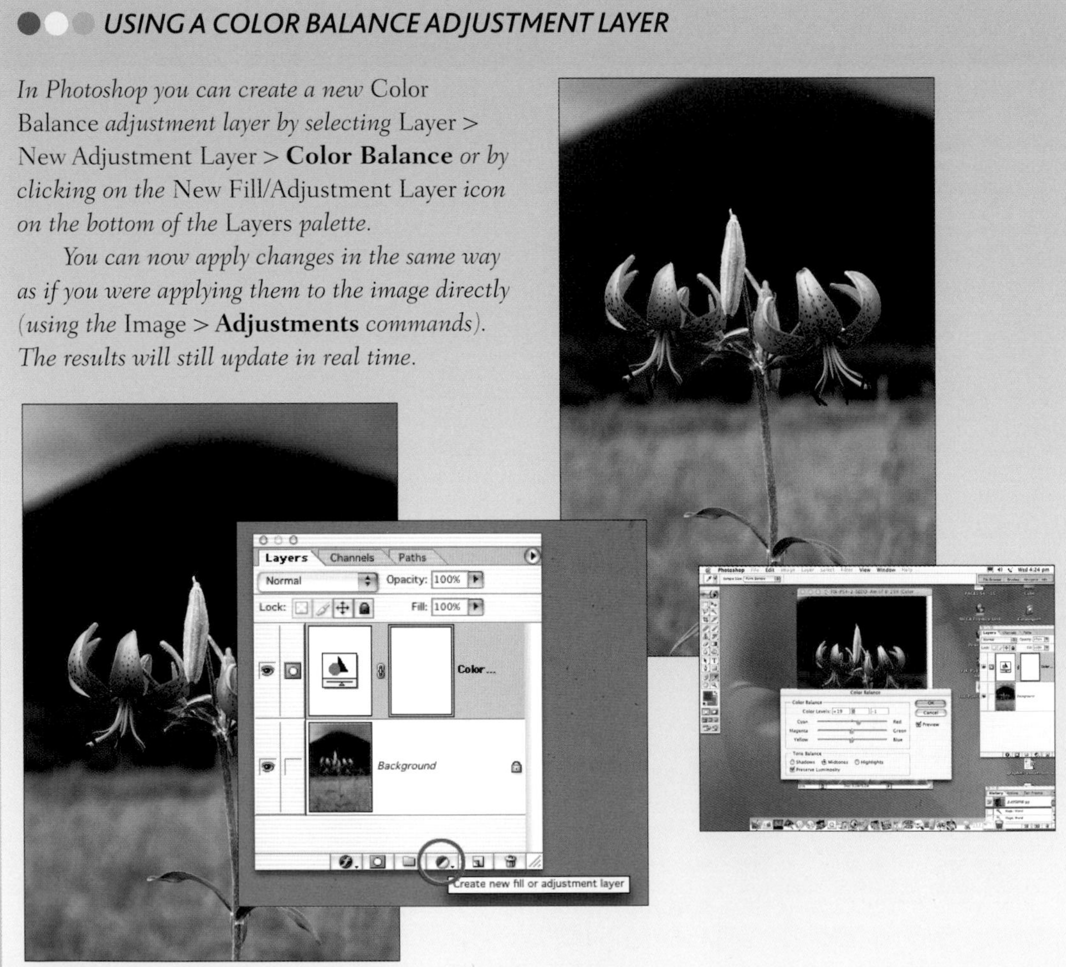

USING A COLOR BALANCE ADJUSTMENT LAYER

In Photoshop you can create a new Color Balance *adjustment layer by selecting* Layer > New Adjustment Layer > **Color Balance** *or by clicking on the* New Fill/Adjustment Layer *icon on the bottom of the* Layers *palette.*

You can now apply changes in the same way as if you were applying them to the image directly (using the Image > **Adjustments** *commands). The results will still update in real time.*

SOLVING PARTICULAR COLOUR PROBLEMS

Applying Colour Shifts to all parts of an image: Use the *Hue/Saturation* control (*Image > Adjust > Hue/Saturation*). Dragging the hue slider changes all the hues by an equal amount; the spectrum lines at the base of the dialog box illustrate the correspondence between the currently displayed hues and the original. Colour shifts are applied to highlights, shadows and midtones equally.

Change only one colour: Use the *Hue/Saturation* control, but select a colour from the pulldown menu. Changes will then only be effected on those colours. Use the eyedropper tool to select a precise colour within the specified range or drag the handles that appear between the spectrum lines to broaden the range included.

Make changes only to shadow, highlight or midtone regions: Use the *Color Balance* controls (as right), but select only the appropriate region using the radio buttons.

Localised Colour Correction: Make a selection first and use either the *Color Balance* or *Hue/Saturation* controls to effect the changes. Better blends can be achieved by using soft-edged selections (*see page 46–47*).

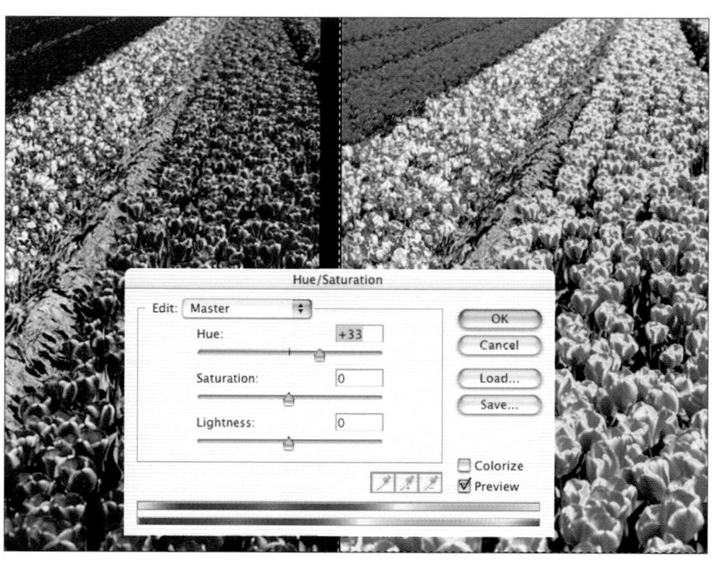

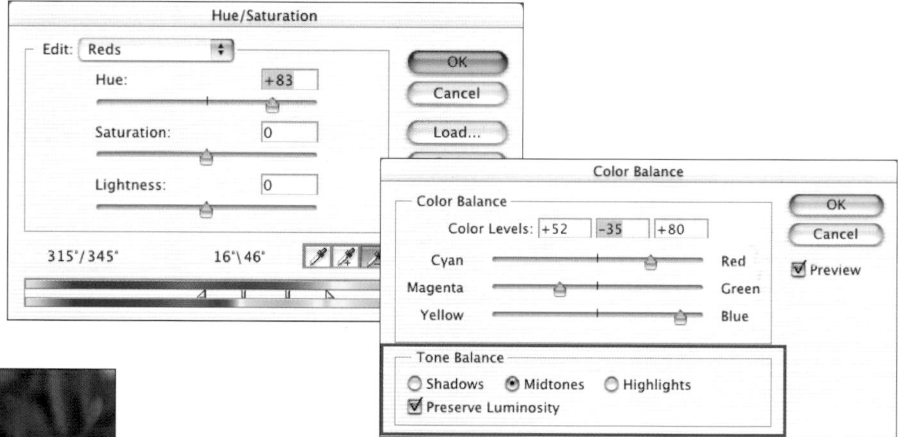

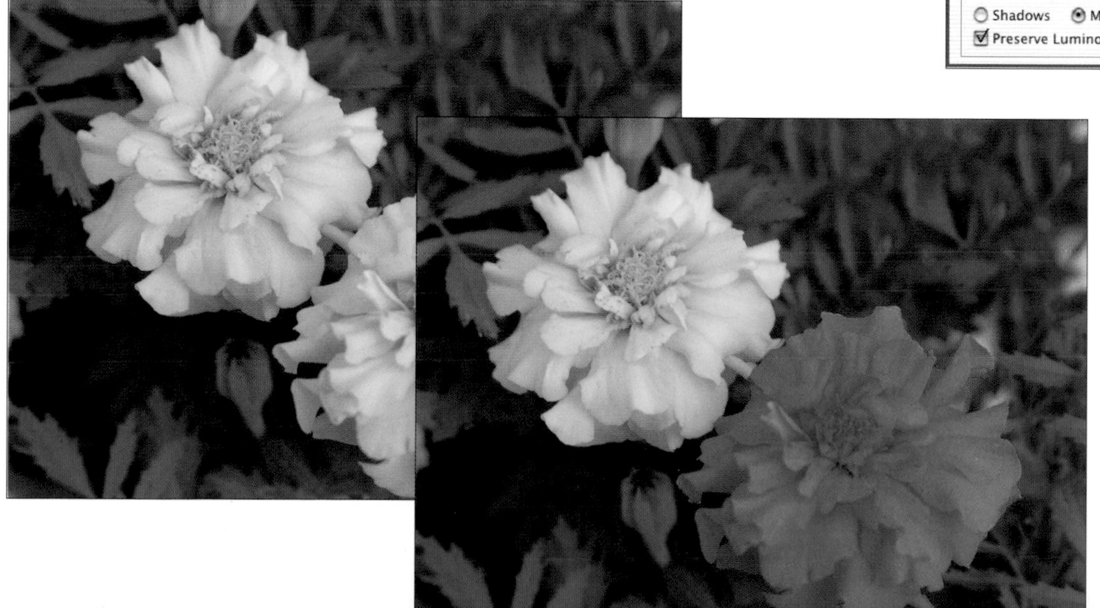

You can use either the Color Balance *or* Hue/Saturation *controls to correct any colour faults. Which you use depends on whether you want to adjust the whole or just part of an image and whether you want to change all colours or just selected hues.*

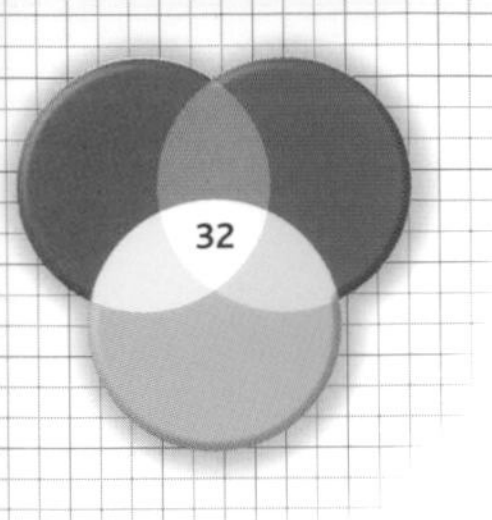

Restoring colours in a faded print

A major use of the colour balance controls in image-editing applications, both in the hands of the amateur user and the professional, is in the restoration of old photographs. Time takes its toll on these in several ways.

First, environmental action – from sunlight and atmospheric chemicals in particular – has the effect of fading and colour shifting. Then the dyes and pigments are prone to colour changes over time. Finally, poor work practices, such as incorrect processing chemical formulation or poor fixing, can leave residual chemistry within the photograph substrate. This will ultimately hasten their degradation.

But with the tools available in the digital darkroom, it is possible to rescue such a shot even when the original negative or transparency is lost. Here are the typical steps in recovering an aged print. With proper care and attention, it is often quite feasible to produce an end result that looks even better than the original.

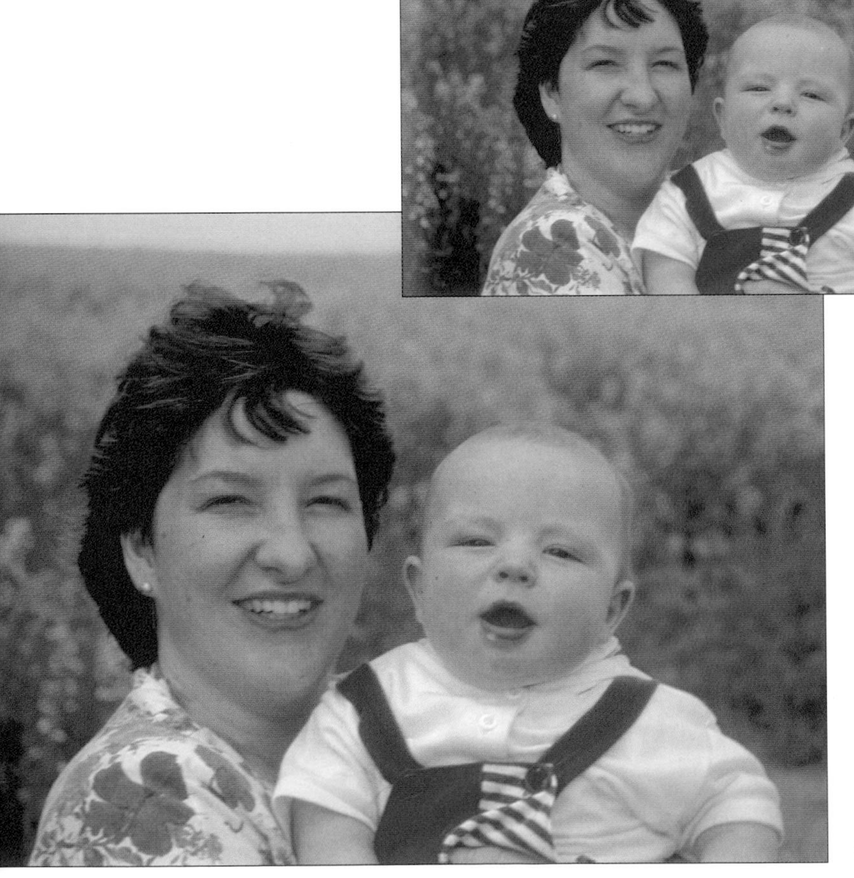

1

2

PUTTING THE COLOURS BACK

1 *Begin by surveying the damage. This image (scanned from the original) shows classic symptoms of ageing along with one or two that are due to mistreatment. Overall, the colours have faded only slightly, but these have taken on a colour cast that tends towards the magenta. There is patchy fading where part of the original has been unevenly exposed to light.*

2 *Despite this, the image is not beyond repair. We can immediately attend to the fading at the edges by using the* Crop *tool to crop the print. In this case, this also improves the composition.*

3 *When people use image-editing applications for the first time to repair faded prints, the instinctive reaction is often to boost the contrast. While this does restore colour to a point, it can also exacerbate colour shifts and can make the image too contrasty. A better way is first to check the* Levels*. Scans from aged prints always tend to be tonally compressed to some degree, and adjusting the white, black and grey points can have significant results.*

4 *In this photo, the magenta colour cast has affected the image evenly, tinting the shadows, highlights and midtones equally. As we discussed on page 31, the best solution is to use the* Hue/Saturation *command to nudge the overall hue from magenta to green. There may also be a need to alter the saturation to make up for the bleaching effect of sunlight.*

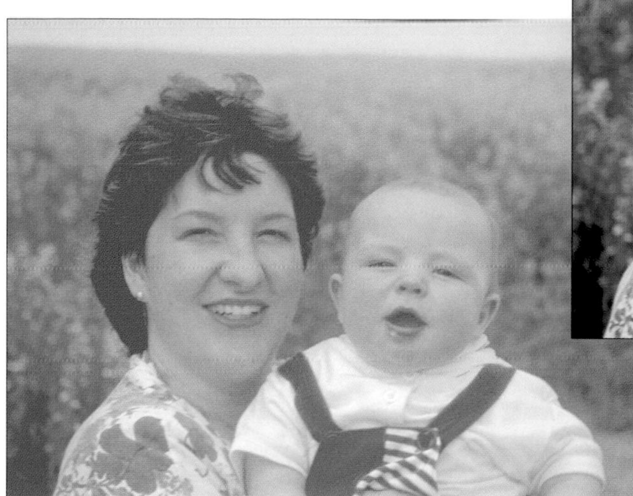

4

5 *Colourwise, the print is now pretty much as it would have been originally. To improve upon this, we need to perform a couple of further operations. First, sharpening: by applying the* Unsharp mask *filter (see page 34), any softness in the image, whether due to poor focus in the original image or the softening effect of the scanning process, can be removed. Some work with the cloning tools helps to clean the image and remove the years of neglect. Compare the original image (left) with the final colour corrected, sharpened version (right).*

5

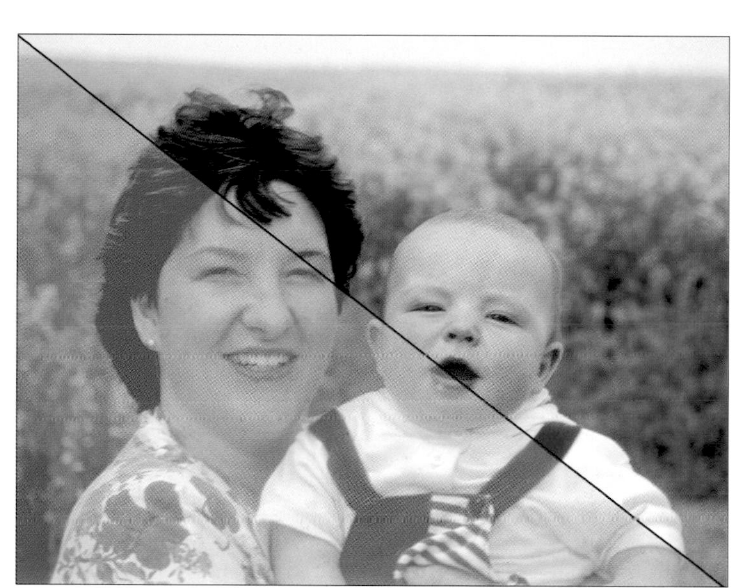

FACE-OFF

Human skin always causes the most difficulty in any restoration project. While our eyes are forgiving of faded colours in nonorganic subjects, we are particularly sensitive when it comes to flesh tones, the natural colours of the grass or sky, or familiar items of clothing. When we need to be more precise, it is best to compare the restored image with others that feature similar tones. Simply open up a more recent or undamaged image, then make your corrections with the two sitting side by side.

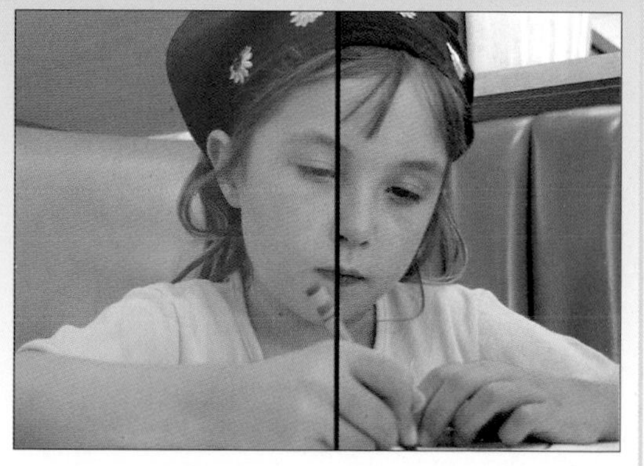

DARKROOM SECRETS

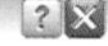

QUICK FIX FOR FADING

If an old print has faded evenly across the surface, those colour shifts can often be corrected by using the *Color Cast* command or the *Set Gray Point* eyedropper. If successful, you may then only need to use *Hue/Saturation* control to give a small boost to the saturation.

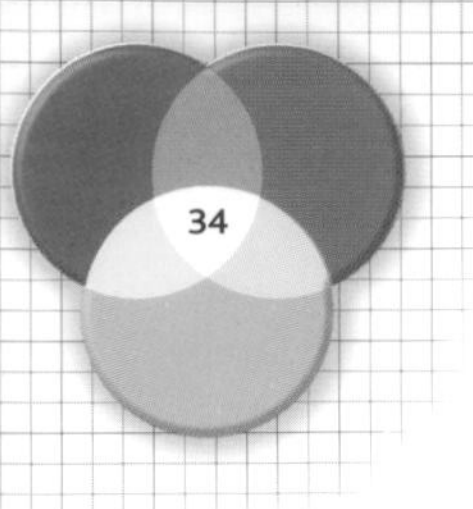

Sharpening an image

1 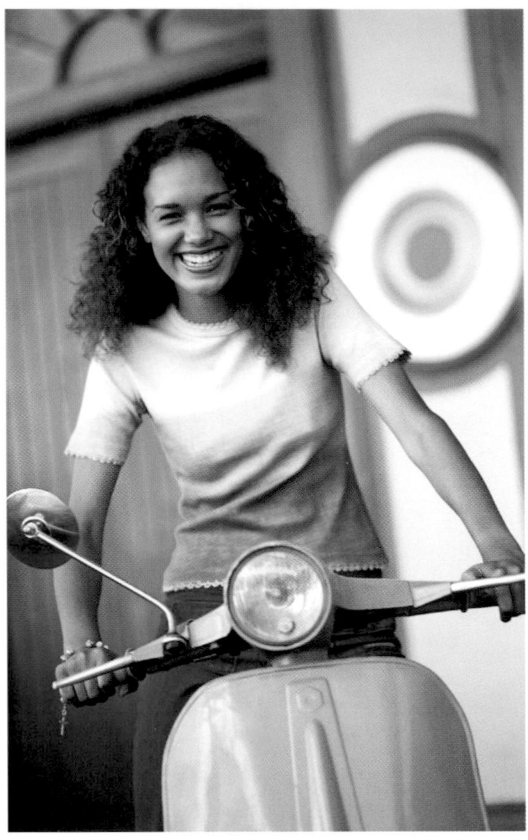

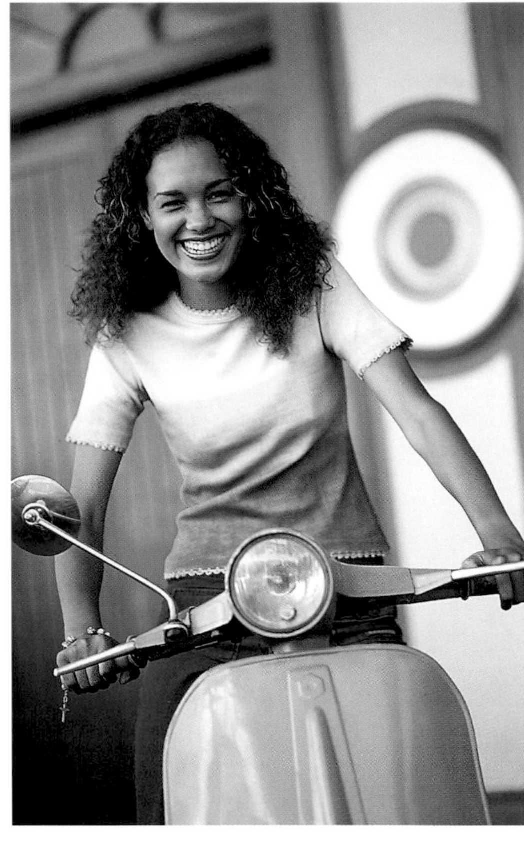 2

Our judgement of the quality of an image is largely based on how sharp it is. If an image is blurred, out of focus or soft, we tend to reject the shot unless there is some clear sign that the effect has been introduced deliberately. This has particular ramifications for digital imagery because of the way images are imported. Inevitably, many scanned images are slightly softer than the originals, due to a combination of the optical scanning process and the methods used to digitize them. Images from many digital cameras also tend to lack the sharp focus you would expect from a high quality SLR, although the advance of technology means that this is rapidly becoming a thing of the past.

In the early days of digital imaging, much was made of the sharpening abilities of image-editing applications. Some protagonists even went so far as to suggest that critical focusing was no longer necessary because we could correct any deficiencies using digital techniques. That, of course, was absurd. These sharpening features can bring out hidden or softened detail, but they cannot produce visual information that was not captured in the first place – correct focusing will remain a vital part of the photographic process for some time to come.

However, while sharpening is not the same as restoring sharp focus, it can at least give an impression of it. Like most image-editing software, Photoshop has several sharpening tools. We recommend only one: the *Unsharp Mask*. It is a more complex tool than the *Sharpen* or *Sharpen More* filters, which are applied without any control parameters, but with only a little more effort it delivers much more satisfying results.

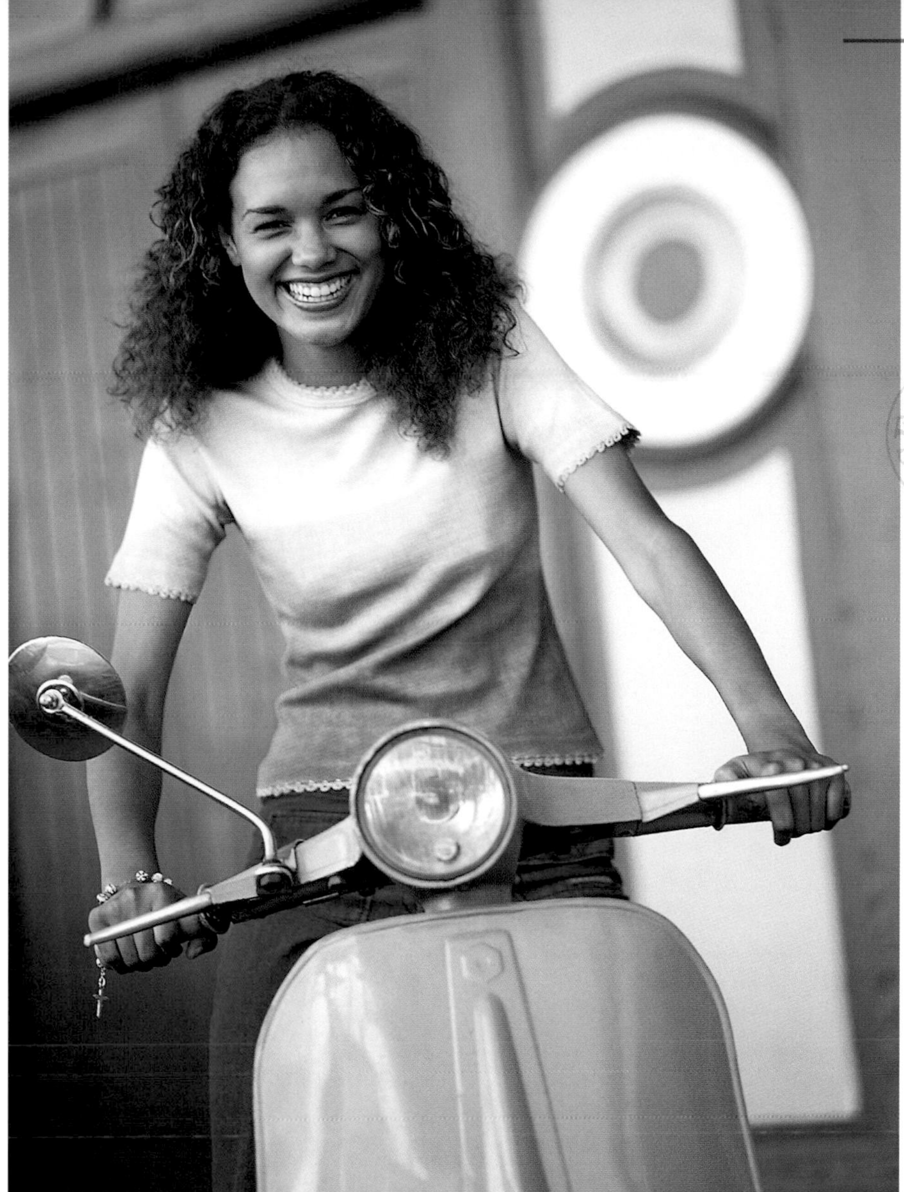

3

ACHIEVING CRITICAL SHARPNESS

1 *This is an image that can be successfully enhanced using the* Unsharp Mask. *Though in focus, it is not critically sharp. This may be due to slight movement during the exposure or the precise point of focus not being on the subject.*

2 *We can apply an Unsharp Mask by selecting* Filter > Sharpen > **Unsharp Mask**. *Using an Unsharp Mask with an* Amount *of 150% and a* Radius *of 3 gives the image that all-important critical sharpness, in particular enhancing the appearance of the hair and some of the detail on the scooter. Setting a* Threshold *of between 5 and 10 will limit the amount of sharpening that occurs elsewhere in the image.*

3 *Oversharpening can be a hazard with this tool, but we can avoid going over the top by fading the filter. Using the* Fade Filter *command* (Filter > **Fade Unsharp Mask**), *we can retain the natural softness in those parts of the image (such as the face) which do not respond well to the sharpening process. This 'sharpen then fade' approach can give more effective control over the final result.*

USING THE UNSHARP MASK

Some tips for getting the best from the Unsharp Mask:

- *Practise, practise, practise. The* Unsharp Mask *is one of the more abstract effects, and experimentation (following the guidelines here) will pay off.*
- *Err on the side of smaller radii rather than larger. A large* Radius *can oversharpen and actually hide some of the detail you are aiming to enhance.*
- *The same sharpening effect can be achieved by a range of different amount, threshold and radius settings, but concentrate on getting the radius right.*
- *Contrary to convention for other filters (including* Sharpen *and* Sharpen More*), you often get better results from the* Unsharp Mask *by applying it twice using lower amount values.*
- *Make the* Unsharp Mask *the last stage of the image-editing process. The artefacts generated by the filter can be enhanced by other operations to the detriment of the image overall.*
- *Don't shy away from high settings. Setting the controls to absurd levels can produce very graphic effects, although the results on portraits are less than flattering!*
- *Use the* Unsharp Mask *to sharpen transformed images. When you rotate or resize or skew an image, softness can be introduced.*
- *Splitting an image into channels* (see page 96)*, then applying different* Unsharp Mask *effects to each channel can help negate the effect of a noisy channel. Use a low* Radius *setting – 1.5 or less – to avoid colour fringing.*

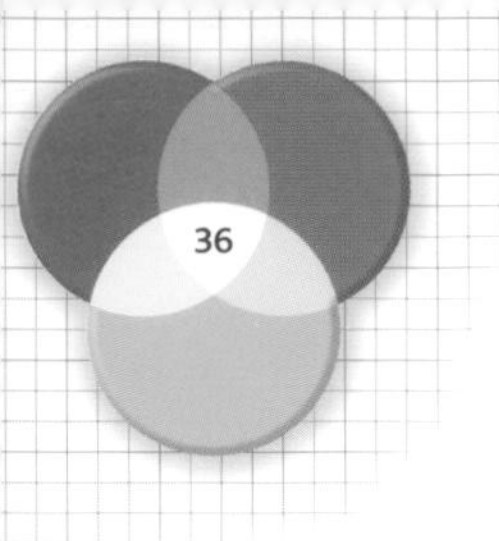

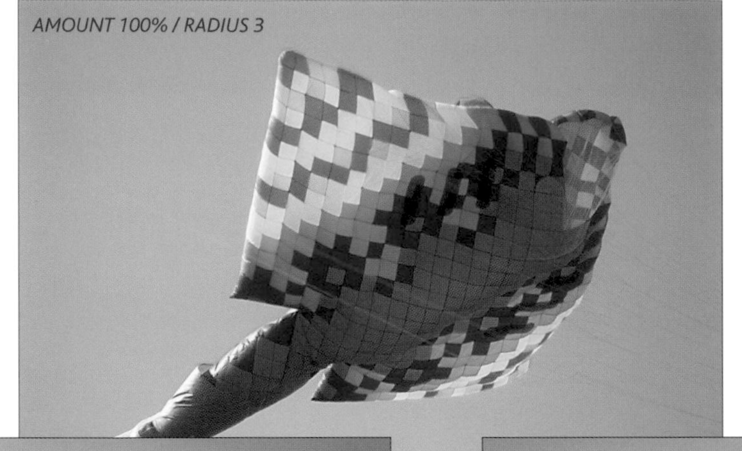

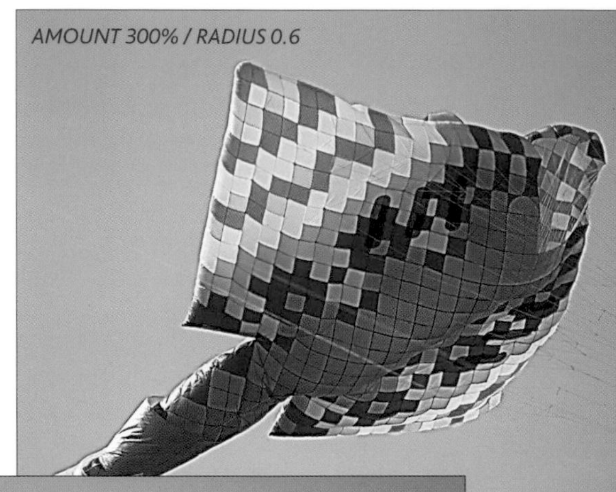

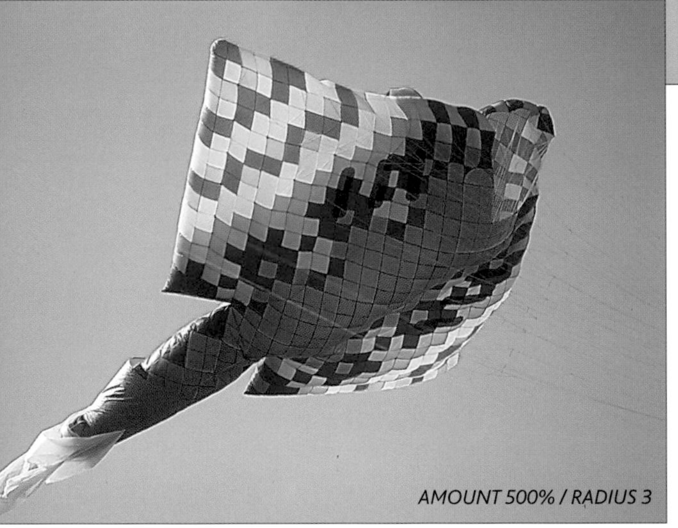

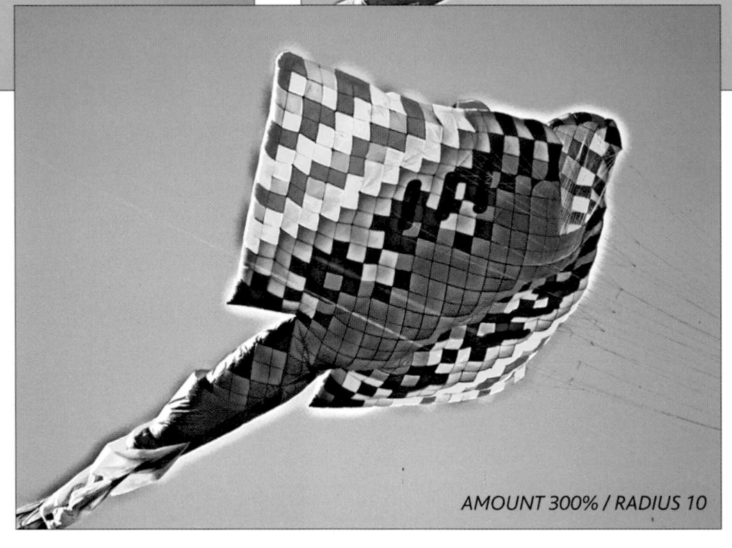

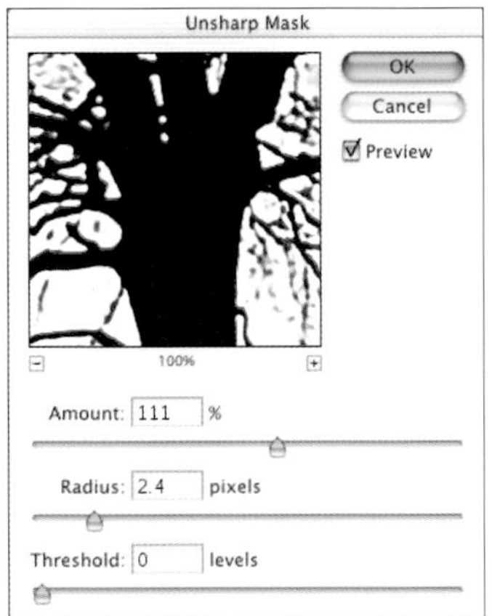

The Unsharp Mask dialog provides sliders for the three control parameters and a preview box for the settings.

To really make the most of the *Unsharp Mask*, it helps to have a sense of how the tool works. In raw processing terms, it's one of the most labour-intensive filters in any image-editing application. It works on a pixel-by-pixel basis, assessing contrast changes and making alterations on the basis of the settings you have stipulated in the dialog box.

Those settings comprise *Amount*, *Radius* and *Threshold*. As you might guess, the *Amount* specifies the amount of sharpening to be applied. The sharpening effectively increases the contrast at the edges and transitional points in an image, adding extra lightness on the lighter side and extra darkness on the darker. Set the *Amount* to a high figure (at the top of the typical 0 to 500% range) and you will have a black and white boundary; 200% is a good working figure in most practical situations.

The *Radius* determines the number of pixels over which this sharpening will be applied. A low *Radius* setting results in tight gradients using the amount specified; higher numbers tend to produce broader halo effects.

Finally, the *Threshold* determines the tonal separation between two values before the effect is applied. With a *Threshold* setting of 10, two adjacent pixels with tonal values of 55 and 65 will be affected. This basically affects the sensitivity of the effect to edges in the image.

You can see how the settings affect an image in the examples above. While the sharpening effect in the top-left image is too subtle to make an appreciable difference, the effect in the bottom right image is excessive. The colours have been affected, and there are clear halo artefacts around the edges. The balanced images in between are far more lifelike.

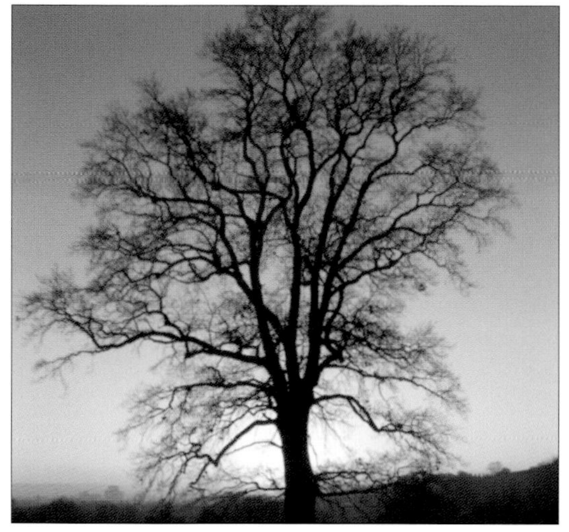

1

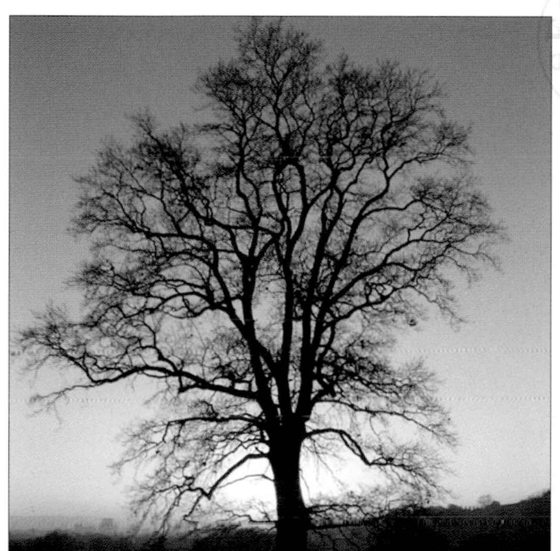

2

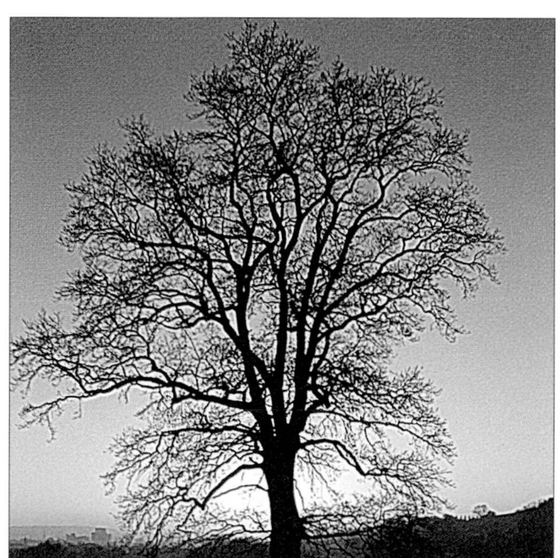

3

USING THE UNSHARP MASK

The settings for the Unsharp Mask will vary according to the subject. We can divide these into two groups, normally described as high-frequency and low-frequency. High-frequency subjects (or images) include a lot of fine detail. Cityscapes, the branches of a tree, and hair are typical high-frequency subjects. Low-frequency subjects include faces and organic subjects.

HIGH-FREQUENCY SUBJECTS

1 *This tree (left) contains a lot of high-frequency detail. Here we need to use a low radius setting to prevent the individual branches from merging into one another, but a relatively high amount setting to ensure a clearer final image.*

2 *With settings of* Radius *1 and* Amount *200%, the image looks commendably sharp. The individual branches are distinct from each other, and the tree stands out more against the sky.*

3 *Increasing the* Radius *to 3, however, has a detrimental effect. While you could argue that the branches are more sharply defined, the clear sharpening halos look ugly and actually reduce the fine detail visible.*

LOW-FREQUENCY SUBJECTS

1 *In this informal portrait (right,) there is little fine detail that requires enhancing, but the image could still do with crisper definition. Like most images involving human figures, it is in need of some low-frequency treatment.*

2 *If we apply the same settings that worked so successfully on the image of the tree, the results are less than perfect. The sharpening is on too small a scale to work effectively.*

3 *With the* Radius *set to 3 and the* Amount *to 200, the result is far more satisfactory. The facial details are clearer, but the image doesn't look artificially 'hard'.*

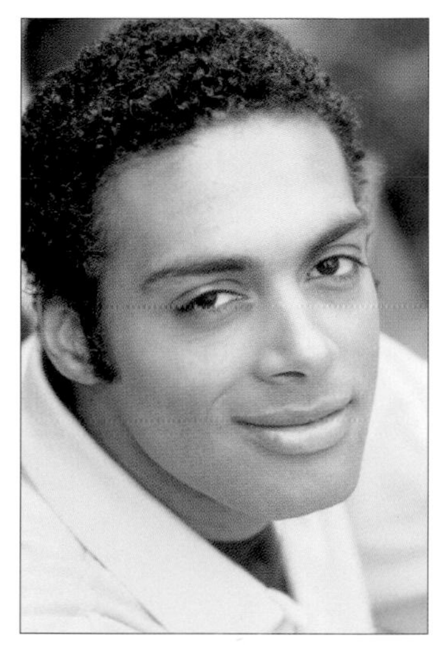

1

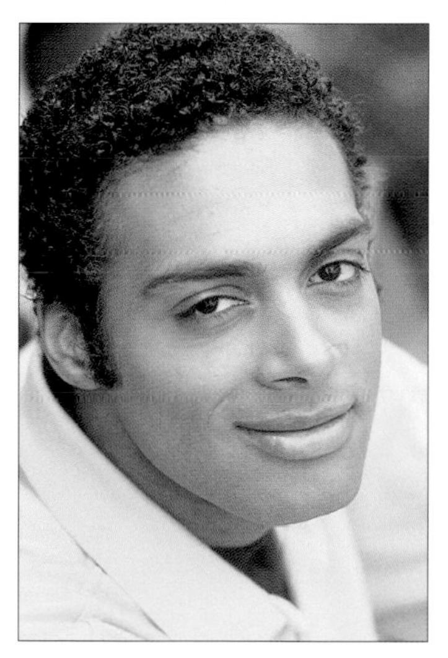

2

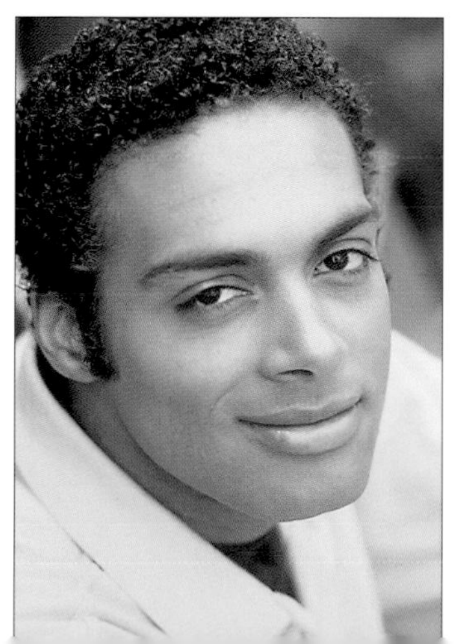

3

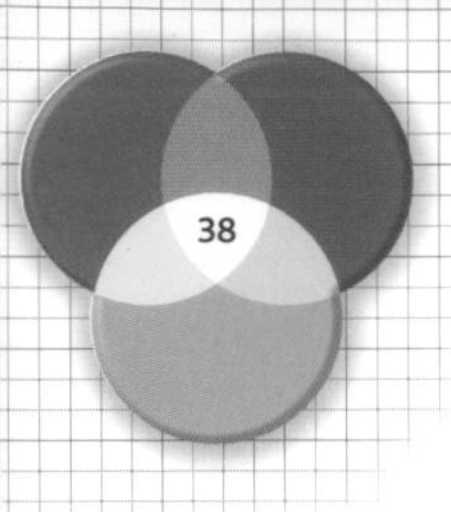

Dodging and burning

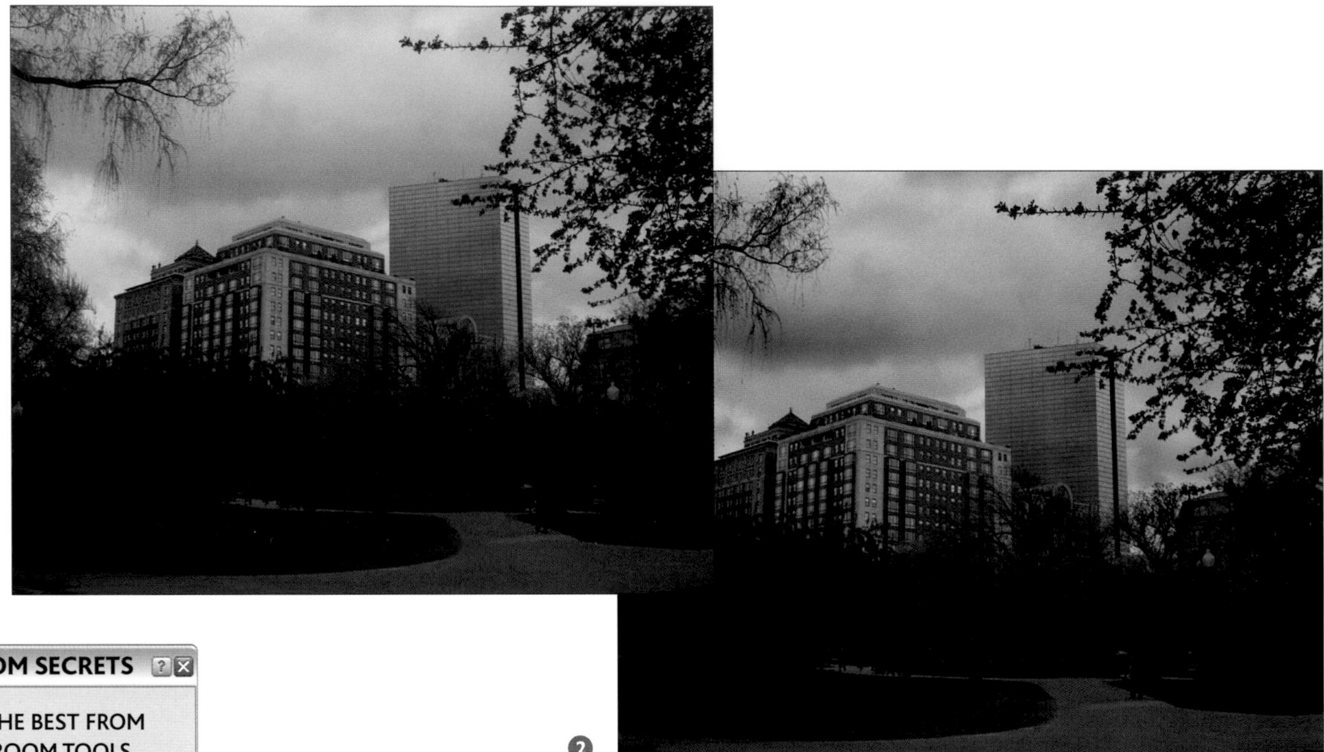

1

2

DARKROOM SECRETS

GETTING THE BEST FROM THE DARKROOM TOOLS

- Unlike their chemical darkroom equivalents, the digital darkroom tools can be rather abrupt in their effect. Hence it's a good idea to use (or create) very soft-edged 'brushes' to apply the *Dodge* or *Burn*.
- Similarly, begin by setting a low *Density* or *Opacity* for the tool and build up the effect gradually.
- Burn in shadows and midtones only. Never burn in highlights. Similarly, don't set the tool to dodge shadows. You'll find that you can get better results by lightening shadows with the tool set to dodge the highlights.

Images taken with digital cameras often suffer from compressed tonality and a lack of contrast. We could correct these deficiencies in the image as a whole by adjusting *Levels*, but we can get more atmospheric results by making localised corrections using the *Dodge* and *Burn* tools.

These are also techniques that have made the transition from the conventional darkroom to the digital. Burning (or burning in) is a process that involves increasing the density of a selected part of the image to create darker areas. Dodging reduces the density to produce lighter, 'thinner' areas. They affect the tonality of the image without affecting the colour component and can be used to correct errors in the original image or to enhance an image that is – exposure-wise – deemed correct.

When we dodge and burn in the conventional darkroom, we use our hands (or specialised tools) to hold back selected parts of the image or give additional exposure to other parts. In the digital darkroom, we use brush tools to 'brush' the lower or higher density into the image, but this method has its limitations. The brushes we use, although variable in terms of shape and density, are fixed during application. The trick is to pause and vary the pressure (*Density*) and brush size and shape during use. It can be better to address tones in the image selectively; dodging or burning only the highlights, then the shadows and then the midtones. This approach also helps to alleviate some of the obvious signs of treatment.

BURNING IN

1 *This image is a typical subject for dodging and burning. The bright overcast sky has lost its detail and at the same time has influenced the image to the extent that the foreground landscape is underexposed.*

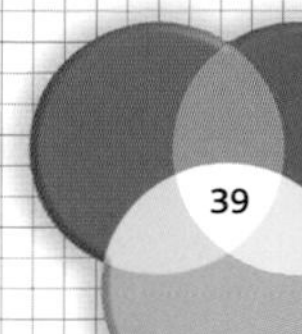

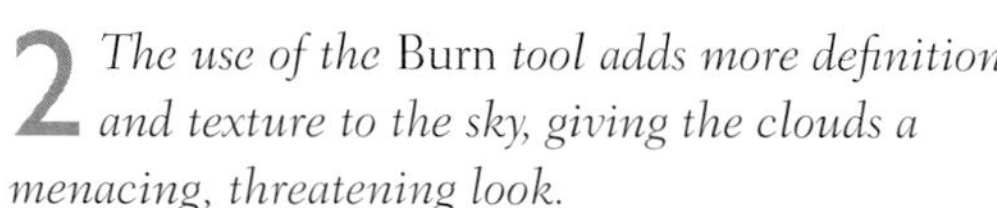

3

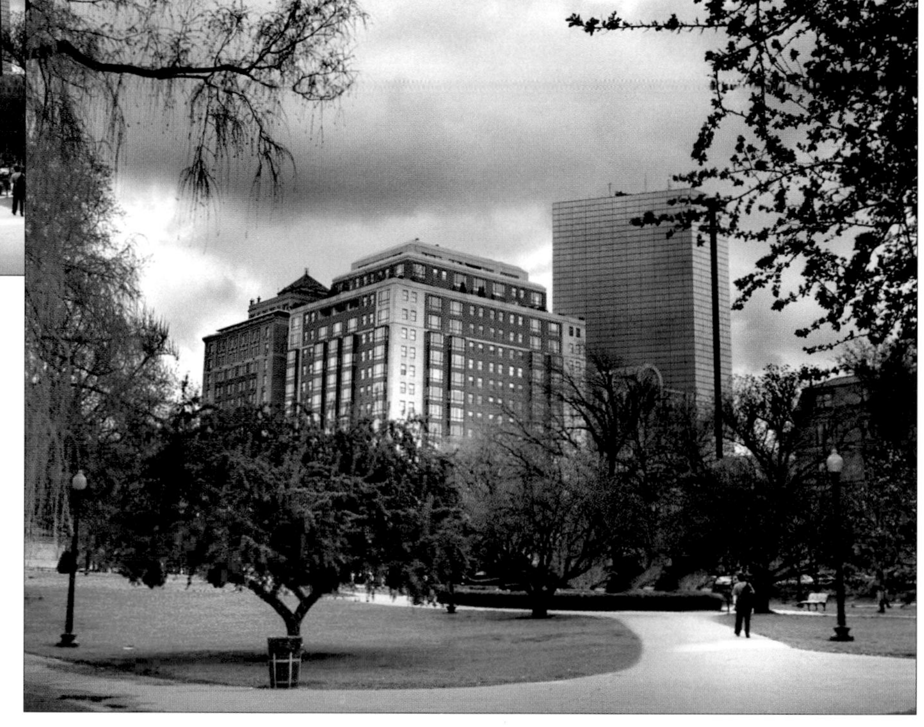

4

2 *The use of the* Burn *tool adds more definition and texture to the sky, giving the clouds a menacing, threatening look.*

3 *Using the* Dodge *tool on the landscape raises the brightness and gives a more balanced result. Do note, however that there can be colour changes. Here in the sky a magenta cast has developed in heavily burned areas.*

4 *We can correct oversaturated colours using the* Saturate *tool. Part of the same suite of tools, this reduces or increases the colour saturation in an image. Here the saturation of the sky has been reduced to zero, leaving it totally monochromatic.*

USING THE BRUSH TOOLS

The darkroom brush tools comprise the Burn, Dodge *and* Sponge *tools. As these work exactly like any other brush, you can set the size, shape and the dynamics as you would the* Paintbrush, *for example. You can also specify which tonal region of an image the tool is to be applied to – highlights, midtones or shadows.*

You can also specify a density – which, in photographic darkroom terms, would be referred to as exposure. Working at 100% exposure is rarely to be recommended. The results will be harsh and, no matter how delicate your touch, obvious. It is better to build up the effect using very modest exposures of perhaps 10%, adding extra strokes as necessary.

The Burn *tool intensifies a region, making it more dark but not affecting the colour saturation.*

The Dodge *tool lightens an area, again without affecting the colour saturation.*

The Sponge *tool alters the colour saturation (you can select to saturate or desaturate), but does not affect image density.*

The keyboard shortcut for all the darkroom tools is O. Press the O key repeatedly to cycle through the three options.

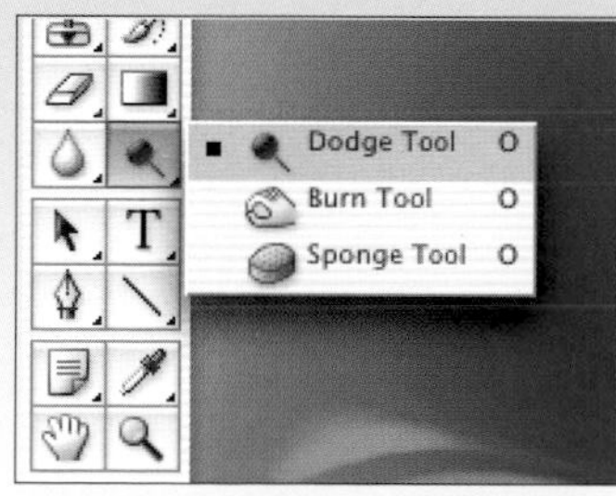

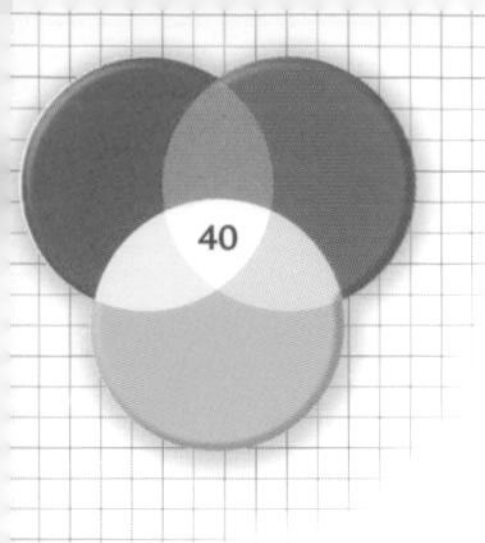

Removing dust and scratches

Though some will argue that proper handling and storage would mean that no image suffered from dust and scratches, those of us in the real world will invariably face both at some point. Dust and scratch marks can accrue at any time – even when the film is still in the camera.

Like most image editors, Photoshop provides a *Dust and Scratches* filter, designed to remove the dust and scratch marks on an image. Sadly, these filters tend to be indiscriminate: they cannot tell the difference between dirt on the image and the fine detail you wish to preserve.

As dust and scratch removal tends to be performed early on during editing, it's wise to save a copy of the original image so you can retrieve it, unaffected by any changes, should these prove detrimental. The tools discussed here work in any recent version of Photoshop, although users of version 7 should know that its *Healing Brush* and *Patch* tools deliver more effective results (turn the page for more detail).

Though excellent at removing dust and scratch marks (including, in this case, mould growth), the filter also does sterling work at removing similarly sized details from the image itself.

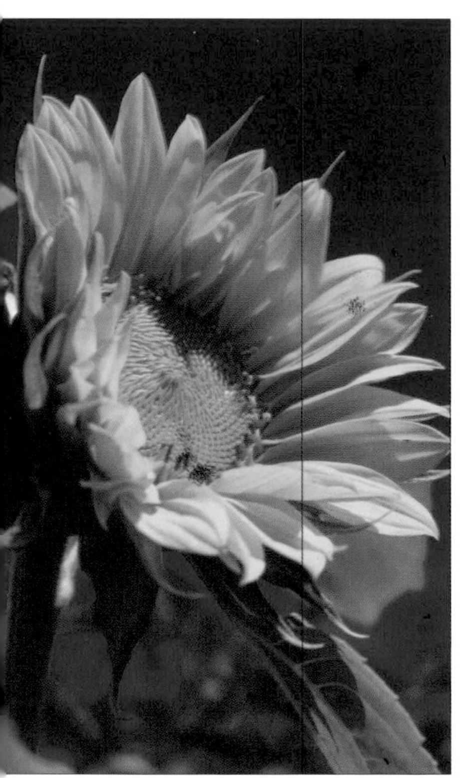

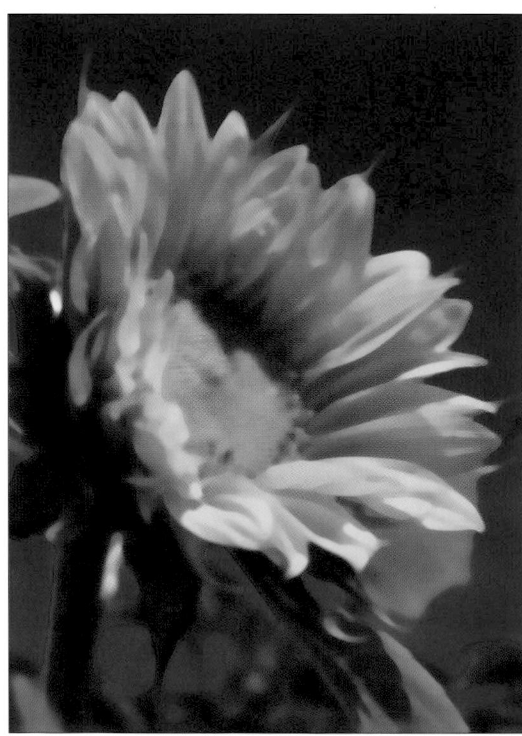

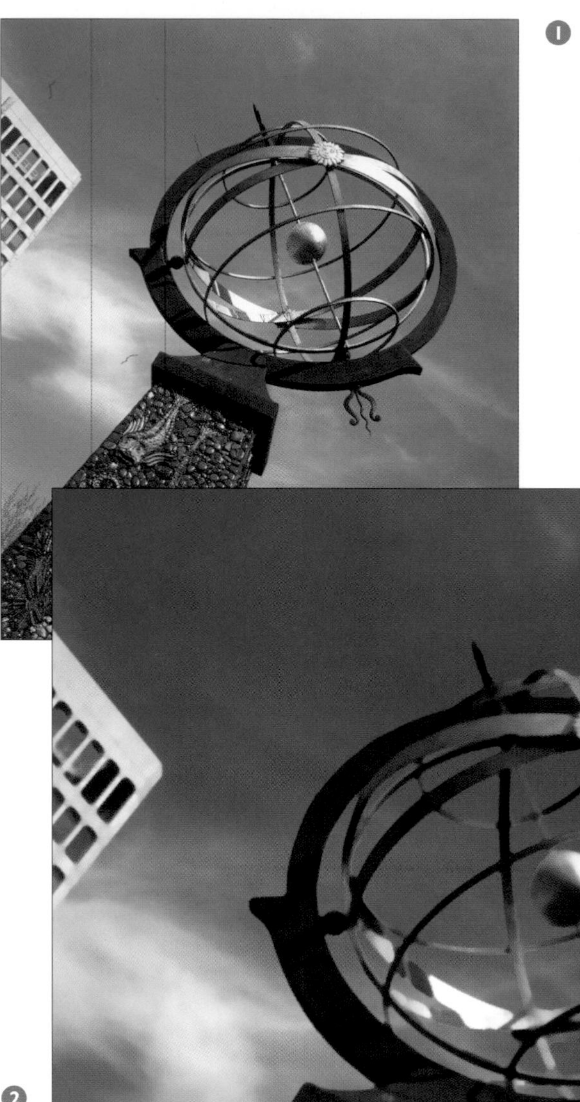

REMOVING FINE BLEMISHES

Instead of using the *Dust and Scratches* filter in a wholesale fashion, you can employ it in a form that protects the image from its softening effect. If you need to remove only some fine blemishes – the kind caused by dust when a large photograph is scanned, or the fine tramline scratches found sometimes on 35mm roll films – use the filter selectively and invoke a *Layer Mask* to control the extent of its reach.

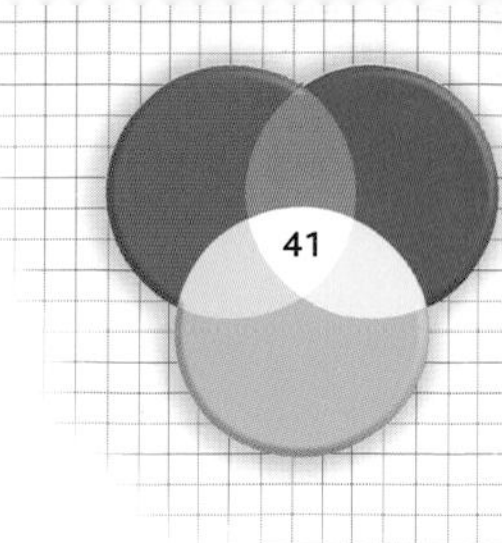

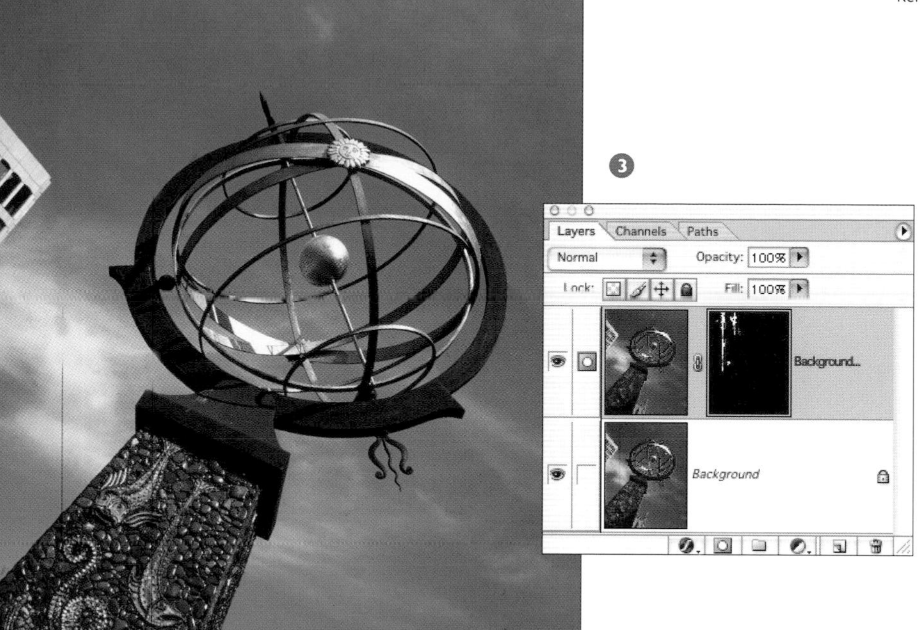

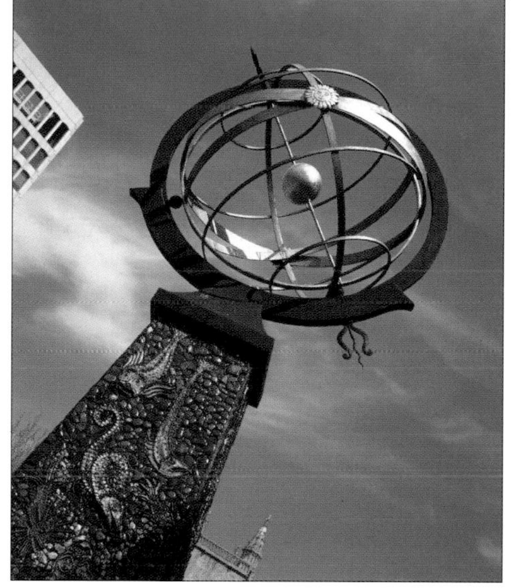

SIMPLE SCRATCH REMOVAL

1 *In this first instance, we will remove the fine blemishes on the image above. The most obvious points of concern are the large vertical scratches in the sky to the left of the image, but there are also a few smaller marks that have appeared on the surface of the print.*

2 *Copy the image into a new layer* (Layer > **Duplicate Layer**) *and apply the* Dust and Scratches *filter to it. Use the radius slider to alter the size of dust or scratch marks to remove, but note how increasing the size also removes the fine detail in the image.*

3 *Add a black-filled* Layer Mask *to the layer* (Layer > **Add Layer Mask**). *This protects the layer from any alteration. Now paint with a fine white paintbrush only where necessary to obscure the blemishes. The white paint produces 'holes' in the* Layer Mask. *These enable the filtered layer image to overlay the original background layer.*

4 *The image is unblemished, but it has not been softened. Zooming in on areas where the cleanup was performed will show only minor artefacts, due to the filter's colour-smoothing effect.*

REMOVING LARGER BLEMISHES

Because of their small original size, any dust marks on negatives or transparencies are enlarged when these are scanned, making them more problematic to remove. In such cases, it is best to use a combination of filtration and the *Clone* tool to remove the blemish, rather than entrust the task to the *Dust and Scratches* filter on its own.

We can, for example, repair the mistreated original slide, showing a sunflower against a deep blue sky. Begin by using *Dust and Scratches* to remove the smallest dust marks, then create a new empty layer (*Layer* > **New Layer**). You can now use the *Clone* brush (*see page 42*) to make corrections, taking care to use a cloning point close to the blemish – this ensures consistent colour – and painting over the affected areas. Ensure the *Use All Layers* box on the tool options bar or *Clone* palette is checked, so that background pixels can be used.

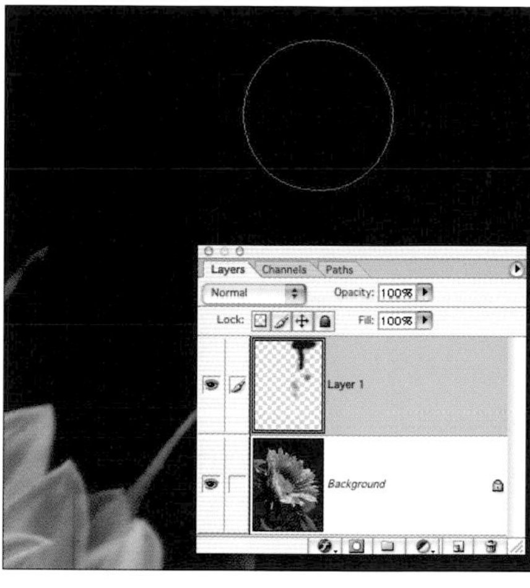

For fine control during scratch removal, use the Dust and Scratches *filter to sort out the smaller errors, then the* Clone *tool on the larger blemishes.*

DARKROOM SECRETS

CLEAN-UP SHORTCUTS

Marks of any kind are more obvious in areas of continuous tone, such as the sky or the bride's dress in a wedding photograph. You can quickly correct these by selecting the affected area using the *Color Range* command or the *Magic Wand* selection tool, before applying the dust and scratches filter to that area only. As the colour in these areas is continuous, any softening will not be visible and any adjacent, non-selected areas will remain perfectly sharp. You can increase the threshold in the *Dust and Scratches* dialog box to ensure that only those blemishes that are significantly darker (or lighter) than the background are removed.

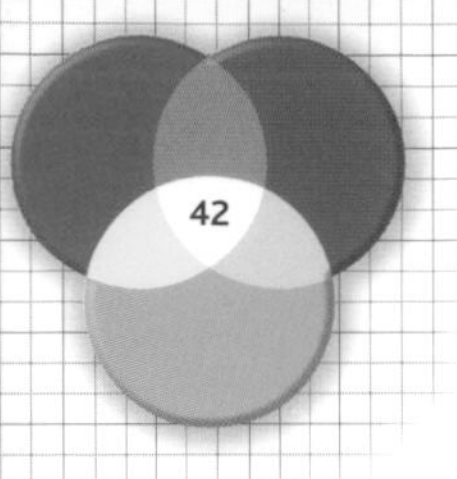

Retouching portraits

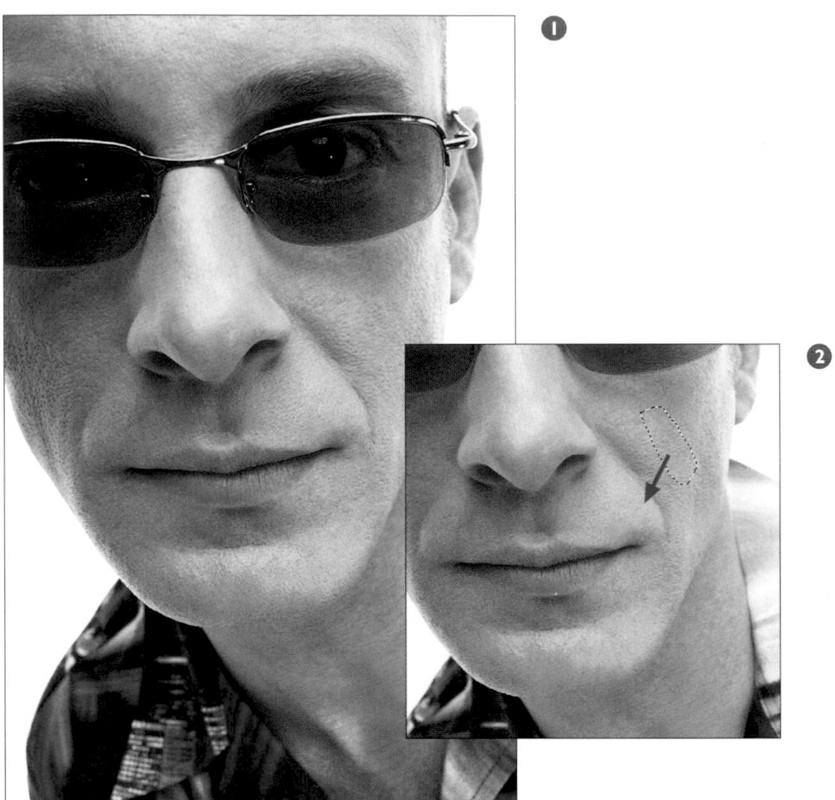

1

2

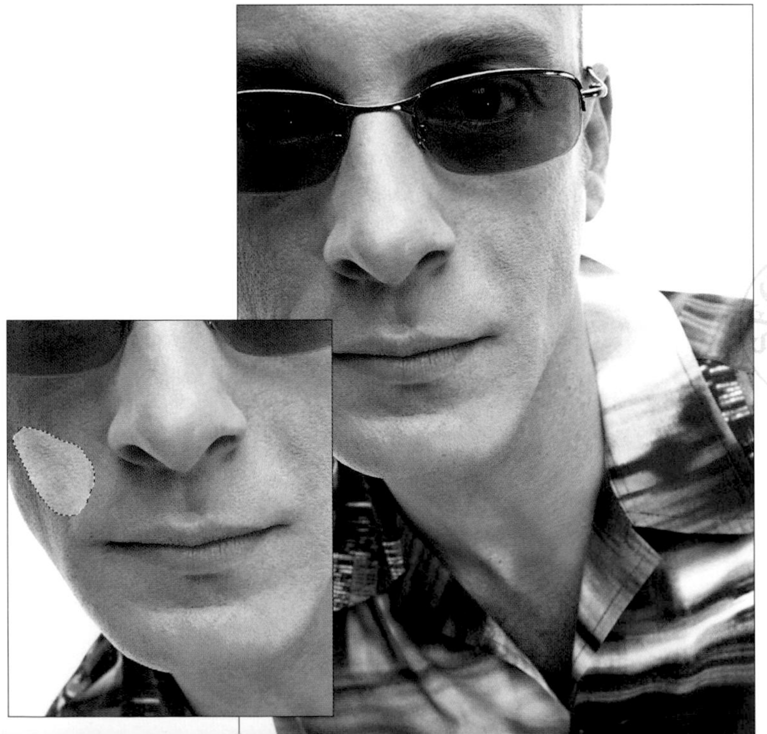

3

4

As adept as it is at removing dust and scratches from photos, the *Clone* tool has another vital use: removing the more natural kind of blemish from your digital images. Retouching has always been a key skill in conventional darkrooms, particularly when applied to portrait photography. With our digital tools, it is much, much easier to get good, flattering results.

The *Clone* tool is just one of the retouching tools in Photoshop. Even those who are adept at using it will tell you how difficult or time-consuming it can be to get a convincing result. Not only do you have to find pixels that match the area being overpainted, you also need to ensure that these are adjusted to match the texture, lighting level, lighting type and shading of those underlying.

To make the process much simpler, Photoshop 7 introduced the *Healing brush*. As if to answer the criticisms of the *Clone* tool, the *Healing brush* paints with pixels sampled from an appropriate part of the image, but it alters their brightness and contrast characteristics, adding small-scale textural variations to create a seamless blend. The *Healing brush* really comes into its own when removing blemishes from skin.

The *Patch* tool does a similar job, matching the shading, texture and lighting of the original pixels. Instead of using a brush, however, you use the tool to define an area that will then be used to 'patch' over the portion of the image that requires modification.

ANTI-AGEING

1 *Careful application of the* Patch *tool can actually reverse the effects of ageing. For a start, we can give our subject a slightly more youthful appearance by eradicating some of the harsh lines and wrinkles from his face.*

2 *Begin by identifying a region of smooth skin texture using the* Patch *tool selector. It is useful if you select an area similar to that over which you wish to apply the new texture.*

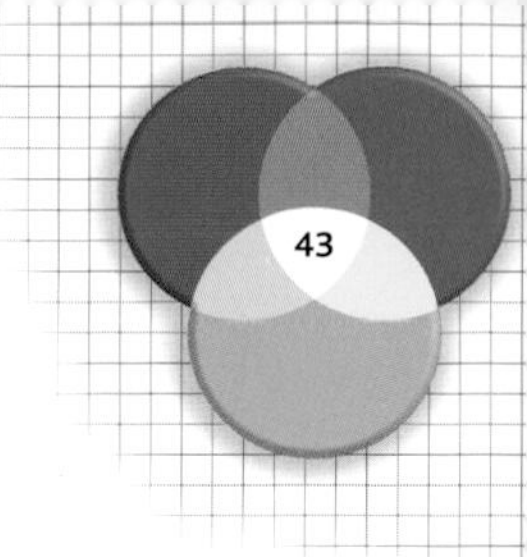

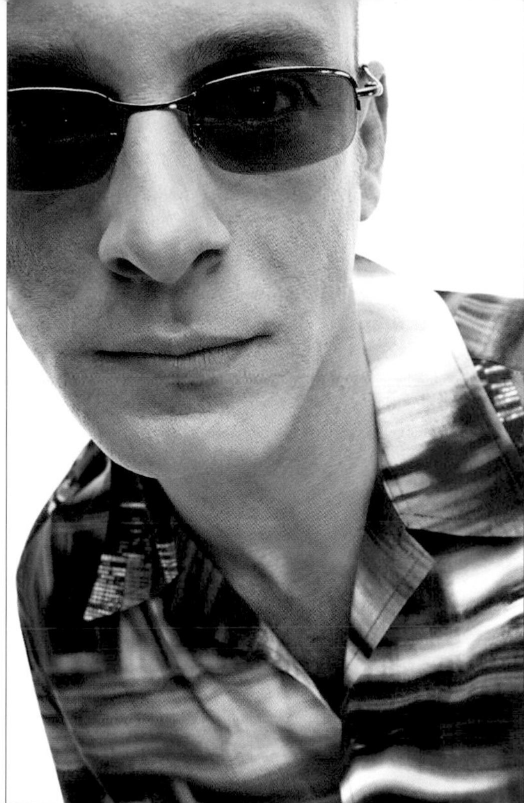

5

3 Drag the selection to the intended position and release the mouse button. The new texture will be laid over the original, but the old brightness values will show through, enabling the new patch of skin to blend in with the old.

4 Repeat the process. In this case, we have dragged a region from the sitter's left cheek to the right. The inherent brightness difference is obvious until we drop the selection.

5 Once finished, the original blemishes and wrinkles have all been removed without compromising the integrity or the original. It is also a much quicker and easier method than trying to use the Clone *tool for the same result.*

CLONING

1 Because the Patch *and* Healing brush *tools retain the underlying brightness, it may sometimes be necessary to use them in conjunction with the* Clone *tool. If we use the* Patch *tool on this female portrait, we would not get a satisfactory result: the spots we want to remove would appear through the patch.*

2 To correct this, first use the Clone *tool to obliterate the spots. This will be successful in removing the blemishes, but your corrections will probably leave some residual evidence behind.*

3 To destroy that evidence, we can use either the Patch *or the* Healing brush *to overlay those areas where the* Clone *brush has been at work. The texture of the patched areas will now take precedence over the original layer and give a more coherent overall effect.*

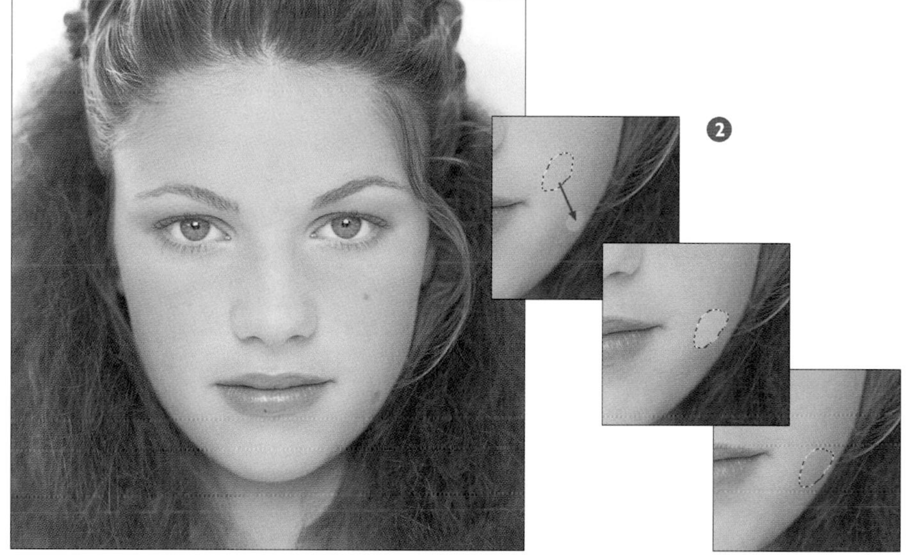

2

1

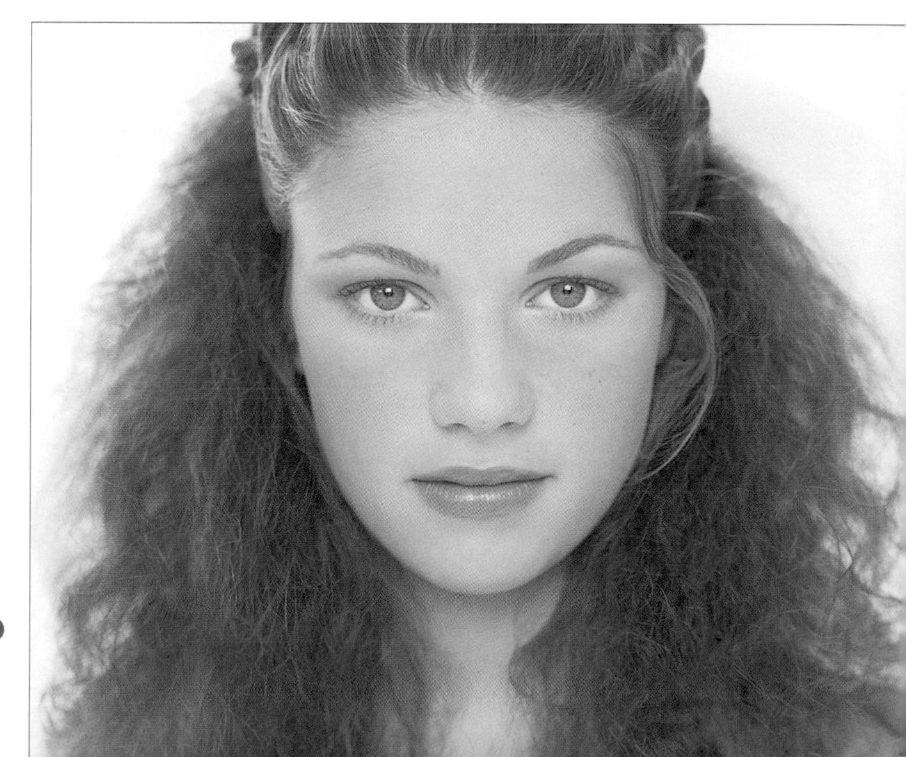

3

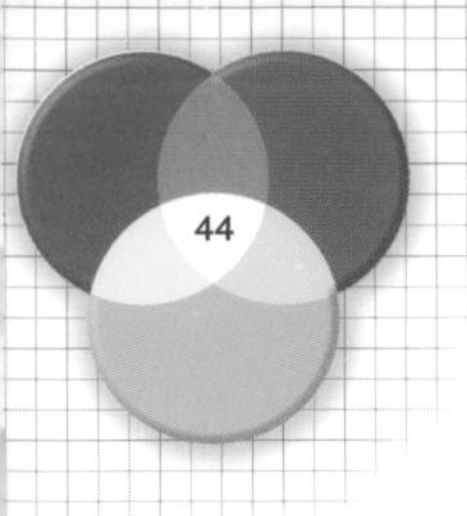

Changing parts of an image

> **DARKROOM SECRETS**
>
> **MOVING SELECTIONS**
> You can drag a selection to another part of the image (or another image altogether) by placing the Move tool's cursor inside the selection and dragging it. If you want to move only the selection boundary – and not any of the enclosed pixels – select the selection tool first and then drag with the cursor inside the selection.

There will obviously be times when we want to make changes to just part of an image, not the whole. In some previous examples, we have already done so by using tools that, like the *Paintbrush* or the *Clone* tool, produce an effect only where the tool is applied.

However, this approach is not as effective if we need to work with larger areas of an image. Luckily, Photoshop offers us a powerful alternative. We can use specialised tools to select an area of the image, and apply an effect only to the pixels in that selection. We can make this selection on the basis of a predetermined shape using the *Marquee* tool, or we can create our own, more complex shape, matching the basic form of our subject, using one of the various *Lasso* tools. We can also make selections based on colour, using the *Magic Wand*. Each of these tools has their own variants and control parameters, making it possible to select diverse subject types with relative ease.

Once we have made a selection, we can alter the pixels within that selection in any of a number of ways. We can change the colour or alter the brightness or contrast. We can even – as in the following example – paste a new image into the selection area.

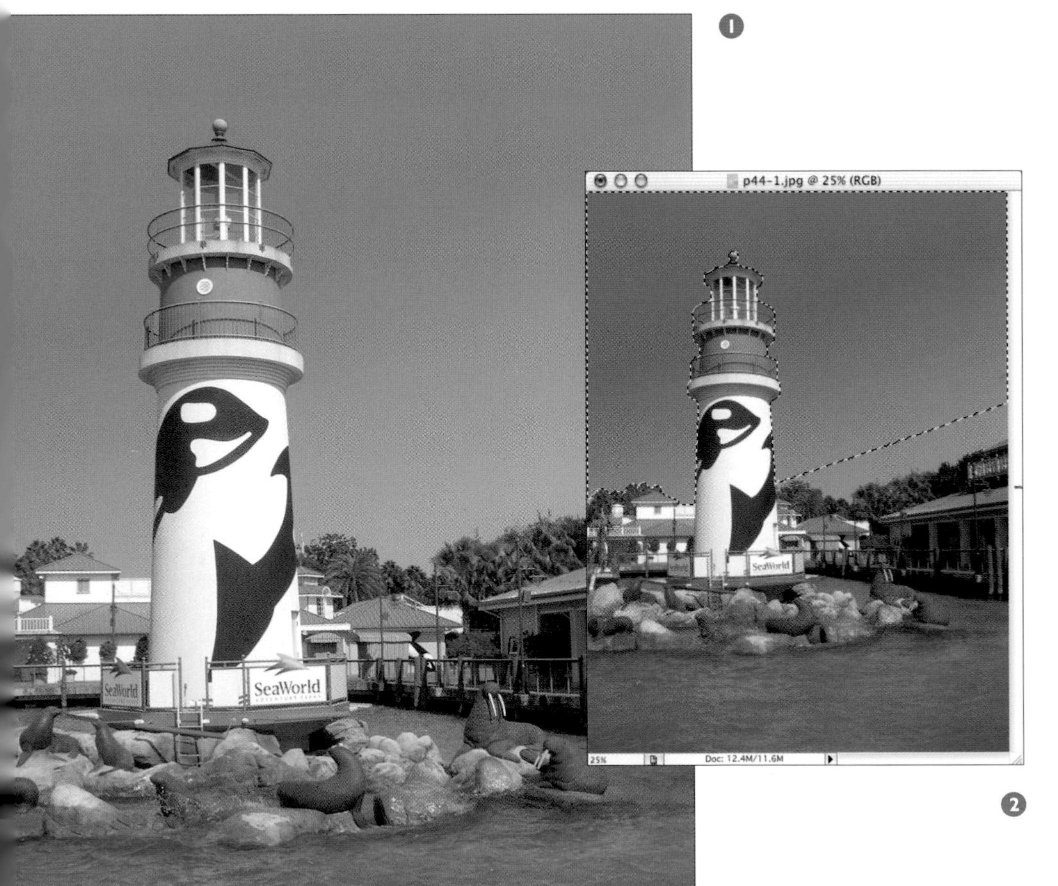

CHANGING THE SKY

1 *This photo of the harbour at Sea World, Florida, is fine, but the sky is a little boring! We will replace it with an alternative that includes a little more detail.*

2 *Begin by choosing the* Magic Wand *tool and selecting the sky region. Don't worry if you cannot select all of the sky with a single application. That very rarely happens.*

3 *Ensure that the* Add to Selection *button in the tool options palette is pressed, and select more of the sky using the* Magic Wand. *Also, make sure that you add any noncontinuous areas of sky, such as the parts visible through the lighthouse railings in this example.*

4 *Open up the image with the new sky, then select and copy an area before pasting it into the first image. It should paste into the selected area, but you need to ensure that the scale of the original image and the sky are broadly similar, or the resulting image will not be effective. To ensure that the effect is totally realistic, adjust the brightness and contrast of the sky so that both parts of the scene appear to be equally bright.*

Don't be fooled into thinking that Photoshop's selection tools are limited to the obvious options: the *Marquee*, *Magic Wand*, *Lasso* and variations. Explore the menus and you will soon discover that there are actually far more.

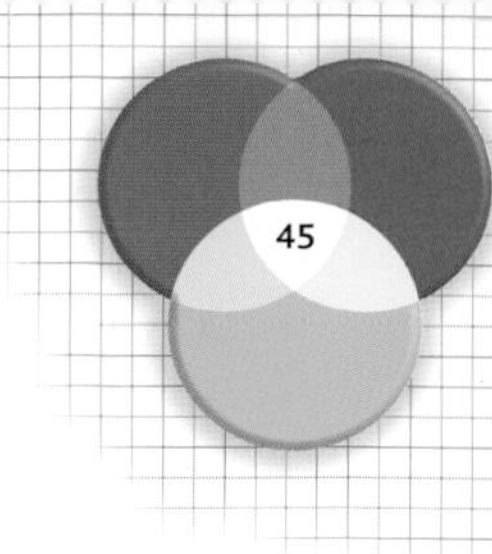

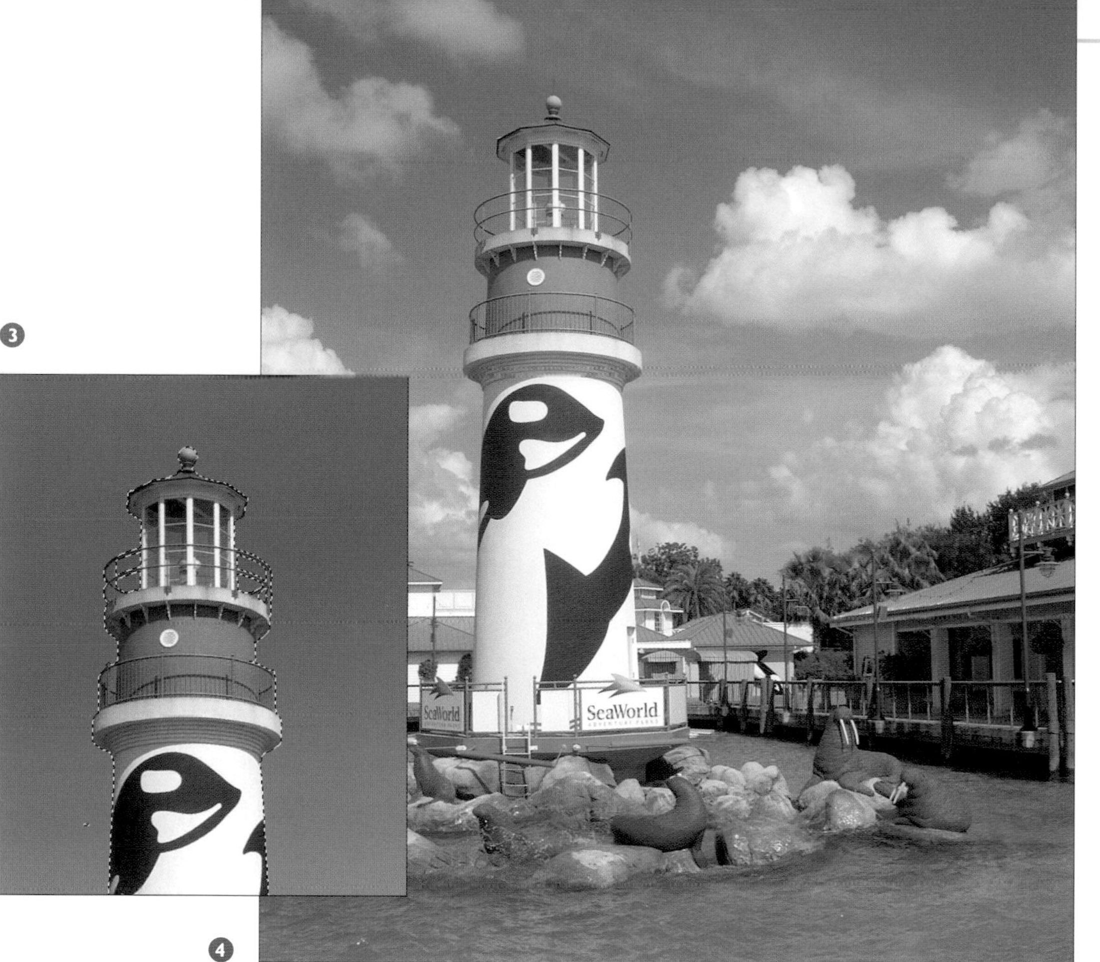

3

4

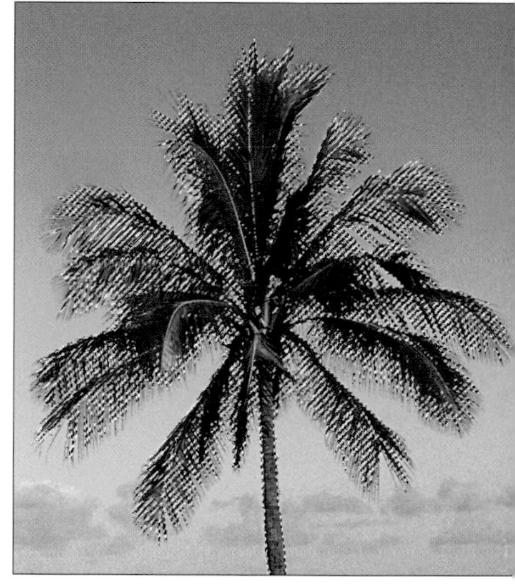

Just as we can use the Magic Wand to select every portion of this tree and seperate it from the background, we can use the Magic Eraser to select and then remove the sky from behind this lighthouse, piece by piece.

There is, for example, the *Eraser* tool. While it might not seem like a selection tool, it has two variations – the *Background Eraser* and *Magic Eraser* – that are very effective when used in this way. Unlike the conventional selection tools, these work by isolating the subject on a transparent layer, identifying and discarding any image elements outside of the subject boundary. You can see this in action in the image to the right. In principle, the erasers work in the same way as many masking and extraction tools, including Photoshop's *Extract* command or Procreate's *Knockout* plug-in tool.

What's more, the 'raw' selection tools are complemented by a host of features that enable us to modify a selection in very subtle ways. We can, for example, nudge selections larger so that the selection can be increased in size by the smallest of increments. We can select other parts of an image that conform to the criteria set for the selection, which can be very useful when, for example, we want to select the sky in an image and make sure that every single piece is selected, or check that our selection captures every leaf and branch on a tree.

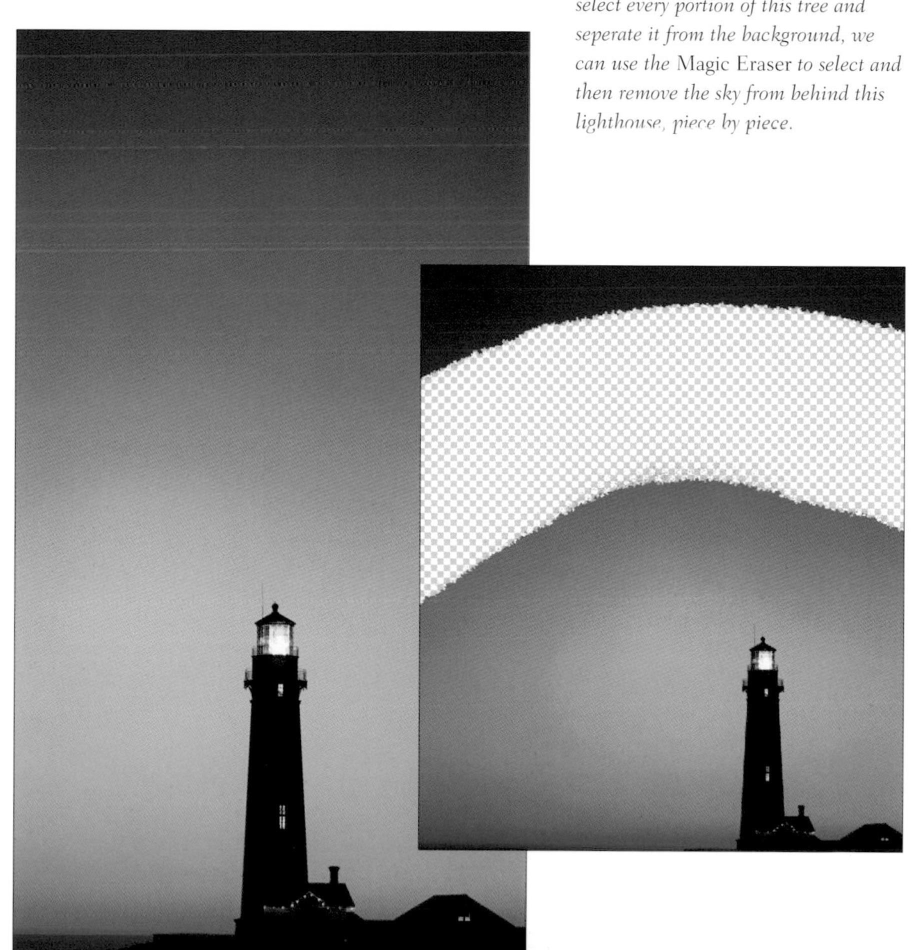

Selections, frames, and vignetting

This framing device uses the marquee to select the central area of the image. By inverting the selection and applying a gentle Gaussian blur to the area outside, this subtle frame is produced.

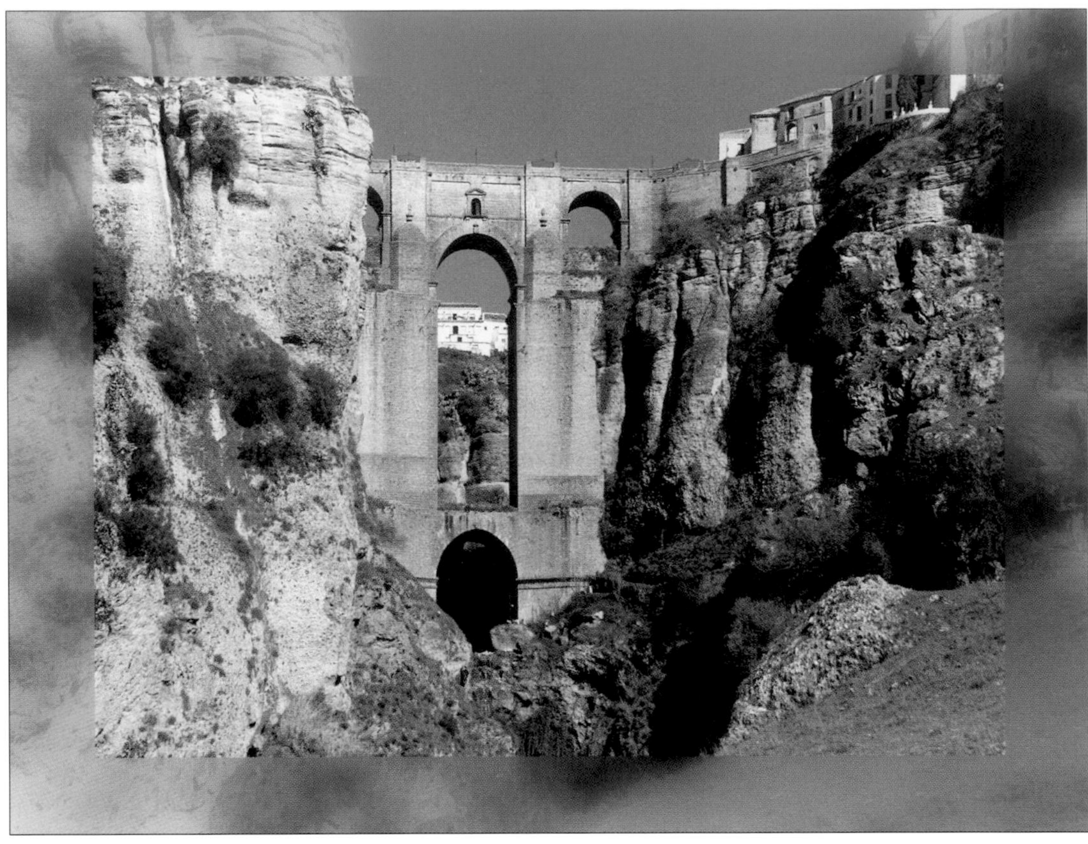

DARKROOM SECRETS

THE SINGLE COLUMN MARQUEE

The *Marquee* tool's curious single line and single column options do have a purpose. They can be used for fine-trimming errant lines from a cropped image – a job they do with ease.

They can also be used to repair screen capture shots, where fine delineating lines can be replaced, or to fix scans where an erroneous line has appeared. Simply copy the scan line immediately below the damaged one and paste it over the blemish.

The simplest selection tool is the *Marquee*, used to select rectangular or elliptical areas of the canvas. To create a selection, you just click where you want the top left corner to be, and drag down and to the right to make your shape. To create a perfect circle or square, just hold down the shift key while dragging the mouse.

Having drawn the initial selection, you can also position it more accurately, either by dragging it around in the image window, or by moving it incrementally up, down or sideways using the cursor keys.

At times, the standard way of forming the marquee, drawn corner to corner, is less than ideal. If you are trying to create a symmetrical selection, it's often best to hold the Alt key (Windows) or Option key (Mac), then 'pull' the selection outwards from a central point.

The *Marquee* tool can also be used to select an area of a fixed size or shape, which may be useful if you are planning to use the selection in another image or on the Web. You can constrain the selection by aspect ratio, setting the ratio between the width and the height, or even define an absolute fixed size. In Photoshop, this is done from the *Style* pulldown menu on the context-sensitive *Options* bar.

As a bonus, when using the square or rectangular *Marquee,* you can easily crop the image to the selection (select *Image* > ***Crop***).

THE MARQUEE AS A CREATIVE TOOL

The marquee comes into its own in the creation of vignettes and frames. Clichéd though some of these effects may be, they can produce attractive images. In the image above, for example, a

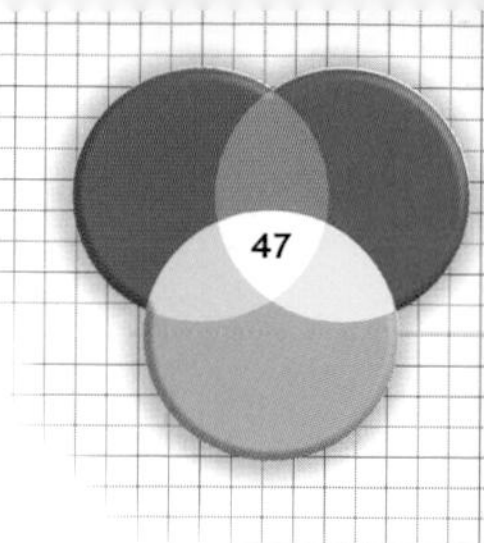

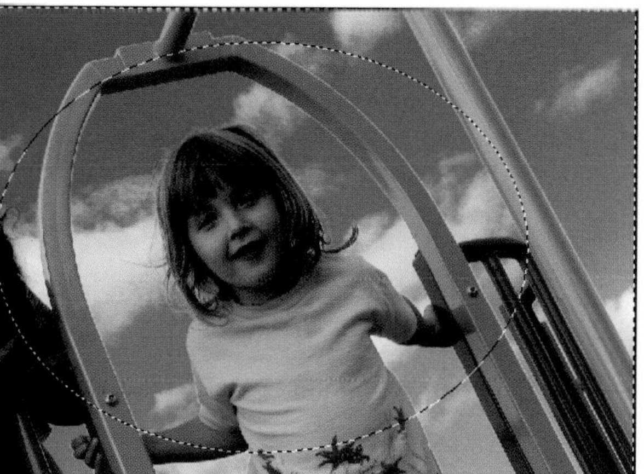

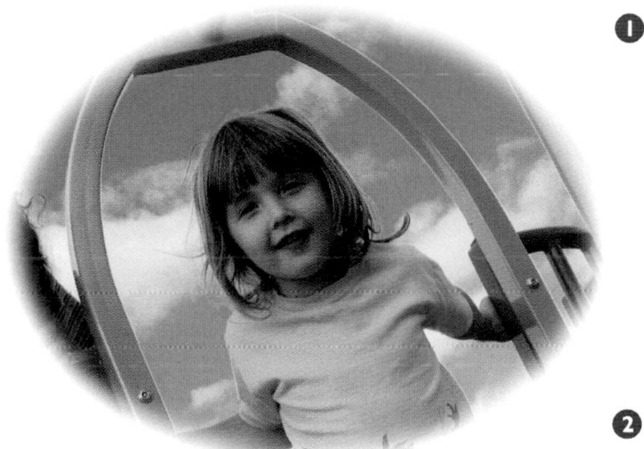

marquee has been drawn around the central image, and that selection has been inverted (*Select* > **Inverse**). With a *Gaussian blur* filter applied, we get an instant and distinctive frame. A simple vignette is just as easy to create.

CREATING A VIGNETTE

1 *Firstly, set a feather radius of around 25 pixels and select the elliptical* Marquee. *Now make your selection, ensuring that the marquee is placed symmetrically over the subject. Either use the Alt/Option-drag method, or create a selection of the right shape and then move it into position.*

2 *Invert the selection* (Select > **Inverse**) *and press the delete key. This removes the area outside the selection and leaves the selection with the trademark soft edge.*

SOFTENING THE EDGE

The hard edges of the standard selection tools are not ideal in many circumstances. When applying a filter or a colour correction to a part of an image, the combination of a visible change with a clean edge can make the affected area stand out from the rest of the image. To blend a selection in, it is best to give it a softer edge through feathering.

A feathered edge fades to transparent over a distance – called the feathering radius – set by the user. You can set a feathering radius prior to making the selection (using the box on the Tool Options *bar). If you make a selection without applying feathering and afterwards decide that you want one, you can apply a radius remedially by selecting* Select > **Feather** *and entering an appropriate radius. The latter is especially useful with tools such as the* Lasso, *when a delicate selection may have taken some time to complete.*

Feathering and image size

It is important to remember that feathering – and the feathering radius – is measured in absolute terms of a finite number of pixels. Hence, when the same feathering radius is applied to images of different pixel dimensions, the feathering effect will also differ.

In the two example images shown here, a feathering radius of 25 pixels has been applied in each case. The first image has absolute dimensions of 250 x 275 pixels. The effect is a very soft feathering in which the image appears to blend gradually into the background.

In the second case, the same image has been reproduced with dimensions of 750 x 825 pixels. The result, when the image is reproduced at the same size, is a much more obvious feathering gradient and boundary.

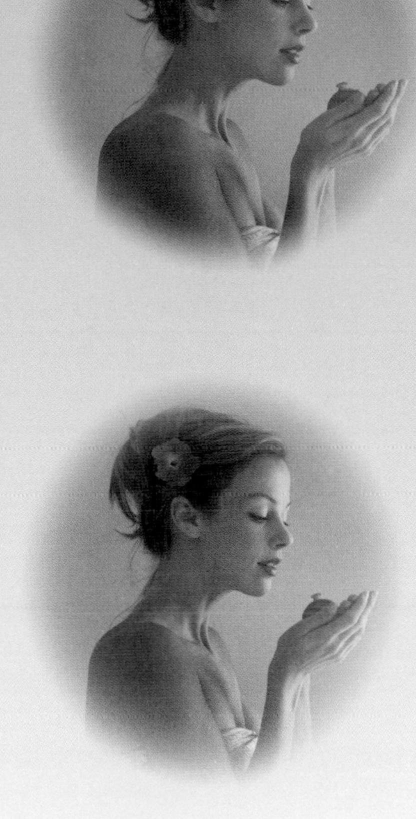

An eliptical Marquee *with a feathering radius of 25 pixels has been applied to two differently sized copies of the same image, one of 750 x 825 pixels (top) and one of 250 x 275 pixels (bottom).*

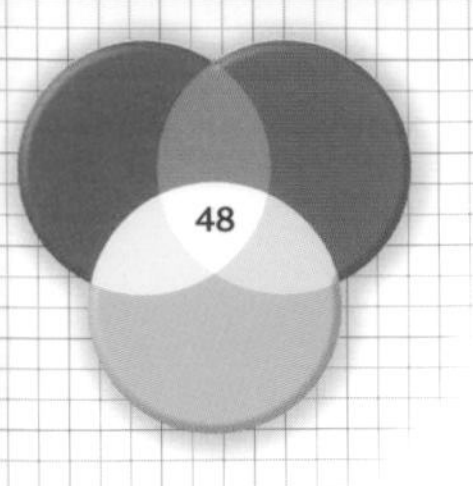

Cutouts and the lasso

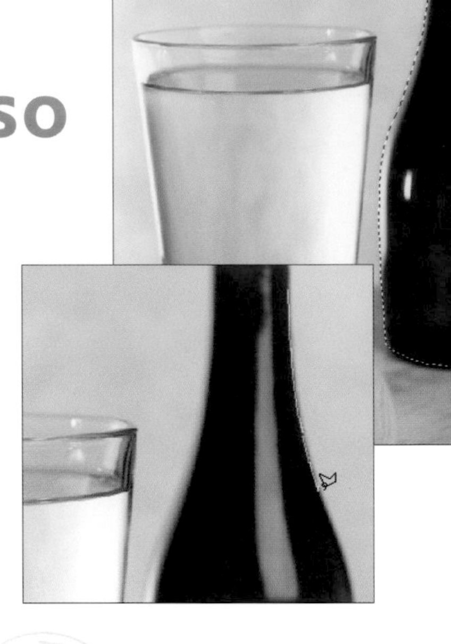

RIGHT
Don't think of the polygonal lasso as being good only for describing rectilinear forms; it is suitable (and quite adept) for selecting curved surfaces, particularly when combined with feathering.

DARKROOM SECRETS

POWER TO YOUR LASSO

The *Lasso's* selection closure that results from letting go of the mouse key – even momentarily – has driven even the most dedicated user to distraction. If only they knew: hold down the Alt key (Windows) or Option key (Mac), and you can release the mouse key to reposition the mouse or take a quick swig of coffee. And when that key is pressed, you can also drag the mouse and draw a dead-straight line. Click the mouse and release the key to continue. This trick works with both the conventional and magnetic lassos. There's no need for this on the polygonal lasso, as all its movements take the form of straight lines.

The marquee tools are fine for regularly shaped objects, but once you start dealing with more complex or irregular forms, you need to reach for the *Lasso* tools. By using the *Lasso* to draw around the outlines of an object, you can use it to describe any shape on the canvas.

So far, so good. However, the *Lasso* is a dumb tool, and will draw a line only where you tell it to. Unless you have a brain surgeon's delicacy and precision of touch, this can be a challenge. Worse, the *Lasso* has one very annoying attribute. Let go of the mouse button and your selection is immediately closed (that is, your current selection point will join to the start point).

Fortunately, the *Lasso* also comes in two other flavours: the *Magnetic Lasso* and the *Polygonal Lasso*. The former tries to intelligently select an object by 'sticking' to the edges as you draw around. The latter enables you to draw in straight lines around the shape, clicking where you want to set a new anchor point.

At first glance, the *Polygonal Lasso* might seem useless on anything except shapes with perfectly straight edges. You can use it, however, to select less regular shapes by defining the edges using very short lines. When combined with a modest feather radius (two or three pixels), you can describe complex shapes with ease.

Don't be disappointed if you don't get a precise selection with your *Lasso*; aim to make a good selection and you can always use other features – such as the *Quick Mask* (*see page 54*) – to make fine adjustments later.

You can also use feathering with any of the lasso types. A small radius (one or two pixels) is often recommended if the selection is to be used in another image as part of a montage to provide a soft, more authentic edge that melds successfully with the host image.

The *Lasso* tools are ideal for creating cutout selections, but these don't just have to be used in photo montage. In this example, we can cut out the main subject of a photo in order to separate him from a distracting background.

PULLING OUT THE SUBJECT

1 *Selecting the background to this portrait is an ideal job for the* Magnetic Lasso. *The boundaries (edges) of the subject are well defined, which will make it reasonably easy for the tool to spot the edge.*

2 *Begin by setting the tool parameters. In Photoshop 6 and later (including Photoshop Elements), the parameters are displayed in the tool options bar. We can set the* Contrast *(the degree of edge contrast detected), the* Line Frequency *(number of samples) and a feathering radius.*

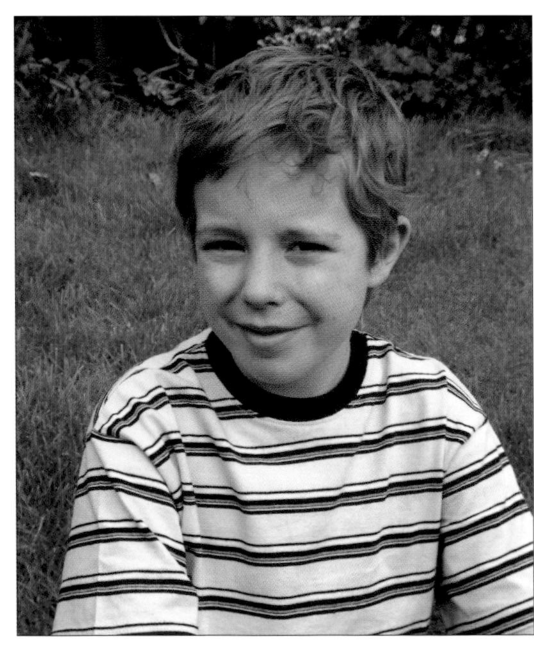
1

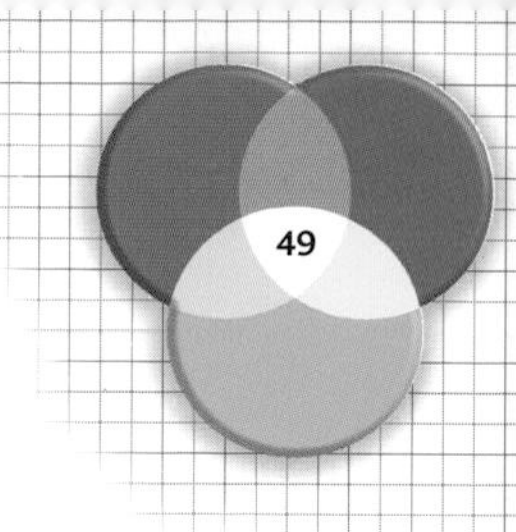

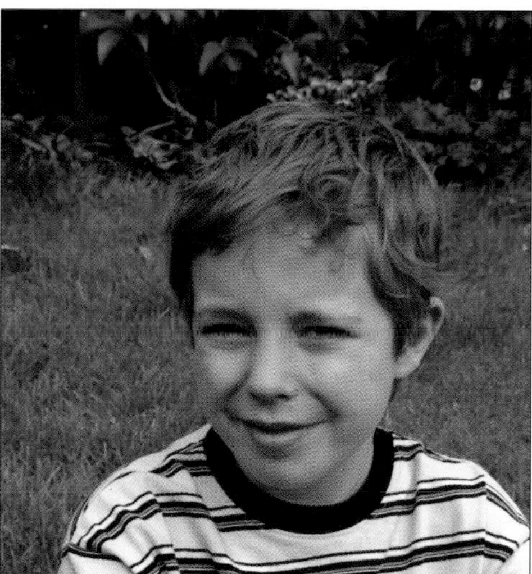

2

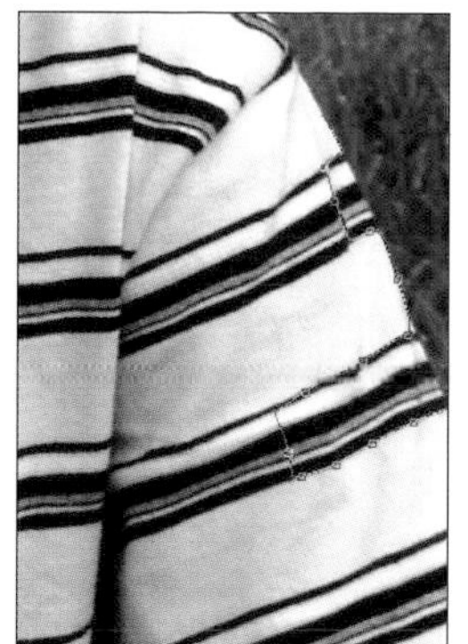

3

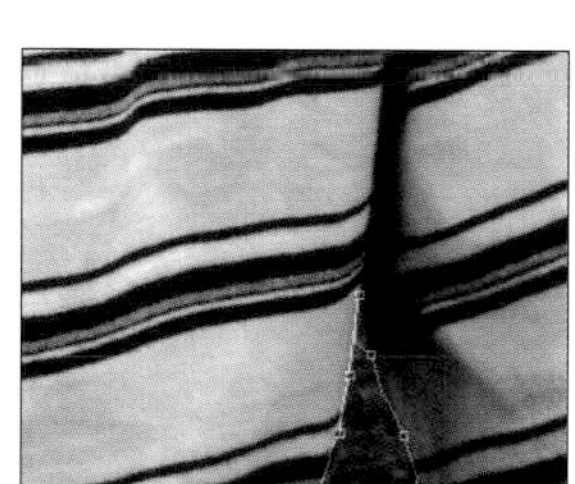

4

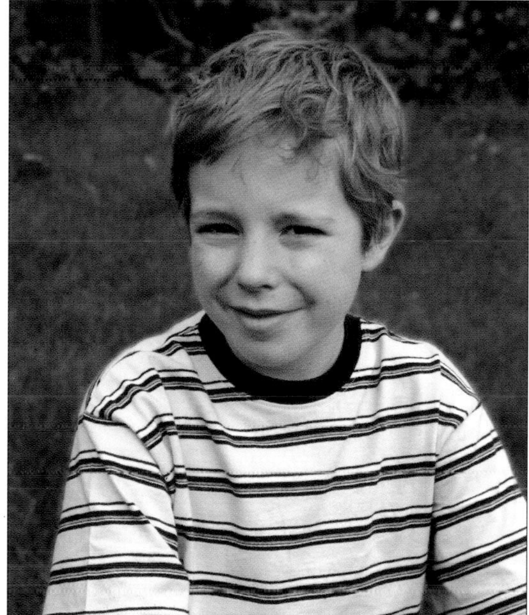

5

3 *Begin drawing the outline of the subject. The* Magnetic Lasso *will automatically attach itself to the edge. If the* Lasso *attaches incorrectly (to the the stripes in the shirt in this example), you can drag it backwards and click along the edge, which 'forces' the* Lasso *to follow your chosen path.*

4 *Continue around the subject. Remember to include any subsidiary areas (such as under the arms) so they will not be included in the selection.*

5 *With our subject selected, we could copy this selection to a new, plain background image. In this case, however, we have inverted the selection, and then desaturated the background with the* Hue/Saturation *tool to make it less distracting.*

MAGNETIC LASSO

The Magnetic Lasso *is an intelligent tool, in that it can identify the edge of your subject and, in response to your crude outline, follow it precisely. Or so the software manuals would have you believe. In fact, it is not always quite that smart. When using it, we tend to be lazy about the outlining, assuming the tool will know our intentions when it won't.*

The Magnetic Lasso *works best with strong outlines, so it is fine when you have a hard-edged object against a plain background. It is not so effective when your intended selection is just one of many objects whose edge the* Lasso *could latch on to. Low contrast also makes the path less distinct in the eyes of the lasso and can result in it going off course. Still, there are some ways of getting the best from it.*

Don't let the lasso do all the work: *By clicking along the path, you can add new anchor points, helping to lock it to the correct edge in areas where there might be confusion.*

Add anchor points to sharp corners: *The algorithm that defines the path tends to smooth acute angles and even some obtuse ones. Add an anchor point to any corner to be sure that the line stays in shape.*

Backtracking: *If the* Lasso *has taken the wrong course, just move the mouse backwards and that section will be deleted. If an automatic anchor point has been dropped and you want to remove that too, use the delete key.*

The magnetic lasso doesn't always correctly identify the edge of your subject. If you're having difficulties getting a clean selection, backtrack and add anchor points where necessary.

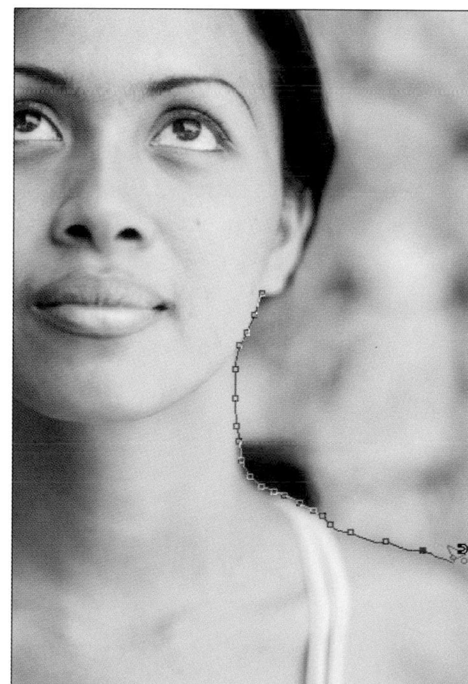

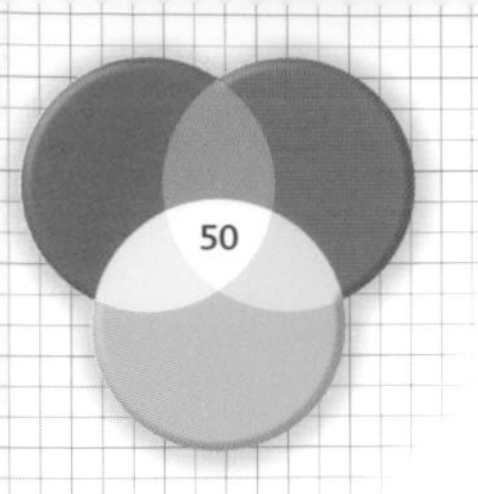

Image extraction

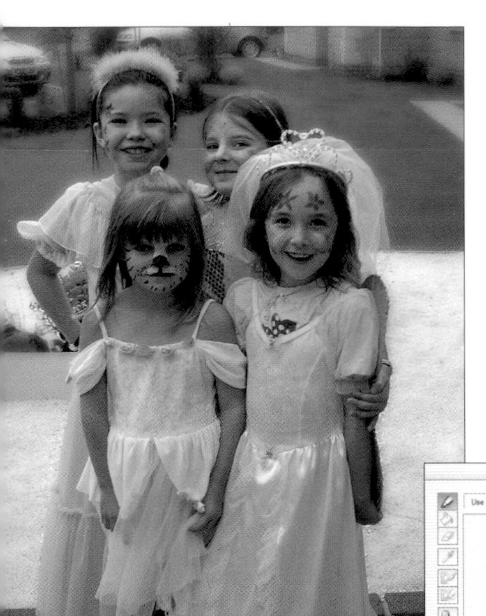

❶

With skill, patience and a little practice, we can create cutouts using the *Lasso* tools, but there can be an easier way. Anyone who has spent any time using the *Magnetic Lasso* will know that some subjects, particularly people and animals, prove difficult to select when they do not have a precise edge. Fly-away hair may by ideal for a shampoo commercial, but it is a nightmare in the digital darkroom!

As accurate image extraction is essential for some tasks, this has given rise to some tools designed specifically for the purpose.

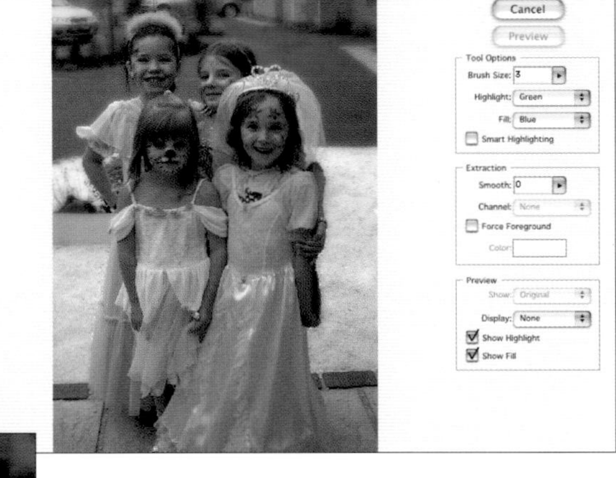

❷

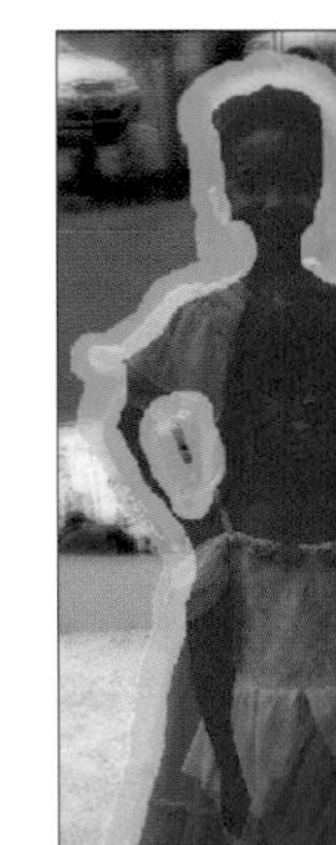

❸

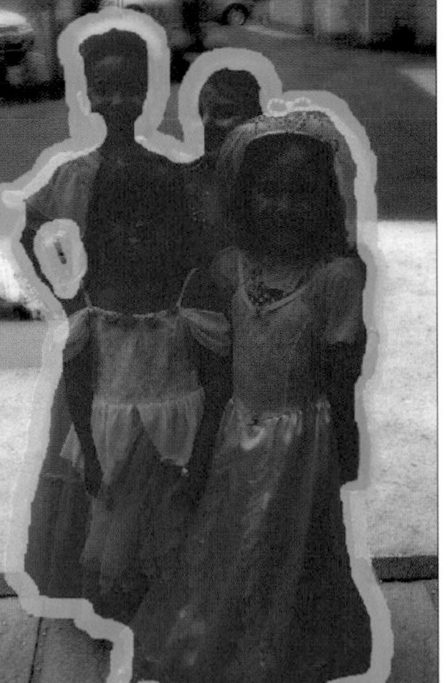

❹

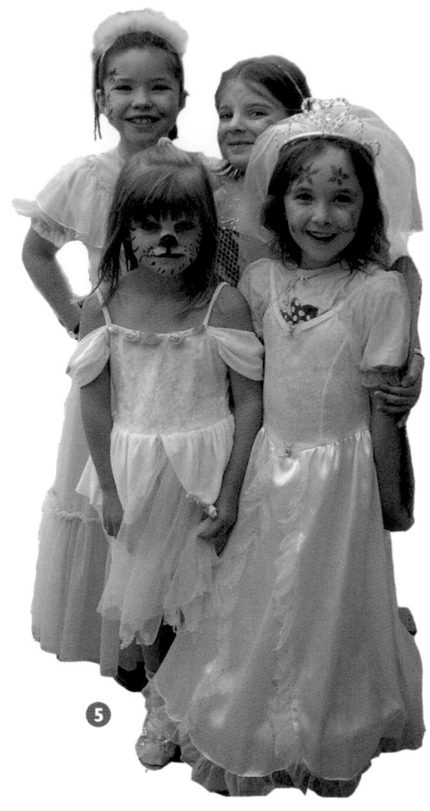

❺

Photoshop Extract

The *Extract* feature in Photoshop (and Photoshop Elements) works by using a 'highlighter pen' to describe a transitional zone around an object. The *Extract* tool then analyses the pixels in the transition zone to determine whether they should be apportioned to the subject or the background. This can be clumsy at first, but refine the selection and you can get a very good extraction that would take hours using the *Lasso* tool.

EXTRACTING THE EASY WAY

1 *This photograph is an ideal candidate for the use of* Extract. *Though most of the subject boundaries are sharp, there are regions of hair and a fluffy headdress that could cause problems for other selection tools.*

2 *The* Extract *dialog box features the control buttons ranged to the left and the settings for these to the right of the image.*

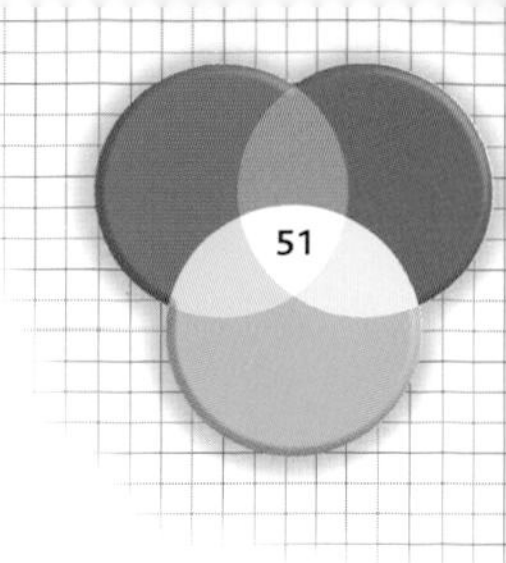

3 *Begin by using the* Smart Highlighter, *which works a little like the* Magnetic Lasso, *to define the edge of the subjects. It is important to subtract any regions (such as inside the arm, to the left) that should be excluded from the extraction.*

4 *Use the* Flood *tool to fill the area with colour. This useful check ensures that the boundaries have been properly defined and that regions not to be included have been discounted. Press the* Preview *button if you are happy with the selection.*

5 *If the preview looks ragged at the edges, use the* Cleanup *tool to add or subtract areas from the edges and the* Edge Touchup *tool to smooth them. When you are happy, perform the extraction. Notice how the tricky hair and headdress regions have been accurately extracted.*

6 *We can now apply the extracted image element to our new image. Here a simple radial gradient has been combined with the* Outer Glow *and* Drop Shadow layer styles.

6

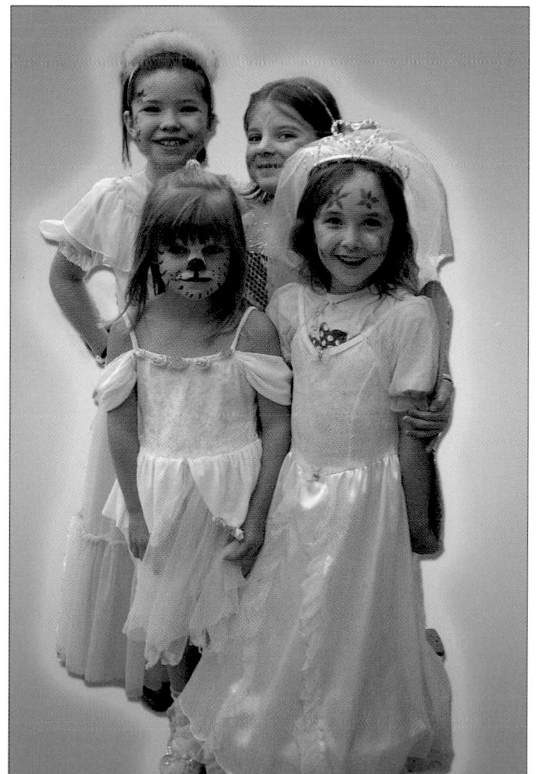

KnockOut

Procreate KnockOut is a commercial plug-in that does a similar job to the Extract tool, and has long been a favourite of professionals. Extracting the owl in this image would be a nightmare using conventional tools: its loose feathers would be too confusing. With KnockOut, it is a simple three stage process.

USING KNOCKOUT

1 *Make a duplicate layer of the image, then choose* KnockOut *from the* Filters *menu of the host application (such as Photoshop). KnockOut starts with the new image layer on the desktop.*

2 *Click on the* Inside Object *tool (a pen in a circle) and draw around the inside edge of the subject. Don't be too precise; we are aiming only to select the colours and contrast levels that make up the perimeter. The* Inside Object Addition *and* Subtraction *buttons can be used to add or subtract areas from the selection. Now select the* Outside Object *tool (pen outside circle icon) and draw close to – but not touching – the outer edge of the subject. There is an option to generate this line automatically, but it normally needs tweaking to produce useful results. Again, you can use the relevant addition and subtraction buttons to fine-tune the perimeter line.*

3 *Having created the transition zone, we need to set a transition complexity setting that will work for the image. The options are relatively self-explanatory. They simply define the number of colours that are identified in the transitional zone.*

Press the process button to make the selection, and your extracted image will appear. By holding down the Command key (Mac) or Ctrl (Windows) and a number key, you can alternate views between the original image, the extracted selection and the border area that separates the two. If you are happy with the final result, just return to your host application with your selection ready to use.

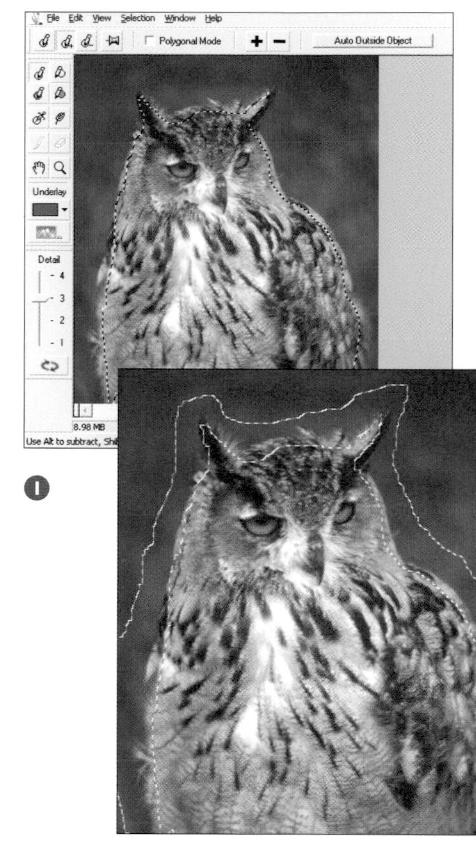

1

2

3

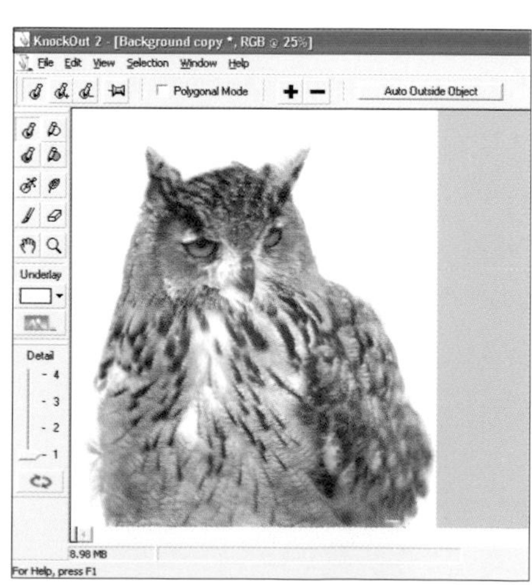

Selecting and changing colour

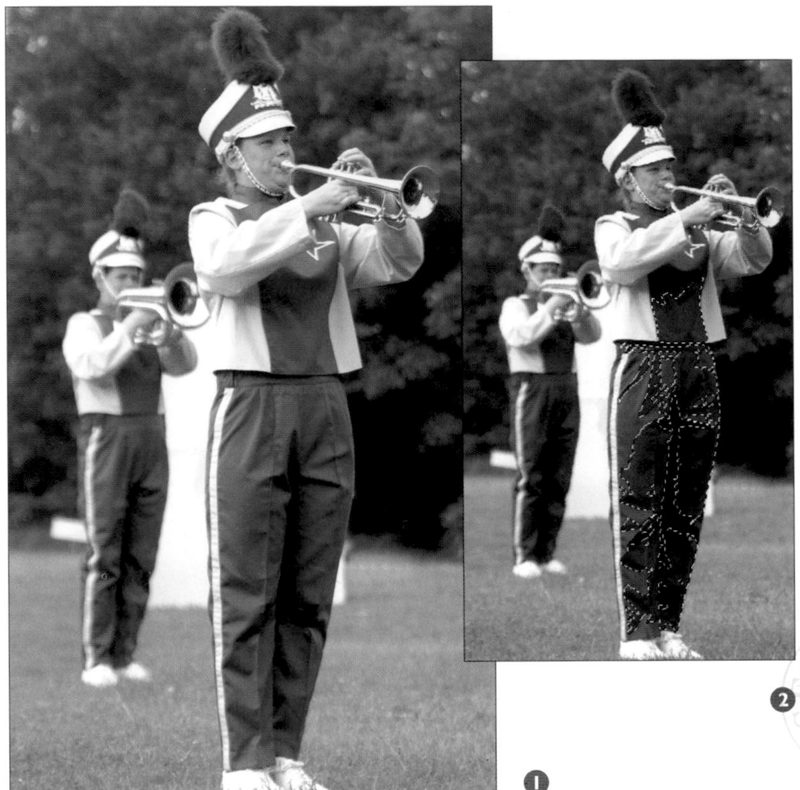

1 2

There is something of a knack to using the *Magic Wand*. Often the first attempt to select an area of colour results in only a partial selection, and the amateur mistake is to increase the *Tolerance*, and try again. This usually ends up selecting the intended area, but most of the surrounding area too! Rather than increase the *Tolerance*, it is better to keep a median value (about 20–30) and make multiple selections, adding incrementally to get exactly what we want. If you overstep the mark, you can simply undo the previous step and try again. Isolated pixels can be pulled into the selection using the *Grow* and *Similar* commands.

The *Magic Wand* can be the easiest way of selecting an object for extraction. As it is based on colour, it also makes sense to use it if we need to change certain colours in an image wholesale.

CHANGING COLOURS BY MAGIC

1 *The colour in these band members' uniforms can be changed from their original blue using the* Magic Wand, Grow *and* Similar *commands.*

2 *Begin by selecting the blue of the uniform on the principal subject. You may need to make repeated selections.*

3 *Apply the* Grow *command to extend the selection to the adjoining pixels. This ensures that those pixels which are partly coloured in the boundary regions are also added to the selection.*

4 *To add the range of blue tones in the second band member's uniform and in the hats, choose the* Similar *command. All blue tones similar to that in the original selection elsewhere in the image will now be added to the selection.*

5 *Now we have all the blue elements selected, we can change the colour. The easiest way is to use the* Hue/Saturation *control. By moving the* Hue *slider, we can change the blue into any other colour, including this charming cerise.*

DARKROOM SECRETS 

TIDYING UP YOUR SELECTION

Grow and *Similar* can also be used as 'tidy-up' controls. When we make colour-based selections, there are often odd pixels that, due to noise or other artefacts, are quite different in colour to their surroundings. These tend to get orphaned by the *Magic Wand*, but become obvious when the selection colour or characteristics are changed. Use the *Grow* and *Similar* commands to add these rogue spots to your selection and make it complete.

As we saw on page 44, selections are not restricted to shapes: they can also be made based on colour. The *Magic Wand* might not be particularly magical, but it is an effective tool for pulling image elements that share tonal values into a selection. Car bodywork and items of clothing are just two examples of subjects for which it is ideally suited.

To make a selection, simply click on the area of tone you wish to select. Any pixels that share the tonal range or a similar value and are conjoined (connected along an edge to the selected pixel) will be included. By similar, we mean areas whose tones are lighter and darker than the selected one but that may vary in precise colour. We can set how much of this variation is allowed before an area is excluded from a selection by setting a *tolerance* setting (measured in tonal values between 0 and 255).

3

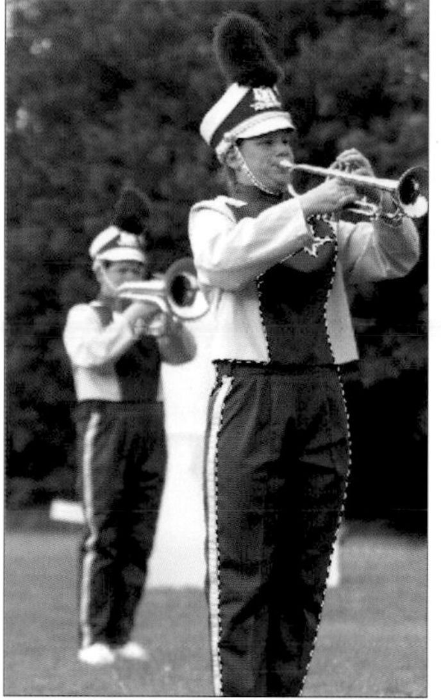

4

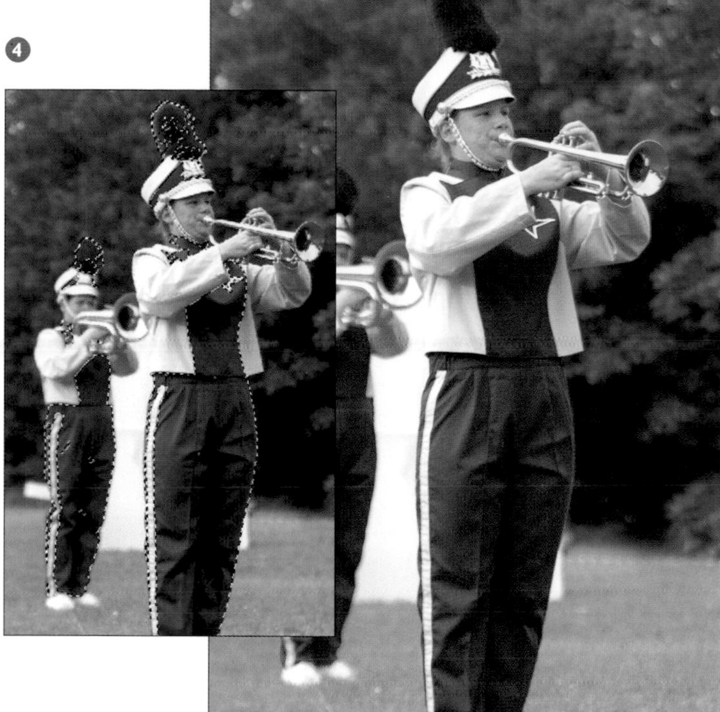

5

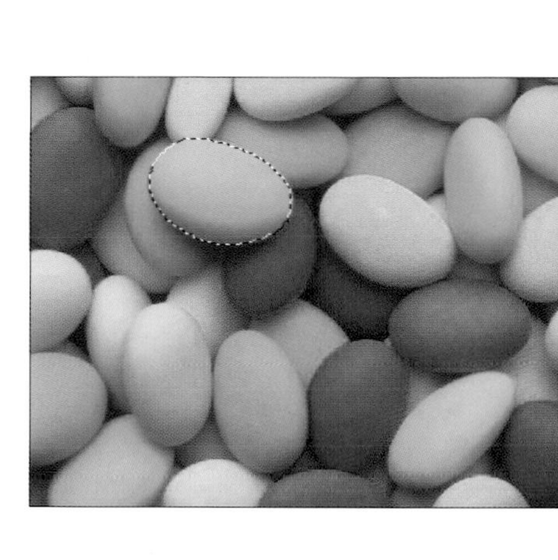

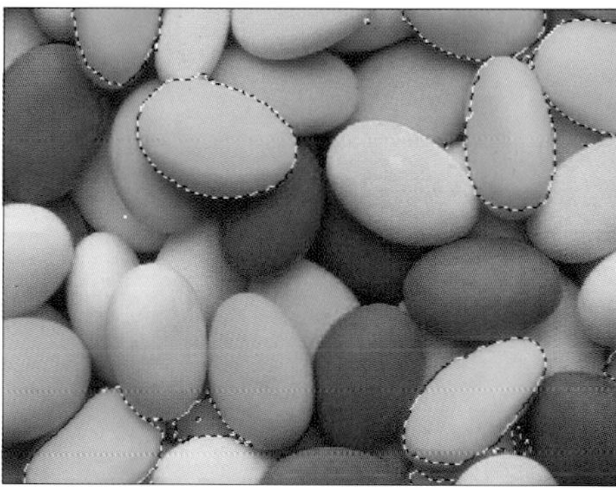

Select one element and it becomes easy to select others of a similar hue using the Similar *command.*

GROW AND SIMILAR

Two commands really come into their own when using the *Magic Wand*: *Grow* and *Similar*. Both can be found in the *Select* menu. *Grow* expands a selection by picking adjacent pixels if they conform broadly to the colour and tonal criterion of the original selection (although the actual assessment method is somewhat more tortuous than it sounds).

The *Similar* command, conversely, selects those pixels similar to those of the original selection that are not physically connected to one of the original pixels. This can be of particular use when selecting similarly coloured objects scattered over an image, such as picking all the red apples on an apple tree or all the green coloured pebbles in the image to the right.

COLOR RANGE

You can think of the Color Range *command* (Select > **Color Range**) *as an amalgam of the* Magic Wand *and the* Grow *and* Similar *commands. From the* Color Range *dialog box, you can select a colour in the image and select all pixels of similar colour. This time you have a* Fuzziness *control instead of the* Magic Wand's Tolerance. *Unlike the* Tolerance *control, the fuzziness setting won't determine which pixels are included and which are not. Rather, it determines how a pixel is selected. Those close to the selected colour will be 100% selected; those further away but still within the fuzziness range will be only partially selected. A partially selected pixel will still be affected by any manipulation applied to the resultant selection, but only in proportion to its degree (or percentage) of selectivity.*

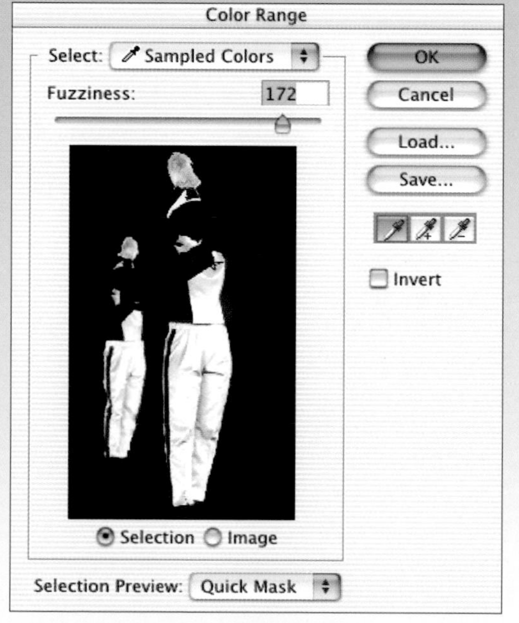

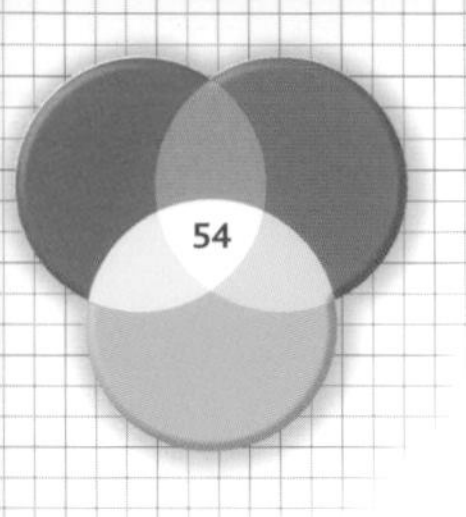

Refining and saving selections

1

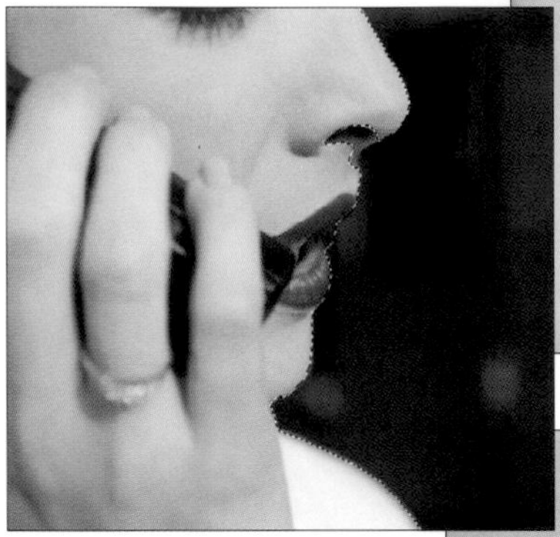

2

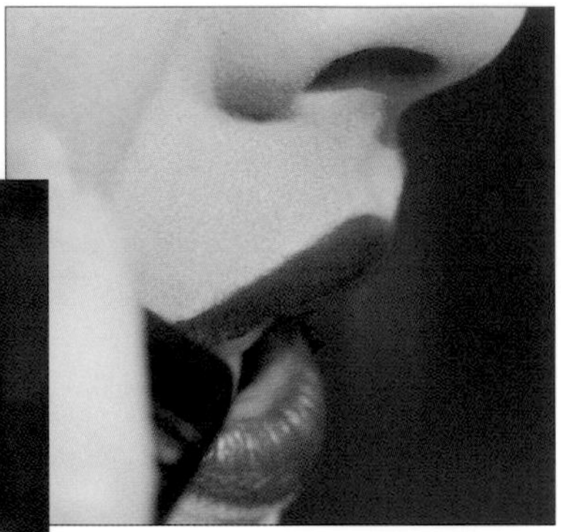

3

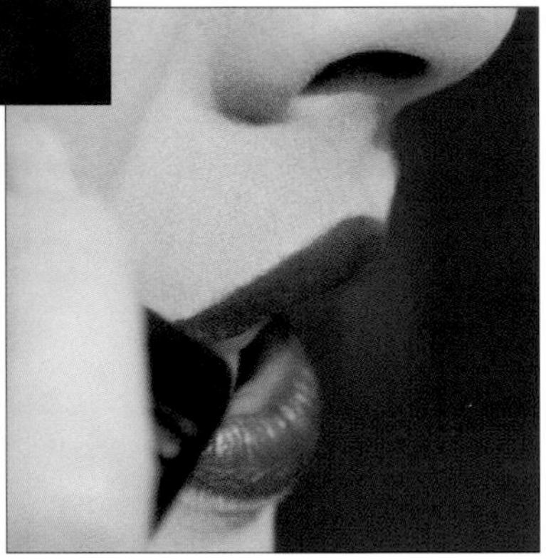

4

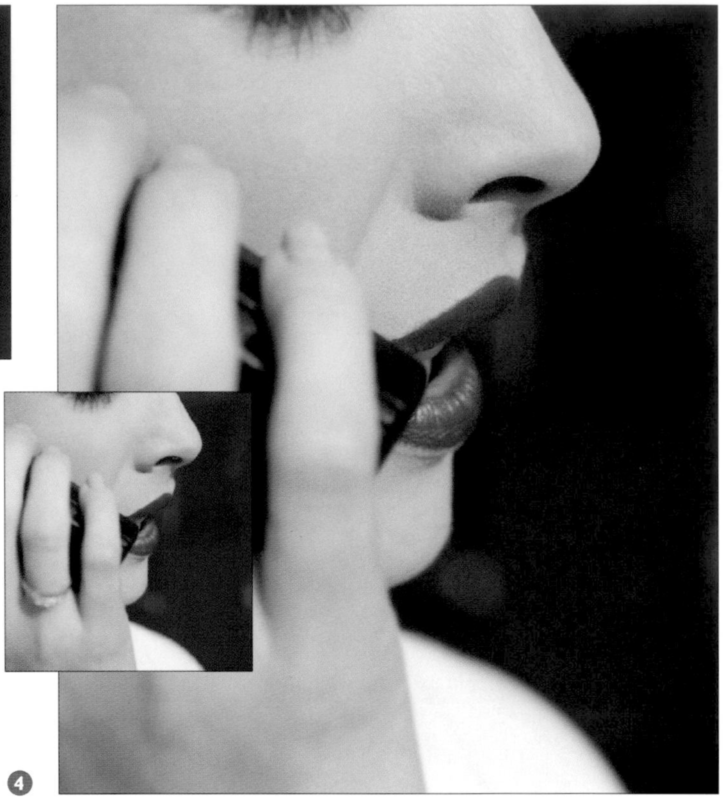

Creating a selection of a complex objects takes time, and the basic selection tools rarely get it completely right in every case. In addition, if you are repeatedly manipulating one or more objects, it makes sense to avoid having to make the same selection again and again. Luckily, Photoshop has tools that can help us tidy selections and then save them for later use.

The trick to refining selections is to get used to using the *Quick Mask*. To start with, press the *Quick Mask* button on the toolbar. The mask appears as a coloured overlay on your image – any existing selection will appear as a clear, 'unmasked' area.

THE QUICK MASK

1 *In this example, the* Lasso *has taken short cuts, leaving areas of background out of the selection, and appending part of the subject's nose.*

2 *Switch to the* Quick Mask, *then select an appropriate brush and the black paint, which adds pixels to the mask and removes them from the current selection. Here, using a fine-tipped brush, we can mask out those areas of the background between the model's lips.*

3 *Similarly, we can use white paint to remove the masking from areas that should not be protected. Note too that if you make a mistake (removing or adding too much mask), you can correct using the opposite paint colour.*

4 *With modifications complete, the mask covers only the intended area. We can press the* Normal *mode button to return to normal mode and make any changes. In this case, we have applied a* Hue/Saturation *change to the background, turning it blue to add a colour contrast to the image.*

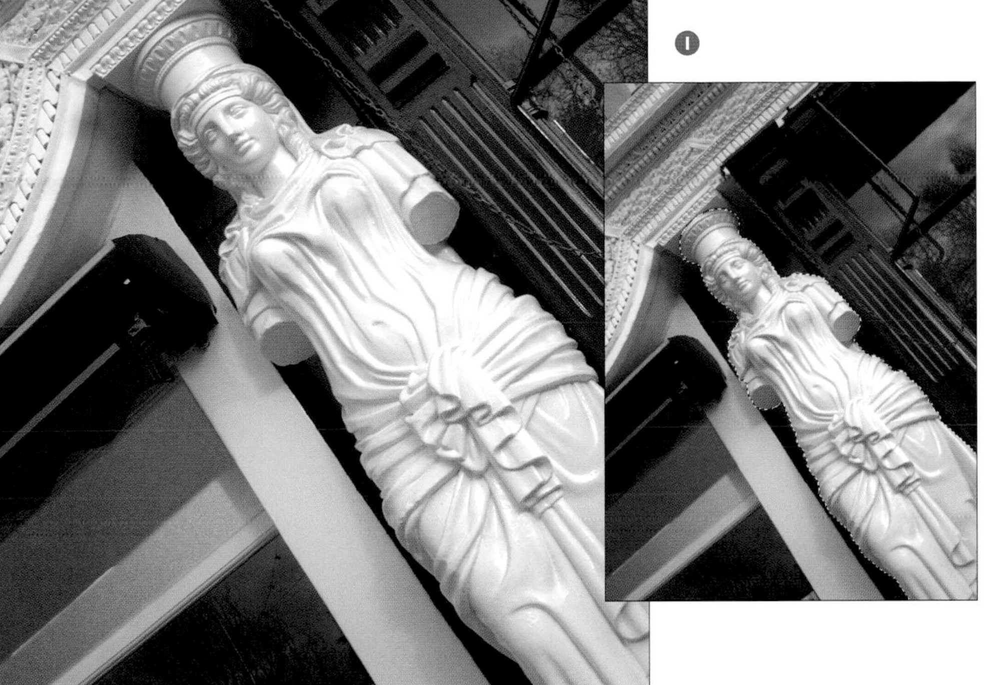

1

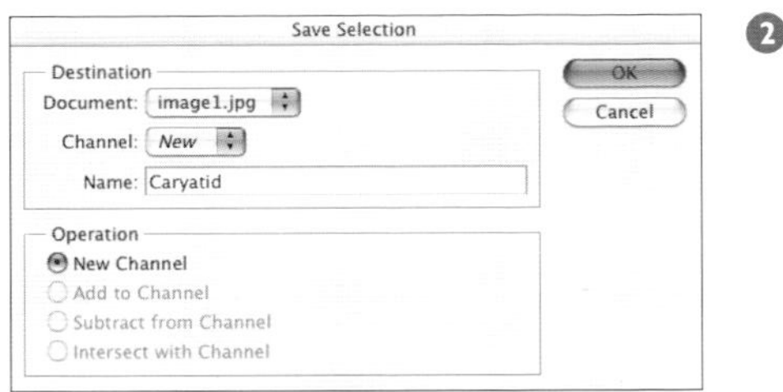

2

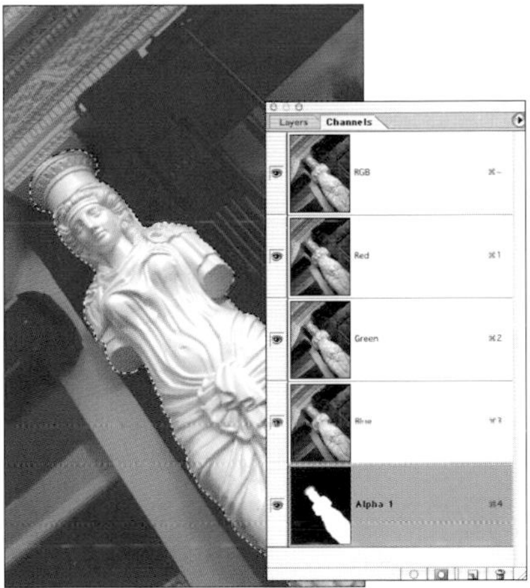

3

If you want to use a selection several times in an image, you don't have to select it repeatedly. Instead you can save it as an alpha channel – an 8-bit greyscale image, stored as an extra colour channel in the image file.

CREATING AN ALPHA CHANNEL

1 *Selecting this Grecian pediment is simple. We can use the* Magnetic Lasso *to select most of the outline, thanks to the high contrast boundaries between the pediment and the background.*

2 *We can convert this selection into an alpha channel by choosing* Select > Save Selection *from the menu or clicking on the* Save Selection as Channel *button on the* Channels *palette. An alpha channel is created, with the channel thumbnail appended to the bottom of the palette.*

3 *Normally an alpha channel is invisible, save for the thumbnail in the* Channels *palette. Click on this to see the area selected. A red masked area represents the alpha channel over the parts of the image that were not part of the original selection. With the alpha channel mask visible, any foreground and background colours automatically change to black and white.*

Like a *Quick Mask*, we can easily add to the masked area by selecting a painting tool and painting with black, or add to the selection by painting with white. Once a selection has been saved as an alpha channel, retrieval is a similar process. Choose *Select* > ***Load Selection*** and then choose the alpha channel from the list.

ALPHA CHANNELS: PRO TIPS

An image can have – within reason – as many alpha channels as we would like or need. Using a number of alpha channels allows us to save multiple selections individually and then create compound selections based on two or more. By doing so, you can apply the same filter or other manipulations to a number of selections in one pass, which can be very useful in, for example, a complex montage.

Also, take note that a stored alpha channel is not tied to the document you originally saved it from. You can take the saved channel and use it on another image. This saves time if the image has similar elements, and it can also open interesting special effects.

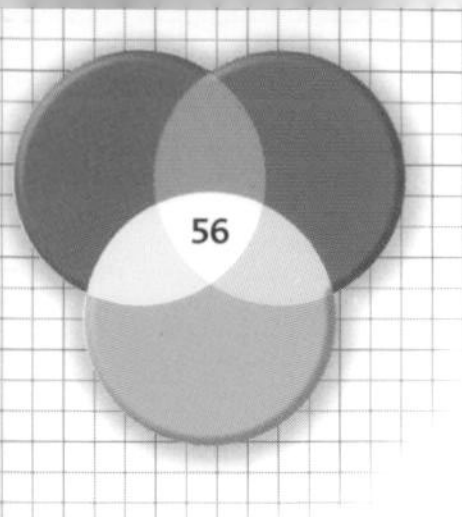

Get creative with selections

DARKROOM SECRETS

TIPS

- You can employ alpha channels as a safety net when making any complex selection. If a selection takes more than a couple of minutes to define, save it regularly to an alpha mask so that, if you make any mistake, you can go back to the previously saved state. As mistakes are easy to make, this will save you some time and frustration.
- If you can, avoid saving files with alpha channels as TIFF files. Although the TIFF format supports multiple alpha channels, the file size will be large. It is usually much more efficient to use the application's native format (such as .PSD in Photoshop).

So, creating an alpha channel is easy, but what can you do when you have got one? The simple answer is that alpha channels do not lend themselves to just one application, but to many.

Obviously, you can perform manipulations on the alpha channel selections just as you would conventional selections. This makes it easy to make new selections by deriving combinations or intersections of existing alpha channels.

COMBINING ALPHA CHANNELS

1 *We make an initial selection, then an alpha channel, of the boy, which call 'Boy in pool'. We then select the air bed, complete with boy, and create a new alpha channel, 'Boy and airbed'.*

2 *Let's make a third selection and alpha channel that includes only the boy's goggles. We'll name this alpha channel 'Glasses'.*

3 *We can now combine and subtract these alpha channels. First, load 'Boy in pool', then use the* Subtract from Selection *button (in the* Load Selection *Dialog) to subtract the 'Glasses' channel. We can alter the boy's skin tone without affecting the neutral colours in the goggles.*

4 *By loading the 'Boy and airbed' channel and subtracting the 'Boy in pool' channel from it, we can use the* Hue/Saturation *command to change the colour of the airbed, without altering any of the other elements in the image.*

Alpha channels are not restricted to saving selections, however. For one thing, alpha channels can also be used to apply different levels of compression to selected parts of an image. This technique is particularly important when images are being saved for use on a web-site or for e-mail; a situation where you need to get your image as small as possible without serious compromise to quality. Normally image compression is applied to the whole image, irrespective of detail or content. But by selectively defining those parts of the image that are of lesser importance (we can compress these more heavily), we can get smaller files while retaining detail where it's important.

In this case the foreground subject is much more important than the background. We can exploit this fact to reduce the file size quite dramatically, while still preserving detail where it's likely to be missed.

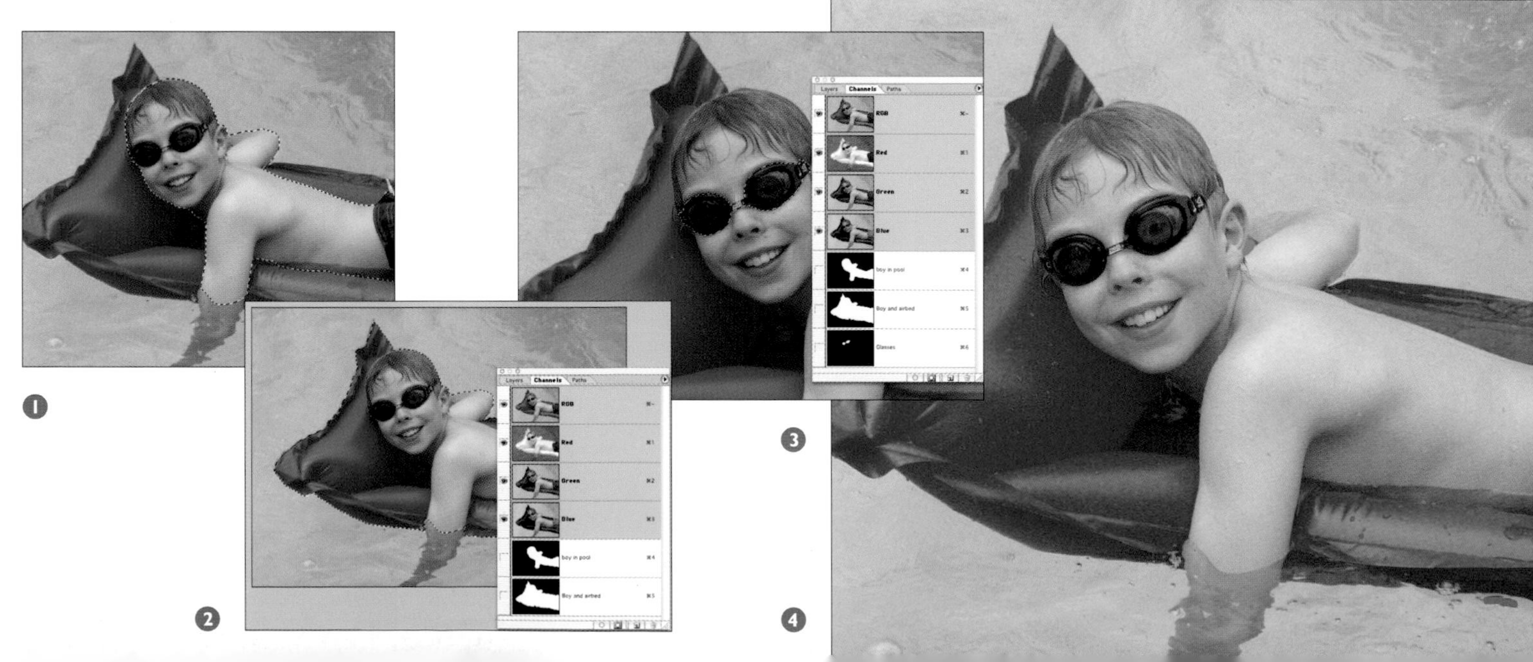

1 2 3 4

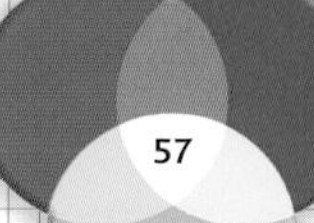

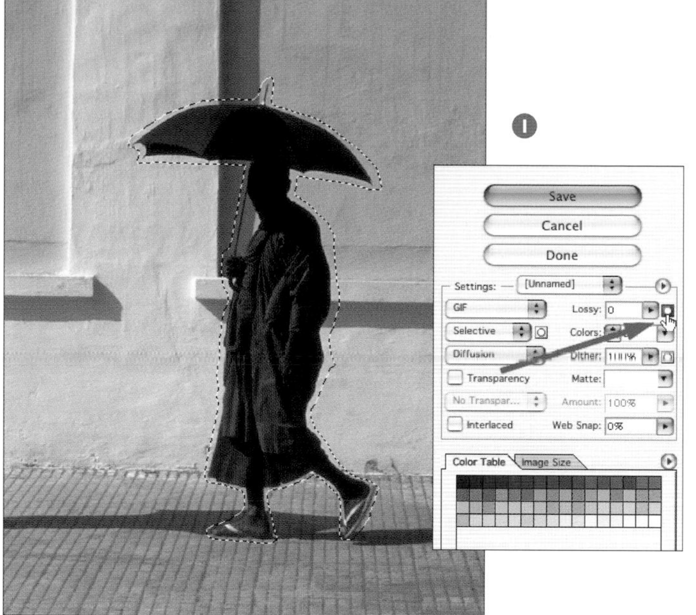

ALPHA CHANNELS AND COMPRESSION

1 *Begin by using the* Lasso *tool to make a very rough selection around the subject. This does not have to be too precise because any changes applied are not as severe as those made when using, say, a special effects filter. Now invert the selection, so that the background is the selected area. Create an alpha channel as before.*

2 *Select* File > **Save for Web** *and in the dialog box click on the* Channel *button (highlighted by the red arrow) to the right of the* Lossy *option box. Choose the new alpha channel from the dialog box menu and adjust the sliders. This enables you to vary the degree of compression while you monitor the effect on the image.*

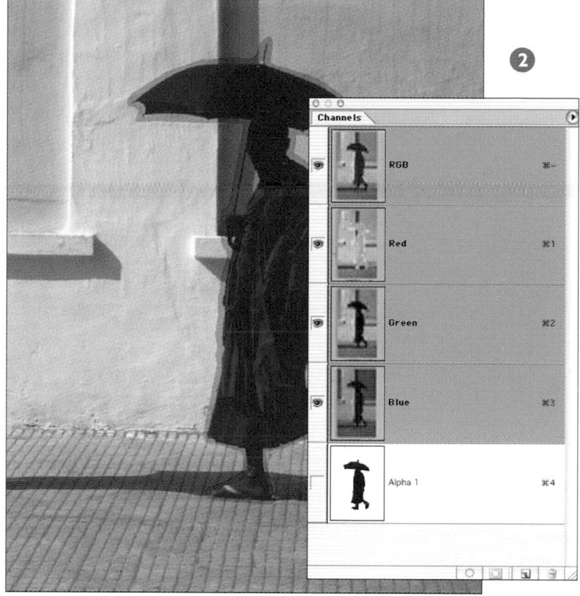

GRADIENT ALPHA CHANNELS

Alpha channels can also be used to apply gradient effects to your image. It is easiest to do this by converting an alpha channel from a *Quick Mask*. Switch to *Quick Mask* mode and apply a *Gradient* to the mask, then return to normal mode and convert the selection to an alpha channel. The principal reason for choosing an alpha channel is that, unlike the *Quick Mask*, it is retained when the image is closed and reopened. This leaves plenty of room for worry-free experimentation.

In this case, we've applied a *Radial Gradient* to the *Quick Mask*, before converting it into the alpha channel. With the latter selected, we can create some interesting effects. Here, we've applied a *Desaturate* command, a *Gaussian Blur* filter with a radius setting of 17, and finally a *Torn Edge* filter to the image.

By converting a quick mask to an alpha channel, we can experiment with a number of interesting gradient effects. In this case we've used the same selection with desaturation (right), a Torn Edge *filter (bottom) and a* Gaussian Blur *(left).*

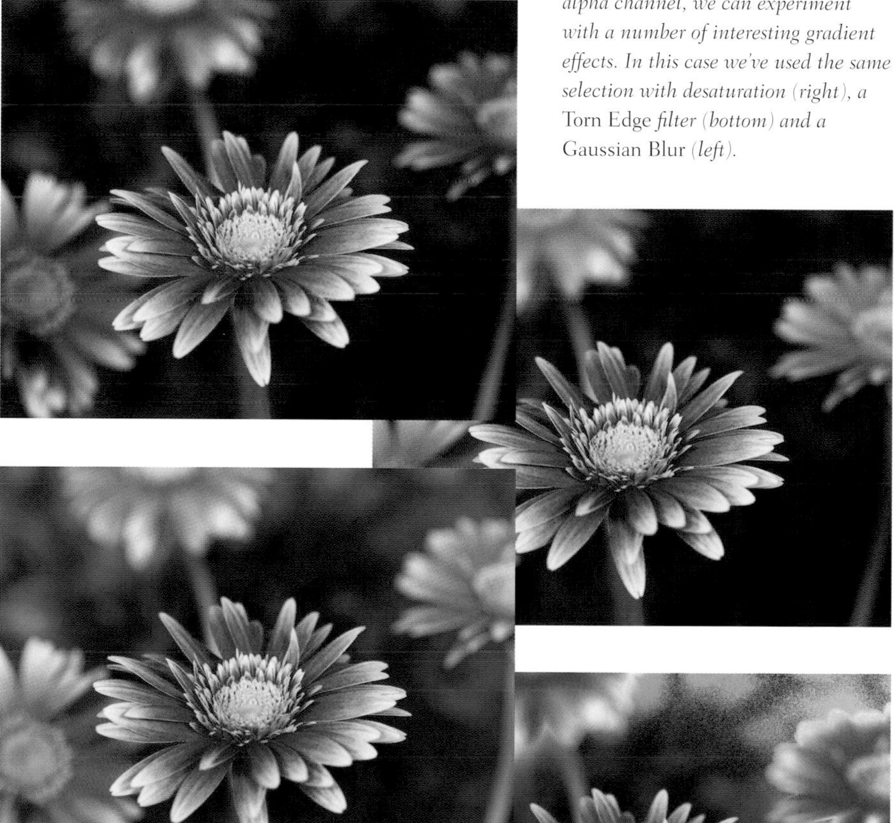

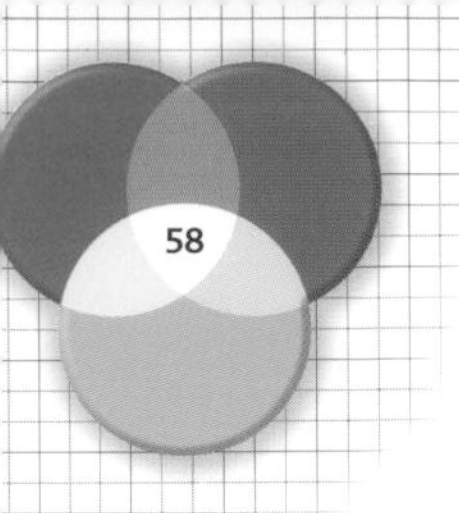

Layers and simple montage

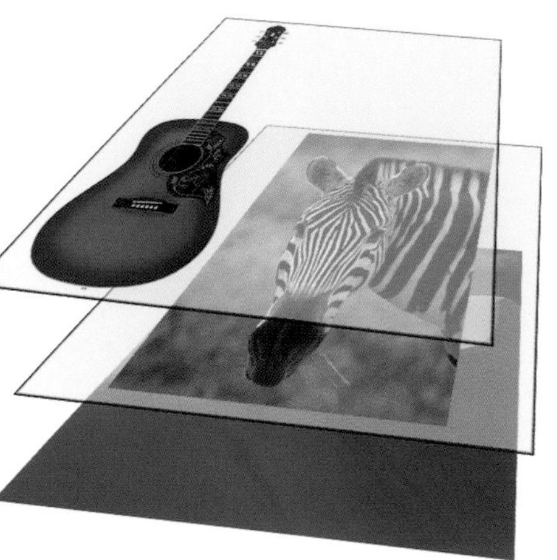

In the conventional darkroom, we created montages by physically cutting and pasting elements of images together. In the digital darkroom, it's not such a messy process, thanks to selections and layers. Layers are a fundamental and important part of any image-editing application. By using them, we can arrange image elements on top of each other, rearrange the stacking order, and perform more complex – but more successful – interactive manipulations.

Imagine layers as sheets of clear acetate placed on top of the basic photo. Image elements from that photo, or from others, can be pasted onto individual sheets to create a montage when viewed from above. But digital imaging methods offer many possibilities for further interactions. We can, for example, change the opacity of a layer so that layers below show through.

Here we've created an image from three layers: the base is the image of a sand dune, the next a photo of a zebra, and the top layer is a cut-out image of a guitar.

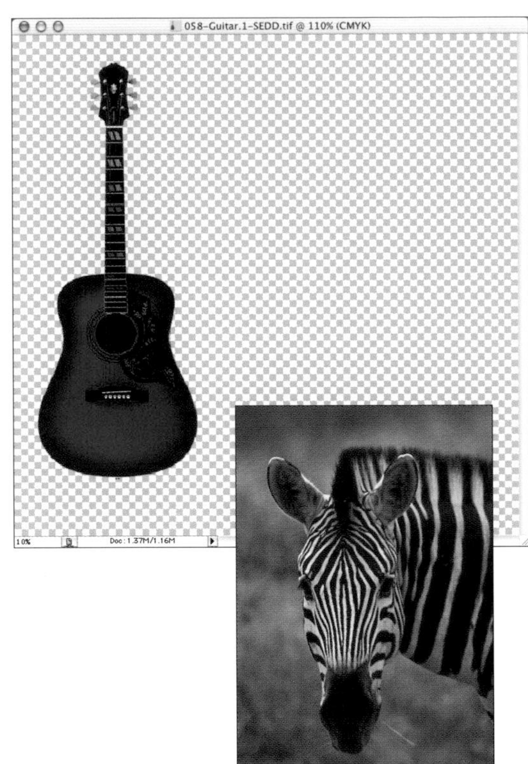

THE LAYERS PALETTE

The Layers *palette displays the image layers as stacked thumbnails with the lowest layer (normally the background layer) at the bottom. Apart from the background, the order of layers can be rearranged at will. Click on any layer you wish to move, then drag to the new position. The currently selected layer is shown highlighted. When it is selected, you can alter the opacity, using the slider at the top of the palette.*

Buttons at the base of the palette allow the creation of a new layer, the application of layer styles or layer masks, and the creation of adjustment layers. By dragging a layer to the trash icon, you can permanently remove it. The pop-up menu gives easy access to many of the grouping and other features also found in the Layers *menu.*

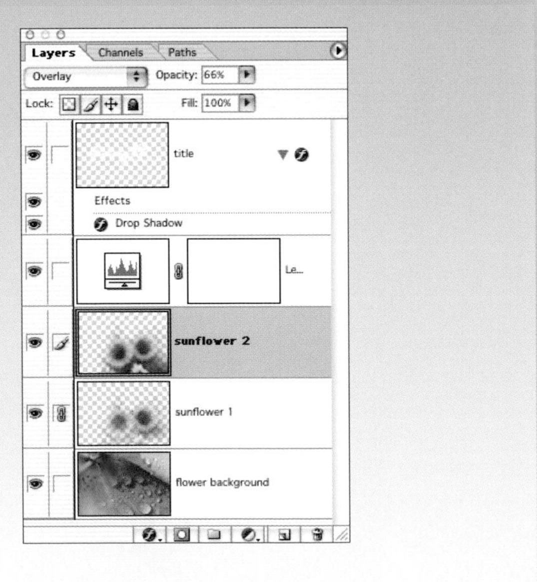

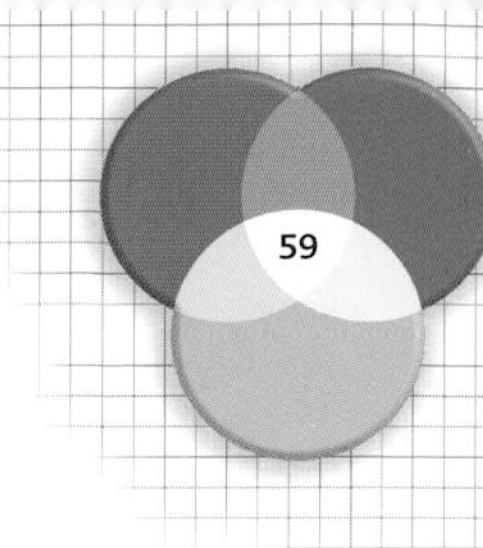

CREATING A BASIC MONTAGE

1 *This is how the three images are represented in the layers palette.*

2 *The resultant image shows the zebra image overlaying much of the background layer. The guitar, uppermost in the layer stack, overlays both.*

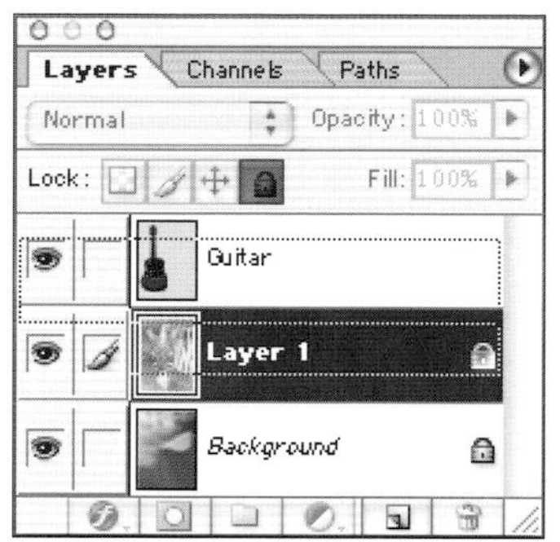

1

2

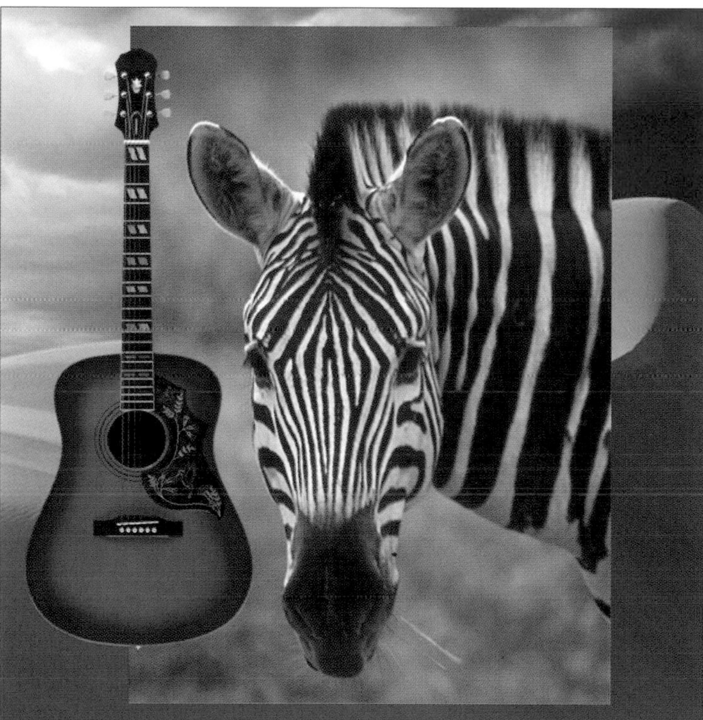

3 *We can now select* Layer 1 *and (using the slider control at the top of the* Layers palette*) alter the transparency of this layer. You will see that the zebra layer becomes translucent and the background layer becomes visible through it.*

3

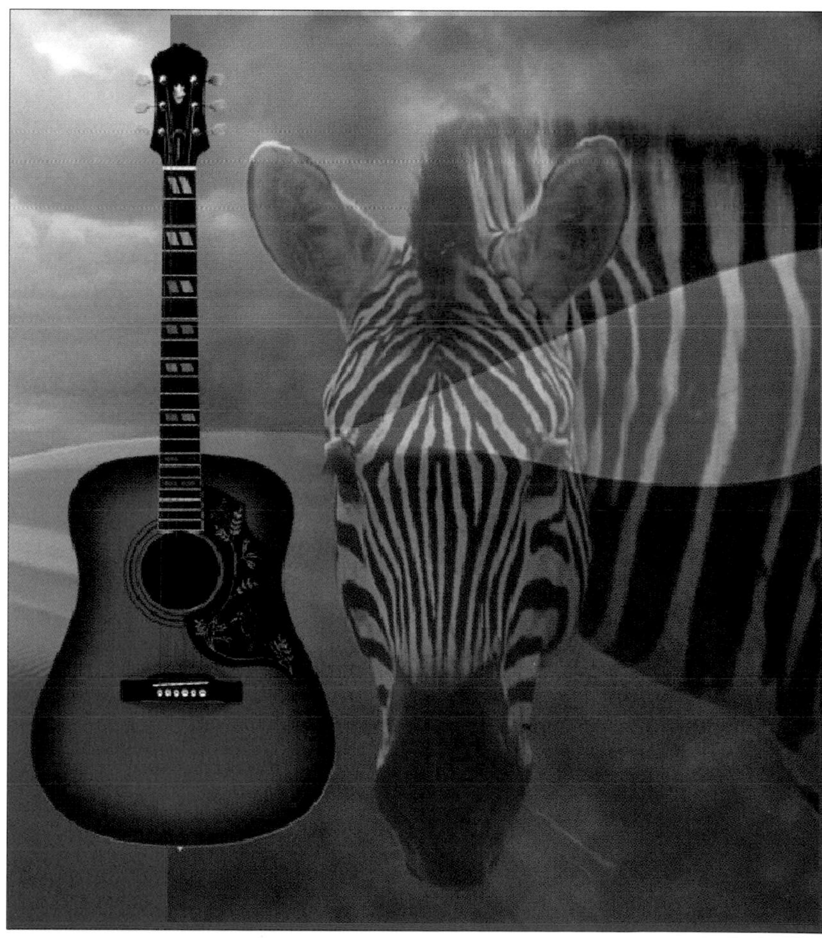

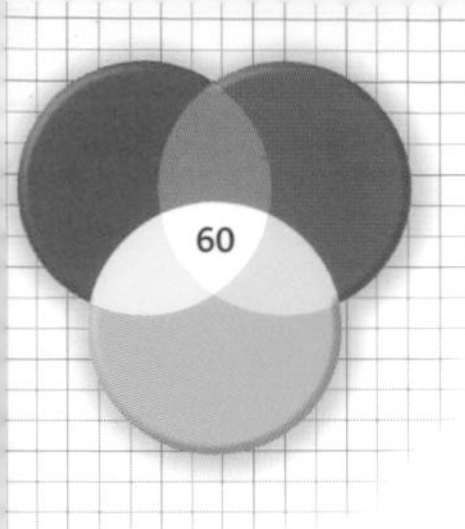

Layer masks and montage

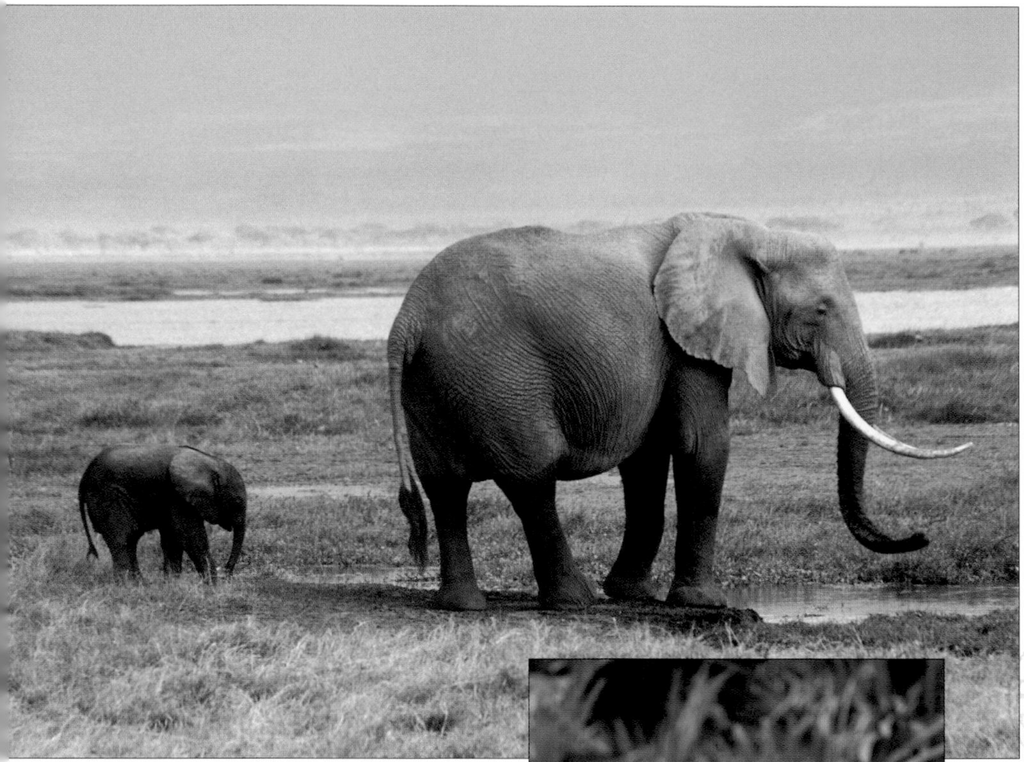

❶

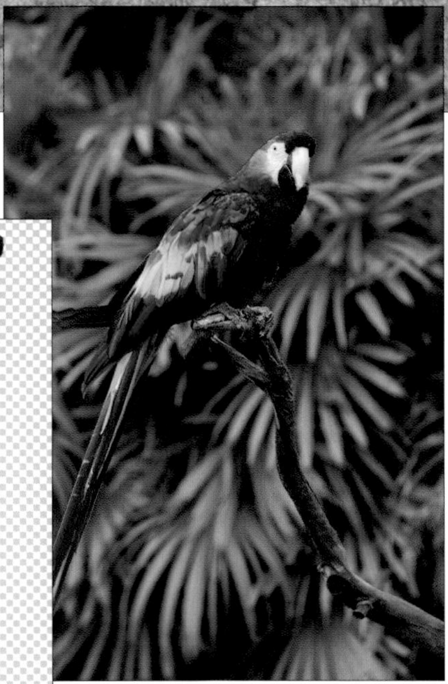

❷

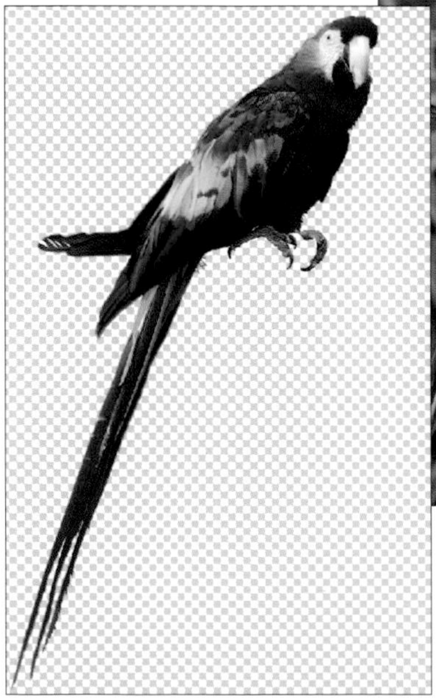

❸

Layers really come into their own when we create more complex montages, where we take elements from a number of images and put them together in a way that suggests that a newly placed object is actually set within the original scene. We can simply use layers to build up the new image, but each element will just sit on top of the elements below it. To combine them in a more lifelike way, we need to make our foreground elements look like they fit behind some portions of the background, but stand out in front of others.

In this example, we bring a parrot out from the jungle and make him sit on an elephant's tusk. While the overall effect is not exactly realistic, the key to making it believable is the fact that the parrot's tail goes behind the tusk, while the rest of the parrot stands forward from the background image.

MANIPULATING LAYERS

1 *We begin with the background image of the elephant. Make any adjustments or corrections you need to make to this image, then open up the image of the parrot.*

2 *Use the* Transform *command to change the size of the parrot, so that it sits roughly in scale with the elephant and at approximately the right size. At the same time, use the* Levels *tool to adjust the parrot image so that it is a close tonal match to the background.*

3 *Now extract the Parrot from its background, using the* Lasso *tools or the* Extract *feature, and paste it as a new layer onto the elephant.*

4 *Apply a layer mask to the parrot layer by selecting* Layer > **Add Layer Mask**. *Select the* Reveal All *option so that we can see the image layers in their original state. Use a hard-edged black brush to paint over the area of the tail in front of the tusk. This makes the mask transparent in those areas. It helps if you reduce the layer opacity so that you can see the tail through the layer.*

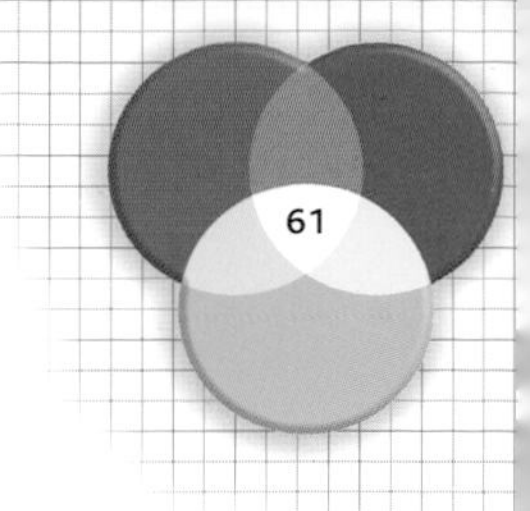

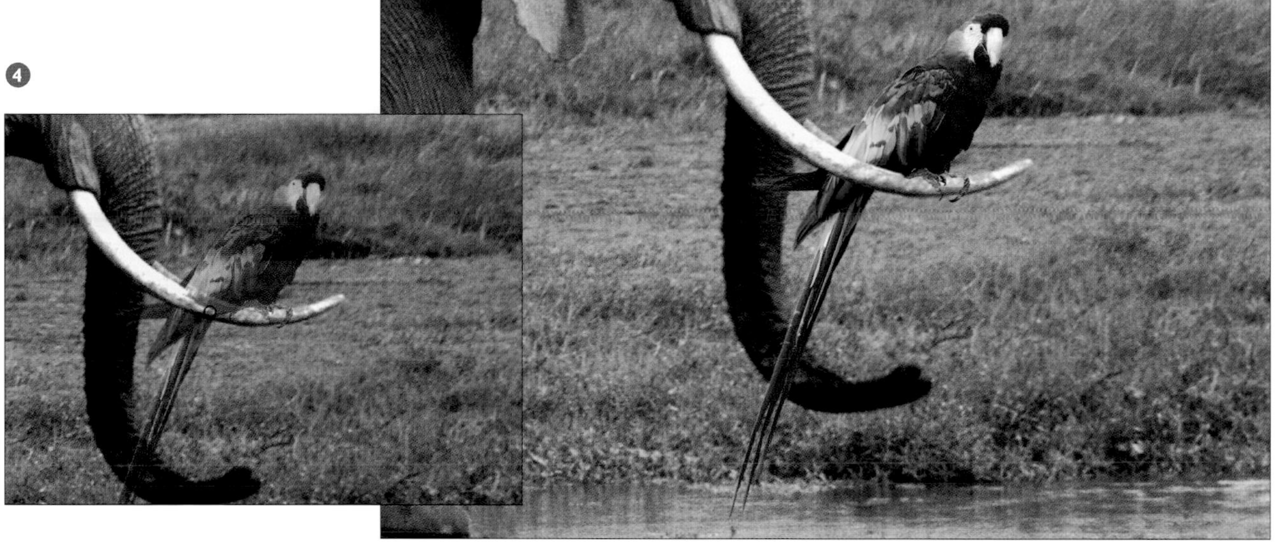

4

5

5 *Once you have finished, restore the opacity to 100% and check that you have included all of the tail beneath the tusk, but no more. If you have strayed over the boundary, change the paint colour to white and paint over those areas.*

6 *Our layer masking is now complete. To finish the image, we need to check that the image elements have successfully knitted together and that edges are neither too sharp nor too soft. We also need to ensure that the colour balance is right. As each element may have been shot under slightly different lighting conditions, there may be colour casts that need attention.*

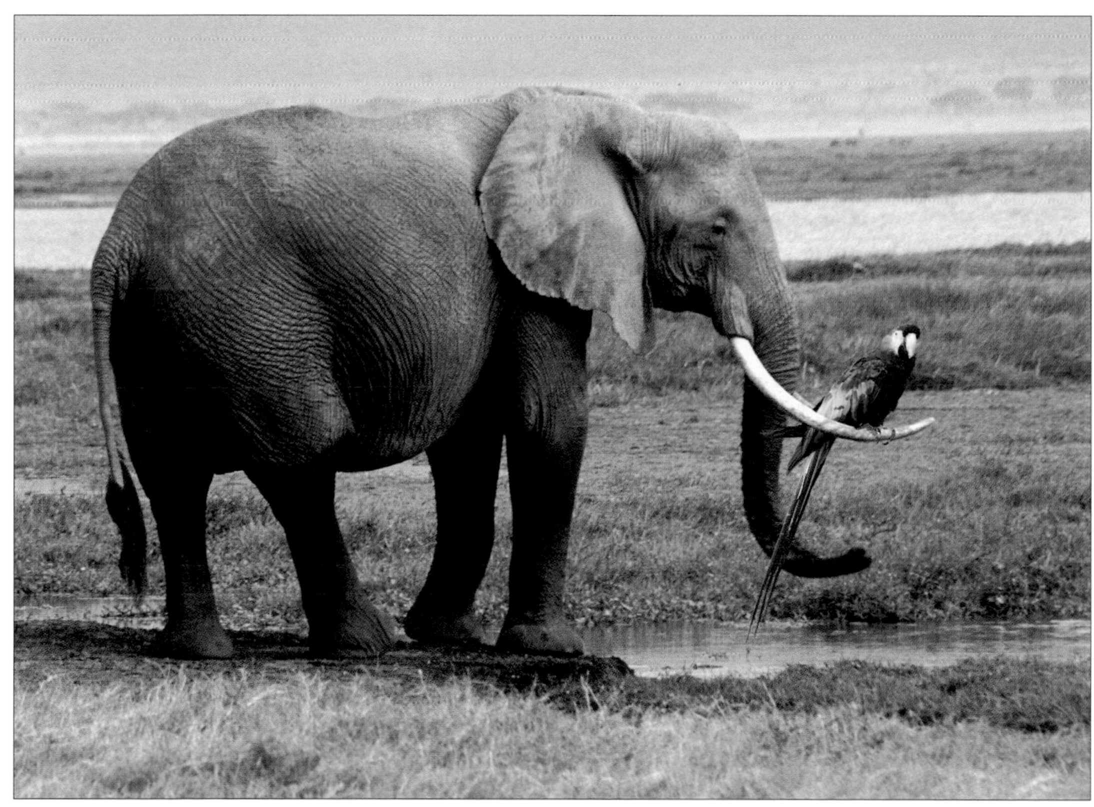

6

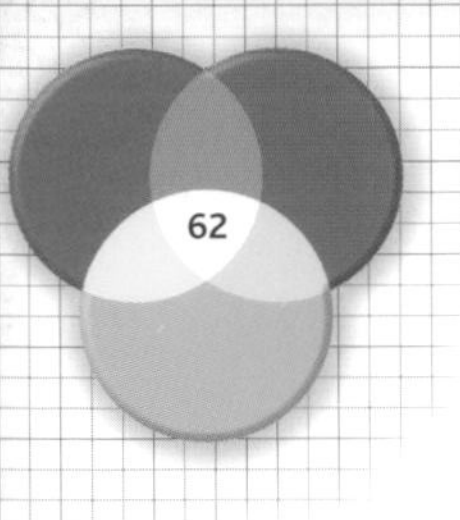

Blend modes

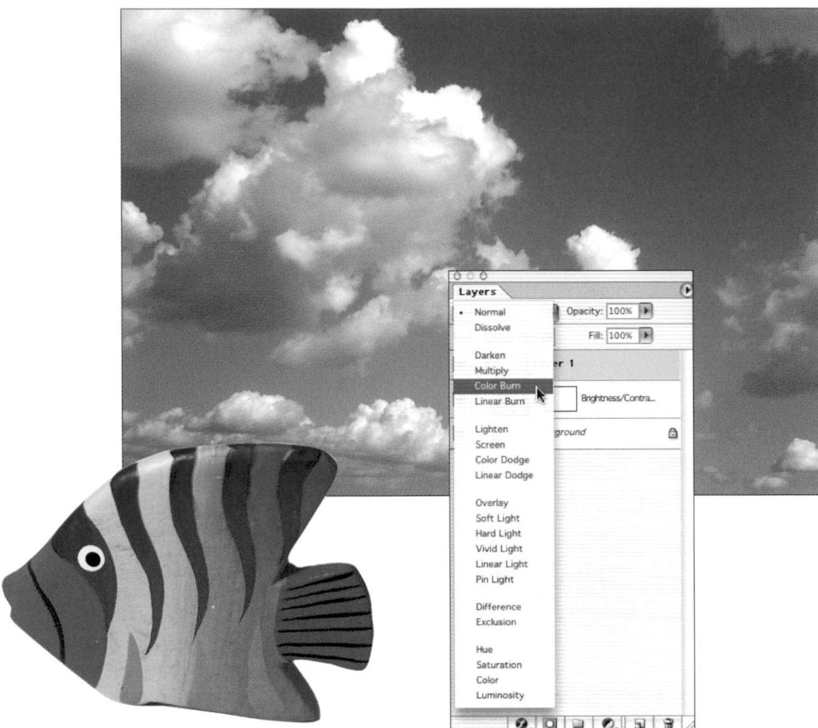

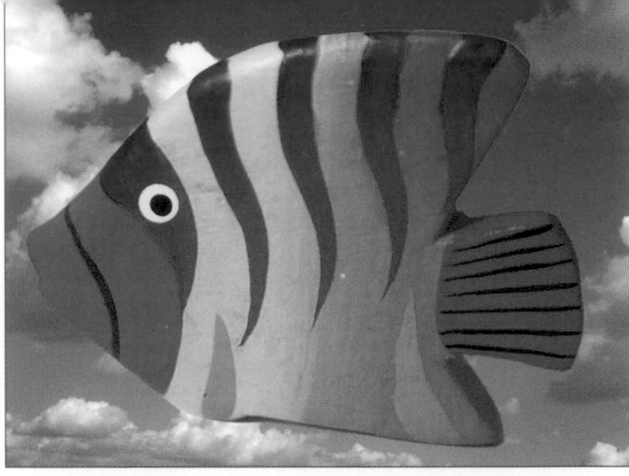

NORMAL MODE

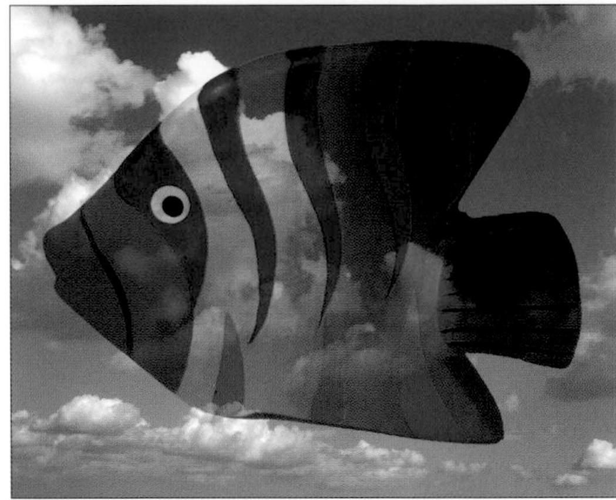

MULTIPLY

In the traditional darkroom, we can create montages in several ways. We can selectively expose parts of the photographic paper to different source images, taking care to assemble each so that there are no obvious joins. We can expose an original image to a second original transparency or negative and add, for example, clouds to a sky. Or we could produce a sandwich of originals and produce our print directly from this. With digital images we have even more options. We can control how image layers – whether components of an image or distinct images in their own right – interact. These often complex interactions are known as blending modes (or merge modes in some applications).

You can set a blend mode at various places in your application, but the most common route is through the *Layers* palette. The dropdown menu gives you access to all of them.

When blending two images or image layers, we describe the lower image as the base layer and the overlaid one as the paint layer. In the examples used here, a paint layer contains a fish, while the base layer is a skyscape background.

The principal blend modes are as follows. Where relevant, the corresponding darkroom equivalent is noted, although, as you might have

DARKROOM SECRETS

SWITCHING BLEND MODES

You can change through the blend mode options in Photoshop by pressing the Shift-minus or Shift-plus keys and scrolling through the options. Or you can hold down the Shift and Option keys and press the first letter of the mode required (Shift-Option-M for multiply). This changes the mode of the layer unless a painting tool is currently selected, in which case the mode of the tool is changed.

EXTRA BLEND MODES

The release of Photoshop 7 has seen the introduction of five new blend modes:

Linear Burn *is designed to darken images. It acts by checking the colour information in each channel and reducing the brightness of the base colour correspondingly.* Linear Dodge *has the complementary effect of reducing the contrast and lightening the base colour.* Vivid Light *combines dodge and burn modes, lightening the base if the blend colour is lighter than 50% grey.* Linear Light *is a subtle variation on this based on brightness levels.* Pin Light *produces more dramatic changes. If the selected blend colour is lighter than 50% grey, then darker pixels are replaced. If darker, then the lighter pixels are replaced.*

expected by now, the range of options available definitely exceeds those possible through traditional means.

NORMAL MODE

The default mode. When the opacity of the paint layer is altered, it simply mixes (by averaging) the colours in the two layers.

MULTIPLY

Multiplies the base layer by the paint layer. The result is always darker (or more dense) than either original. This is similar to sandwiching two transparencies and printing the result.

SCREEN

Creates a lighter result by combining the inverse of the paint layers with the base layer. A similar result to sandwiching two negatives together and printing the combination.

OVERLAY, SOFT LIGHT AND HARD LIGHT

These three modes give a similar result to printing an enlarged image from the paint layer and base layer consecutively. *Overlay* gives a median result, multiplying or screening the paint colours depending on the base colour. *Soft light* gives a less intense result while *Hard light* gives a more pronounced effect.

HUE, SATURATION AND LUMINOSITY

The *Hue* mode keeps the original luminance and saturation of the base image, but replaces the hue with that of the paint layer. Likewise, *Saturation* mode preserves luminance and hue while replacing the saturation, and *Luminosity* keeps the hue and saturation of the base while replacing the luminance with that of the paint layer.

COLOR

Color keeps the luminance values of the base while replacing the hue and saturation with that from the paint layer.

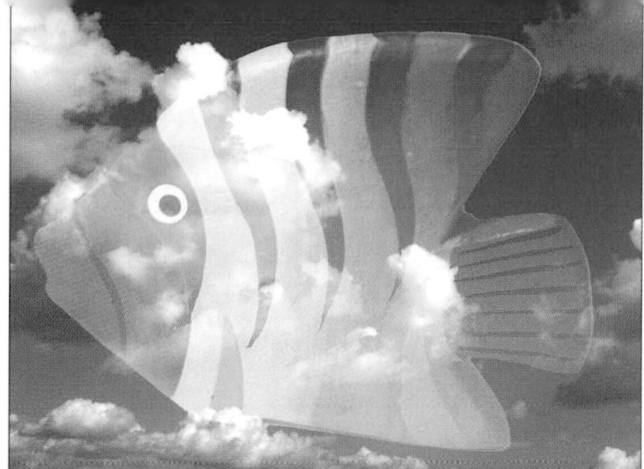

SCREEN

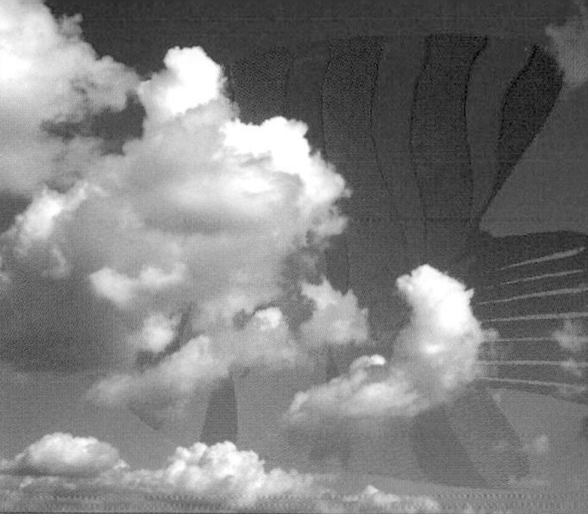

HUE

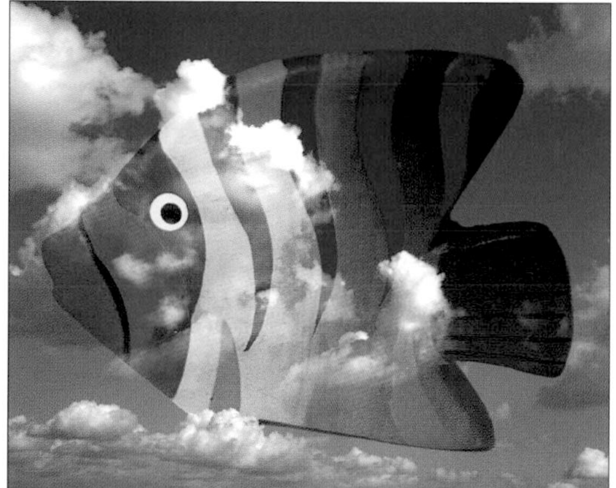

OVERLAY

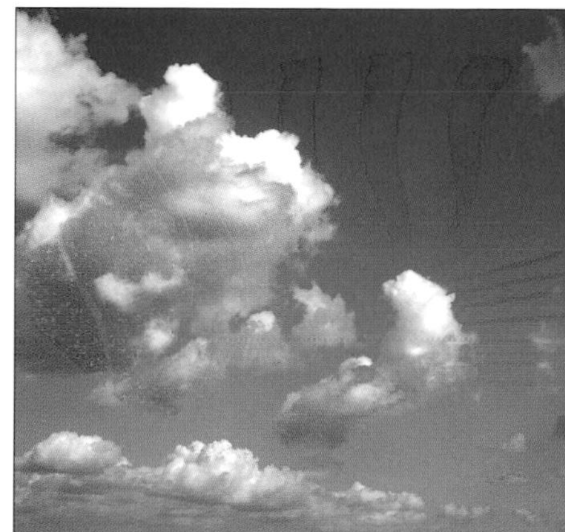

SATURATION

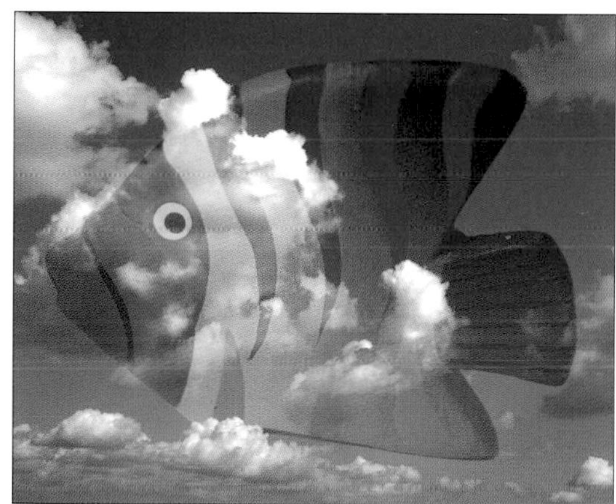

SOFT LIGHT

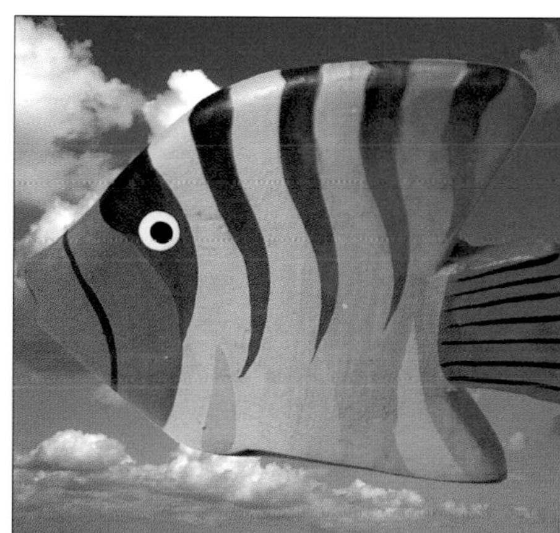

LUMINOSITY

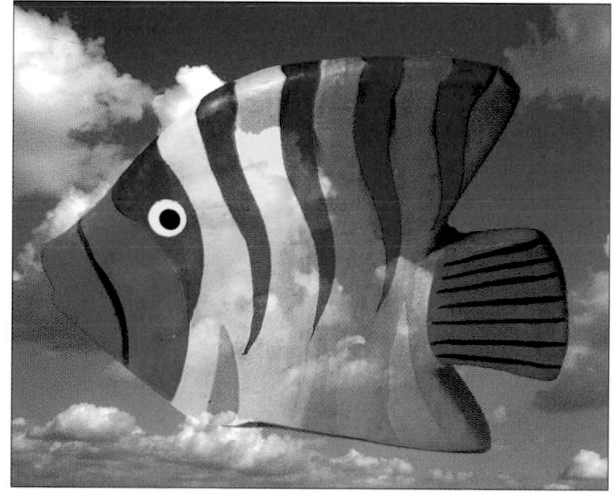

HARD LIGHT

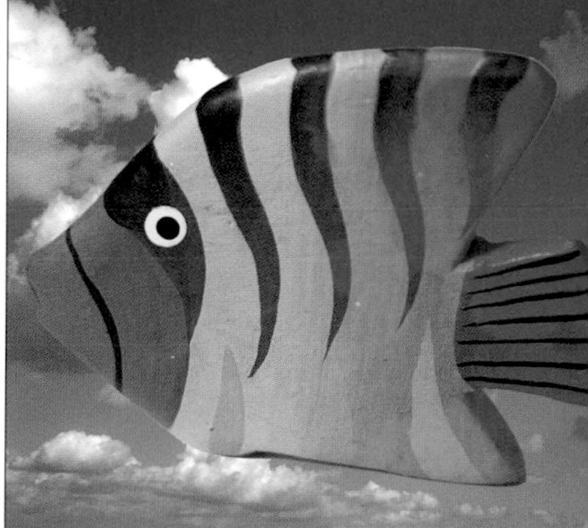

COLOR

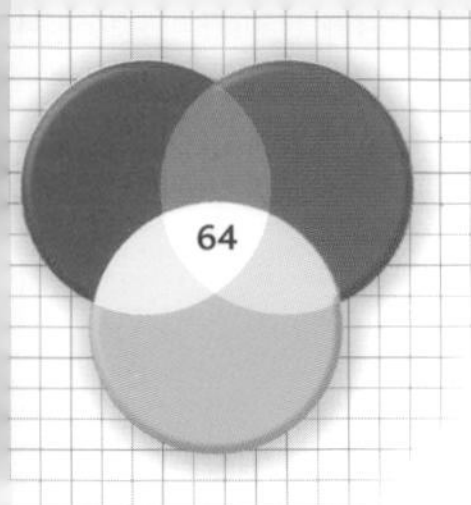

Blend modes and montage

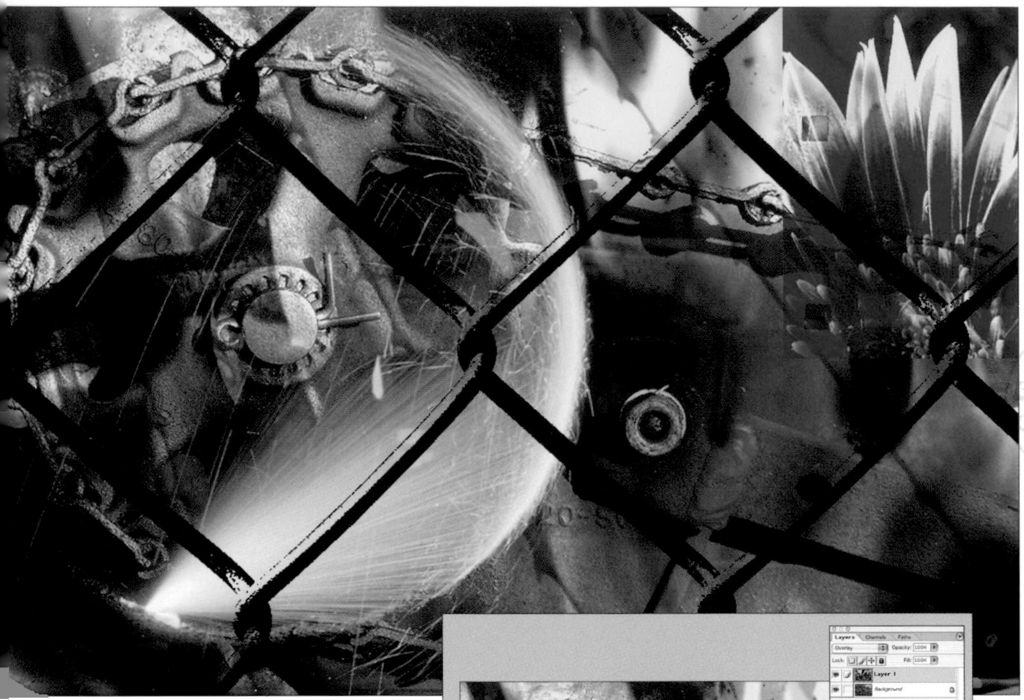

Blends always have their uses when you are creating montages, but these are not limited to hiding the joins or creating particular textures. It is possible to use them to create richly textured multi-element montages without ever reaching for selection tools or masks. Simply experiment with layer blending options, blend modes and opacities to build up an image that ends up being more than just the sum of its parts.

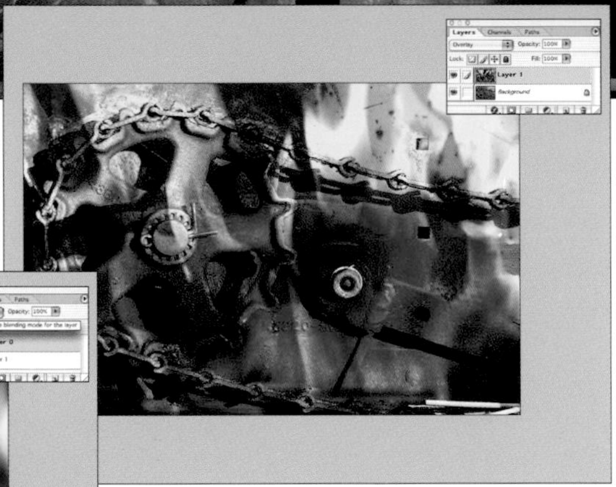

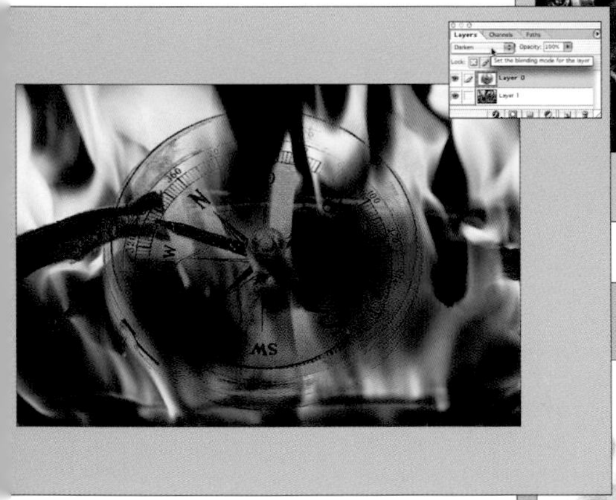

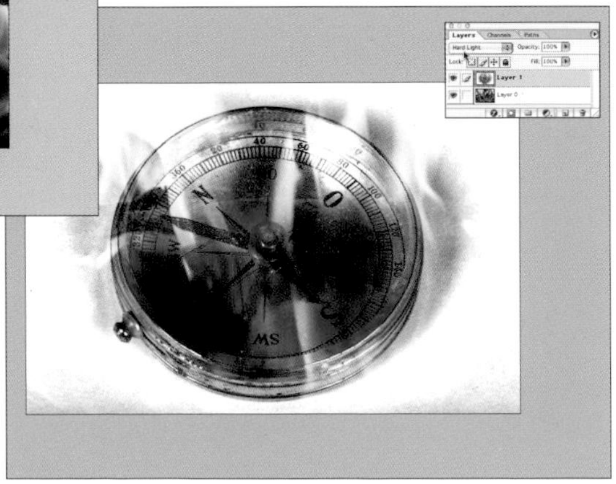

MONTAGE USING BLEND MODES

1 *This image has been built from a combination of six different layers, each scaled to an appropriate size and moved into position, with a variety of blend modes and opacity settings. There are no cutouts or masks to worry about, and the whole thing took minutes.*

2 *By adding a layer containing an image of flames and changing the blend mode to* Overlay, *the detail of the original underlying image combines with the colours from the flames. This kind of technique is useful for adding an overall texture to an image with very little effort.*

3 *Experimenting with blend modes never takes much time, and you can get effective results with very little real effort. In this example, we have used two different blend modes on a simple two-layer image – it is surprising how different the results can be. In* Darken *mode (left),the detail on the compass seems to be pushing through the flames. In* Hard Light *mode (right), the flames add colour to the compass image.*

Blend modes also have other uses. By using them in conjunction with multiple adjustment layers, we can add tonal richness to a dull or faded image. Take this heirloom photo, for example. Like many prints of a certain vintage, it has lost both contrast and density. Fading, as a result of poor storage or intrinsic chemistry, has left the subject hard to see. Boosting the contrast using the *Brightness/Contrast* controls will improve it, but using blending modes can be more effective.

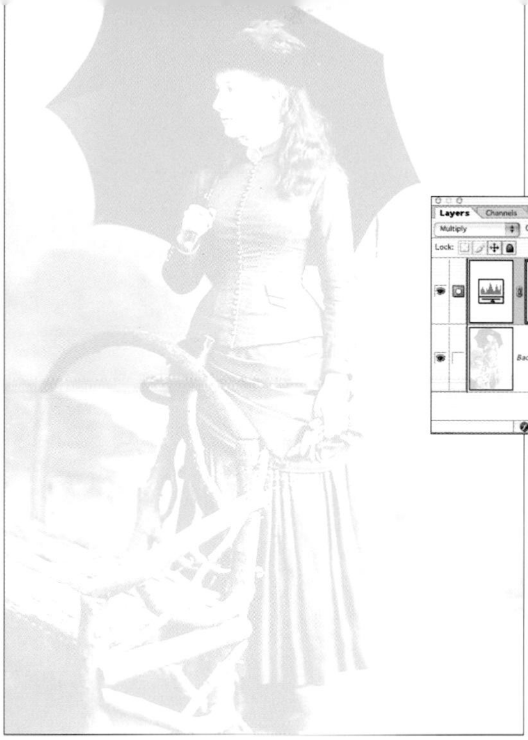

ENHANCING HEIRLOOM PHOTOS

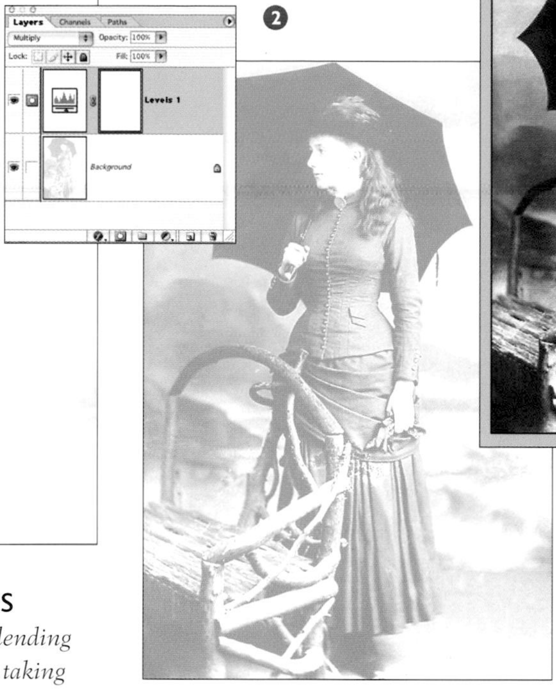

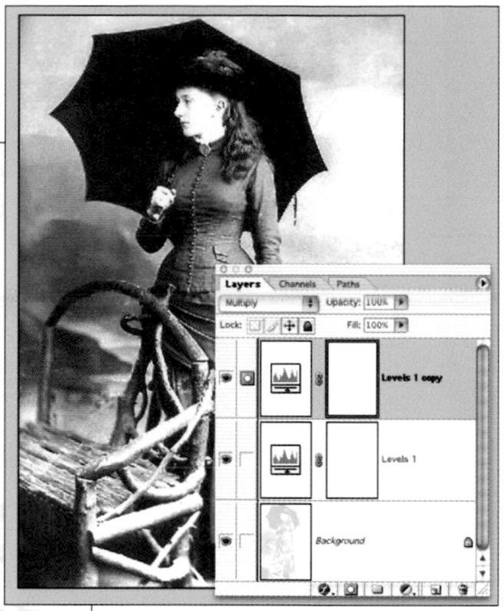

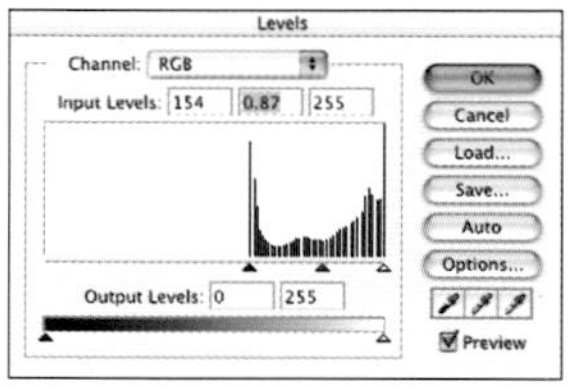

1 *In this case we will use the Multiply blending mode. The net result will be similar to taking two transparencies of the original image and combining them in a single 'sandwich'. Add a Levels adjustment layer, as there is no need – at this stage – to make alterations to the actual layers.*

2 *Select the adjustment layer and then change its blending mode from* Normal *to* Multiply. *The image becomes darker and more dense.*

3 *In the case of many faded images, this will be sufficient to restore sufficient density. If not, you can add a second adjustment layer. It is easiest to do this by duplicating the existing one.*

4 *Alternatively, you can adjust the levels. Click on the thumbnail* Levels *icon to open the* Levels *dialog and then move the sliders, the start and end of the actual tonal range, as indicated here.*

5 *Whether by duplicating the layers or adjusting the levels, you will ultimately achieve a result that features the full contrast range and brings this image back to life.*

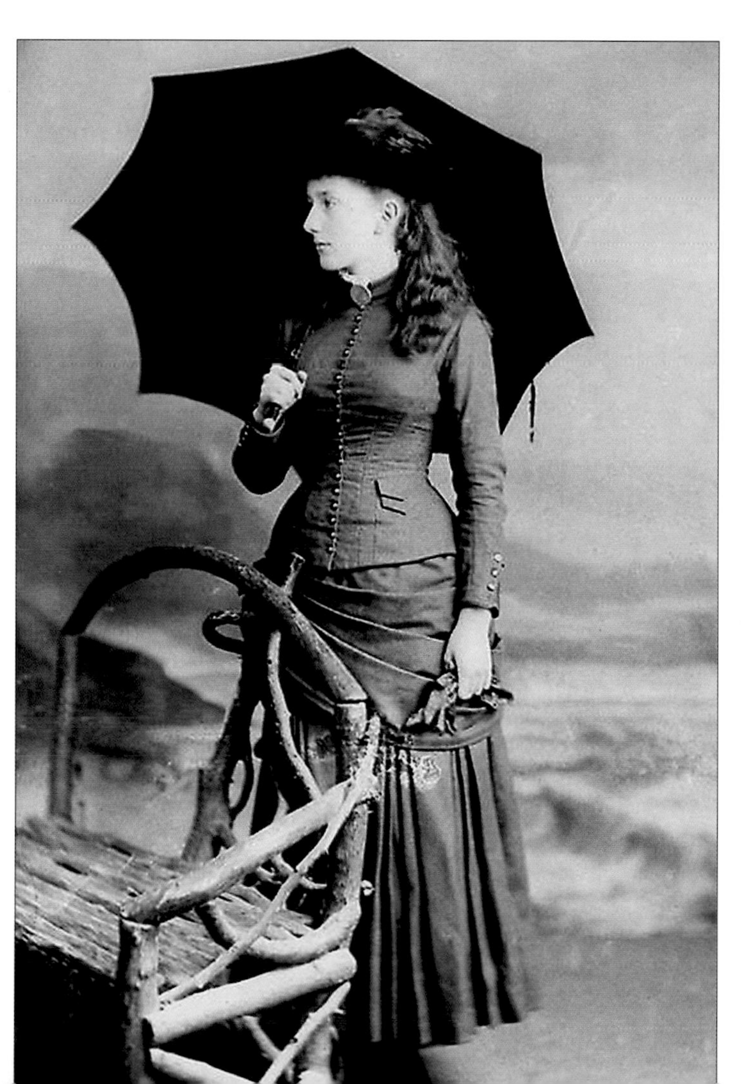

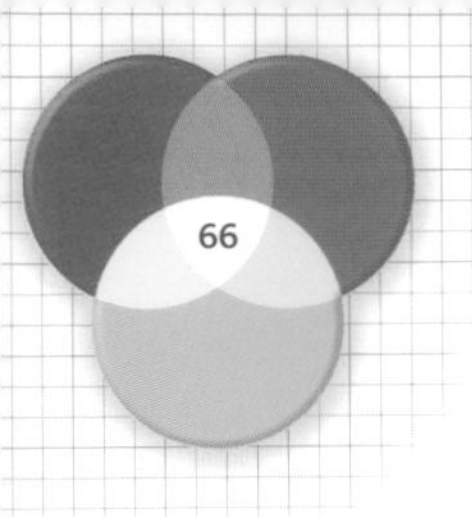

Adding text to enhance an image

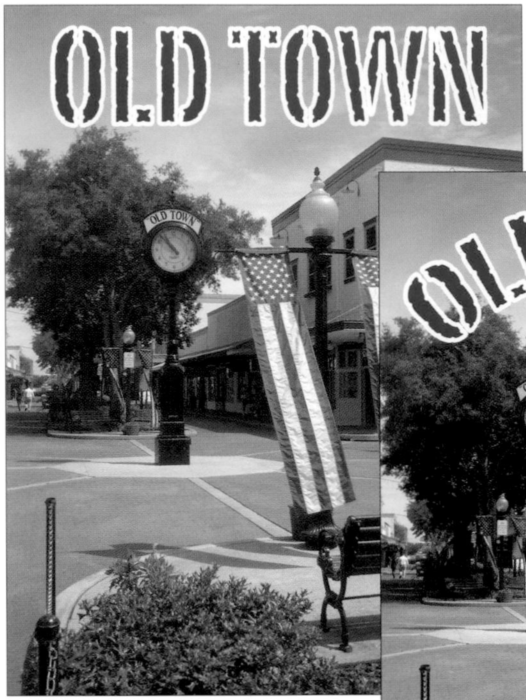

Though often considered the preserve of the graphic designer, type and text effects still have a place in the digital darkroom. Adding simple text to caption images is easy, but with care and imagination you can make text a prominent and compelling part of your artwork.

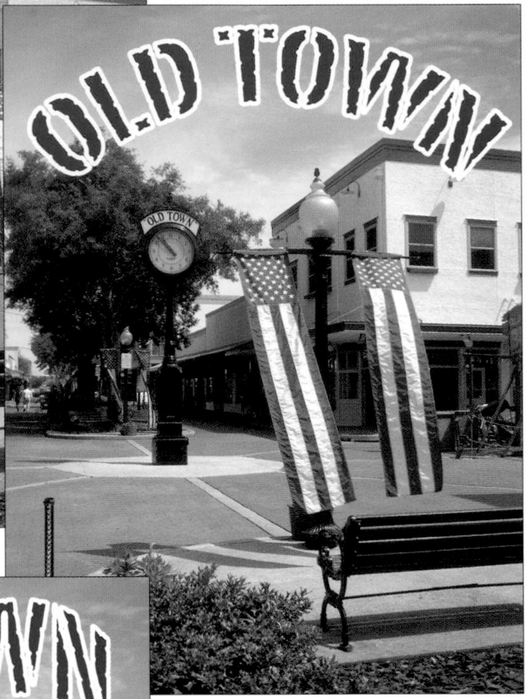

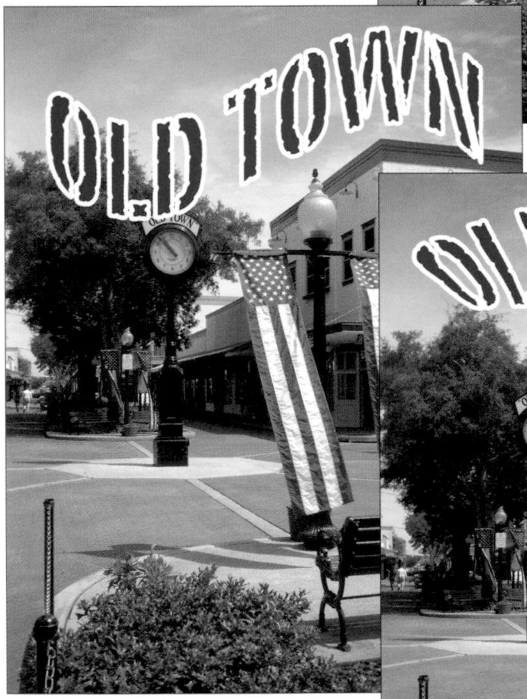

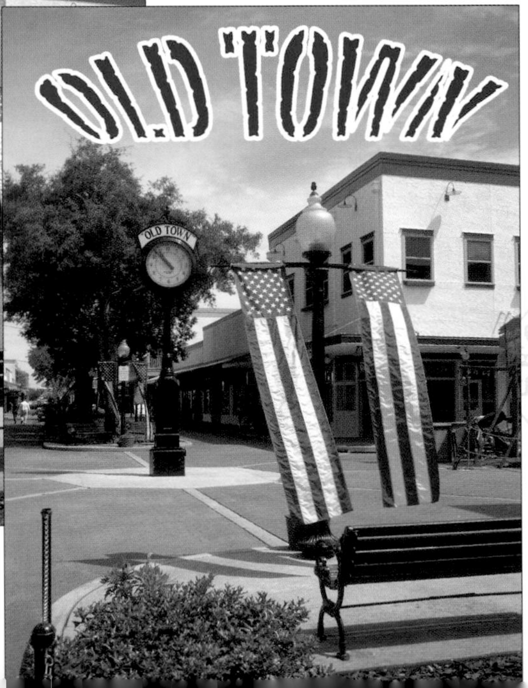

When you work with text, you do need to be aware that it is – in virtually all applications – a vector graphic rather than a bitmapped pixel-based image element. This means that, unlike pictorial elements in your image or montage, you can enlarge or reduce the type almost at will without affecting the quality.

LAYER STYLES

The first step towards making text exciting is to experiment with *Layer Styles*. The simple *Drop Shadow* is the most commonly used – and can be very effective – but it's not the only one. Combine a *Drop Shadow* with an *Inner Shadow*, and your text takes on the appearance of having been 'cut-out' of the background with a pastry cutter to reveal the colour behind. Changing the shadow colour to white produces a 3D effect, with the text a rising from the background.

A more pronounced three-dimensional effect can be achieved when the *Bevel and Emboss* layer style is applied. In the variation to the right an *Outside Bevel* has been applied, giving the text the appearance that it has been stamped through the background, like text on a credit card.

For more complex effects, we can turn to the *Type Warp* commands. These allow you to adjust the text and make it appear as if it is waving, expanding or otherwise distorted.

USING TYPE WARP

1 *For this shot of Kissimmee, Florida's, Old Town, a title has been added using an appropriate typeface (Portago ITC) and given a white* Stroke *(found with the* Layer Styles*). A* Stroke *is a perimeter outline that can be applied inside, outside or across the perimeter of the type, and is another way of making text stand out.*

1

2

3

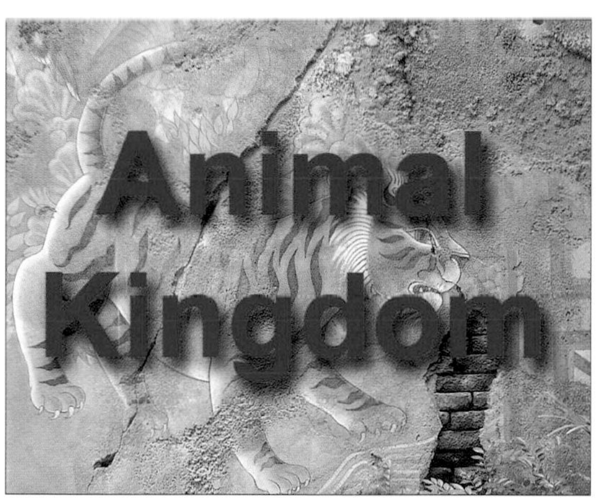

2 *Using the* Arc warp *option of the* Type Warp *feature, the type can be given an arched appearance that helps frame the subject better than the 'straight' text.*

3 *Selecting* Flag *(left) and* Shell Upper *(right), we get two more, quite different effects.*

With the *Type Mask*, the letter shapes can be filled with your paint selection, gradients or even imagery. Using the *Type Mask* is simple.

THE TYPE MASK

1 *To use an image to fill in your type, open the image that you want to use, then select the* Type Mask *tool along with your choice of font and font size. Type the words and select the move tool. In Photoshop, you'll see a conventional mask appear when entering text. This changes to a selection marquee when you select the* Move *tool. Move the selection area and you will see your text filled in with the desired image.*

2 *Drag the text to the image upon which you wish to place it (or use* Edit > Copy *and* Edit > **Paste** *to paste it into a new image).*

3 *When the text is in the new image, it is stored in a layer so you can then apply any* Layer Styles *and effects that you wish.*

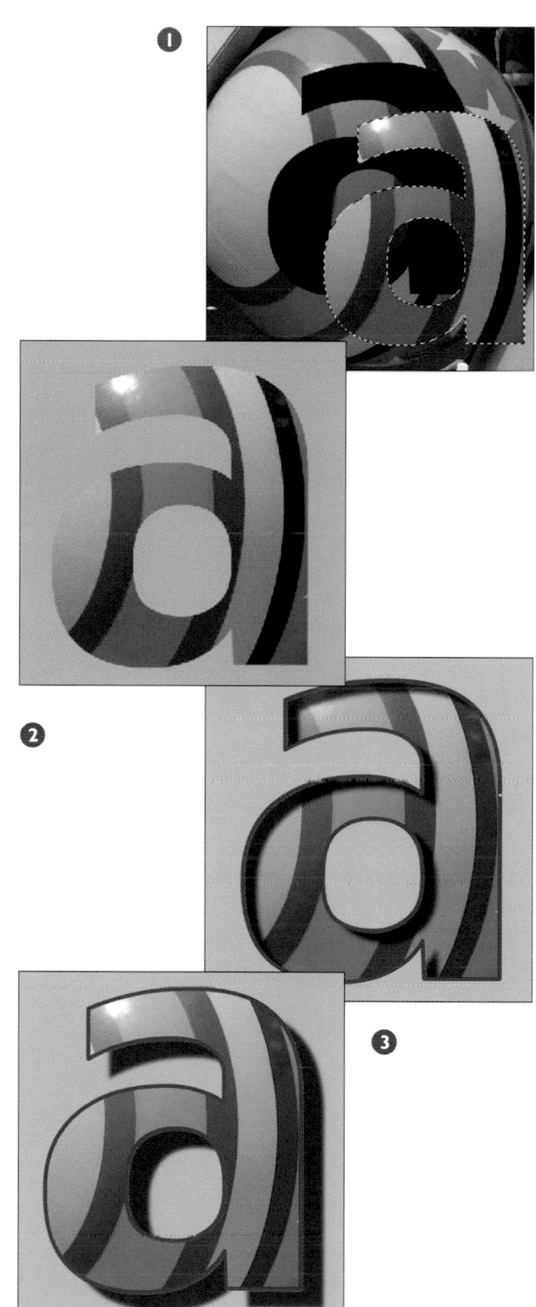

1

2

3

DARKROOM SECRETS

TYPE AND TEXT HINTS

- Keep your text as vector graphics (in its own layer) until you have completed (or at least finalised the size) of your print. If you make changes to the size of an image after flattening the image, there is a risk that the text will become ragged and show the characteristic jagged edges.
- In many applications, you cannot use certain effects filters while the type is still a vector graphic. You will either be prevented from using the filter or will be prompted to rasterize – or convert to pixels – the text layer prior to application. Remember that, once your text is converted, you cannot convert back to vector mode.
- When using a Type Mask, use a bold typeface and a simple image to avoid a cluttered or confusing result.

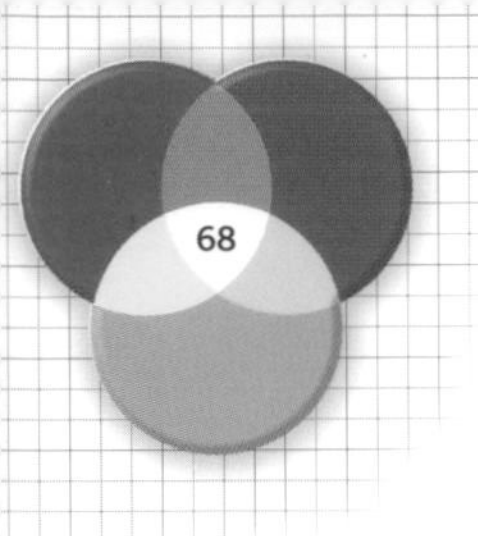

Filters and effects

> **DARKROOM SECRETS**
>
> **KEEP EFFECTS SPECIAL**
> The clever digital darkroom worker is economic with the use of manipulative effects. One carefully selected effect applied to an image often delivers a far more potent result than the application of several. Try to think of manipulative or filter effects as you might focal points in an image – if there are too many, the viewer's eye will jump around the image, diluting the impact overall.

All image-editing applications include a collection of effects filters that can deliver subtle or dramatic changes to an image. In fact, the term 'filter' covers a range of features that are actually quite disparate. Sharpening and blurring tools, painting and natural media effects, and transformational tools all qualify as filters.

Filters can be thought of as small subprograms that interface with the host application. This modular nature has made it possible for adept programmers to develop new filters that further enhance the range of effects on offer. You don't need to be content with the effects filters supplied with Photoshop, Painter or Paint Shop Pro; you can also choose from the countless plug-ins available from Alien Skin software, Xaos Tools, Andromeda and others. As many applications and plug-ins now feature Photoshop compatibility, you can use most filters with most image editors or share them between applications if you use more than one.

Many filters are so extreme and compelling in their effect that it can be tempting to overuse them. However, filters are never a quick fix for a mediocre image, and with more experience you will learn to take care with the more overpowering effects. Still, to neglect effects filters is to do them a disservice. They provide us with important and significant functionality as long as they are used wisely.

The old wisdom goes that using more than one filter on an image is the road to disaster, but this should not be taken as gospel. Slapping filter after filter on a poor image only makes it worse, but layering filters on a good image can create some super artistic effects.

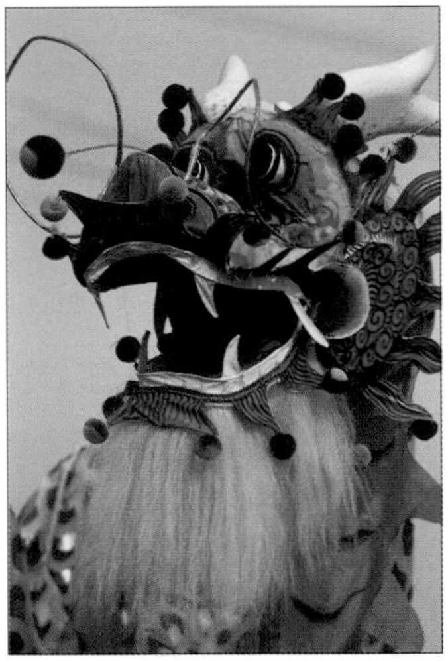

1

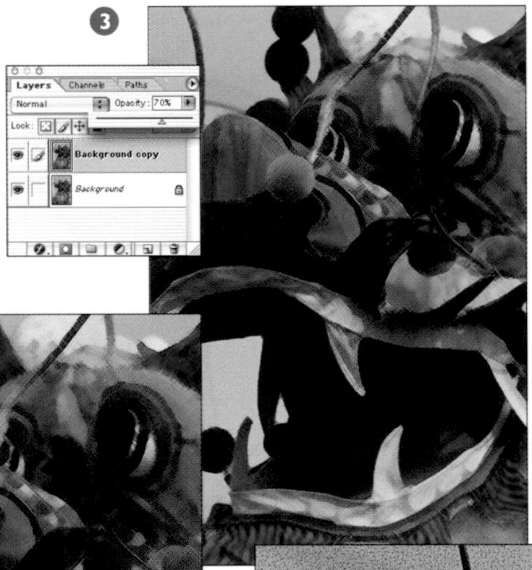

2

3

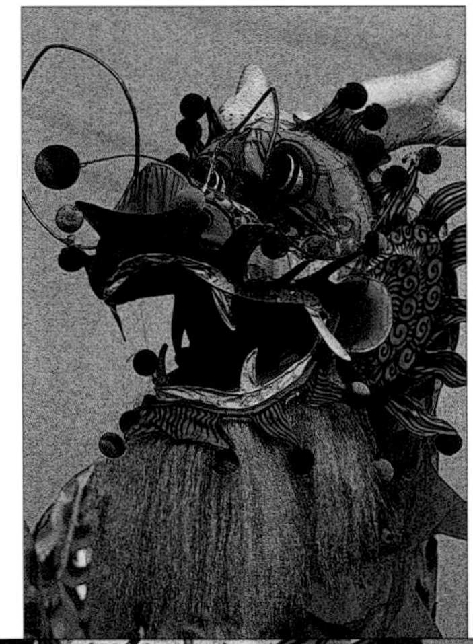

4

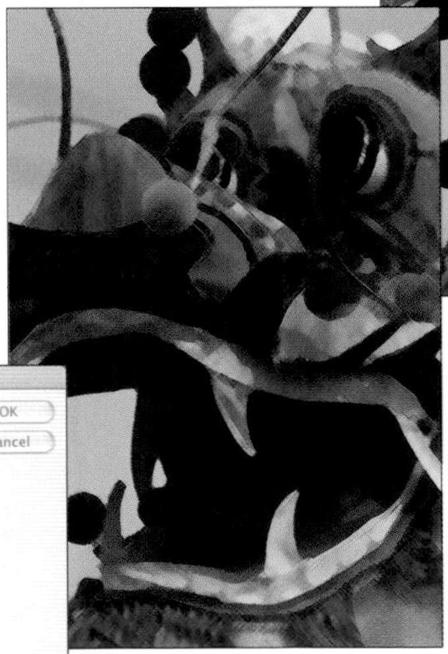

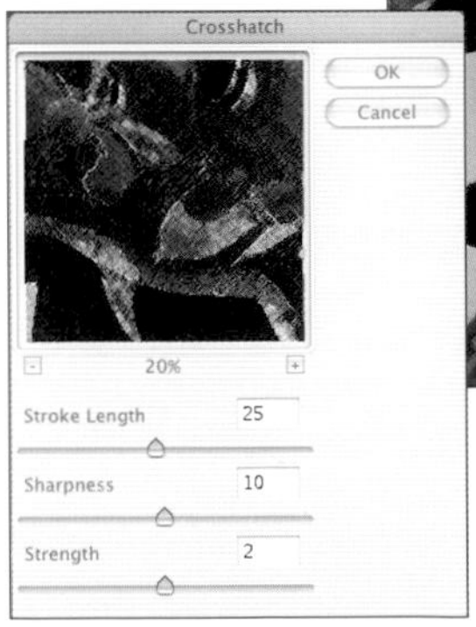

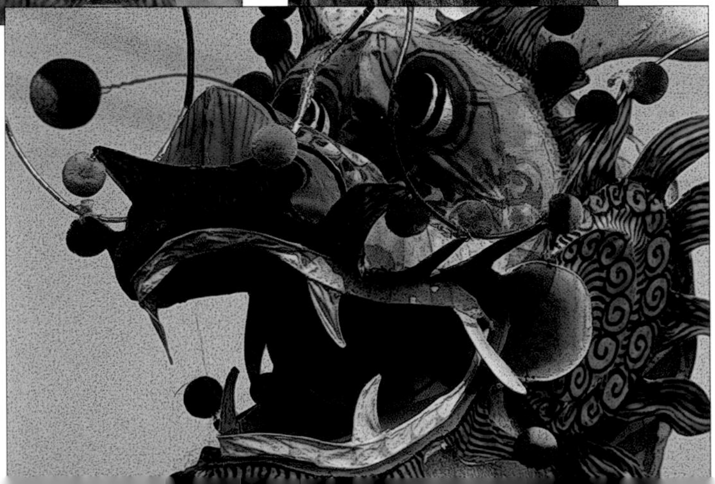

5

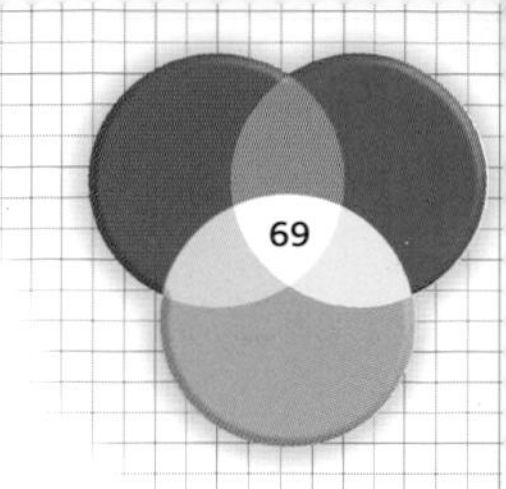

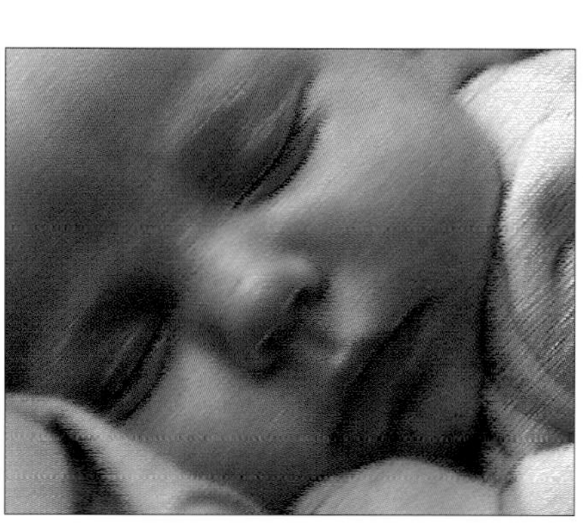

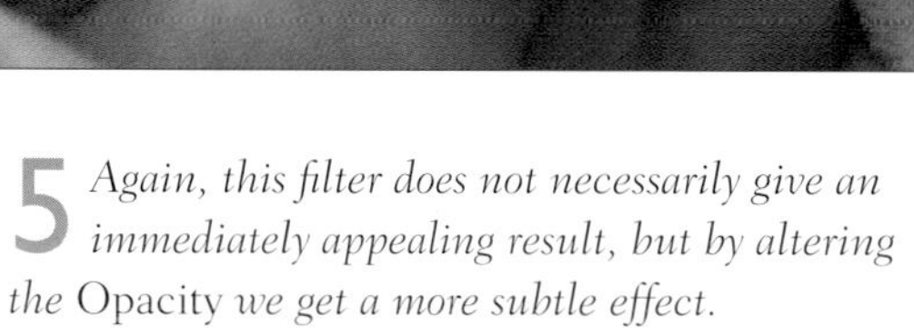

FILE SIZE MATTERS

An original Hasselblad 6 x 6 cm transparency was scanned to produce a high-resolution file size of 52MB and a smaller, medium resolution 7MB version of this snoozing infant.

The Rough Pastels *filter has been applied (using the default filter settings) to the high-resolution image. Note how fine the pastel textures are in the close-up of the central area.*

Using the same filter settings on the lower resolution version produces a more dramatic pastel effect. Neither is 'correct': the best settings and image size will depend on other factor. These would include the proposed printed image size and the viewing conditions.

LAYERING MULTIPLE FILTERS

1 *When combining more than one filter effect on a single image, you should apply each filter in an individual layer. By copying the image to new layers, the effects can be applied and then varied in strength by using the opacity control.*

2 *Create a duplicate layer and apply the chosen filter. Here we have used the* Crosshatch *brush stroke filter. As it is, the effect is rather severe and too graphic to be of any real use.*

3 *By altering the layer* Opacity *to 70%, we allow some of the original detail of the image, which was lost when the filter was applied, to appear through. The result is still a painterly effect, but with a greater amount of detail.*

4 *Make a second duplicate layer from the background. By applying a second filter, this time* Poster Edges*, we get a different interpretation.*

5 *Again, this filter does not necessarily give an immediately appealing result, but by altering the* Opacity *we get a more subtle effect.*

FILTERS AND IMAGE SIZE

Many effects filters work at pixel level. Whether the effect is to create a patch of colour by averaging underlying pixels, or – as in the case of some of the painting effects filters – to produce the effect of brush strokes, every filter works its magic by moving or otherwise transforming finite groups of pixels.

As a result, the visual effects of a filter will vary according to the size of the image. Applying a filter to a high resolution, 60 MB image will produce a different result from that produced when the same filter is applied to a 1 MB version. Though many filters offer changes options that enable you to scale the effect to suit the size of image, this characteristic is still an important one to bear in mind.

DARKROOM SECRETS 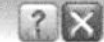

FILTER SHORTCUTS

Applying filter effects is simpler if you remember these shortcuts:

- Control/Apple-F applies the last filter used using the same settings as the previous time.
- Control-Alt-F (Windows) or Apple-Option-F (Mac) opens the dialog box for the last filter, allowing changes to be made to the effect settings before you apply it again.
- Control/Apple-Shift-F opens the *Fade* dialog box for the last applied filter, which allows the intensity of the effect to be altered as needed.

Filters and their secrets

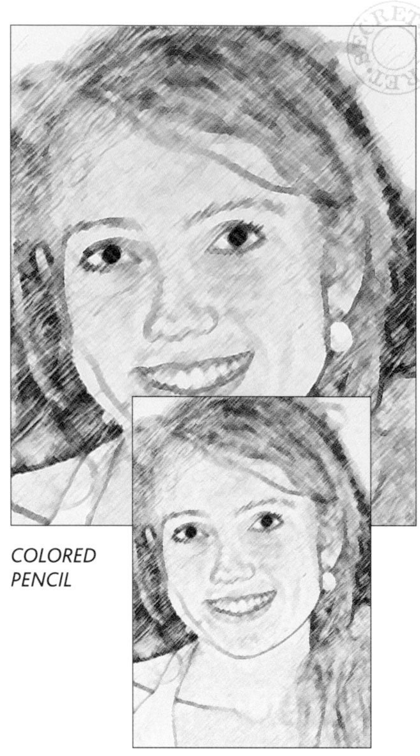

COLORED PENCIL

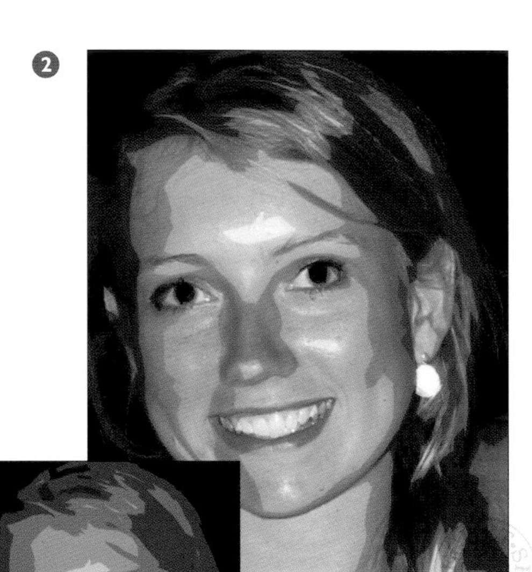

CUTOUT

When you bear in mind that there is always a temptation to treat filters as a quick fix for a failing image, it is no surprise that many newcomers to image-editing don't spend the time needed to learn how to get the best from them. Some filters are more useful than others – particularly when it comes to photographic work – but with some tweaks to the settings or a little work after the application, many become far more effective. We discuss many filters elsewhere, but the next few pages cover those that are most useful in the digital darkroom, and offer a few tips on how to deploy them.

❶ ARTISTIC > COLORED PENCIL...

Typical of the drawing type filters, the *Colored Pencil* recreates the image as if it had been sketched using coloured pencils on flat, even media. The dialog box permits the adjustment of the paper brightness. At a higher level the paper becomes white; at lower levels, grey.

Secret: The result can often look a little washed-out, but using *Edit* > ***Fade Colored Pencil*** to apply a *Color* blend mode will restore a little colour and detail.

❷ ARTISTIC > CUTOUT...

This filter recreates the image as if it were made from torn pieces of coloured paper. The result is similar to posterization but often the effect is more graphic and more illustrative. As with the *Posterize* filter, you can specify a number of levels but these tend to be quite sharpely defined.
Secret: Although this can produce a pleasing graphic effect, a subject will sometimes benefit from a little more of the original being visible. In this case use *Edit* > ***Fade Colored Pencil*** to apply the *Overlay* blend mode – but you may also need to desaturate the result (*Image* > *Adjustments* > ***Hue/Saturation***).

❸ ARTISTIC > FRESCO...

The *Fresco* filter applies large, sloppy dabs of paint to the image based on the underlying image. Small details tend to get lost, so this filter is best used with bold, graphic images in which elements tend to be reduced to bold graphic shapes. Setting the sliders to their maximum value

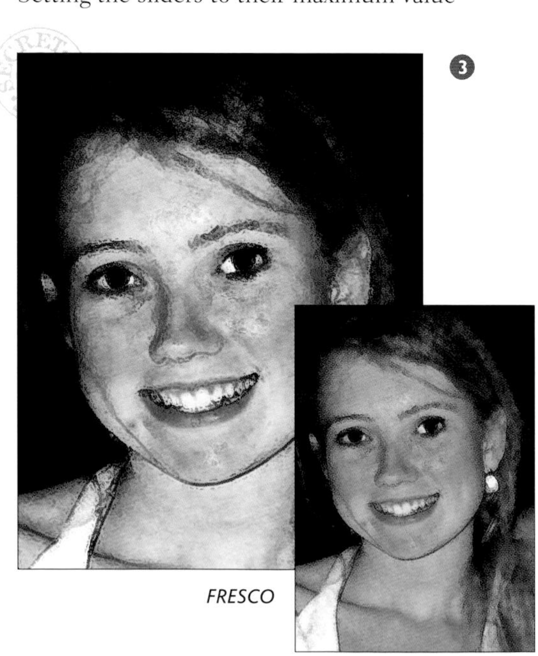

FRESCO

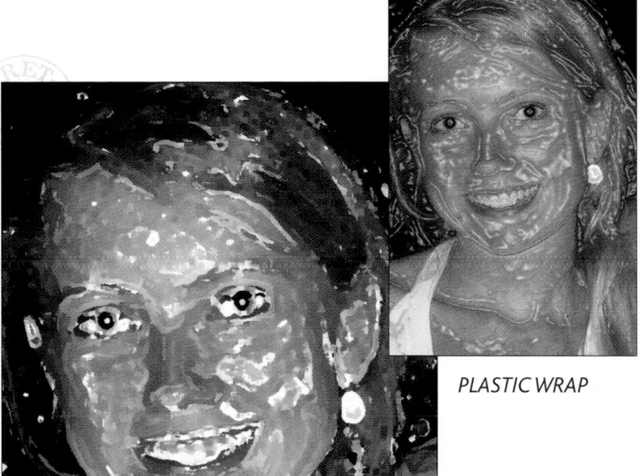

PLASTIC WRAP

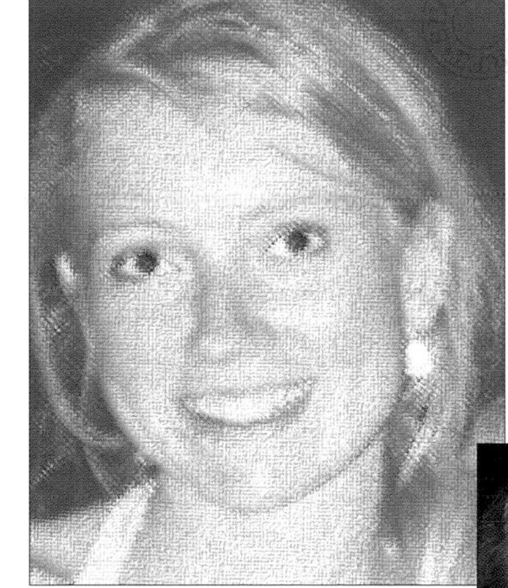

ROUGH PASTELS

generates a bold, slightly blurred result. Setting them to minimum produces a more refined result **Secret:** Although decribed as *Fresco,* this filter can generate an effect more like an oil painting by using *Edit > **Fade Fresco*** with a *Hard Light* blend mode.

❹ ARTISTIC > PLASTIC WRAP...

Gives the impression that the image has been placed behind plastic film and vacuum-wrapped. It is particularly useful for giving a fluid texture or appearance to image elements.
Secret: This is one of those filters on which the result depends entirely on the subject of the original – portraits, for example, usually look appalling. However, you can sometimes use the filter to produce a loose, painterly image by using it in combination with the *Dry Brush* filter.

❺ ARTISTIC > ROUGH PASTELS...

Uses the original colours of the image but represents the image as if it were drawn using pastel crayons on a textured surface. The type of surface and the roughness of the strokes can be specified by the user. Gives a hand-drawn result.
Secret: To avoid making the picture look too blurred, set the *Stroke Length* to 0. This filter can sometimes increase colour saturation, in which case, desaturate the picture (*Image > Adjustments > **Hue/Saturation***) before running the filter. You can produce a softer result by reducing the contrast of the original before running the filter. Then, for an even softer image, run the filter twice, but – and here's the trick – before running it the second time, rotate the canvas 90° clockwise (*Image > Rotate Canvas >* **90°CW**). Finally, having run the filter for the second time, restore the picture to its original orientation by choosing *Image > Rotate Canvas >* **90°CCW**.

❻ ARTISTIC > POSTER EDGES...

This filter first posterizes the image (to a predetermined number of levels) and then applies a fine black line around the edges. The intensity and thickness of the defining lines can be specified to produce several different effects. The result is similar to *Cutout*, but with a slightly less graphic appearance.

PERFECT POSTER EDGES

The Poster Edges *filter can sometimes produce a rather dirty image, but experimenting with different blend modes on duplicates of the Background layer can often produce more interesting results. This example uses a combination of the* Color Dodge *and* Exclusion *blend modes applied to duplicate layers of the original background. The layer with the* Exclusion *blend mode is also inverted. The filter was finally applied to yet another duplicate of the original, to which a* Linear Dodge *was then applied.*

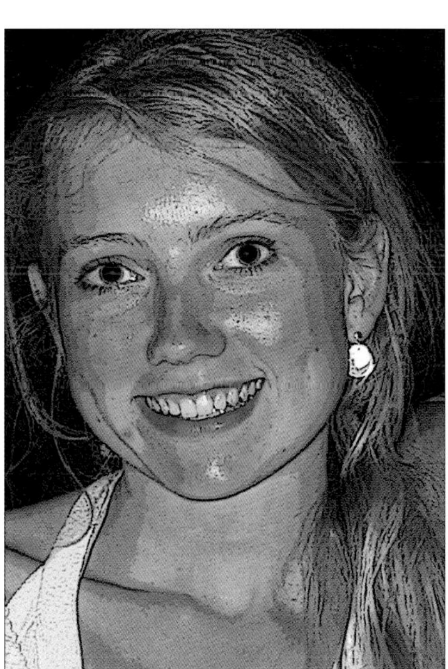

POSTER EDGES

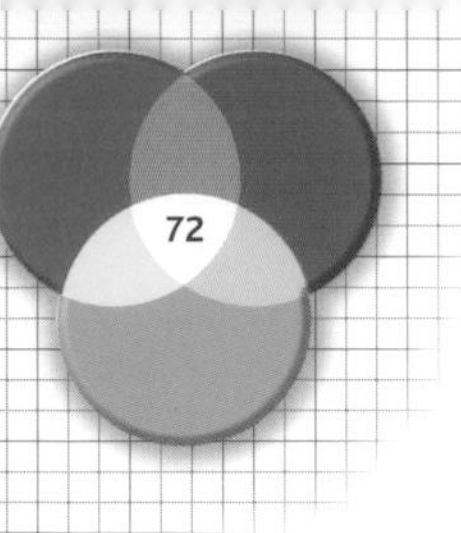

Filters and their secrets

7

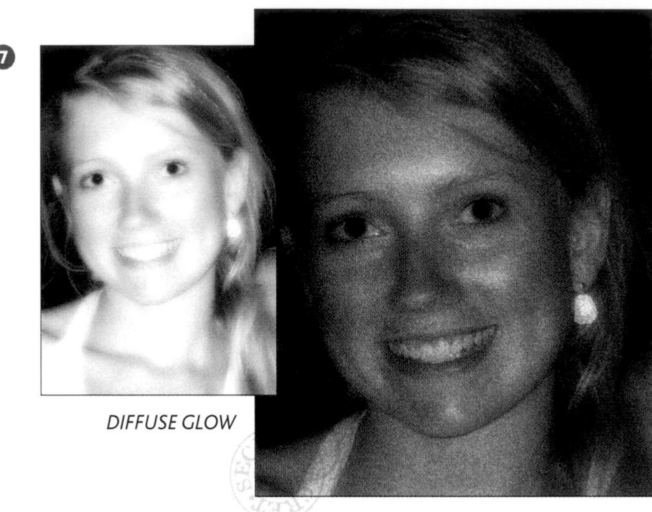

DIFFUSE GLOW

7 DISTORT > DIFFUSE GLOW...

This gives an effect like a diffusion or soft-focus photographic filter, but with added noise. The effect is stronger on brighter areas of the image. **Secret:** The 'glow' is determined by setting the background colour, with white usually giving the best glow. However, an almost opposite effect of a 'glow' can be applied to the darker areas by choosing black as the background colour and applying the filter to a duplicate layer, then setting then blend mode to *Difference*.

PAINTING WITH GLASS

*You can also use the Glass distortion filter to give your image an attractive, painterly texture. First of all, create a duplicate layer of the original image, then apply the Glass filter using the Tiny Lens texture. When that's done, invert the duplicate layer (Image > Adjust > **Invert**). Now set the blend mode of the duplicate layer to Color Dodge and you should get a result like this. You can get a further effect, resembling a watercolour, by simply giving the duplicate layer a Gaussian Blur.*

8 DISTORT > GLASS...

The Glass filter simulates the placement of different types of glass over the image. Preset glass types are provided, and you can also create and save custom versions. This example uses the Frosted texture with a low percentage of scaling.

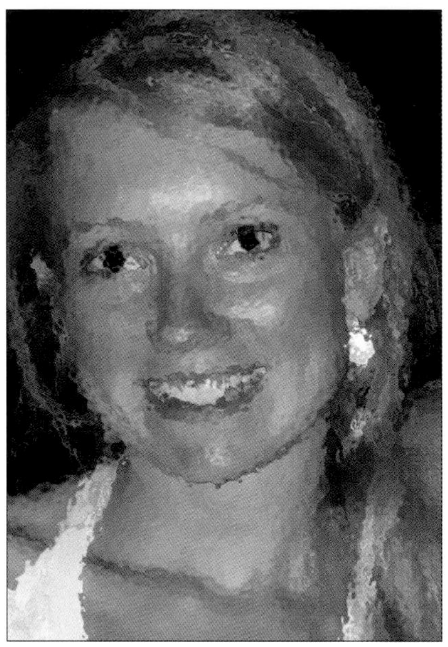

8

GLASS

9 PIXELATE > MEZZOTINT...

Using lines or dots, this simulates the effect of the mezzotint printing technique. However, when the filter is applied to an unmodified colour image, it can produce a rather dead result. You will invariably produce a more interesting result by increasing the contrast of the original before applying the filter.
Secret: You can get a more dramatic graphic effect by thresholding each of the colour channels in turn, then applying the filter to each individually.

10 PIXELATE > MOSAIC...

This recreates the image using square mosaic tiles averaged from the underlying pixels, resulting in an effect usually described as 'pixelated'. Mosaic tile sizes can range between 2 and 200 pixels.

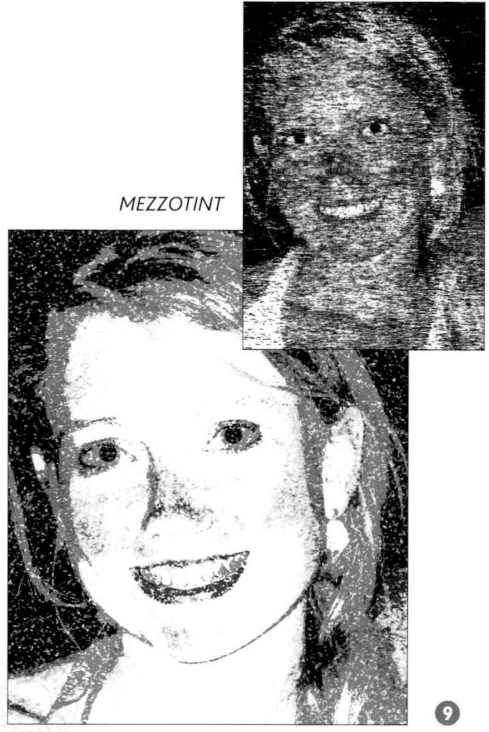
MEZZOTINT
9

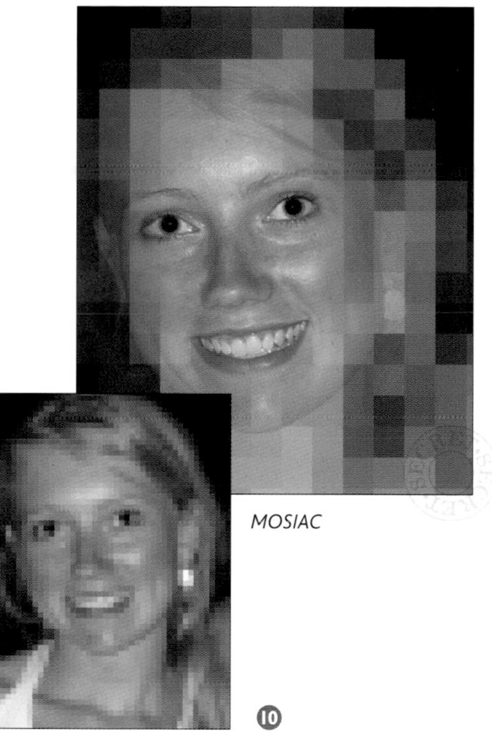
MOSIAC
10

Secret: You can create a graphic effect by protecting part of the image and then applying the filter to the unprotected part. In this example we drew an oval around the face, feathered the resulting selection, inverted it and then applied the *Mosaic* filter.

11 RENDER > LENS FLARE...

Lens Flare introduces the internal reflection patterns that are produced when a shot is taken towards, or close to, a bright light. This can add drama and impact to a shot. Patterns corresponding to wide-angle, telephoto and zoom lenses are provided.
Secret: This filter works better on darker images, so, if necessary, darken your image before application. If your picture is of a person, make sure that the *Flare Center* is not within the shape of their figure.

12 PIXELATE > POINTILLIZE...

This filter simulates a painting in the style of Seurat, Sisley or Signac, by recreating the image in pointillist dots. When using *Pontillize*, your choice of background colour is particularly important. As the filter generates the dots, it leaves spaces between them, the colour of which is determined by your background colour. In the top example shown here, the background is 100% magenta, but another colour might suit your image better.
Secret: You may want your image to be made entirely of dots, without any background colour showing through. In this case, simply make duplicate layers of the original image (about four will do) and apply the filter to each, giving each layer a *Darken* blend mode. As the filter generates a different, random pattern each time it runs, the gaps between the pixels should be filled.

12
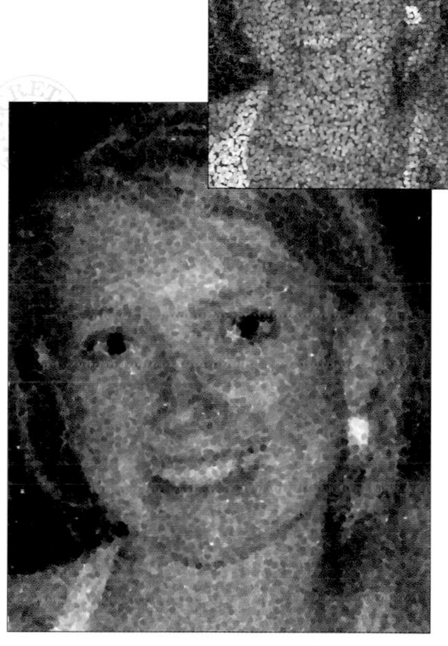
POINTILLIZE

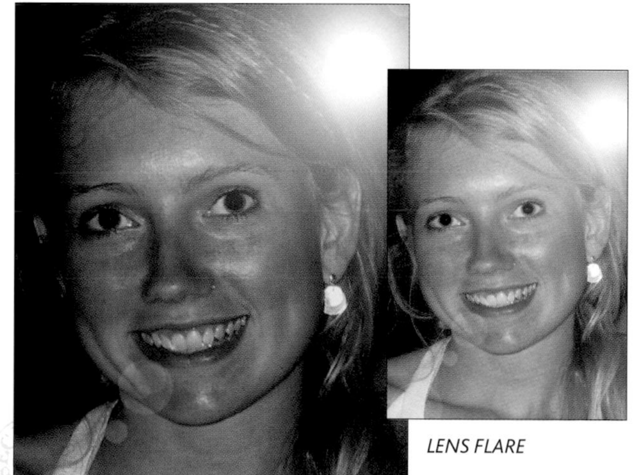
LENS FLARE
11

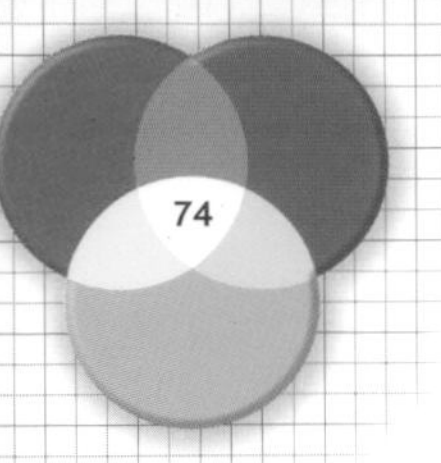

Filters and their secrets

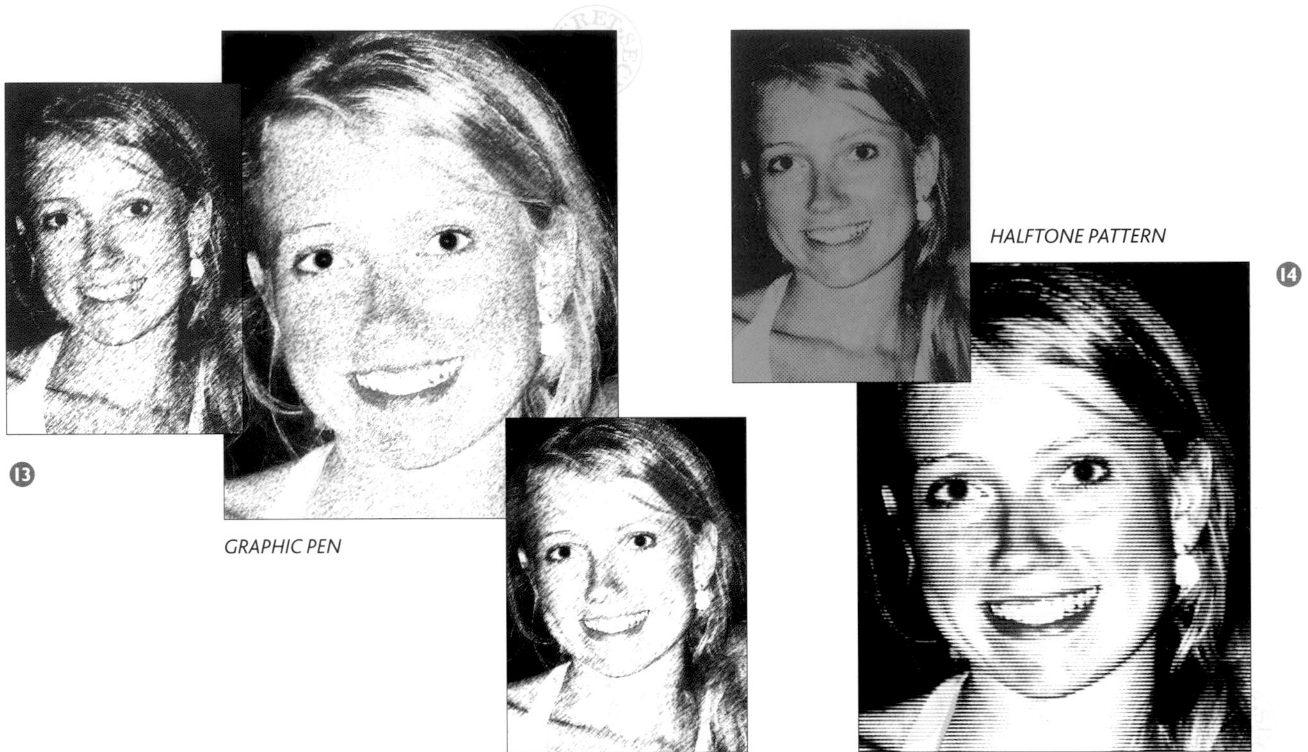

GRAPHIC PEN

HALFTONE PATTERN

⓭ SKETCH > GRAPHIC PEN...

A sketching filter that renders an image as if it were drawn with a graphic pen. Used on its own it generates very powerful black-and-white images, but fading the effect can add colour to create a hand-drawn, hand-tinted effect.

Secret 1: For a subtle result, *Fade* the *Graphic Pen* and use the *Overlay* blend mode. You can also fiddle with the *Opacity*, but the effect will depend on your image – for this image, we chose to leave it at 100%.

Secret 2: Duplicate the background layer of the original image and then apply the filter to each of the colour channels (try different settings for each). This creates a colour image. Set the blend mode to *Color Dodge* with 50% *Opacity*.

⓮ SKETCH > HALFTONE PATTERN...

While *Pixelate* > ***Color Halftone*** provides a means of simulating the printing process used for color images, *Sketch* > ***Halftone Pattern*** offers far more creative possibilities, providing options for dots, lines and circular lines. Essentially, when applied to a colour image the filter generates a monochrome result, the colours of which are determined by the background and foreground colours (make sure that your background colour is lighter than the foreground or the resulting image will be in negative).

Secret: By applying the filter to each of the colour channels in turn, you can create an interesting four-colour effect.

⓯ SKETCH > RETICULATION...

This mimics the effect of large changes of temperature or acidity on film emulsion, and generates a monochrome stippled image, the colours of which are determined by your choice of foreground and background colors.

Secret: You'll get a more colorful result by using the *Fade* command to reduce the opacity, and choosing *Luminosity* as the blend mode.

16 STYLIZE > EMBOSS...

The edges in the image are identified and then given an apparent raise or depression. The result is an image that appears to be imprinted on a flat (normally grey) surface.

Secret: You can combine the *Emboss* filter with a *Fade* command and the *Luminosity* blend mode if you want to retain some colour detail.

17 STYLIZE > WIND...

A simple filter that can be used to suggest motion. Edge highlights are drawn into short or long lines. The direct application is rather crude, but it can be combined with the *Fade* command. Use the *Stagger* option for the random ripples shown in the portrait here (right).

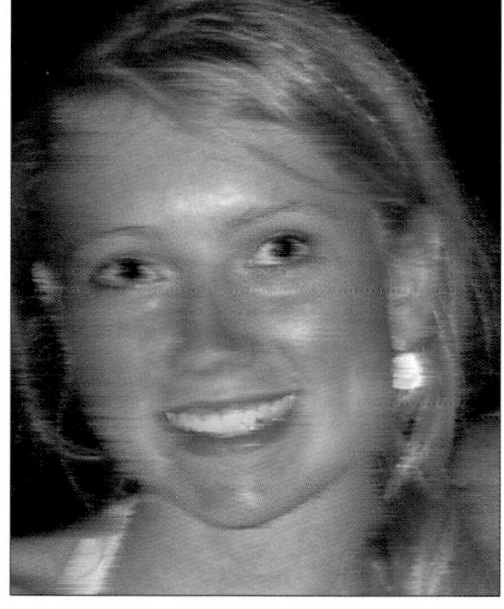

15

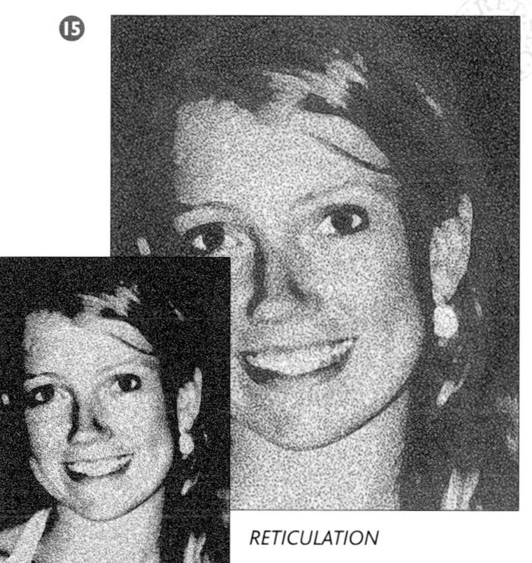

RETICULATION

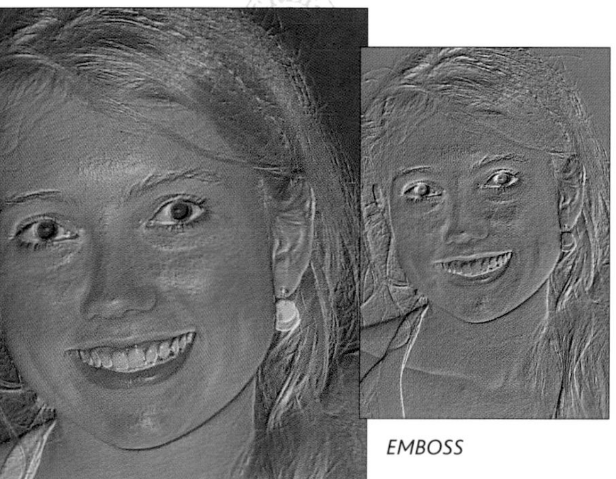

EMBOSS

16

MAKING WIND WORK

Wind doesn't always do much on its own, but try this little expert tip. First of all, duplicate the background layer of your image. Having done so, run the Image > Adjust > **Threshold** *command on the duplicate layer, with a 128* Threshold *level. Now apply a* Gaussian Blur *to the image with a* Radius *of 3.*

Now you need to apply the Distort > **Polar Coordinates** *filter, selecting the* Polar to Rectangular *option, then use* Edit> Transform> Rotate Canvas > **90° CW** *to turn the image on its side. Now pick* Filter> Stylize > **Wind** *to apply the filter with the* Wind *option. It doesn't matter whether the 'wind' effect comes from the left or the right. Now use* Edit> Transform> Rotate Canvas > **90° CCW** *to rotate the image back to its start position, then Apply the* Polar Coordinates *filter once again, this time with the* Rectangular to Polar *option selected. You should get an effect like the one above right, although it's worth experimenting with the blend mode between the two layers. Here we used the* Screen *blend mode at 90% opacity.*

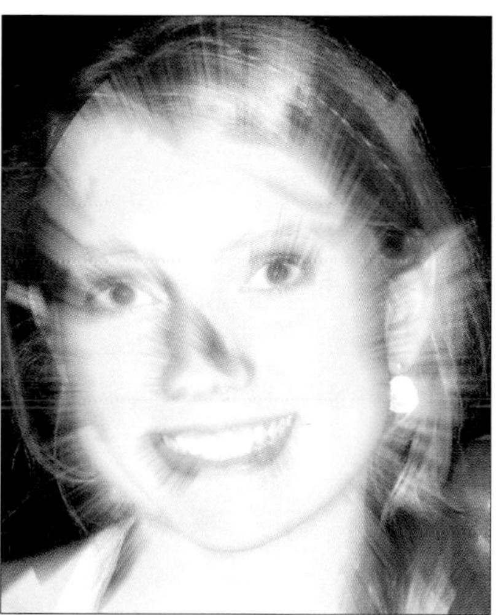

WIND

17

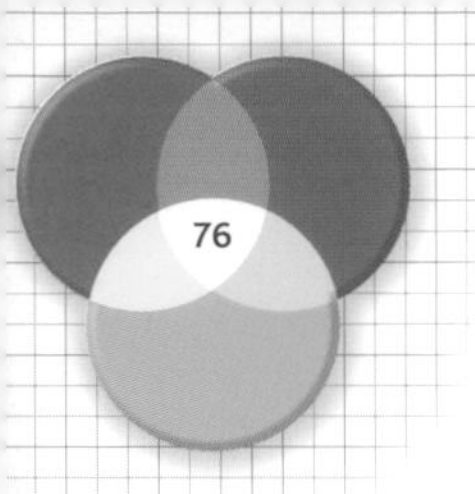

Motion effects and selective blurring

We often use blurring to cover faults in an image or to differentiate a subject from its surroundings. However, we can also use blurring to give a still image an impression of rapid movement, in the same way that we might use a long exposure in a conventional photo. To do so, we use two of the other filters in the *Blur* suite: *Motion Blur* and *Radial Blur*.

We can interpret motion effects in two ways. We can create an effect similar to panning the camera to track the car in motion, where the subject appears sharp but the background is blurred. Alternatively, we can give the vehicle the motion, keeping the surrounding landscape sharp. In this example we will try and give the image a panned effect.

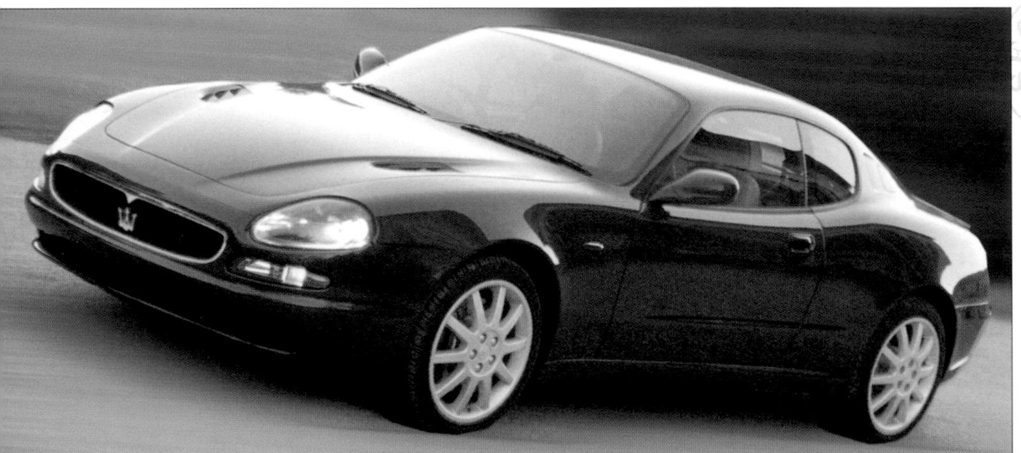

1

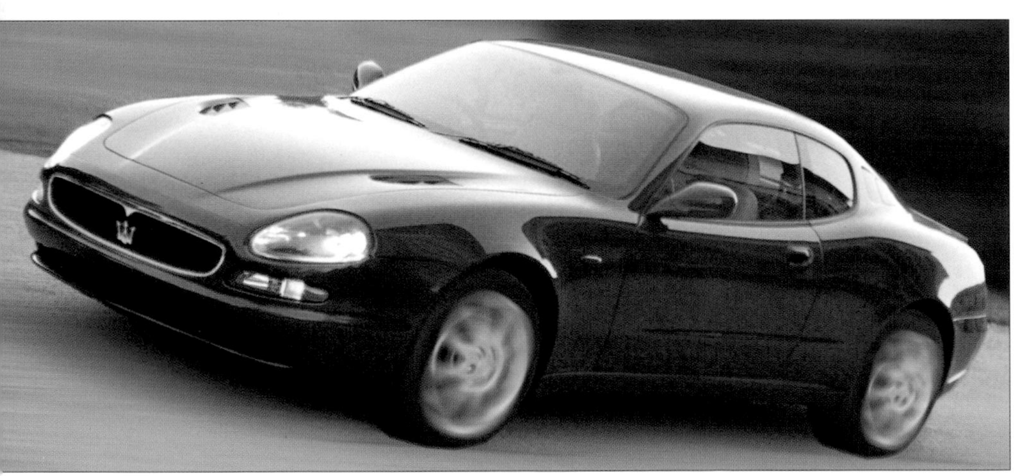

2

GETTING A MOVE ON

1 *Begin by selecting the subject, using any of the appropriate selection tools. Copy the selection to one layer, and invert it so that the subject's surroundings are selected. Now copy this selection to another layer. We will first apply the blur to the background without the subject included: the* Motion Blur *filter drags the layer's contents in the direction of the blur and, if we used the background layer itself, the subject will smear as well. You will also need to adjust the angle of the* Motion Blur *so that it aligns with the direction of the car's movement if you want the effect to succeed.*

2 *Now we need to work on the wheels. Notice how the car appears to be in motion but that the motionless wheels betray the conceit. Select each wheel in turn and apply the* Radial Blur *filter to it. Ensure that the* Radial *mode, not the* Zoom *mode, is selected. This can be difficult to perform successfully, but see the text insert for a useful tip. With all in place, the finished car appears to be tearing along the road!*

3 *For some added drama, we have added a lighting effect. By selecting* Filter > Render > **Lighting Effects** *and then the* Blue Omni, *you can change the ambient lighting from a cold blue to warm red, merely by sliding the Intensity slider. The final result is a much more dynamic image with a genuine feeling of speed.*

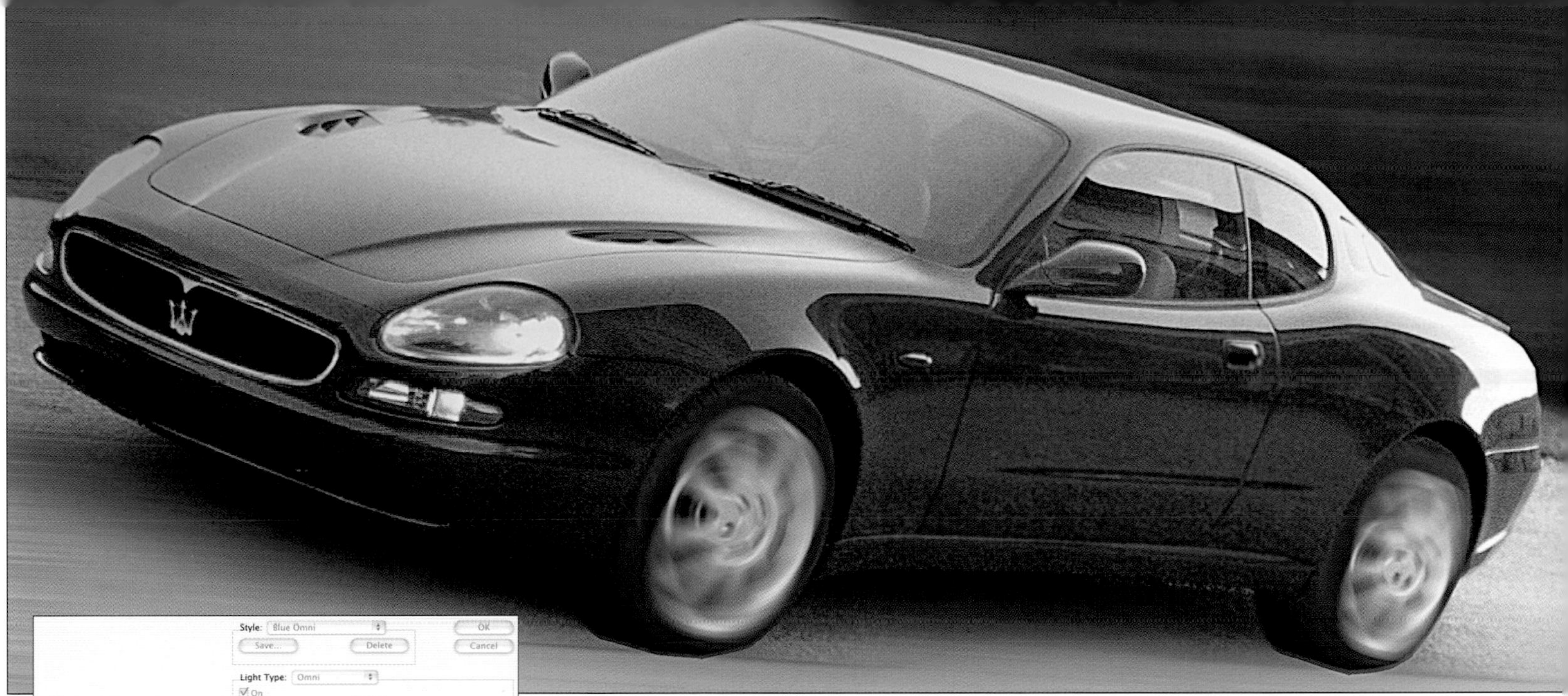

3

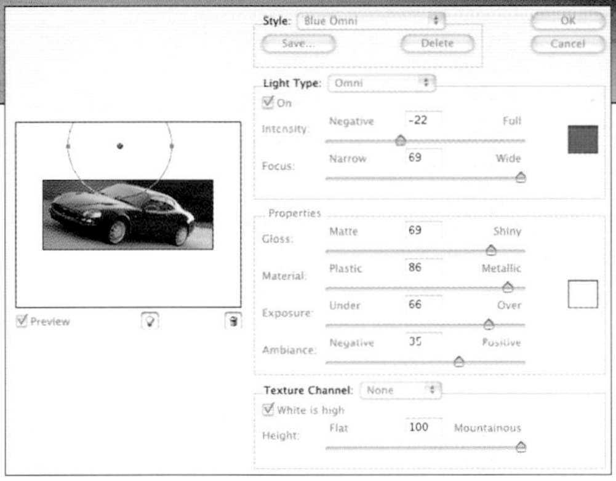

ZOOMING WITH THE RADIAL BLUR FILTER

Change the mode of the *Radial Blur* filter to *Zoom* and we can also create very effective zoom effects, akin to those produced when a camera's zoom control is operated during exposure. It is an excellent technique for isolating a subject and focusing attention.

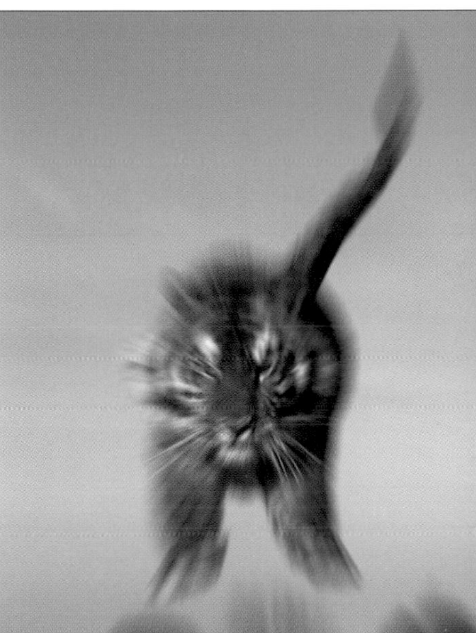

The zoom effect works best if the subject is selected and the filter is then applied with a large feather radius to the surroundings. This prevents the subject from becoming unduly blurred.

GETTING RADIAL BLUR JUST RIGHT

The Radial Blur *filter normally applies the blur from the centre of the image. Though you can move this centre point anywhere on the image, you do so using the dialog box display rather than the image itself. This makes it difficult to get the precision necessary to produce a* Radial Blur *centred on the wheel centre.*

To achieve the necessary accuracy, use a selection tool to select the wheel and, where appropriate, the tyre too. Copy this selection and then open a new image. When you select File > New *in Photoshop, the new image will be the same size as the copied selection.*

Paste *in your selection and perform the radial blur on this large, centred image. Once applied,* Paste *the image back into the main image. The* Radial Blur *should look realistic, precise and effective.*

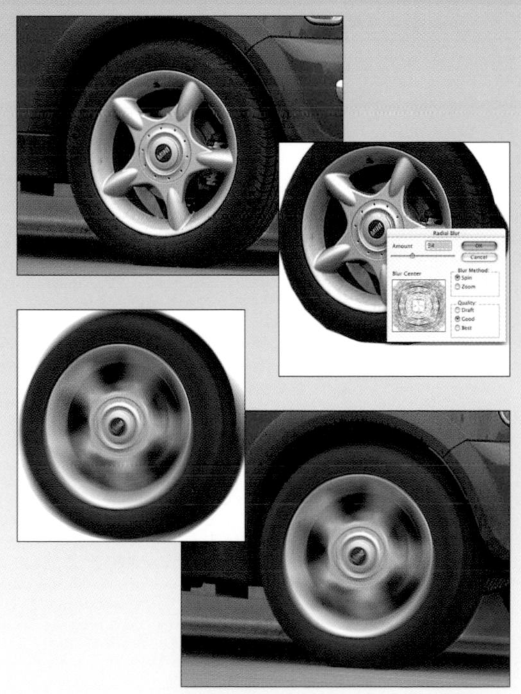

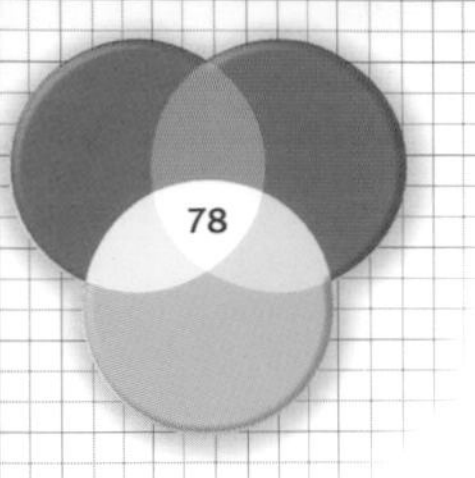

Adding grain for impact

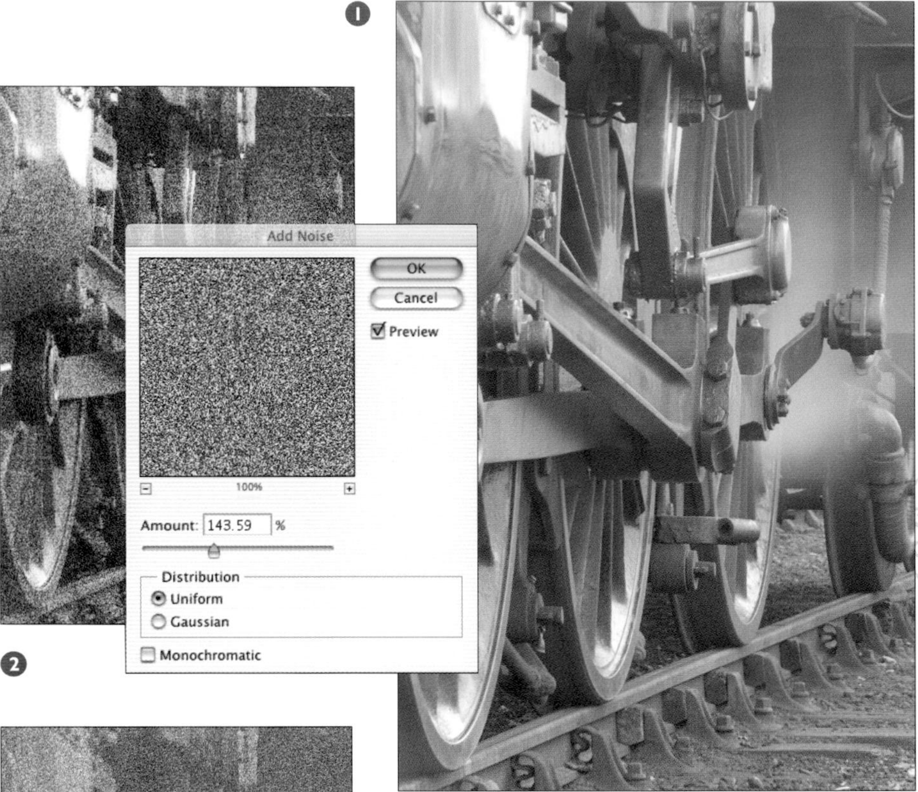

3

Despite the fact that film manufacturers spend millions to produce film stock with increasingly fine grain, many photographers still take pains to enhance the grain in their shots. Using film known for its grain structure – particularly the fast monochrome films – they exaggerate it in the darkroom to achieve gritty, atmospheric results.

Although digital images have their own grain structure – the pixel pattern – this doesn't give quite the same effect. Fortunately we can use our effects filters to introduce artificial grain into any image that demands it. As a bonus, this 'fake' grain is a lot easier to control than the real thing.

PRODUCING ARTIFICIAL GRAIN

1 *Although there is an element of cliché, grain effects work best with gritty, industrial images. This cropped-in photograph of a train's wheels is a perfect example.*

2 *Rather than apply the grain directly to the image, we will apply it in a layer. This will allow changes to the blend mode (and other parameters) if we need to alter them later. Select* Layer > **New Layer**, *and choose* Overlay *as the blend mode. Set a 50% neutral grey fill too.*

We can now add a grain texture to this layer. Instead of using a film grain filter, we will use the Filter > Noise > **Add Noise** *command. The dialog lets you set the amount of grain using a slider, and choose from* Uniform *or* Gaussian *and* Chromatic *or* Monochromatic *noise.*

3 *When the* Monochromatic *box is unchecked, you get a multicoloured grain effect. This works well when combined with very fine grain structures, but the coloration tends to dominate at larger settings. Until you become practised in the use of this filter, it is best to keep the box checked.*

4 *Selecting* Gaussian *for the noise type alters the distribution so that there is more noise in the midtones and less in the highlights and shadows. Now adjust the amount of grain until you get the*

ACHIEVING AUTHENTICITY

Authenticity is a perennial problem for digitally manipulated images. The techniques involved enable any one of a range of effects to be applied to an image in seconds, and this simplicity often leads to their inappropriate use. In our digital darkroom work, we need to establish a rationale. Does the effect enhance the image? If it does, what does it bring to the image that was not there originally?

When using effects, we must be sure that we achieve a result that improves on the components. Does this mean that we should never use a gritty, masculine effect on a portrait of, say, a young girl? Maybe, but if the results will be effective and make a statement, do so!

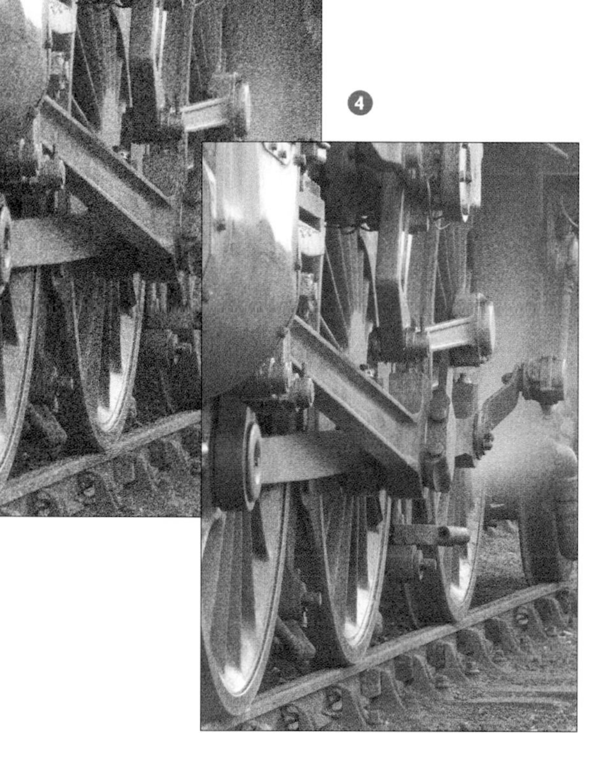

4

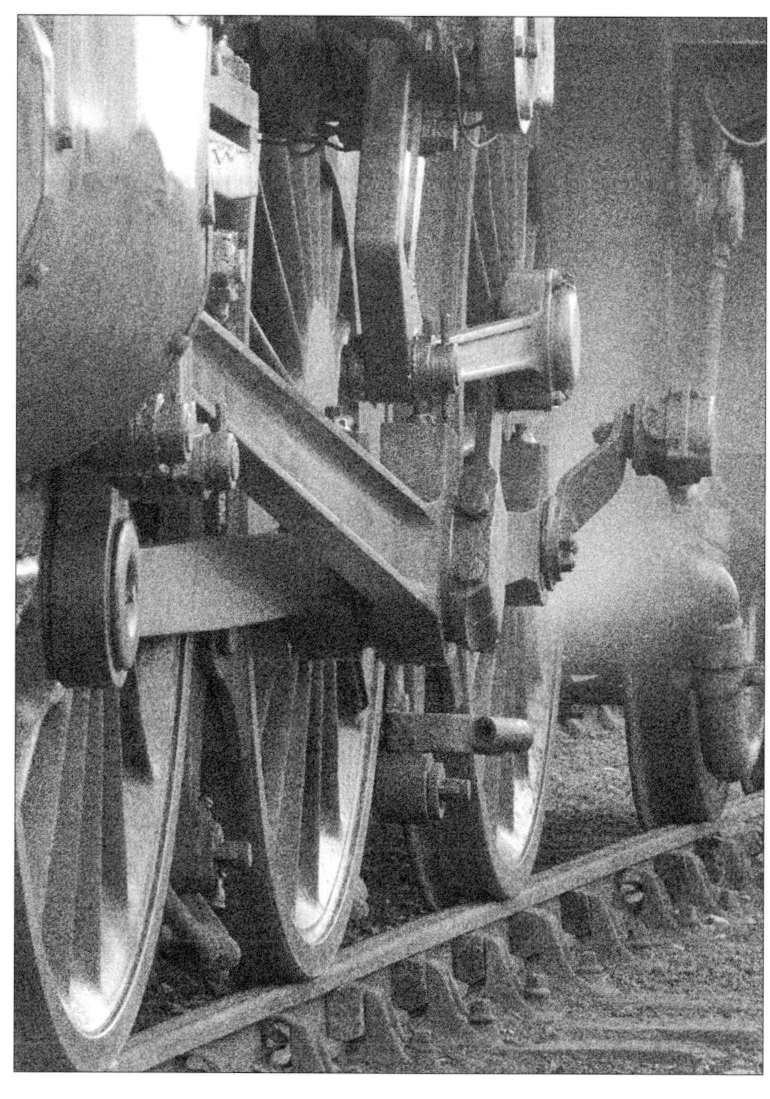

5

effect you desire. Note that the noise filter effects are based on pixel dimensions and therefore the amount of noise that needs to be applied varies according to the size and resolution of the image. For this 4.5MB image, noise settings of 25% (left) and 50% (right) have been applied.

5 *If the grain size is okay but the effect dominates the image – or if you want to use a high noise level that might do so – use the* Opacity *slider for the 'grain' layer to give the effect a slight fade. As an alternative, try changing the blend mode to emphasise or soften the grain.*

TRUE GRIT

It might seem strange, but in most image editors the Add Noise *filter does a better job of creating grain than the dedicated* Grain *filter. This filter isn't superfluous, however. The alternate textures provided allow the production of other gritty textures that are useful in, amongst other things, simulating aged photographs.*

This image has been treated with Horizontal Grain. *To enhance the effect, the* Hue/Saturation *tool has been used to reduce the* Saturation *by 30% and the* Hue *by 10%.*

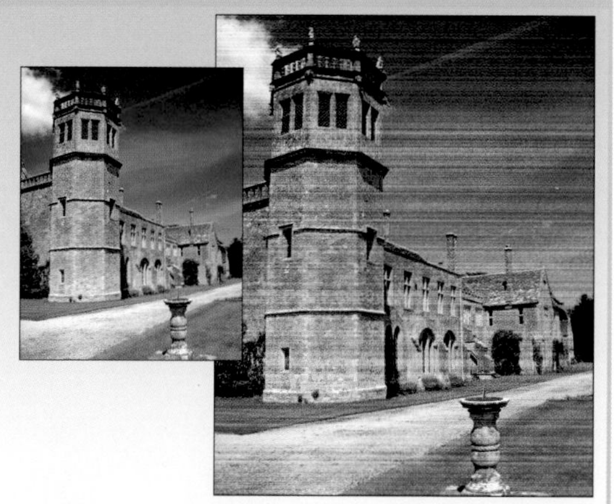

DARKROOM SECRETS

USING GRAIN IN MONTAGE

Grain can have other uses too. When we use montage to combine image elements of differing original resolutions and grain patterns, any new or transplanted elements can be obvious, wrecking the unity of the image. Adding a modest amount of grain across the composite can restore it.

SECTION THREE

pro techniques

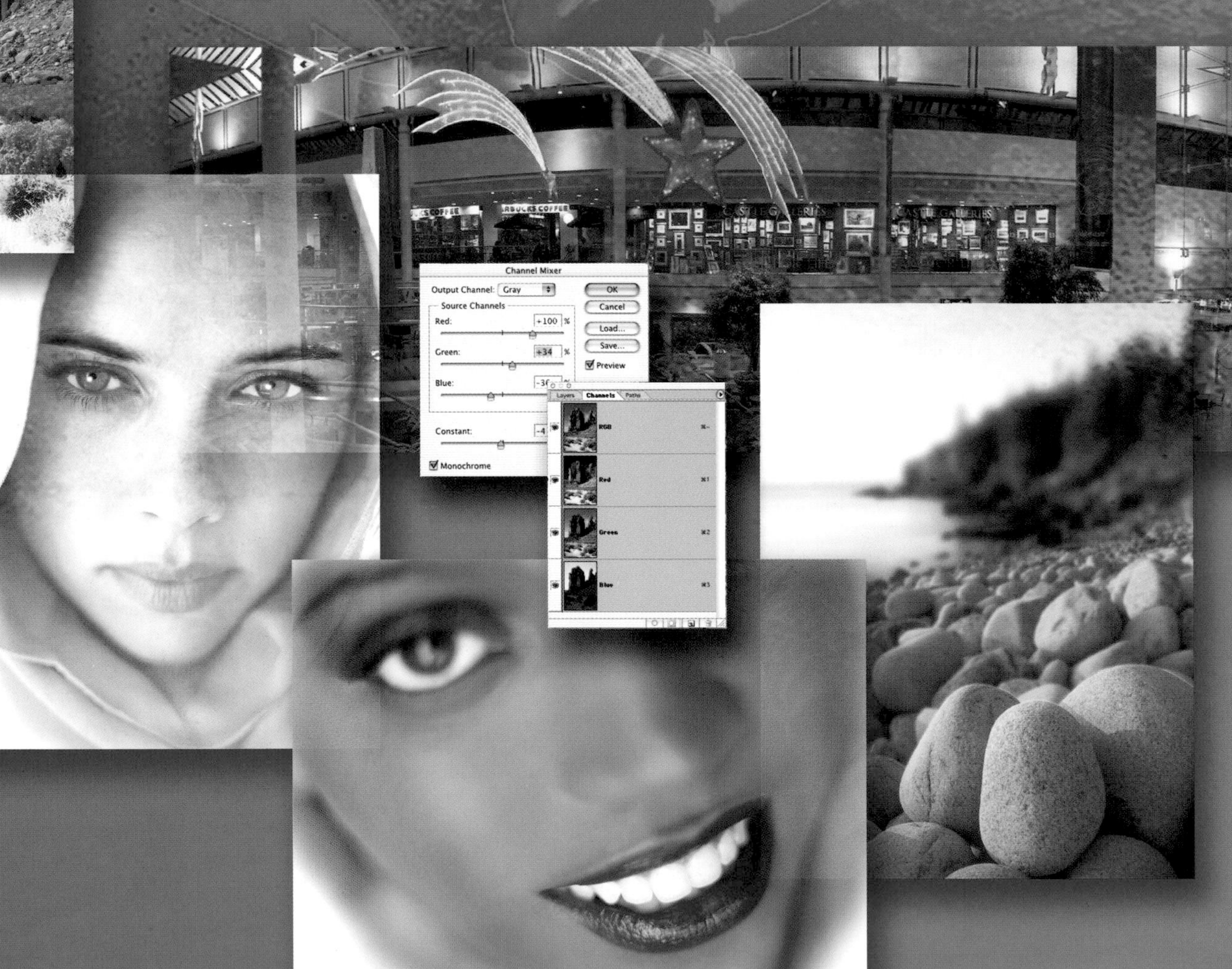

If you've come this far, you probably have a taste for the power of the digital darkroom, but there's still plenty more to discover. By using either basic tools in an advanced form, or by creating composite effects, we can achieve some far more intriguing results.

In some cases, these effects don't need to be obvious. Sometimes, we actually want to produce images that look like they were produced in-camera. In the following pages, you'll find out how to use blur filters to simulate depth of field, how to create perfect soft-focus portraits through a mixture of blurs and blend modes, and how to produce brooding black-and-white landscape shots without losing any tone. You will see how we can emulate the effects of light and shadow, recreate the look of standard photographic filters and turn a set of photos into a wide-angle panorama.

Other projects are more audacious. If you want to know how to turn day into night, transform photos into paintings or even create images that travel back in time, this chapter will show you the secrets. Little is impossible in the digital darkroom, and with confidence and experience you will soon discover other exciting ways of moulding reality to your own devices.

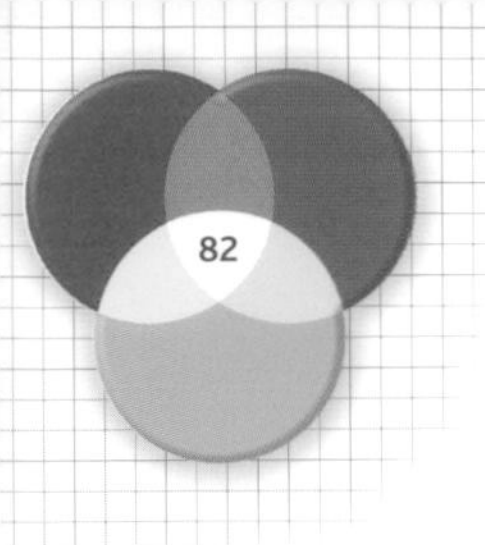

PRO TECHNIQUES

Correcting errors of perspective

Having learned the basic techniques of the digital darkroom, it's now time we put them to more good use. By applying or combining tools, we are able to correct the more troublesome faults that plague all photographers, or to simulate a range of photographic effects. We can easily emulate soft focus or high-key techniques, add artificial lighting to our images, create rich black-and-white tones from colour images or produce photos with a hand-tinted look. We can turn our photos into paintings, mosaics or panoramas, and we can even turn back the hands of time. You have already had a glimpse of the power of the digital darkroom – now prepare to see the bigger picture.

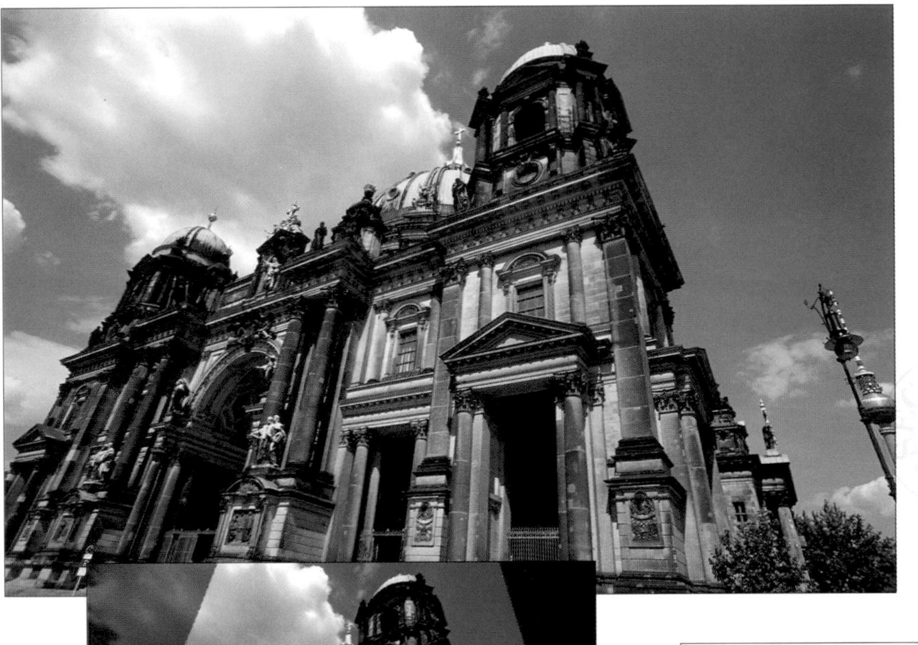

1

2

Perspective effects have plagued photography since its earliest days. Expensive specialised lenses made it possible for professional photographers to make in-camera corrections, but otherwise the darkroom worker had to solve these problems by tilting the enlarger baseboard. With Photoshop 6 and above, the task is much easier. The *Crop* tool has a *Perspective* option, which allows us to adjust the boundaries of the tool to compensate for perspective and convergence.

USING CROP IN PERSPECTIVE

1 *This image shows perspective effects typical of those that result when a conventional camera is used to photograph a building from ground level.*

2 *We can now use the* Crop *tool to make the corrections. Drag the* Crop *tool across the*

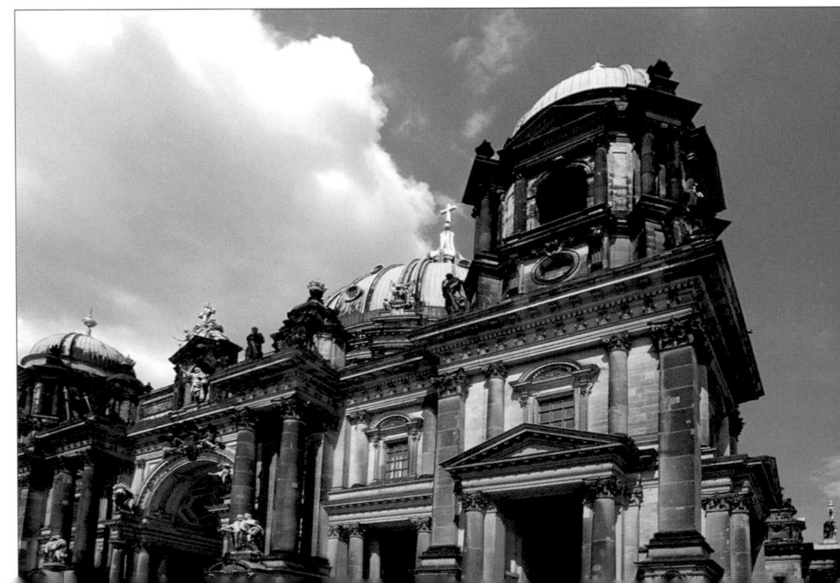

3

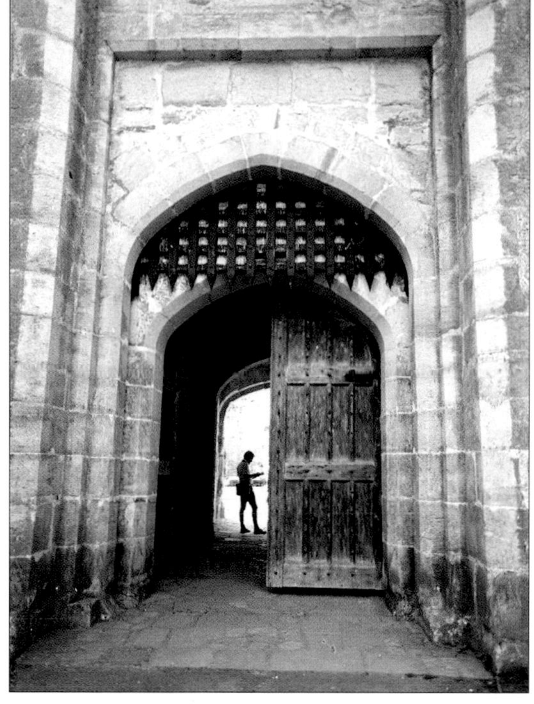

1

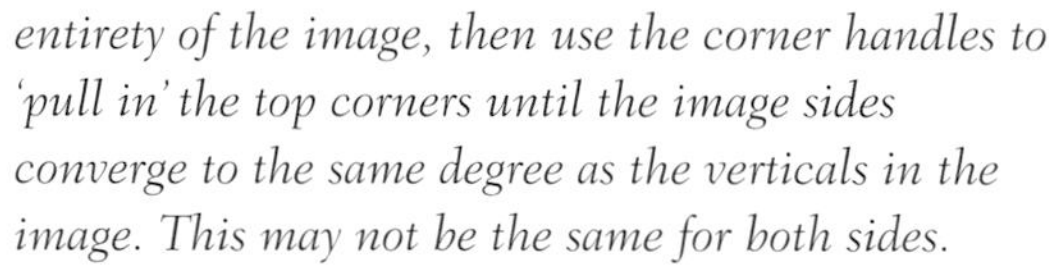

entirety of the image, then use the corner handles to 'pull in' the top corners until the image sides converge to the same degree as the verticals in the image. This may not be the same for both sides.

3 *Apply the* Crop *as normal and the image will appear with the errors of perspective corrected.*

If you have problems making the crop, or if you use an earlier version of Photoshop, you can achieve similar results by using the *Free Transform* command. Here we are using it to correct vertical and horizontal convergence in a castle gatehouse.

USING FREE TRANSFORM

1 *Begin by drawing a selection over the image. Then select the* Free Transform *tool to convert the selection into a* Transform *frame.*

2 *Hold down the* Command *(or* Control*) key and drag the corners to give the required correction. You can move any corner independently.*

3 *You can turn on the grid to help compose the image. The grid will remain fixed to the original image boundaries.*

4 *When you accept the corrections (by clicking on the check mark in the* Tool Options *bar in Photoshop), your image is left with gaps and will need cropping. Some detail may be lost, but the corrected image is much more satisfactory.*

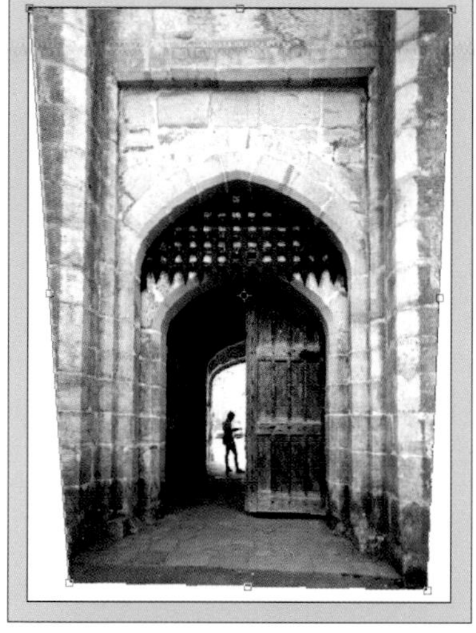

2

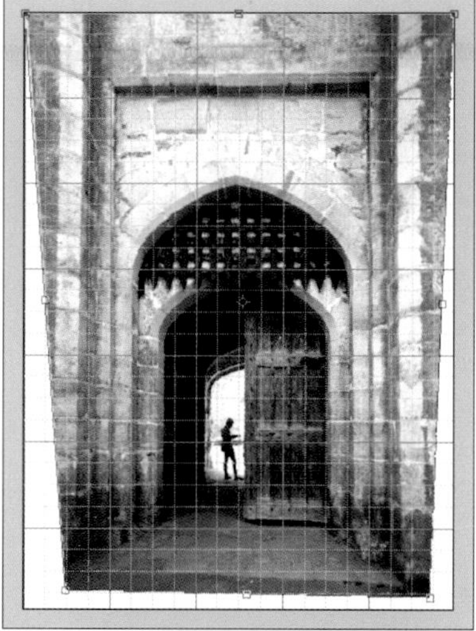

3

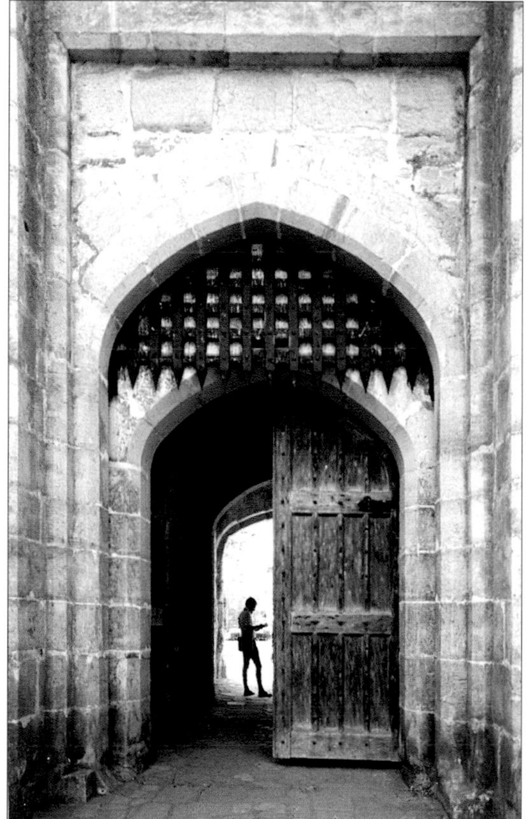

4

DARKROOM SECRETS

You may need to alter the proportions of a perspective cropped image, as there is a tendency for the corrected image to look stretched in the direction of the original convergence. For instance, shortening a corrected image of a building can preserve a natural look. You can adjust the proportions from the *Image Size* dialog – uncheck the *Constrain Proportions* box and reduce the appropriate dimension by 10%.

Correcting perspective effects does mean cropping (quite heavily in some cases) into the image extremes. Where there is insufficient image at the edge of the scene, your subject could be compromised. If you envisage needing to correct the perspective later, it's a good idea to shoot a little wider than would normally be the case to give leeway during the final correction.

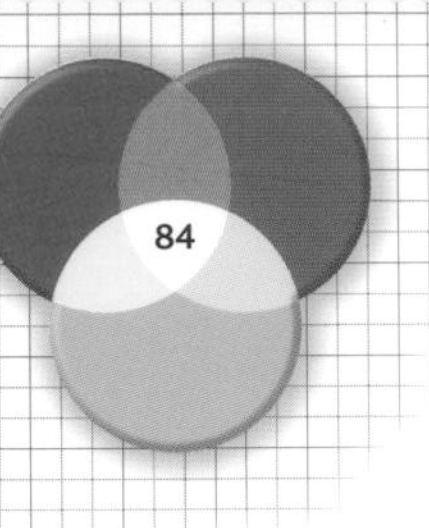

Altering depth of field

DARKROOM SECRETS

DEPTH OF FIELD TIPS

- To be effective, blurring should simulate the result which would have been achieved if a wider aperture had been selected at the time of exposure. If too extreme, the effect separates the subject from its surroundings.
- Consider using the *Film Grain* filter on your finished image. The blurring process obliterates any grain or texture, which can deliver an obvious mismatch.
- It may sound obvious, but don't use this technique when you want to keep both the subject and the background in focus.
- If you find that you have not properly selected your subject and that there is a fine fringe of focused background, you can use the *Blur* tool (with a fine brush size) to gently blend this into the blurred background. To fine-tune your selection, however you originally made it, zoom in close and use the *Quick Mask*.

Depth of field – the measure of the distance over which objects are acceptably sharp in an image – is something the photographer likes to have control over. A wide depth of field delivers images that are sharp from the foreground through to the distance. A narrow depth of field will capture only the subject in sharp focus and blur everything – or everyone – in front and behind. This is a very powerful tool for isolating a subject from surroundings that would otherwise be confusing or that might compete with them for our attention.

Depth of field is controlled in camera by altering the aperture. Small apertures (indicated by high f-stop numbers) give greater depth of field, wide apertures narrower. In practice, many of our photographs may not have been checked for depth of field; indeed, many cameras do not give sufficient control to be able to assess it prior to exposure. Digital cameras are often particularly limited in this respect and tend to deliver exposures that are sharp over an extremely wide range, often wider than the lens geometry and aperture would suggest. This is because post-processing of an image tends to increase its perceived sharpness. Luckily, digital editing can put the control firmly back in our hands.

USING BLUR TO ADD DEPTH OF FIELD

1 *In order to emphasise the importance of a subject or subjects, we can use* Blur *filters and effects to alter the depth of field in an image that has a very wide range of in-focus objects. In this example, we want to give the pebbles in the foreground precedence over the background detail.*

2 *Begin by selecting the principal subject. This is the object or person that you want to remain in sharp focus. Use the appropriate selection tools to extract the subject – here, the pebbles in the foreground – and copy them to a new layer. Take care that the subject is precisely defined. If there is an overlap into the surrounding landscape, this will also remain in sharp focus and seem obvious later.*

3 *Depth of field works by keeping planes in focus, not individual objects, so ensure that you also include in your selection any contiguous items. In this example, we would just be careful to ensure that all the pebbles on the same plane are selected.*

Now invert the selection and copy the surroundings to another new layer. Pull this layer down (using the Layers *palette) so that it is below the subject layer. This multilayer approach ensures that our blurring process does not result in parts of the subject or the background spreading into each other. It also gives us more flexibility later to fade the blurring effect later on.*

4 *For the sake of clarity, turn the visibility off for the subject and background layers. Now select the layer with the surroundings in it and apply a mild* Gaussian blur, *sufficient to just soften the focus across the layer as a whole.*

5 *Now select only a slightly smaller portion of the surrounding layer, so that only the middle distance and distant parts are now selected. With a feather radius of around 25 pixels, apply a stronger* Gaussian Blur. *Having done so, reduce the selection so that it now includes only the far middle distance and distant parts. Apply the* Gaussian Blur *filter for a third time.*

6 *Finally select only the distant parts of the image and give this a final blur. You should see that the four blurring stages have blended seamlessly to give a steady increase in blur proportionate to the distance.*

7 *Turn on the visibility for all layers (including the background layer) to fill in the boundary areas between the subject layer and the layers that have been softened by the blurring process.*

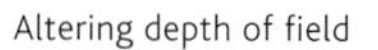

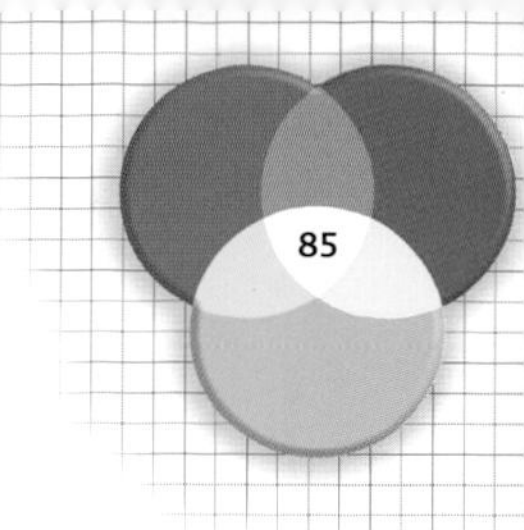

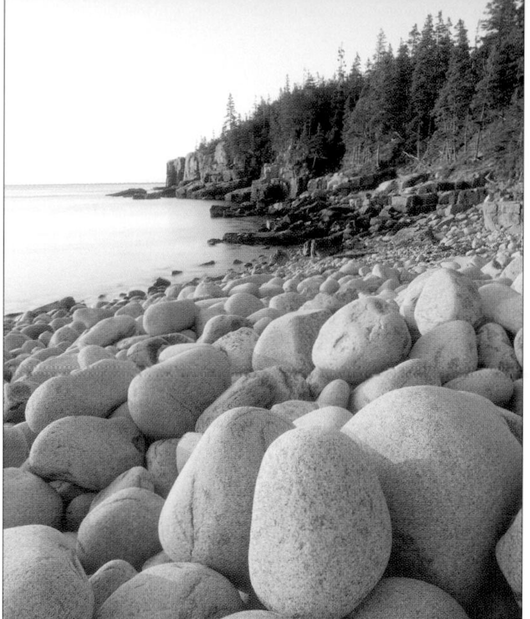
1

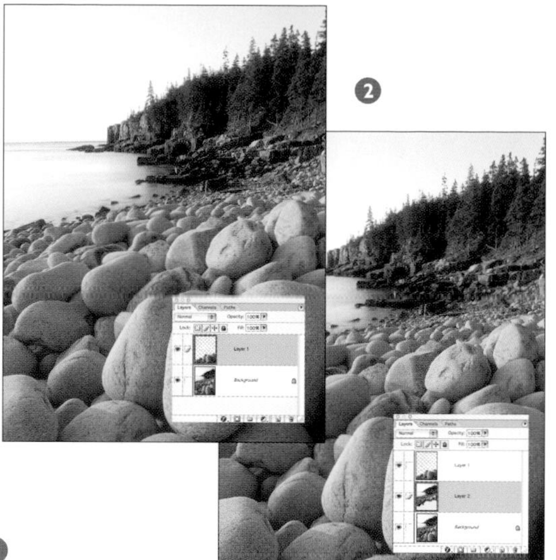
2
3

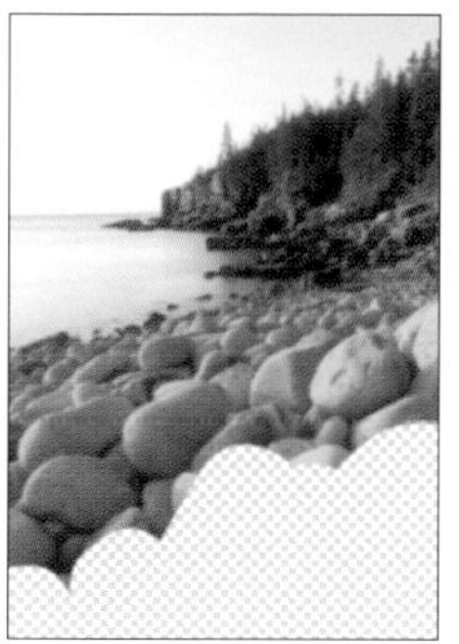
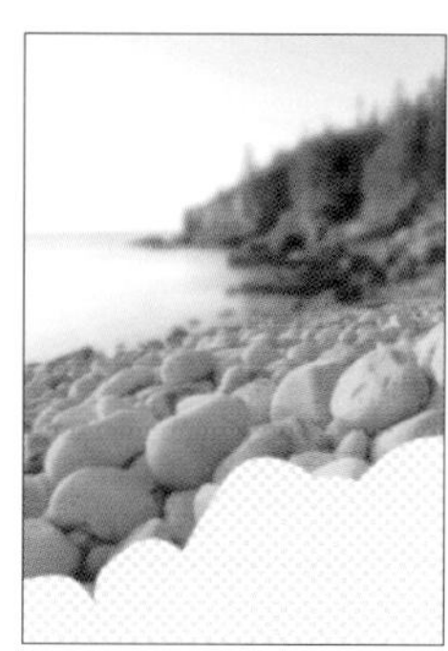
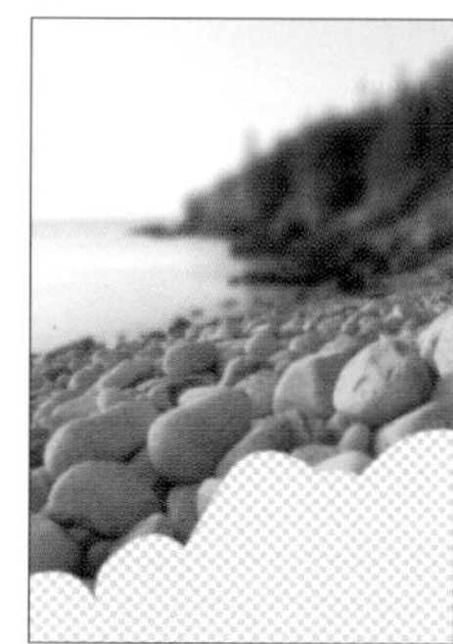
4 5 6

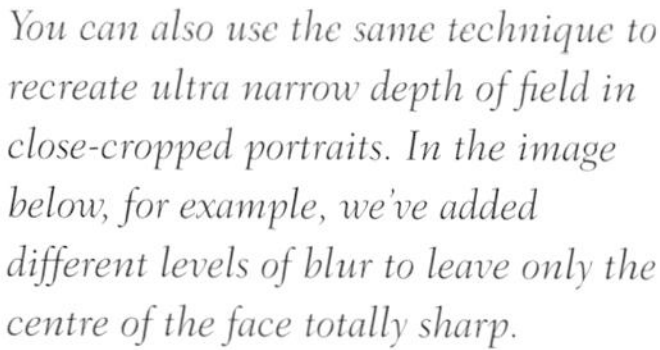
You can also use the same technique to recreate ultra narrow depth of field in close-cropped portraits. In the image below, for example, we've added different levels of blur to leave only the centre of the face totally sharp.

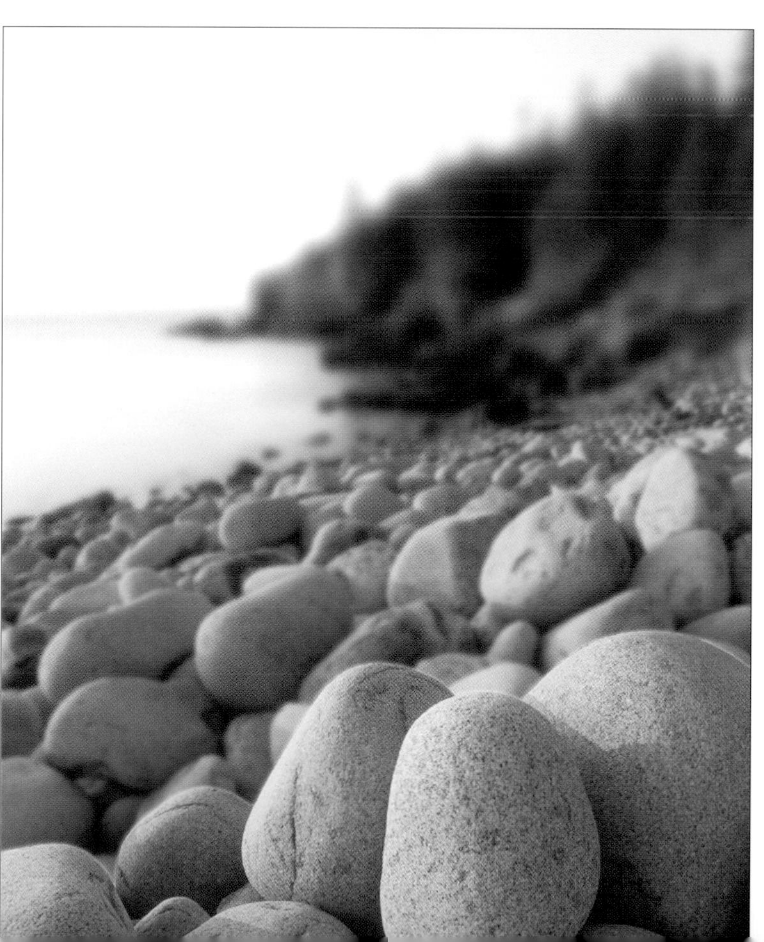
7

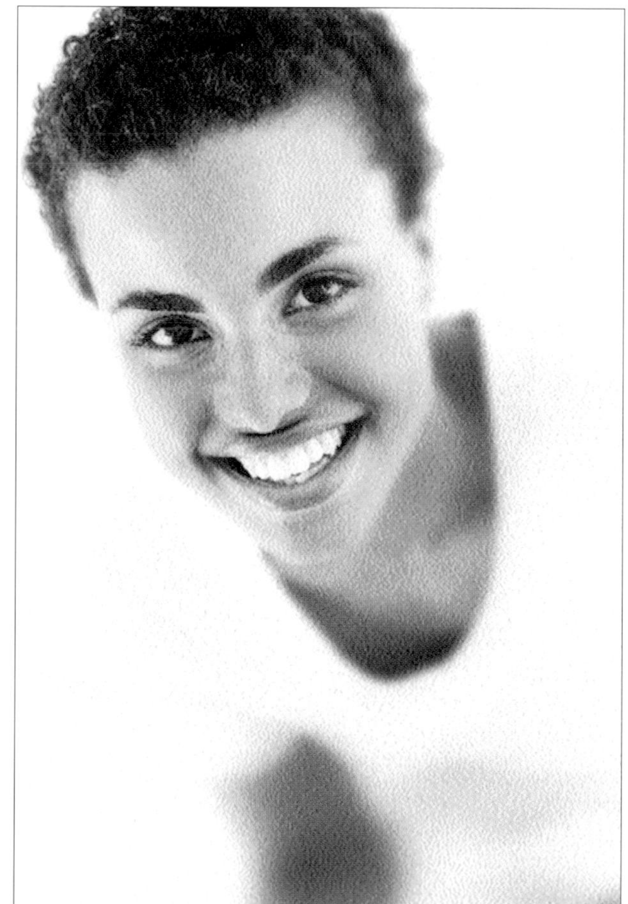

The real route to soft focus

DARKROOM SECRETS 

SOFTEN THE BACKGROUND
The potency of soft focus effects can be enhanced if the image background is blurred. Because applying a soft focus effect tends to slightly flatten the depth of field, one unwanted effect of doing so can be to add emphasis to a distracting background.

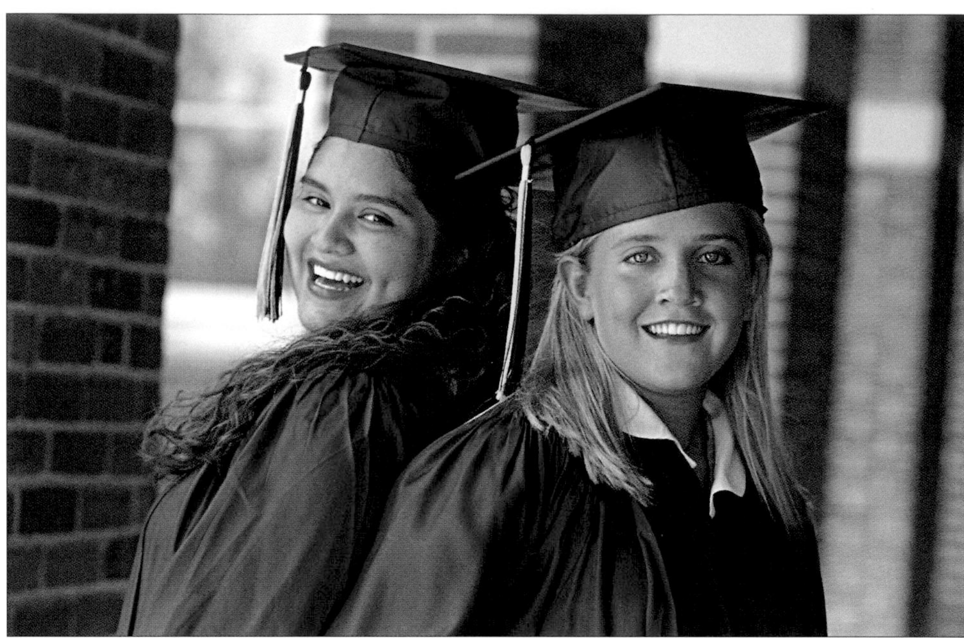

1

Where some effects, such as grain, are ideal for masculine subjects, feminine subjects have often been associated with another treatment: 'soft focus'. This term is actually much abused, with images that are slightly out of focus described as 'Soft Focus', although they are really just blurred. True soft focus requires the image to be in sharp focus, but with the fine detail smoothed out. The soft haze of the resulting effect lends itself perfectly to flattering, romantic portraits.

In conventional photography, soft focus is produced in-camera through specialised filters, of which the Softars – promoted by Hasselblad – are the exemplars. Softar filters are made of perfectly clear, flat glass on which a pattern of fine 'drops' is placed. The number and size of the drops determines the degree of 'softness' produced.

Digital image-editing is ideal for emulating this effect because we can easily create a softened picture and then combine it with the sharp original.

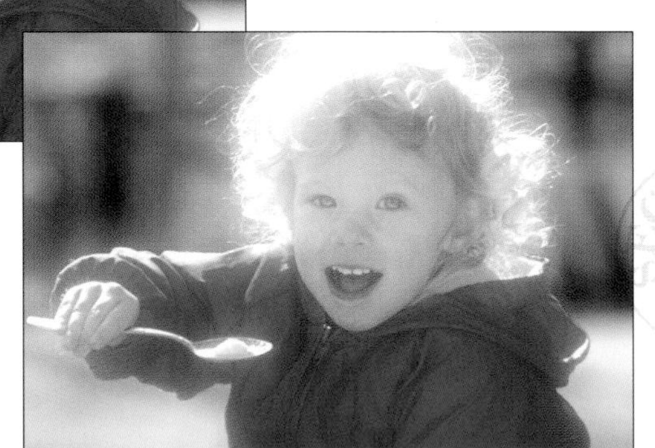

When using the Screen *blend mode, you can apply the* Gaussian Blur *a second or even a third time to achieve a lighter, softer effect, as the examples here show.*

EMULATING SOFT FOCUS

1 *Begin by editing your image. If it needs any sharpening to make it pin sharp, apply an appropriate amount of unsharp masking. Because we will be overlaying the image with a softened version of itself, we can get away with slightly more sharpening than would normally be the case.*

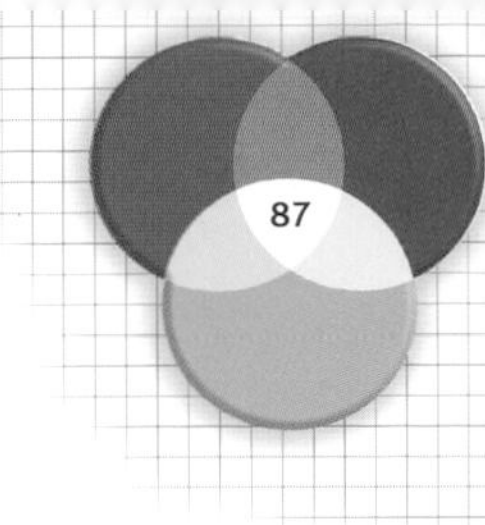

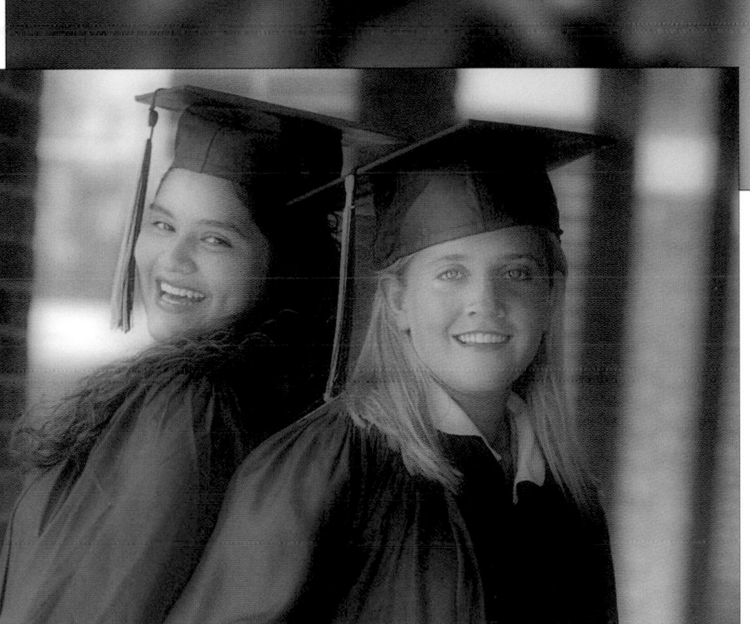

MASKED SOFT FOCUS

Applying a mask to the central part of an image will restrict the softening to the edges of the image. In keeping with the soft nature of this effect, any masking should have an equally soft edge – in the manner of the soft vignettes we looked at on pages 46 and 47.

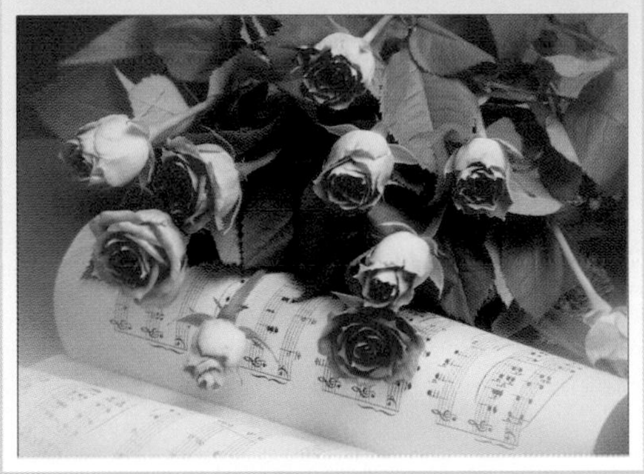

2 *Make a duplicate layer from the image and apply the* Gaussian Blur *filter* (Filter > Blur > **Gaussian Blur**) *to it. You need to apply sufficient blurring to soften all features of the original. As with many effects filters, the effects of the* Gaussian Blur *will be directly proportional to the image size. A large, high-resolution image will require higher blur settings than a smaller one. Bear this in mind, as you are meant to be softening the detail rather than obliterating it entirely.*

3 *Now reduce the opacity of the blurred layer to 50%. This combines both the layers so that the details in the sharp background layer are blended with the softened haze of the blurred layer to simulate the soft focus effect.*

4 *You can just leave things there if you want, but why not try changing the blend mode to* Screen, *then increasing the blurred layer's opacity by a slight amount? This adds some extra brightness to the image and creates the flattering, high-key effect shown here.*

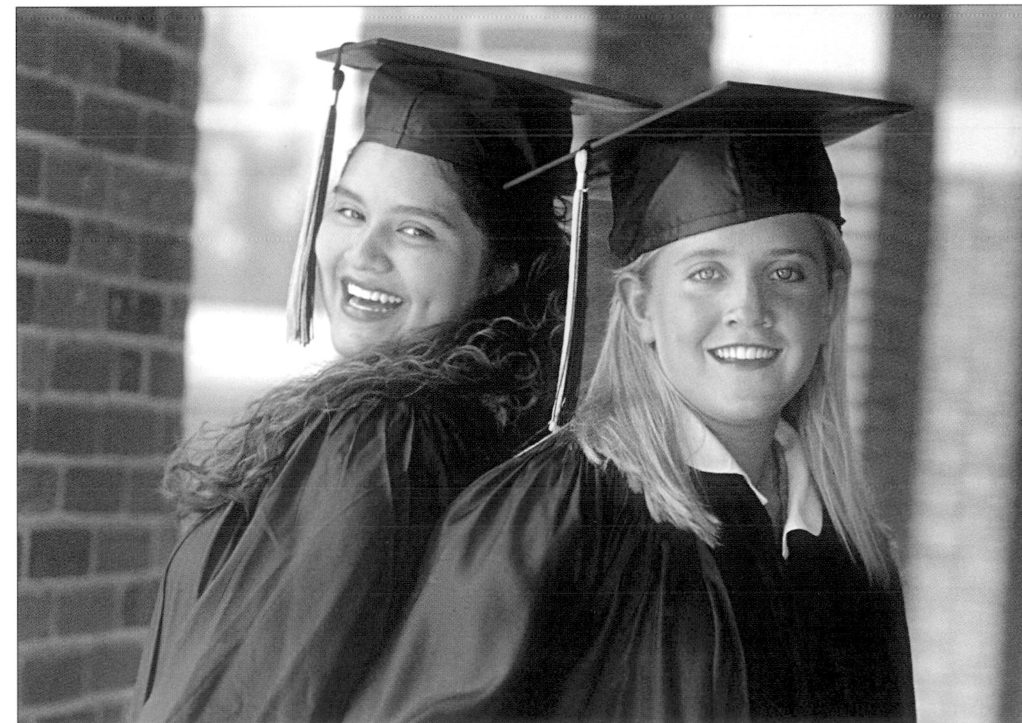

High-key portraits

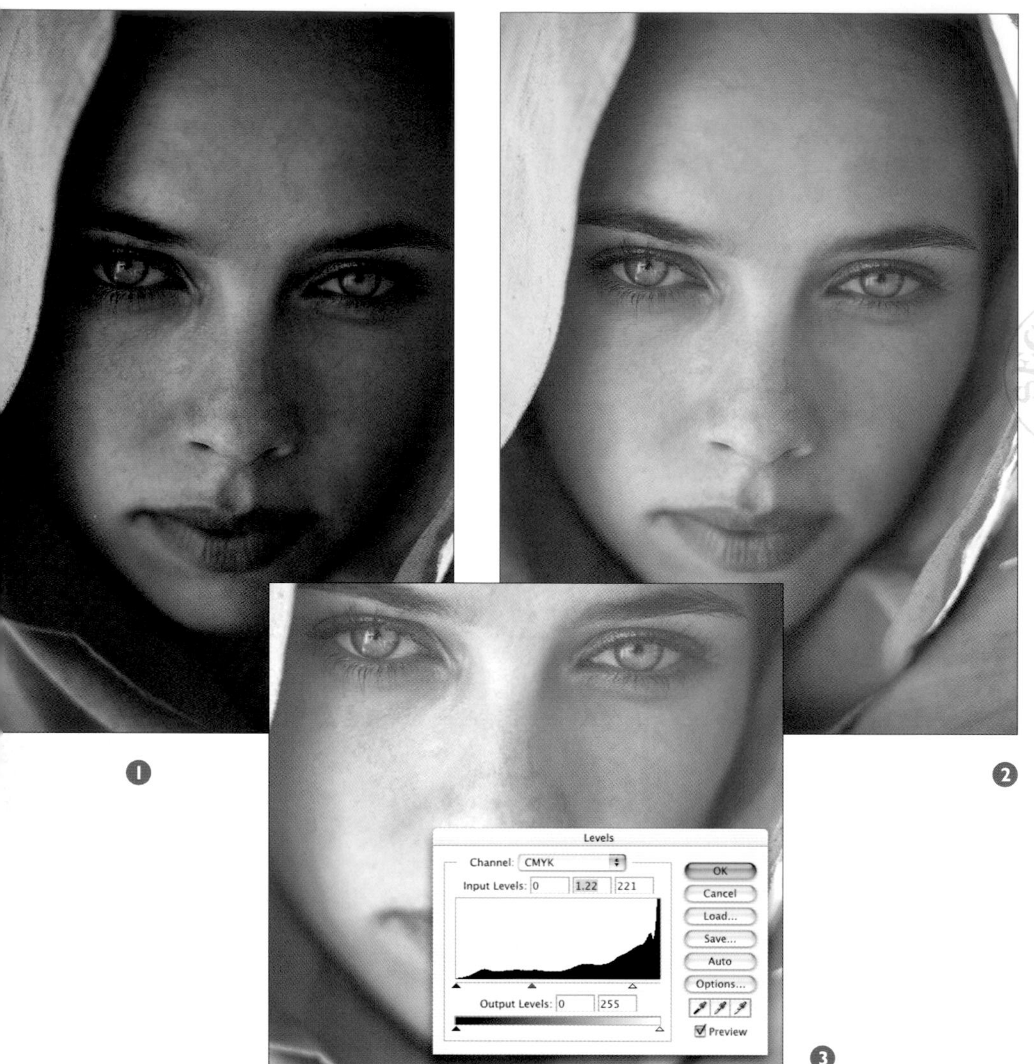

High-key portraiture is one of those classic darkroom techniques that makes the transition to digital media in a somewhat looser and more versatile form. A high-key image is merely one in which the lighter tones – particularly those close to white – predominate. In the darkroom, we would achieve the effect by holding back (dodging parts of the image) while allowing a very limited part to be exposed to normal density. The result is a light, dreamlike image that flatters and complements female portraits.

CREATING HIGH-KEY PORTRAITS

Of course, there is more to creating a successful high-key portrait than adjusting the tonality. Many proponents believe that portraits must be specially shot in order to produce the effect. However, using digital means we can create high-key from almost any original portrait. In this example, midtones and darker tones dominate but we can still successfully create a high-key result.

1 *Begin by making any basic adjustments you feel necessary. Here, modest corrections have been made to the contrast and brightness. Also the colour – a very overt magenta – has been supressed by reducing saturation by about 15%.*

2 *Now we change the tonal balance. Open the* Levels *palette and move the* Black Point *slider to the left. Don't slide it too far, or you will lose image detail in the highlight areas. Then drag the* Gray Point *(midtones) slider to the left. You should have slightly more room for manoeuvre, here.*

3 *The image has been lightened, but there are still some areas of dark tone that can be removed to improve matters further. Begin by drawing a vignette around the face using a* Lasso. *Set a large feathering radius so that the vignette will be very gentle. Invert the selection to make the border areas active, then press delete. Ensure that the background paint colour is white to get a clean white background to the vignette.*

4 *The eyes are the most important part of any portrait – in a high-key portrait even more so. The earlier steps may have resulted in eyes that are tonally soft and dull. We need now to restore some of the original quality. Use the* Burn *tool and a soft brush to paint in the eyebrows and eyelashes. Set a low amount (15%, say) so that the amount builds gradually. By selecting* Shadows *on the* Tool Options *bar, the* Burn *will be applied only to the hair, not the surrounding skin. Switch to* Midtones *to darken the area below the eyelashes.*

4

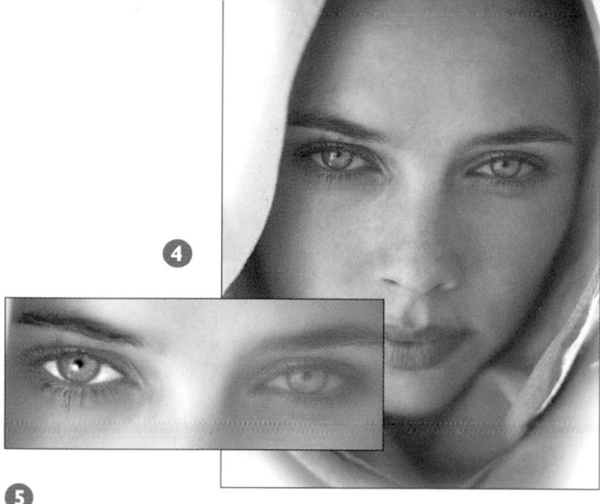

5

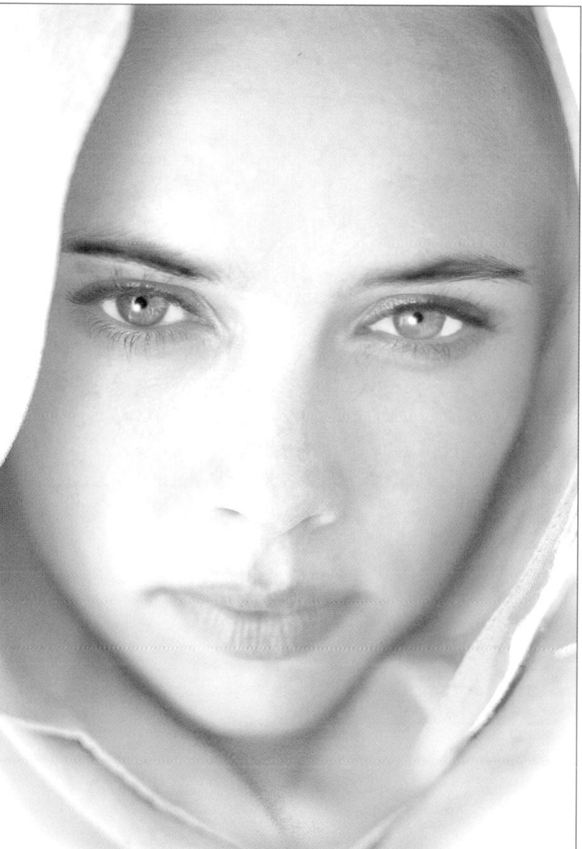

Using the Dodge *tool (selecting* Highlights*), whiten the white parts of the eye. Bright eyes and bright teeth are key to the success of this technique. Note how we have darkened the pupil of the left eye and added a bright 'catchlight'. This allowed us to attend to a reflection of the photographer that had crept into the original!*

5 *To finish, use the* Dodge *tool, again at a low setting but with a very broad, diffuse brush. Use broad strokes to lighten the scarf and outer parts of the face. Producing high-key portraits is never an exact science, so use as much or as little lightening as you need.*

High key or low key?

High-key techniques should not be confined to images with soft tones and light colours. In this example, critical focusing on the right eye of a high-key portrait makes the result very powerful and, as you can see, the technique is equally applicable to black skin tones. In cases, where you are dealing with more vivid colours, you may find it easier to achieve a high-key effect if only the mid-tone is used to adjust levels. Using the black slider can cause adverse colour banding.

As you might deduce, low-key portraits are the converse of high-key. With dark tones predominating, the results can be dark, brooding and ominous. As such, the technique tends to be reserved for male portraits. To create them, adjust the sliders in the *Levels* palette to the right, then use the *Dodge* and *Burn* tools to mark out the shadow and highlight levels by hand.

By adjusting the Levels *and using the* Dodge *and* Burn *tools to boost the darker tones and shadow areas, a more gloomy or even ominous atmosphere can be created.*

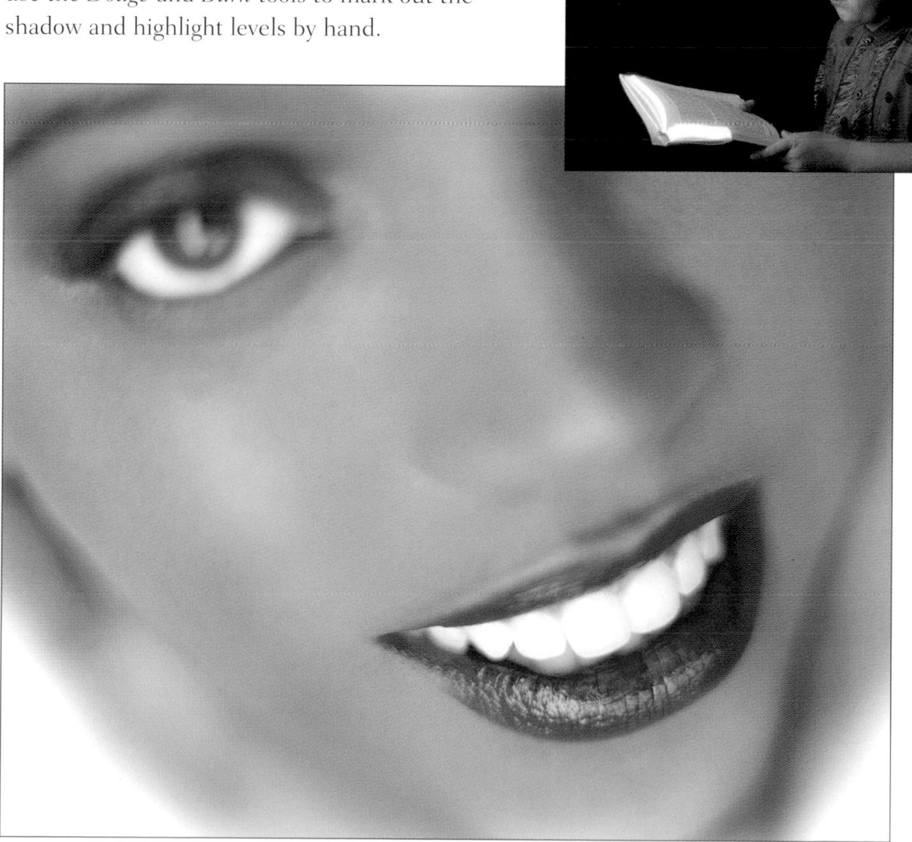

Artificial lighting

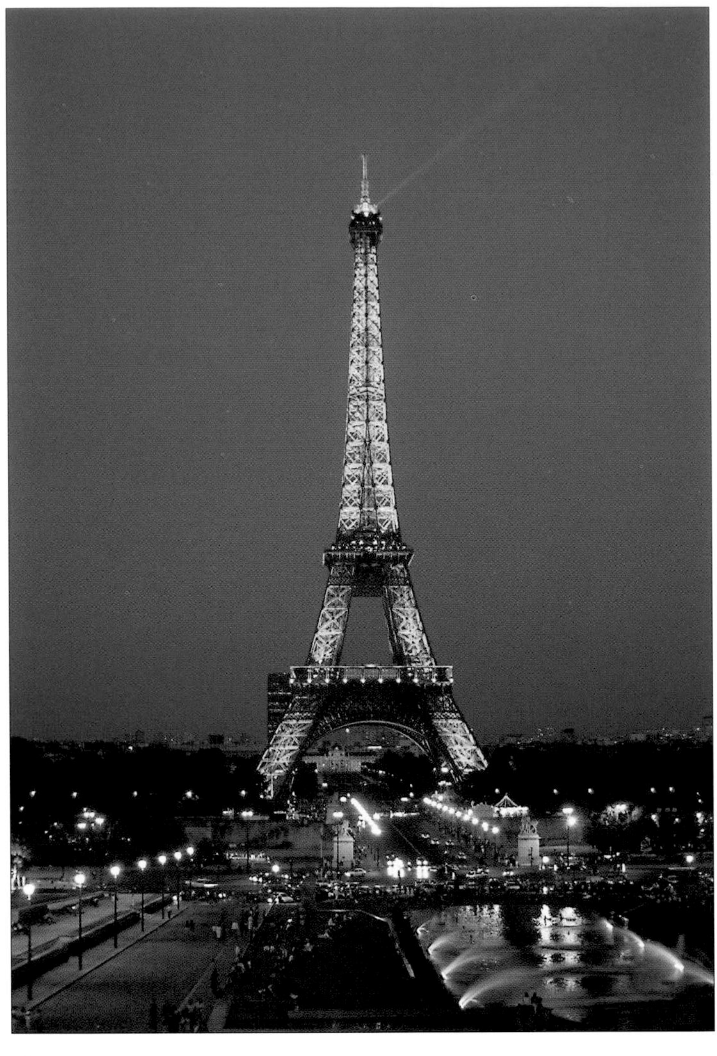

1

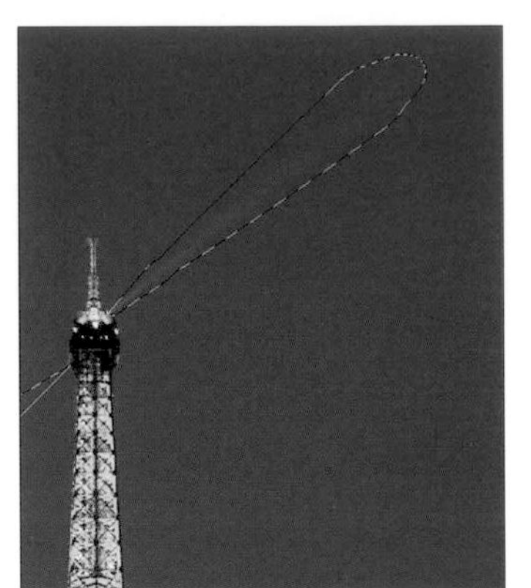

2

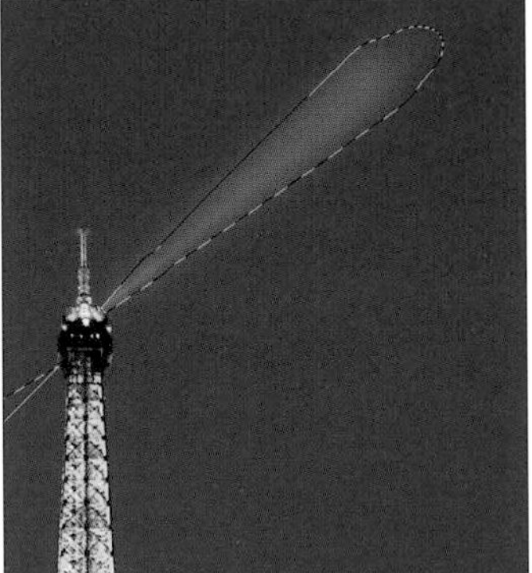

3

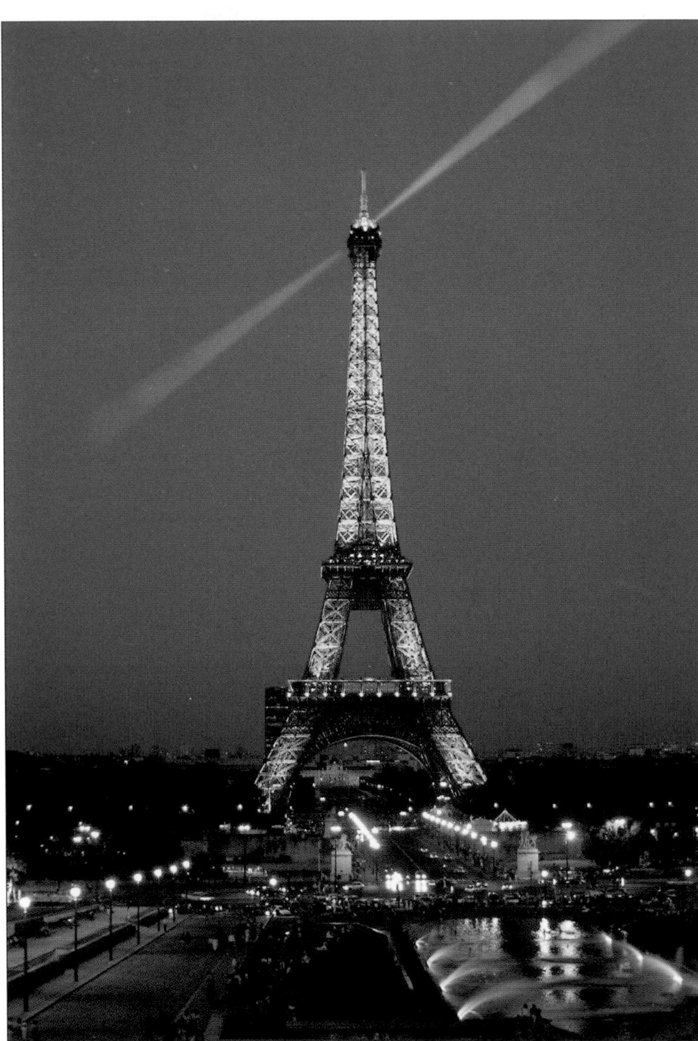

4

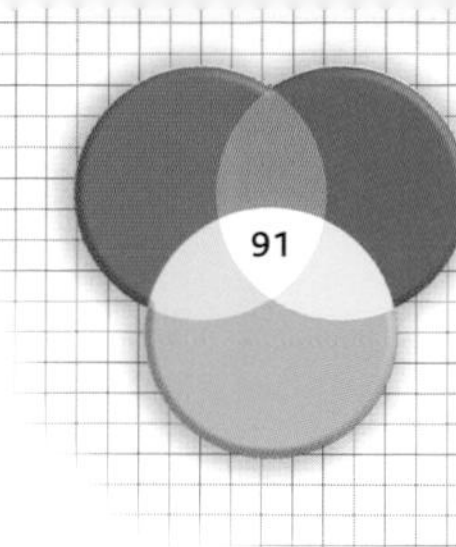

Photography is, according to many, about playing with light. It is unsurprising, then, to find that Photoshop has many controls and effects designed to alter the lighting conditions in a scene, or to add an impression of luminance to elements within an image.

In most cases, you will find these controls under *Render* in the *Filters* menu. The most important of these filters, *Lighting Effects*, is also one of the most complex in Photoshop – the kind of tool that takes time to learn but rewards practice and experimentation. However, when we think about lighting effects, we should not just think in terms of the filter. We can also use more prosaic tools – such as the paintbrush – to add new lighting dimensions to our shots.

SEARCHLIGHTS

1 *Lighting is not just concerned with changing the lighting in a scene. We can also create the effect of different lights to enhance a scene. This photograph of the Eiffel Tower required an exposure that was too short to capture the searchlight beams radiating from the top of the tower.*

2 *Luckily, we can easily add beams of light, emulating the original. Use the* Polygonal Lasso *to draw in the shape of radiating beam patterns from the tower. Apply a large* Feather *amount to give them soft edges.*

3 *With the selections active, use a white paintbrush (or airbrush) with the* Opacity *set to a very low amount (around 5%). Also set the* Flow *to around 40%. This will help give diffuse results. Make short sweeps along the light beams.*

4 *Gradually build up the intensity, keeping in mind that the beams should get more diffuse with distance and also wider if the effect is to look realistic. Aim for the beams to fade away completely at their furthest point from the tower. The gentler the fade, the more effective the result.*

A little more flare

Don't forget that the *Lens Flare* filter is also a lighting effect. This can be used to great effect when applied more than once to an image. In this case, the flare elements will build in strength. To get more drama, apply the filter using two (or more) of the lens settings. This will give you even more flare points.

This Grecian ornament is already an evocative image, but the application of a Lens Flare *filter adds an extra sense of mystery.*

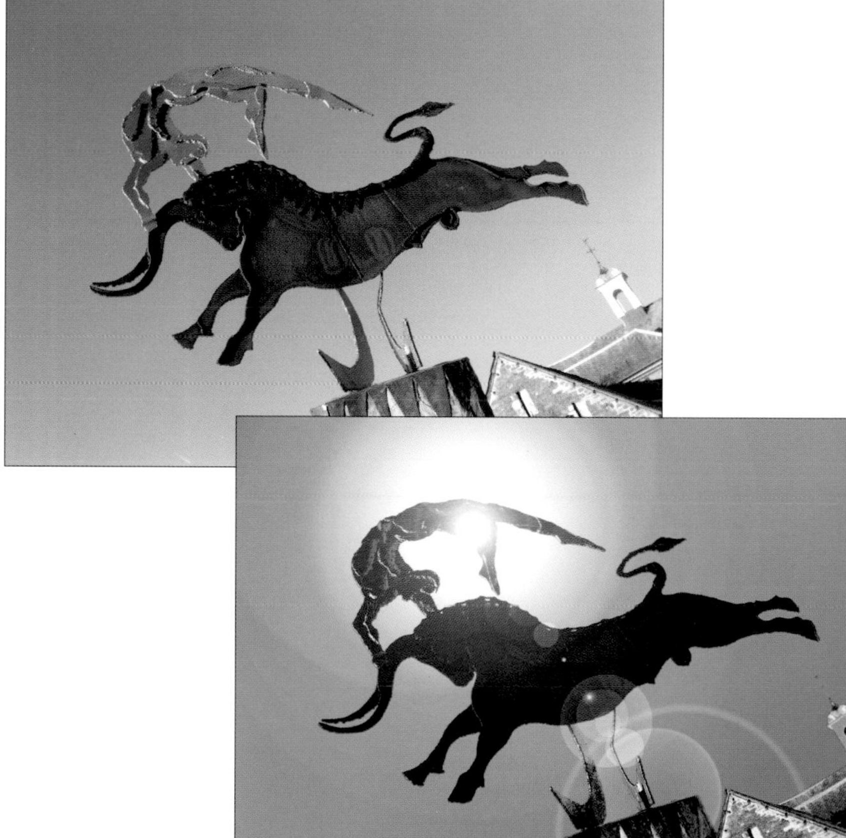

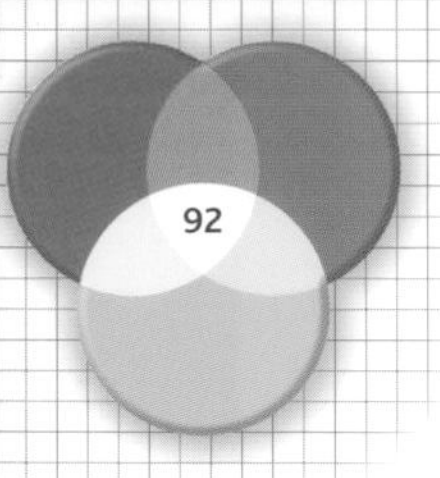

Lighting effects

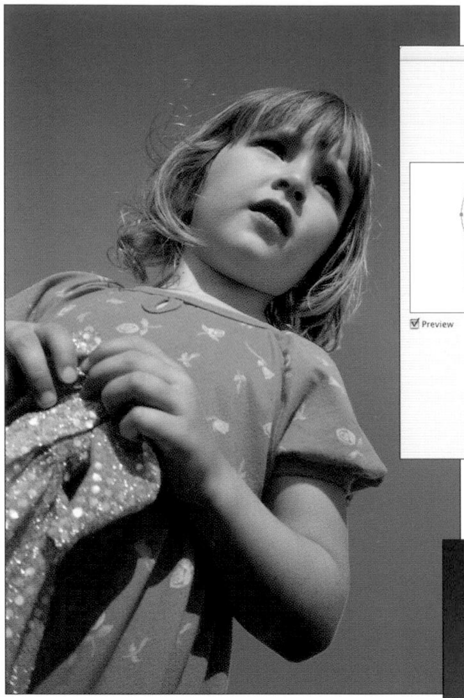

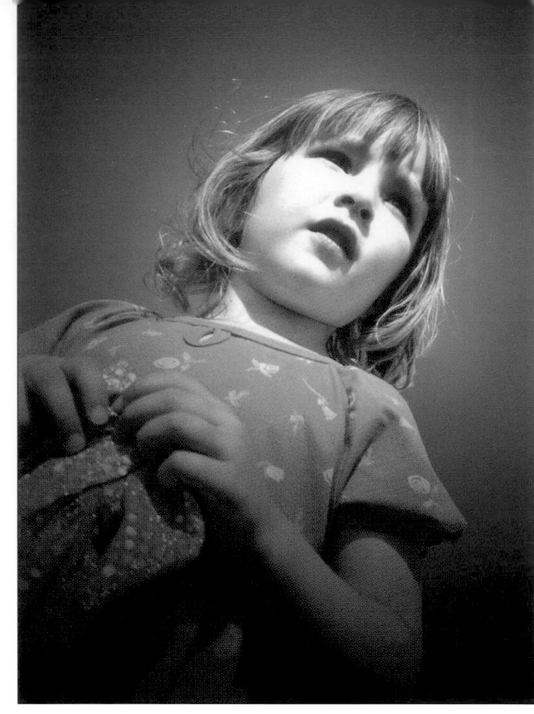

While most filters provide just one effect with a few variations, *Lighting Effects* offers a whole range of effects to enhance or change the lighting in an image. These include effects designed to deliver subtle alterations in ambient lighting conditions – such as modifying the direction of the principal illumination – all the way through to more obvious or theatrical efforts. We can, for example, use the filter to add emphasis to the subject of a shot.

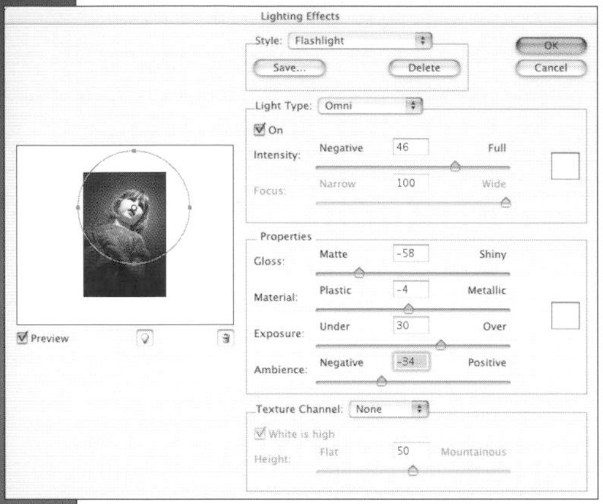

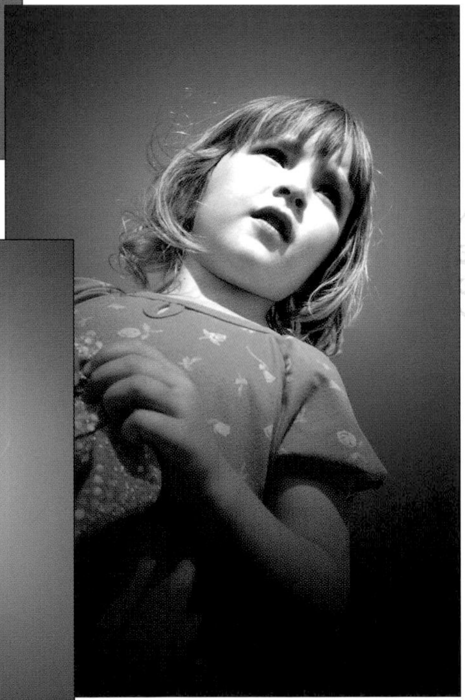

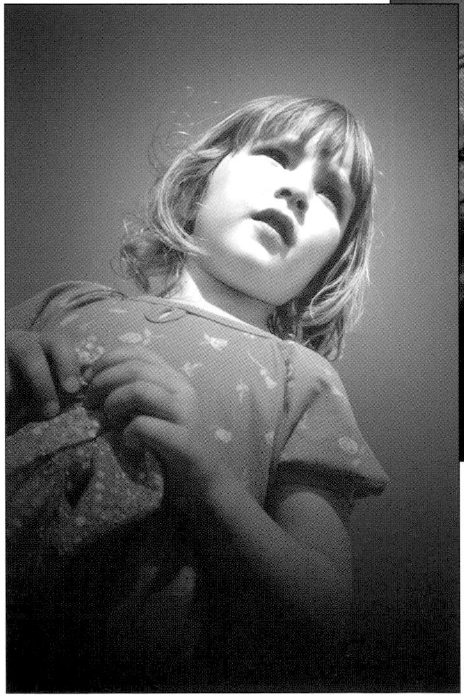

EMPHASIS LIGHTING

1 *This shot of a girl has been taken from a low angle for impact, but the natural sunlight doesn't quite bring the image to life. On a less spontaneous shot, we might use reflectors, but we can get similar results with* Lighting Effects.

2 *Using the* Flashlight *lighting effect, we can give the girl's face a spotlight treatment. The amount of spotlighting can be adjusted using the handles on the thumbnail image. The wider the spotlight, the greater the central brightness.*

3 *Other lighting properties can also be adjusted. Moving the* Material *slider to the* Metallic *end (left) creates a harder reflected light. Moving it toward the* Plastic *end creates flatter, more diffuse reflections (far-left).*

4 *To get the best effect to flatter the girl's skin tones, we should use a neutral setting, which delivers this highlighted result.*

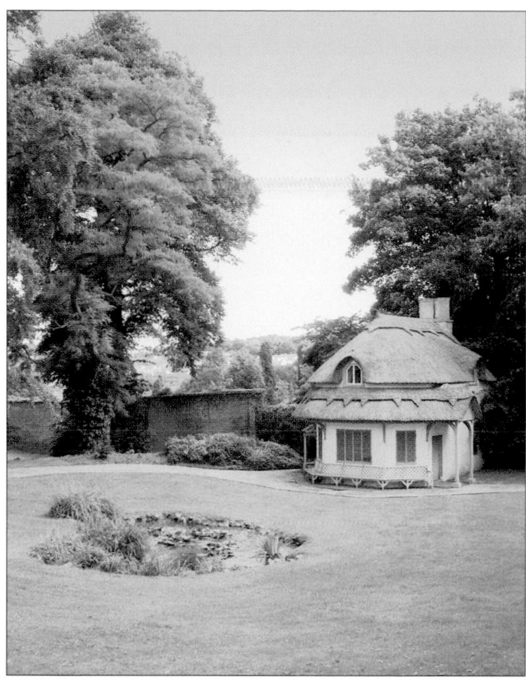

1

2

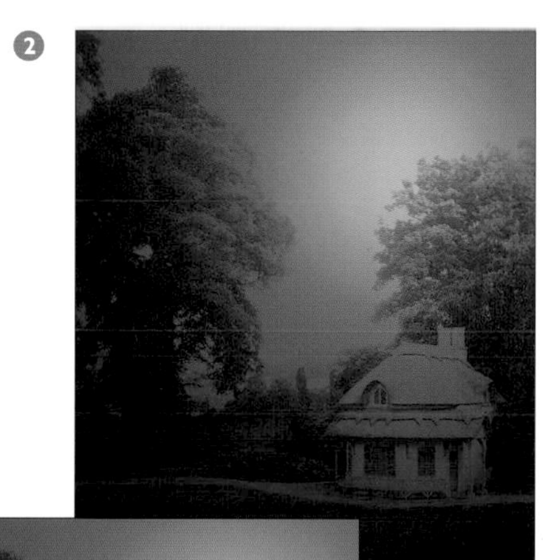

DARKROOM SECRETS

A TOUCH OF THEATRE

Several of the *Lighting Effects* deliver stage spotlight effects. Used in their default configurations, these can look a little clichéd and undoubtedly artificial. But with a little adjustment and fine tuning, they can work very well. The result will still be somewhat theatrical, but if the image works, why not?

3

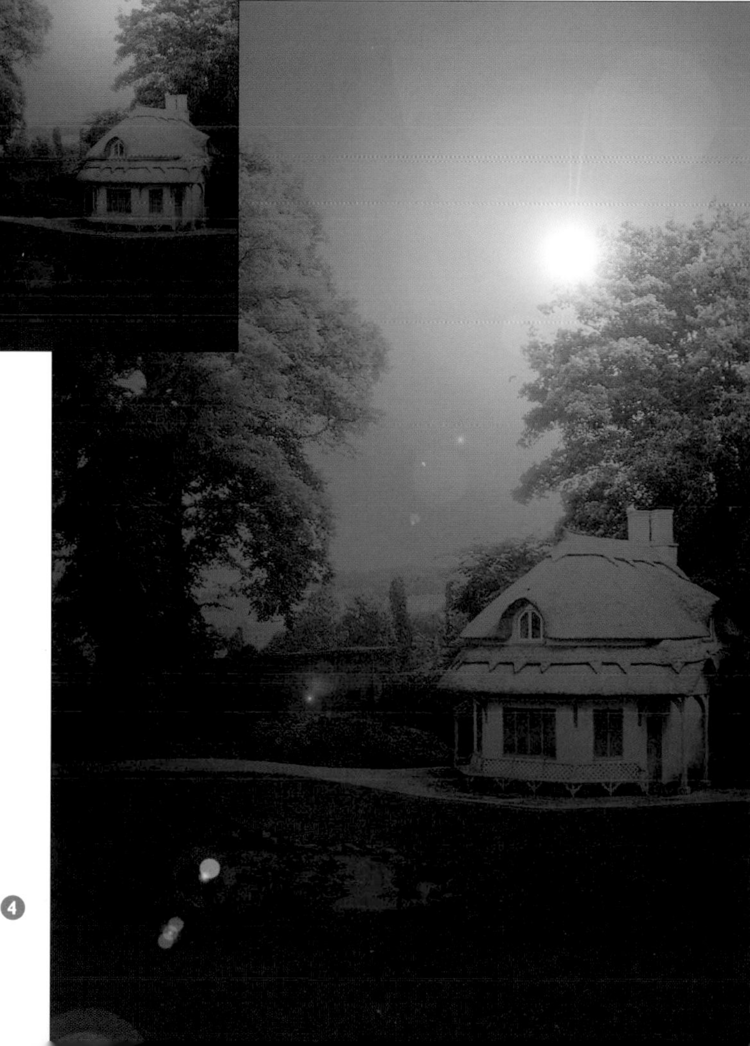

4

The *Lighting Effects* filter does not have to be limited to realistic effects, like those we might achieve through conventional methods. It can also be used to create something fantastic or otherworldly or even to create dramatic changes in the lighting conditions.

DAY INTO NIGHT

1 *This daytime scene can, as here, be transformed into a nighttime scene, complete with moonlight!* Lighting Effects *provides all the tools we need to turn day to night.*

2 *Begin by applying the* Blue Omni Lighting Effect. *Position the centre of the omidirectional light effect appropriately in the sky. You will need to carefully adjust the exposure controls to get the best 'night' effect.*

3 *To retain some of the original colour of the scene (rather than the rather harsh overall blue delivered by the effect), select* Edit > Fade Lighting Effect *and reduce the amount to around 90%.*

4 *To add a convincing moonlight effect to the sky, use the* Lens Flare *filter and position the central flare point on the centre of the* Blue Omni *light.* Fade *the effect for an more appropriate result.*

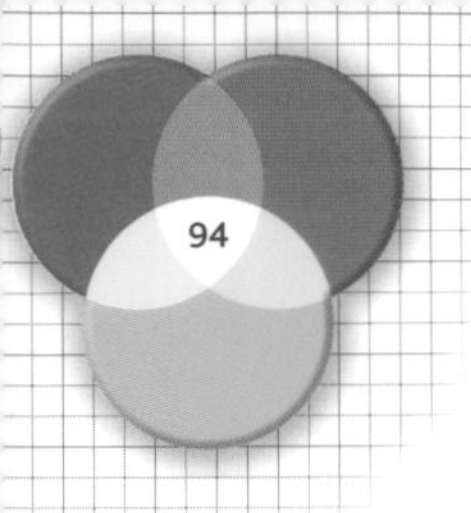

Simulating photographic filters

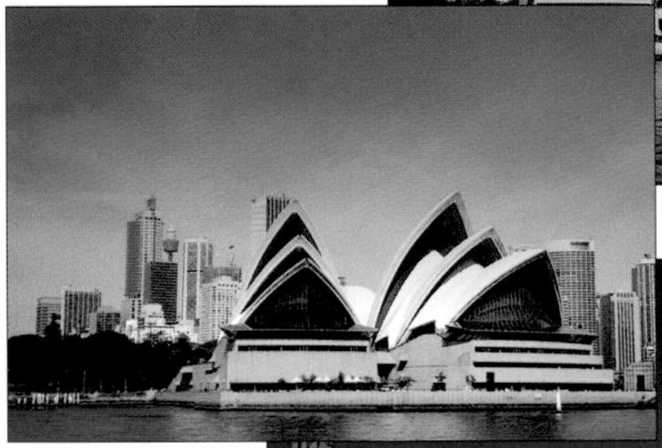

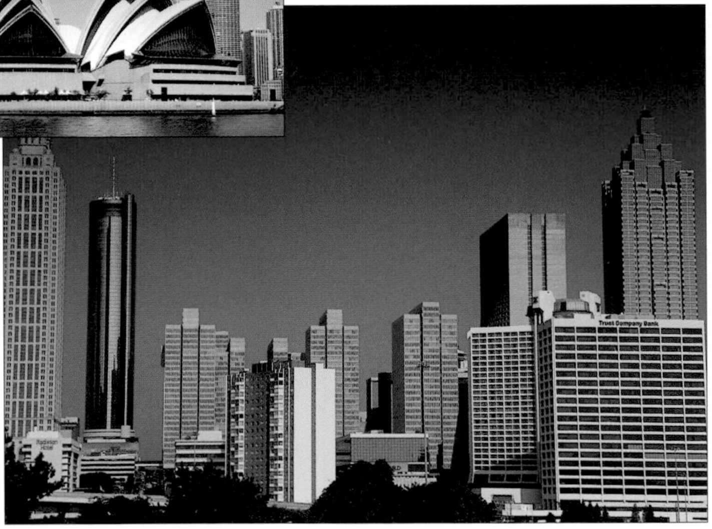

Given the breadth and variety of effects filters that come with image-editing applications, it is perhaps surprising that some of the filters which we have come to know and love on-camera are not reproduced in the standard effects filter libraries. Such common devices as the cross screen, colour graduates, colour spot and mist filters are not to be found. However, it is possible to simulate these – and most other effects – with just a little computer dexterity.

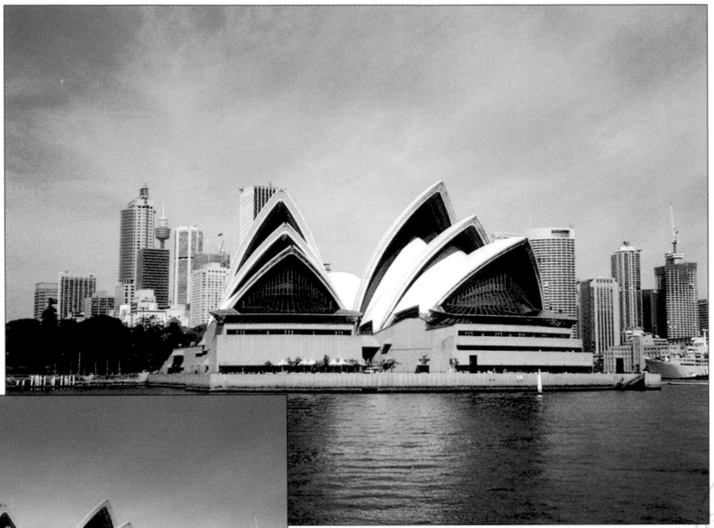

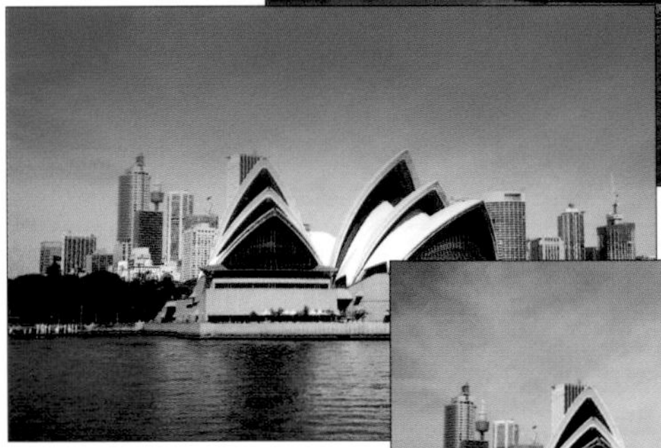

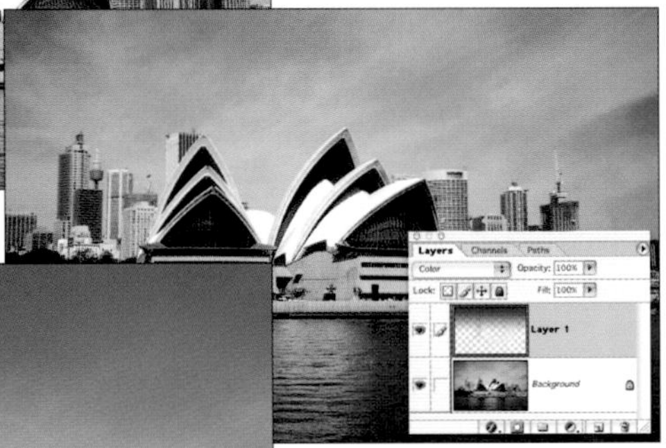

Colour graduated filters are ideal for adding impact to lacklustre skies, using either authentic or wildly absurd colours.

COLOUR GRADUATES

1 *Select your original image. This scene has a good sky, but it could be made even more effective by the application of a colour graduate.*

2 *Create a new image layer. Use the* Gradient *tool to produce a gradient, from top to bottom, using the* Foreground color to transparent *option. Here we've chosen a dark indigo colour sampled from the blues of the sea. You can vary the layer transparency for best effect.*

3 *More subtle or unusual effects can be produced by altering the blend mode of the graduated layer, such as here where* Color *has been selected. This adds the colour of the original image to that of the graduate without obscuring anything in the background layer.*

4 *By changing the graduate layer colour, you can experiment with different effects. When you change the colour in images that feature water, keep the reflections in mind and make sure that you also apply appropriate coloration to the water too.*

When choosing colours for this technique, it's easy to forget that black and white can also be used. In this example, using black as a graduate colour has produced a strong cityscape image.

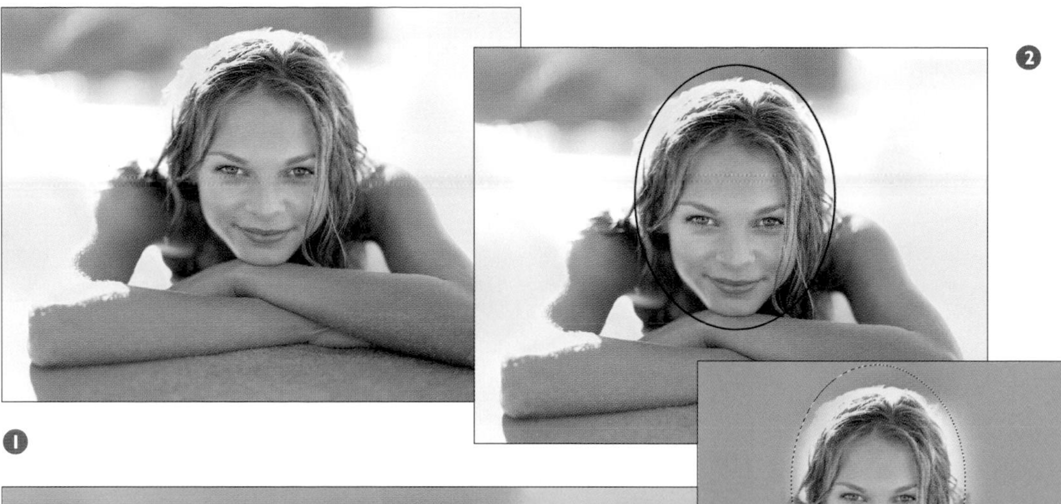

1

2

3

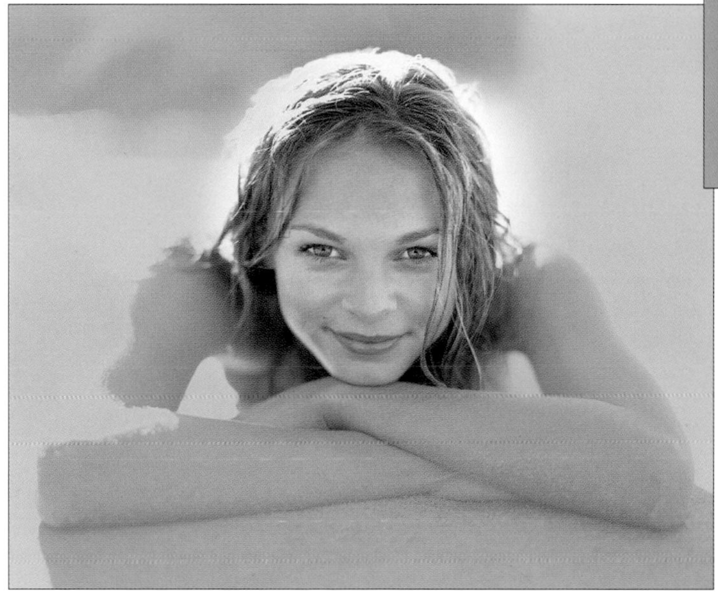

4

Spot filters are often used to distinguish a clear, central area – where the image is displayed normally – from a surrounding area which is coloured, misty or some combination of the two. The success of the effect in-camera is due to the boundary between both regions being blurred. Digitally we can create this effect using coloured layers, and produce the soft boundary between the two areas using selections and feathering.

CREATING SPOT FILTER EFFECTS

1 *This is the portrait to which we will apply our simulated spot filter. By using a semi-opaque colour we can also reduce the brightness range. This helps to overcome the burned-out highlights of the original image.*

2 *Create a new layer. This will, as in the case of the graduated filters, enable us to adjust the effect, using the layer controls. Set a feather radius. This will vary according to the image size, but a setting of 50 makes a good starting point for a 2 megapixel image. Draw an elliptical* Marquee *over the surface of the image.*

3 *Now invert the selection* (Select > **Inverse**) *and use the paintbrush to paint over the selected area.*

4 *Use the* Opacity *slider to make the paint layer translucent. If you want a more subtle effect, just turn the* Opacity *down. You can also use blend modes here to produce colour combinations.*

DARKROOM SECRETS

THE POLARIZING FILTER

Perhaps the most commonly used filter in color photography is the Polarizer. By removing reflected light (whether as direct surface reflections or random air-particle reflection), it produces images that have better colour saturation and better contrast. Simulating the effect with image-editing tools is therefore a two-step process. Colours can be enhanced – given greater saturation – using the *Hue/Saturation* control, but when only this command is used, the result can be unnaturally garish (top). To make the effect 'work' (bottom), increase the *Saturation* by about 10%, and then boost the contrast by 5% using the *Brightness/Contrast* tool. The result looks more natural.

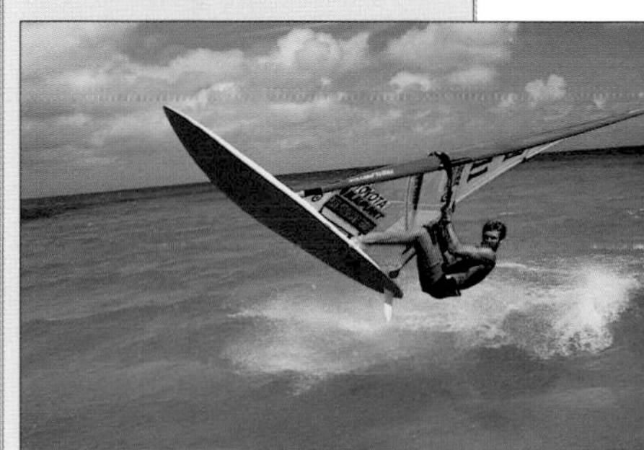

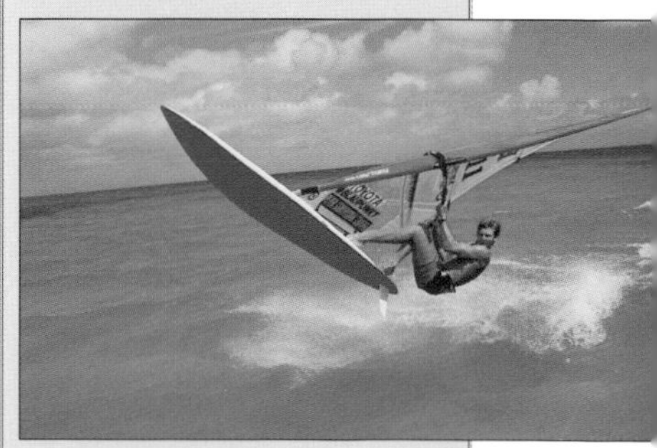

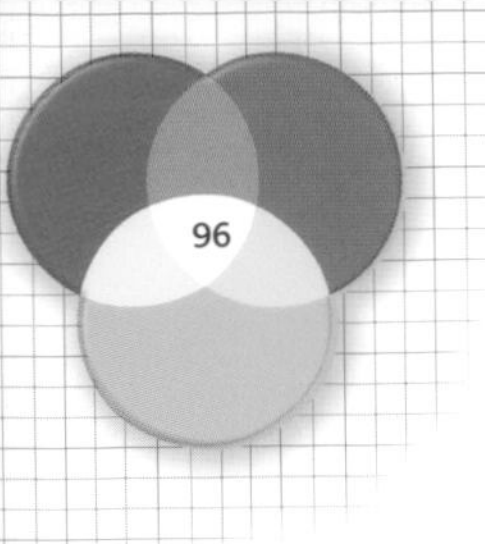

Full-tone monochrome from colour

DARKROOM SECRETS

THE LAB ADVANTAGE

One of the channels in the Lab colour mode (found in many image-editing applications) is L, which contains lightness information. If your image is converted to grayscale, you can select and manipulate the L channel, which now contains all the significant image data. By using the *Levels* or *Curves* command, you have precise control over the qualities of the image. Your image will probably also be sharper than when an RGB or CMYK channel has been isolated, because it contains all the image information, rather than just that of a selected colour. Usefully, the resulting file is also only one-third of the size of the colour original.

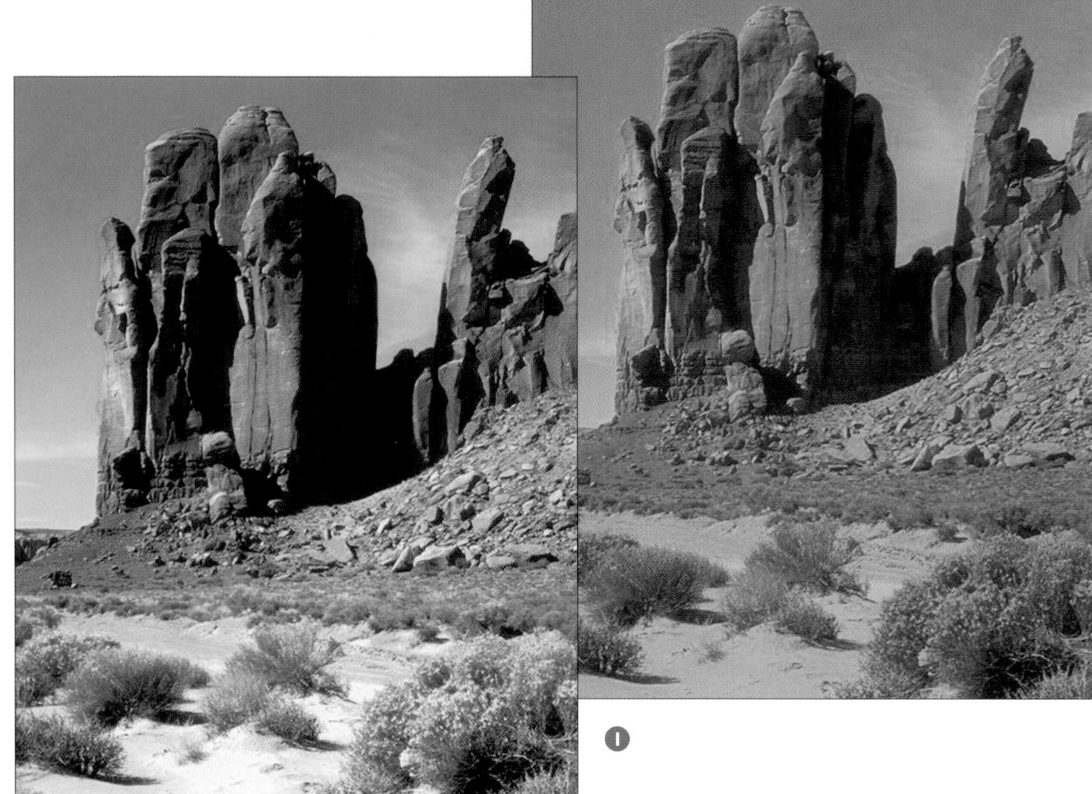

1

There is no doubt at all that black-and-white photography is still – and will always remain – an important branch of the art. Monochrome images can have a very powerful impact and are important when creating character studies. Though they are rarely encountered by the colour photographer, there are a wide range of black-and-white film emulsions available, and many have characteristics that make them particularly suitable for a certain type of subject.

In the digital environment, we can emulate all these and more, but we have to take care that, in producing a monochrome image from colour, we get the best results. Straight desaturation of a colour image rarely delivers a mono image as potent as the original. Don't, either, select the monochrome mode on your digital camera. It is much better to shoot in colour and convert the image later. In this way we can, should the need arise, still use the colour image, perhaps interpreting the image as a toned print or using some other effect.

MONOCHROME BY CHANNEL SEPARATION

In Photoshop, a colour image is composed of three or four channels (three in the case of RGB mode images, four for a CMYK image). Each channel represents the component of that image viewed in the corresponding colour light. Most of the time there is no need to worry about them, but at times channels do prove useful. For our current purposes, think of each channel as a shot taken of a scene using the corresponding colour filter on monochrome film. We can select just one and use this as the basis of our image.

2

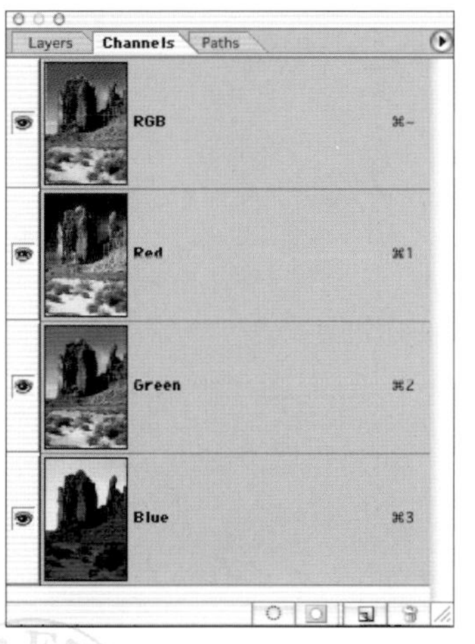

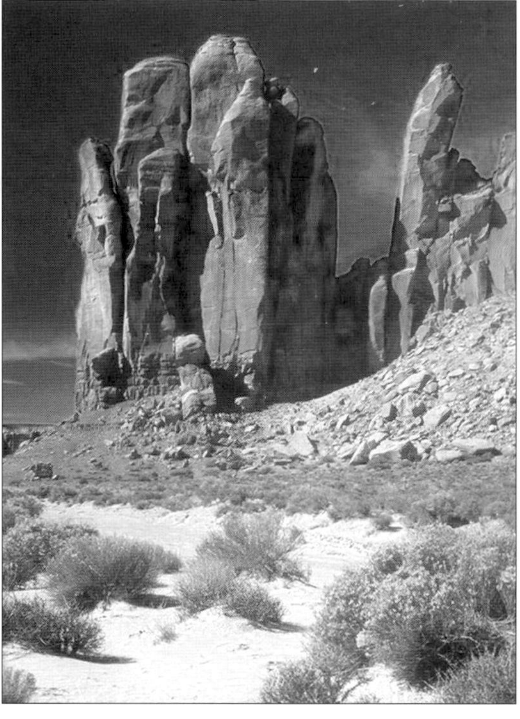

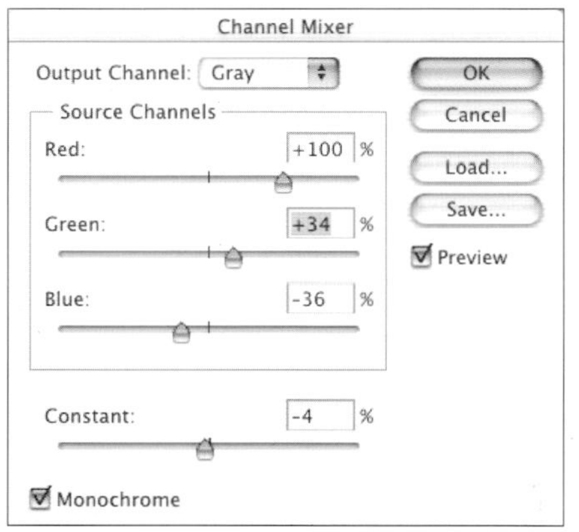

4

1 *This RGB mesa-scape would, if converted directly to a greyscale shot* (Image > Mode > **Grayscale**)*, look rather uninspiring; not the type of image Ansel Adams would approve of!*

2 *If we display the* Channels *palette for the original colour image, we see, from the thumbnails, that each channel presents the image slightly differently. We can turn off the visibility for each channel just by clicking on the eye to the left.*

3 *Here's the red channel. This gives the most saturated and imposing skies, but is the result too dramatic? For our purposes, yes.*

4 *Luckily, there is another way that works better with some images. Using the* Channel Mixer (Image> Adjust> **Channel Mixer**) *lets us overcome some of the harshness of using separate channels, yet still gives impressive results.*

5 *We can use the* Channel Mixer *to take most of the red channel, reduce the blue partially and increase the green. The result has dark skies, but with more detail and better contrast – less of the image is lost in highlight or shadow. Check the* Monochrome *box, then click* OK *to finish.*

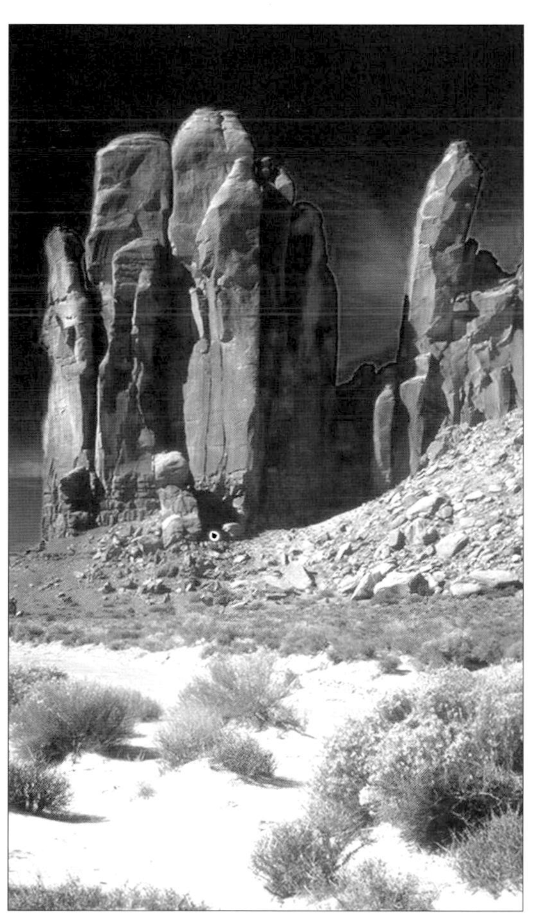

5

DARKROOM SECRETS

PRINTING MONOCHROME IMAGES

For the best results when printing monochrome images, specialised ink sets can be used in most conventional inkjet printers. We look at this option in more depth on page 172.

For the ultimate quality, monochrome prints, particularly those destined for fine art applications, are printed using the duotone process. This enables a greater range of tones to be printed, extending the normal range substantially. We examine the duotone process on page 121.

Colouring a black and white image

1
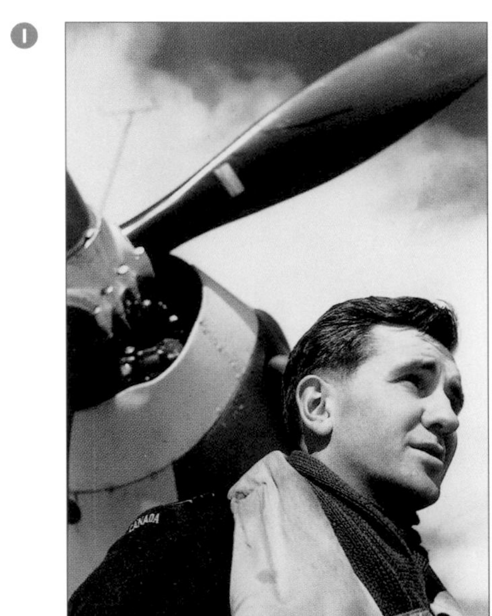

2
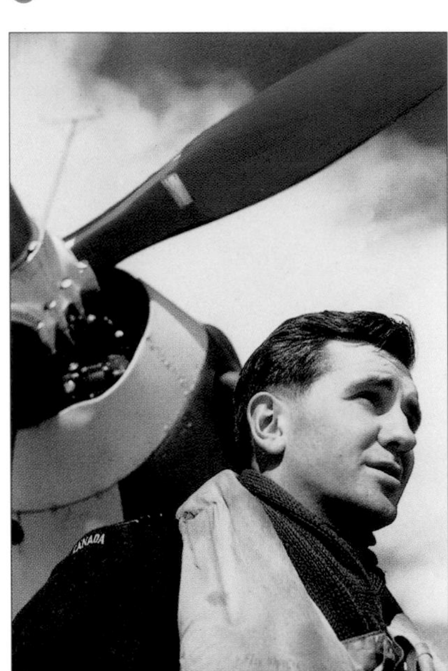

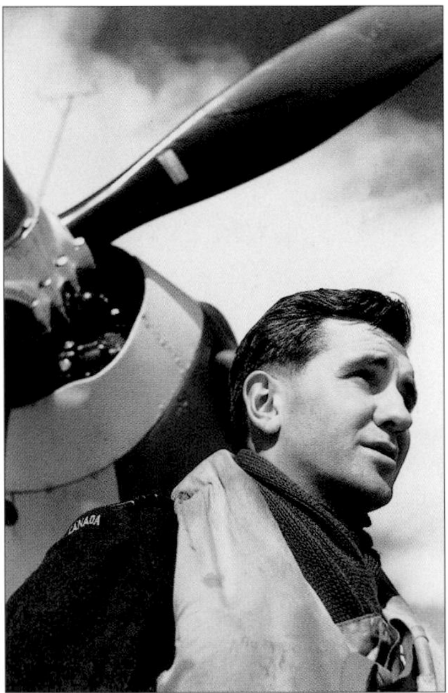
3

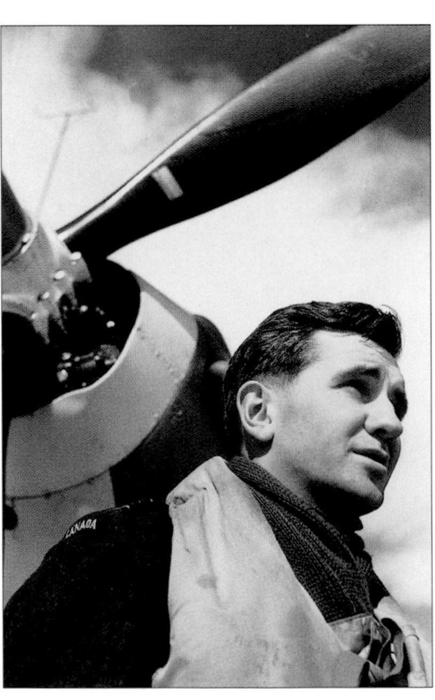
4

Hand-colouring and hand-tinting black-and-white photos has been popular since the earliest days of photography. In the early days, the process was born out of necessity – there simply weren't any colour emulsions that could deliver colour images reliably and directly.

Despite the ubiquity of colour film in more recent times, hand-coloured prints are still prized for their unique subtlety.

Recreating the same effect digitally requires the digital equivalent of hand-tinting dyes. While a paint is opaque, dyes are usually transparent and let the original image show through. When we use the painting tools in any image-editing application, we are still using an opaque medium. True, we can alter the opacity by using the opacity or transparency sliders, but we are still working with paint that is – for the want of a better description – cloudy.

To achieve the classic hand-tinted look, we need to paint onto a layer and use the colour blend mode. This takes the colour – rather than the paint texture – painted in the layer and combines it with the original image. This is the technique used here to colour this monochrome portrait of a Royal Canadian airman.

HAND-TINTING

1 *Create a duplicate layer from the background image. It will be this layer to which we apply the colour. Colours do not have to be authentic; some licence has been used here – as those familiar with military regalia might notice!*

2 *Begin with the propeller, painting over it with an appropriate shade of brown. Try to be precise but don't worry if you stray slightly. Our eyes are very forgiving of any slivers of colour that might be in the wrong place.*

3 *The result when viewing the painting layer and background with the blend mode set to* Normal *is rather abrupt and unsatisfactory. That changes, however, the moment we switch to the*

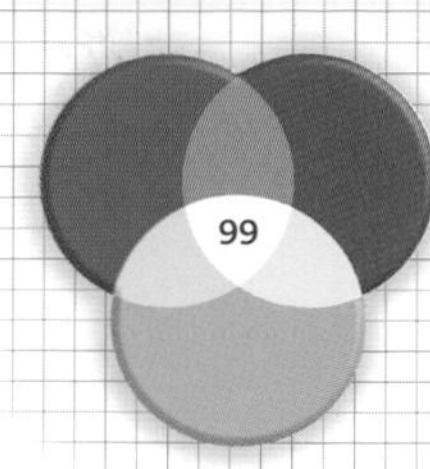

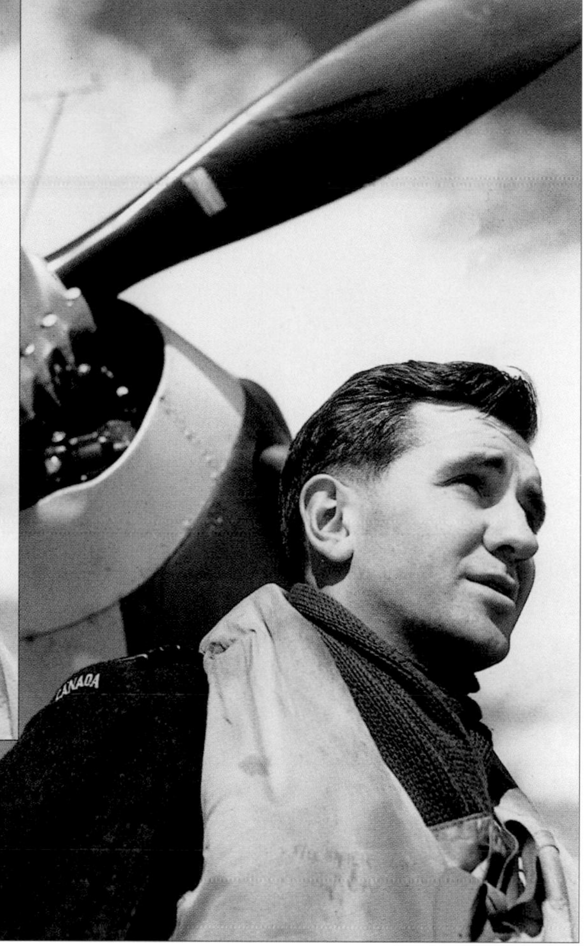

6

Color *blend mode. We now get the sought-after tint with the underlying detail showing through.*

4 *Add a blue wash all over the sky, using a greater opacity for the 'clear' sky and a paler one for the clouds. It might not be photographically accurate, but it helps to make the sky recede into the background.*

5 *Colouring the other parts of the scene, where the original colour is not obvious or unknown, just improvise or choose colours that work in the composition. Flesh tones are notoriously difficult to formulate. Here, Photoshop colour swatch* Pale Cool Brown *has been used at 40% opacity and then painted over with* Pure Red *at 4%. You can always mix colours on the image.*

6 *If your results are too bold, use the paint layer's* Opacity *slider to reduce the amount of tint. Here is the same image at 40% opacity. It is clear that the painting process does not have to be precise or even to achieve an acceptable result. Close examination of hand-tinted photos from a century ago would reveal a similar lack of accuracy, and that's actually part of the charm!*

TIPS FOR TINTING

You do not need to work with an original black-and-white image. You can use a colour image and convert it to greyscale. You can even use an original colour image and add further colour tints to this. In this example, the gilt mask on this sculpture was selected and the rest of the image desaturated to give a black-and-white image. The appropriate green and magenta tints were then added to give emphasis to the subject and de-emphasise the background.

Selective tinting – the tinting of only one part of the image – is a good way of giving more prominence to the subject.

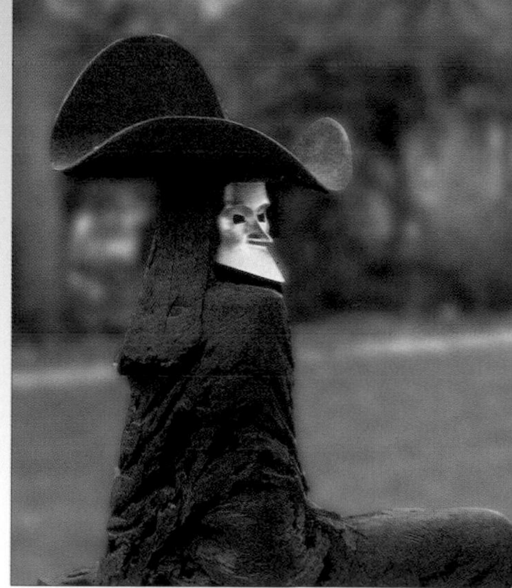

Repairing an old image

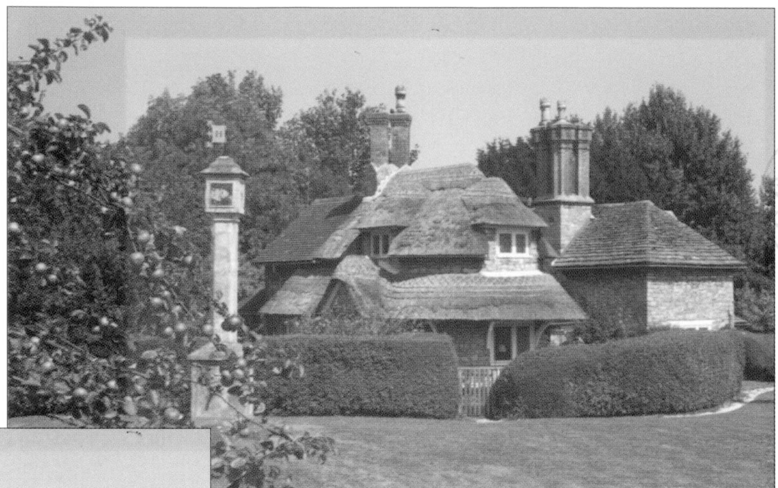

One of the early wonders of digital imaging was its ability to repair old photographs. Images thought lost to time could be brought spectacularly back to life. This used to require high levels of expertise, but it is no dark art. In fact, it is a task that anyone can undertake with just a little knowledge and some experience with the techniques involved.

The print on this page dates from the 1950s and was originally printed – and framed – using high-quality materials. Sadly, the ravages of time, moisture and subsequent handling have taken their toll. The mounting adhesive had also broken down, further exacerbating the problems. We probably all have images that show some, if not all of these faults.

ASSESSING THE PRINT

Though this appears to be a major job, there are only a few problems that need addressing. First is the obvious bleaching effect caused by the framing. The part of the image open to light has very obviously been bleached. In the non-frame areas, colour saturation is better, but chemical action has caused a colour shift towards magenta.

Looking closer, we see two further problems. Since being taken from the frame, some dust has become embedded in the print's surface and the image is not critically sharp by today's standards. Incidentally, one of the chimney pots in this heritage building appears to have been lost!

DARKROOM SECRETS

GO FOR OLD

If you find that your print doesn't respond well to your corrective measures, you can still get a very worthwhile result by giving it an artificially aged effect using vignette and colour-toning effects.

REPAIRING THE IMAGE

1 *We will work on colour and contrast first, paying particular attention to the area of the print protected by the frame. Firstly, we use the* Variations *command to dial in more (or less) of a colour to achieve a colour cast-free image. To overcome our magenta cast, we add more green, and we do so selectively to the highlights, shadows and midtones. In a case like this, where chemical action has been at work, the shift in colour tends to be proportionate to the amount of colour in the scene, so the shadow areas need slightly more correction.*

2 *The bleached area needs more consideration. First we use the marquee tool to select it, setting a feather radius to give a softer transition between selected and unselected areas. Then we adjust the* Hue/Saturation, Color Balance *and* Brightness/Contrast *commands. A degree of fine tuning is required, making it easier to concentrate on a single area – such as the sky.*

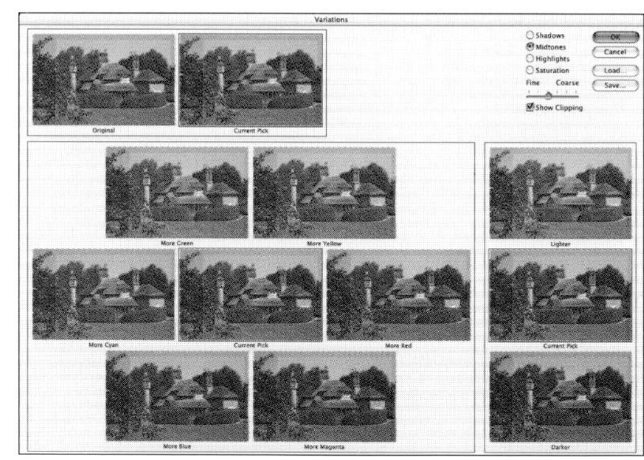

1

2

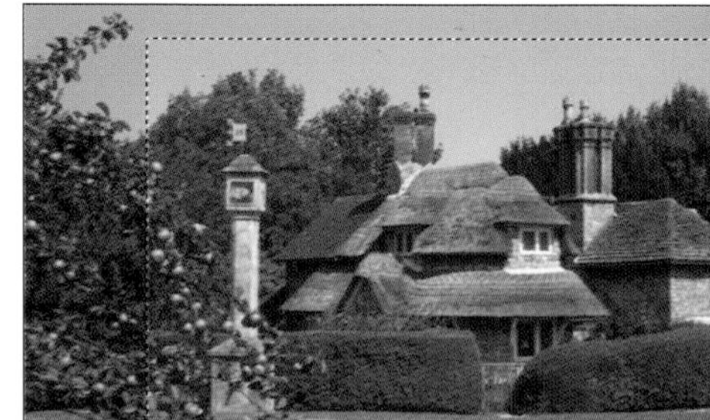

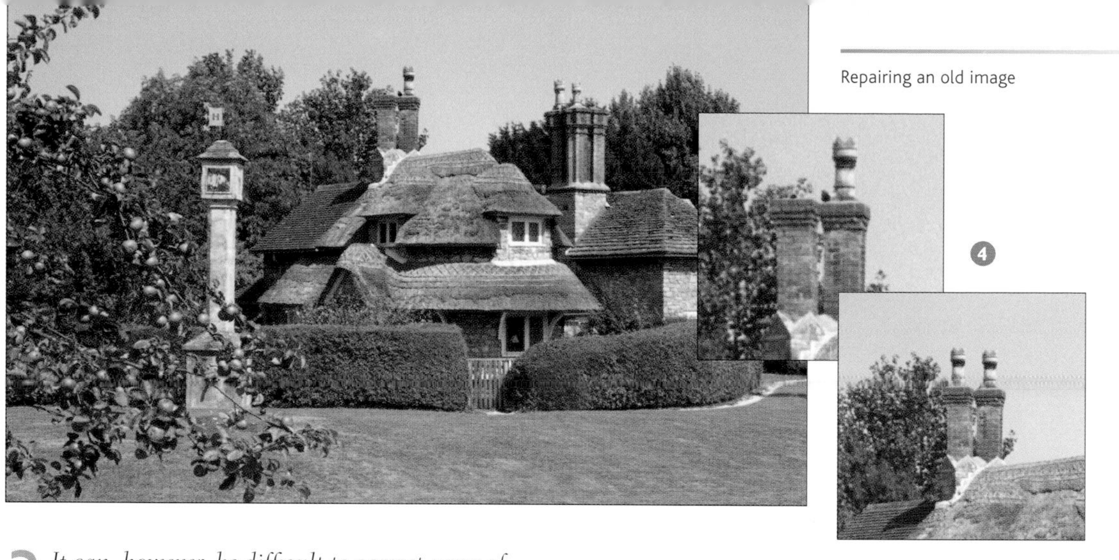

3

4

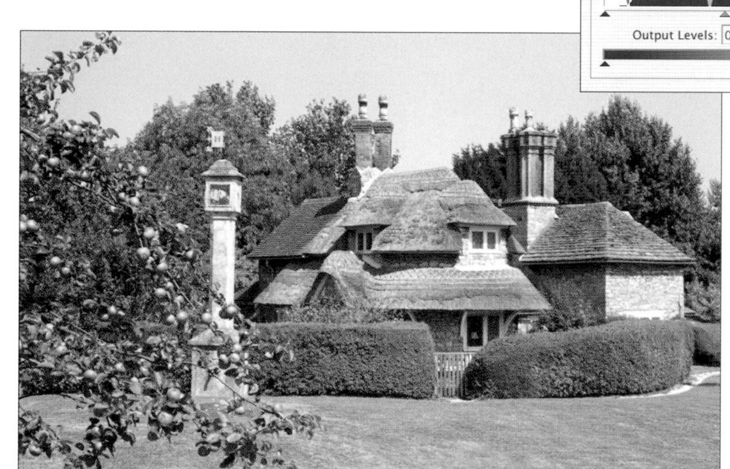

5

3 It can, however, be difficult to correct areas of continuous tone, such as the sky, so that the joins are seamless. In this particular case, it works better if we replace it entirely. The Magic Wand *tool is used to select the sky, both inside and outside the framed area. Then the* Eyedropper *tool is used to select foreground and background colours based on the sky colour in the frame area at the horizon and the top of the frame. Finally, a gradient is applied to the selected sky area, using the foreground and background colours. The result is a continuous, seamless sky, without the dust and scratch marks that were so obvious in this area.*

4 That missing chimney is easily restored by using the Clone *tool to copy the adjacent chimney pot. Just set the remaining chimney pot as the point to clone from, and then paint the new one into place. If only all house repairs were so easy! We can also employ this tool to tidy up any other parts of the image where time has taken its toll.*

5 We can now adjust the Levels *in the image. Adjustments here involve moving the outer sliders to the start and end points of the histogram curve respectively, then moving the midpoint slider until we have a satisfactory result, with brighter colours and increased the contrast. We could have made these changes earlier, but doing so may have had a detrimental effect on the* Levels *distribution.*

6 The final stage is to sharpen the image. We apply the Unsharp Mask *filter with the* Amount *set to around 120%, the* Radius *to 2 pixels, and the* Threshold *between 5 and 10. This gives an impression of sharpness in the fine detail but will not introduce any noticeable sharpening artefacts. Our final image has a much more natural look – it could have been taken yesterday.*

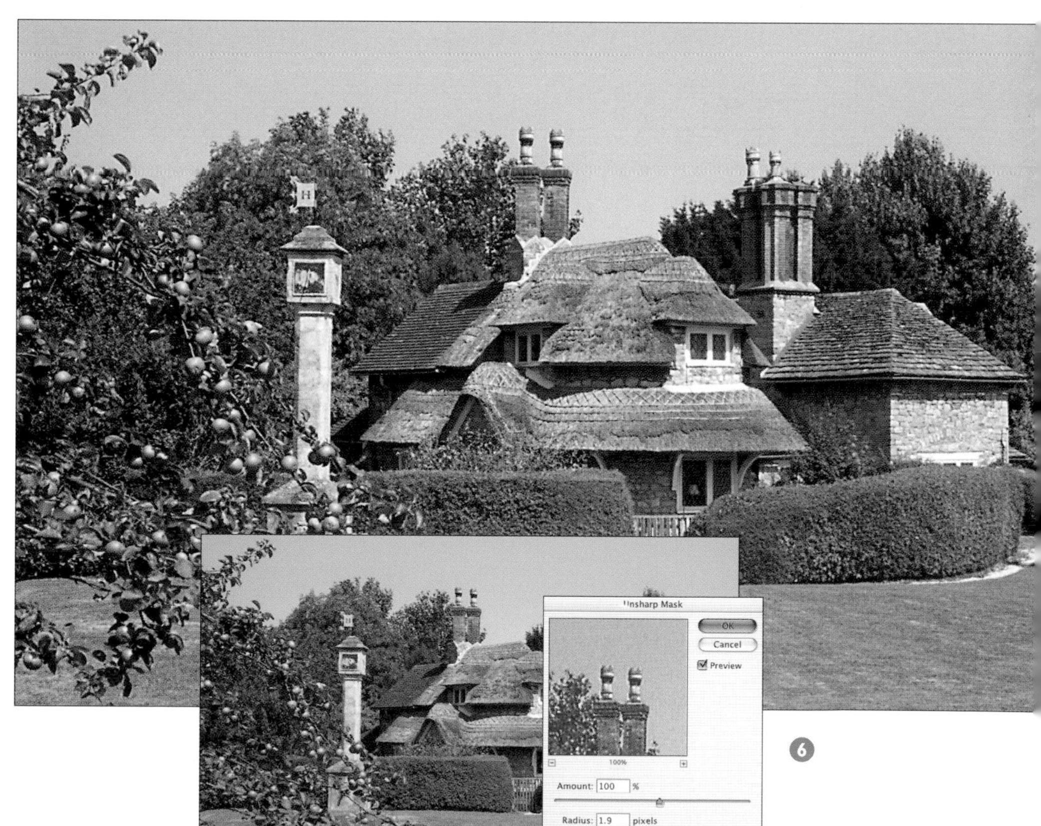

6

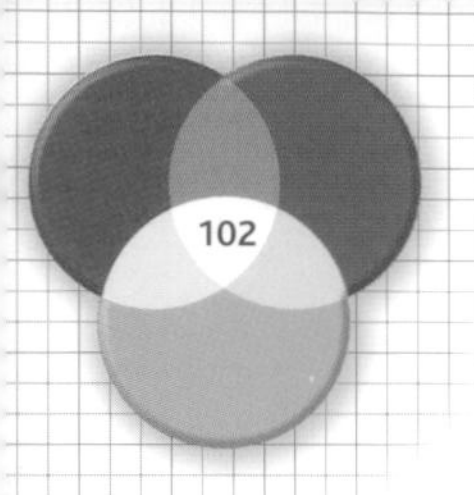

Travelling back in time

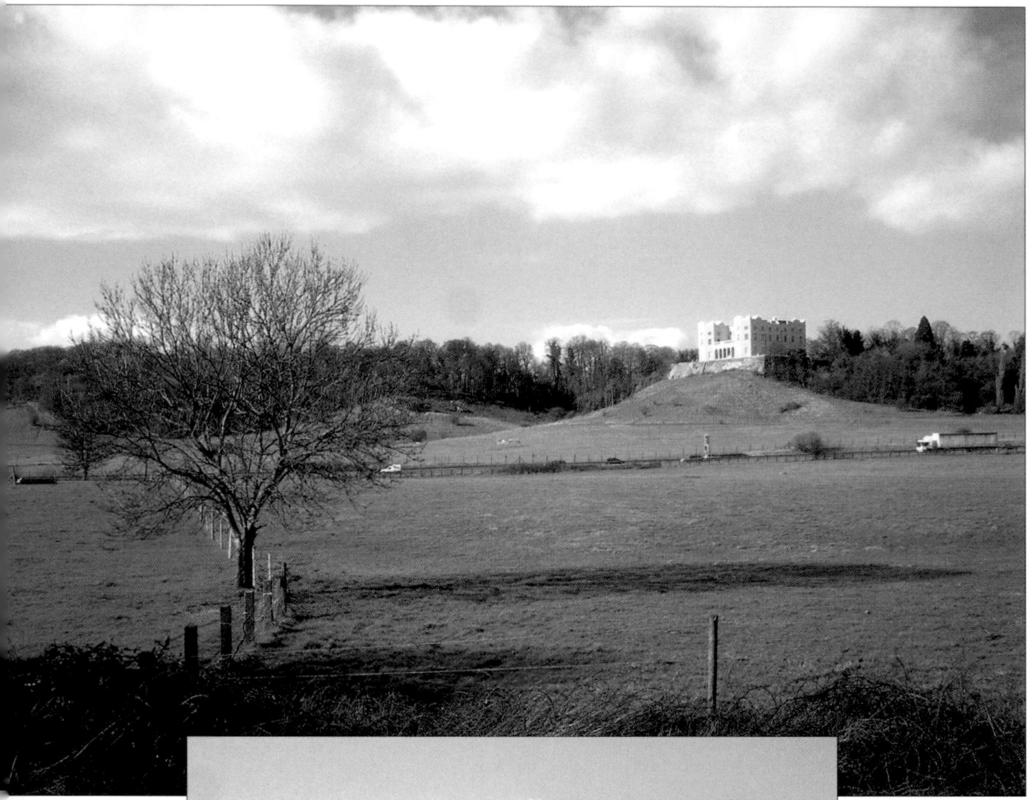

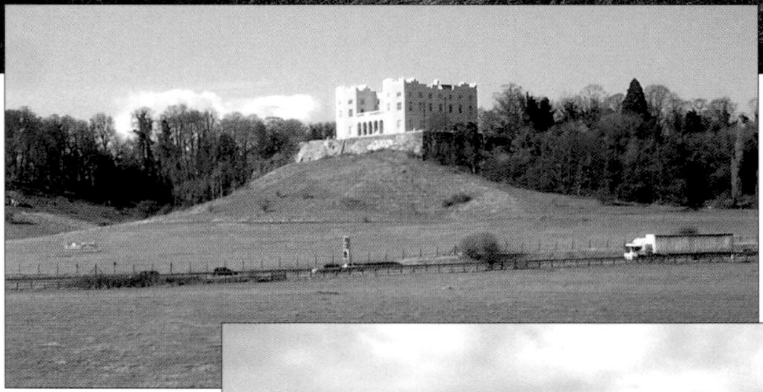

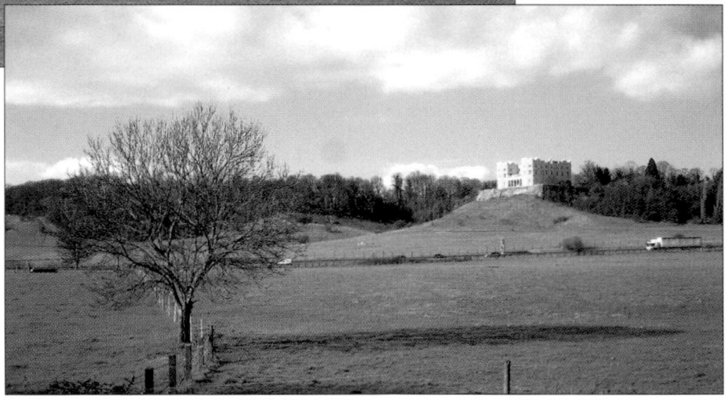

Rescuing old images is one thing, but we can also move time in the opposite direction, restoring contemporary scenes to the way they would have appeared in the past. We can even give them the look of a photograph that might have been taken at the time. In this example, we will take a fairly ordinary scene of a landscape with an old house in the background, and convert it so it looks the way it may have done to a photographer of the nineteenth or early twentieth century.

ASSESSMENT

As in the previous project, we need to assess the image before we do anything else. We need to look very carefully at the image and determine what exactly needs attention. The most obvious element in this particular scene is the road that bisects it. This will clearly have to go. There is also some fence work that should probably disappear. Whether it does go or stay will depend more on composition than authenticity; there would have been fencing here a century ago, but that does not necessarily make it picturesque!

The colours in the image are equally contentious. There were some colour emulsions around at the time our ideal photo would have been taken, but the colours that they would have presented would not be as strong or as realistic as those we see today. Many black-and-white images would have been hand-coloured, and this too would give interesting but less authentic tones.

So far we have established that we want to remove the roadway all across the scene and also the 'Apartments for Sale' signage on the hillside: it's amazing what close inspection of an image reveals. We will also crop away some parts of the foreground that don't really add much to the image or the composition. It is normally a rule to include foreground interest, but as there's little of interest in this particular foreground, it is one rule that we are right to break.

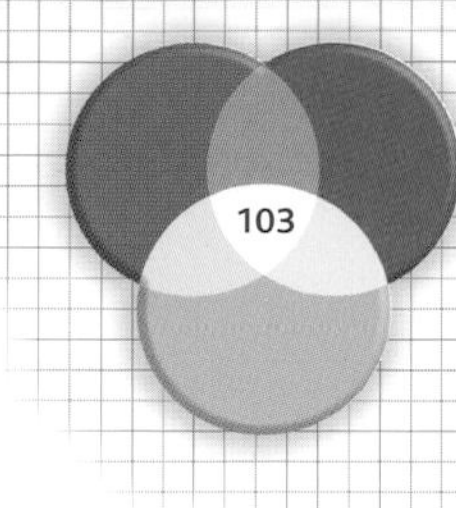

1

2

3

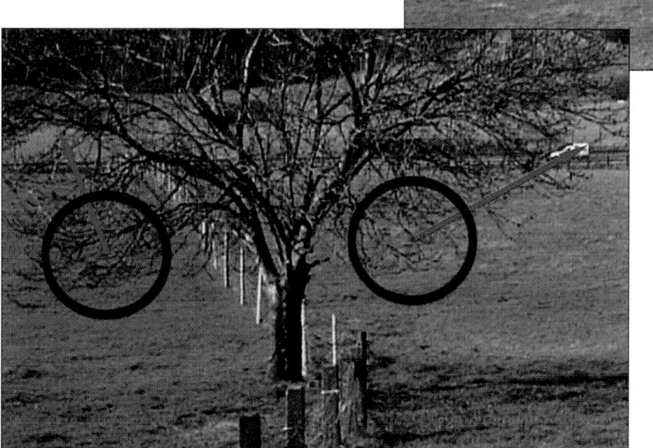

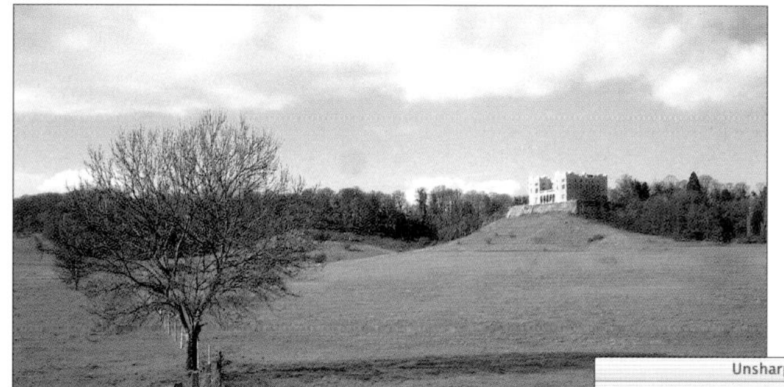

4

RESTORATION: STEP BY STEP

1 *Begin by taking out the roadway by using the* Clone *tool to clone grass land (taken from in front and behind it) over the roadway. In this case, the cloning is pretty simple, as the texture of the grass lends itself to seamless cloning. Remember to vary the clone position now and again to prevent repetition of the cloned material producing a zebra-stripe effect.*

2 *Periodically stop your work and examine the* Clone *work in detail. Remember that the results will generally look better onscreen than they will when the image is printed out. Even if everything looks fine from a glance, zoom in close and make sure that you have not made any weird mistakes or left anything obvious behind!*

3 *You will notice that the road passes behind a tree in one part of the image. You might imagine that we need to be a little more precise and a little more deft when cleaning this part of the scene, zooming in to pixel level and making precise clones between the branches. If so, you would be mistaken. While that approach would work, it would take a great deal of time without being particularly effective. Instead, we're going to cheat, taking advantage of the fact that the human eye can be fooled by fine detailing. We can use other parts of the tree to clone directly over the roadway sections and achieve a convincing result with the minimum of effort. Though you may be aware of the duplicity, you can be assured that others will not be so bothered! Just a couple of minutes work reveals a much more tranquil landscape.*

4 *It is normal to apply sharpening only if it adds something to the image, and to do so at the end of the project. Any earlier and we might find that subsequent edits enhance and exacerbate any artifacts introduced by the sharpening process. In this case, we can break this rule as our subsequent work won't affect the image quality. As ever, do not go straight for the* Sharpen *command. Instead, select the* Unsharp Mask *filter and begin with an* Amount *setting of 100%, a* Radius *of between 1 and 2, and a 0* Threshold. *Check the results using the* Preview *window on the dialog box to prevent oversharpening. This image is now halfway through its journey back in time.*

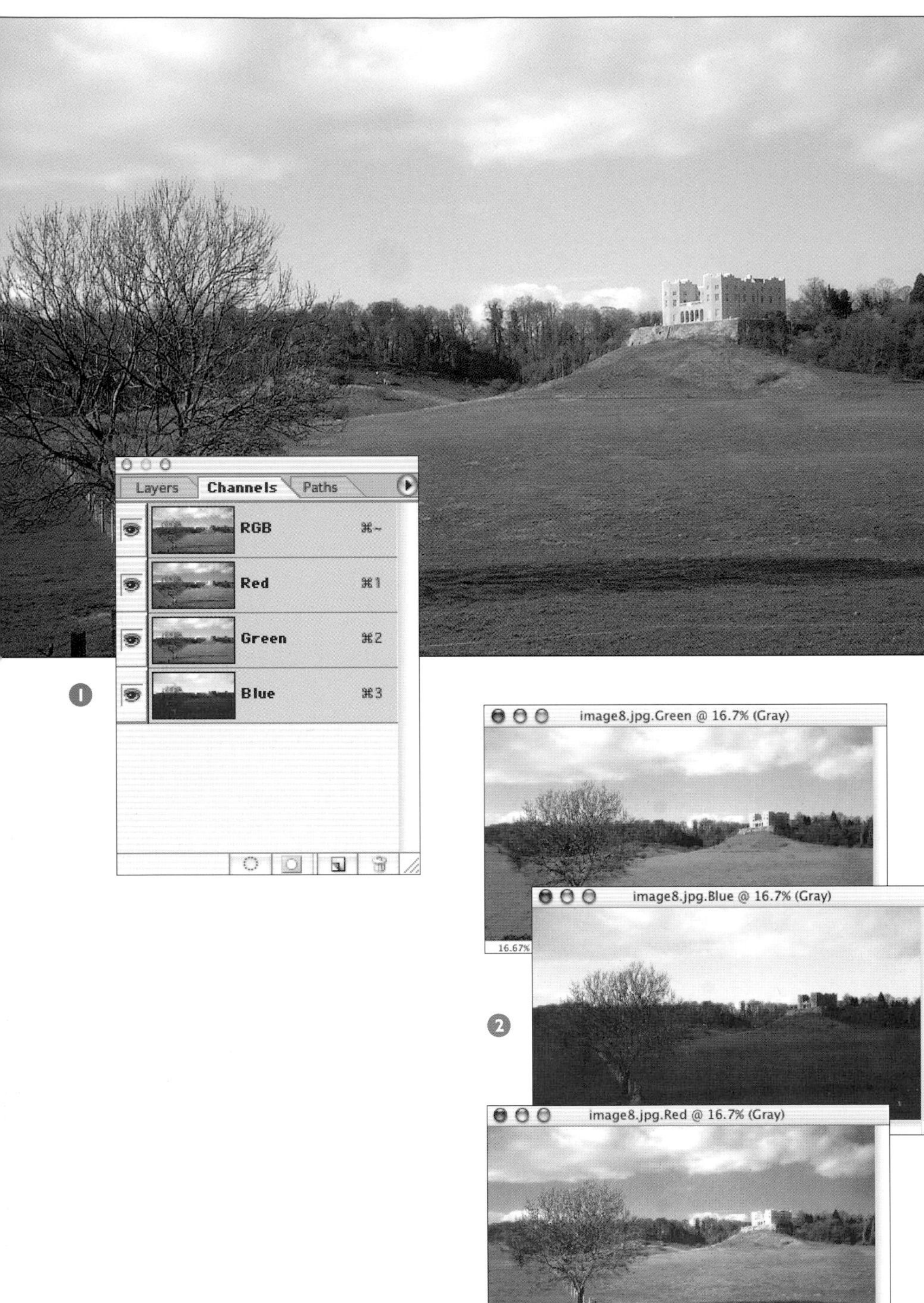

COLOUR AND FINISHING

1 *The film stock popular a century ago tended to be orthochromatic, exhibiting an overt sensitivity to red light. This proved very successful for landscape photography because the results tended to emulate the use of a deep red filter with standard contemporary monochrome emulsions. Blue skies become a very dark grey against which clouds are clearly defined while foliage is lightened. We can achieve a similar result by splitting our colour image into its component channels, as we did in the example on pages 96–97. Doing so gives us three greyscale images, one each of the scene in red, green and blue light. This solution is far more satisfactory than using* desaturate, *which tends to give a flat, low contrast result. The* Channels *palette gives us a thumbnail overview of what we can expect from each one.*

2 *Save a copy of the image in a safe place, and then split it into three channels by using the palette's pop-up menu and selecting* Split Channels. *Our original image now becomes three separate images, one in each colour light. As you can see, it is the red channel image (the bottom image) that gives the best result.*

3 *If we now take a look at that image in close-up, we can see that it is a much stronger result than a simple greyscale conversion. All the same, it still needs some work to pep it up. We can use the dodge and burn tools to add further enhancement. First, burn in the sky area to increase the contrast between the clouds and background sky.*

4 *Now dodge the middle landscape to add depth. It's a good idea to use a large, soft-edged brush when doing this to prevent obvious hot spots or burns. Take your time.*

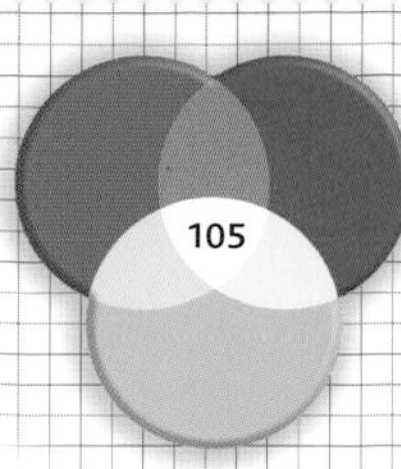

3

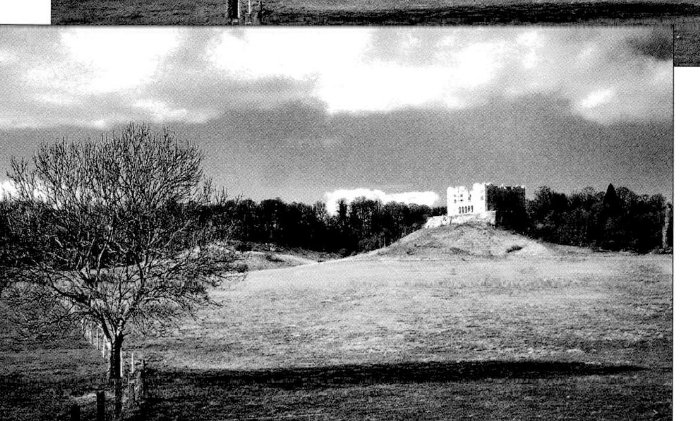

4

5 *Finishing the print provides us with several opportunities. We could use that old stalwart, the sepia tone. It's not that authentic, but many people accept it as a sign of age. Why question their judgment? If you do apply a sepia tone, make sure that you do so in a light-handed way, applying a gentle tone rather than a heavy colour.*

6 *Alternatively, we could apply a grain filter to simulate the grain that would have appeared in a contemporary photo. Remember that grain should not blur the image but add texture, so be careful not to overdo it!*

7 *For our final flourish, we have created a graduated effect in which the restored image from step one is blended seamlessly with our artificially aged result. This has been achieved by creating a new layer in the original and copying the aged image to this. Then a* Quick Mask *gradient is applied across it. When switched back to standard mode, the selection made by the* Quick Mask *is deleted, revealing the underlying image. For extra effect, we used the* Horizontal Grain *option of the* Grain *filter to add a striated effect. It's been a long haul, but the final result makes it all worthwhile.*

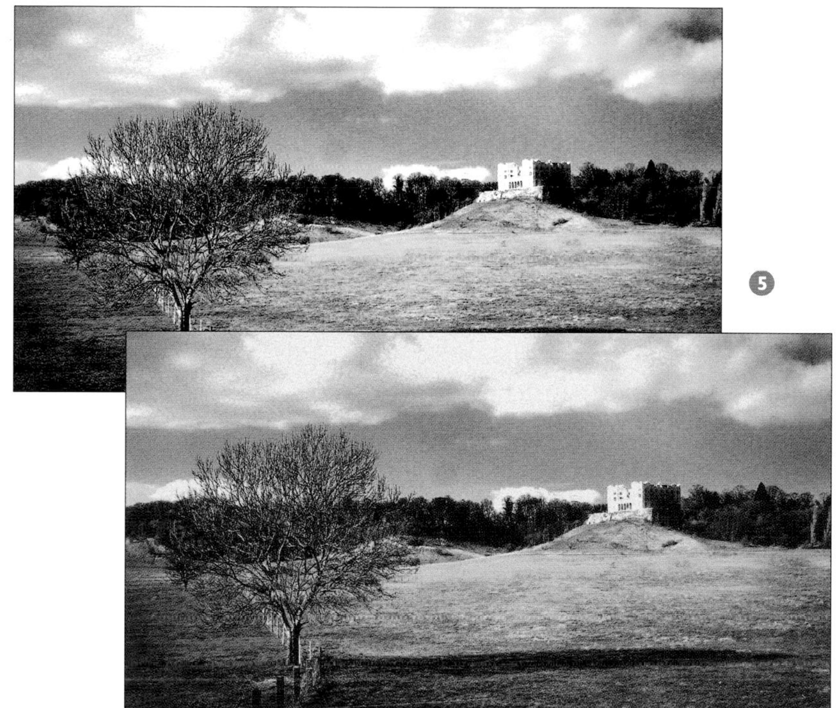

5

6

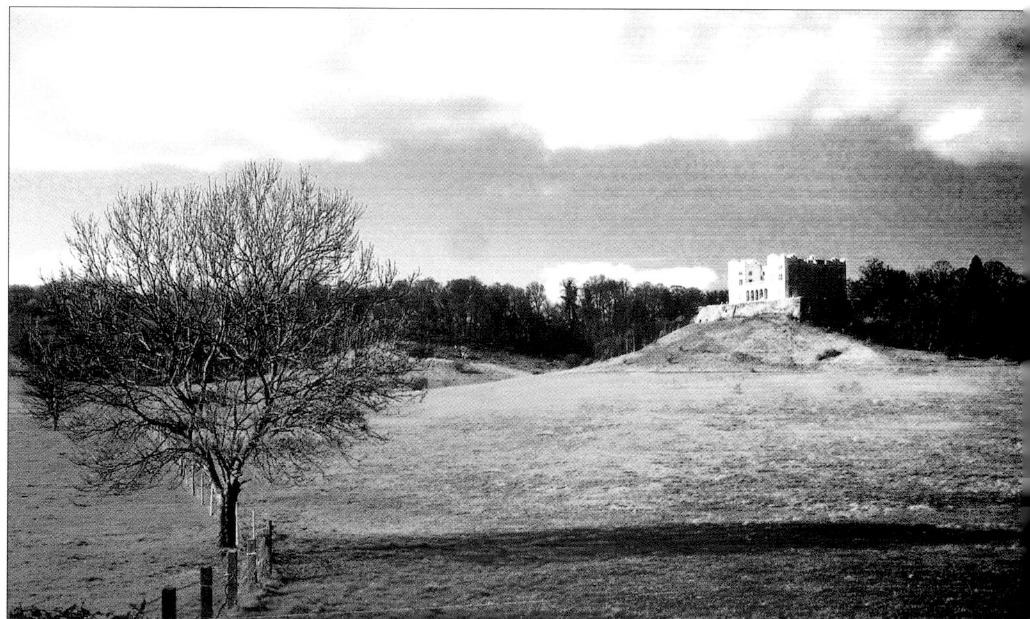

7

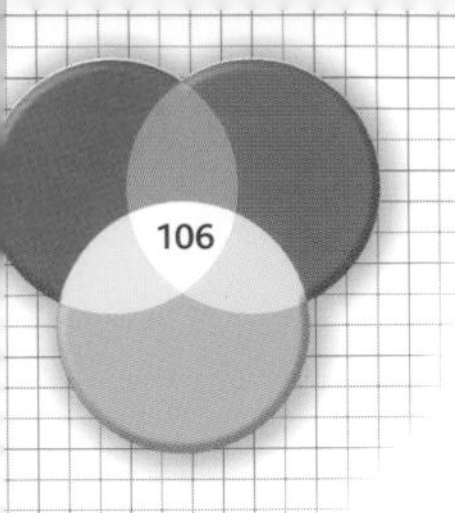

Panoramic photography

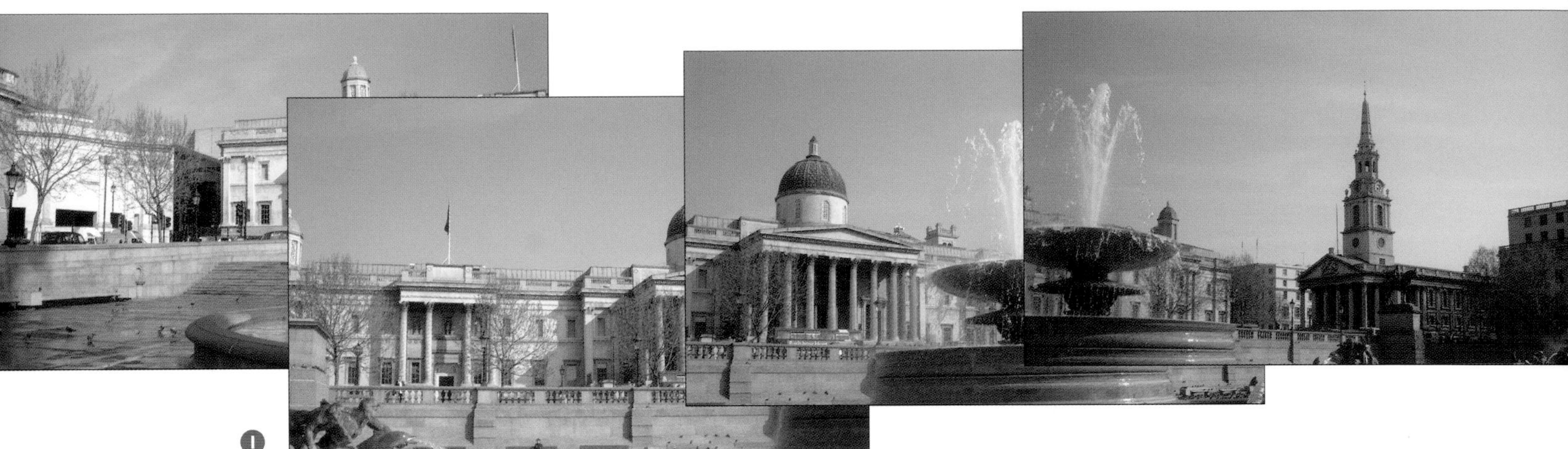

1

Panoramic images are virtually as old as photography. Early pioneers created bespoke cameras that were the forebears of today's swing lens models while others used super-wide lenses to take dramatic, wide views. Others perfected the art of montage, joining – almost invisibly – multiple shots into a sweeping view.

Digital techniques enable us to take those processes a stage further, melding multiple component shots into join-free panoramas that can be as much as 360° wide.

Some digital cameras include in-camera software that will join shots as they are taken, but as with so many things, a software alternative offers more flexibility. There are specialized options available, such as PhotoVista from ISeeMedia, while Photoshop Elements and Corel Photo-Paint include their own stitching module.

Many successful panoramic images are created by directly submitting the images to the panorama application or module, but you can improve your chances of success by following a few simple guidelines. First, check urban landscape shots for linearity and convergence. Converging verticals – even if the effect is mild in individual shots – can cause problems when the shots are assembled to create the panorama: the software finds it difficult to reconcile them. Correct any convergency beforehand, taking care to apply similar degrees of correction to each shot. That aside, leave further editing until after the images have been stitched together. The stitching process can introduce distortion, and contrast, brightness and saturation adjustments are better attended to in the final image.

Let's explore further by creating a panorama from these four images of London's Trafalgar Square. Note that the original images feature a substantial overlap. Creators of panoramic software recommend an overlap of around 30% between adjacent shots, and we would certainly concur with that.

STITCHING IMAGES TOGETHER

1 *The four images are loaded sequentially into the panorama-generating software. In this case, it is PhotoVista, an effective specialised package.*

2 *To get the application to interpret the perspective correctly, we need to select the lens that was used for taking the original photographs. If you used a digital camera to take the original images, you will need to convert this to a 35mm equivalent focal length. Presets are included for certain digital models, and others can be downloaded from the Web. The same dialog box also advises on the number of shots that are required to take a complete 360° panorama.*

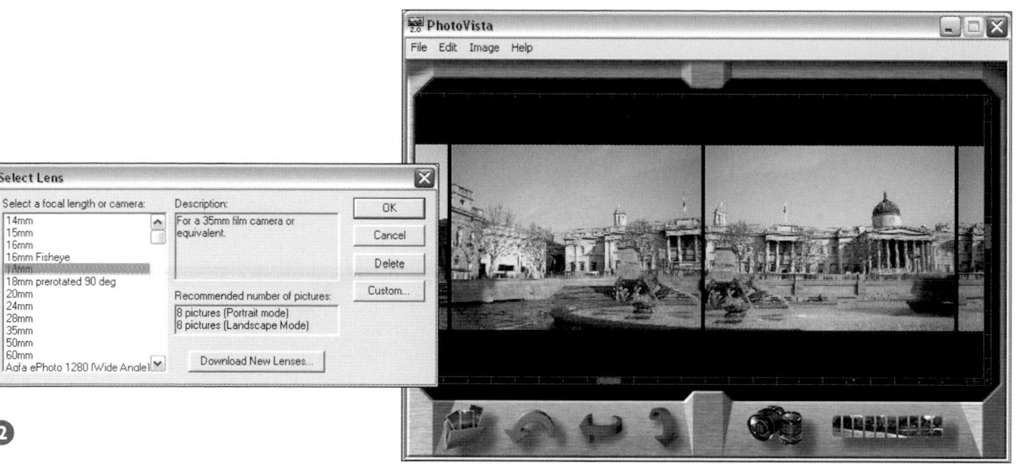

2

3

3 Pressing the Stitch Panorama *button gives us the opportunity to produce a preview stitch. A low resolution surrogate, the preview is a good test of how well the software has coped with the images, and takes considerably less time than a full stitch. You can also, at this stage, select whether the scan should be a full 360° panorama. If all is okay with the preview, you can progress to the full scan. As the stitching process is a complex operation, you should expect this to take some time, particularly with high resolution source images.*

4 You will still need to examine the panorama closely for discontinuities. Even the best panoramic software can be confused by patterns or areas where convergence has taken its toll, and some faults don't always show up during the preview stage. A close examination of the original panorama showed this problem, with a ghost image appearing behind the central dome.

This fault was corrected in the final version by selecting a different lens (replacing the 50mm lens originally selected for a 35mm lens) and by making fine adjustments to the positions of the separate images by hand. Take time to iron out any such defects and it will be hard for anyone viewing your image to spot the joins.

DARKROOM SECRETS

TIPS FOR SHOOTING PANORAMAS

For best results, avoid wide-angle lenses (or wide-angle zoom ratios) when shooting panoramas. The distortions produced by these lenses make it difficult for the panoramic application to effectively stitch the overlapping areas. Standard focal lengths (50mm, 35mm equivalent) or even slimline portrait ratios (70mm) are better.

Shoot in portrait (upright) format to get the required vertical reach in individual shots.

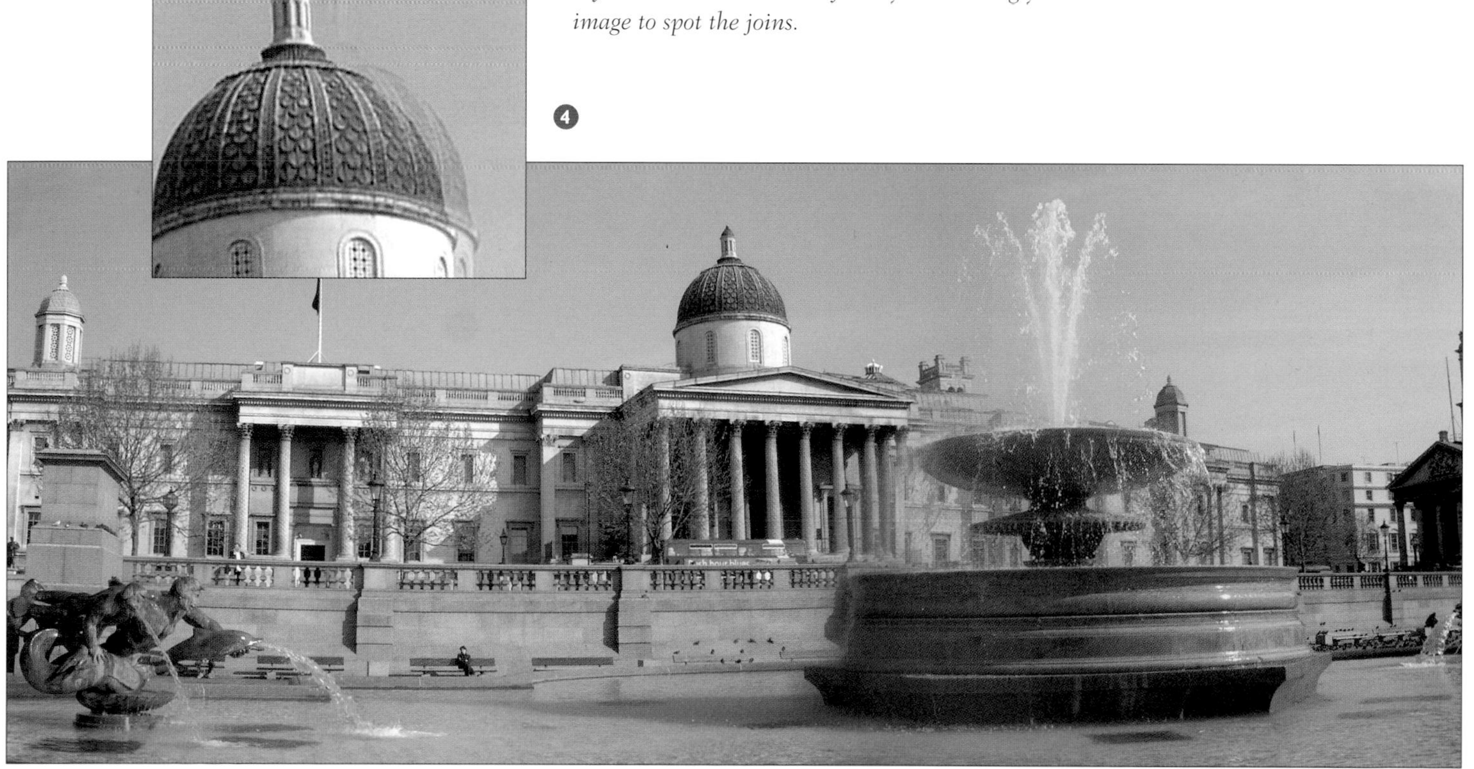

4

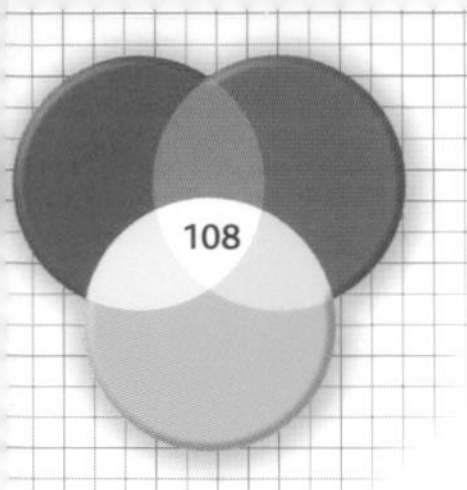

Interior panoramas

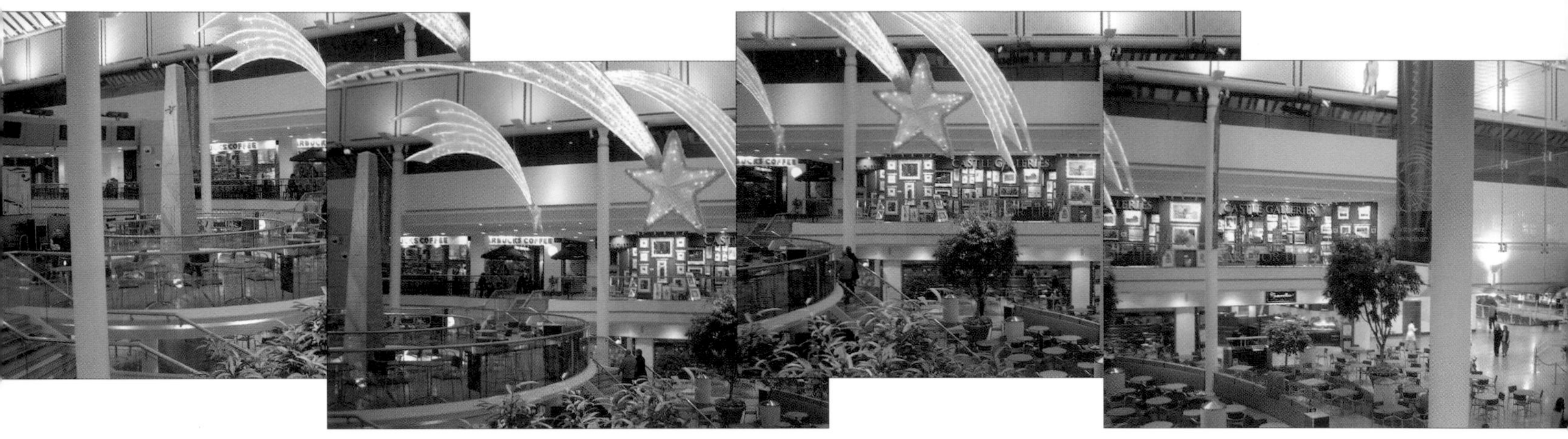

DARKROOM SECRETS

TIPS FOR SHOOTING PANORAMAS

If possible, use a tripod when taking the photos for your panorama. Doing so will help to keep your angles and levels consistent, and allow you more precision as you rotate around the central point. Unless you're shooting in bright sunlight, use a fixed exposure to prevent unusual (and unwanted) variations in brightness across the panorama. These techniques are not – and should not be – limited merely to the creation of panoramas. We can use the processes to create wide-angle shots that are wider than the lens or camera is capable of, and tall shots where we turn the panorama through 90°.

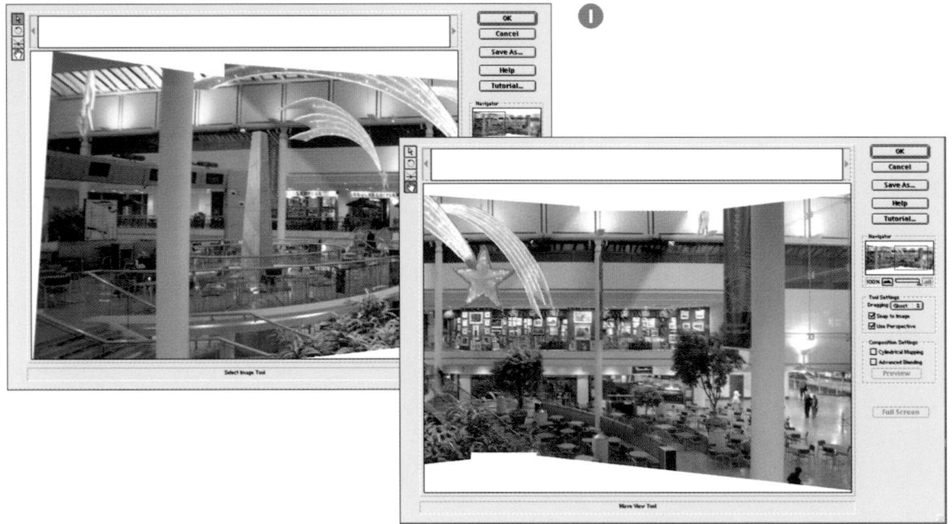

1

2

While panoramas are particularly effective for landscapes – urban and country – they can also be used to bring the insides of buildings to life. This does involve some new potential problems – interior lighting can throw up inconsistencies that the software finds hard to deal with – but these aren't difficult to resolve. For this interior panorama, we have used Photoshop Element's *Photomerge* panorama creator. This is especially useful for interiors, enabling us to retain perspective so that we do not get the distortion common in panoramic photographs.

CREATING AN INTERIOR PANORAMA

1 *Load the images into* Photomerge (Edit > **Photomerge**). *The images are stitched together, then displayed in the main window.*

2 *Notice that, in preserving the perspective, the images have been stretched at the outer limits of the panorama.*

3 *Close inspection also shows that the brightness levels in the blend areas differ across image boundaries, and colour consistency is poor. We need*

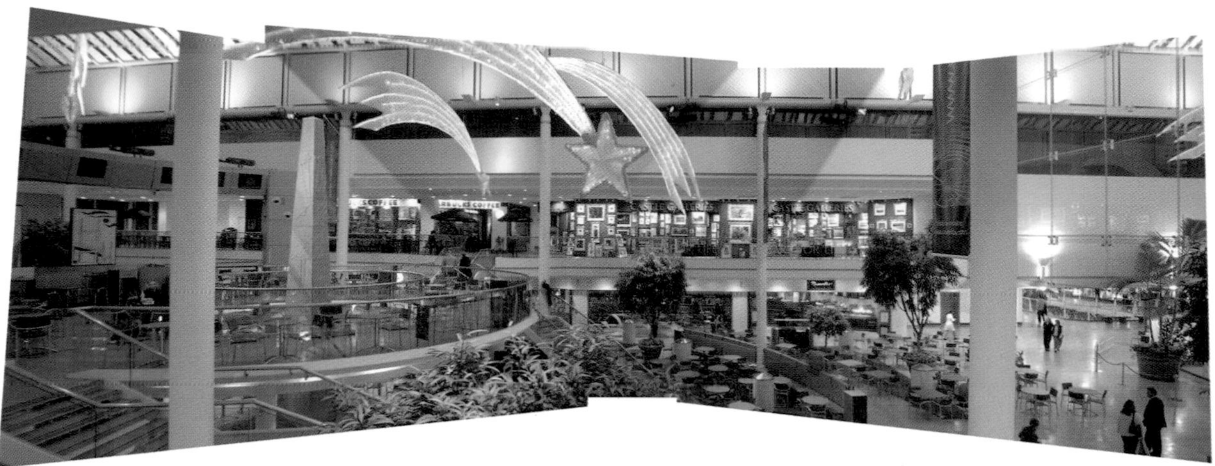

3

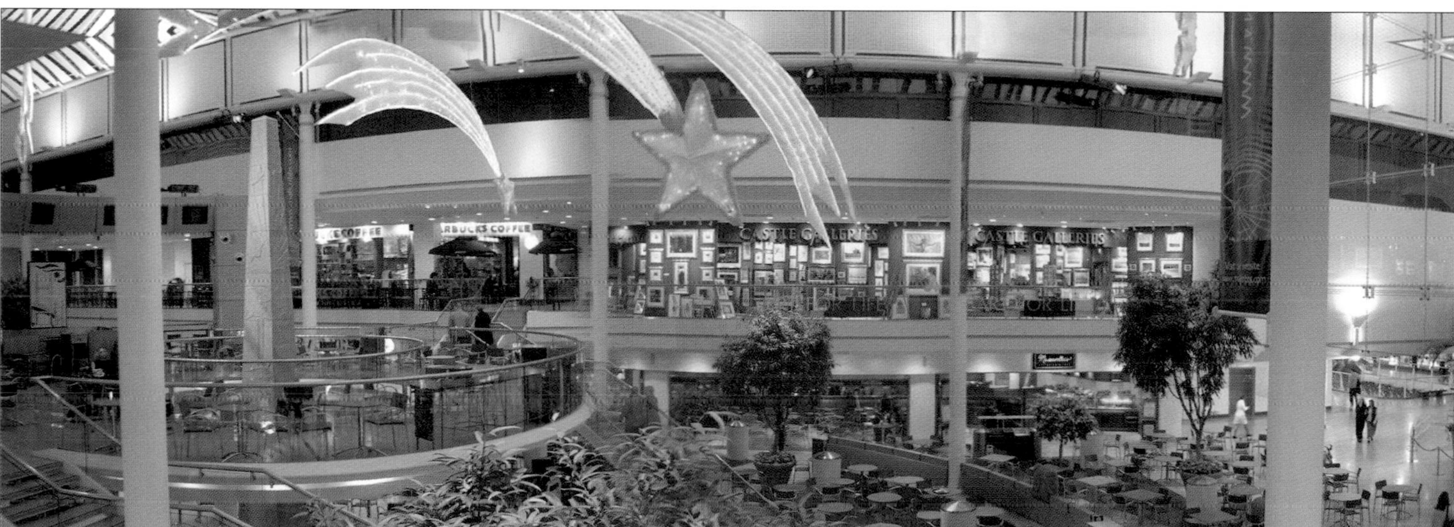

4

to correct these manually by using a Gaussian blur *filter across the boundaries selections, or using the* Clone *tool to clean up disjointed areas.*

4 *We can now crop the panorama to provide a conventional rectangular print, or tidy the image areas to produce a 'Cinerama' effect. If, in the* Photomerge *dialog box, we uncheck the* Perspective *box, the stitching can be more accurate, but this accuracy comes at the expense of image linearity. Note the slight distortion in the lines of the pillars in this example.*

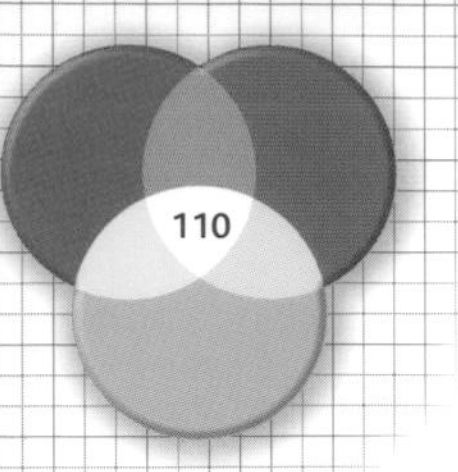

Photomosaic

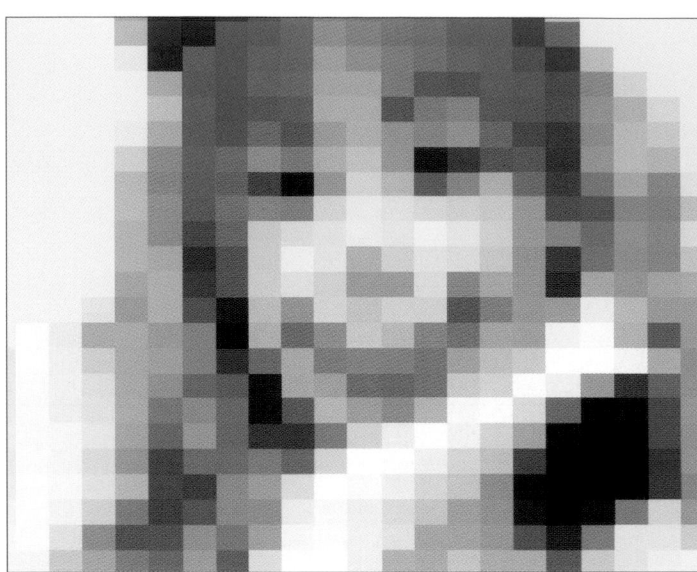

1

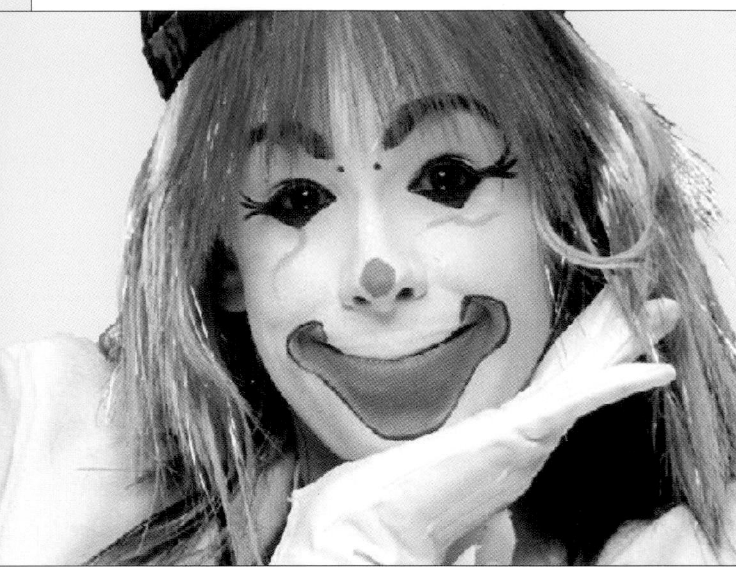

2

Photomosaic – sometimes called phototapestry – is a technique where a large image is constructed from a large number of smaller, thumbnail-sized images. The technique is an old one, but it came to particular prominence in the mid-1990s, when a rash of images – including advertising posters, fine art prints and even jigsaw puzzles – adopted the technique. After a short period in vogue, it has now returned to relative obscurity

You can create a photomosaic entirely by hand – selecting thumbnail images and matching their colour and brightness to discrete areas of the main image – but fortunately there is a more expedient alternative. Some image-editing applications include a routine to produce photomosaics directly. They require you only to specify the number of thumbnails to be used and then select the gallery of small images that will be employed to produce the end result – the software may even provide the gallery by itself. Both roxio's Photosuite III and ArcSoft's PhotoMontage provide all the tools necessary.

BUILDING A PHOTOMOSAIC

1 *The process of building a photomosaic begins by selecting a main image. This is the image into which all your other images will be converted. Photomosaic works with any image, but those with bold, graphic shapes and simple forms tend to produce the best results.*

2 *You then need to determine the number of thumbnails that will be combined into the final image. The greater the number, the smaller each will be and, consequently, the more detail the resulting image will contain. With a smaller number, detail is coarser and the result more abstract. You will also need to specify a gallery of images to be used as thumbnails.*

3 *The application divides the image into a number of discrete blocks, of a size determined by the number of thumbnails to be used. Each is assigned the average colour value and brightness level of the underlying pixels. For each of these blocks, a thumbnail of similar colour and brightness*

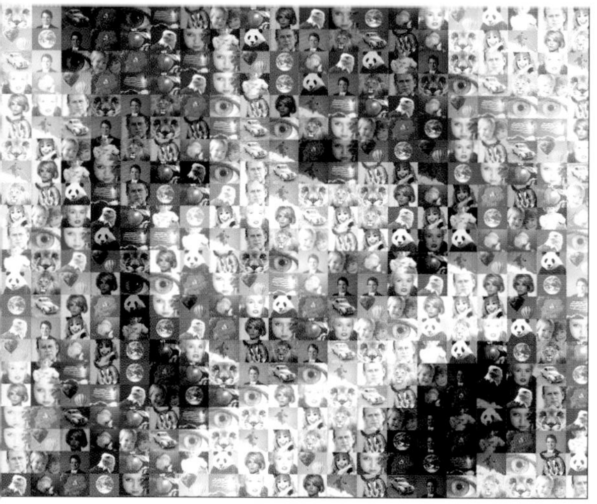

3

is applied. In practice, to have a gallery of images with sufficient variety and range of colour and brightness is virtually impossible, so the tonal values of the thumbnail images are adjusted to suit those of the final photomosaic.

4 *Increasing the number of thumbnails used has an obvious effect on finished picture. Here, we have used 2000 thumbnails instead of the original 600, with the result that more detail in the clown's face can be reproduced.*

Dominant colour images

You can successfully apply the photomontage process to high- or low-key images and also to those featuring a dominant colour. This image of a Florida sunrise has an overt blue bias. When the thumbnails are applied, the result retains that colour dominance even though there is a wide range of coloration at the macroscopic scale.

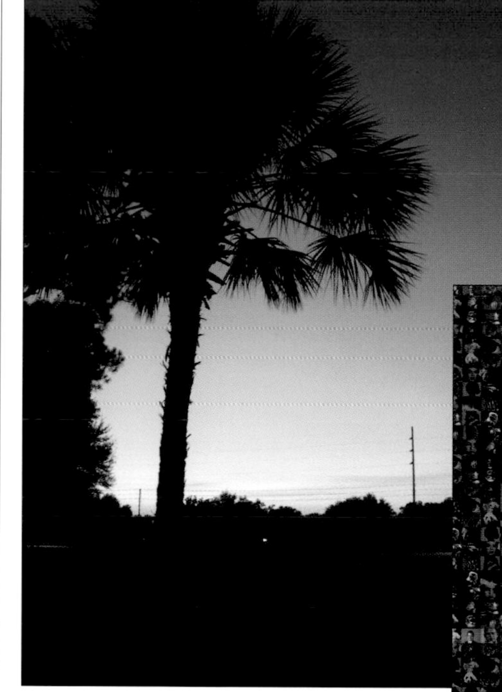

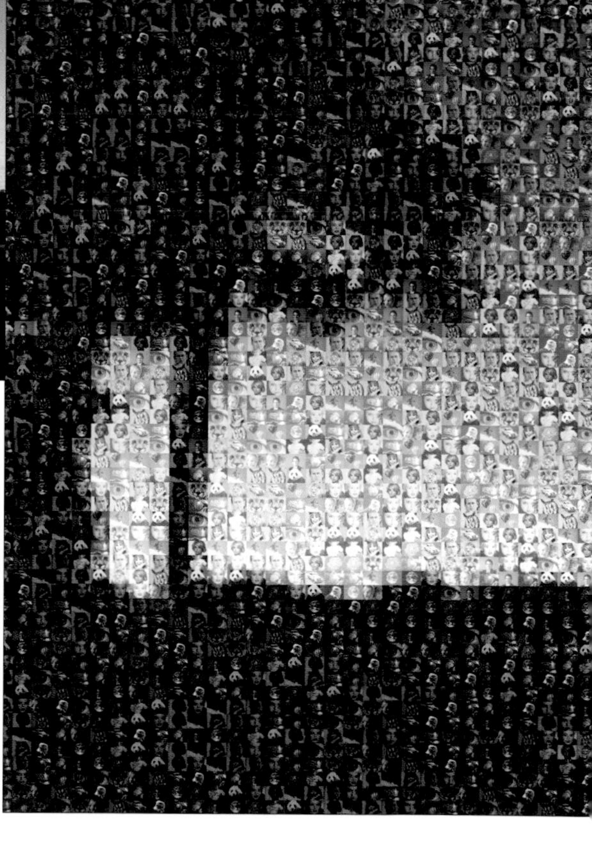

From photo to painting

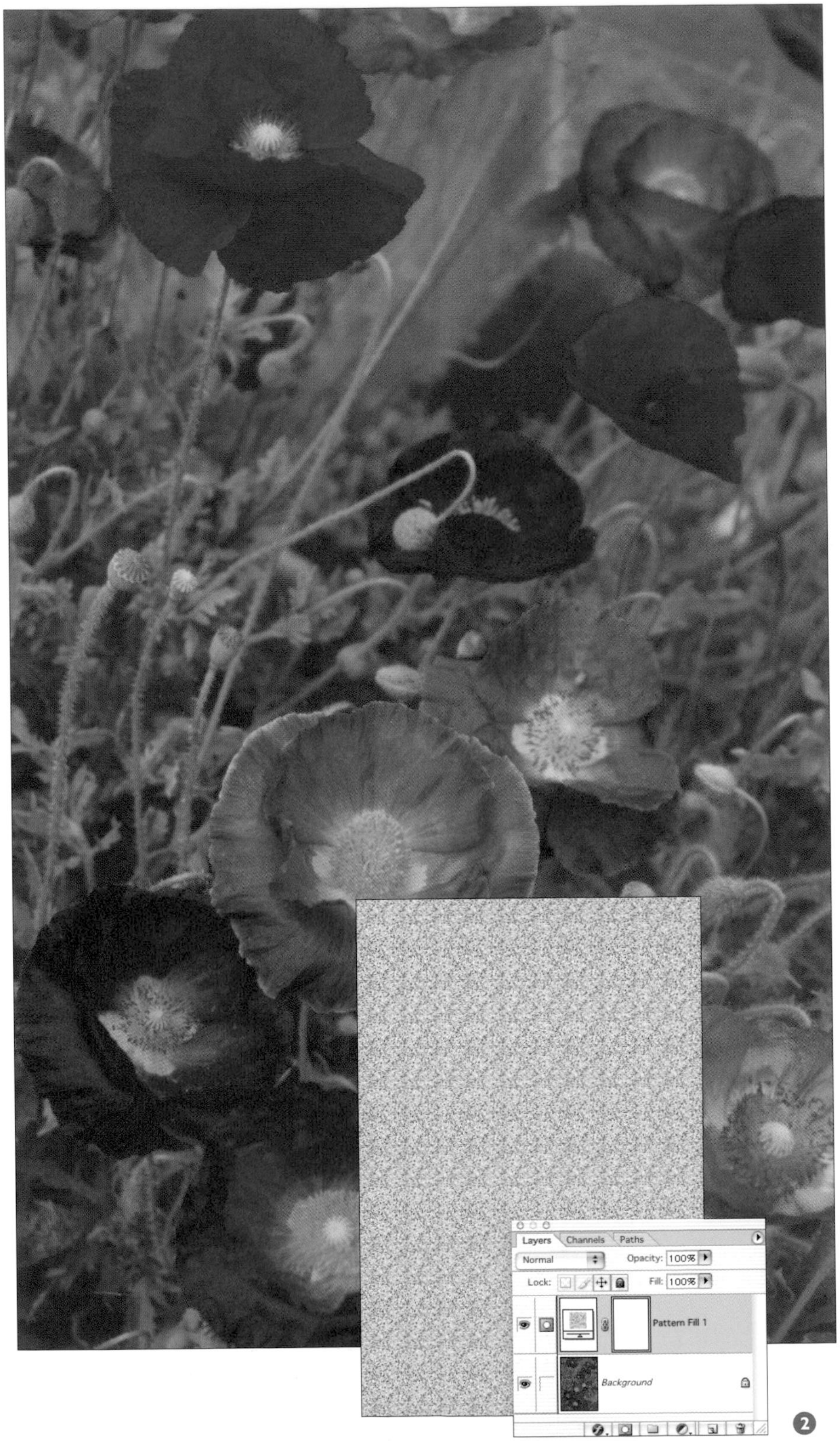

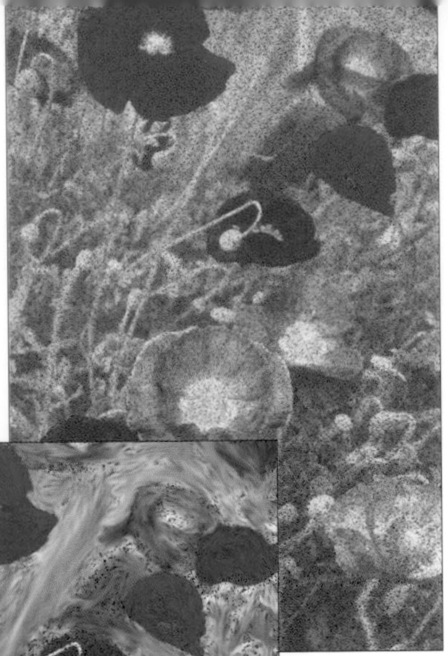

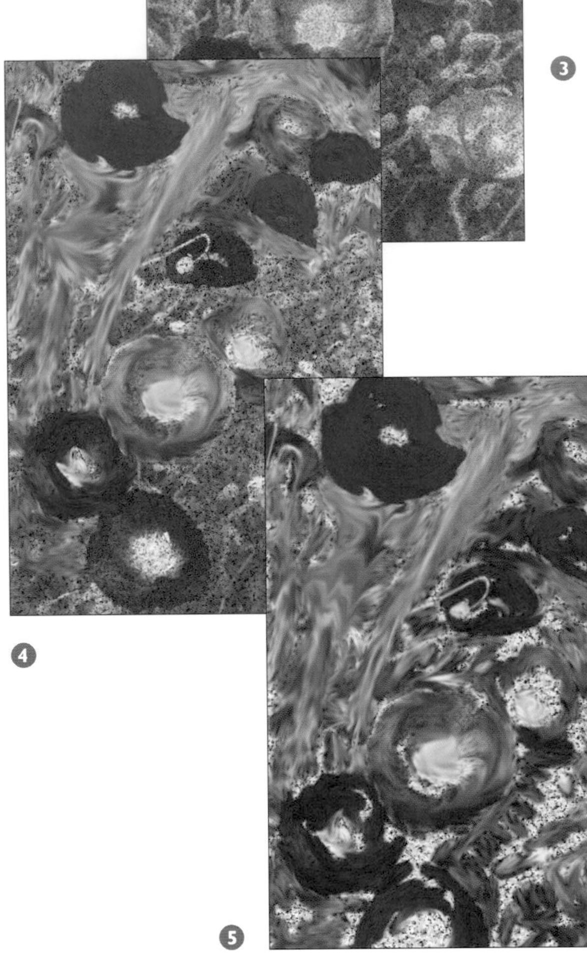

3

4

5

1

2

The artistic filters provided in Photoshop and Photoshop Elements can automatically produce convincing painterly effects from an image. However, what they can't give you is the same degree of control that you would expect from a specialist natural media application, such as Procreate Painter. Painter is still the professional choice for those who want to recreate 'natural media' via digital means, and rightly so: the results can look exactly as if they were painted the old-fashioned way. However, with adept use of some standard Photoshop tools and filters, we can simulate some of those techniques.

The potency of painting, whether using conventional oils or even acrylics, is in the way wet-on-wet brush strokes behave on the canvas.

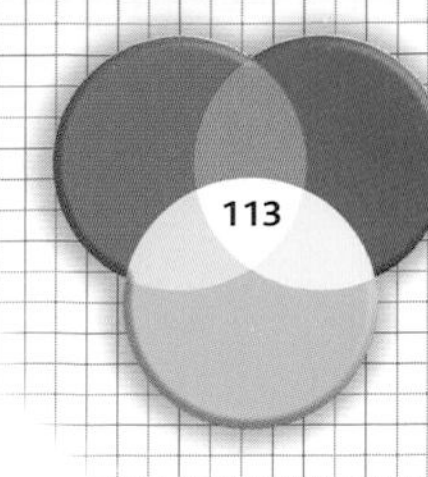

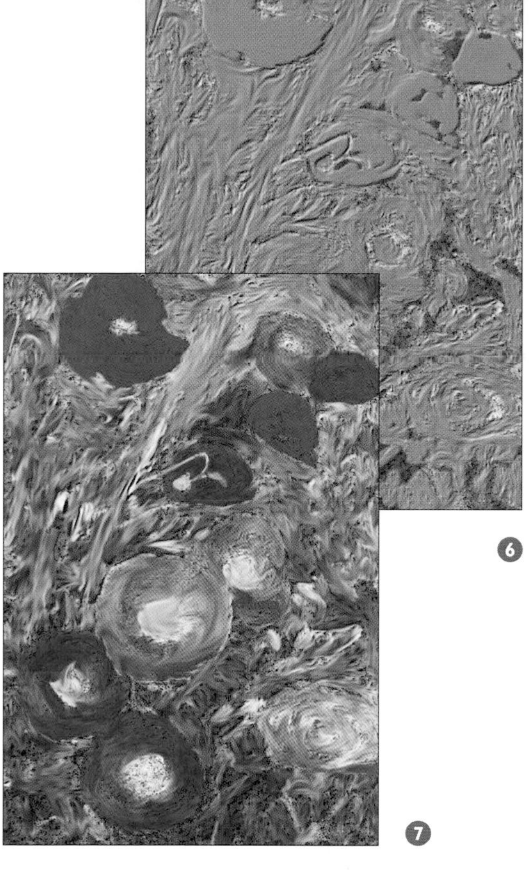

6

7

With a loaded brush, a swathe of colour is laid down that also mixes with the original paint layer to produce intriguing colour blends. To get the same effect on a digital image, we need to first give our image some texture – a variation in colour – that will respond to our brush strokes to give the textured paintwork. Those brush strokes will then be provided by the smudge tool.

PAINTING WITH PHOTOSHOP

1 *This method works best with images that feature large areas of bold colour. This floral study is a perfect example.*

2 *Before painting, we need to give the image some texture. We can use the* Grain *or* Craquelure *filters, but for a more regular texture we use a* Pattern Fill. *Select* Layer > New Fill Layer > **Pattern**. *While there's no 'correct' pattern, those in the* Stone *collection work well.*

3 *Now change the blend mode from* Normal *to* Overlay. *The image should take on a mottled, heavily textured finish.*

4 *Add a new empty layer and name it 'Painting Layer'. This is where our painting effects will be laid. Now select the* Smudge *tool and a reasonably broad brush size. Remember to check the* Use All Layers *button to ensure that both the original artwork and the texture layer are affected.*

5 *Begin painting. Your technique should emulate that of the oil painter, with brief strokes following the colour and shape of the original. Don't be too precise. We are aiming for a painterly effect, not a textured photograph.*

6 *To monitor your progress, periodically turn off the original background layer. You will be able to see how much of the image you have painted.*

7 *Now give the paint some texture. Create a duplicate of the painting layer and apply the* Emboss *filter. Combine this with the original layers by changing the* Color *mode to* Overlay.

8 *The result is a very well-textured paint based on our* Smudge *strokes. You can experiment with different textures and* Pattern Fill *layers to get a range of different effects.*

8

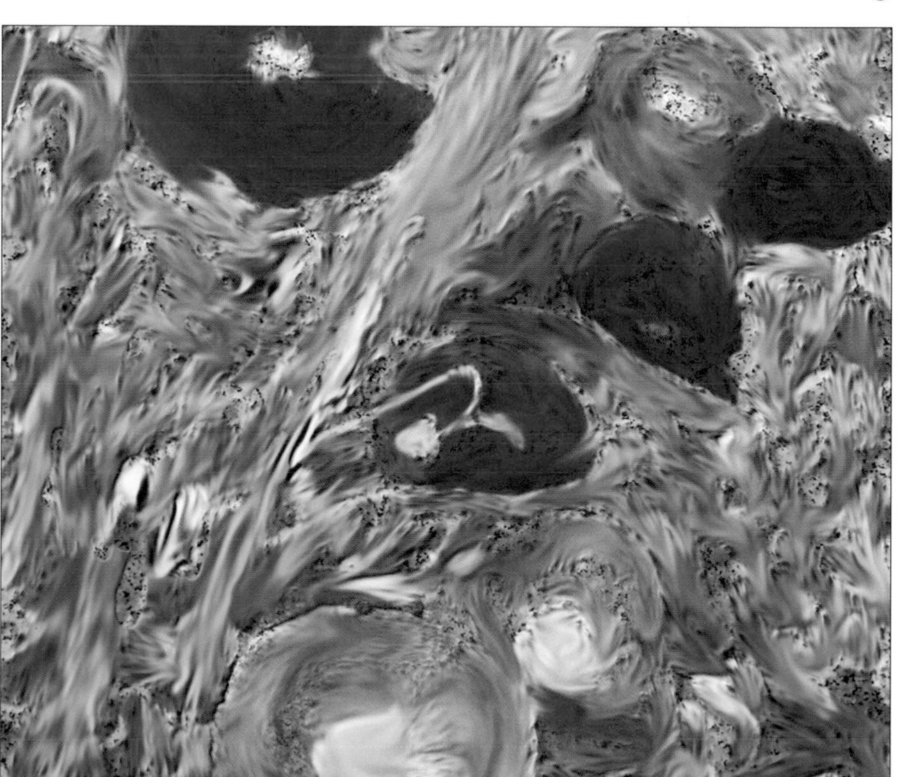

Non-destructive montage

Earlier, we created montages by placing cutout selections onto layers. This is a perfectly valid method, but it does have disadvantages. In image manipulation, it is nearly always better to use methods that avoid permanently altering or deleting the original pixels in the picture. If you retain information, you give yourself more options should you choose to return and rework the montage later on. Instead of using cutouts, it can be better to use *Layer Masks* – masks that hide or protect selected areas of the layer.

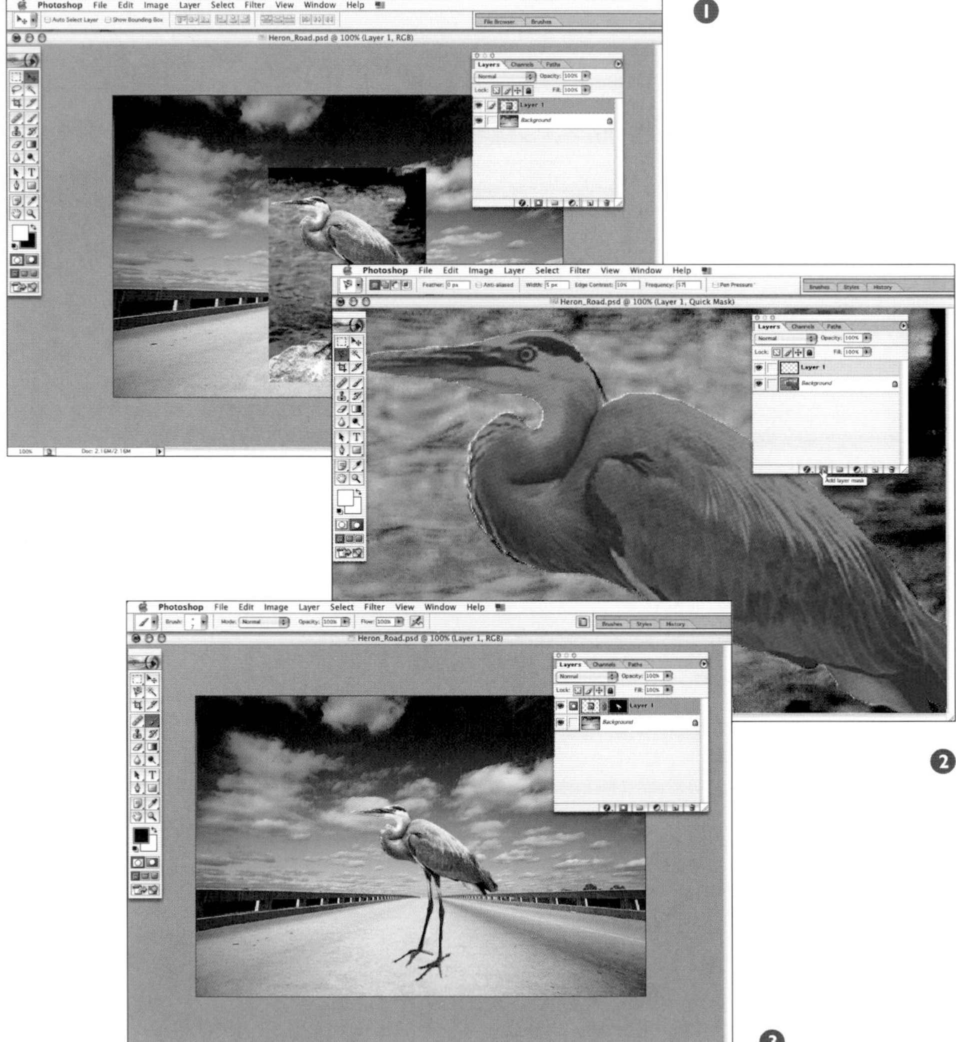

MONTAGE WITH LAYER MASKS

1 *In this example, we will create a montage without ever permanently altering a single pixel. We start with two photos saved as separate layers in a single Photoshop document.*

2 *Start by using the* Magnetic Lasso *to make a rough outline of the bird, then clean up the selection in the* Quick Mask *mode. Once you are happy, quit* Quick Mask, *then click on the* Add a Mask *icon on the* Layers *palette.*

3 *A* Layer Mask *will be created, hiding all of the pixels outside of the current selection. Zoom in and check the edges of the cutout. You can edit the layer mask (and its edges) by clicking on the black-and-white* Layer Mask *icon on the* Layers *palette.*

4 *Use a paintbrush with white paint to remove areas of the mask, or black to extend its reach. In this way, you can get the cutout of your selection exactly right without losing a single pixel. If you need to see the layer without its mask, simply right-click (control-click on a Mac) on the layer and choose* Disable Layer Mask.

5 *To add extra realism, we are going to add a shadow to the bird. First duplicate the layer, then delete the* Layer Mask *for the original (lower) copy by dragging the mask thumbnail to the trash icon on the* Layers *palette. Click on* Apply *when the warning message appears. Now, turn the lower copy of the bird into a shadow by distorting it with the* Edit > **Free Transform** *controls, then turning the distorted image to black using the* Image > Adjust > **Threshold** *command. Finally, blur it using the* Gaussian Blur, *change the* Blend mode *of the shadow layer to* Multiply, *and adjust the* Opacity *until it looks natural.*

6 *To add some final touches, create a new empty layer, then set its* Blend mode *to* Multiply *and the* Opacity *to around 50%. Move the new layer to below the bird and the shadow layers. You can now*

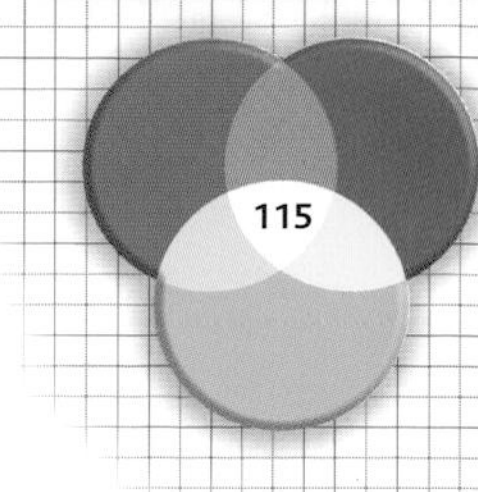

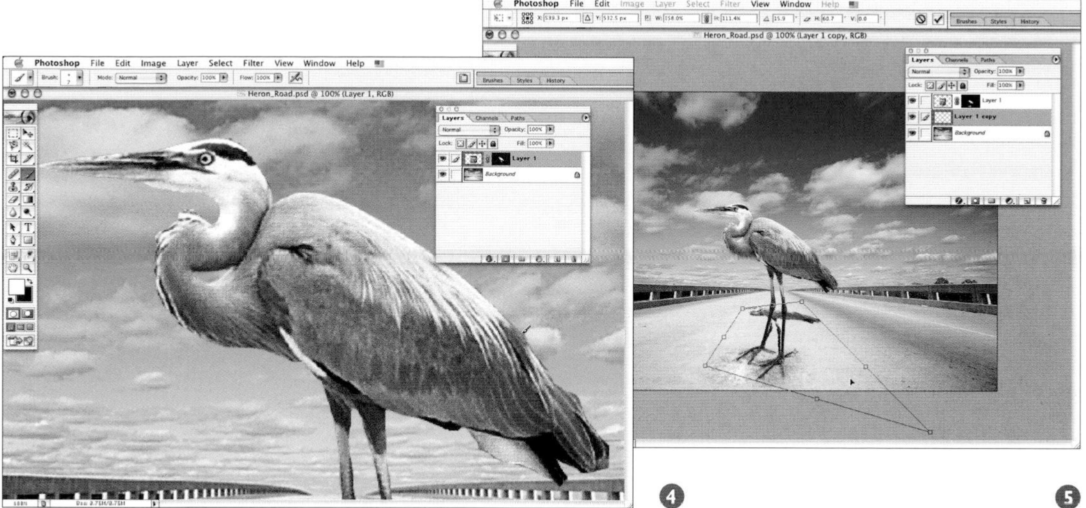

4

5

use a small, soft paintbrush with black paint to add shadows under the bird's feet. Because you are working non-destructively – in a separate layer – you can easily delete any mistakes and start again.

7 The result is made up of five layers and none of the pixels in either of the original images have been touched. By using layer masks for cutouts, and separate layers for painting and effects, we ensure that the entire composition, including any edits and effects, remains fully editable – as long as you save it as a Photoshop file with all the layers intact.

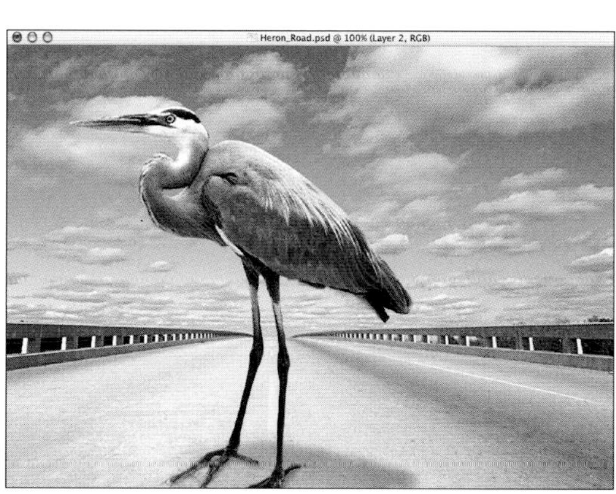

6

DARKROOM SECRETS

HIDE JOINS WITH NOISE

Adding noise to a montage often helps to even out any inconsistencies in tone – especially when the elements come from different sources (PhotoCD and a scanned print in this case). To add noise to a multilayer image nonpermanently, create a new layer using the *Layer>New Layer* menu. Set the mode to *Overlay* and check the box for *Fill with Overlay-neutral color (50% gray)*. Click on OK and you will see no difference. You can now run the *Noise>Add Noise* filter on this layer. You can vary the strength of the effect by altering the layer's opacity, or you can remove it altogether by deleting the layer. By erasing areas of the layer, you can even alter the level of *Noise* applied to different areas of the image.

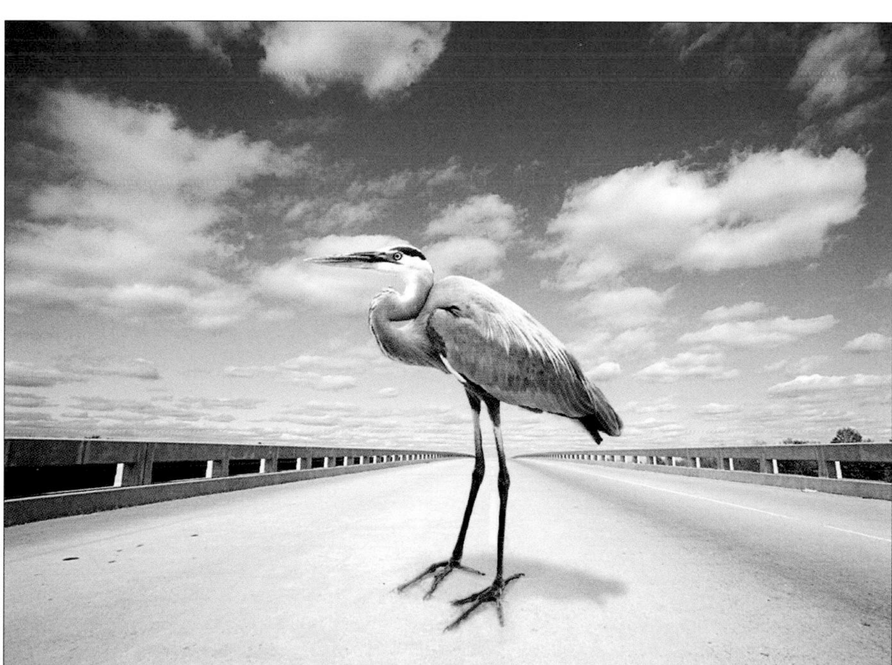

7

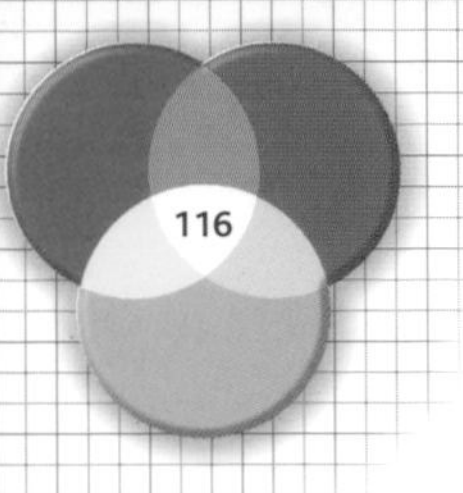

Montage with transparency

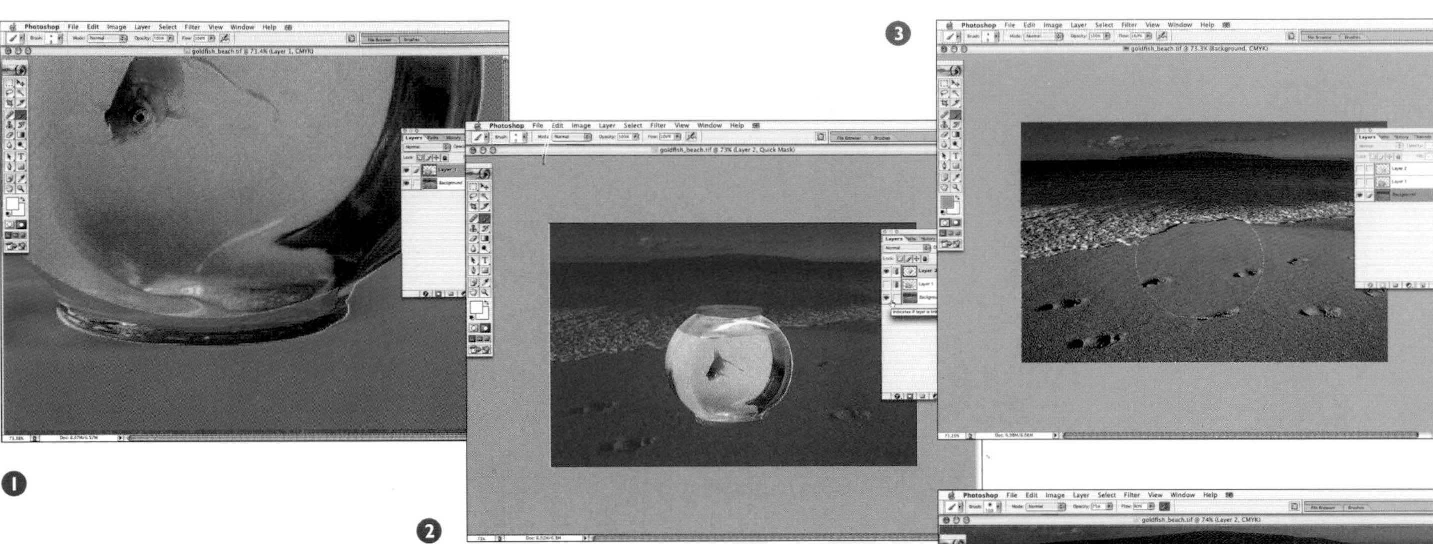

Anyone who has experimented with multilayered compositions is aware that you can easily make layers semitransparent by altering their opacity. But what if we want to make just part of a layer fully transparent? Once again, masks come to our rescue, as you can see in this montage of two very separate images.

HANDLING TRANSPARENCY

1 *Drag the bowl image onto the landscape, which creates a new layer. Select the layer, then cut out the goldfish bowl itself. The easiest method is to start with an oval marquee that matches the edges of the bowl as closely as possible, then to tweak the selection using the* Quick Mask *mode. Alternatively, use the* Extract *tool.*

2 *Turn your mask back into a selection, and create a new layer containing a copy of the area you have just selected (the goldfish bowl). Hide the original layer (layer 1), but don't delete it – we will need it later. Now hold down the command (Mac) or control (Windows) key and click on the layer's name in the* Layers *palette to select all non-transparent pixels. With the selection still active, click on the background layer in the layers patette. Go back into* Quick Mask *mode and – using black as your foreground colour – paint over the top and bottom of the bowl-shaped mask (as above). Now exit the* Quick Mask *mode.*

3 *We now have a selection that we can use to recreate the effect of refraction caused by the water in the bowl. Making sure that the background layer is still the active one, choose* Spherize *from the* Filter > **Distort** *menu.Set the amount to anything from 50 to 100% (the higher the figure, the more the image will be distorted).*

4 *Now to make the bowl transparent: activate the layer containing the cutout bowl, then control-click on the layer to create a new selection based on it. Now click on the* Add a mask *icon at the bottom*

5

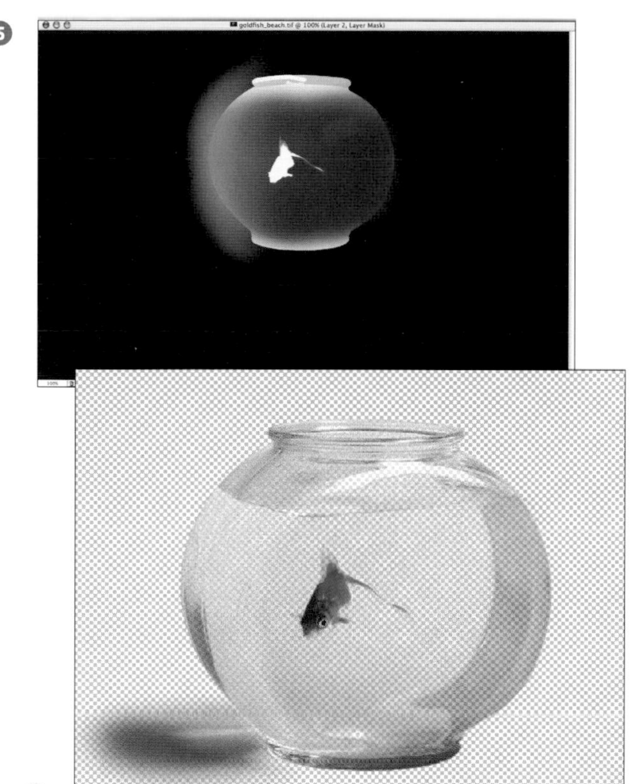

6

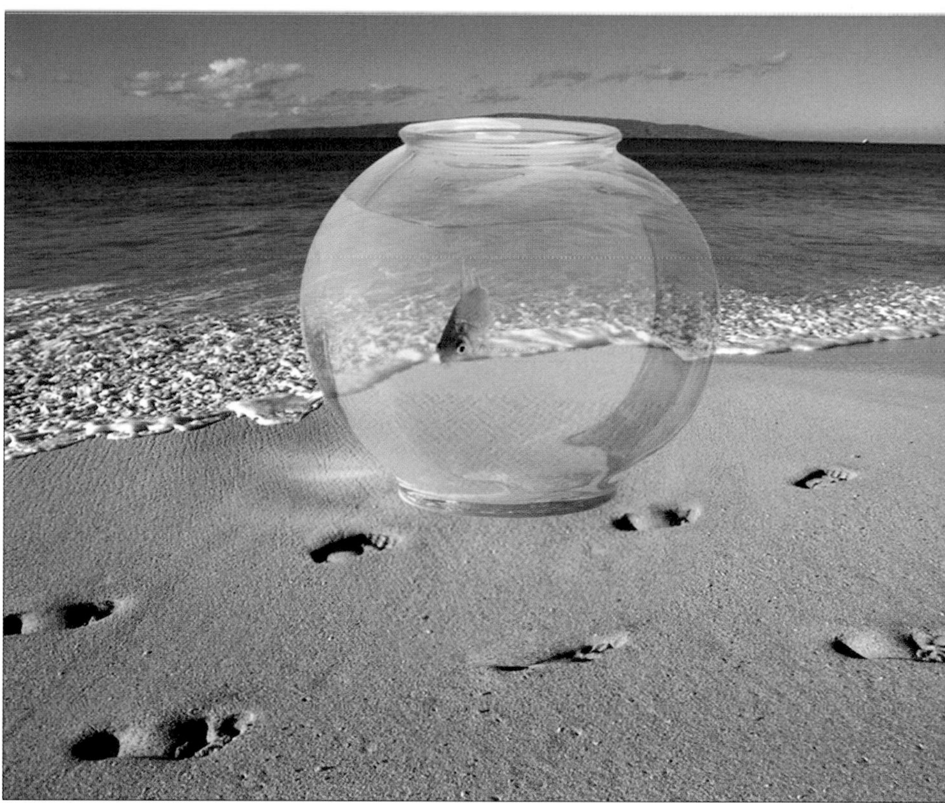

7

of the Layers *palette. Your* Layers *palette should now show a mask applied to the uppermost layer. The transparent (white) area exactly matches the edges of the bowl. Make sure you are working on the mask (click on the mask icon in the layers palette). Select a large, soft-edged paintbrush and change the paint opacity to about 30%. Carefully paint over the bowl area. You will see the bowl gradually turning transparent.*

5 *Obviously we don't want a transparent fish, so we need to erase the mask completely in that area. Change the paint colour to white, and using a smaller, hard-edged brush, carefully paint the mask to match the fish. Now is also a good time to paint over the base and rim of the bowl, which should not be as transparent as the main bowl. Using 20% paint on the right-hand side of the bowl will also make it slightly less transparent. After a bit of work, this is what the final final mask should look like. White areas have no effect on the corresponding pixels in the layer, black areas mask it completely, and the the grey parts are more or less transparent, depending on how light or dark the grey.*

6 *Show the hidden middle layer (layer 1) and use a soft* Eraser *to get rid of everything except the shadow area (which also contains a small highlight caused by light refracted through the water). Change the* Blend mode *of this layer to* Overlay*. Here you can see the upper two layers with the background hidden.*

7 *To finish the image, use the* Burn tool *on the background to strengthen the shadows. If the image still looks disjointed, try using a subtle* Gaussian Blur*, or add some noise to further blend in the two elements.*

SECTION FOUR

classic techniques

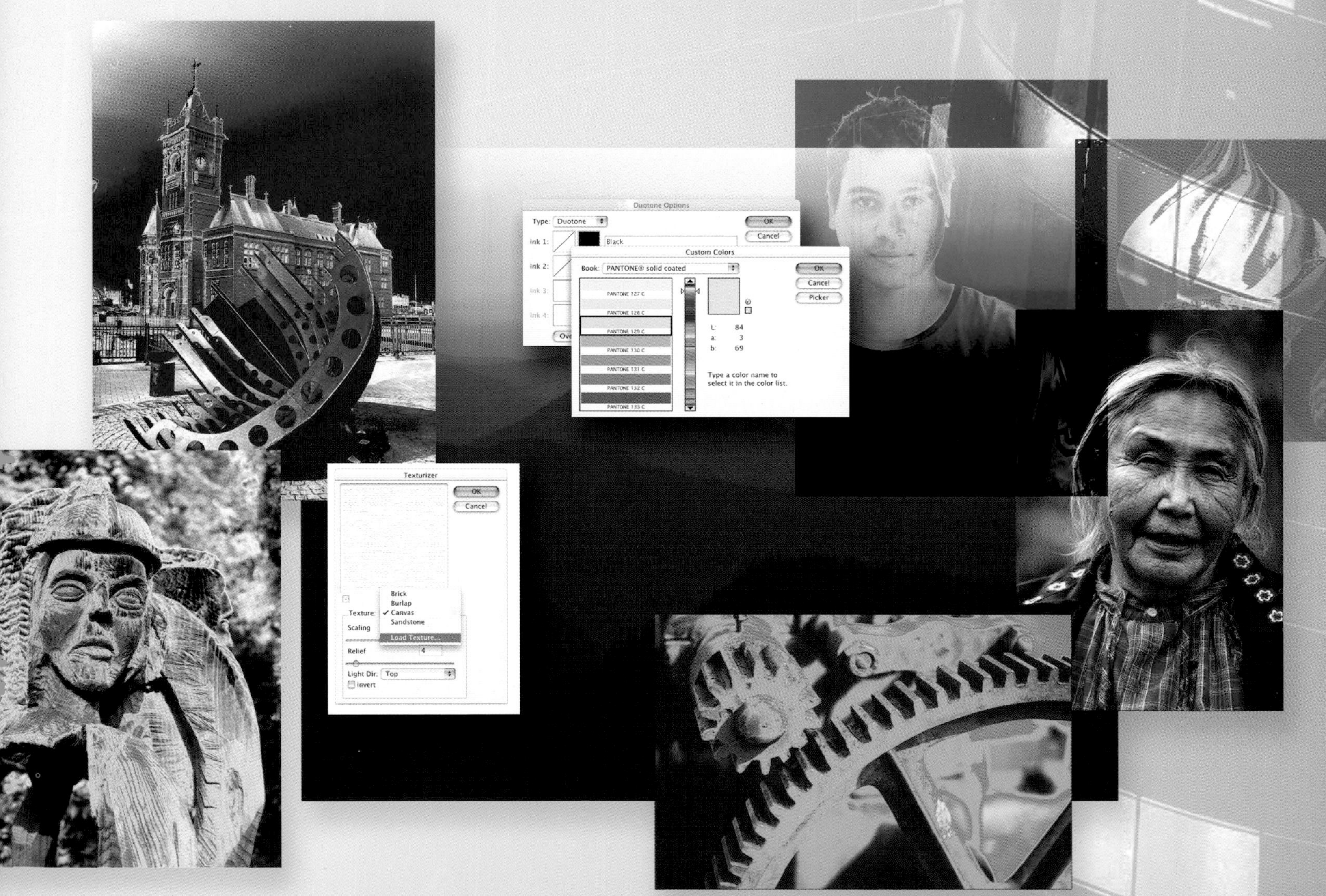

It might seem strange to link the latest development in the history of photography – the move towards digital imaging – with the earliest development techniques, yet the tools of the digital darkroom are surprisingly adept at recreating styles from the earliest days. These pioneering techniques emerged more from necessity than from artistic consideration; they were the best processing methods available at the time. But even now, and perhaps because of their age, they have a character that lends itself perfectly to certain types of image.

When it comes to recreating a 'vintage' look, the standard response is to reach for the nearest sepia filter. While a cliché, it's a valid style and one that this chapter will show you how to do properly. Go beyond sepia, however, and there are several other techniques that might work better. In the next eighteen pages we'll also cover duotones, serigraphs, lith and line images, gum dichromate and Van Dyke brown printing techniques, kallitypes and cyanotypes. We'll also show you how you can recreate the classic 'psychedelic' looks of solarization and the sabbatier effect.

Master these techniques, and you can turn even mediocre photos into graphic images with a real personality. After all, if you can fake age, then you can also fake respectability.

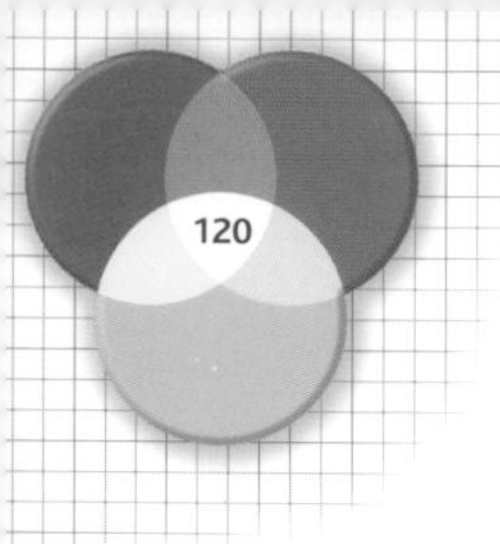

CLASSIC TECHNIQUES

Duotones

As you have already seen in a few of the previous projects, our work in the digital darkroom isn't just concerned with the latest, modern effects – it can also provide a means of bringing back classic darkroom techniques in digital forms. Many of these old-school favourites used to take a considerable amount of time, patience and talent, but with digital tools, we can recreate them with real consistency and control. This is what this chapter is all about: making old-fashioned pictures the new-fangled way.

1

Duotones are often described as toned images: monochrome images with a modest amount of colour added. That description, though accurate, does a great disservice to a technique that is as subtle as it is powerful. What makes a duotone so different from a simple toned image is that it hails from the printing industry where there is a need – particularly in the production of 'fine art' books – to deliver images with a greater tonal range than the printing process will normally provide. By adding a second ink stage to the printing sequence – often a dark brown or other 'warm black' – the tonal rendition is improved and the range of discrete tones possible enlarged.

In most cases, duotone images are given additional warmth by the use of a suitable second colour. Some applications, however, may require a

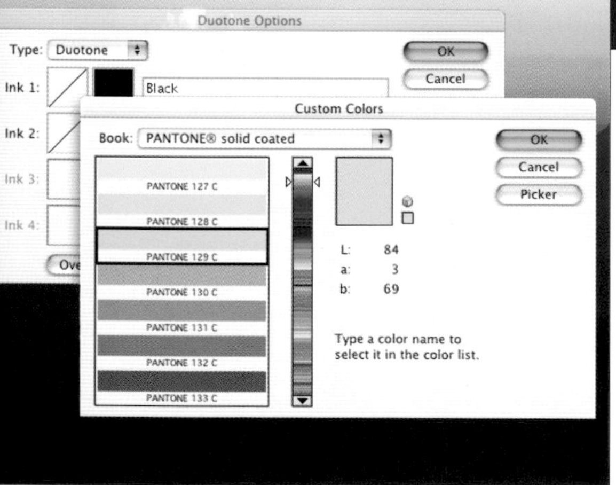

2

3

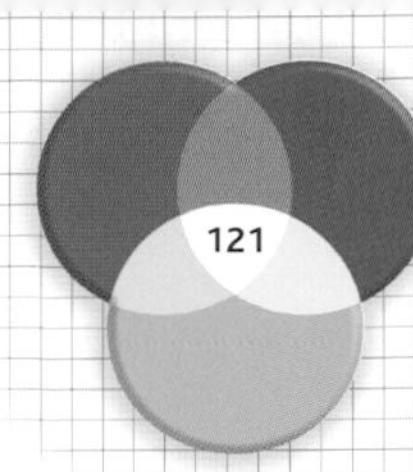

third or even a fourth extra colour. Called tritones and quadtones respectively, the additional colours are used to further increase the tones available or to create more specialised false-colour effects.

CREATING A DUOTONE

1 *Open up your choice of image and save a copy. You can use a colour image, but as soon as you transform it into a duotone, you will lose all of the colour information – which is one good reason to keep your original safe. Now select* Image > Mode > **Grayscale** *to change the image mode to* Grayscale, *and select* **Duotone** *from the drop-down menu in the dialog box. Converted from an RGB colour image, our greyscale image shows a tonal range typical of those taken with panchromatic film.*

2 *Photoshop provides a range of preconfigured duotone settings that include some extended black tonal ranges and PANTONE colours. These are ideal for producing specific duotone effects (such as the warm blacks of the art book), but are also useful if you want to take a closer look at the way in which duotones (and, indeed, tritones and quadtones) are constructed.*

To create your own duotone, click on the coloured box in the dialog to the right of Ink 2. This will open a selection palette, from which you can choose a second ink colour; PANTONE colours are displayed by default, but you can substitute alternate regimes by making a selection from the drop-down menu.

3 *A light ochre (such as PANTONE 129C) will give a warm sepia tone; a deep, warm brown (PANTONE 7519C) gives the tonally enriched image so sought-after by the printing industry. Note that the effects of your duotone selections will be displayed in real time on the image. You'll also see that the ink colour doesn't necessarily impart a corresponding tint in the image. Orange inks, for example, will often produce pink or salmon tones. Once again, it's a good idea to experiment.*

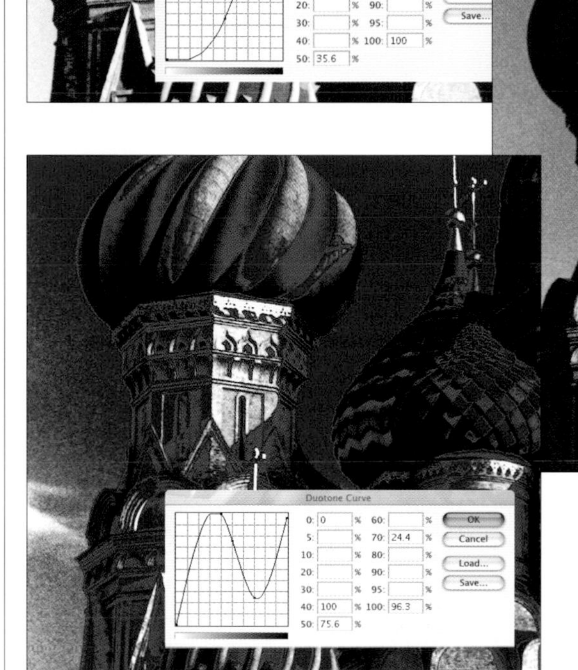

Selecting a rich fuchsia as the second duotone colour, different and dramatic effects can be achieved by altering the curves to boost the colour in the shadows and the highlights. The use of a bell-shaped curve inverts some of the tones to give the solarized effect shown in the bottom image.

Duotones: fine tuning

Duotones are the antidote to the simple toned image effects so beloved by the creators of budget image-editing software. Sepia filters? Forget them; they provide an effect that never existed in photography, only in the minds of those who believe it reflects the way that photographs used to look. The less extreme sepia tone discussed on the next page is a much better way to create an antique look for prints.

You can further modify the way in which the ink colours are used by altering the *Curves* graph for the ink colour. Click on the small graph window (to the immediate right of Ink 2) and the *Curves* dialog will open. Altering the shape of the curve changes the distribution of ink in the image. By dragging the curve upwards in the shadow areas to the right of the graph, for example, you can ensure that they will be more strongly coloured with that ink.

DARKROOM SECRETS

SAVING DUOTONES

Once you have produced a duotone effect you really like, you can save the settings – the curves and the sets of colours – so that you can then apply them to other greyscale images. You can then produce your own collections of duotones. Press the Save button in the Duotone Options dialog box to save the settings. You can retrieve them later using the Load button.

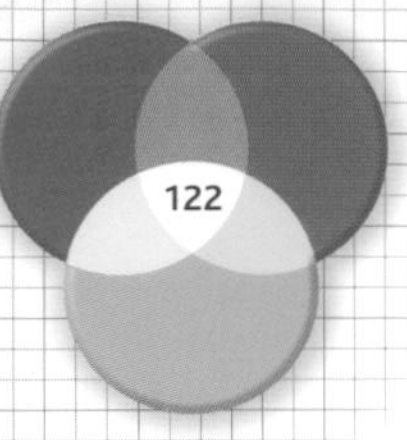

Sepia tones

1

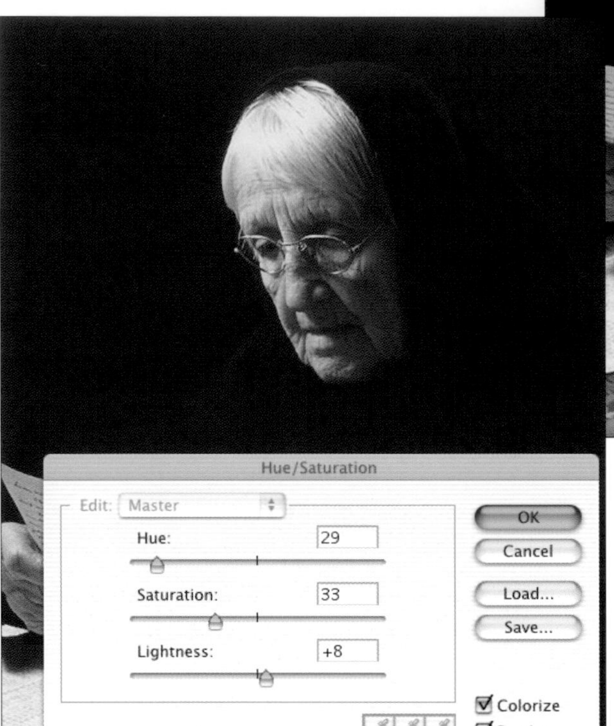

2

Nostalgia is a curious thing. With rose-tinted glasses in front of our eyes, we hanker after elements of a bygone world – usually the elements that the residents of that world would be only too happy to divest themselves of!

In photography, this is seen in the desire to create – or re-create – antiqued, sepia-toned prints. Condemned to watch their pictures fade from the combined effects of chemicals and the environment, the earliest photographers would have sold their souls for the stable chemistries we enjoy today.

Yet, despite our cynicism, toned prints – which need not be restricted to the ashen glow of sepia – can be highly evocative. The traditional darkroom worker has succeeded in producing chemical toners capable of delivering a range of colours, or even colour-coupled toners that allow several different tones in the same print.

Like many darkroom techniques, the ingenuity that evolved the chemistries for these effects is compromised by practicalities. Precise toning effects can be difficult to reproduce where small changes in the chemistry, the timings or even the temperature can deliver distinctly different results. Digitally we have no such limitations and can produce repeatable results with a much wider range of control. We can also achieve toning effects that just aren't feasible in the darkroom.

DARKROOM SECRETS

BEYOND SEPIA

The term 'toned print' is often regarded as synonymous with sepia, but some subjects suit an alternative treatment. For example, blue tones suit harsh landscapes, while a harder grey-blue can give very evocative monochrome portraits.

CREATING A SEPIA-TONED PRINT

1 *Creating a sepia-toned image is not technically difficult, but this is one effect in which the choice of subject is vital. Perhaps due to the association of sepia-toned prints with heritage subjects, the effect can be somewhat incongruous when applied to more contemporary subjects. This portrait is ideal.*

2 *Begin by selecting the* Hue/Saturation *command* (Image > Adjustments > **Hue/Saturation**) *to open the dialog box. Now Click on the* Colorize *button and the image will change from a full colour image into a tinted monochrome. By adjusting the* Hue *slider, you can now change the hue to the characteristic brown of sepia. To get a less brazen effect, try reducing the* Saturation *and increasing the lightness. We are*

3

aiming to give a hint of the tone rather than a completely coloured image. Altering the lightness control can give the shadow areas a slight tint when increased, or reduce them to black when lowered.

3 *Click* OK *when you are satisfied with the settings. There is no right or wrong with toned images. Some settings 'work' better than others, but what is most important is for your final image to reflect your own personal preference, and your chosen tone to work with the content of the photo.*

Colour judgment

Image-editing applications not only give us more control over effects, they often give us alternative ways of achieving an effect. Sepia tones are a very good example, and here are some alternative methods. The results of each are rarely identical, so this is a good opportunity to explore the nuances of each and judge which gives you the most pleasing result. We'll apply alternative toning effects to this portrait.

To create a conventional sepia tone, begin by creating a new layer known as a *Color Fill* layer (*Layer > New Fill Layer >* ***Solid Color***). This produces a layer filled with a single colour of your own choosing. We'll choose a pale brown. Change the blend mode of this layer by using the pull-down menu and selecting *Color* mode. To alter the tone, simply click (or double-click) on the small colour pane in the layers palette. The colour picker will open and allow the selection of a new colour. Experiment to find one that works.

Now try a tinted rather than toned image, in which the original image colours remain. Create a *Color Fill* layer again and this time choose a bold, deep brown on the colour picker as your fill colour. Now select *Hue* as the colour blend mode on the *Layers* palette to blend the two layers. You can also use the *Opacity* control to vary the amount of sepia tinting in the image.

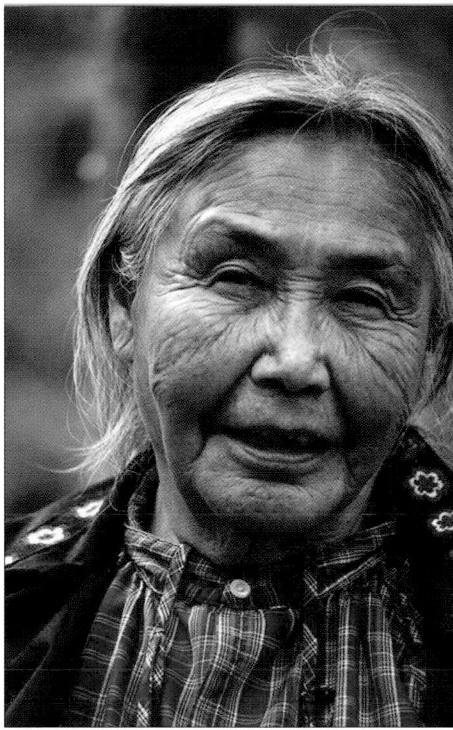

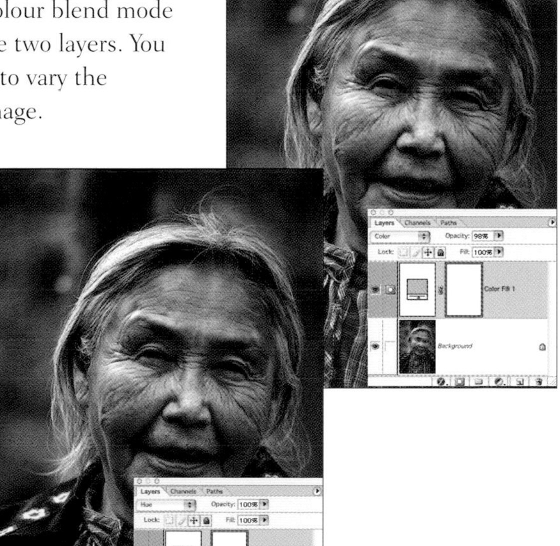

More colour effects

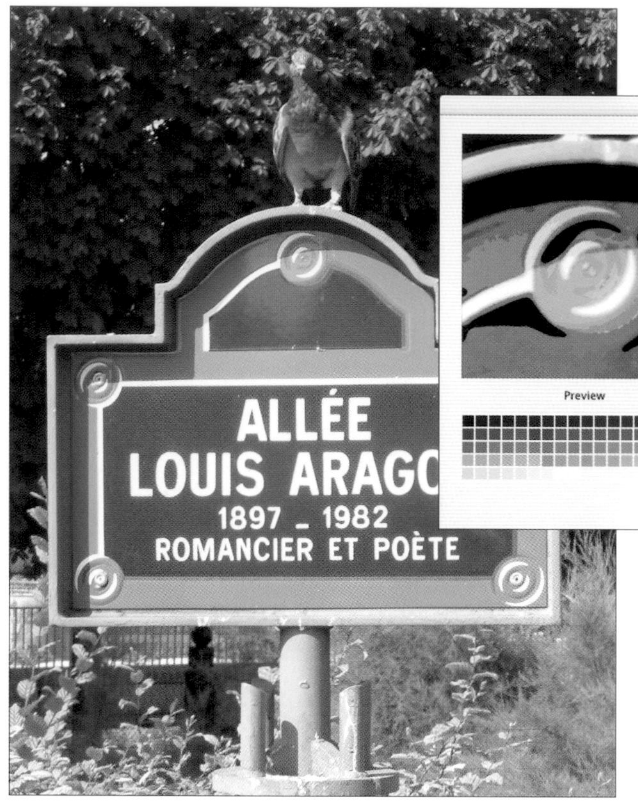

> **DARKROOM SECRETS**
>
> **PUSH THE LIMITS**
> It's always a good idea to push slider controls to their absolute limits when first using a feature. Though the results at the extremes are often absurd and unusable, seeing them is useful in unambiguously displaying the net effect of a control.

It may sound a little strange to want to reduce the number of colours in a colour image, particularly when hardware and software designers have laboured long and hard to give us a full range of lifelike tones. Yet, just as some images still benefit from a monochrome or duotone treatment, so there are some that work best with simple blocks of colour that emphasize graphic form.

Colour reduction has been around a long time in the form of posterization. The name itself gives an indication of the origins of the technique and the destiny of many of the resulting images – posters. With limited colours, posterized artwork was ideal for creating bold posters cheaply.

The photographic posterization effect has not made the transition to the digital darkroom as successfully as some others. One reason is that the banded, reduced colour effect creates images that look very similar to those produced when printing a full-colour image on a low-quality inkjet printer. Another is simply that the effect no longer has the appeal that it once had, given the emergence of some more impressive reduced colour effects.

Two of those, Woodcut and Serigraphy, are expertly implemented in Procreate's Painter (as shown here). There is nothing to stop you getting similar results using Photoshop, but it will take a little more skill and ingenuity. Painter isn't alone, however, and some other image-editing applications can also produce similar effects.

WOODCUT EFFECTS

The woodcut effect renders images in a similar manner to those once produced by hand-cut blocks of wood or linoleum. An early example of relief printmaking, the process can be traced back 1500 years or so to a small province of China.

Of course, the modern way is easier and more versatile. In Painter you can apply a traditional black or white finish to the blocking or use different colours. The number of colours included and the sharpness of the 'woodcut' edges can both be precisely controlled, and you can even determine whether it's a detailed representation of the original or something more abstract.

PRODUCING DIGITAL WOODCUTS

1 *Open your image and make an identical copy using the clone tool* (File > **Clone**). *This will preserve the original image and enable us to erase back to the original image in selected areas. When working in Painter, save your work in progress as a RIFF file. This is the native Painter file format (the equivalent of the PSD format in Photoshop) and ensures that the unique image data generated in Painter is preserved.*

2 *Select* Effects > Surface Control > **Woodcut** *to open the* Woodcut *dialog box. Choose either* Output Black *or* Output Color *to determine whether a colour or black-and-white transformation will be produced. Experiment with the four sliders (two will be greyed out when working with* Output Black*), observing the results of your actions in the* Preview *window.*

3 *Set the sliders to more modest levels. Note that you can turn* Output Black *on for a colour image to produce a black overlay.*

4 *If you are satisfied, save the result* (File > **Save**). *If you propose to use the image later in, say, Photoshop, save a copy in a Photoshop compliant file format, but retain the original RIF file so that you can make changes later, if required.*

SERIGRAPHY

The technical name for silkscreen printing, serigraphy was traditionally used for producing art posters and limited edition artwork. It still works well today, particularly in cases where an identical design is reproduced in different colours – just think of the Warhol portrait of Marilyn Monroe.

CREATING A SERIGRAPH

1 *Begin as with the woodcut image, but select* Serigraphy Effect (Effects > Surface Control > **Serigraphy Effect**). *The Spot Color dialog will open, as the effect produces layers based on selected spot colours in the image.*

2 *Click to select one from the image, then use the dialog's sliders to vary the effect. The* Threshold *slider is the most critical – small changes to its position cause large changes in the image.*

3 *Click the* Create Spot Layer *button when you are satisfied with the effect. Simply repeat the process if you want additional colours.*

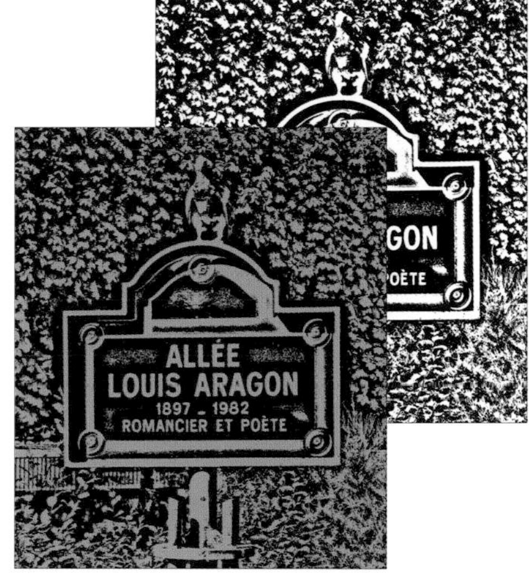

A black-and-white transformation can produce a very bold graphic image. Changing the control parameters produces results that vary between hard blocks of black and marks more like those from a graphic pen. Here, the original (top) has been imported into Photoshop with a colour applied to the white areas (bottom).

1

DARKROOM SECRETS

BE SELECTIVE

Vary the *Serigraphy Effect* by turning selected spot layers on or off. Use the eye icon in the Layers palette to toggle layer visibility.

2

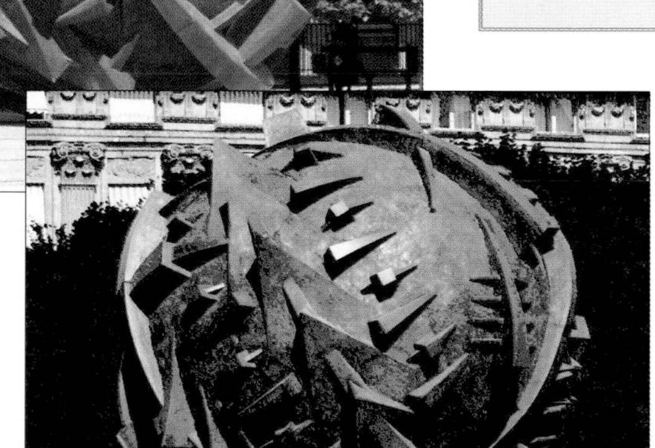

3

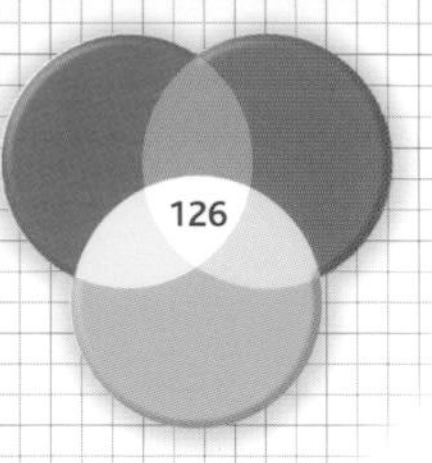

Creating line and lith images

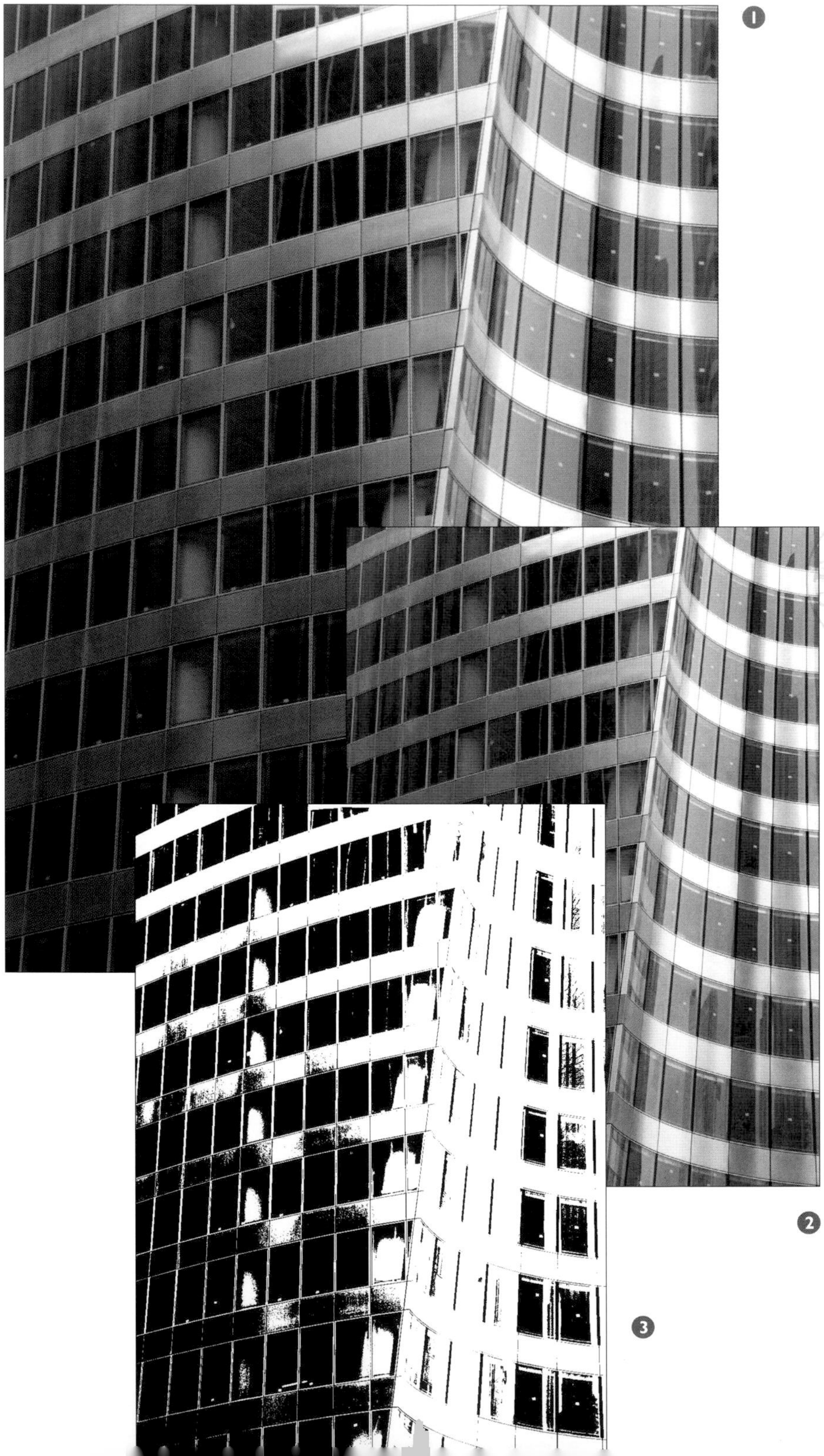

1

2

3

Though not strictly just 'old' techniques, lith and line images are characterised by a very high contrast that virtually eliminates any intermediate tones. High-contrast films are available for use in camera, but their purpose is more easily seen in the darkroom, where they can be used to produce high-contact or enlarged negatives. Lith film tends to produce the most stark results and the deepest blacks, though it does require specialised processing chemistry.

Digitally we can achieve lith results very simply and, as you might expect by now, we can extend the repertoire to further develop the effect. This can include the creation of colour liths, where the result can be likened to extreme posterization.

CREATING A LITH IMAGE

1 *Lith images – of whatever type – work best when the original image itself is a strong, bold graphic. Here is a good example. It already has strong, contrasty elements, but there remains a significant amount of intermediate tone.*

2 *Colour information at this stage is irrelevant, so it's best to discard it. You can use the* Desaturate *command or use the* Image > Mode > **Grayscale** *command to convert the image directly, but it can be more effective to open the* Channels *palette and use the channel split method we talked about on page 96-97. The Red, Green and Blue channels can each give a different starting point to a lith image. A bright blue sky will appear light in the blue channel and become white when the lith effect is applied. The same colour in the red channel will be dark, tending to black, and will become pure black when the process is completed.*

3 *Now select the* Contrast *slider in the* Brightness/Contrast *dialog box. Drag the slider to the extreme right (high contrast) to give the lith effect. Although this is close to the true lith effect, you might decide that the result a shade down from the maximum is more acceptable.*

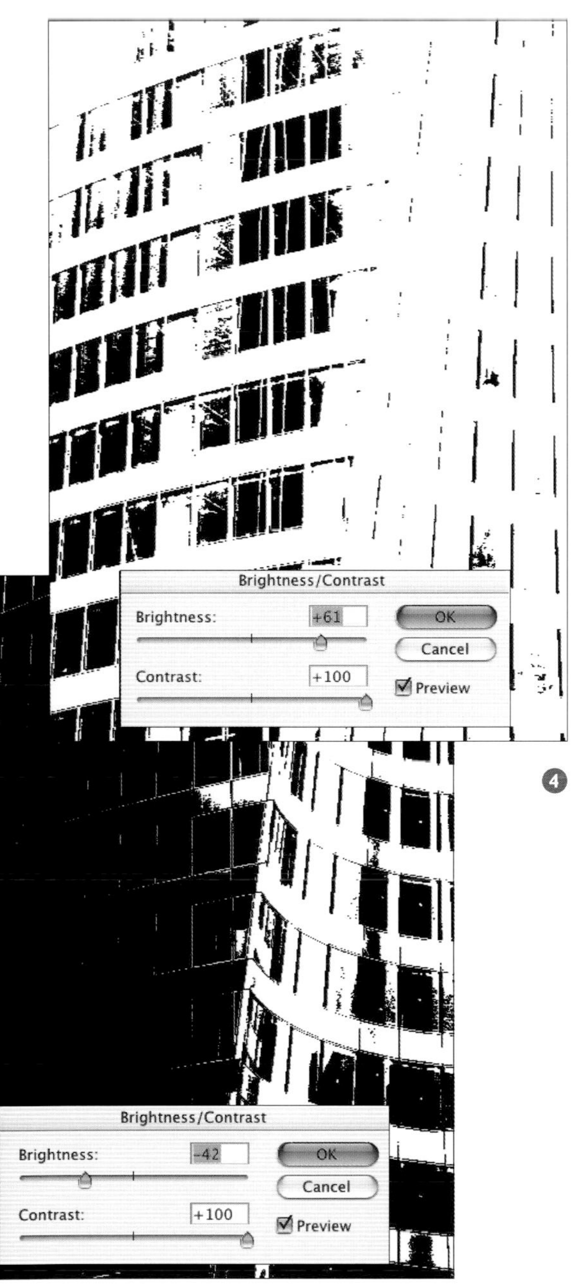

4 *If you want to further refine the precise point of the boundary, which defines the tones that will be represented by black and those that will be represented by white, experiment with the brightness slider until you get the desired result.*

Colour lith

Once you have created your lith image, there is no reason that it should stay black-and-white. By colourizing, you can convert it to a two-colour image or, if there are intermediate tones that need to be preserved, three-colours.

Colour your image by first converting it from *Grayscale* mode to *RGB Color*. Then select the black or white regions, using any of the appropriate colour-based selection tools, and apply a colour to the selection.

DARKROOM SECRETS

THE QUICK LITH METHOD
In Photoshop, the *Threshold* command produces controllable lith imagery at a stroke. The dialog box (Image > Adjustments > **Threshold)** lets the threshold between black and white be set at any one of the 255 tonal levels of the colour image.

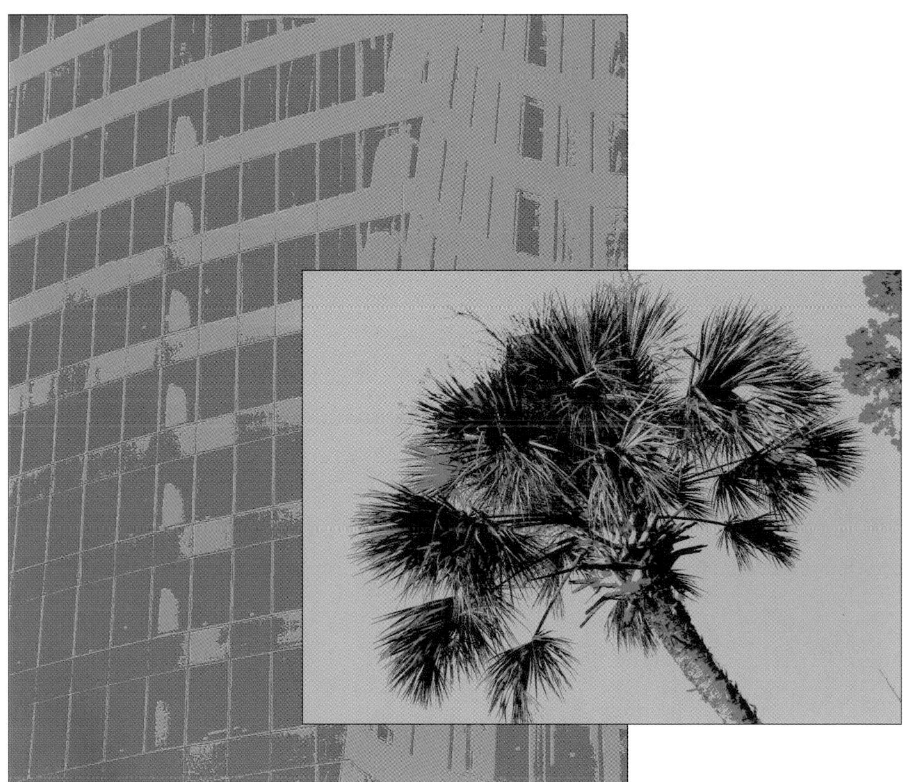

Applying the lith effect to this photograph of a palm tree resulted in three tones. The dark tone was coloured chocolate brown; the intermediate tone, olive green; and the light tone, blue.

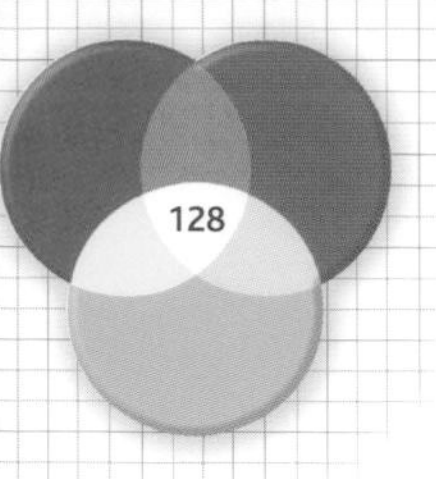

Gum dichromate

1

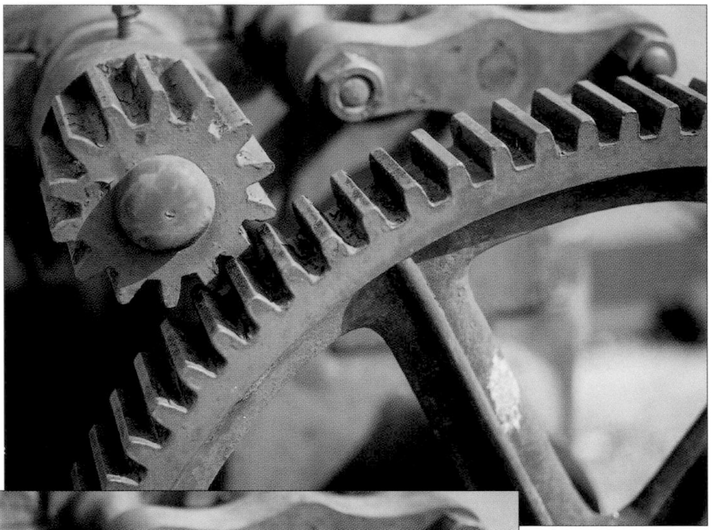

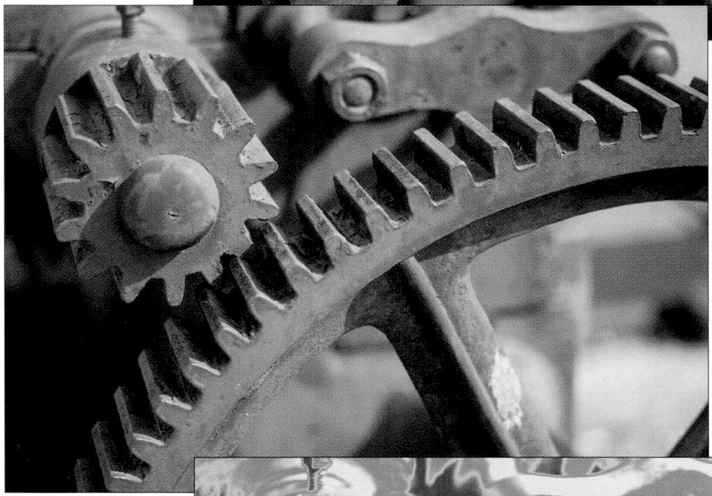

2

3

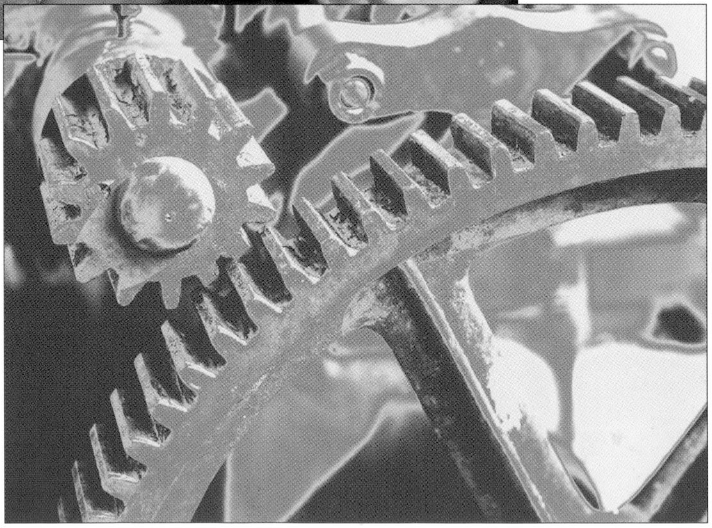

On the tourist trails through Cairo, you may still be lucky enough to chance upon a street photographer who will take your portrait using the gum dichromate process. If you get the opportunity, take it. The result will hardly be flattering, but it will give you first-hand experience of this curious process. If Cairo isn't on your itinerary, you can emulate the effect through digital means.

Popular at the turn of the last century – though first used fifty years earlier – the process uses dichromated gelatine, a light-sensitive compound, along with a colour pigment. After exposure, the unexposed gelatin is flushed from the paper surface and the remaining image is contact-printed in bright light. Skilled artists can add a second, differently tinted layer to build up multicoloured composite images.

Visually, the effect delivers strange, muted colours. In fact, it is less a colour process, more the precise coloration of a greyscale image with a limited tonal range.

THE GUM DICHROMATE EFFECT

1 *Gum dichromates were originally photograms rather than photographs, but any bold image is a good starting point. Still lifes and portraits work best, as this abstract view of a gear mechanism will demonstrate. It already has a restricted tonal range, so we need not make any changes to the tonality.*

2 *Convert the image to greyscale by selecting* Image > Mode > **Grayscale**. *Discard the colour information, and then change the mode back to* RGB Color. *We need a greyscale image as our start point, but we need to add colour later.*

3 *Using* Select > **Color Range**, *select an area of midtone and set the fuzziness to around 80. This amount will vary according to the image. Aim to select most of the midtone greys in the image. Paint this selection using your first colour. Feel free to experiment with any colours you wish, but muted colours work best, such as the grey blue used here.*

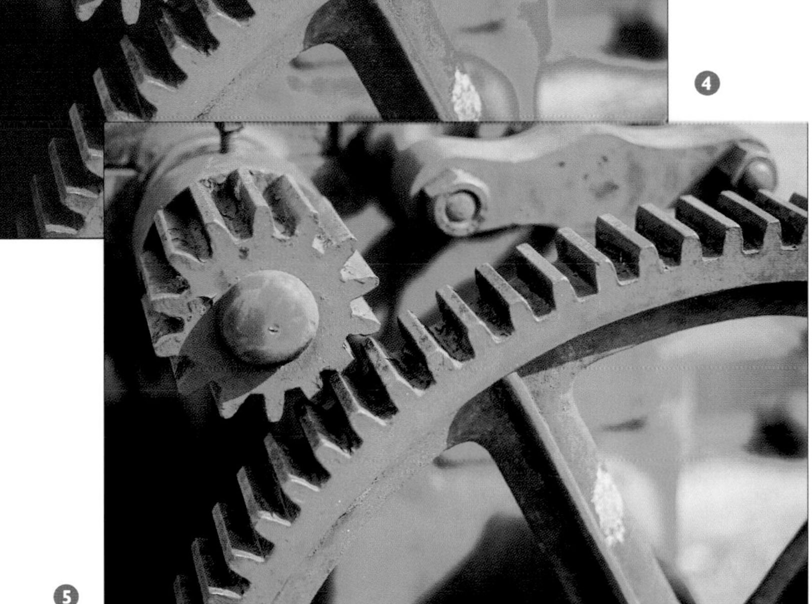

4

5

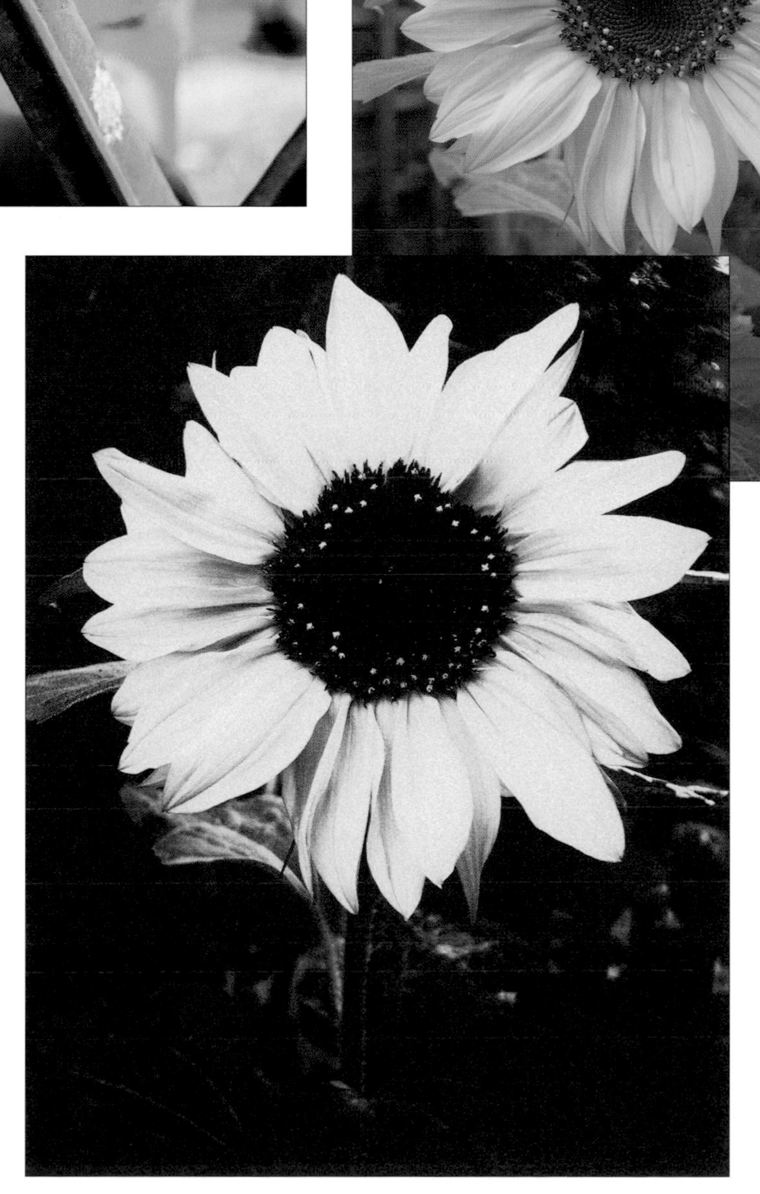

4 Repeat the process for the highlights (pink) and the shadows (maroon). In an authentic dichromate image, there would only be pigmented areas. Better results can be achieved by using separate layers for each tone, then fading the layer's Opacity *to let the background image show through.*

5 For a more authentic result, paint the colours in a new layer. Here is the same image with a different colour selection and with the colours painted to a new layer. The original background has then been replaced with an off-white base.

HIGH-IMPACT BLACKS

In a variation on the technique, darkroom workers combined gum and pigment with lampblack to produce deep blacks and dark colours. This method can also be replicated using digital means. For this picture of a sunflower, we use black for the shadow colour but increase the fuzziness so that the selection takes in some of the midtones. For a more authentic, gritty appearance, we can add a mild amount of grain.

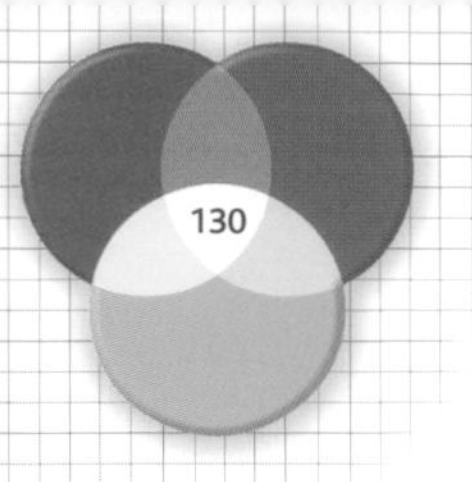

Van Dyke brown

DARKROOM SECRETS 

VAN DYKE BLUE?

The Van Dyke brown process is a very subtle one that introduces a soft warm neutral tone to the image, but in the digital domain there is no reason why you have to stick to this colour. You can use the *Hue/Saturation* dialog to alter the hue, taking care that the Saturation is also altered to give just the merest hint of coloration.

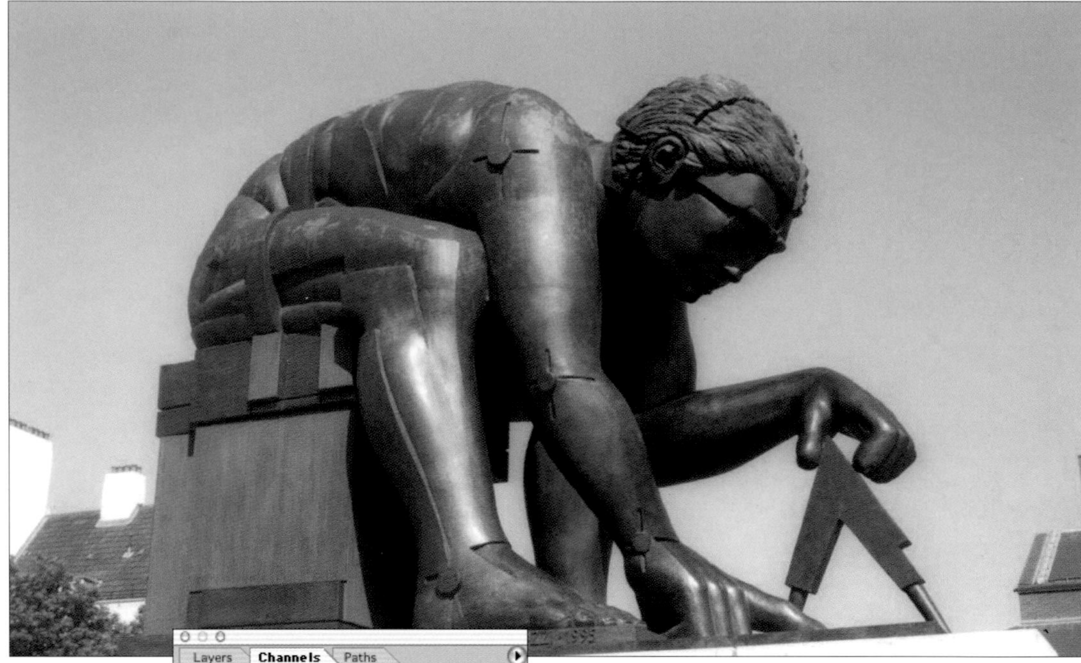

1

2

Variously described as 'Van Dyke printing' or 'brown printing', this process uses the effect of light on iron-based ferric salts with conventional silver nitrate salts to produce images with a very pronounced brown hue. Many early prints produced in this way have a sepia tone. In fact, much of the belief that old prints are sepia-coloured comes from the use of this process.

Early prints tended to use paper as the substrate, but by the end of the nineteenth century the process was also being used on canvas and linens for creative effect. The paper (or cloth) was contact-printed using a light source rich in ultraviolet light, and then processed using a mild borax solution.

The result is a gentle, brown print that looks tonally compressed rather than faded. However, it does not suit all subjects: heritage subjects and simple graphic shapes are most suitable.

CREATING VAN DYKE BROWN PRINTS

1 *Choose a suitable image, such as this Eduardo Paolozzi sculpture in London, then make any contrast or brightness corrections.*

2 *Desaturate the image by selecting a colour channel (as on pages 96–97). Van Dyke brown prints really are brown, and they must begin with a monochrome image. Try to choose the colour channel that best represents the tones in the print.*

3 *Compress the tones in the image. This is most easily done by using the* Levels *dialog. Use the sliders to trim the extremities of the tonal range and*

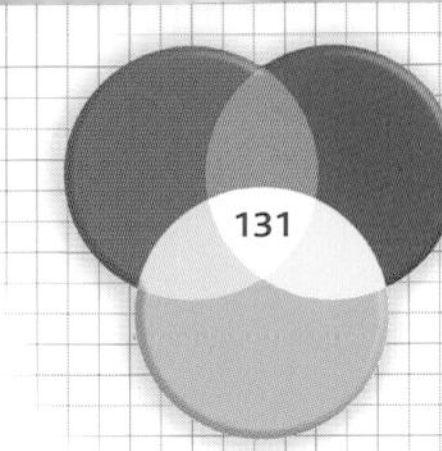

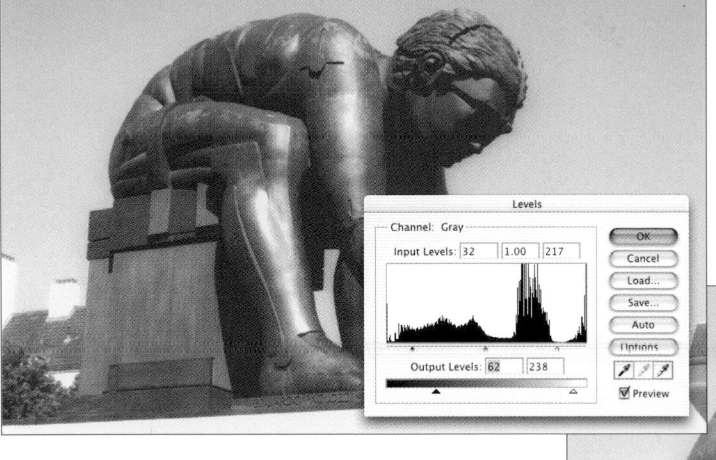

3

4

ALTERNATE EFFECTS

Canvas: *A Van Dyke print has been given a canvas texture. Afterwards a chalk brush is used (with 20% saturation) to give a loose, 'brushed on' finish.*
Water Paper: *Applying the Water Paper filter gives a strong perpendicular structure that again gives the impression of emulsion embedded in a textured substrate.*

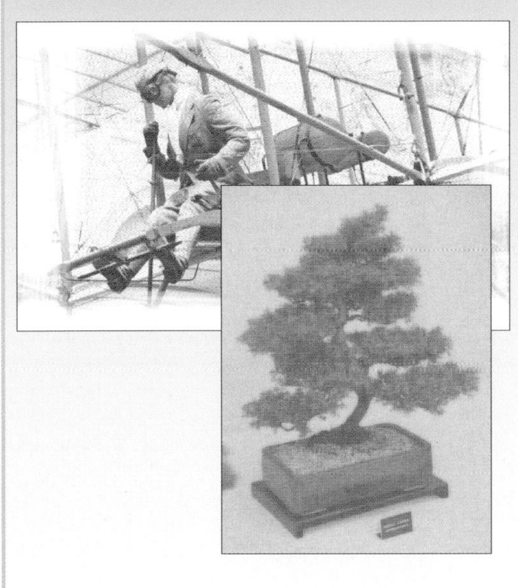

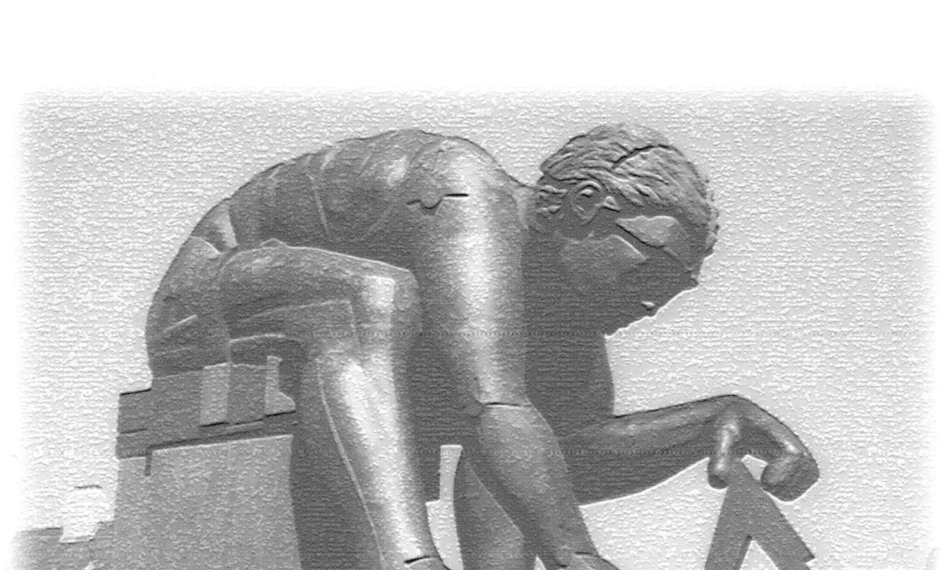

5

then do likewise to the Output *levels. To get the tonality that will best represent this technique, you will need to slide the left* Output *slider to between levels 50 and 75 and the right slider to between 225 and 250.*

4 *If your image is not in* RGB Color *mode, reset the colour mode now and then select* Hue/Saturation. *Check the* Colorize *box. Set the* Hue *to a mid-brown (Hue 35 in Photoshop), and reduce the* Saturation. *True Van Dyke prints include a degree of black in the overall brown colour (due to the silver nitrite salts).*

5 *To finish the image, you can give it a texture to emulate the traditional process of painting the emulsion on a textured substrate. Here the* Craquelure *filter gives a different look in which the applied texture follows some of the structure of the image, giving an illusion of slight relief.*

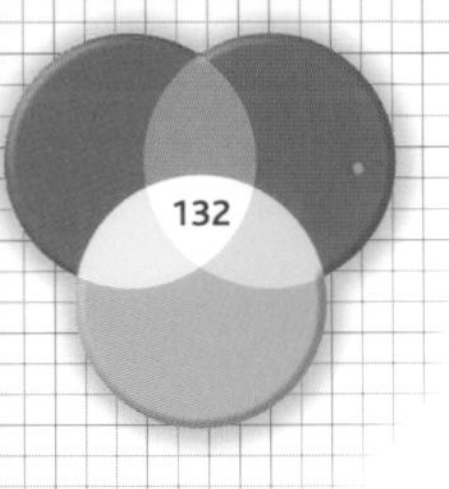

Cyanotypes and kallitypes

DARKROOM SECRETS

ADDING EMPHASIS

Both kallitypes and cyanotypes are great for providing subdued-background effects, where you need to 'lift' a subject from a background but still show that subject in context. Just mask the subject and then apply the processes as described here.

Cyanotype (or blueprint) is another early process, invented by the British astronomer and photographer Sir John Hershel in the 1840s. As the story goes, Sir John did not trust his assistants to transcribe his mathematical formulae, so he developed a process to yield sharp copies of his handwritten originals. The characteristic Prussian blue print comes from the combination of ferrous salts with potassium ferricyanide.

Kallitypes result from the combination of ferric salts with silver salts (as in Van Dyke brown prints), but rely on a different processing chemistry capable of delivering neutral black, sepia and blue prints. The blue colour tends to be a less saturated Prussian blue.

Prints of both processes exhibit high contrast, and therefore contrast-increasing techniques (rather than contrast reduction as with Van Dyke brown) are employed.

PRODUCING CYANOTYPES

1 *The basis of our cyanotype is this architectural shot. In cyanotype the black elements are replaced with Prussian blue, so we must emphasise as much of the image as possible, rendering it in black, white and a few intermediate greys.*

2 *Apply a* Solarize *filter to the image. This will convert most of the light areas to dark and improve the balance of the final image.*

3 *Now use the* Brightness/Contrast *control to boost the image contrast. You should aim to create a scene where the majority of tones are black or white, with as few midtone greys as possible.*

4 *In a true cyanotype, there is nothing darker than the Prussian blue, so some of our areas are still too dark. Select these areas using the* Magic Wand *and paint over them with the Prussian blue paint colour to produce the authentic cyanotype.*

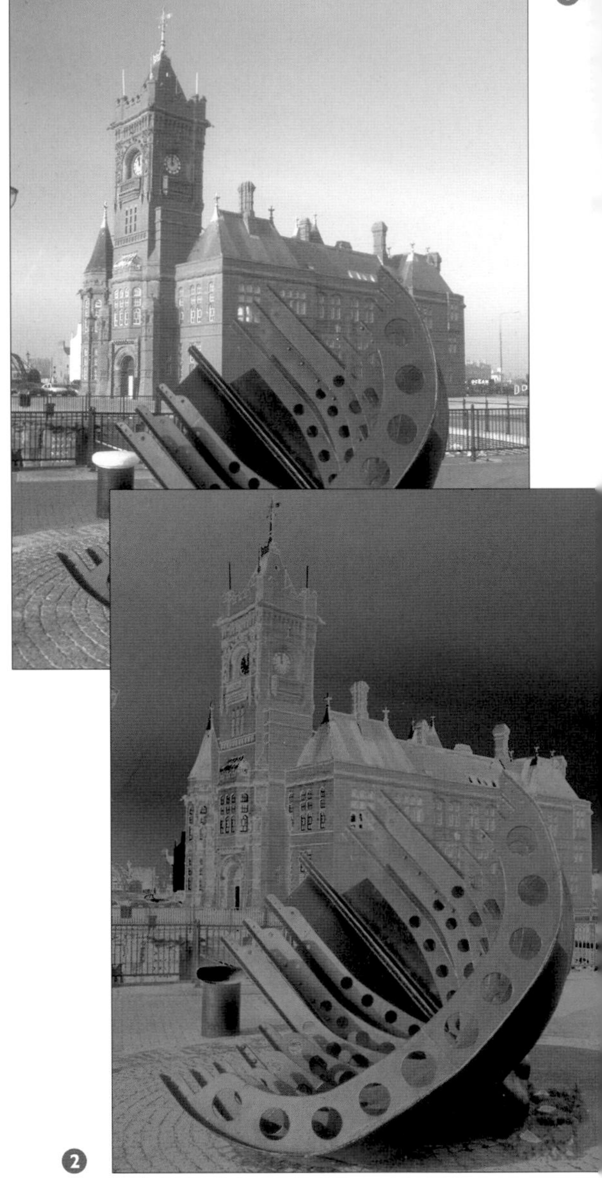

1

2

5 *Now use* Color Range *to select the black and, with the fuzziness slider set to around 50, pick up virtually all the grey tones too. Paint over the selection produced, using the blue paint colour.*

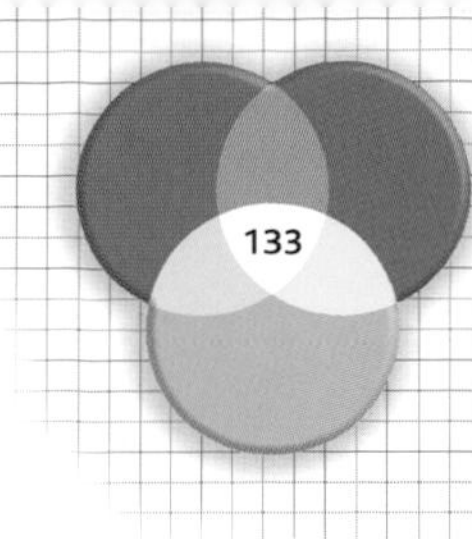

3

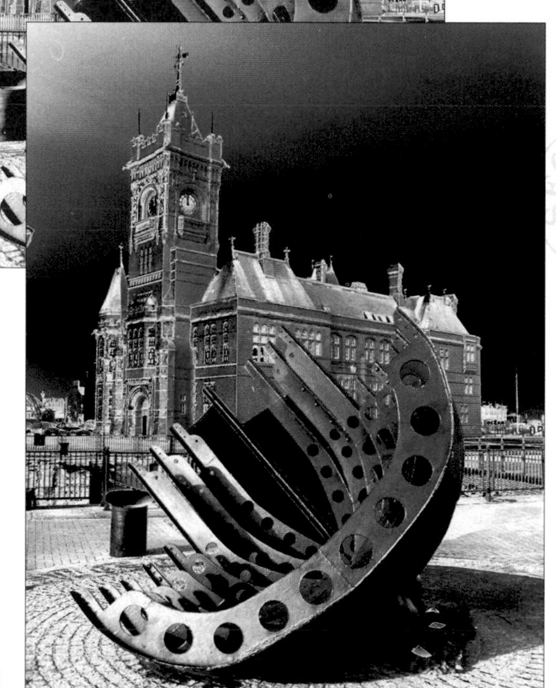

4

The kallitype process is broadly similar but uses even higher contrast original imagery. Here we will convert an original image of an Art Nouveau Paris Metro station entrance.

PRODUCING KALLITYPES

1 *We begin by applying the* Threshold *command, reducing the image to pure black and pure white. In this case, the threshold is set to around 50 so that the image is well balanced and not too heavily shaded.*

2 *Use the* Color Range *command to select all the black areas. As traditional kallitypes feature grey, sepia or steel blue coloration, you may want to choose one of these for the paint colour, but don't feel constrained to do so!*

3 *Grittiness is another feature of the kallitype, so add some grain. Use the monochromatic grain option to ensure that the strong coloration is not compromised in the process.*

1

2

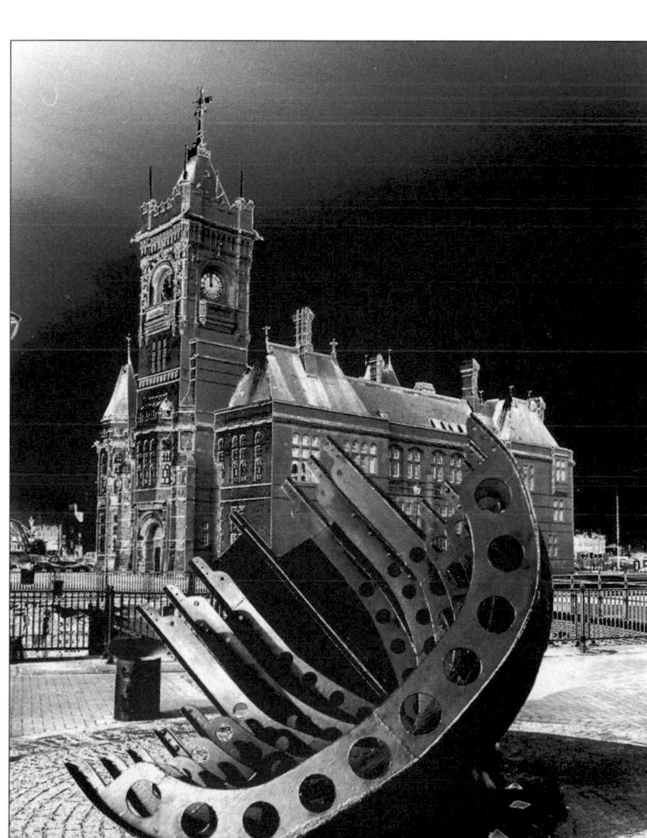

5

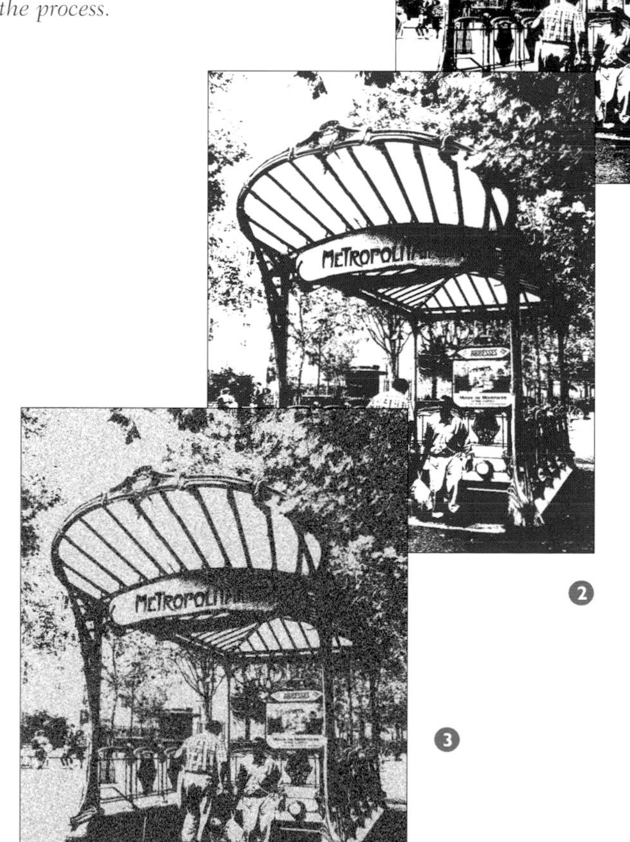

3

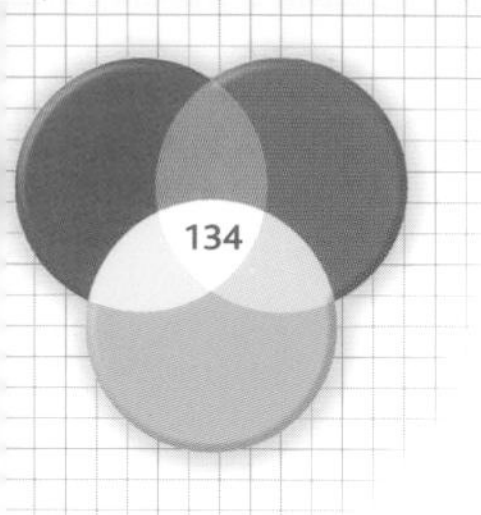

Reticulation and solarization

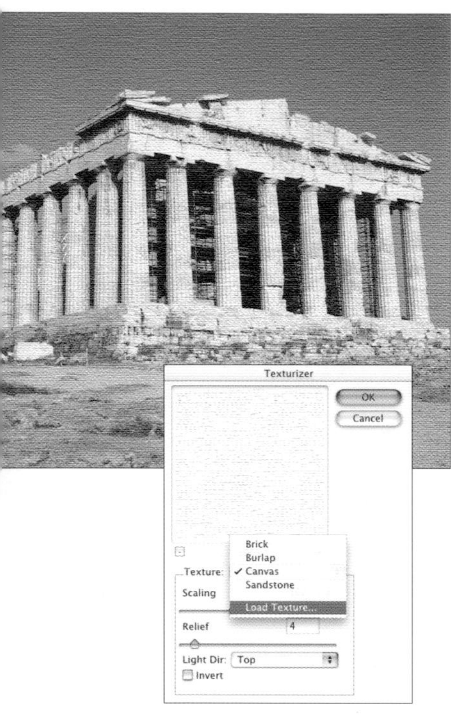

For decades, reticulation was considered a symptom of bad darkroom practice. The fine crackling of the film surface was nothing but a fault caused by large changes in temperature or acidity levels between consecutive processing stages. Since then, it has been used creatively for the delicate and natural texturing it gives images.

Through digital methods, we can not only recreate the textured finish characteristic of reticulation, but also any number of alternatives. Plug-in filters are available to recreate reticulation or other specific effects, or we can use standard Photoshop filters, such as *Craquelure*, to simulate them. Otherwise, we can use the *Texturizer* (*Filter > Texture >* **Texturizer**).

The *Texturizer* features a group of standard textures, but you can load others. A number are included in Photoshop's *Presets* subfolder.

Begin by opening your image and selecting the *Texturizer* filter. Select *Load Texture* from the dropdown *Texture* menu, then navigate down to the *Textures* folder in the Photoshop *Presets* subfolder. Click on a texture to select it. You can use the dialog sliders to convert the basic texture by varying the scale, amount of relief and the lighting angles. In the example to the left, the texture *Rust Flakes* has been applied using scaling and relief of 25% and 20 respectively for the left-hand side and 150% and 50 for the right.

You can create and add your own textures for overlays, but with those already on offer and the amount of variation available, there's really very little need to do so.

Textured images work best when printed using matt finish papers (glossy papers give incongruous results) and when used with suitable subjects such as the historic building shown here.

SOLARIZATION

In the darkroom, solarizing a print involves deliberately fogging an image through exposure to bright light part way through processing. The result is a darkening of those areas undeveloped at the time of the exposure and the reversal of some other tones. Characteristic fine lines, called 'Mackie lines', are produced at the border of those areas that were originally light and dark.

Solarization effects sit a little uneasily in our brave new digital world. On the one hand, it is considered to be an established, if challenging, darkroom process that (as darkroom colour effects go) delivers surprising colour consistency (it is repeatable) and creates some very graphic images. On the other, its potency has slipped in the digital darkroom, where the 'anything is possible' ethos can deliver colour and tonal effects that are much more dramatic and less proscribed.

Darkroom workbooks generally include solarization in their advanced techniques section. Digital image-editing applications conversely (and almost contemptuously!) regard it as a simple effects filter. Grouped with the *Stylize* filters, it offers no user interventions. The filter is simply applied to the entire image or selection within the image. To get more subtle effects and gradations, we can manually invert the tones by using the *Curves* command.

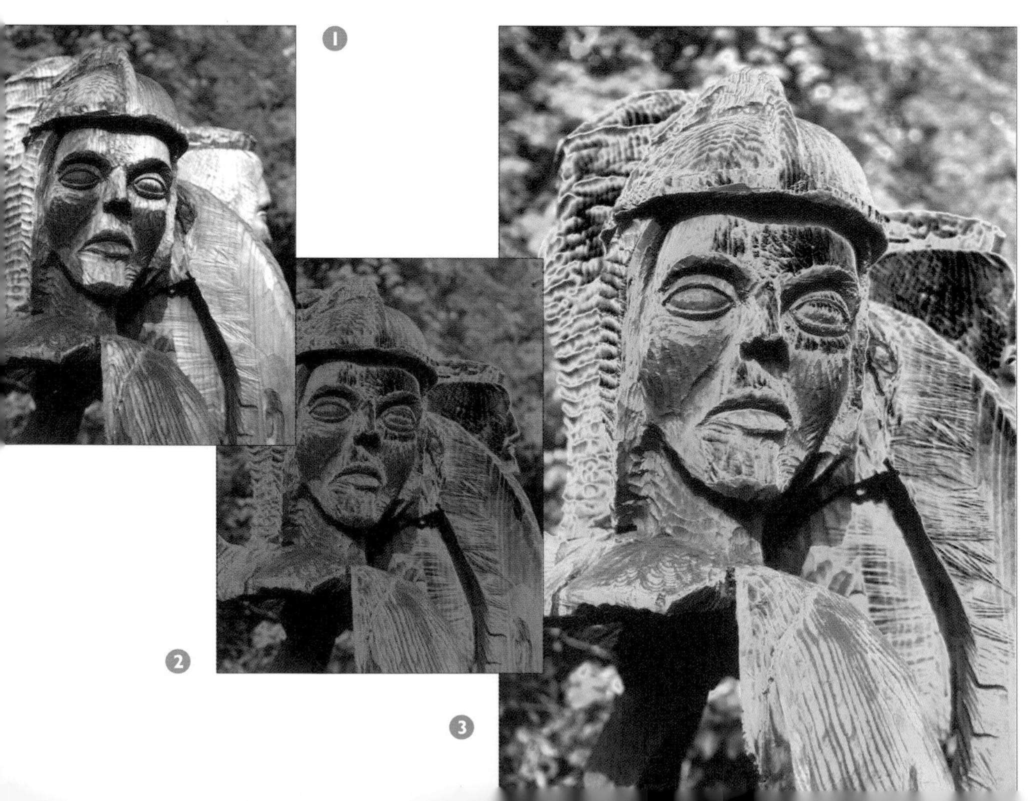

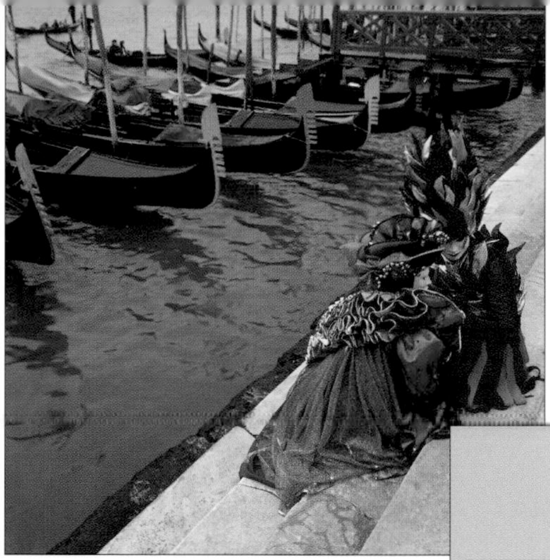

SOLARIZING AN IMAGE

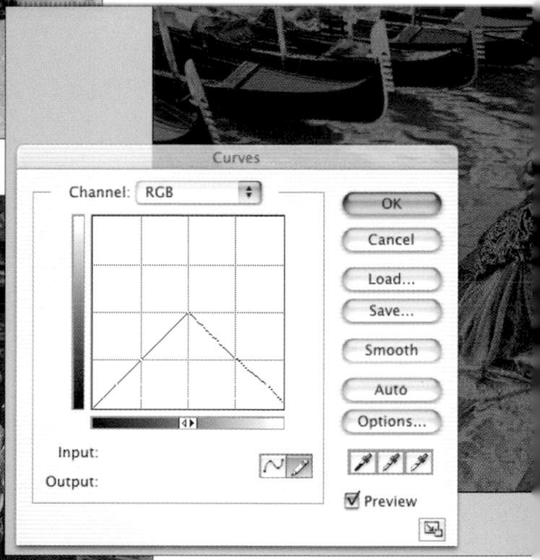

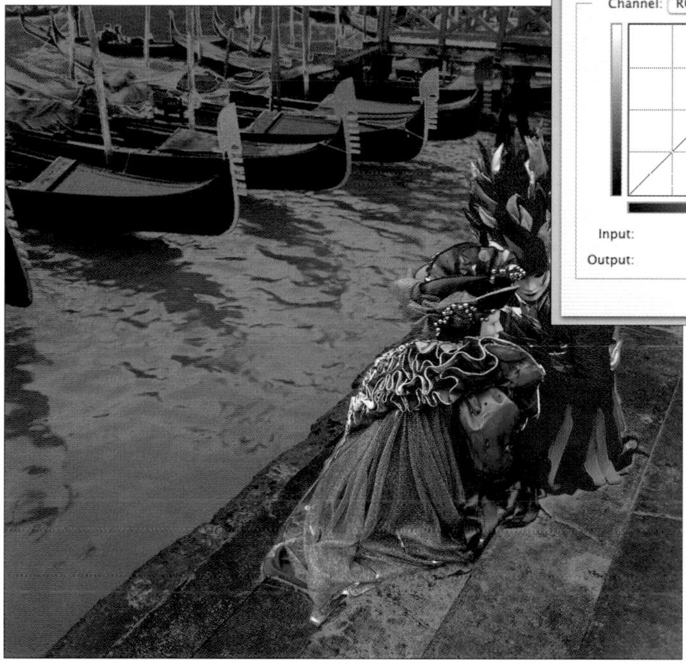

1 *As the results of solarizing are a little unpredictable, the effect can be attempted with almost any image. Those with bold graphic shapes and good tonal range respond best. Select* Filters > Stylize > **Solarize** *to apply the filter.*

2 *'Psychedelia, the morning after' is an apt description of the standard implementation of the* Solarize *filter. It is somewhat brusque, and characteristically delivers muddied, dull colours often dominated by maroons and olive greens.*

3 *Applying* Auto Levels *can deliver a much more satisfactory and tonally enriched image. The* Auto Colors *and* Auto Contrast *can also help. Because the colours in a solarized image are not precisely defined, it matters little if the tones shift. This gives you a degree of freedom you would not have with a normal photographic image.*

SOLARIZATION OR SABATTIER?

The Sabattier effect (*page 136–137*) is often confused with solarization. Indeed, many authoritative manuals regard the two terms as synonymous. In a strict interpretation, the term 'solarization' should be reserved for those images in which gross overexposure has resulted in tone inversion, before any secondary exposure to light. In an image subject to the Sabattier effect, partial solarization occurs during processing.

In any case, the creators of digital image-editing applications have blurred this already fine distinction to the point where the Sabattier effect is normally reserved for the more dramatic colour and tonal inversions possible through adjustments to the image curve.

SOLARIZATION WITH CURVES

1 *While we can use just the* Solarize *filter to recreate the effect of massive overexposure, making adjustments to the* Curves (Image > Adjust > **Curves**) *offers us more precise control over the process. By creating a new* Curves *adjustment layer* (*Layer > New Adjustment Layer >* **Curve**), *we can also apply the solarization via the layer, making it easy to remove the effect from all or selected parts of the image later on.*

2 *In this example, reversing the gradient of the upper part of the* Curves *graph has generated a simple tonal inversion. Do this yourself by clicking on the arbitrary map tool (the pencil icon to the lower right of the curves) and describing a shape similar to that shown. Solarization is not – and has never been – an exact science, so do not be too concerned about absolute precision.*

3 *Our use of an adjustment layer for the* Curves *enables us to selectively apply the solarization to the image by masking those areas that we do not wish to be solarized.*

DARKROOM SECRETS

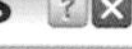

NO REVERSALS

When you use extreme *Curves* effects on colour images, the colours will be reversed. If you want to avoid this, change the image colour mode to Lab and apply the effect only to the L channel. Colour authenticity (if not fidelity) will be preserved.

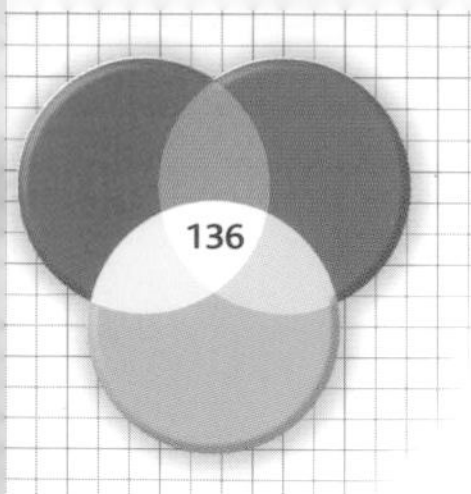

The Sabattier effect

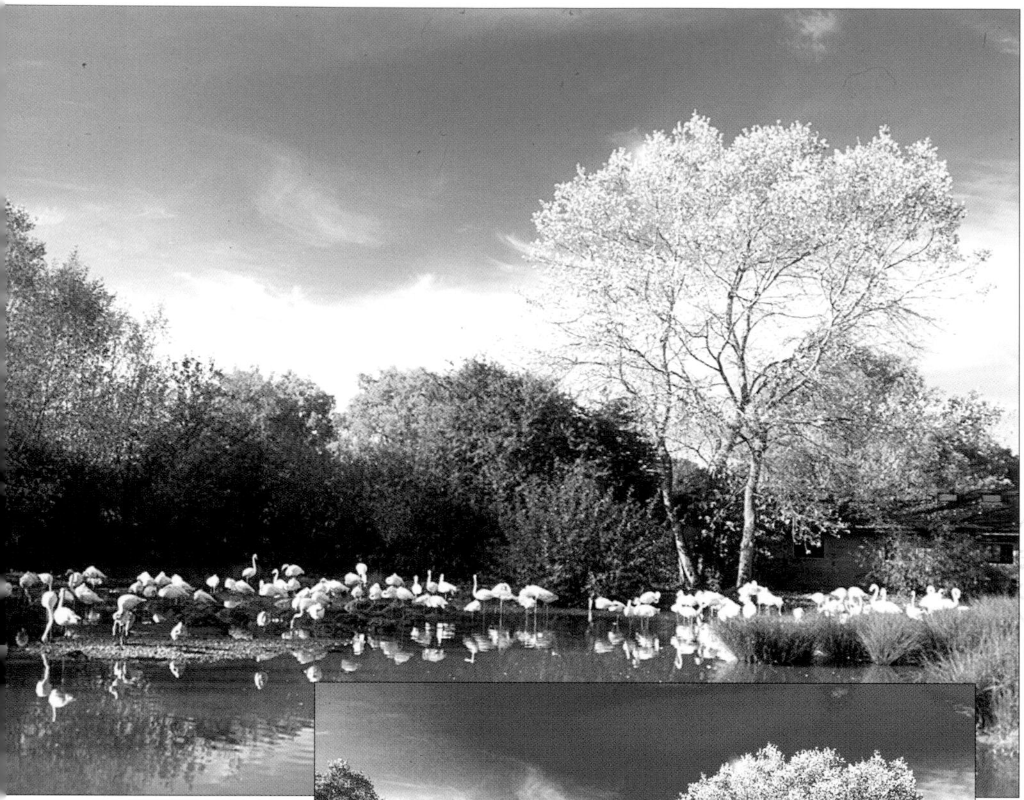

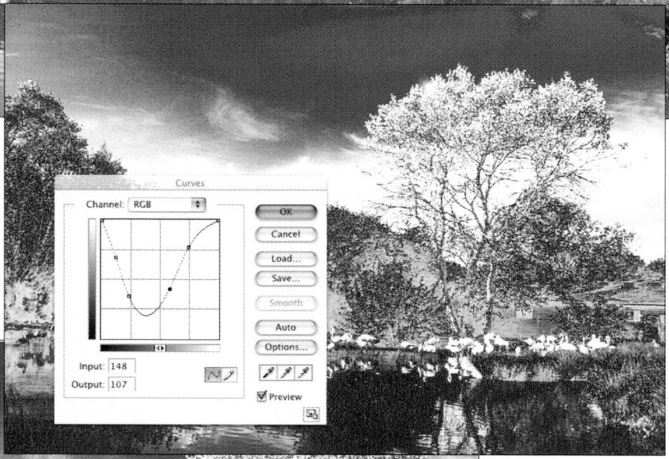

What distinguishes Sabbatier from Solarization is that that the former is the result of gross overexposure of film emulsion to light, while the latter (in simplistic digital terms) is the result of inversion of the curves in the *Curves* dialog. This creates the effect of making tones that should logically be lighter than their neighbours, darker, such as a dark sky above a bright landscape.

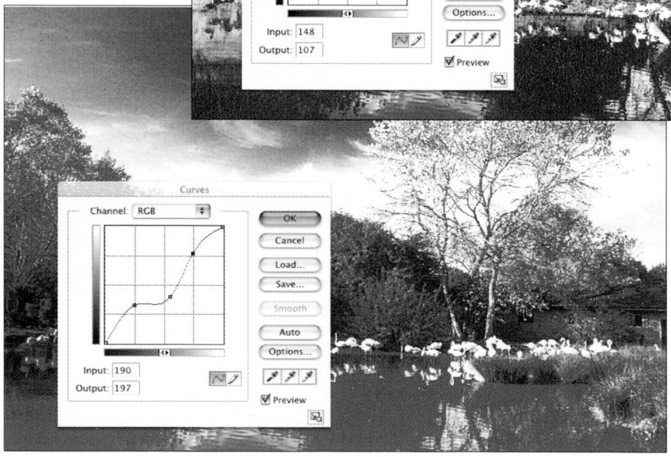

Many photographic manuals will simply describe Sabattier as any tonal inversion. This perhaps harks back to the darkroom days, where the effect was notoriously difficult to control and chances were minimal of producing two prints with even the semblance of similarity.

ACHIEVING SABBATIER EFFECTS

1 *To create a more effective Sabattier print, which may be consistently repeated or fine-tuned, it is best to work with a dual layer image, with each layer featuring the original image.*

2 *Select the upper layer and then open the* Curves *dialog box. Conventionally, as we have seen earlier, the graph line runs diagonally from the lower left to top right. If we pull or push the line in any way, the correspondence between input and output levels changes.*

3 *For a Sabattier effect, we need to make a curve that is substantially negative. Most workers suggest making a gentle catenary curve from top left to top right with the lowest point in the catenary located reasonably central.*

4 *As we have suggested, there is no definitive look to a Sabattier, so you will need to make fine adjustments to the curve, depending on the tonal and colour composition of the image. The examples here show how divergence from the conventional diagonal curve affects the degree of the effect. A partial divergence creates an image in which there is only partial tonal inversion, with the other parts of the image almost unaffected. Something more dramatic creates a surreal or hyper-real coloration.*

1

2

❸

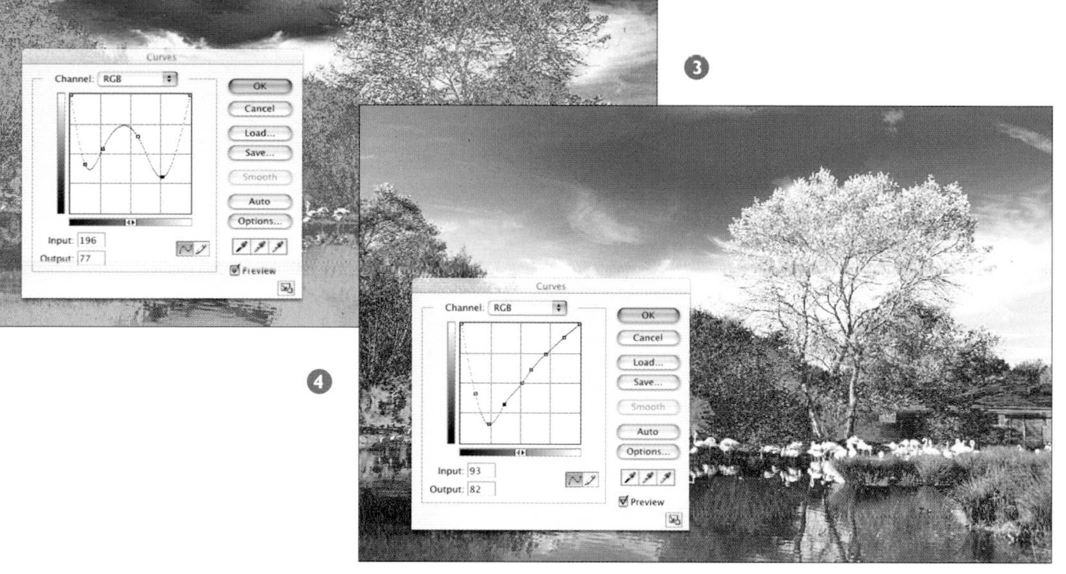

❹

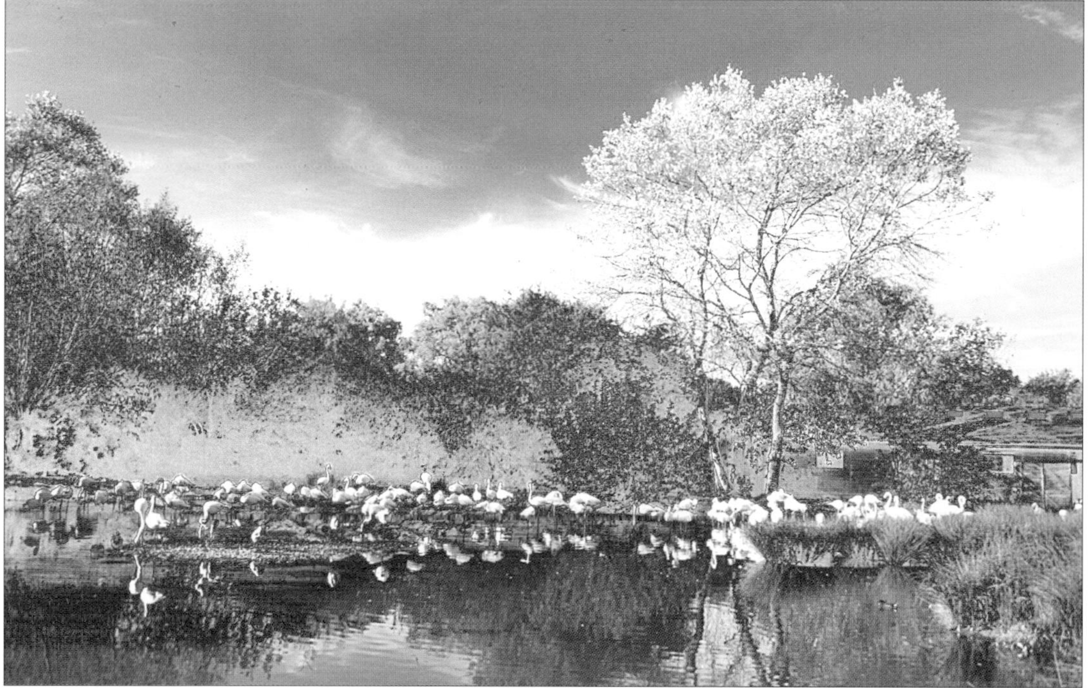

DARKROOM SECRETS

SABBATIER TIPS

- You can also create Sabattier (and Sabattier-like) effects by changing the layer blend modes. *Exclusion* and *Difference* will produce dramatic effects, while an *Inverted Adjustment* Layer gives a negative image. Use a layer mask, and you can create areas that are positive, negative or even transitional.
- The Sabattier effect works better on some subjects than others. Abstract landscapes work better than formal portraits.
- As a guide, the deeper the curve, the more intense the colour.

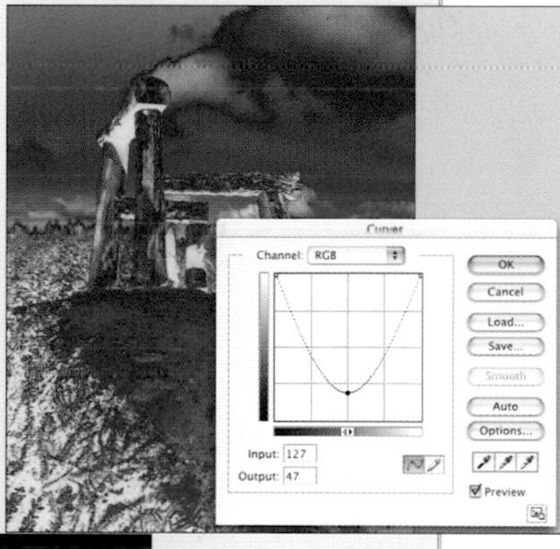

MONO IMAGES

Applying Sabbatier effects to greyscale images – as in the image to the right – can also work very well indeed. It is worth noting that simpler, more graphic subjects (such as a face) will often produce better results.

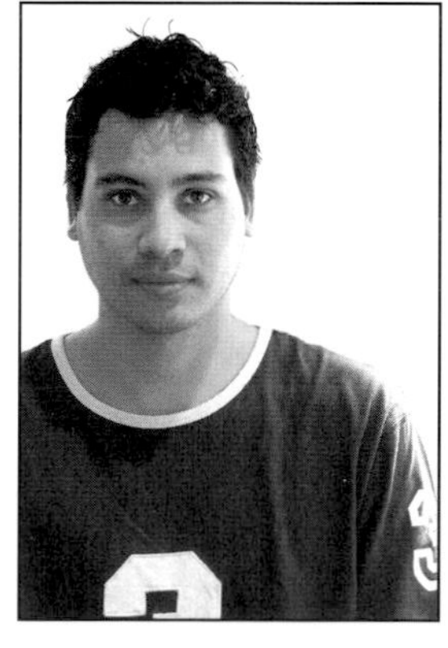

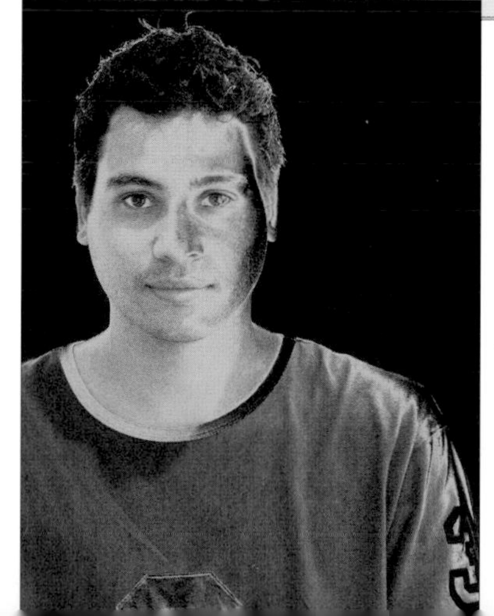

SECTION FIVE

creating a digital darkroom

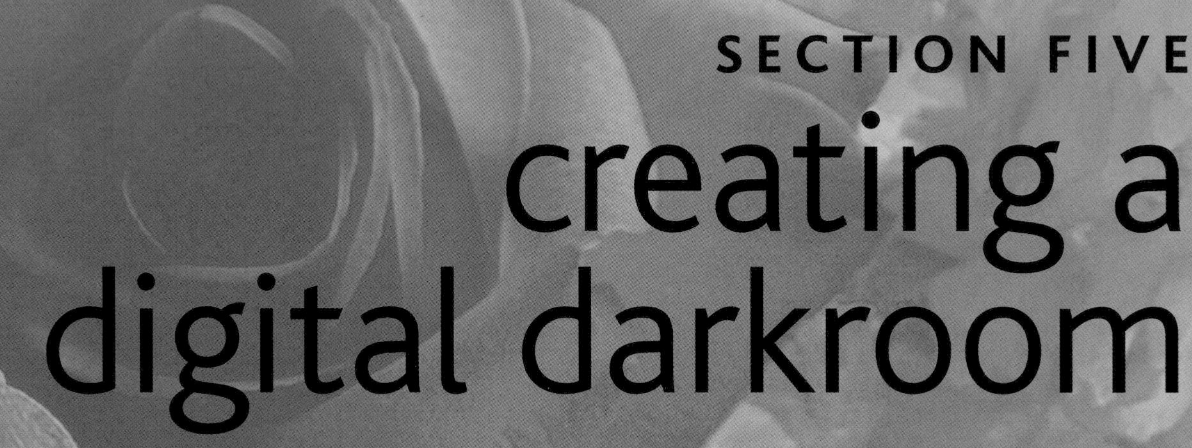

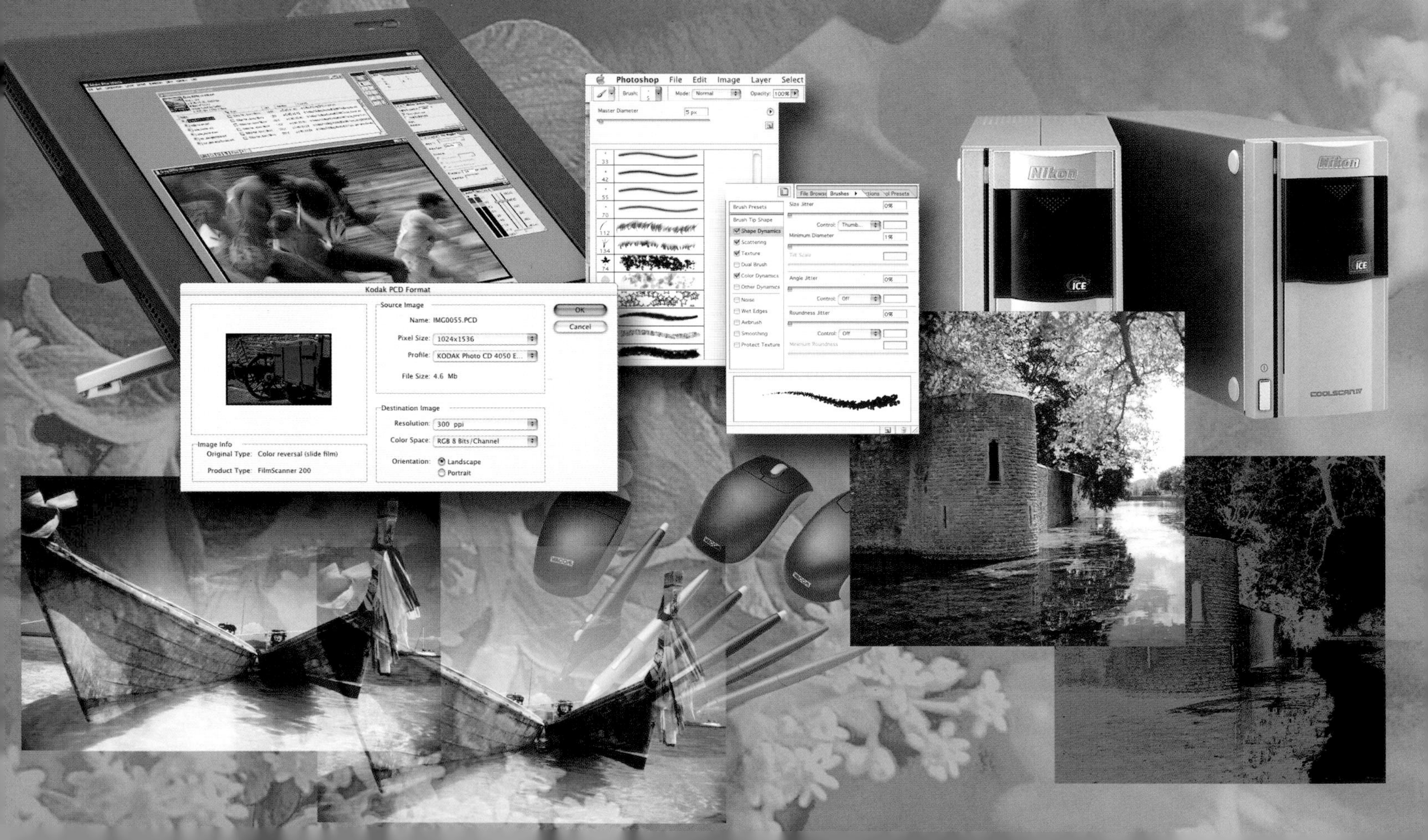

This chapter is intended as a reference, covering the hardware and software that might go into your digital darkroom, more options for gathering images, and background information that can make your work easier. It's not a tutorial in using computers or a shopping list of equipment to buy – there are plenty of other books and magazines that do that sort of thing – but it will give you a basic idea of what you are going to need and how to get the most from it.

We start with a rundown of what to look for in your home computer, whether it is a Windows PC or an Apple Mac, and the accessories that you will need to make your digital darkroom work. The art of scanning is also discussed in depth, so you can make sure that you get the best possible image before you start work on it.

We then cover the wide range of image-editing software that's available. We've used Photoshop – the industry standard – for the majority of the examples in this book, but there are several other applications that have their own, individual strengths to offer. We follow on with a discussion of file formats and their uses: essential reading if you're serious about your digital images. We'll also show you how to make dealing with files less of a chore, and how you can automate the most tedious tasks in Photoshop.

Finally, we'll give you some ideas on how to share and show your efforts. Printing is still a popular way, but you'll also find out about digital slideshows and simple websites that allow you to display your work to anyone with an Internet connection.

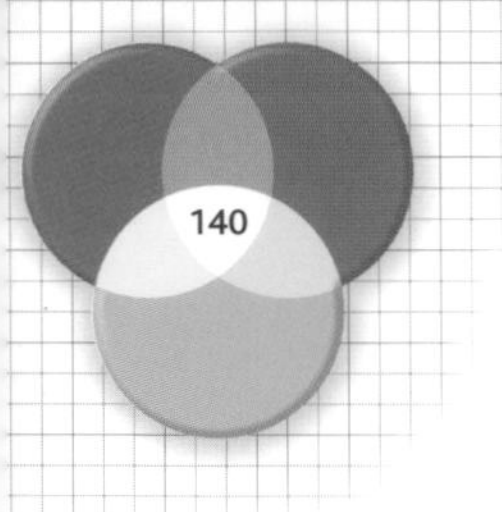

CREATING A DIGITAL DARKROOM

Basic requirements

Preparing your digital darkroom does not have to be an expensive or onerous task. The same computer that you use to write letters and manage accounts can be the core, with just a few upgrades if necessary. Image-editing applications can push computing resources to extremes, but – with a few caveats – most computers you can buy today are reasonably well specified to handle them. Once you have your basic system ready, you just need to find the right mix of additional hardware and software to get images on and off your computer; this might include a scanner, a digital camera and a printer. You will also need the software to work with your images while onboard. In the examples in this book, we have mostly used Photoshop and Photoshop Elements, but there are alternatives that might better suit your needs or budget. This section is all about helping you to make all those decisions.

DARKROOM SECRETS 

DOUBLE YOUR DISKS

Many imaging professionals use computers with second hard disks that are reserved for image-editing purposes. This ensures that you have a disk which is not sharing its time and resources with other processes. Large hard drives are getting cheaper all the time, and are not too difficult to install yourself. Just check that your computer has a space for a second drive before you buy.

GRINDING HARD DISKS

When your whisper-quiet hard disk starts making crunching noises while running your image-editing application, it isn't necessarily a sign of anything terminal. Check your computer's memory and, if appropriate, the virtual memory settings. If your computer doesn't have enough 'real' RAM memory, it could be making use of the hard disk as virtual memory, writing parts of your image to and from the disk as it processes commands. There's nothing wrong with this – but swapping to disk like this is painfully slow, as you will have no doubt noticed. The solution? Add more RAM. Be aware that most systems – even those with substantial quantities of RAM – will use virtual memory now and again, if only for a little occasional elbow room. Don't be too concerned with the occasional grind!

Image files are, by their nature, large. Go for the best in quality and resolution and you will find them getting larger still. Manipulate them and the size escalates: your finished image file will often be larger than the original, with each adjustment or effect only adding to the data.

Processing an image is a mathematical process. In its raw state, a digital image is just a long continuous string of binary code, and it is upon this code that your manipulations – whether you are applying a filter or changing a colour – are interpreted and applied. All these calculations make incredible demands upon your computer and, in particular, its central processor.

As a result, the specifications of computers designed for image editing are high, but there's no need to go straight to the top of the range. Most of us live in the real world (without a corporate account) and just need a good working system.

KEY REQUIREMENTS

CPU: Windows XP users should go for a PC based on an Intel Pentium 4 or AMD AthlonXP. Users of a Macintosh system (the designer's choice) can get away with using a G3 iMac or iBook, but we recommend looking at a G4 Mac running OS X. Apart from being faster, the latest processors also feature advanced technology (such as the G4's AltaVec), which accelerate the performance of image-editing applications.

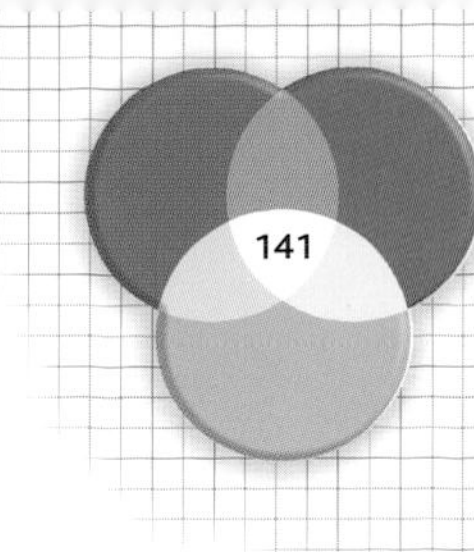

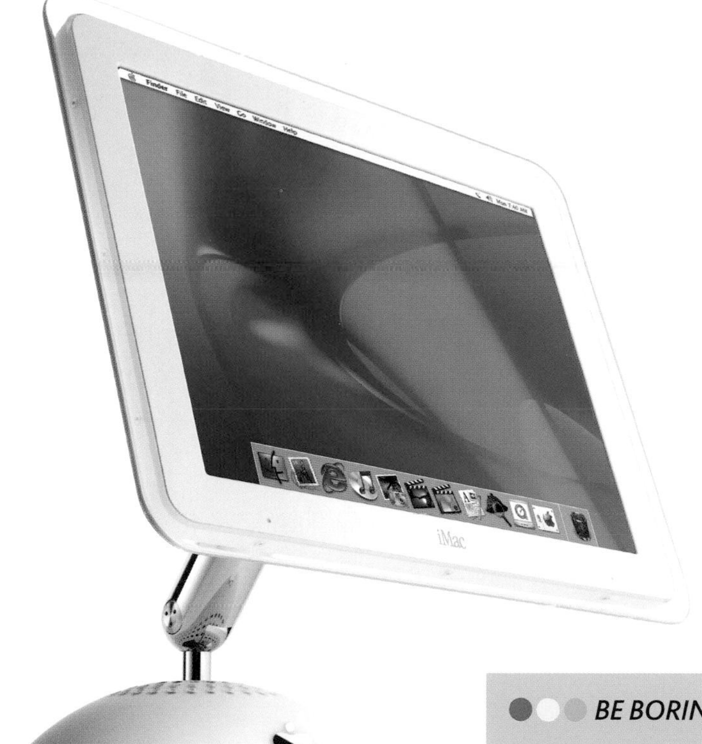

Apple's Macintosh, in its various forms, remains the designer's choice of computer, but the majority of Windows PCs are equally capable of handling the demands of your digital darkroom.

RAM: The software manufacturers suggest 64MB or 128MB as a minimum, but we would suggest that you aim for 256MB or even 512MB. Applications will run on less, but you need to ensure that there is sufficient memory for the application, the operating system and any other processes to run concurrently. Though the price of RAM fluctuates wildly, it's never too expensive, and you can never have too much.

Free Hard Disk Space: At least 2GB is recommended. With 20GB and 40GB hard disks now standard, this is less of an issue than it was, but remember that you will need space for your downloaded and edited files.

Monitor: 800 x 600 pixels is the minimum, and 1024 x 768 is standard for 17-inch (43-cm) monitors and 15-inch (38-cm) LCD screens. Go for larger screens and larger resolutions if you can, as you will be able to see more of the image at a time, and you will also be able to place floating palettes more efficiently.

BE BORING!

For best results, think about your desktop. Try to avoid those multicoloured nature images supplied with OS X or the latest download from your favourite TV character desktop wallpaper site. Stick to a plain grey background. We won't patronise you by explaining how to properly calibrate your monitor (after all, that's what the assistants and wizards for), but be assured that any gains you make through proper calibration will be prejudiced if you are constantly viewing your images against a multicoloured background. Photoshop – and other applications – can be configured to display a neutral grey background. If you are unwilling to lose your desktop image, use this option.

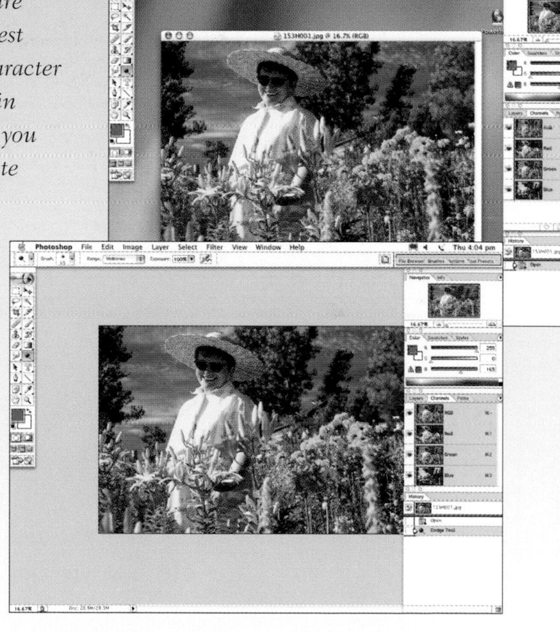

Keep your computer in shape, making sure that the hard disk is kept tidy, and that all of your software is up to date. Apple and Microsoft update MacOS and Windows on a regular basis, so try to keep pace with the the free downloads from *http://windowsupdate.microsoft.com* and *www.info.apple.com*.

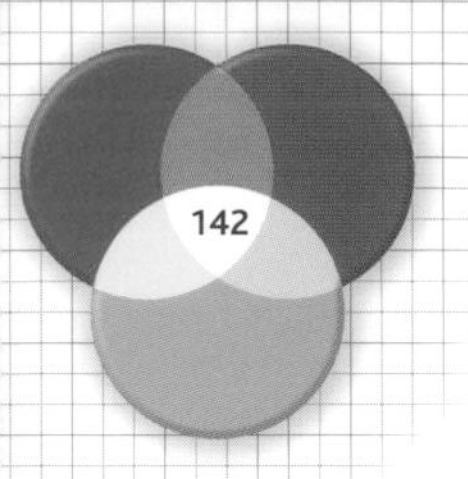

Additional equipment

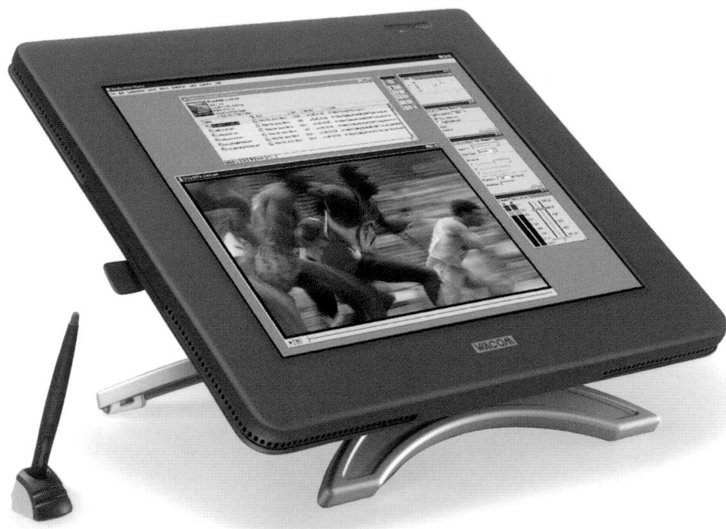

Giving the best replication of a drawing environment in everything but texture, the interactive pen display makes it possible to paint directly onto the LCD 'canvas'.

Of course, there is more to our digital darkroom than just the computer. Though it plays a more pivotal role than any single piece of conventional darkroom component, it needs the support of some ancillary equipment to have the requisite versatility. The need to first input images in a digital form requires that we have the means to do so. The equipment required will vary according to the image type. Scanners will deliver digital files from flat artwork and transparent media; card readers service the digital camera market (as an alternative to direct connection); and the humble CD drive will give us access to any CD based images.

SAFE STORAGE

Apart from the limited number that you may commit to print, digital images exist only in the ethereal memory of your computer. Should anything happen to our computer – even something comparatively minor – these images could be at risk. It makes sense to keep tabs on your virtual collection and to keep copies. Like negatives and transparencies, your digital archive is a valuable asset that contains both original images (and artwork) and the results of your image-editing projects.

In fact, a CD-R (or even DVD-R) drive is pretty much essential for any image worker. If you don't want to lose work, it pays to be scrupulous about file storage and back-up.

Even recordable CDs, once the paragon of computer storage, have somewhat limited capacity when it comes to complex images. Multilayer images can be very large and even a CD can hold only a limited number. DVD-R is a high-capacity alternative, but there are drawbacks. With several competing recordable DVD standards on the market and many older CD-R drives still around, compatibility can sometimes be an issue.

IMPROVING THE WORKING EFFICIENCY

The interaction with the computer – a task usually delegated to the mouse and keyboard – is one that also needs more discussion. The ubiquitous mouse is still the means by which the great majority of us use image-editing applications. As a general-purpose tool, equally at home making menu selections, painting, cloning and drawing selections, it knows no peer, but when it comes to specific actions it can be a little lacking in control. For one thing, a mouse is a truly digital tool: it is either off or on. In practice, this means that you cannot (without clever software to simulate complex brush dynamics)

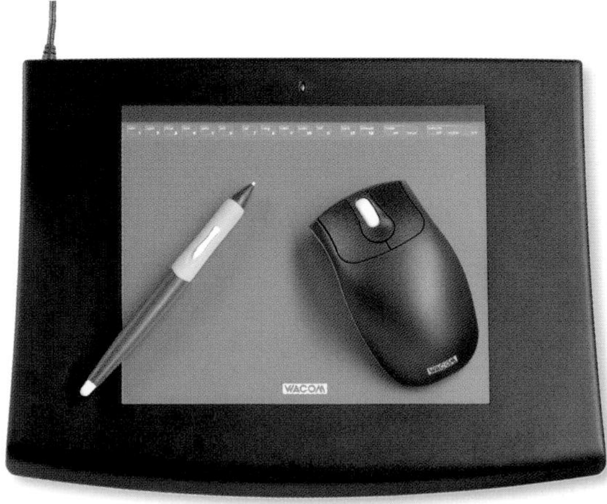

use it as you might a brush, varying the pressure or angle to adjust how the digital paint is applied.

Professional users, who need to have that sort of additional control close at hand, will use graphics tablets: pressure sensitive drawing surfaces equipped with pens – styli – that can emulate a range of painting and drawing techniques much more successfully than a mouse. A good graphics tablet will include a range of productivity features that will include:

- A large (or reasonably large) working surface. A5 (7 x 6 inches) is normally the smallest successful size.
- A range of pressure sensitivity levels (1000 or more is desirable).
- Tilt sensitivity to apply different strokes with different pen angles.
- Customisable buttons (to reduce the need to use the mouse to change modes).
- Alternate pen types to use for painting and airbrushing.

An evolution of the graphics tablet is the interactive pen display. Combining the active surface of a graphics tablet with a high-quality LCD panel, this gives arguably the most authentic painting experience, enabling direct interaction with the screen. Though designed for laptop or tabletop use, these devices can also function as conventional monitors.

VIDEO ACCELERATION

The 'bigger is best' philosophy that we have applied to hard disk, RAM and virtually every aspect of our optimised computer should logically also apply to the video board. The presumption is often made that an accelerated board, fully loaded with video RAM, or VRAM, will make your screen-intensive application run faster because it can redraw the monitor screen faster. Unfortunately (unless you count millisecond improvements as significant), this will not be the case. Video boards are rarely pushed to their limits by image-editing applications and spend most of their time waiting for data from the main RAM or even the hard disk. Buying a graphics board packed with the latest graphics technology and high-speed VRAM will give you a tremendous advantage when it comes to playing the latest Quake variant, but it will have no visible impact on your image editor.

DARKROOM SECRETS

BRUSH DYNAMICS

If you do not have a graphic tablet, you can still simulate many of the effects using the Brush Dynamics feature found in image-editing applications. As well as the fundamental Airbrush tool (a variant of the Paintbrush tool in later Photoshop versions), brush dynamics enable the rate of flow, dissipation and many more parameters to be adjusted. Using the brush dynamics control isn't as slick as using a tablet but can achieve many of the same effects.

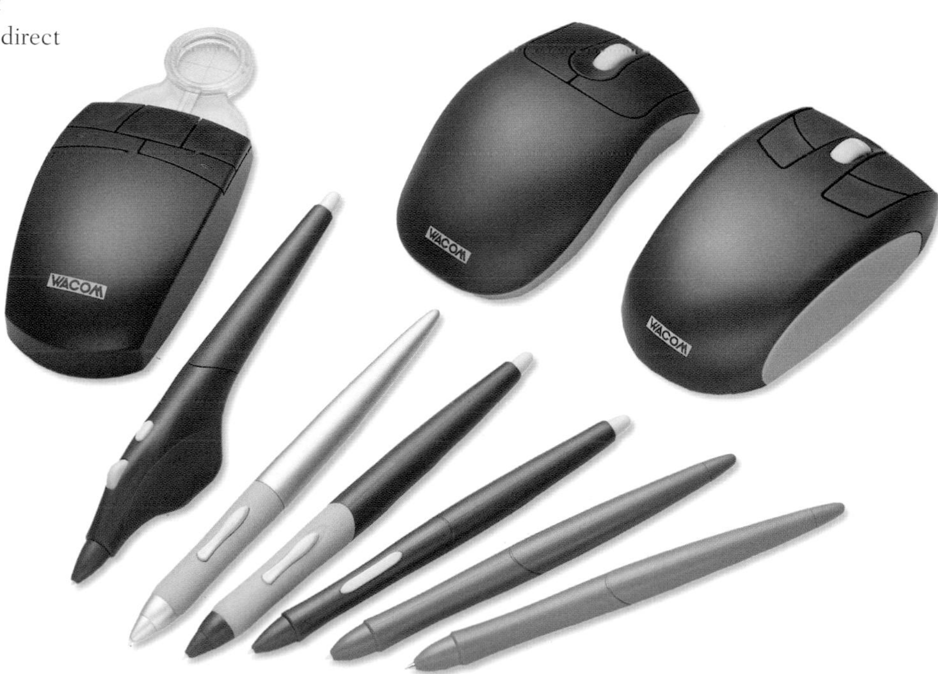

A range of styli (and mice) add to the versatility of graphics tablets. They offer an even wider range of effects, particularly when they are used with calligraphic pen and airbrush tools.

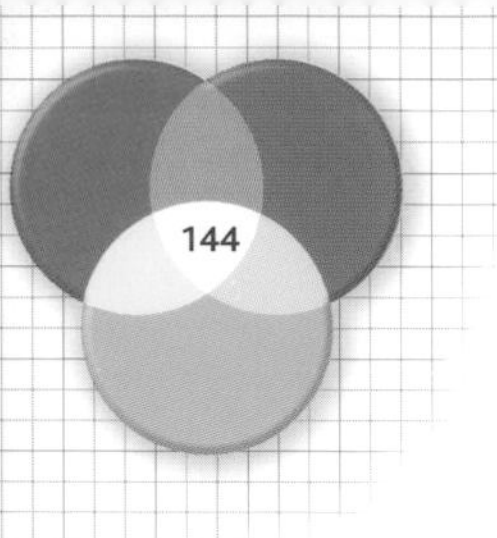

Image acquisition

The images we work on using our computer and image-editing software are digital. Many will come straight from a digital camera, but not all of them. In particular, we need a way of taking older photographs and transferring them into the digital domain. In the latter case, the desktop scanner provides the most convenient and – for most media – most effective way to digitize images or artwork, whether from prints, transparencies or negatives. But it is not by any means the only method. Your image portfolio may include images downloaded from the Internet, those put onto CD by a photo lab, or those converted to digital form by a professional service.

It would be nice to think that once your images – from whatever source – were transferred to your computer they would all be equal. Sadly, that proves not to be the case. Each capture system tends to impose its own characteristics on the images it produces, and you need to be mindful of this during the acquisition. As with the film processing stage of work in a traditional darkroom, it is in the image acquisition stage that we begin to determine the quality of the results possible from our image. In other words, we need to get things right from the outset.

A standard flatbed scanner (top) will handle a variety of material, and ever-increasing resolutions mean that many can handle negatives or transparencies. For the best results, however, try a specialised film scanner (bottom).

SCANNERS

Scanners take images and convert them to pixel-based digital files. The actual method of scanning is basically the same whether the scanner is a standard office flatbed device, a film scanner or a high-end drum scanner of the type used in professional publishing.

However, if we want to describe scanner performance unequivocally, we need to understand a complex set of specifications that seem to have been devised to enthrall and baffle the potential purchaser rather than give a clear indication of the actual performance. To get a good idea of how effective a scanner actually is, you should take a slightly jaundiced view of the published specifications and understand a little of the theory underpinning it. In particular, this means revisiting two concepts we examined earlier in the context of the digital image – resolution and bit depth – in order to see how these contribute to scanned image quality.

PPI OR DPI?

The resolution of a scanner should be described in ppi (points per inch), a term used generally to describe the resolution of an input device and that indicates the number of samples taken per inch. Confusingly, some scanner manufacturers insist on describing scanner resolutions in dpi (dots per inch), a measure that is more appropriate to output devices, such as inkjet printers.

A single screen pixel can represent any one of millions of colours, but a single printed dot can only represent one of four or six. Only by printing the dots in patterns can a printer simulate the full range of screen colours – up to 24 dots may be needed to represent the same colour as a single pixel.

RESOLUTION

Scanner resolution is undoubtedly at the top of peoples' list of specifications when shopping for a scanner. Unfortunately, it is also the most misunderstood. Scanner brochures often provide attention-grabbing figures, with resolutions as high as 9600 ppi or more. However, a closer look at what we call the optical resolution will reveal that the CCD array that scans the image has a resolution of only, say, 1200 ppi. The scanner software can deliver image files with a 9600 ppi resolution, but only by interpolating the smaller, 1200 ppi file size. New pixels will be added, but no extra detail. Leave interpolated resolutions alone and focus in on the true, optical resolution.

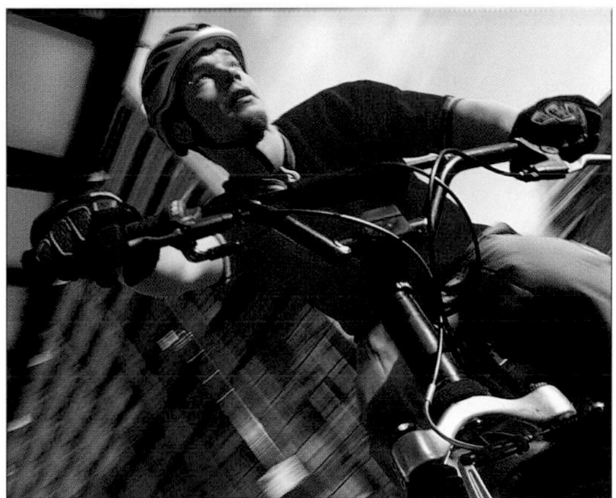

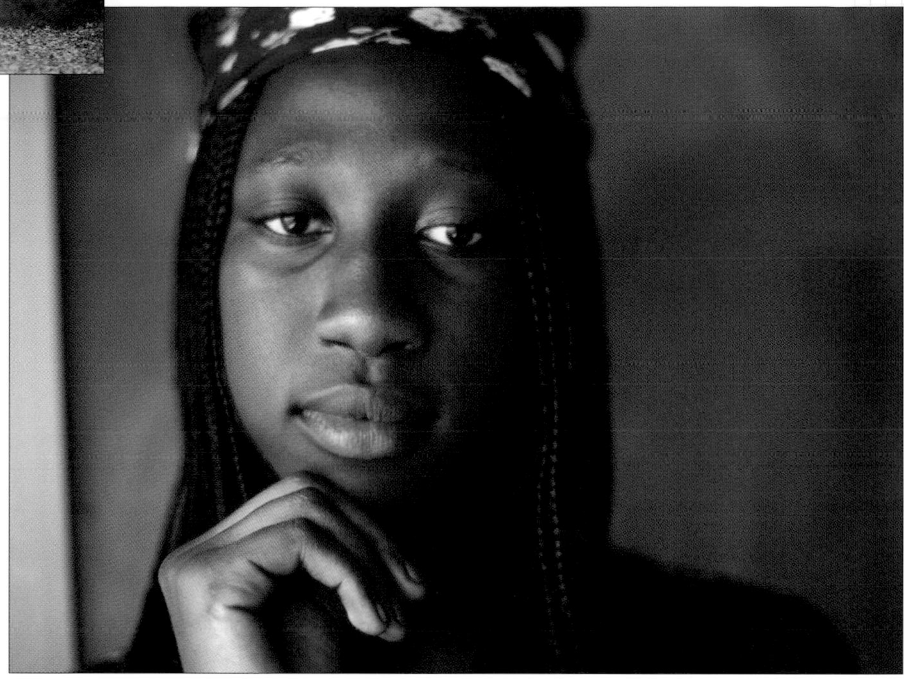

To add to the confusion, some brochure specifications will quote two optical resolutions. These devices, which are becoming rarer as basic scanner resolutions increase, use a dual lens system. The lower figure describes the resolution with which the entire image area can be scanned. The higher figure, which applies only when the alternate lens system is used, can be used only over a smaller area – usually a central pane or strip of the scanning window. This is used for scanning transparencies and negatives, which need to be scanned at higher resolutions, thus saving the need for a separate, specialised film scanner to handle this sort of material.

The most confusing aspect of resolution is the inference that it is a measure of image quality. Though it is the case that higher resolution scanners are capable of delivering more detailed images, absolute image quality is determined by a combination of factors, including bit depth, dynamic range and the performance of the actual scanning mechanism. Unless every part of the scanner works together to optimise image quality, it's unlikely that you will see the full benefit of its resolution, no matter how high that might be.

There are times when you won't want to scan at full resolution, anyway. Scanning at a very high resolution makes sense if you are planning to crop in tightly on a small area of a frame, but if you continually scan at maximum resolution, you are going to run out of hard-disk space pretty quickly.

As with most computer-related purchases, it is best to take the sales brochures, advertising and quoted specification with a grain of salt and take advice from magazine reviews and Web forums instead.

While resolution is a key factor in getting the most from your scanned images, it does not tell the whole story. Unless your scanner's grasp of colour and dynamic range is equally good, it won't capture the rich potential of the original print or negative.

UPPING THE RESOLUTION

Is there a practical limit to the resolution of a scanner? Yes, there is. Over 4000 ppi, a scanner will be capable of resolving the grain structure of most film emulsions and those of a photographic print. In many cases, the resolution of the original artwork will have already been exceeded. There is little purpose, then, in moving much beyond the 4000 ppi level; you get larger files sizes with improved resolution, but you will not get any true improvement in the detail.

DARKROOM SECRETS

SCAN THEN DOWNSAMPLE

To get a scan of a specific resolution, it is usually best to scan at the scanner's highest optical resolution and then downsample in your image-editing application. This is because the algorithm that changes the size within the application is generally more effective than that of the scanner, although the process will take longer.

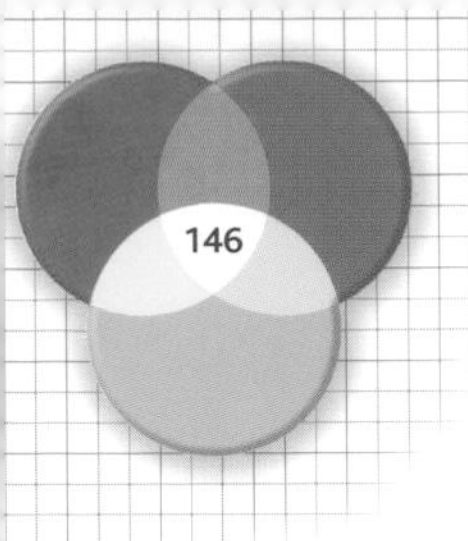

Capturing colours

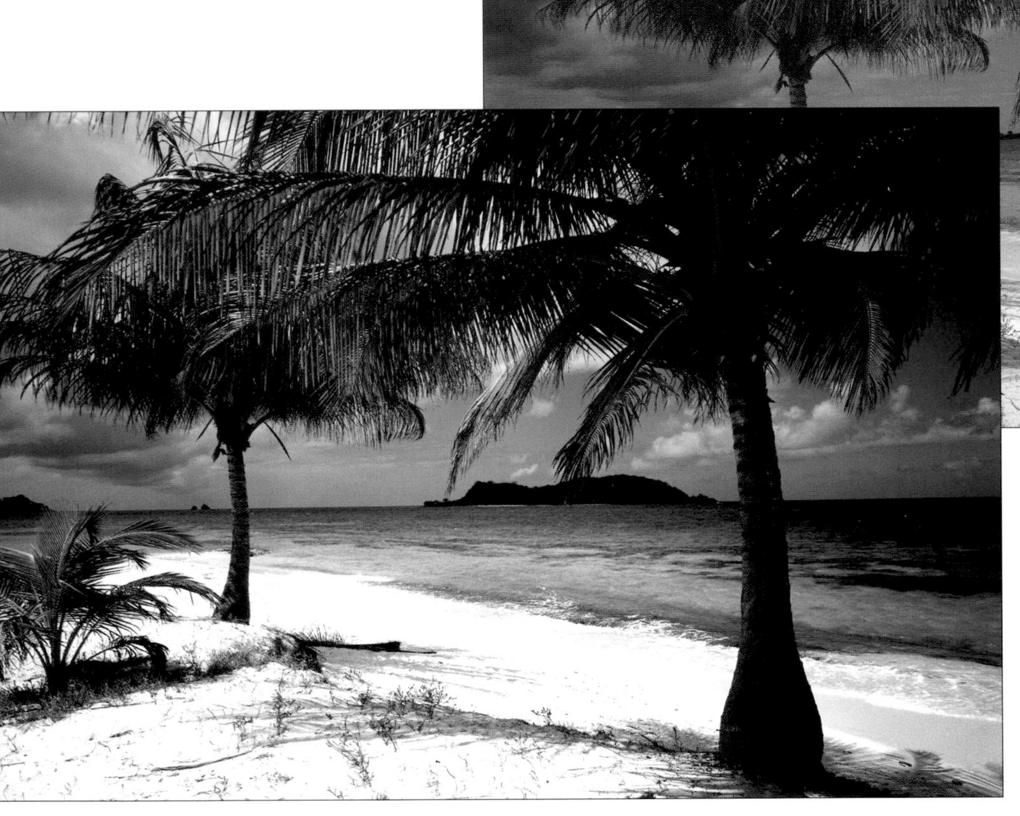

With the black point set incorrectly (top), the whole image suffers from a lack of tonal richness. Set correctly (bottom), the dark tones stand out and there's improvement across the range.

BIT DEPTH

For many professional users, high-resolution scanners have been commonplace – albeit at a price – for some time. For them, the resolution improvements in mid-range machines have been less significant than the improvements in bit depth capture. The bit depth, you will recall, determines the number of discrete colour that can be recorded: the higher the bit depth, the better. Good scanners will offer bit depths of 36 (12 bits per colour channel) or even 48 (16 bits

WHITE AND BLACK POINTS

The dynamic range and dMax become critical when setting the black and white points in the image. The black point represents the tones in the image that (either manually or automatically selected) are to be reproduced as black; the white point, those tones to be represented as white. When performing a scan, we need to ensure that we do not set a black point so low (that is, in the deepest shadows) that it becomes impossible, given the dynamic range, to properly represent the bright highlights. Consider this example: if we set the black point to the darkest shadow (dMax of 3.9) and the dynamic range is 3.7, we'll find any light tones of 0.2 (dMax – dynamic range) will be clipped. Clipping, in this context, means that any highlights above this level will be totally washed out.

per channel). Ultimately, you will downsample your image to 24 bits (8 bits per channel), and this extra capacity may seem a little superfluous. Not so. If you were to begin with a 24-bit image, you would lose tonal information when you performed certain image edits (such as tonal corrections) and end up with a 24-bit image that featured less than 24-bit tonality. Perform the same corrections on a 36-bit image, and you'll find that, when you downsample, you still have the same range of tones that you started with.

DYNAMIC RANGE

The dynamic range is the range of densities that a scanner is capable of recording. It is one of those important performance-defining parameters which manufacturers of some scanners have been very happy to bury out of sight, largely because the figures are so poor. However, now that improved electronics have made better dynamic ranges possible, even with budget scanners, the figures are coming out of the shadows.

Dynamic range figures on their own are somewhat indecisive. They need to be given more precision by defining the darkest shadow area that can be recorded. This is represented by the so-called dMax. Typical dynamic range and dMax figures might be 3.7 and 3.9.

SCANNER TYPES

The workhorse of most digital darkrooms, the flatbed scanner needs little introduction. It is just as much at home performing scans of black-and-white office documents as it is scanning photos and artwork. All but the lowest-priced machines now come complete with – or at least offer the option of – document feeders and transparency hoods that further enhance their capabilities.

Many flatbed scanner models, by virtue of improvements to their resolution and dynamic range, are now adept at scanning transparent media such as slides and negatives. Those with the highest resolutions of 2400 ppi or more can even produce effective scans from 35mm media.

SERVICE BUREAU SCANS

The service bureau makes a great alternative source of digitized images for those requiring only a limited number of scans. You'll need to brief the bureau on what you want from your scans – bureaus, with the best of intentions might convert your image to CMYK or even sharpen your images prior to returning them to you. As scanners scan in RGB, you would do better to request an unconverted file and perform the conversion, if required, later. The same goes for any enhancements. If in doubt, just ask for an unfiltered RGB scan.

But for really superb results, particularly if you have a large number of images to scan, a dedicated film scanner is a better bet. Optimised for transparent media, they are virtually all capable of handling 35mm negatives and (usually via an adaptor) processed APS films. Some models are also capable of scanning medium format and even large format transparencies. Designed to scan small images at very high resolutions, the best of them scan to a level where even the tiniest scratch or speck of dust becomes a problem. As a result, most include software or hardware to intelligently remove such glitches.

Few of us will own a drum scanner, but if we submit material to a pro lab for scanning, chances are that the resulting scans will have been produced on one. They produce the best results, but are not nearly as easy to use as either of the previous types. Have your images scanned in a drum scanner, and you will have absolutely noiseless shadows and nearly perfect colour fidelity. There are, however, restrictions on the media that can be scanned. Originals (reflective or transparent) have to be wrapped around the drum, instantly precluding mounted images or pages from books.

DARKROOM SECRETS

CALIBRATION TARGETS

An accurately calibrated scanner is a prerequisite for high scan fidelity. Though most scanners are precisely configured out of the box, you can use for critical work a standard target image such as the IT 8.7/2 designed for colour prints. Your local camera shop can order these for you. Detailed instructions should accompany the target image.

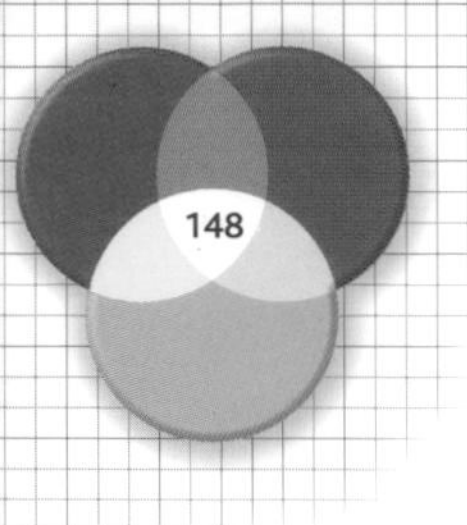

Performing a scan

DARKROOM SECRETS 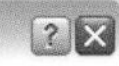

GETTING THE BEST FROM YOUR SCANS

- Ensure that your originals are flat and free of creases and kinks.
- Clean both the scanner plate and the originals using lint-free cloths or photographic brushes.
- Take glass-mounted slides out of their mounts to avoid interference fringes ('Newton's Rings').
- Select only well-exposed originals, if at all possible. Underexposed transparencies can be problematic.
- Prints made on glossy paper work best, particularly if the original is small. Satin-finish or textured papers should be avoided if possible.
- Avoid using filters such as *Sharpen* during the scan; the sharpening filters of your image editor are at least as efficient (and probably more so), and sharpening during the scan adds to scanning time.

Your scanner will have been shipped with driver software, an application that controls the scanner, comprising a stand-alone program or a plug-in for your image-editing application. In the latter case, you can launch the software from within the image editor, usually by selecting either *File > Open > [scanner name]* or *File>Import>[scanner name]*, depending on the program. With some scanner models, you may even be able to launch the scanner software just by pressing a button on the device itself.

However you invoke the scanner, you will need to use the driver to acquire your image and, by making adjustments to the driver's settings, ensure that you get the best capture possible.

While all scanner driver software does approximately the same job, there is a large amount of variation when it comes to features. Some include additional proprietary tools, such as automatic enhancements or dust and scratch removal filters, while others offer high levels of intervention controls.

The first step when scanning is to perform a prescan. This is a quick, low resolution scan that is normally conducted using default settings. It enables you to see your originals within the whole scanning area, then crop the area so that you only scan what you actually need.

LEVEL CONTROLS

If you are really fortunate, your driver will feature a histogram and densitometer. The histogram shows the tonal distribution of the image, illustrating in graphical form the number of pixels in the image at each grey level (there are 255 from deepest black to whitest white). From the histogram you can tell, almost at a glance, whether your scan will contain the required full tonal range. If the histogram is missing any components, the final image could be compromised. Some drivers will let you correct for discrepancies in the histogram. You can make changes in much the same way that you would in the *Levels* dialog box (*see page 26*). In the case of

SCANNERS: TESTING TIMES

Using a black-and-white print is a good way to test the quality of any scanner. Colour images often look good, even if just superficially, because the colour components to the image dominate.

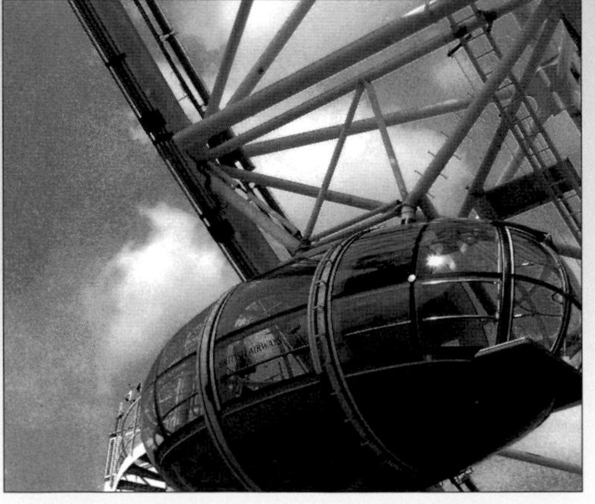

Scan a good black-and-white print and examine it closely. The characteristics of poor performance are posterization in tonal gradients and gaps in the tonal range. The bad news is that you won't be able to 'fix' these images, or at least you won't be able to do so without an unreasonable amount of remedial work. The best solution is to scan the photo in colour (if at all possible) and desaturate the resulting scan in your image-editing application. In this way, you'll end up with a better print that will better respond to a little intelligent post-production.

This example illustrates such faults in the continuous tonal areas. Though other areas seem unaffected, the sky towards the left of the image shows all of the obvious signs of banding.

GAMMA ADJUSTMENT

Gamma adjustment involves making changes to the midtones of an image without affecting the shadows and highlights, as long as those changes are not too large. Few scanner drivers permit 'live' gamma adjustments, relying on users to make these adjustments post-scan using the Levels *controls. This is something of a shame, as most scans need some gamma correction. Scans typically have over-dark midtones that correspond to the scanner's direct reproduction of the original: a gamma of 1:1 or 1.0. Though technically authentic, our eyes (and, indeed, the computer monitor) interpret brightness in a nonlinear way that points to a gamma of around 1.8 or even 2.0 as an appropriate value.*

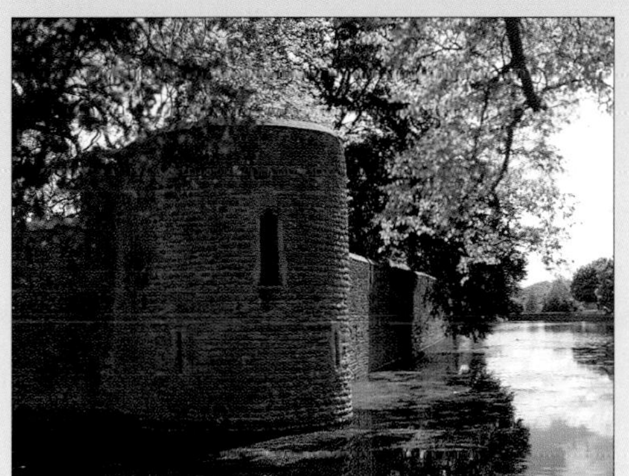

GAMMA 1.0

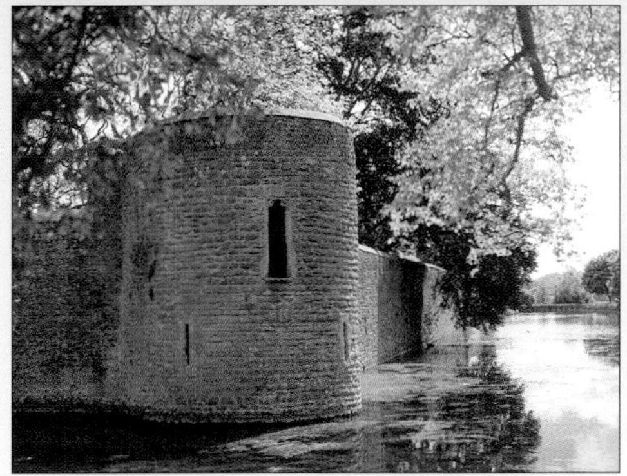

GAMMA 2.0

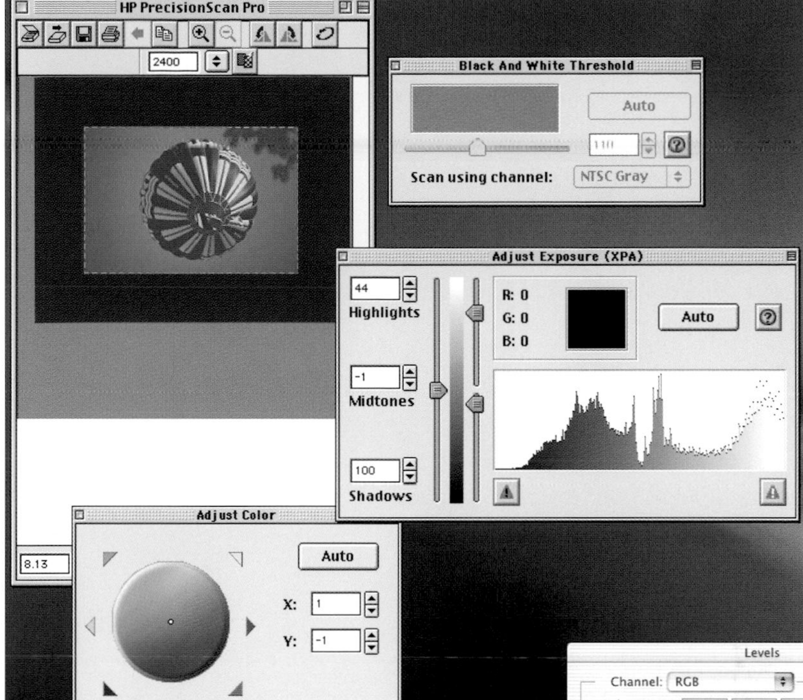

the driver shown above (HP's Precision Scan Pro), we are able to make adjustments to the histogram and even the hue and saturation, using the appropriate supplementary dialog boxes.

Though not many drivers feature all the control shown here – which in many ways is unforgivable – some do at least feature black-and-white point settings. With these, you can manually configure the tonal range by selecting those pixels you wish to define as black and those you want to represent as white. Again, the process is similar to that explored with the *Levels* feature. Some drivers even feature histogram and slider controls identical to those of the *Levels* dialog, while others make do with the slightly more rudimentary eyedroppers. If at all practical, it is important to choose a neutral black-and-white point, because selecting one with a colour cast could compromise the colour fidelity of the image as a whole. If your driver includes one, a densitometer is ideal for identifying whether your chosen point is truly neutral, so avoiding any danger of tainting the colours in the final capture. If not, you will just have to make a 'best guess'.

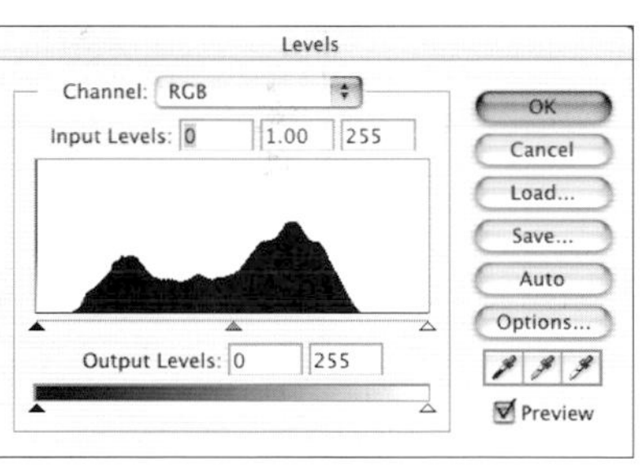

The Levels palette for a good scan (top) and a bad one (bottom). The histogram in the good example shows that the scan has captured the full range of tonal levels. In the bottom scan, levels are clumped together in the middle, and less data has been captured.

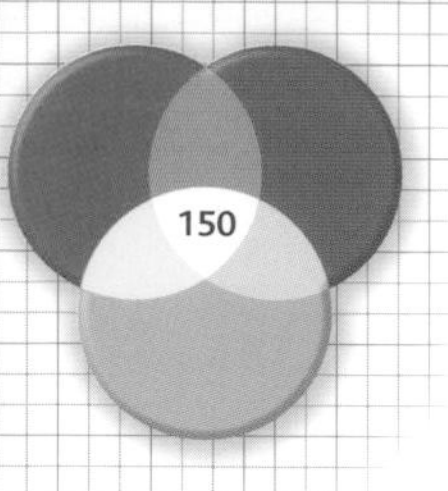

Other input options

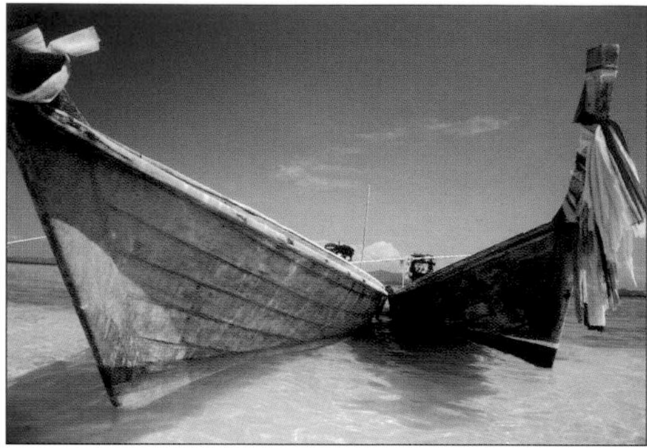

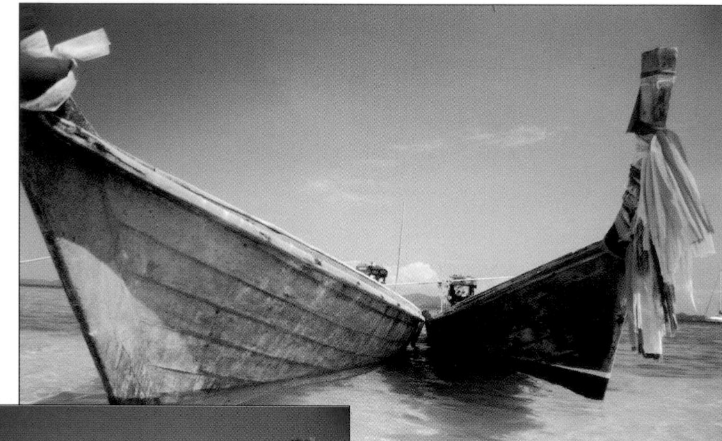

In-camera effects are no substitute for their image-editor equivalents. With an effect applied, digital camera images can be even more compromised in terms of tonal and contrast ranges.

IMAGES FROM DIGITAL CAMERAS

In a few short years, digital cameras have come up from the back of the pack to vie with digitized film stock as the principal source of digital images. Granted, despite all the advances in resolution and performance over the past few years, digital cameras are still some way from matching the ultimate versatility of their film-based stablemates, but to denigrate digital cameras purely because they do not match these characteristics is to do them a great disservice. In fact, we could put the argument in reverse and suggest it will be some time – if ever – before conventional cameras match the more advanced characteristics of digital models.

Anything we say about digital cameras will be something of a sweeping generalisation. The range of types and formats far exceeds that of conventional cameras, and the technology advances almost daily. Nonetheless, we can highlight a few issues relating to the use of images direct from nearly any digital camera.

Compression: The size of high-resolution digital images means that the images need to be compressed if the camera memory cards are to hold more than a handful of images. Sadly, compression is generally of the lossy JPEG type, which does, to some degree, compromise image

DARKROOM SECRETS

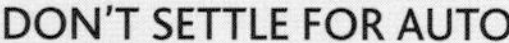

DON'T SETTLE FOR AUTO

Digital cameras feature a white balance control that ensures the scene will be free of colour casts. In most cases, the control includes presets for a range of common lighting conditions, including sun and blue sky, overcast sky, tungsten lighting and a range of fluorescent lighting types. In general, you will find that you get more satisfactory results by selecting one of these presets over the auto setting.

TIPS FOR BUYING PICTURES

- *Assess your need. Do you really need to buy a picture? Have you got something already that would work just as well?*
- *Survey the marketplace. Some libraries and agencies are better disposed towards the casual purchaser than others that are better geared for the professional.*
- *Check the stock photos that come with some image-editing applications. Quality can be variable, but they can often provide useful images for free.*
- *If you do buy, or are using free stock photos, check any restrictions on use. You may be limited in terms of how you ultimately use the images, and you might find there are stiff guidelines on the ways you can edit them!*

BUYING PICTURES

If you find that you need to use images from other photographers, you have a choice of options. That choice is an important one. Images are now available from a wide range of sources and vary almost as much in quality and price as they do in subject matter.

Photo libraries represent the most comprehensive source of good quality material. All the large libraries are aware of the needs of the digital darkroom worker, and images are generally optimised for those requirements. You'll often be able to choose from a range of image sizes and qualities; there's no point in paying for a high-resolution image if you intend to use it only as a thumbnail. Purchase options frequently include anything from whole CDs of images grouped by thematic subject, down to galleries of selected images and an individual shot. Pricing varies enormously and in many cases depends on the intended use of the image. Major commercial applications often command high pricing regimes, whereas noncommercial ventures will attract lower payments. Shop around to avoid paying through the nose.

quality. Some cameras permit the saving of data using the more satisfactory TIFF format or even as raw image data. Use these options for important images and whenever space permits.

Dynamic range: The dynamic range of many cameras (particularly low-budget, consumer models) is lower than ideal. The pictures produced will be tonally compressed and lacking in highlight and shadow detail. Try to avoid using *Auto Levels* (or similar) to correct these. Opt instead for the finer control of *Levels* and *Hue/Saturation*. Where tones are unduly compressed, auto controls tend to produce banding effects that are minimised when the alternate manual controls are used.

In-camera effects and corrections: Many digital cameras offer a range of special effects that can be applied to an image. Stay well clear of them! None of these effects is particularly effective and, once embedded in your image, they are impossible to remove. If you need one of these effects, take a straight shot and apply the same effect later in your image-editing application. You'll have much more control. The same advice goes for any sharpening effects. Though a sharpened image may look better when downloaded, it contains no more picture detail than would an unsharpened copy. And the sharpening tools your image editor puts at your disposal are far more effective.

Tone controls: Some cameras – and these tend to be the most expensive professional models – also offer tone curve control. This is a feature that – if your camera possesses it – can be used to great effect. We won't go into detail here, as the workings will be more better described in the camera's manual, although most tone controls let you alter the gamma, brightness and contrast.

Using the camera's white balance control correctly can avoid colour casts such as these (due to using a tungsten setting outdoors). Note how the sky colour is fine but the stonework and foliage have taken on a pallid appearance.

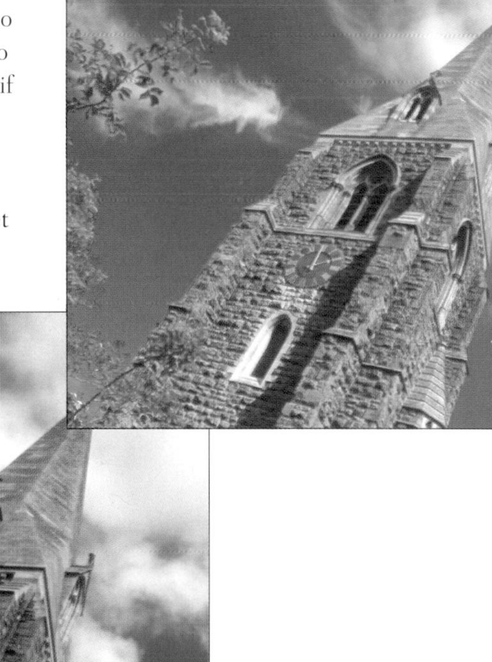

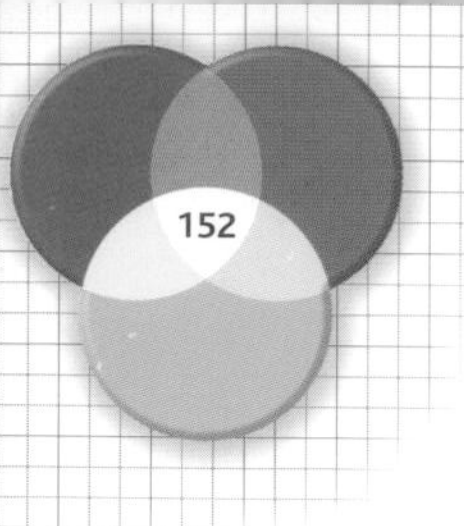

Images on disk

Photo CD and image CD are the two principal ways in which conventional images are written to CD. The term 'image CD' covers a range of proprietary formats, of which the most widely available is probably Kodak's PictureCD.

The idea behind the PictureCD was to scan 35mm films during processing and supply the digital images on a CD along with any prints. As well as the images, the CD usually includes some simple image-editing and cataloguing software.

The only drawback of this process for the more serious user is that the scanning is, by necessity, a fast, automated process resulting in average rather than good scans. In addition, the resulting digital files are stored as compressed JPEG files. Hence the image files (around 6MB per 35mm original) do not really capture their full quality, although they are generally good enough for most purposes.

The somewhat better Photo CD format was launched in the early 1990s as both a way of providing high-quality digital images for computer use and a way of presenting these images in a domestic environment. Enhanced CD players could play back Photo CDs as slide shows through a conventional television and the viewers had the opportunity to review, zoom and crop selected images live on screen. This element of the format floundered somewhat, but Photo CD has been pretty successful otherwise.

The unique feature of the Photo CD is the image file format. Called Image Pac, it records each image at five different resolutions, ranging from the thumbnail-size (128 x 192 pixels) Base/16 through to 16 Base (2048 x 3072), but only 16 Base and 4 Base (1024 x 1536 pixels) are of practical use. The files for each image are stored using a lossless compression regime, while a nifty technique means that the different file resolutions are stored as changes, or 'residues' (Kodak's term), from the base resolution.

AVOID THE PICT!

A word of warning. If you are using a Mac, it is tempting to open the Photo CD, then open the Photos subfolder and select your image. Though the image will look fine whether viewed from within Photoshop, or even when opened by Picture Viewer or Preview, these copies are actually PICT format images designed only for on-screen use. Though they can look as good as the 'real' images, the dynamic range used often results in clipped, washed-out highlights. Avoid!

The Photo CD dialog box is packed with options, enabling you to choose a colour profile, mode and resolution that best captures the qualities of the original image.

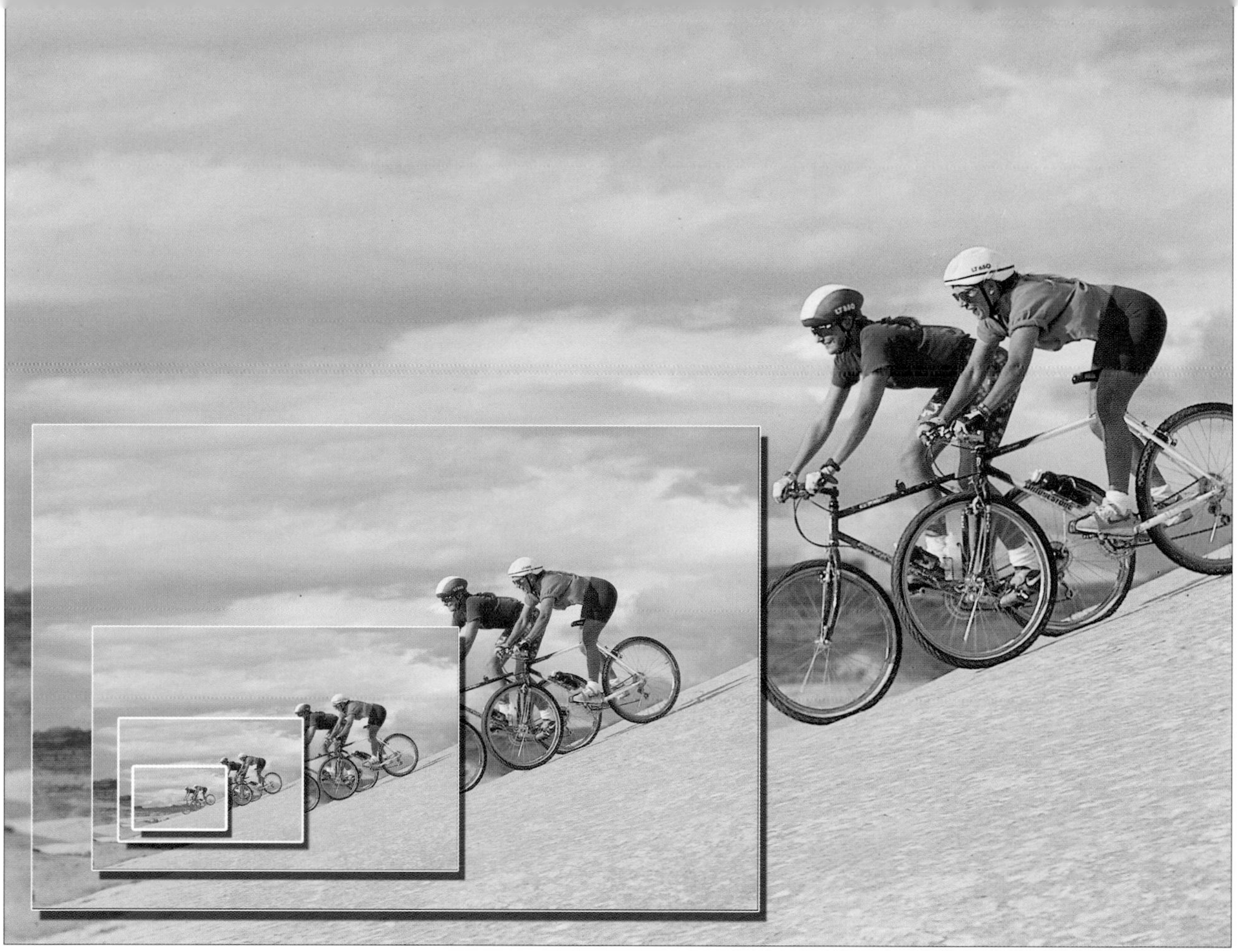

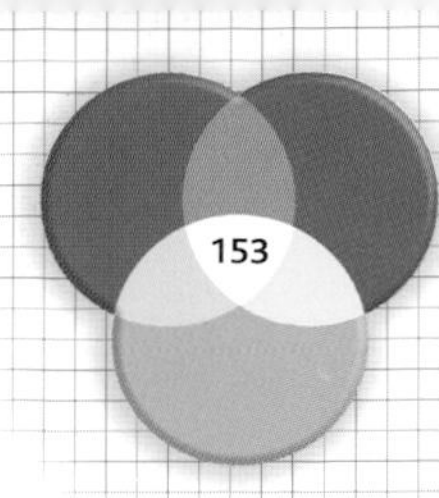

USING PHOTO CD IMAGES

Photo CD disks can be loaded onto any modern computer platform, and virtually all image-editing, illustration and painting applications will read and understand the format.

You select an image as you would any other, navigating through the Photo CD folder, and then through the Images folder to the relevant image number. Click on this to open the Kodak PCD Format dialog box.

The dialog allows the selection of any of the Photo CD resolutions from the Pixel Size drop-down menu. You can also choose a colour profile. If possible, choose one that most closely matches that of the film stock used to take the original image. Where uncertain, or the information in the *Image Info* window is vague, use the Universal E-6 for slide originals and Color Negative for negative originals.

You can also choose to open the image as a 24-bit (8 bits per channel) RGB image, 48-bit RGB, or a Photoshop Lab colour mode image. Lab was once the preferred option because RGB Photo CD images tended to look clipped, but now both are equally valid.

Note that, once you edit your image, you won't normally be able to save it back in PCD format. In most cases, you'll be prompted to save it as a TIFF, which, as you don't lose any image data, is usually a better choice than a JPEG.

PHOTOCD QUALITY

How good is a PhotoCD image? Kodak introduced the format to achieve the highest practical quality from the originals and they have worked hard with the licensed laboratories to maintain quality. But Photo CD scanning is a semi-automated process and subject to the same limitations as other scanning processes. A good PhotoCD scan is very good, but average-quality scans are also widely encountered. Professional Photo CD (Pro Photo CD) is one solution for those needing the best quality at all times. You pay a premium price, but images are of higher quality and feature a sixth, larger (18MB) image version.

Image Pac provides multiple resolutions. It is best to regard the smaller ones as thumbnails and use only the larger two for your image manipulations.

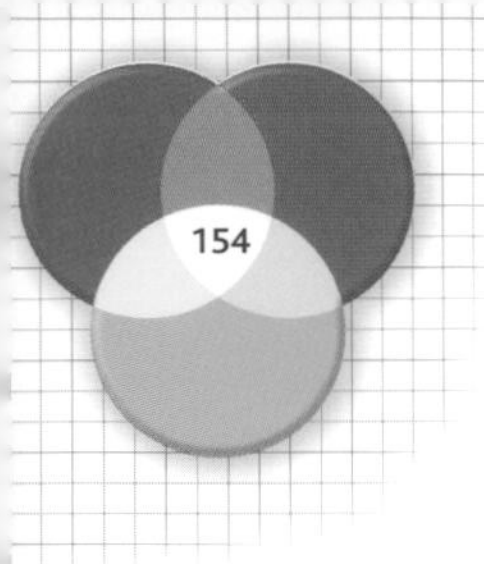

Image-editing applications

To take in the comprehensive nature of Photoshop's abilities, you need only to take a look at the myriad options and combinations offered by the Layers *palette on its own.*

Image-editing applications are as important in the digital darkroom as the camera that took the images in the first place. And, like cameras, there are countless options vying for your attention, ranging from the software equivalent of the disposable APS camera through to the top of the range professional SLR.

Let's take a look at the essential requirements of an image-editing application and also the important areas in which the first rank applications differ. We will also look at those applications that we would call 'accessories'. Not designed to be your front line in image manipulation, these tools give added firepower to your arsenal and will ultimately help you to create more stunning imagery.

In the right hands, virtually any application is capable of being used to produce impressive images. Having said that, there are some applications that enforce a working methodology which is just not appropriate for the serious digital darkroom worker. Designed for the casual consumer, they are designed to make simple image enhancements and corrections as easy as possible. Once you start using the tools in the more creative or abstract ways required for intensive image manipulation, you might find your way fraught with problems. As in any other work, we need to find tools that are appropriate to our needs, and this can limit our choices.

For many of us, those choices have already been made. We might look over our shoulder at times and examine the alternatives favoured by our peers, but once you learn one application, you will more easily find further ways of exploiting it. The good news – particularly for those who might fear that they have made the wrong decision – is that all contemporary products are packed with useful features and very powerful.

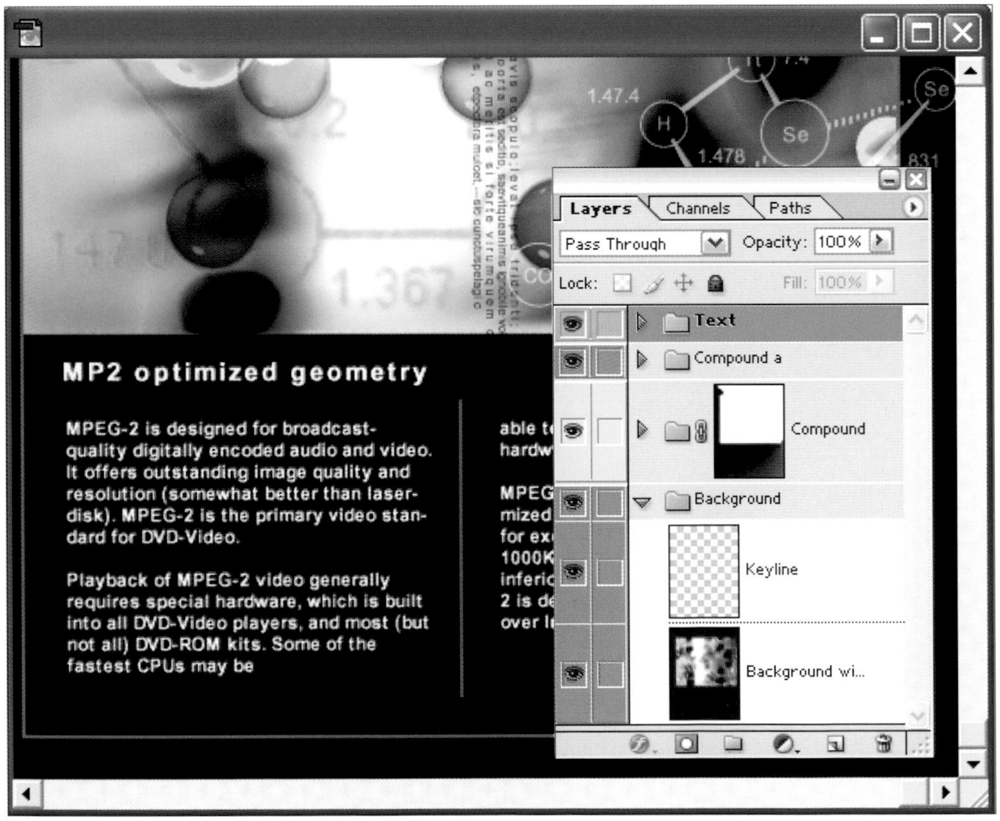

SOFTWARE: THE UNIQUE SELLING PROPOSITIONS

Ask the image-editing professional or digital artist which product they use, and they will be likely to tell you 'several', though each would have a favoured application upon which most of their work would be done. The nature of the professional's work is such that even the most extensive image-editing application will not feature all the tools and options which would be required for them to meet their clients' or their own design criteria.

Most of the principal image-editing applications boast the same core image-editing tools. However, for many users the subtle unique features of each become increasingly important. To use the jargon of the software houses' marketing departments, each has unique selling propositions (USPs) that make them special. To really understand an application, you need to look at it in that sort of context.

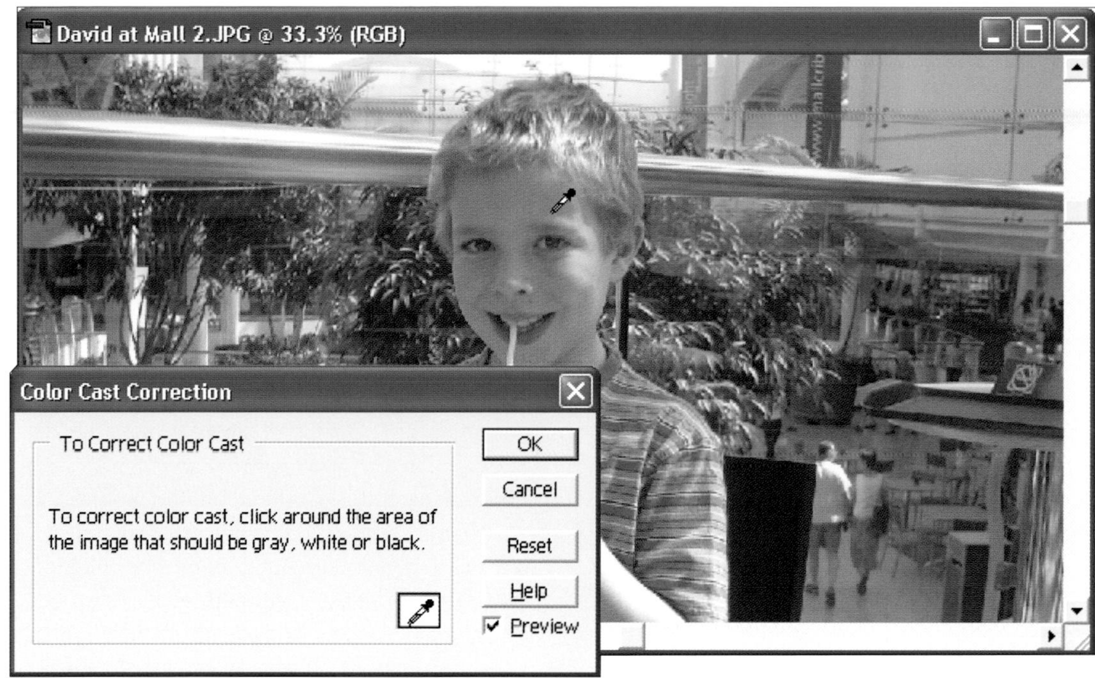

Photoshop Elements includes some features that can not be found in the parent application. Most are specifically designed for the enthusiast digital photographer, such as this colour cast 'quick fix' tool.

PHOTOSHOP (Adobe Systems)

Throughout the 1990s, Photoshop was the exemplar image-editing application by which all potential pretenders were judged. It retains that position today and is the accepted industry standard. Photoshop has managed this by offering a specification to the photographer, pre press worker and Web designer that makes it practically impossible to better, plus an interface that makes working with it as fast and slick as possible.

A number of Web tools (such as image slicing and optimization features) are included in Photoshop, but many more are provided in ImageReady, a sister product that combines all the essential Photoshop image-editing tools with a full range of Web tools. ImageReady now comes supplied with Photoshop, and documents can be quickly shuffled between the two when necessary to exploit the unique powers of each.

TOOLS OF THE TRADE

Our comparison of some image-editing applications to a professional SLR is quite apt. Professionals tend to use top-specification SLRs because they can be configured – by interchanging lenses, adding filters and other accessories – precisely to meet the demands of the current job. Likewise many software applications have some degree of flexibility in their configuration. Not only can you customise the workspace according to your needs, you can also install software plug-ins (the equivalent of new lenses) that will add general or specific functionality to the host program.

PHOTOSHOP ELEMENTS (Adobe Systems)

Photoshop has a drawback, and it is a big one: the price tag. This price precludes many serious amateurs or enthusiasts taking advantage of it. Photoshop Elements is Adobe's solution. You retain the slick interface and all the key image-editing features, but lose the pre-press tools and some of the Web functions. As recompense, you get some unique, easy-to-use tools covering the most common image-editing operations.

DARKROOM SECRETS 

THE BARGAIN BASEMENT

If you need a particular feature that is included in an image-editing package which is not your 'native' application, you may find it cheaper to buy the previous version of that software, assuming those features are also available on this. Previous versions can often be downloaded from the vendor's website, in some cases at no charge at all!

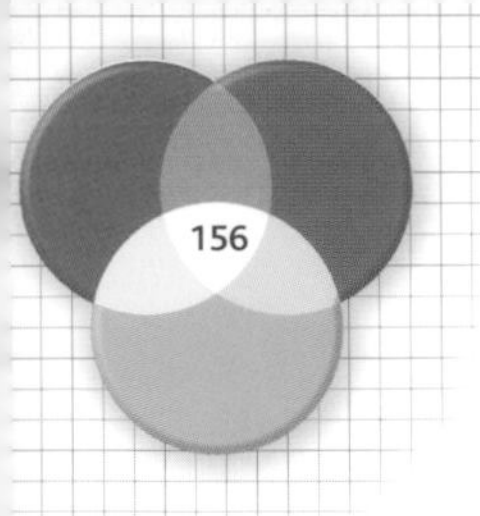

Paintshop Pro's advanced features are ideal for working with scanned images, and its low price makes it an attractive choice for Windows users.

PAINTSHOP PRO (Jasc Software)

Though it originated as a painting tool, Paintshop Pro is now a very comprehensive image-editing tool in the mould of Photoshop but priced for the enthusiast. It is hard to think of a decisive USP that would place Paintshop Pro ahead of the competition. Instead, think of it is a great all-rounder that is widely used (meaning help and support abound) and capable of creating stunning imagery. It is supplied complete with Animation Shop, an application designed for the creation of Animated GIFS for websites.

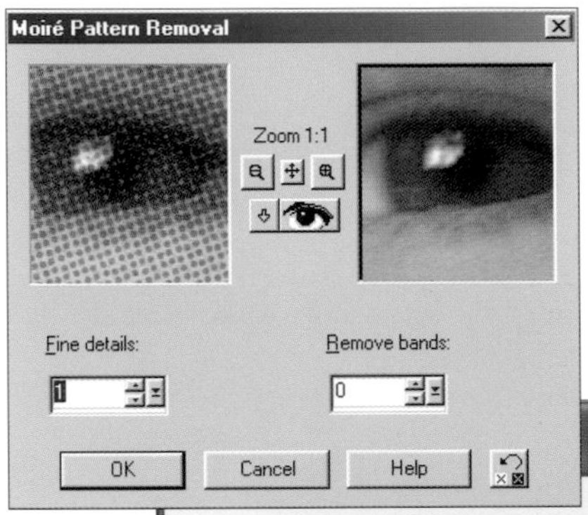

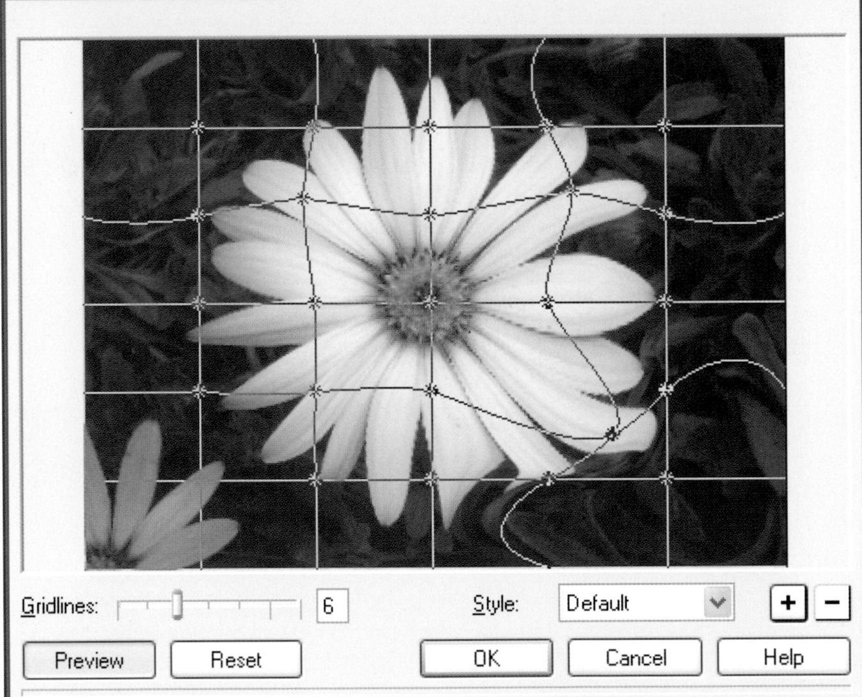

Though similar in many respects to other high-level image-editing applications, a few features such as the Mesh Warp (shown here) have established Photo-Paint as a leader rather than a follower.

PHOTO-PAINT (Corel)

Though overshadowed by CorelDraw (Corel's graphics mammoth), of which it is only the image-editing element, Photo-Paint is another superbly specified image editor. It is preferred by many workers on account of the close integration

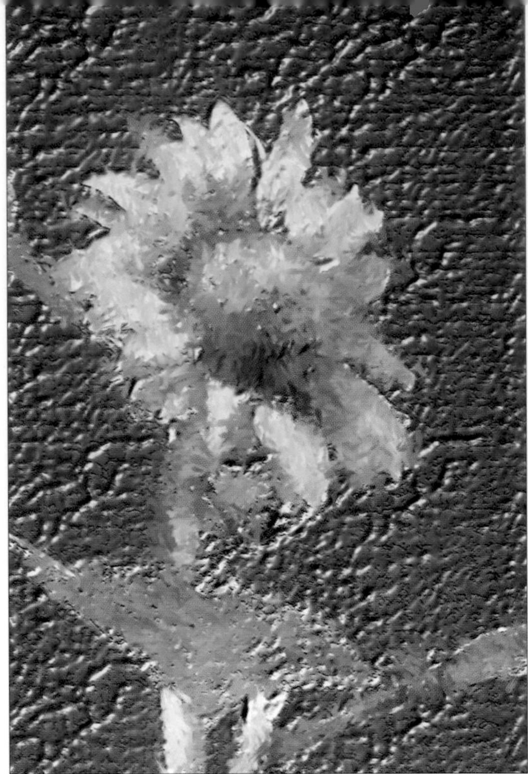

between it and the other CorelDraw components, simplifying any illustrative work that needs to combine painting, image-editing and vector-based illustration. It is also available as a standalone-package, and also as a component of Corel Graphics Suite for Macintosh.

CorelDraw Essentials is a pared down version of the 'full' CorelDraw application and includes version 9.0 of Photo-Paint. Given that the latter was itself a far-reaching and effective tool, this Windows-only application is an economic way of entering the Corel graphics environment.

PAINTER (Procreate)

As you might expect, Painter's forte is the way that it simulates the use and effects of traditional media – paint, pastels and crayons – letting users create artwork with a very high level of realism. It offers a wide range of painting tools, along with an equally extensive number of textures and paper finishes that can be used as painting surfaces. Later versions of Painter have added some more digital art tools to further increase the range of effects possible.

With further enhancements to its image-editing tools, Painter's versatility has grown even more. Now workers can prepare their images from a scanned photograph or digital camera and then convert them into artworks within a single program environment.

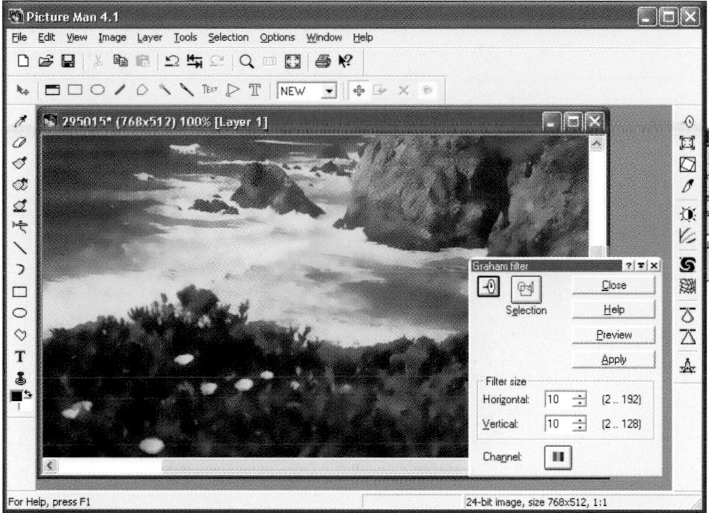

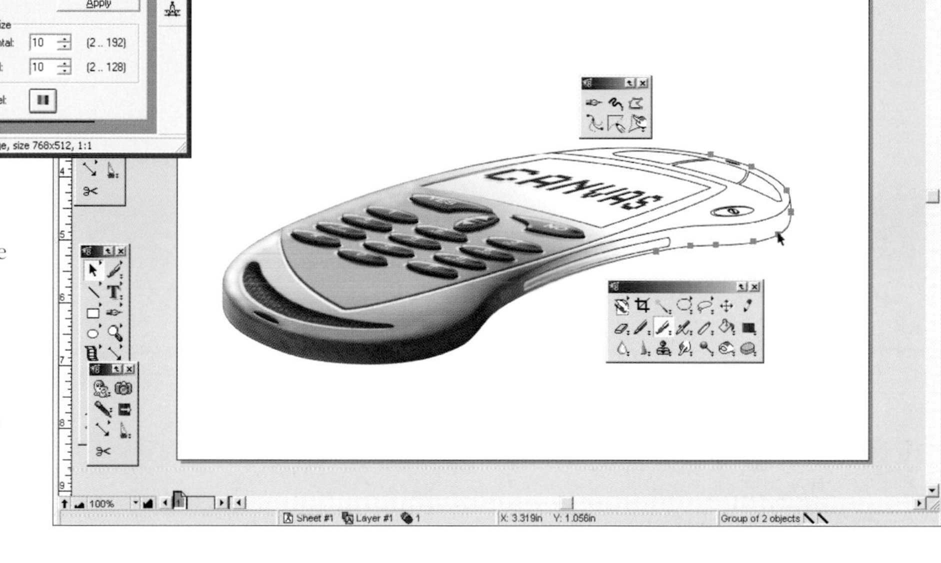

PICTURE MAN (Stoik Software)

The little known Picture Man from Stoik software is an idiosyncratic application that, with some amount of lateral thinking, delivers a working environment that is subtly but fundamentally different from virtually any other. Most obviously, Picture Man uses a nonmodal interface. This lets users run several instances of the same tool concurrently on the desktop and also keep (and adjust) multiple tools simultaneously on your working canvas. This mimics 'real world' situations, where we rarely perform one task to the exclusion of all others.

Furthermore, brushes are used throughout, including the application of filters. The brush can be defined in any way that you wish (as with an advanced painting brush tool) so that the effects filter can be applied in a very precise and controlled way. As well as boasting a conventional raft of effects filters (and compatibility with Photoshop plug-in filters), Picture Man includes some unique and useful tools, such as a sigma filter and Graham filter. These additional effects alone have won this application many converts.

Another intriguing feature of this application is that it can run in automatic mode. This is, in effect, an animated tutorial, which proves useful if you need to understand how complex retouching techniques are applied. An effective camera noise suppression facility completes a potent specification.

CANVAS (Deneba)

Whereas Painter has successfully married a painting environment with an image editor, Deneba's Canvas combines image-editing tools with vector graphic illustration tools that are normally the preserve of illustration applications. To this mix it adds for good measure a selection of painting media and textures. Photorealistic and pure vector illustrations can be produced from imported images, but the most interesting effects are the hybrids that call on the use of features from both camps.

This dichotomous approach has led to Canvas being adopted by many graphic design professionals, who appreciate the fluidity of working with both pixel-based images and illustrative elements. Another powerful feature, DenebaShare, makes it possible for several artists to work on the same artwork across a network or Internet connection at the same time.

TOP LEFT

The singular approach taken by Stoik in their Picture Man software means that a number of idiosyncratic but useful features are included that you will not find elsewhere. The Graham filter, shown here, is a good example.

ABOVE RIGHT

Illustrator or image editor? It's hard to categorise Canvas. It's a powerful application, combining successful elements of each plus a few novel touches for good measure.

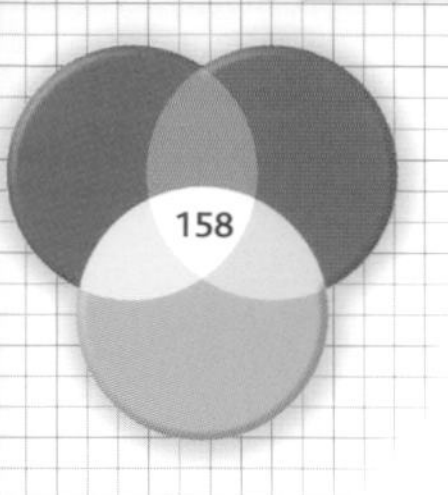

Software accessories

Though it is a term rarely applied to software, accessory is an apt description for a range of packages that work as supporting acts to your main applications. Some of these are complete stand-alone products, others are modules that fit into your image editor. Either way, they can provide extra creative tools or functionality that you would not normally find elsewhere.

You will find the Internet is awash with image-editing applications, filter plug-ins, cataloguing software, and more that can lay claim to your attention. Some of these are just digital white elephants, the equivalent of the multiprism-rainbow polarizer filter you bought once but have never used. Some, however, could become an essential part of your digital darkroom. They might give your work a real creative edge, or they might just make it easier to get the dull grunt-work done more rapidly. The following list is not exhaustive, by any means, and does not suggest that any alternatives are inferior. Instead, it simply points the way to some of the most useful accessories around.

PIXELNHANCE (Caffeine Software)

The Internet offers tons of image-editing programs of varying degrees of efficiency, often offered as shareware or freeware. None truly match the power of Photoshop or its rivals, but there are some gems that excel in limited areas. PixelNhance is one: a Mac OS X-only application features a range of image enhancement tools, including a five-point histogram tool.

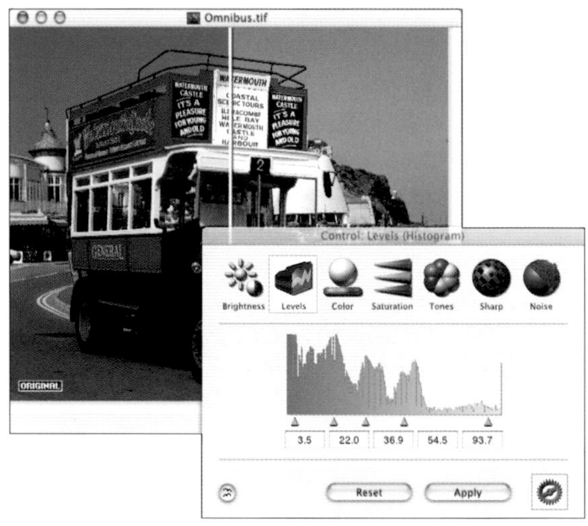

BRYCE (Corel)

Not a product for the photorealist, Bryce's *raison d'être* is the creation of landscapes or 3D terrain. Used commercially to visualise bizarre and alien landscapes, Bryce can also render real landscapes when supplied with appropriately encoded terrain data. But it earns a place in the photographer's tool chest as an easy way to produce skyscapes and seascapes. Once Bryce has rendered its final image, the resolution and level of detail will be equivalent to that of anything you can capture with a digital camera or scanner, and fantasy landscapes are just as easy.

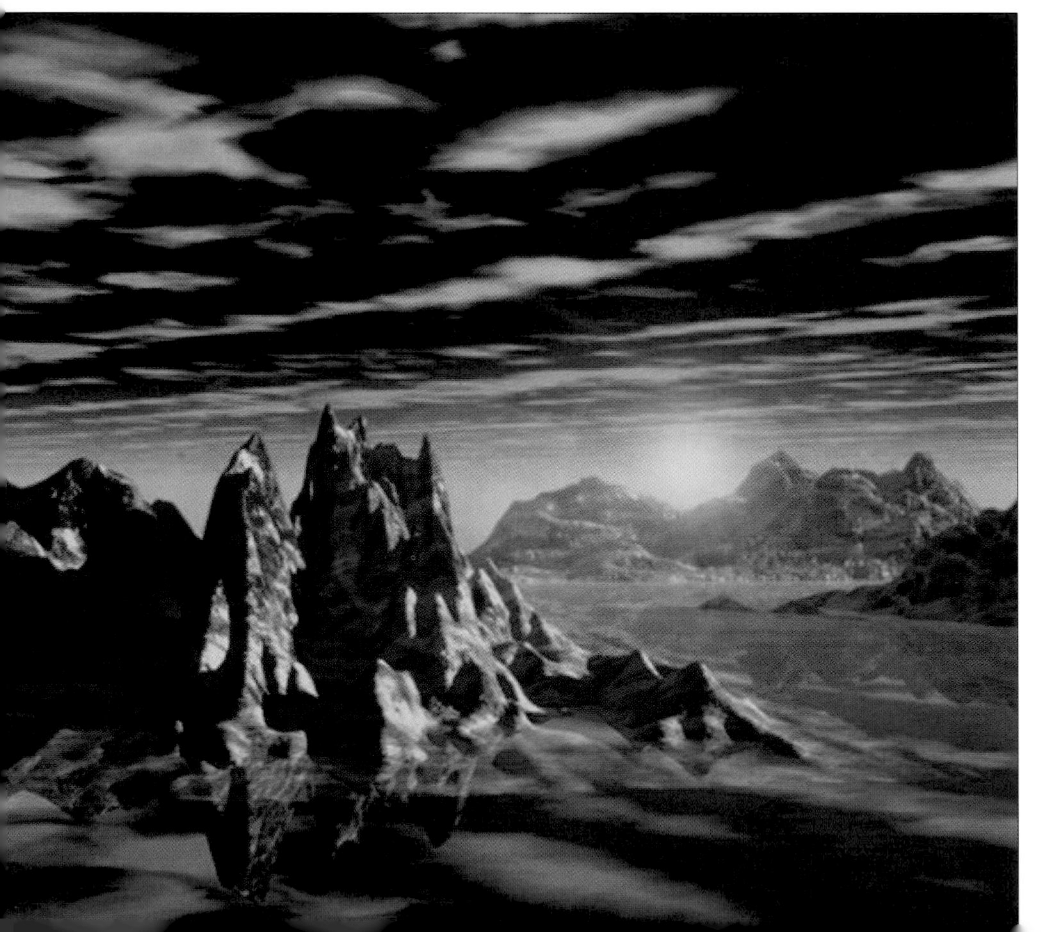

Bryce is capable of rendering skyscapes in as much detail as required. The user can vary the angle, lighting and colour ad infinitum, starting from any one of a library of presets. Once a skyscape has been rendered, it can be combined with an image to replace the existing sky.

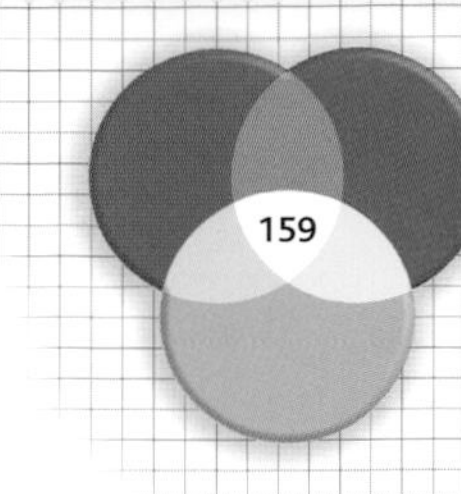

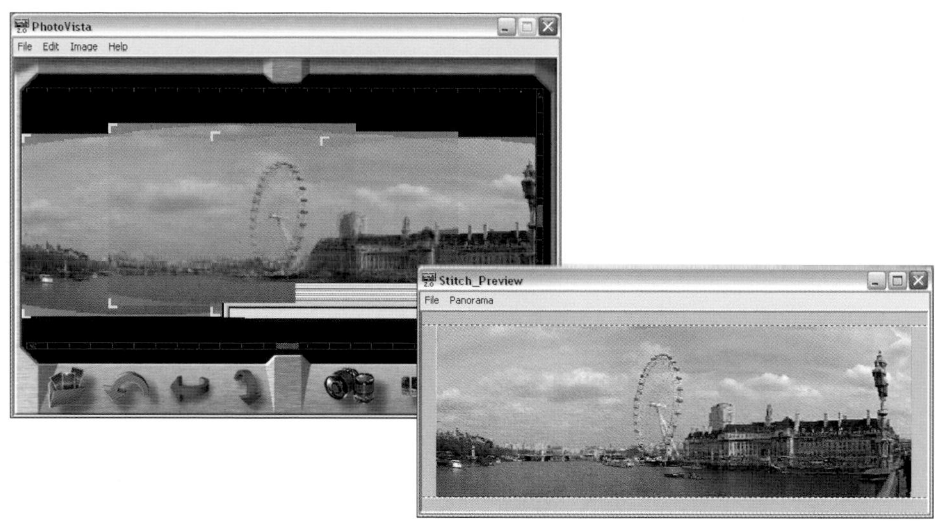

ABOVE LEFT

Panorama generators (such as PhotoVista) can create true 360° panoramas or wide-angle views that are beyond the usual scope of the camera. This is particularly useful when used with digital cameras, many of which have restricted wide-angle focal lengths. In the example shown here, four photographs (with an overlap of around 40% between each) have been combined to give a panoramic image of London's South Bank.

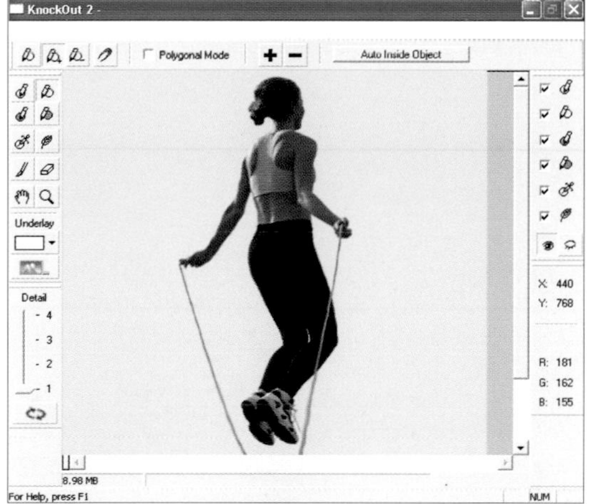

MIDDLE LEFT

Separating a subject from the background is often difficult, particularly when the boundaries are very blurred. KnockOut makes the process comparatively simple by identifying and allocating every pixel to either the background or foreground.

BELOW

Once you have digitized your images, there's a chance that you could easily lose track of them. As a result, a good cataloguing application like Portfolio is pretty much essential.

PHOTOVISTA (ISee Media)

For those applications that don't include facilities for creating panoramic shots (*see page 106-109*) PhotoVista will do the job. It is a good example of a stand-alone panorama generator, and while the mechanics of stitching are complex, the results achieved can be very good indeed. For those who take panoramic shots only occasionally, the results stand up well against those from a professional panoramic camera. Images created by PhotoVista can even be used (with the appropriate player and viewer software) in QuickTime VR (Virtual Reality) environments. Sadly, the latest version is Windows only.

KNOCKOUT (Procreate)

The selection of an image element is one of the most common tasks in image-editing. When the subject is a simple shape, this process is usually straightforward, but when the subject is more complex – such as a person, or a plant – it can be more problematic. For success you will need to draw precisely around the subject's edge. Luckily, there is an alternative to tracing around every hair and struggling to avoid the selection of background areas between hair strands. It is much easier to use a masking tool such as Procreate's KnockOut, which will preserve the fine image details that would be impossible to mask using conventional selection or masking tools. Even fine filamentary subjects, such as smoke and fur, can be isolated. The same goes for liquids, which are easily separated from their containers.

KnockOut is a Photoshop plug-in that can be used in any compatible application, including Corel Photo-Paint or Paintshop Pro.

PORTFOLIO (Extensis)

Nothing to do with image manipulation per se, Portfolio is a popular image database, essential for keeping track not only of your images but of all your other media resources. Portfolio will also produce image previews, slideshows and custom layouts that can, depending on the program version, be shared across a network or the Internet. Obviously, that is of more use if you're working within a large team, but some form of image catalogue system is a must for any serious user.

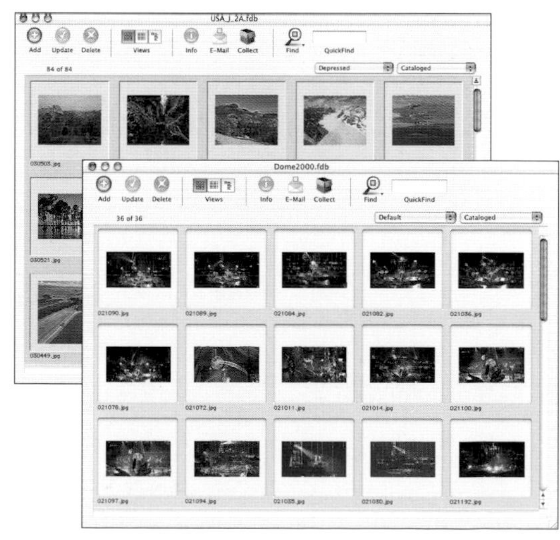

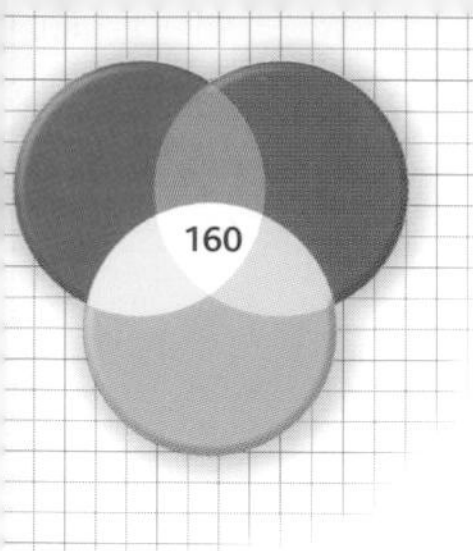

Interfaces and tool box

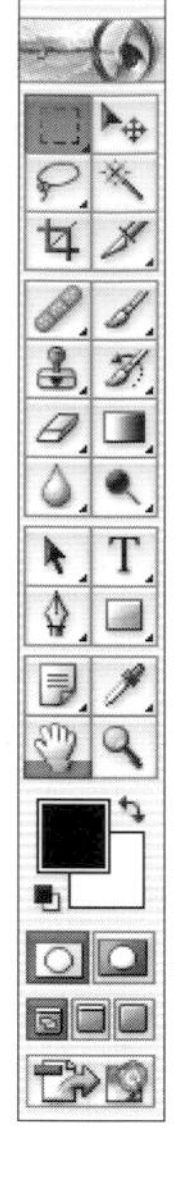

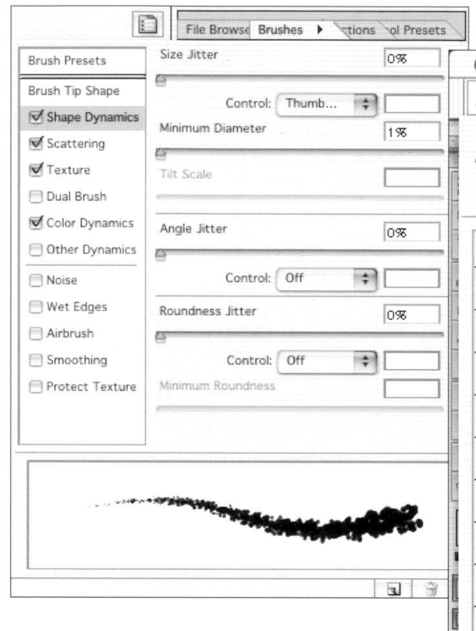

ABOVE RIGHT

The main Photoshop tool palette, containing the most-used brushes, selection tools and other features. More detailed options palettes allow more control over how each tool behaves in practice.

Whatever your favoured application, the interface will broadly follow a similar layout and feature similar components. The interface, if it has been successfully created, should be the feature of the application that you pay least attention to, the enabler that places all the tools and features of the application if not at your fingertips, at your mousetip. Software engineers have laboured long and hard – with varying amounts of success – to create interfaces that are slick and efficient. Image-editing and painting applications rely more than most on an efficient interface, and it is in these that you see some of the best examples of their art. Though Photoshop is generally acknowledged to have the slickest of interfaces, competing products are not far behind. The different ways in which they handle the principal components have helped them find favour with many users.

In any interface, the most important element is the tool box, where the principal tools for painting, selecting, adjusting and manipulating your image will be found.

PAINTING & DRAWING TOOLS

Comprising the obvious tools – the *Paintbrush* and *Pencil* – and the less so – the *Clone*, *Gradient fill* and *Vector* shape tools – the painting and drawing tools are used to draw on or add to the existing pixels of the image. Constraints can be placed on their application by the creation of a selection (using one of the selection tools, for example). In painting applications, these tools have a more prominent position and you will find additional tools such as those required for emulating painters' pens, brushes and textures.

BRUSHES: MORE THAN A PAINTING TOOL

Brushes are key to many image-editing functions and a number of tools. Their use isn't limited to painting; they can also be used with the *Clone*

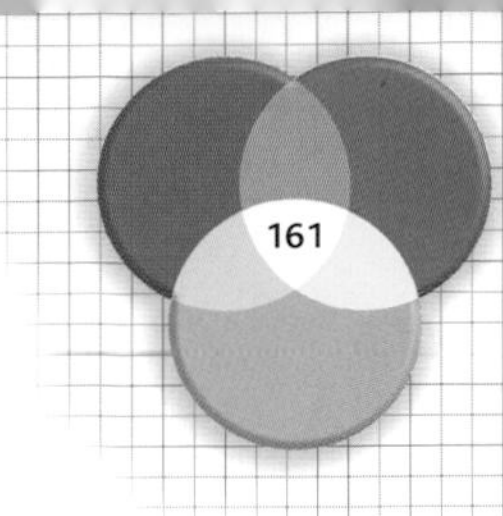

tool, to saturate and desaturate colours or even for erasing pixels. PictureMan, as we mentioned earlier, also employs brushes for all of its filter applications. Hence the brush settings in image-editing applications enable brushes from any number of presets to be used to apply paint or an effect. If the precise brush tip is not available, you can create a new one, either based on an existing definition or from scratch.

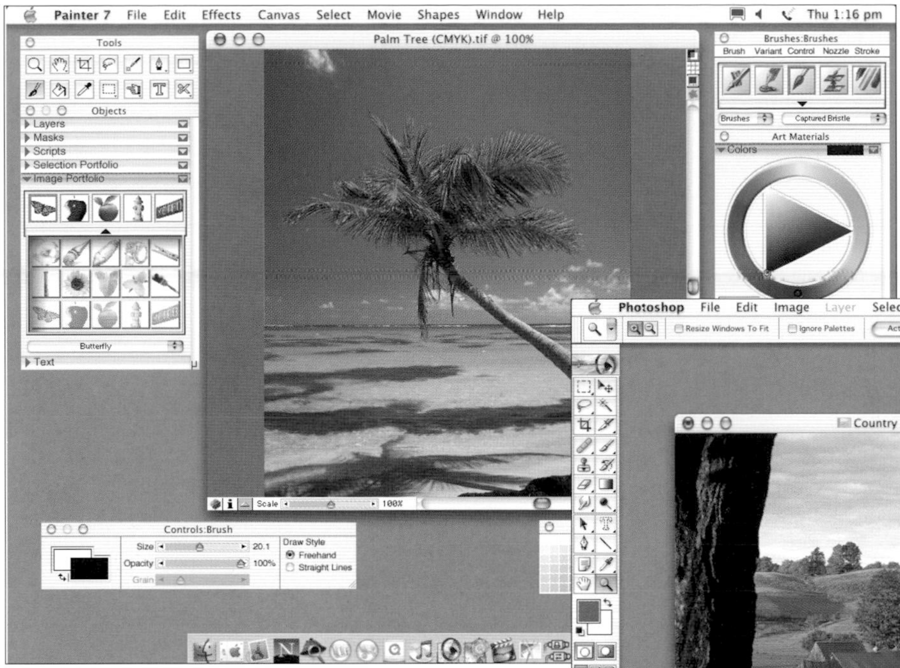

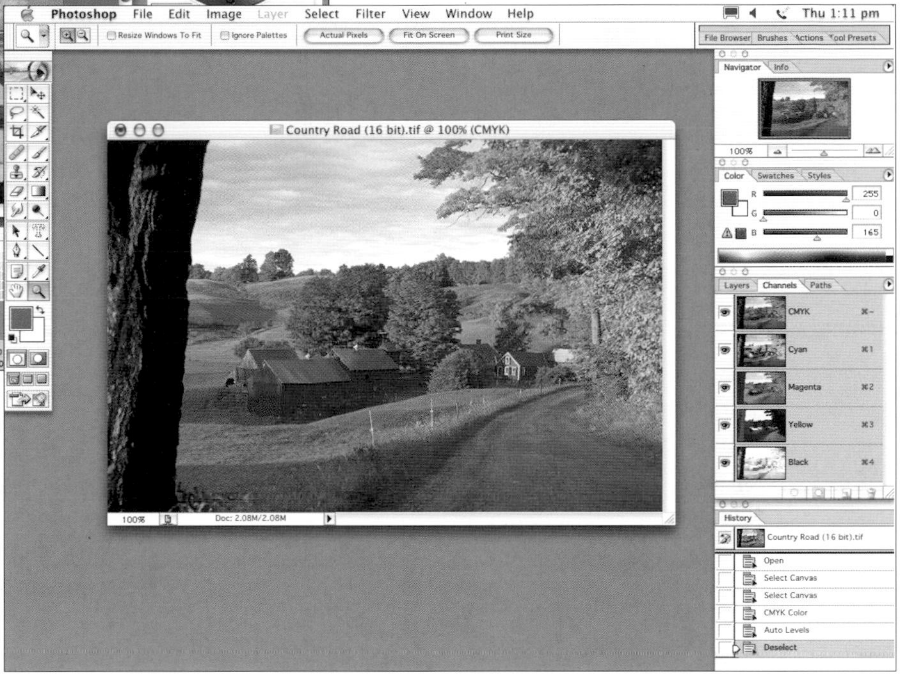

SELECTION TOOLS

Though many corrections or effects need to be applied to an entire image, it is more usual to apply them to a more limited area. The selection tools make it possible to select an object from within an image using different selection criteria. We can, for example, select on the basis of shape (using the *Lasso*), colour (*Magic Wand*), or arbitrary regular shapes (*Marquee*). Boolean operands make it possible to produce composite selections using more than one tool.

DARKROOM TOOLS

Darkroom tools work in the manner of their darkroom namesakes. The *Dodge* tool is used to dodge areas of an image to lighten it, the *Burn* tool is used to darken and so enhance areas of shadow, while the *Sponge* tool can saturate or desaturate the colour in the image. The size of these tools is determined by selecting an appropriately sized brush.

TEXT TOOLS

The text tools make it possible to add text to an image as a feature or caption. Text features vary significantly between applications, but most offer the option of choosing fonts and sizes, along with some elementary formatting functions. Text can also be enhanced by using *Layer Effects* to outline the text (*Stroke*), give it an inner or outer glow, or even add a shadow behind (*Drop shadow*).

VIEWING TOOLS

The *Hand* and *Zoom* tools make it possible to navigate quickly around the image and examine details of it in depth. The *Move* tool, however, is more active, shifting selected parts of the image from one location to another.

OTHER TOOLS

These will vary from application to application, but this category can feature specialist tools as diverse as a *Layer Adjuster* (Painter) through to *Image Annotation* (Photoshop).

TOP LEFT

Painter's interface takes a different approach from Photoshop's, but it still shares the general principles – palettes, toolbars, menus and so on.

ABOVE

Photoshop's interface has had time to mature and has helped it to become the industry standard, to the extent that other image-editing applications use it as a model.

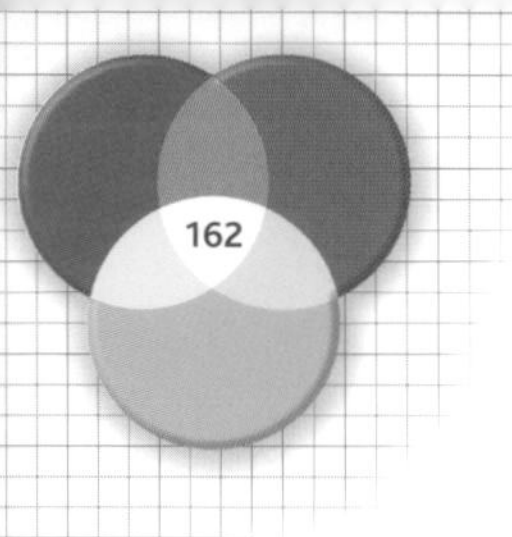

File formats

The need to share and distribute images, and the demands of the professionals who work with them, have given us a wide range of file formats in which we save them. We don't need to know the history or technology behind these file formats, but we do need an understanding of how using them affects our images for better or worse. Even common image file formats have their drawbacks, and it pays to know what these are.

JPEG: It's hard to get away from the JPEG file format. It is used as a convenient storage format in digital cameras and forms the basis of image storage and distribution on PictureCD and the Web. This comes down to its compression technology, which enables a JPEG file to be compressed to as little as 5% of its original size. But while JPEG is virtually the standard image file format, it isn't always the best. The algorithm that achieves compression does so by discarding image data and averaging much of the remainder, which can result in a reduction in image quality.

A CONFUSION OF OPTIONS

Standard image-editing applications, such as Photoshop, tend to offer all – or most – of the file formats listed on these pages, and little else. If you need to open or save in any of the dozens of more esoteric image file formats in existence, you'll need a specialized application, such as Graphic Converter (Macintosh) or Graphics Workshop (Windows). Luckily, both of these programs are widely available as shareware on the Internet.

Though you will find yourself using JPEG images, you should always save original copies in an alternative, lossless format such as TIFF. Not only does JPEG compromise image quality, it does so cumulatively. Edit your image and resave and you'll find further degradation.

JPEG 2000: Aiming to address the failings of the basic JPEG file format, JPEG 2000 uses fractal and wavelet technology to produce images that do not suffer compressional losses yet can still be compressed for distribution and storage.

JPEG files suffer from deterioration on saving and resaving after editing. The averaging technique used by JPEG tends to cause 'buzzing' around sharp or high-contrast edges, as you can see below. The original image is a TIFF file, the JPEG copy has been saved once at 90% compression, resized slightly and saved again.

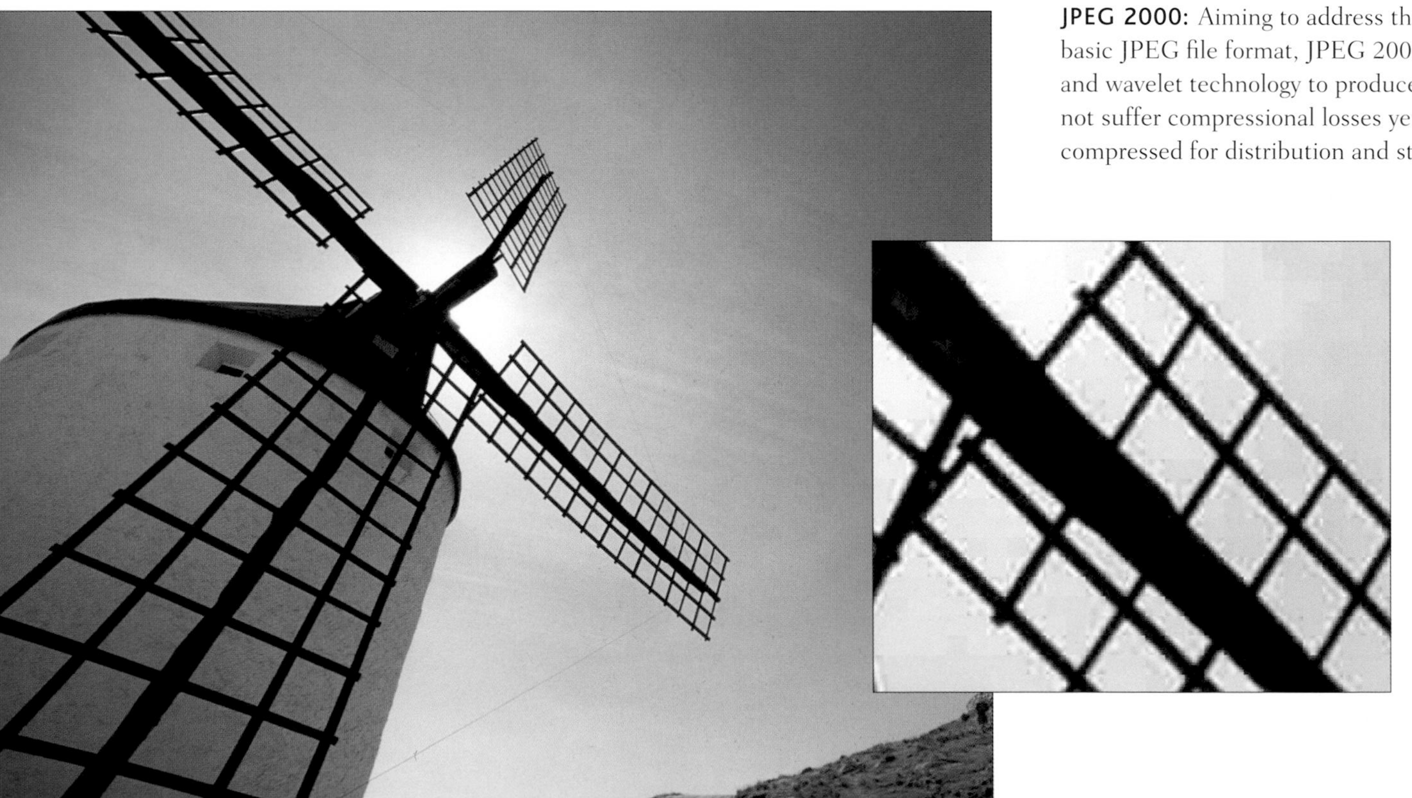

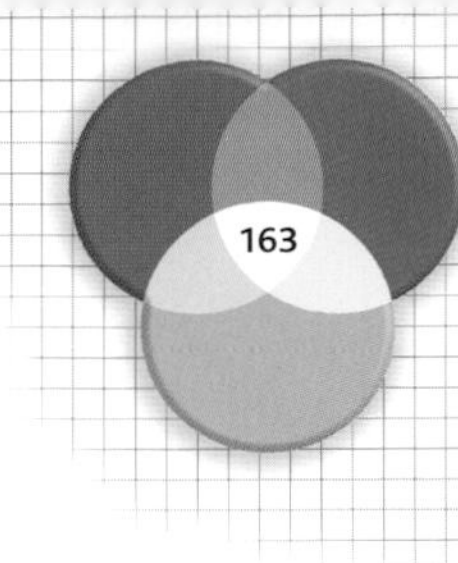

TIFF: The Tagged Image File Format is used by many digital cameras to store uncompressed files and is widely support by applications. It supports 24-bit colour and can also be compressed, using a lossless system known as LZW, by up to 60%.

BMP: The standard Windows image format, but one with a few shortcomings. Some applications can't interpret compressed BMP files, and BMP doesn't support features such as alpha channels.

PICT: A standard for image-editing on Macs, but one that's been superceded by other formats. The enhanced form, PICT2, supports 32-bit colour.

Photo CD: Photo CDs use a proprietary file format for encoding images known as Image Pac. Images are made available at five resolutions (six on 'Pro' Photo CDs). When you open a Photo CD image, a dialog will prompt you to select a resolution.

POSTSCRIPT AND PDFS

The Encapsulated Postcript format – EPS – is yet another format that can support vector information in its original form (without it being 'flattened' into the image). The Portable Document Format – PDF – lets your artwork be viewed by anyone with a PDF viewer (which, in general, means Adobe's Acrobat). The Photoshop variant (Photoshop PDF) retains most of the image information and any vector data. Use this with the Embed Fonts box checked and any text you use will be preserved and accurately reproduced, even if the host computer does not include your font selection. You can also import PDF documents into Photoshop as PDFs, with multipage documents converted into separate images.

GIF: A GIF image can contain only 256 colours, but some Web images are stored in this format. It has the bonus of supporting transparent areas and animation, and can therefore be used for the creation of web-based animated graphics.

RAW AND NATIVE FORMATS

Every image-editing and painting application has its own native file format. In the case of Photoshop it's the Photoshop PSD format, but Paintshop Pro uses PSP, and Painter, RIFF. Each of these formats preserves all the features (such as layers, masks and paths) that are associated with the image and that can be lost where a more generic format is used. Some of these native formats can be opened in other applications, but not all; if you are planning to share images with friends or colleagues, then you should check compatibility first.

Some digital cameras also have their own native file formats. These 'Raw' files deliver the best quality, and can be smaller in size than an uncompressed TIF, but they often need proprietary software to open and read them. In some cases, plug-ins make it possible to use Raw files directly from an image-editing application.

WEB FILE FORMATS

If you're sending images by e-mail or using them on a website, then smaller files are a must. As a result, JPEG is used extensively, despite the concerns about image quality. Luckily, the 'save to JPEG' option in most image-editing programs allows you to adjust the degree of compression and preview the effects, so that you can achieve an effective compromise between keeping file sizes low while maintaining image quality.

As an alternative, you could try the Portable Network Graphics (PNG) format. While not as widely used as GIFs or JPEGs on the Web, PNG files can be saved and opened by most applications, and the format offers an attractive combination of lossless compression and support for transparency and 24-bit colour.

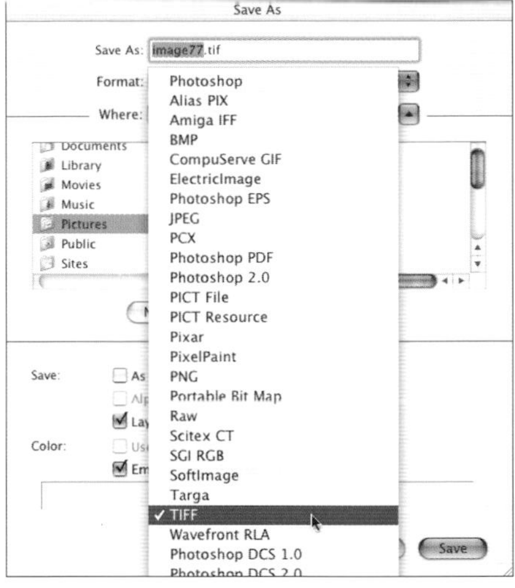

Graphic Converter 'save as' options for an image. These can include some pretty obscure formats, including those used by PDA's and long-obselete computer systems.

DARKROOM SECRETS

SAVE FOR SAFEKEEPING

You will need to determine the file format of every image that you save. It is generally safest to use the TIFF format, but it can be a good idea to keep a version of the image in the original, native format for safekeeping. That way, you can make quick adjustments and reuse it at a later date.

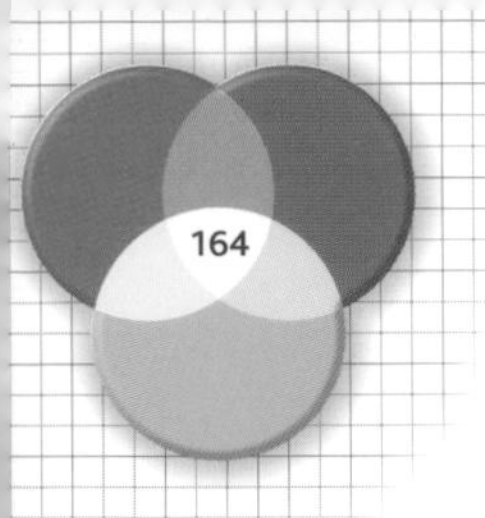

Converting image files

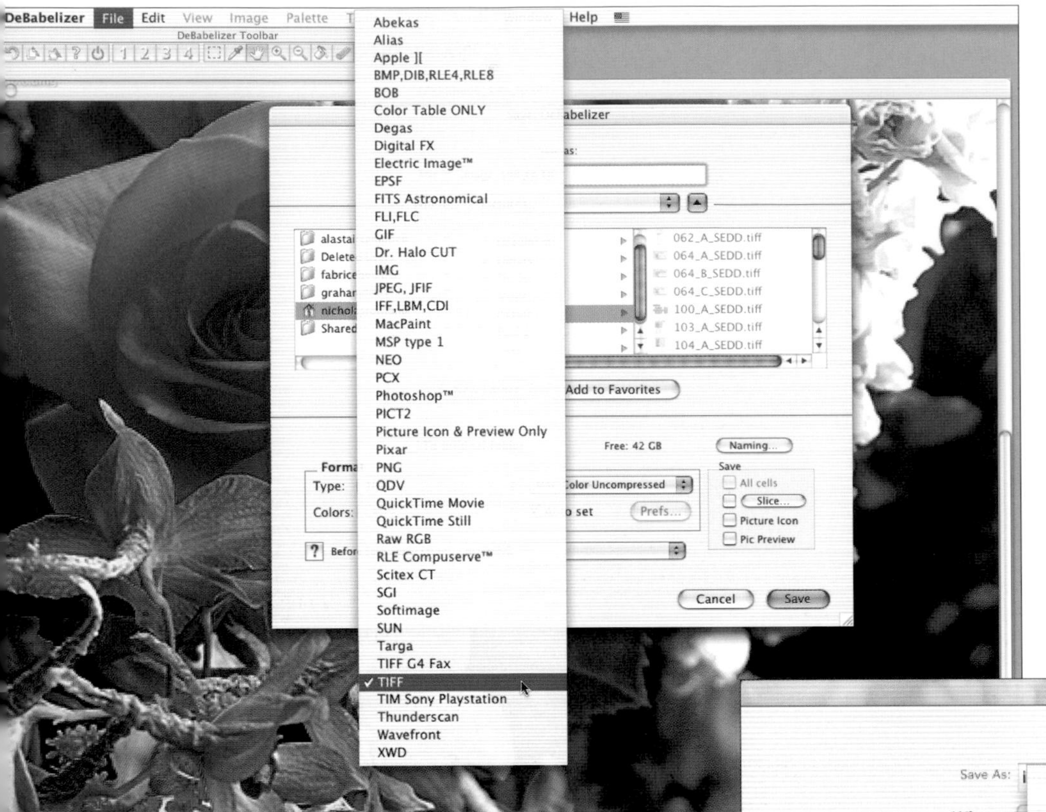

Image-editing applications are adept at being able to recognise many file types, including those that may have been created on a platform other than the host. There could still be situations, however, in which you wish to use an image file without having an application that can open it, or where you want to convert a file from its original format so that someone else can view and edit it.

DeBabelizer is an image and graphics tool that not only converts from one format to another, it also lets changes be made during the conversion. For example, you can optimise images for subsequent use on the Web, change the orientation, crop or even resize.

Simple conversions are achieved by first selecting *File* > **Open** to load the original file and then using *File* > **Save As** to save the file in the chosen format. You will find that the list includes many file formats you may never have heard of!

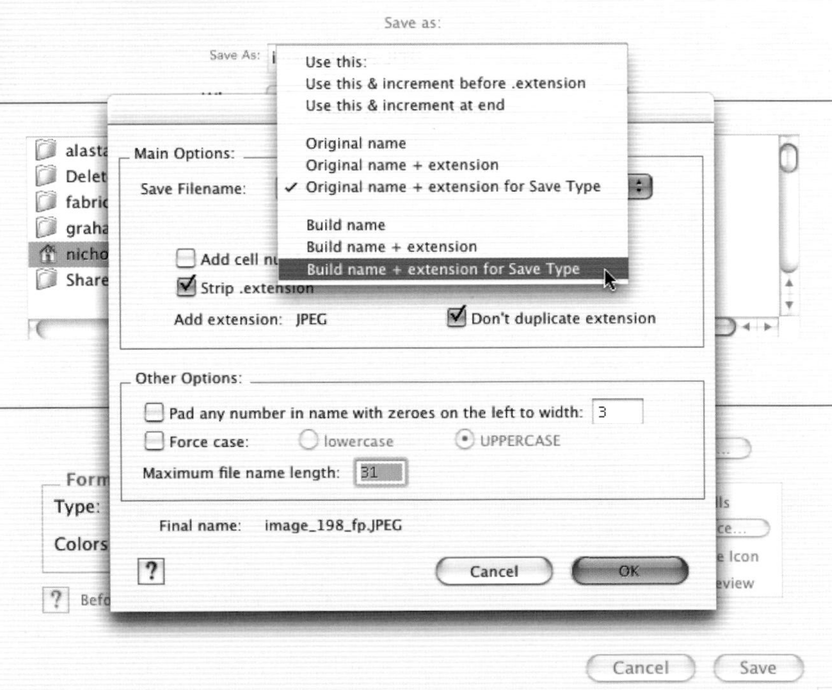

DeBabelizer has a simple slider control for JPEG compression, but it also gives you other options to reduce your image file size as much as possible while keeping the quality in balance.

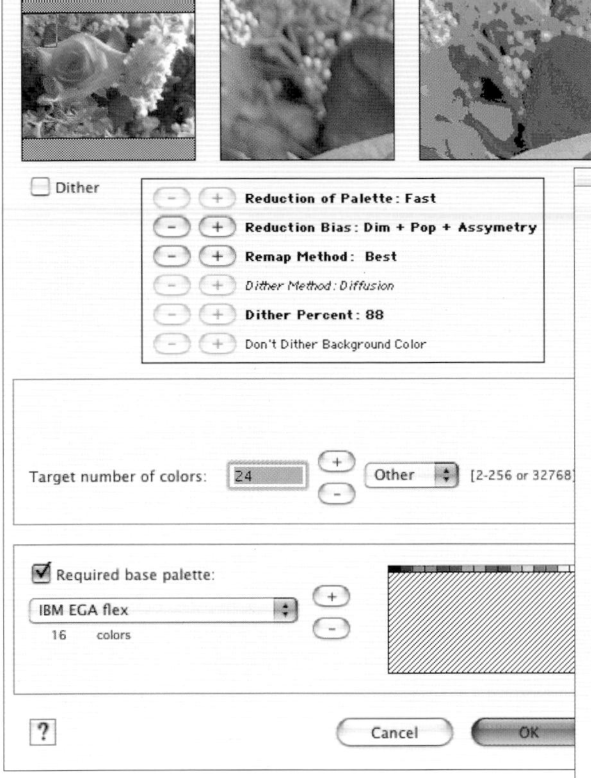

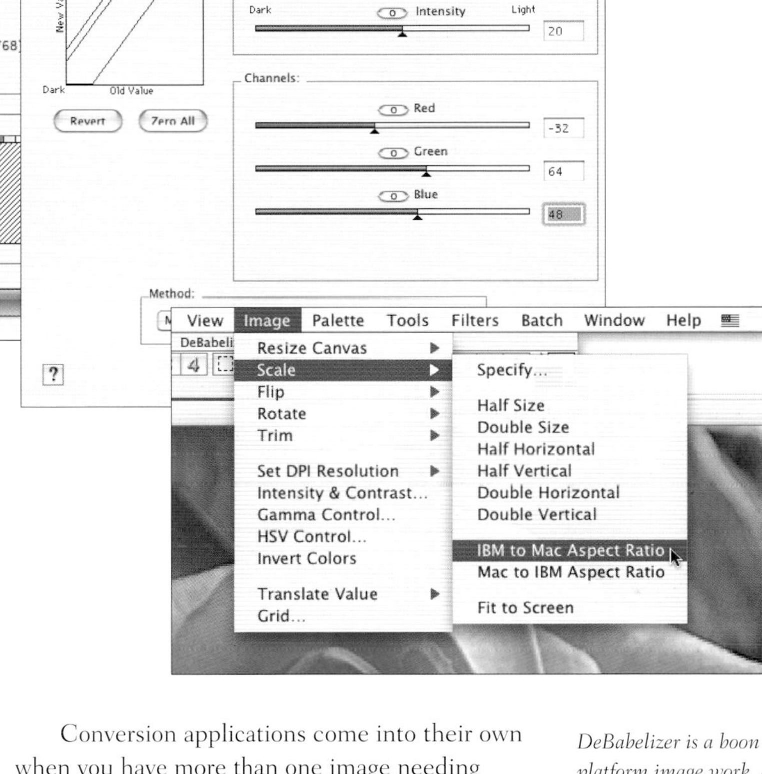

While the conversion is in progress, you can determine the output file size as well as type. When using JPEG as the output file type, for example, you are not restricted to the standard compression ratio Quality slider. DeBabelizer permits a far wider range of conversion changes.

For instance, you can reduce the file size by limiting the number of colours that are used to create the output image. The colour reduction can reduce the output colours all the way down to two. A live preview screen enables you to assess whether the amount of colour reduction is acceptable or not.

Though not designed to serve as an image editor, DeBabelizer can alter some other fundamental characteristics during conversion. The *Intensity/Contrast* command allows changes to be made to the brightness, contrast and individual red, green or blue colour saturations. Select *Image* > ***Intensity/Contrast*** to make these changes.

Similar tools are provided in the Image menu to crop, rotate and even change the output resolution. More significantly for cross-platform users, it is possible to change characteristics of an image that would differ between platforms.

Conversion applications come into their own when you have more than one image needing attention. Although many image-editing applications feature batch commands that can be applied to a set of images, the features are often restricted to those directly related to image processing and image manipulation. With a conversion application, however, you could convert a set of digital camera TIFF files to a set of JPEG images that have been orientated, cropped and optimized for use on a website. You can even work with frames from a digital video, not only converting consecutive frames to layers in an animated GIF, but also processing frames as individual images. It might not be particularly creative or exciting, but it will save you time.

DeBabelizer is a boon for cross-platform image work, enabling all the standard file conversion features plus some fixes for less obvious problems. One of these is the slightly different aspect ratios used by many Windows and Mac screens.

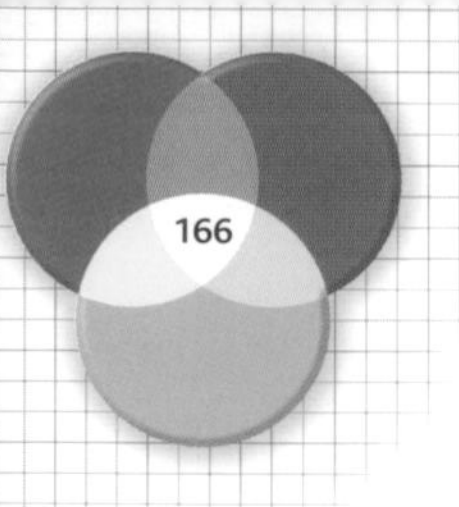

Understanding and using actions

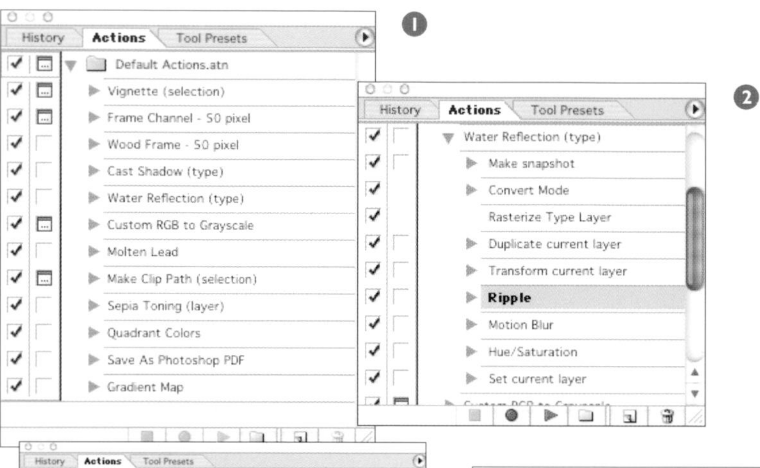

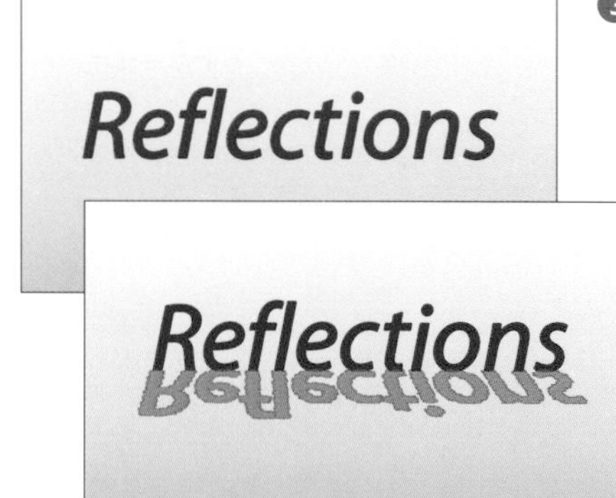

Photoshop's Actions – and most image-editing applications have an equivalent – are one of those Cinderella features. Most people know broadly what they do, but few exploit their true potential.

In essence, an action is just a macro: a series of commands work automatically. You might want to apply the same set of corrections to several images in exactly the same way; resizing them, applying a sharpening filter and then adding a frame. Create an action, and you can apply it to an image or group of images with a mouse click. Actions can even be used to batch process whole folders of images unattended, leaving you free to do something more rewarding.

Virtually all of Photoshop's image-editing commands can be recorded as actions. Where user input is required, perhaps to define a parameter or apply an effect using a painting tool, stop points can be incorporated. You can choose to see actions in component form, so that each step of the action is displayed, or in button form, where simple push buttons are substituted.

Running a preconfigured action is simple. In this example (left), we have employed the default action *Water Reflection*. This is an action that is enacted on the type layer in an image and creates a fairly realistic water reflection.

RUNNING AN ACTION

1 *Create your starting image. Here, it comprises a gradient background with some stroked text applied in a text layer. Now open the* Actions *palette, select the action* (Water Reflection) *and click on the* Play *button.*

2 *If you click on the small arrowhead to the left of the action, you can open the action and see the steps involved. You'll see the commands highlighted as they are enacted on your image.*

3 *Simply wait and your image will be displayed complete with reflection.*

DARKROOM SECRETS

ACTION TIPS

- If you need to add a command to an existing action, go to the *Actions* palette. Select the action and then the command that immediately precedes the one that you wish to add. Click on the *Record* button, add the command (or commands) and then click stop.
- Slow down! Debugging a long and complex action can be tricky. Select *Playback Options* in the *Actions* palette menu and you can progress through the action step by step or with *Pause* for each command.
- Keyboard shortcuts can be set for useful actions. After selecting *New Action*, you can choose any function key combination along with Ctrl (Windows), Command (Mac) and the shift key.

ACTIONS AND DROPLETS

Photoshop and ImageReady also feature Droplets. These are small, distinct applications that feature a series of actions. When an image file – or a group of files – is dragged on top of a droplet icon, the actions of that droplet will be applied. Droplets can be saved direct to the desktop for further ease of use.

Creating a Droplet from an action is simple:

1 *Select* File > Automate > **Create Droplet**.

2 *Select a location to save the Droplet in.*

3 *Choose the appropriate set and action from the* Set *and* Action *menus.*

4 *Set a play option and destination for the processed files.*

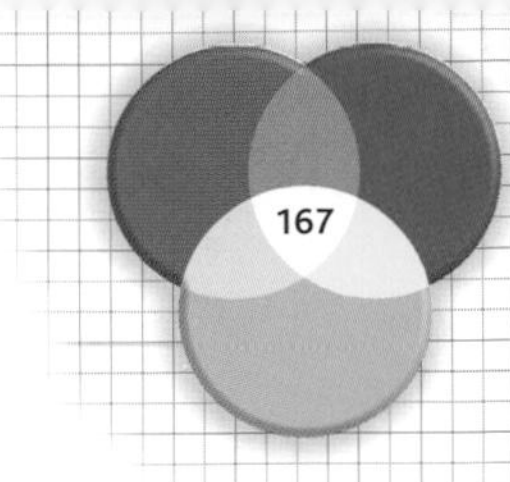

CREATING A SIMPLE ACTION

Although actions can be highly complex sets of commands designed to completely transform an image, they are most commonly used to automate repetitive tasks, such as resizing all the images on a camera card. Here, we will create a simple action to change the size of a JPEG image to 200dpi, run the auto levels and unsharp mask filters, and resave as an uncompressed TIFF in a specified location. We will then run the action on a whole batch of JPEGs.

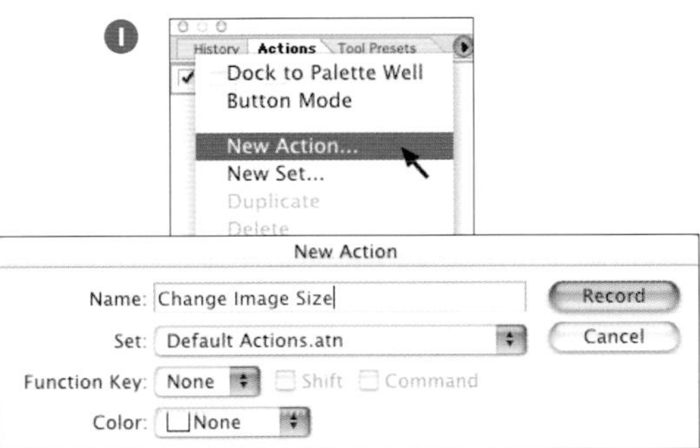

2

1 *The first step is to open a single, sample picture. Now open the* Actions *palette and choose* New Action *from the drop-down menu*

2 *The* New Action *dialog appears; give it a name and – if you wish – assign a Function Key and colour to the new action.*

3 *Click on the* Record *button and you will be returned to the image. Run any filters or other changes you want to the image. In this case, we change the image resolution to 200 dpi (without resampling) and run the* Unsharp mask *filter and the* Auto levels *command.*

4 *Choose* Save As *from the file menu and choose* TIFF *as the file type. Save the new file and close the image.*

5 *Click on the* Stop recording *button at the bottom of the Actions palette.*

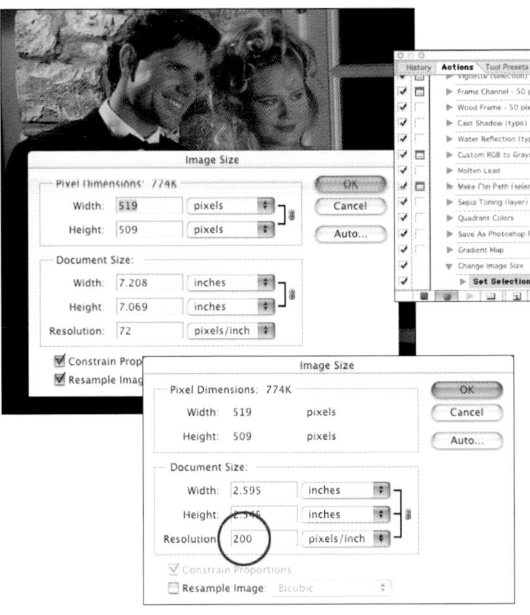

3

6 *To run the action on a whole folder of images, choose* File>Automate>**Batch**. *You will see the dialog on the left appear. Select your new action and use the* Choose *button in the* Source *section to browse for the folder of images you wish to batch process. The* Destination *section allows you to choose a new place to save the altered files. Check the* Override Action Save As Commands *option if you want to use a different location than that specified in step 4. Click on OK and you can sit back as Photoshop does all the boring work for you!*

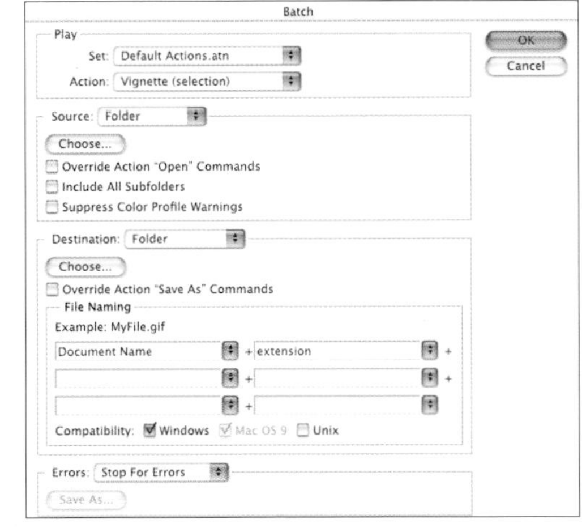

6

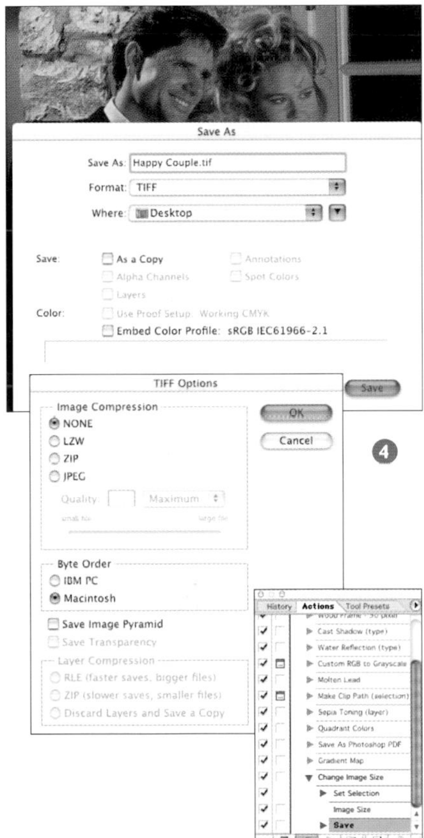

4

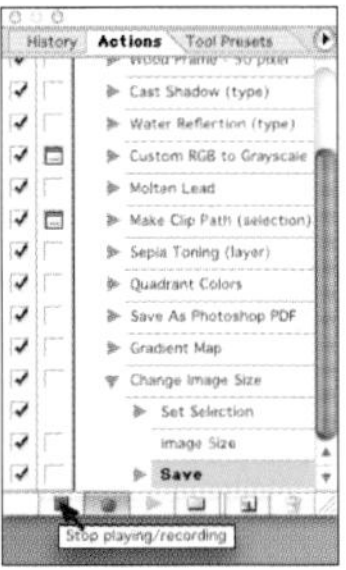

5

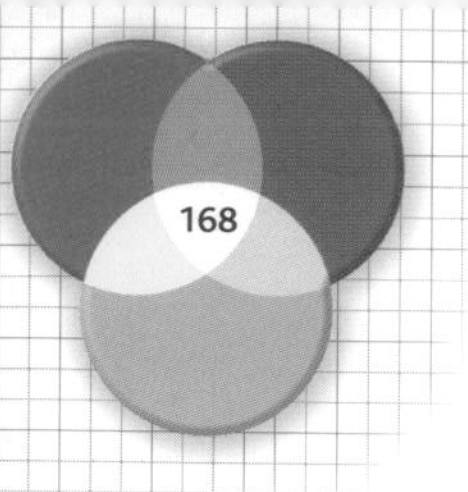

Printing and outputting

The process of printing digital images is fundamentally the same as when traditional techniques are employed. The most obvious difference is in the equipment.

TOOLS OF THE TRADE

Though by no means the only solution, the majority of nonprofessional users print with inkjet printers. Having evolved from the early, somewhat crude alternatives to the first daisywheel and dot matrix contact printers, the inkjet is now capable of the best of photographic results. But not all inkjet printers – indeed not all photo-quality inkjet printers – are created equal. To be effective, an inkjet printer needs to be able to reproduce not only the obvious characteristics of an image – the colour – but also its full tonal range. The measure of a good printer is the ability to capture this as accurately as possible, without truncating the tonal range and losing precious detail in the highlights and shadows. Six-colour printing technology and high resolutions help.

RGB vs CMYK

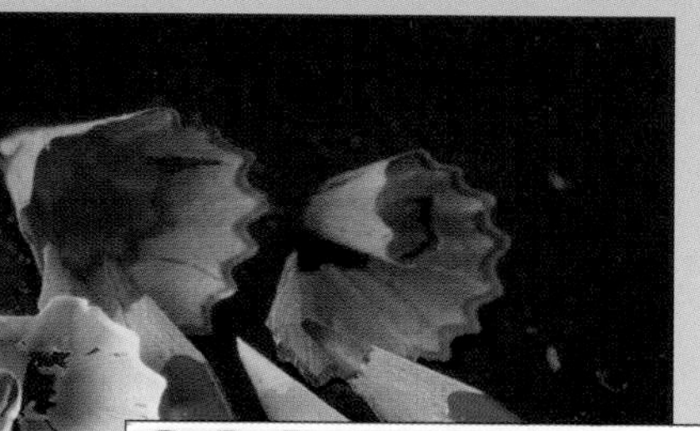

Top-level image-editing applications are able to work in either RGB or CMYK colour modes. Which is the best to work with? Although colour management is an exacting science, most people tend to work with RGB as their default colour mode, even when virtually all printing processes use CMYK inks. In some applications, you'll find there is a CMYK Preview mode that permits the previewing of an image in CMYK while you carry on editing in RGB.

The critical worker will insist that work destined for CMYK output should be edited in the same mode. Leave them to it. Unless your system's colour calibration and colour consistency are absolutely spot-on, any differences will be inconsequential at the editing stage at least.

Most inkjet 'photo' printers use six or even seven ink colours to produce a full colour print. The addition of pale cyan and pale magenta inks improves pastel tone reproduction, but a standard CMYK conversion (as offered by Photoshop, for example) doesn't take them into account. For this reason, it is usually preferable to leave your images in RGB mode (which offers a wider range of colours, or gamut) and leave the complex matter of converting to CMYK to the printer software. CMYK images are usually needed only when they are destined for publication in a magazine or book – and even then it is often advisable to leave the final conversion from RGB to CMYK to a professional unless you are totally confident that you know exactly what you are doing!

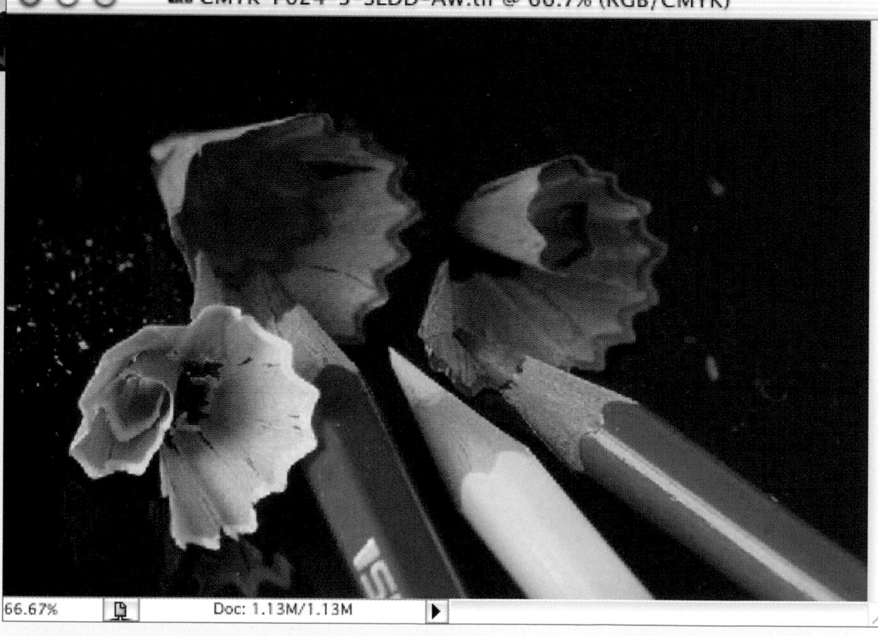

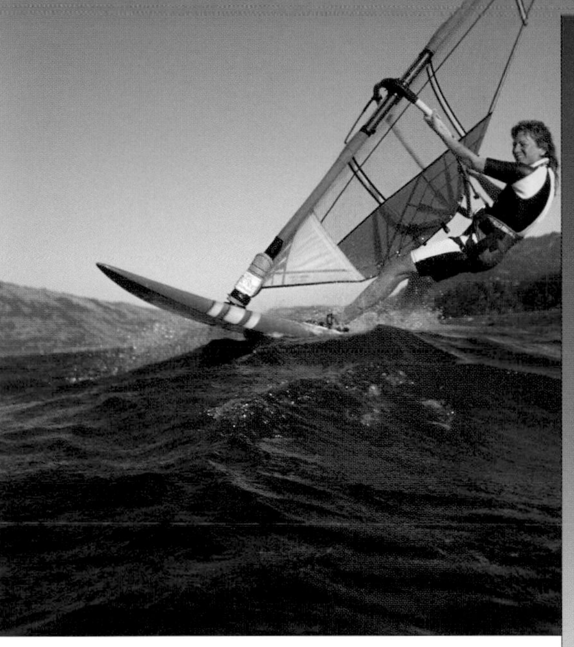

A MATTER OF BALANCE

It might seem obvious, but there is no escaping the fact that the best prints are the results of good original images. This maxim is as true in the digital world as it is anywhere else. To produce a good digital image, you need an original with a high resolution and bit-depth. However, such images also tend to be very large – a detailed image consisting of over 16 million colours needs a lot of digital data to store and reproduce it, and will also be slow to work with when manipulating.

To work effectively, we need to strike an acceptable balance between our need for good image quality and our need for a file size that is small enough to work with. At the least, we need to find a file size that delivers an image which when printed at the intended size, does not end up looking blocky or pixelated.

Remember that the key is to make sure that any image which you want to print will fill the required area at 300 dpi, and the best way of doing this is to have a source image – whether a scan or a digital photo – that closely matches these dimensions already.

Not all inkjet printers are created equal. Six-colour photo-quality printers can capture the detail and the full range of tones in an image (above left). Other inkjet printers struggle, and the output suffers from overt colour casts (above right).

DARKROOM SECRETS

KEEP CALIBRATING

While dull, printer and monitor calibration are key to getting results on paper that reproduce those on screen. Calibration routines are included with many computers, monitors and applications. Try to recalibrate your whole system periodically.

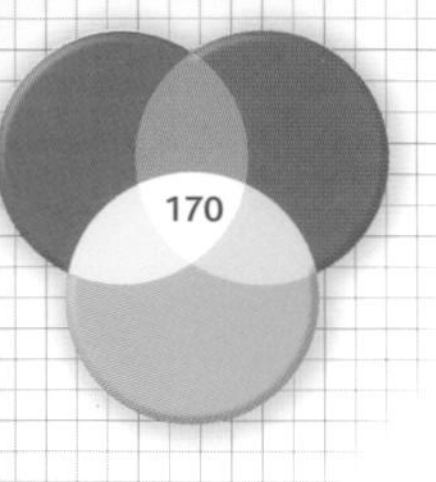

Printing using specialist inks

TOP LEFT AND RIGHT
Images with little natural colour but a significant amount of detail should be ideal for printing in monochrome. However, converting the image to greyscale and printing it gives rather lacklustre results.

BOTTOM LEFT AND RIGHT
Using a Small Gamut ink set gives better tonal reproduction, especially in the shadow and highlight areas. It is a trivial matter to add a subtle tint. This sepia tone was produced using the Hue/Saturation *control.*

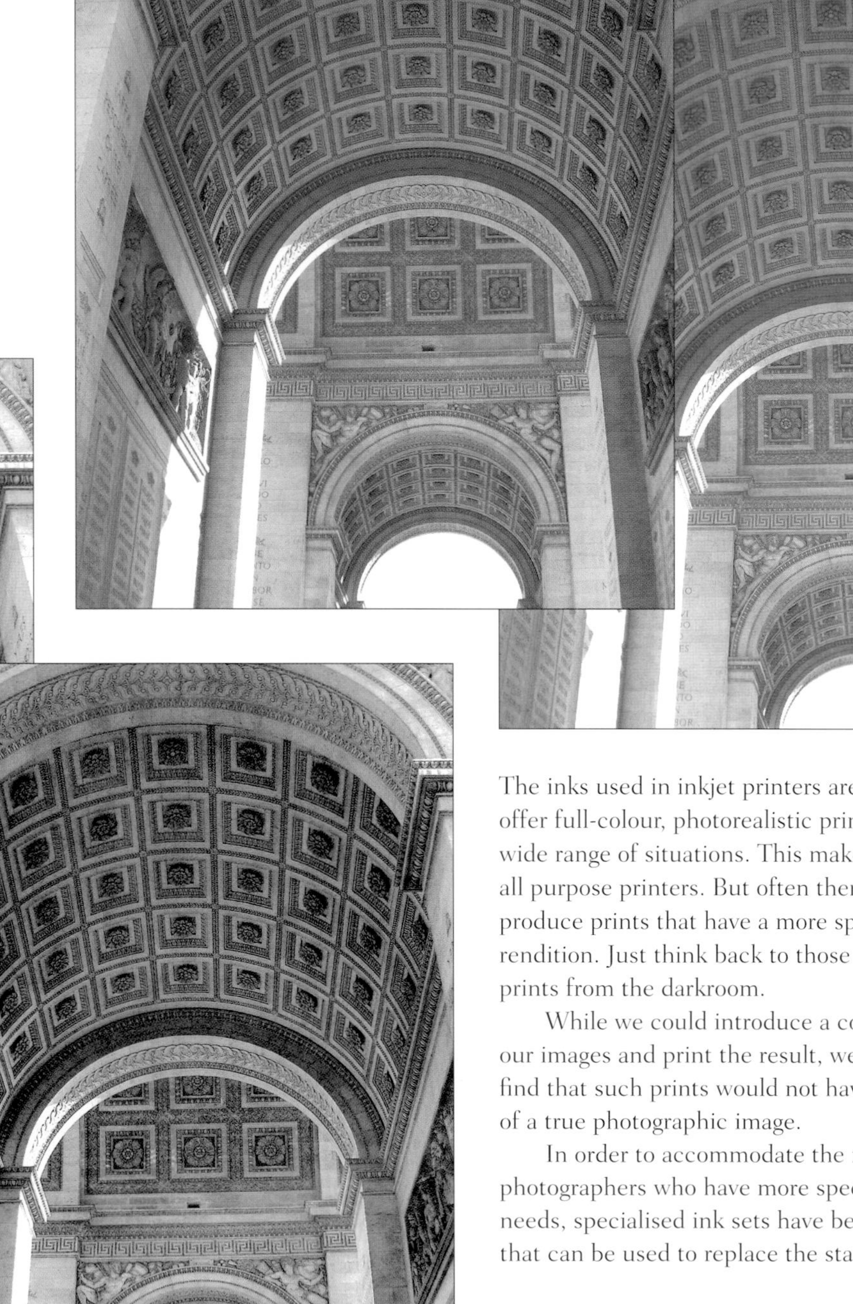

The inks used in inkjet printers are optimized to offer full-colour, photorealistic printing across a wide range of situations. This makes them ideal all purpose printers. But often there is a need to produce prints that have a more specific colour rendition. Just think back to those warm bromide prints from the darkroom.

While we could introduce a colour cast to our images and print the result, we'd probably find that such prints would not have the impact of a true photographic image.

In order to accommodate the needs of photographers who have more specific colour needs, specialised ink sets have been developed that can be used to replace the standard colour inks. They overcome the problem of printing black-and-white images using full colour inks. Unlike the polychromatic inks that are usually used, they can produce monochrome images without colour shifts.

Small Gamut ink sets are a typical example. Produced by companies such as Lyson, these feature a much reduced set of colour tones, making it easier to print monochrome images without any colour cast creeping in. In addition, the inks are designed to reveal a significant amount of detail, particularly in the highlight and shadow areas.

The drawback with specialised inks is that the printer used with them needs, ideally, to be dedicated to them. Switching between conventional and small gamut inks requires you to flush and clean the ink mechanism between each set. This is laborious and time-consuming, but also expensive if you need to change inks more than occasionally.

Small gamut inks not only produce great monochrome images, they can also produce the most authentic of toned prints. The techniques used to add tone to an otherwise monochrome image are the same as those we have explored on previous pages. You would still use adjustment layers and the *Hue/Saturation* control. Only the final printing method needs to change.

Professional printing

Go beyond the inkjet and you have a range of equipment to consider. Your local or online print bureau will feature some, if not all the following.

LARGE FORMAT INKJETS

Taking the inkjet concept to large paper sizes, wide format printers work in essentially the same way. Print resolutions are lower, but as the prints are designed for viewing from a greater distance, this isn't a serious concern.

PICTROGRAPHY

Using a technique akin to that of the laser printer, these printers use laser diode technology to create large, photographic quality print with high resistance to fading and atmospheric damage.

IRIS PRINTERS

Using a high resolution inkjet system, Iris prints can be produced on a very wide variety of media including specialised fine-art papers. Many photographers use Iris printers when producing limited run fine art reproductions of their images, as the results are superior to any alternative print production method.

DARKROOM SECRETS

MATCH PAPER TO PRINT

Expensive, glossy papers are ideal for many images, particularly wide landscapes or attractive portraits. When you print an image with a rough or textured finish, however, use a plain, high quality matt surface, which will emphasise the texture of the image.

By replacing coloured inks with different densities of black, even more potent monochrome images can be printed.

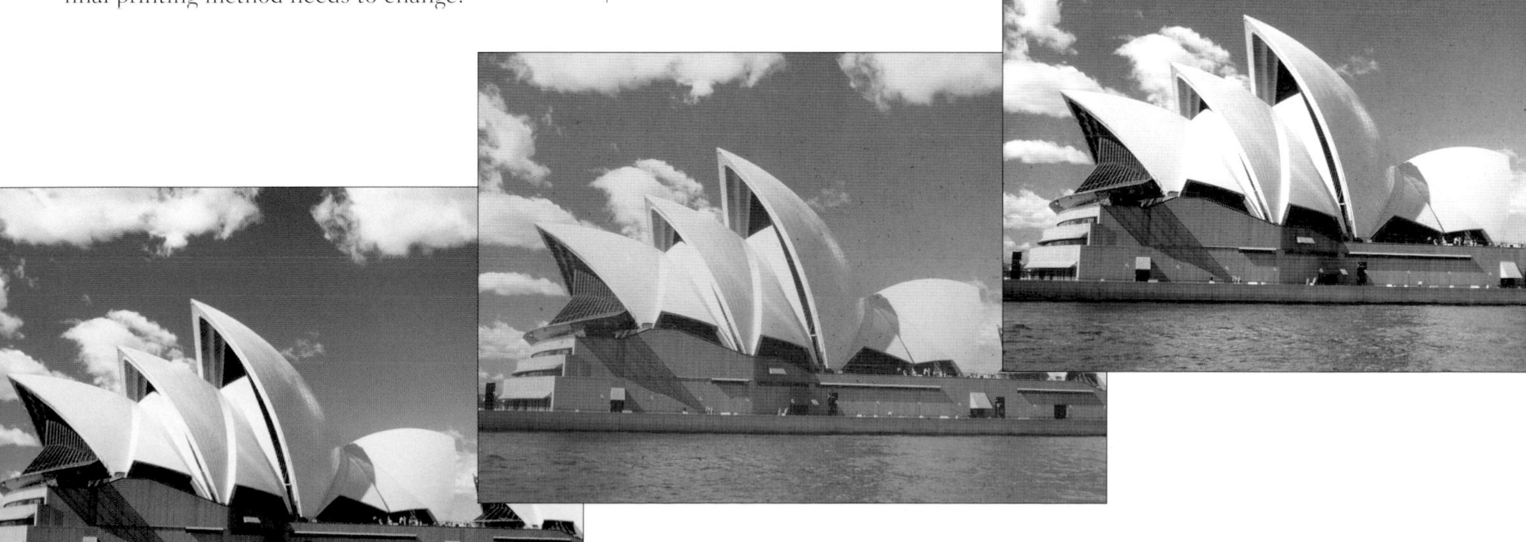

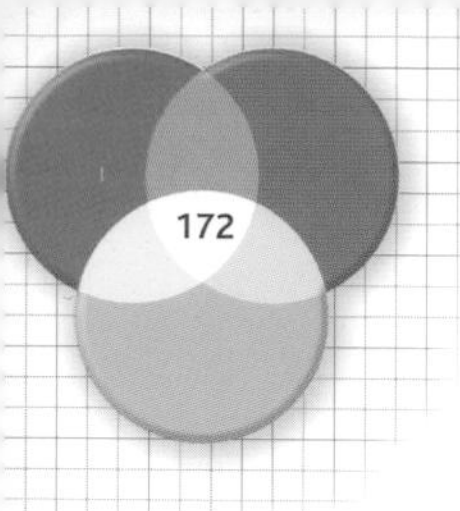

Saving and publishing to disk

TOP LEFT TO RIGHT
roxio's VideoWave treats film footage and still image similarly, enabling you to compile a film from your still images or even combine them with the .AVI files generated by the movie function found on many digital stills cameras. iMovie and Windows Movie Maker, bundled with Apple OS X and Windows XP, offer similar features.

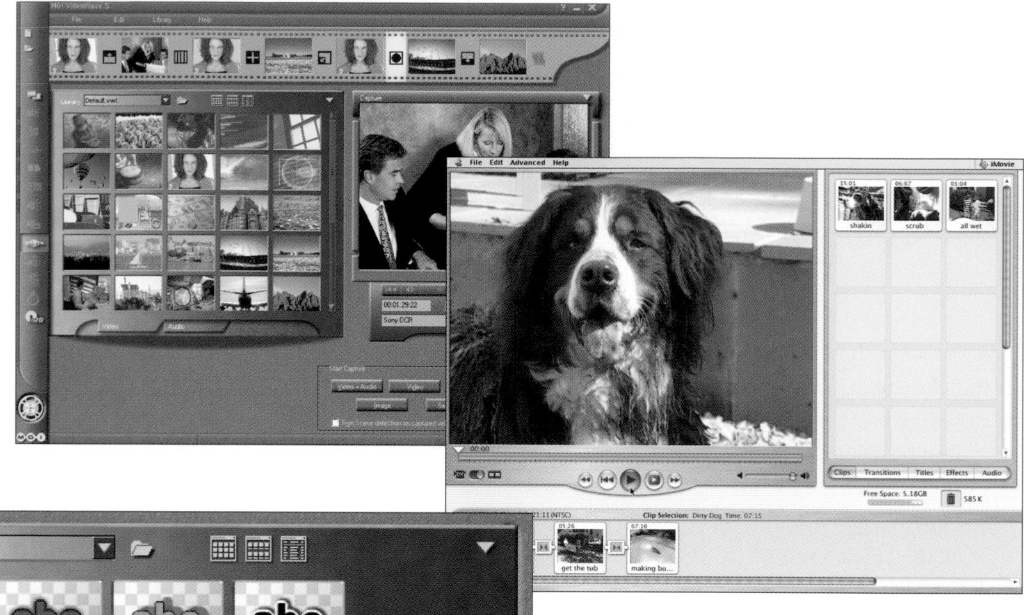

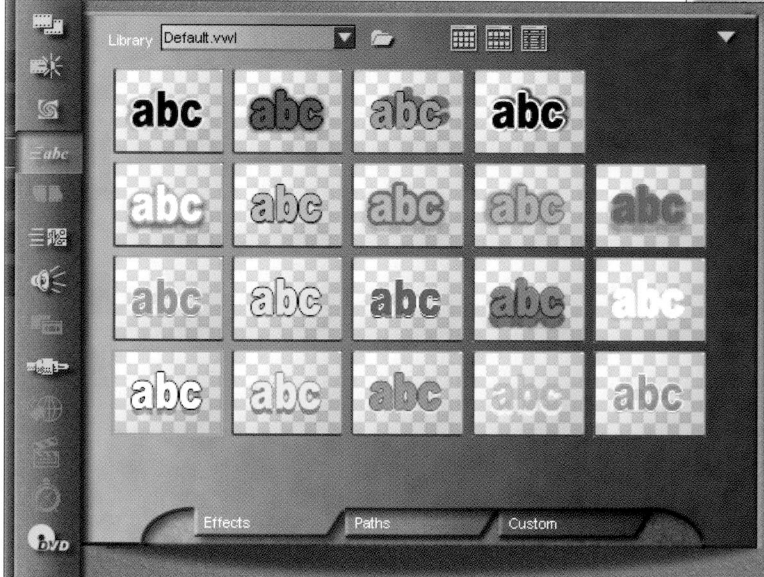

In VideoWave you can add text to your images in any form and font that you care to use. Good titles can enhance the look and feel of your slide show.

Thanks to the onward march of file sizes and the efforts of Apple with the original iMac, the floppy disk as an image file-sharing medium has long been consigned to history. The all-pervasive nature of the net, too, has produced a strong alternative delivery method with an immediacy not shared by any tangible medium, but the need for smaller file sizes will always mean a compromise in terms of final quality. Where quality is paramount, CD and DVD provide the ideal means for sharing your images.

CREATING SLIDE SHOWS AND SHOW REELS

Saving a collection of images to a CD-ROM disk is easy, and is usually achieved using simple CD-burning software such as roxio's Toast (for Macintosh) or Easy CD Creator (Windows). This makes a convenient way to store images as a back up or archive. But what if you wanted to do something more special with your collection?

For example, you can create slide shows of your image collections that can easily be replayed by anyone you choose to share the disk with. Many image-editing applications provide the tools

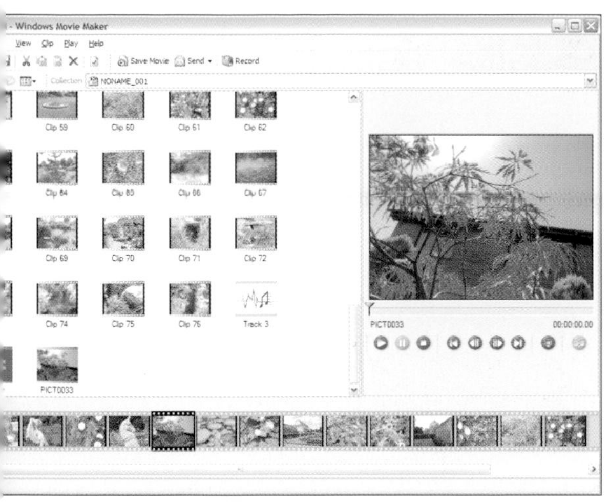

to create such a slide show, but you can often create more elaborate and interesting presentations using basic video editing software. iMovie, included free with Macintosh operating systems, Windows Movie Maker (supplied with Windows ME and Windows XP) and roxio's VideoWave will all do the job.

In each case, you import still images, which are then regarded by the video applications as separate video clips. You can then determine how long each one appears on screen and what sort of transition is applied between each. The beauty of using these applications, which can be much simpler to use than image-editing applications, is that you can easily embellish your production with titles, commentaries and background music.

SAVING YOUR CREATION

Once you have produced your film, you can export it to disk as a QuickTime movie or equivalent format. You can even save a small copy that can be e-mailed, although it should be pointed out that film slide shows are not the most expedient way of sending photos to your friends. You can also save the film to video tape (miniDV provides the best quality and most robust storage) or if your computer is equipped with the appropriate AV sockets, to VHS. Applications such as VideoWave and Toast also permit (again assuming you have the correct hardware) the conversion of the production to an MPEG1 stream that can be burned to DVD or CD-R as a Video CD for high-quality playback on some standard DVD players.

Making a Quicktime movie from your photo collection

If you are a Mac user, you can easily make a slide show film from your photo collection and share it around. It can be replayed by anyone with an application (such as a Web browser or graphics program) that supports QuickTime. Better still, as it uses Apple's free iPhoto, you don't need to purchase any software!

The process is straightforward. Simply select the album or collection of photos that you want to include and select Export from the File menu. Choose QuickTime as the export file type.

Set the maximum dimensions of the film and the duration that each image will be displayed for. You can also specify background colour and even a background image. To make a full multimedia production, select some background music. When you are finished, just click on export and give the new film a name.

DARKROOM SECRETS

WATCH IT ON TV

If you save any slide show in MPEG1 format (either in the creating application, or a video editing application), you can burn the file to a CD in VideoCD format. The main advantage of doing so is that VideoCDs can be replayed on most domestic DVD recorders.

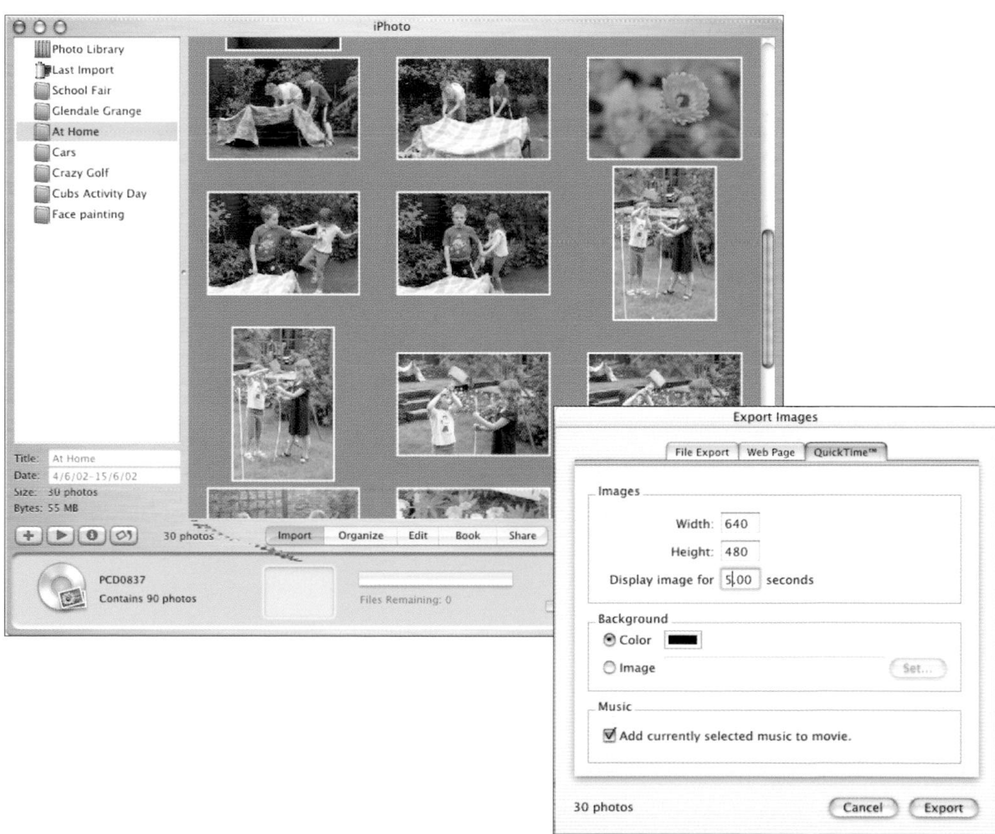

iPhoto: It's no Photoshop, but iPhoto is great for creating basic slide shows that act as showreels for your photographic prowess.

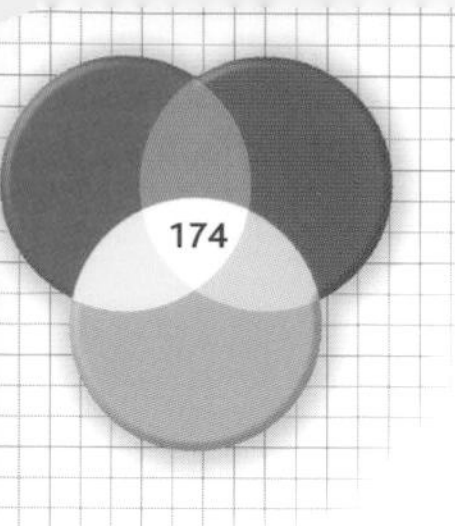

Images for the Web

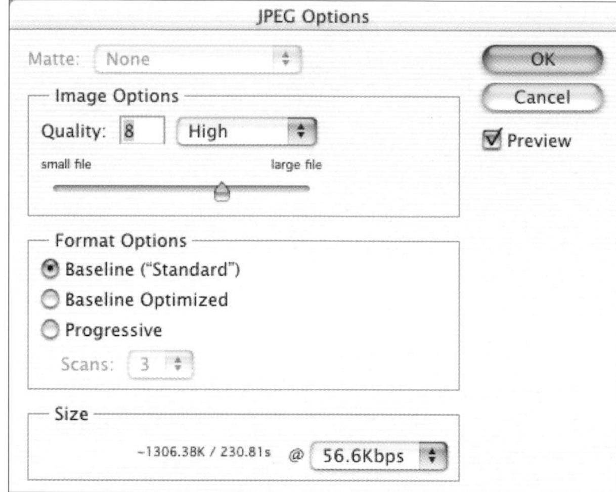

Altering the slider determines both the file size and the image quality. In basic terms, you play one against the other.

Most of the effort we place in getting our images perfect is concerned with the resolution and overall quality. More pixels, conventional wisdom dictates, gives better results. And when we prepare images to be printed, whether on our home office inkjet or through the more colour-wise systems offered by our local repro house, those qualities are very much to the fore.

When it comes to preparing images for the Web, however, other considerations come to the fore. Sure, we would love to be able to send our greatest high-resolution images to all who would appreciate them, but getting the corresponding digital file across the Web would prove at best problematic and, in practice, impossible.

No, for distributing images over the Web – whether for e-mail or placement on a website – a whole new set of considerations come into play. Just as there are optimum ways to get an image onto the printed page, so there are optimum ways to prepare that same image for the Web.

A MATTER OF BALANCE

Getting an image right for the Web is a matter of achieving a balance between file size and image quality. A large file size offers better image quality (all other parameters being equal), but by virtue of its size will take longer to send. A smaller file size will be more expedient to send, but will have a lower quality. By a lower quality, we mean that there is likely to be less visual detail in the image and that noticeable artefacts – electronically induced image defects – are also going to make an appearance.

Most images destined for Web use are saved in the JPEG or GIF formats (*see page 162–163*), both of which feature compression capabilities that allow the final file sizes to be reduced.

DARKROOM SECRETS

THE POSITIVE SIDE OF JPEG COMPRESSION

In some situations JPEG compression can be a friend. If you want to protect your images from misuse, using heavy JPEG compression can compromise the image quality to the extent that it makes them unusable for any unauthorised purpose.

SAVE FOR WEB DIALOGS

As we mentioned, it can be difficult to gauge the trade-off between quality and file size. Some image editors include a feature that permits side-by-side comparison of images at different file sizes. In the case of Adobe's ImageReady 7, seen here, equivalent download times using a range of modems are also given. You can see the download times in seconds listed underneath the file size, along with the number of colours that are being used – reducing the colour palette is another good way to shrink file sizes down.

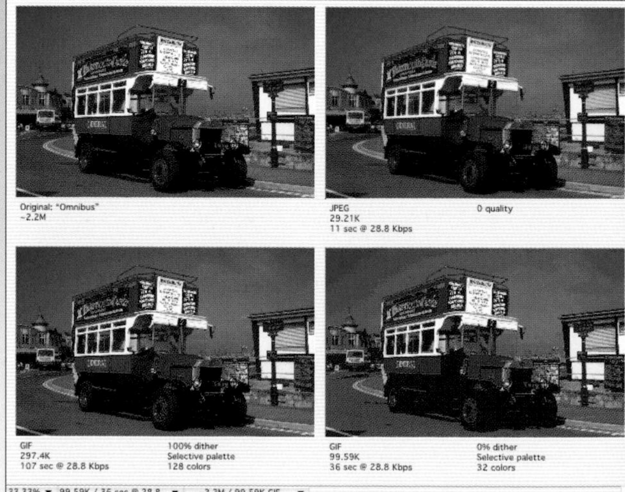

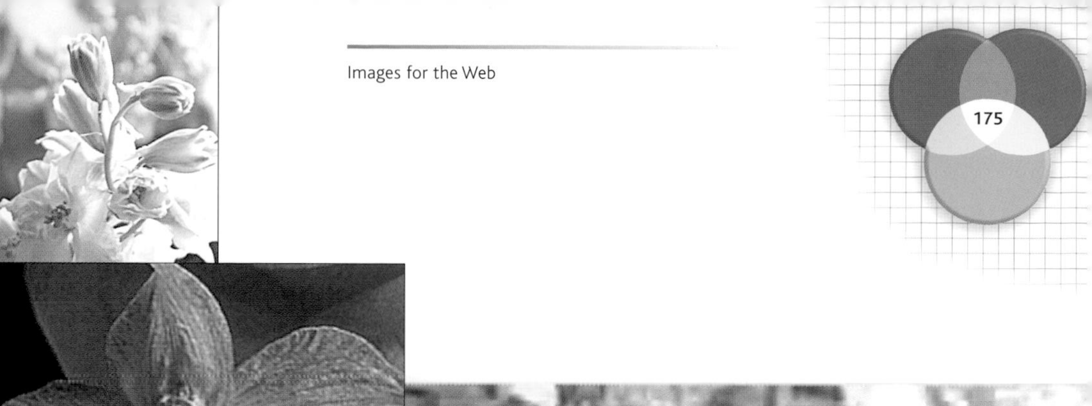

GIF files, as most Web experts will concede, are best suited to producing images from graphics or simple images. This is because the format supports a maximum of only 256 colours. This can lead to posterization effects, where it proves impossible to provide sufficient colours in, say, a graduated sky.

JPEG files, therefore, tend to be the type most commonly used on the Web. As we saw earlier, JPEGs can be reduced to around 1 percent of the original size (although this will compromise quality significantly) and still retain the full tonal variation and extent of the image.

When images are saved in the JPEG format, the quality/file size can be specified, using a linear scale. Sadly, only some image editors illustrate the corresponding quality when a file size is changed. In this case, it's a good idea to save a copy of important Web images at different settings to compare the results.

A good rule of thumb? To e-mail good quality images that may still be successfully printed by the recipient, a setting of around 80% can be used. File sizes are still pretty compact. Images for on-screen use can be compressed further without obvious degradation – often to settings of 30% or even less.

CONNECTION SPEED

It is important to remember at this point that we may have the fastest of broadband connections, but those that we might e-mail our work to or those who might choose to view it on a website may not. While it would be equally unwise to work to the lowest common denominator (that is, the slowest of modems), we must make a sensible assumption about the modem that our typical recipient is likely to use. For most purposes this can be a 56K modem, single channel ISDN, or equivalent.

ABOVE
At the 'Large File' setting (top), the image quality hasn't seriously changed from that of the original. Move the slider to 'Small File' (bottom), and the level of detail falls significantly while artefacts appear.

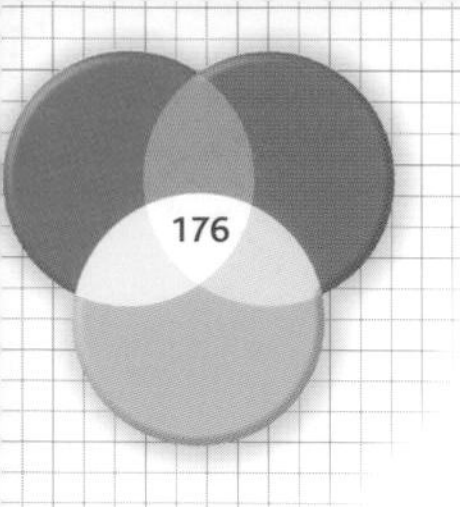

Creating and launching Web galleries

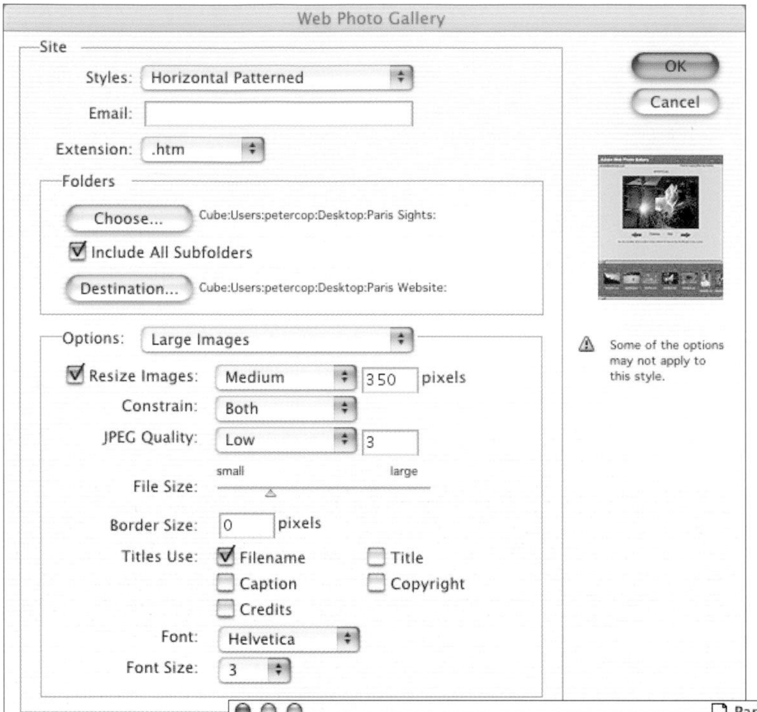

Once you have saved your images in a Web-savvy format, you will probably want to make them available for all to see. Luckily, getting images on to the Web has never been easier. Specialised website packages can be used, but many graphics packages include built-in modules that do the same basic job. Here, we will use the tool provided in Photoshop and Photoshop Elements.

The Web Photo Gallery option can be found in the *File* > ***Automate*** submenu. In the dialog box, you will find around ten options for the layout of the page, plus ways to customise the content to a limited degree. For our gallery, the layout is not crucial in the way it is for a regular website, as the emphasis is on making the photos accessible rather than creating a slick, eye-catching design.

Specify any titles you wish for the webpage, choosing any suitable font. Just remember that clearer fonts will work better than complex or

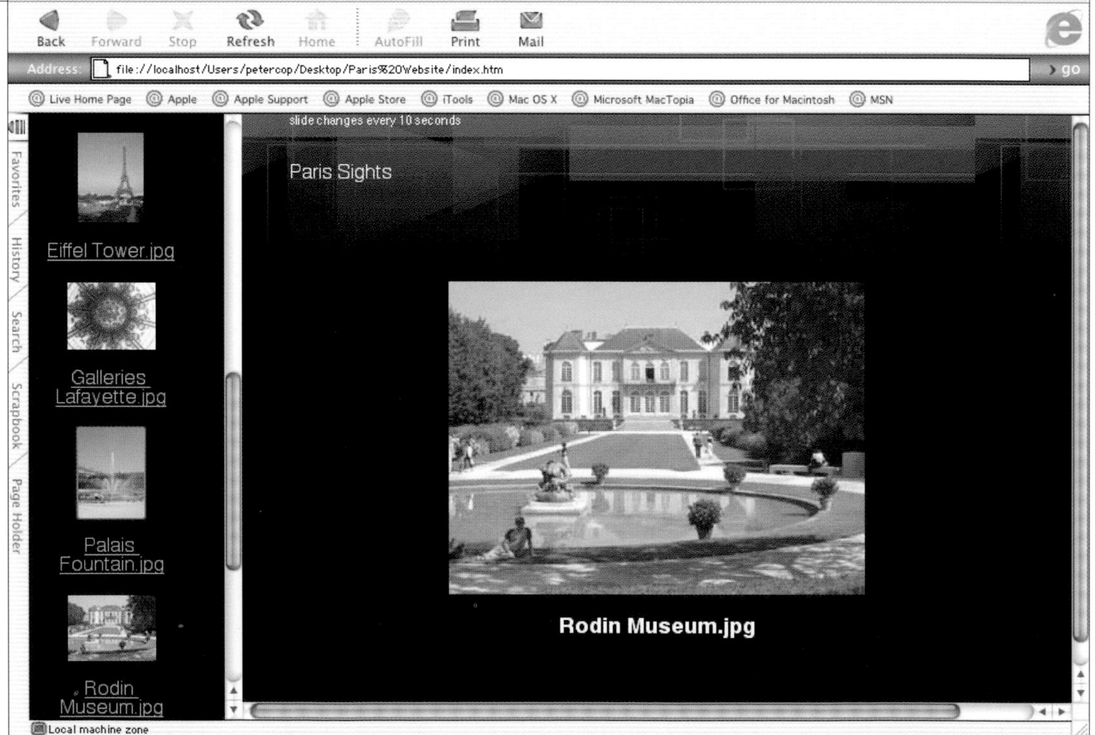

Photoshop's Web Photo Gallery feature makes it very simple to create an online gallery of your photographic works. The layout will be more functional than stunning, but it is an effective way of sharing your images with a wider audience.

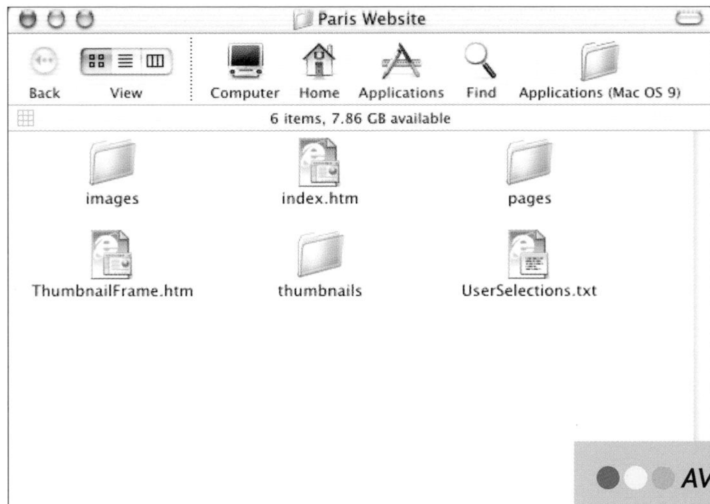

flashy options. In most cases, it is best to retain the default values provided. Adobe knows best!

The same can be said for the file size options; unless you have experience of optimizing images you should let the application take care it. All images – no matter what the original file format – will be converted to JPEGs, so you will still have the option of altering the compression ratio and the final on-screen pixel dimensions.

Finally, select the folders from which images will be taken and to which the webpage files will be written. Keep them separate. It is also essential that you check all of your original images and make sure they are correctly oriented. It is irritating to discover that some of the images on your webpage have been displayed in portrait format when they should be in landscape.

Start the process by pressing OK. Depending on the number of images, this may take some time but you can monitor progress onscreen. Once completed, your webpage will be automatically displayed in your chosen browser.

You will notice that a number of files will have been saved to the output folder that you specified earlier. These should include the JPEG versions of the original images, thumbnail versions and the necessary HTML files. Don't touch these, for the moment at least.

AVOIDING TROUBLE

When you use FTP to upload the files in your newly created webpage folder, make sure that you upload all of them. Don't alter the layout of the folder or the arrangement of the subfolders. The HTML code behind the site, and the browsers reading it, expect to find files in specific places. Be just as careful not to change the name of any of the files within.

GOING ONLINE

So far, we have created everything that we need for the webpage. We now need to get it all online. There are no hard-and-fast rules for how you go about this, and your first port of call should be your Internet Services Provider (ISP) – the company that provides your connection to the Internet. They can tell you how much Web space you have available and how to upload the files that comprise your Web gallery. The usual method, FTP or File Transfer Protocol, is not difficult to handle and you should get plenty of help from online tutorials.

DARKROOM SECRETS

CHANGE YOUR LAYOUT

If you aren't crazy about your chosen layout, there is no need to recompile your entire webpage contents. Simply return the Web *Gallery Page* dialog and select an alternative. When you select OK, the new layout will be displayed almost immediately.

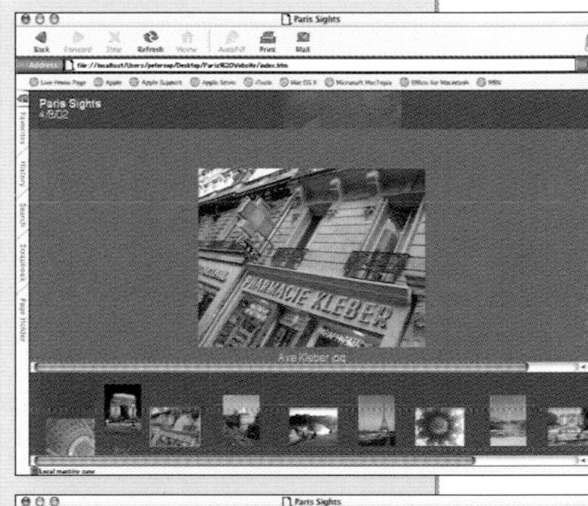

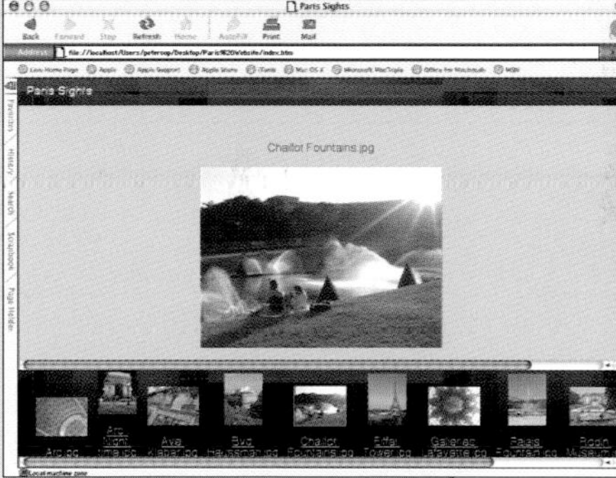

SECTION SIX

reference

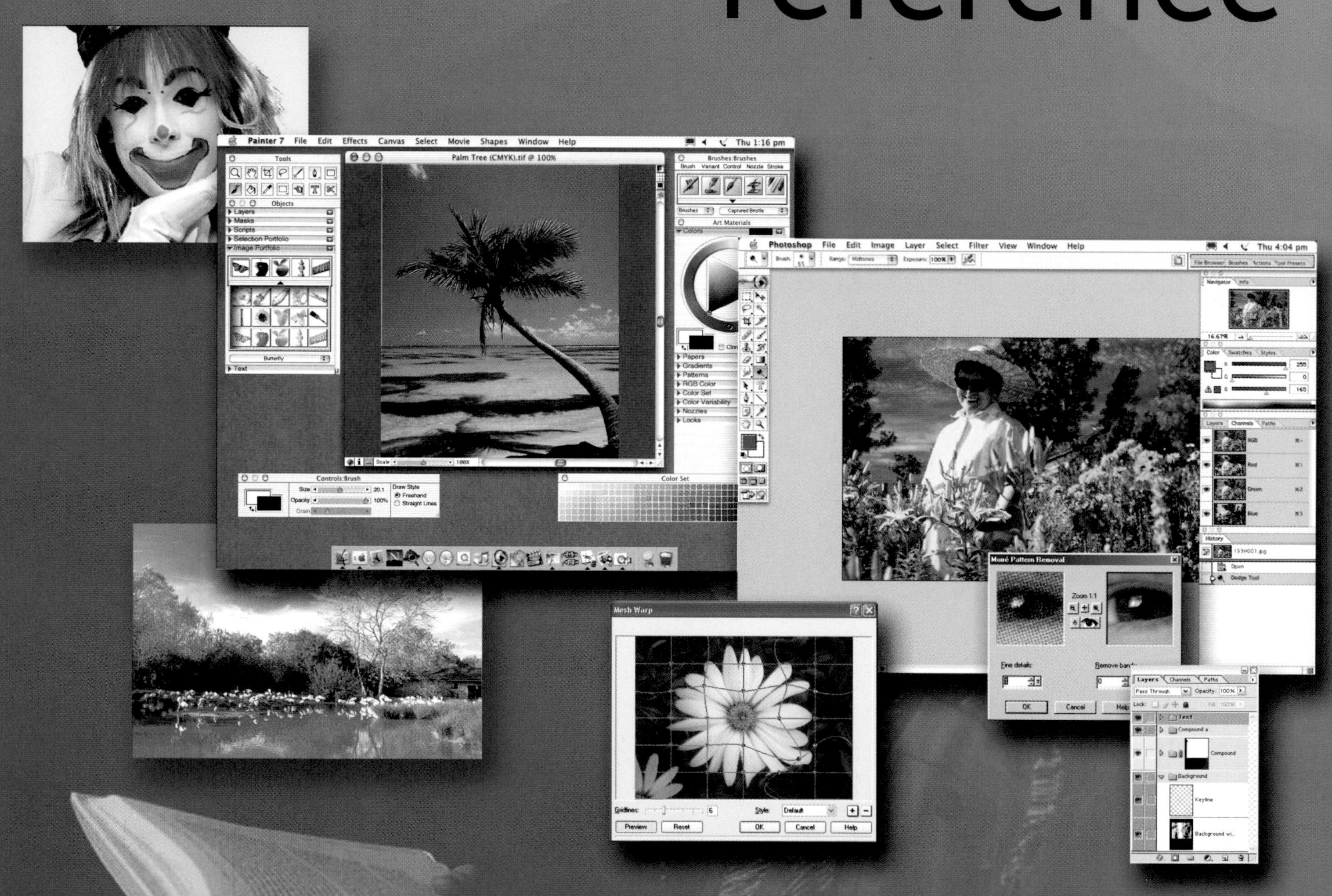

So, you have discovered how many of the image creation skills that were once the preserve of the darkroom expert are now simple to replicate on a computer. And, furthermore, that in the digital domain you can extend the range and possibilities almost without limit. You have created images that you are happy with, and you have received the plaudits from family, friends and colleagues. What do you do if you want to take your skills and ambitions one step further?

Even the most seasoned of professionals will agree that the key to success is to keep studying and keep practising. Other books and monthly magazines can teach you new techniques and time-saving tips, while the Internet contains a mass of advice from professional and amateur image workers.

Over the next few pages, we have gathered together a collection of resources that will enable you to take your interest further. Just starting out? We have also included website addresses for most of the hardware and software manufacturers. Though their websites are ostensibly designed to promote and sell their products, you will also find that many provide useful information on getting the best from them. Some even include additional collateral – including image editing plug-ins and extension applications that you can download for free. And, just for those terms that we all tend to forget now and again, we've included a comprehensive glossary.

The digital darkroom is a great place not only for creating exciting imagery but also for keeping at the cutting edge of digital media. We wish you every success.

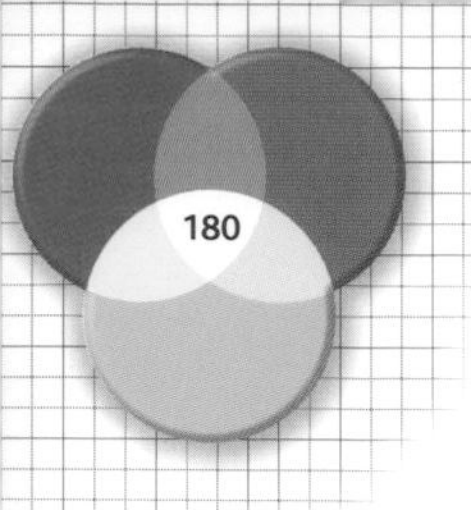

Glossary

8-bit: Of display monitors or digital images – the allocation of eight data bits to each pixel, producing an image of 256 greys or colours (a row of eight bits can be written in 256 different combinations: 0000000, 00000001, 10000001, 00111100 and so on).

24-bit colour: The allocation of 24 bits of memory to each pixel, giving a possible screen display of 16.7 million colours (a row of 24 bits can be written in 16.7 million different combinations of 0s and 1s). Eight bits is allocated to each of the three RGB colour channels.

alpha channel: A place where information regarding the transparency of a pixel is kept. In image files this is a separate channel – additional to the three RGB or four CMYK channels – where 'masks' are stored.

antialias/antialiasing: A technique of optically eliminating the jagged edges that appear when bitmapped images or text are reproduced on low-resolution devices such as monitors. Achieved by blending the colour at the edges of the object with the background by averaging values of the pixels involved.

archive quality: Any print, mounting board or storage medium that is designed to last (almost) indefinitely. In practice it describes printing inks that don't fade rapidly, and mounting boards and storage materials that don't give off gases or seep acids that will be detrimental to the imagery mounted on (or stored in) them.

artefact: A visible flaw in an electronically prepared image, usually occurring as a result of imaging techniques. JPEG compression, for example, reduces image data in square blocks of pixels, and these can become clearly visible, particularly when high contrast or colour effects are applied.

aspect ratio: The ratio of the width of an image to its height, expressed as x:y. For example, the aspect ratio of an image measuring 200 x 100 pixels is 2:1.

bas relief: An image that is embossed, so that it stands out in shallow relief from a flat background and gives an illusion of further depth.

bevel: A chamfered edge applied to type, buttons or selections to emphasise a three-dimensional effect.

binary: Literally, two outcomes or two components. The binary number system has the base 2 and so all values are expressed in terms of combinations of 1 and 0, including logical states (true/false). These states can be represented in computers as on/off or circuit closed/circuit open. As a result, the binary system underpins digital computing.

bit depth: The number of bits assigned to each pixel on a monitor, scanner or image file. Most systems can now handle 24 bit, or up to 16.7 million, colours. In contrast, the GIF file format can support only eight-bit colour, or 256 different hues.

bitmap: A bitmap is a 'map' describing the location and binary state of 'bits' that define a complete collection of pixels or dots in an image. The term is also used to refer to pictures that have only black and white pixels.

brightness: The strength of luminescence from light to dark.

burn: A method used in the conventional darkroom to darken areas of an image. Often simulated in digital image-editing packages.

calibrate, calibration: The process of adjusting a machine or piece of hardware to conform to a known scale or standard so that it performs more accurately. In graphic reproduction it is important that the various devices and materials used in the production chain – such as scanners, monitors, imagesetters and printing presses – conform to a consistent set of measures in order to achieve true fidelity, particularly where colour is concerned. Calibration of reproduction and display devices is generally carried out in software, or by using specialised tools, such as 'densitometer'.

capture: The action of 'getting' an image, by taking a photograph or scanning an image into a computer.

CCD (Charge Coupled Device): A component used in digital imaging hardware to turn beams of light into an electrical signal that can then be converted to digital form.

clipping: Limiting an image or piece of art to within the bounds of a particular area.

CMYK: Colour model describing the primary colours of reflective light:

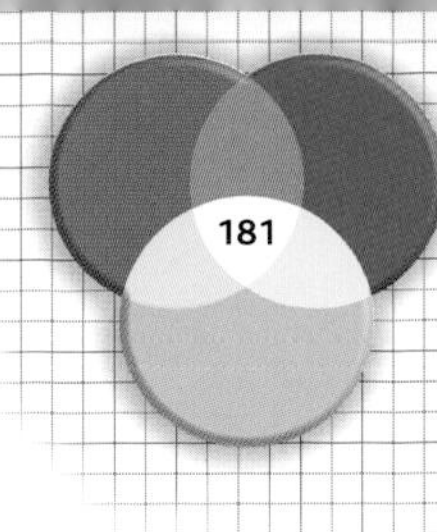

cyan (C), magenta (M) and yellow (Y). Together with black (K), they are used in most forms of printing. The letter K is used rather than B to avoid confusion with blue.

composition: The effective arrangement of elements in the scene captured in the photographic frame.

compression: The technique of rearranging data so that it either occupies less space on disk or transfers faster between devices or on communication lines. Different kinds of compression techniques are employed for different kinds of data – applications, for example, must not lose any data when compressed, whereas photographic images and films can tolerate a certain amount of data loss. Compression methods which do not lose data are referred to as 'lossless', whereas 'lossy' is used to describe methods in which some data is lost. There are many proprietary utilities for compressing data. Typical compression formats for images are LZW (lossless), JPEG and GIF; (both lossy). The latter two formats are commonly used for files transmitted across the Internet.

constrain: In digital imaging, to ensure that an image maintains a particular aspect ratio or proportions during resizing or resampling.

continuous tone: An image that contains infinite continuous shades between the lightest and darkest tones, as distinct from a line illustration, which has only one shade. A photographic print or slide would be an example of continuous tone, but a photo printed in a magazine would not, as its colours would have been broken down into patterns of tiny CMYK dots for the mass printing process.

contrast: The degree of difference between adjacent tones in an image (or computer monitor) from the lightest to the darkest. 'High contrast' describes an image with light highlights and dark shadows, but with few shades in between, while a 'low contrast' image is one with even tones and few dark areas or highlights.

crop: To trim or mask an image so that it fits a given area, or so that unwanted portions of the image are discarded.

definition: The overall quality – or clarity – of an image. In a photo this is determined by the combined effects of graininess and sharpness. In a digital image resolution would also have a part to play in the mix.

densitometer: A precision instrument used to measure the optical density and the other properties of colour and light in positive or negative transparencies, printing film or computer monitors.

density: The darkness of tone or colour in any image. In a transparency this refers to the amount of light which can pass through it, thus determining the darkness of shadows and the saturation of colour. A printed highlight cannot be any lighter in colour than the colour of the paper it is printed on, while the shadows cannot be any darker than the quality and volume of ink in the printing process will allow.

density range: The maximum range of tones in an image, measured as the difference between the maximum and minimum densities (the darkest and lightest tones).

desaturate: To reduce the purity of a colour, thus making it greyer.

diffuser: Any material that scatters transmitted light, thus increasing the area of the light source.

digital: Anything operated by or created from information represented by binary digits. Distinct from analog, in which information is a physical variable.

digital data: Information stored or transmitted as a series of 1s and 0s ('bits'). Because values are fixed (so-called discrete values), digital data is more reliable than analog data, as the latter is susceptible to uncontrollable physical variations.

digital image: Image converted to (or created in) the digital domain. Elements of the image are represented by groups of pixels, each with their own discrete colour and brightness values.

dithering: A technique of 'interpolation' which calculates the average value of adjacent pixels. This technique is most often used to add extra pixels to an image – to smooth an edge, for example, or to simulate a large range of hues from a smaller selection.

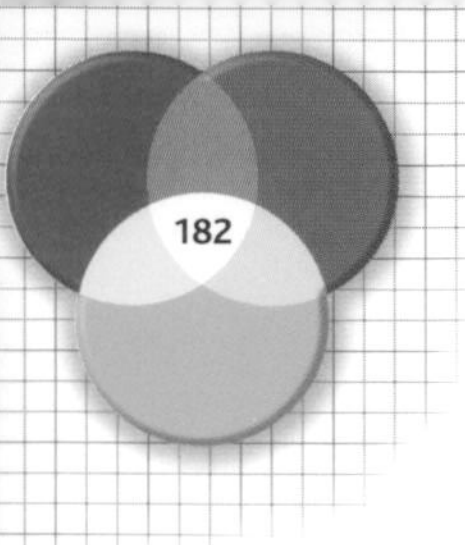

dodge A method of obtaining lighter areas in a photographic print by selective masking. Many image-editing applications can simulate the effect through digital means.

dots per inch (dpi): A unit of measurement used to represent the resolution of devices such as printers and imagesetters. Also applied, erroneously, to monitors and digital images, where the resolution should be more properly be expressed in pixels per inch (ppi). The closer the dots or pixels (the more there are to each inch), the better the quality. Typical resolutions are 72 ppi for a monitor, 600 dpi for a laser printer and 2450 dpi (or more) for an imagesetter.

duotone: A monochromatic image combining two halftones with different tonal ranges made from the same original. When printed in different tones of the same original, a wider tonal range is reproduced than would be possible with a single colour. Special effects can be achieved by using the same technique and printing with different coloured inks.

dynamic range: In electronic imaging, the range of light levels recordable by a CCD (charge-coupled device) or other electronic device.

feathering: A similar process to antialiasing, this blurs the edge pixels of a selection to give a soft border.

filter: Strictly speaking, a filter can be any component in a software program that provides the basic building blocks for processing data. In image-editing and drawing applications, the term usually refers to the advanced features used to apply special effects to an image.

fractal: Infinitely variable shapes characterised by (often) extreme irregularity and defined by complex but precisely defined mathematical expressions. A principal characteristic is self-similarity, wherein a magnified part of a fractal appears identical to the 'parent' shape and has identical visual and mathematical properties. Some Photoshop filters make extensive use of fractal mathematics and patterning, allowing users to make bold graphics from scratch and use image elements as the basic element.

gamma: A measure of the contrast in a digital image, photographic film or paper, or processing technique. Gamma curves are sometimes found in the software that comes with scanners, allowing users to preset the amount of light, dark and contrast on input.

GIF: The Graphics Interchange Format, or GIF, is a format designed specifically to produce very small, optimized image files for the Web. GIFs also provide basic inbuilt animation features. The format allows for simple transparency but can only contain up to 256 colours.

graduation / gradation: The smooth transition from one colour or tone to another.

grain: The density of light-sensitive crystals in a photographic emulsion. Fine grain allows more detail, but the film is less light-sensitive. Coarse grain is sometimes used for a graphic effect, and this can also be simulated using digital means.

graphic: A general term describing any illustration or drawn design. Can also refer, more specifically, to 'graphic' images where the emphasis is on high-impact visuals with strong lines and dramatic tones at the expense of realism or fine detail.

greyscale: The rendering of an image in a range of greys from white to black. In a digital image and on a monitor, this usually means that an image is rendered with eight bits assigned to each pixel, giving a maximum of 256 levels of grey.

highlight: To mark an item, such as a section of text, icon or menu command, to indicate that it is either selected or active.

HSB: A colour model based on the variables of Hue, Saturation and Brightness.

hue: A colour as found in its pure state in the spectrum.

image library: A source of original transparencies and pictures that can be used for virtually any purpose on payment of a fee, which usually varies according to usage – a picture to be used in an advertisement will invariably cost a great deal more than the same picture for use in a school textbook. Many libraries specialise in various subjects, such as garden plants, wildlife and fine art.

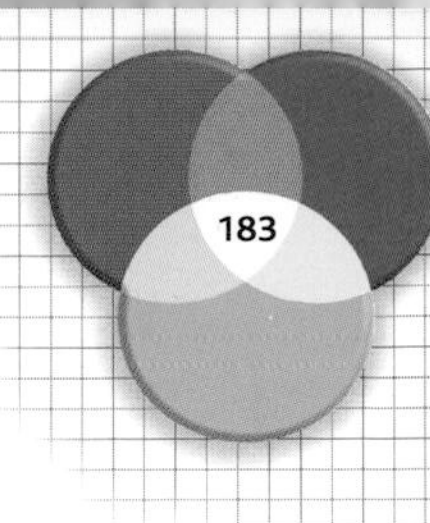

image size: A description of the dimensions of an image. Depending on the type of image being measured, this can be in terms of linear dimensions, resolution or digital file size.

import: To bring text, pictures or any other form of data into a document.

interface: A term most often used to describe the screen design that links the user with the computer program or website. The quality of the user interface often determines how well users will be able to access and use all the features in the program, or navigate their way around the pages within the website.

interpolation: A computer calculation used to estimate unknown values that fall between known values. This process is used, for example, to redefine pixels in bitmap images after they have been modified in some way, such as when an image is resized or rotated, or if colour corrections have been made.

JPEG (Joint Photographic Expert Group): A digital image file format that is particularly suited to continuous tone images such as photographs. It uses a lossy compression algorithm to squeeze large images into smaller, more compact files. The Joint Photographic Expert Group first created the format.

Kelvin temperature scale (K): A unit of measurement that describes the colour of a light source, beginning with absolute darkness and rising to incandescence.

landscape format: An image or page format in which the width is greater than the height. Also known as 'horizontal format'.

layer: In some applications and webpages, a level to which you can consign an element of the design you are working on. Selected layers may be active (meaning you can work on them) or inactive. Some applications may not provide a layers feature, but will still allow you to lay items one on top of another in the order that you created them – and in some cases will allow you to send items to the back or bring them to the front.

lasso: A freehand tool used in image-editing applications to select a portion of an image. In Photoshop this also comes in a magnetic variety, which identifies the edges of a particular element, and a polygonal version, which creates straight-edged selections around an object.

light table: A table or box with a translucent glass top lit from below, giving a colour-balanced light suitable for viewing transparencies and, if necessary, colour-matching them to proofs.

lightness: The tonal measure of a colour relative to a scale running from black to white. Also called 'brightness'.

line art: Diagrams and graphics comprising (normally) black lines on a white background.

lossless / lossy: Refers to data-losing qualities of different compression methods: lossless means that no image information is lost; lossy means that some (or much) of the image data is lost in the compression process.

magic wand: In image-editing applications, a tool used to select those areas of an image which possess similar brightness or colour values.

marquee: A selection tool used to make selections based on simple rectangular or elliptical shapes.

mask: Originally a material used to protect all or part of a image during photographic reproduction. In image-editing applications, a mask is used to prevent alterations from affecting the masked portion of an image.

master: An original item from which all copies are made, or upon which any changes are marked or made.

midtones / middletones: The range of tonal values in an image anywhere between the darkest and lightest – usually those approximately half-way.

moiré: An unintended pattern that occurs in professional halftone reproduction when two or more colours are printed with the dot screens at the wrong angles. Can also appear when a magazine print is scanned into a computer, due to inteference between the scanner's resolution and the halftone resolution. Scanner software and some image-editing applications contain filters to counter such defects.

monochrome: An image of varying tones reproduced using inks of a single colour. While this is usually black ink on white paper, this isn't necessarily the case.

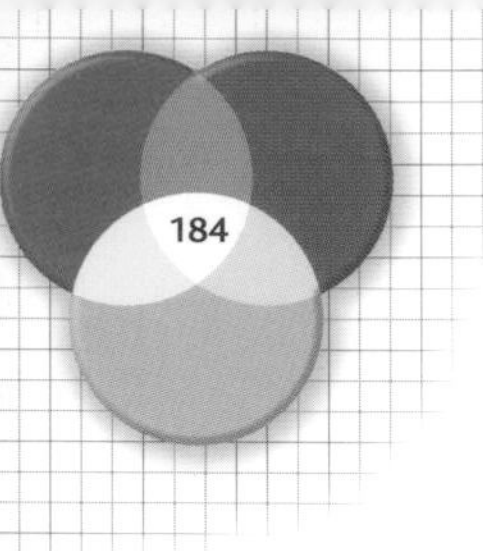

multimedia: A generic term used to describe any combination of sound, video, animation, graphics and text incorporated into a software product or presentation.

palette (1): The subset of colours needed to display an image. For instance, a GIF image has a palette containing a maximum of 256 distinct colours.

palette (2): A part of the interface in many image-editing and visual-design applications, a palette is a window that contains features such as tools, measurements, options or other functions. In most applications, palettes can be moved, hidden and even docked together if desired.

perspective: A technique of rendering 3D objects on a 2D plane, duplicating the 'real world' view by creating an impression of the object's relative position and size when viewed from a certain point. The perspective gets narrower as the distance increases.

picture skew: The distortion of an image by slanting the two opposite sides of the image rectangle away from the horizontal or vertical.

pixel: Acronym for picture element. The smallest component of a digital image – a single block in the bitmap grid, with its own specific colour and brightness values.

plug-in: Subsidiary software for a browser or other package that enables it to perform additional functions, e.g., play sound, films, or video.

PNG (portable network graphic): A digital image format that uses a highly sophisticated compression technique, which is said to result in file sizes typically 30 per cent smaller than those for comparable GIFs. The PNG format can also support the full 24-bit colour palette, and as a lossless format is less likely to cause artefacts than using JPEG.

polarizing filter: A popular photographic filter used to remove polarized light, including reflected light, resulting in brighter colours and richer skies.

portrait format: An image or page in a vertical format. Also called 'upright format.'

posterize/posterization: To divide, by photographic or digital means, a continuous-tone image into either a predefined or arbitrary number of flat tones. Also known as tone separation.

proprietary: A design, product or format developed, marketed and owned by a company or person, rather than one defined by a standards organisation.

QuickTime: Computer movie software developed by Apple, but now also in use on PCs.

RAM: (Random Access Memory) The memory 'space' made available by the computer, into which some or all of an application's code is loaded and remembered while you work with it. Generally speaking, the more, the better. Imaging software such as Photoshop needs up to five times the size of the files that you are working on in memory in order to process images.

refraction: Light that is bent, typically when passing through one medium to another, such as air to water.

rescale: Amending the size of an image by proportionally reducing or increasing its height and width.

resolution: The degree of quality, definition or clarity with which an image is reproduced or displayed. In a photograph this would be the result of focus, clarity and grain structure. In a digital image, resolution refers directly to the numbers of pixels contined within a finite area of the image.

restore: To restore something to its original state or, in the case of a document, to its last 'saved' version. Also called 'revert.'

reticulation: An effect of photographic processing where the film emulsion adopts a distupted or crazed pattern. While usually undesirable, the effect is simulated in some image-editing applications as a quick means of artificially aging an image.

retouching: Altering an image, artwork or film to modify or remove imperfections. Can be done using mechanical methods (knives, inks and dyes) or digitally, using Photoshop or a similar image-editing program.

RGB (Red Green Blue): The primary colours of the 'additive' colour model, used in video technology, computer monitors, and for graphics such as for the Web and multimedia that will not ultimately be printed by the four-colour (CMYK) process.

saturation: A variation in colour, affecting hues of the same total brightness, ranging from none (grey) through pastel shades (low saturation) to pure (fully saturated) colour.

scanning: An electronic process that converts a hard copy of an image into digital form by sequential exposure of a CCD to a moving light beam or laser. The scanned image can then be manipulated.

sepia: A shade of brown, which lends its name to the sepia tone, a rich monochrome print in which the normal shades of grey appear as shades of brown.

shadow areas: The parts of an image that are darker or denser than the majority.

soft focus: An effect that softens or diffuses the lines and edges of an image without altering the actual focus. Usually used to confer a romantic feel to portraits.

thumbnail: A small representation of an image used mainly for identification purposes in an image directory listing or, within Photoshop, for illustrating channels and layers. Thumbnails are also produced to accompany PictureCDs, PhotoCDs and most APS and 35-mm films submitted for processing.

tonal compression: The effects on an image, usually caused by scanning or printing, where the range of tones, from light to dark, is reduced to the detriment of the picture as a whole.

tritone: A halftone image that is printed using three colours. Typically, a black-and-white image is enhanced by addition of two colours. For example, when added to black, process yellow and magenta will produce a sepia-coloured image.

unsharp masking (USM): A traditional film-compositing technique used to 'sharpen' an image. This effect can also be achieved digitally. Most image-editing applications contain a USM filter which can enhance the details in a scanned or digital photo, and give an impression of improved clarity.

USB (Universal Serial Bus): A port (socket) for connecting peripheral devices to your computer which can be daisy-chained together. These can include devices such as scanners, printers, keyboards and hard drives.

vector: A mathematical description of a line that is defined in terms of physical dimensions and direction. Vectors are used in drawing and image-editing packages to define shapes (vector graphics) that are position- and size-independent.

vignetting: A noticable fading at the edges of an image caused by a reduction in light levels at the edges of the frame. While a problem if caused by deficiencies in a camera, vignetting can also be used to positive effect and simulated via digital means.

virtual: Any thing that, while it doesn't exist physically, can be made to appear as if it does. For example, virtual memory is a simulation of RAM on the hard disk, which the computer uses as if it were physical RAM.

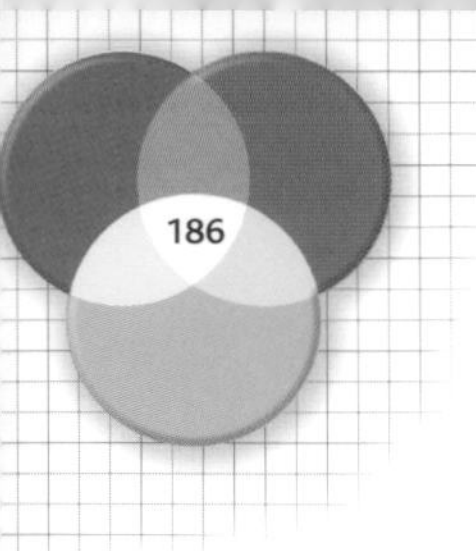

Resources

The Web abounds with sources of information, tutorials and help on all aspects of image-editing. You'll find sites such as About.com are great for comparative reviews of software and giving both general and specific advice. The manufacturers' websites are also a very useful source of information and many include useful resources for your applications.

Photoshop Specific Sites

NAPP: National Association of Photoshop Professionals

The leading resource for Photoshop news and training, it operates for anyone - not just professional users - who is serious about image manipulation using Photoshop, though it does operate as a 'trade body' for users of the product.
www.photoshopuser.com

Photoshop Hall of Fame

A hall of fame created to recognise the people (and their work) who have had a significant impact on Photoshop use, either because of the novel nature of their work or the impact of their techniques upon the development of the product.
www.photoshophalloffame.com

Photoshop World

An annual convention for users of Photoshop. Now the largest Photoshop-only event.
www.photoshopworld.com

General Sites

The Complete Guide to Digital Photography

www.completeguidetodigitalphotography.com

CreativePro

News, information and resources designed for the creative professional.
www.creativepro.com

ePHOTOzine

Everything to do with photography, digital imaging and image-editing.
www.ephotozine.com

The Imaging Resource

News and reviews and general help/information.
www.image-resource.com

PhotoLink International

Education and training in photography and imaging.
www.photoeducation.net

Photo Net

Major photographic resource site with advice, tutorials and galleries.
www.photo.net

Short Courses

Shortcourses in digital photography, digital video and other related fields.
www.shortcourses.com

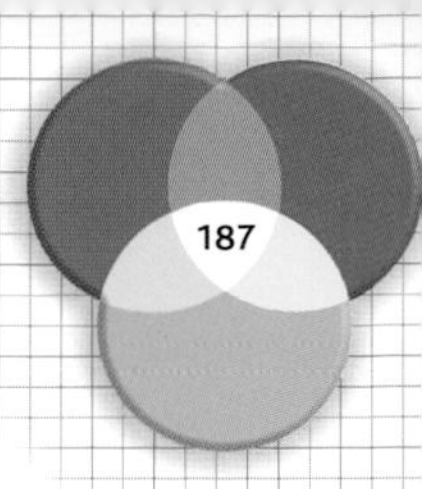

General Web Resources and Contacts

Adobe
www.adobe.com
Alien Skin (Plug-ins)
www.alienskin.com
Andromeda (Plug-ins)
www.andromeda.com
Apple Computer
www.apple.com
British Journal of Photography
www.bjphoto.co.uk
Compaq
www.compaq.com
Connectix
www.connectix.com
Core
www.corel.com
Deneba (Canvas)
www.deneba.com
Extensis
www.extensis.com
Ferrania (inks)
www.ferrania.it
Formac
www.formac.com
Fujifilm
www.fujifilm.com
Hewlett Packard
www.hp.com
Iomega (storage)
www.iomega.com
Jasc Software
www.jasc.com
Kingston
www.kingston.com
Kodak
www.kodak.com
Lexmark
www.lexmark.com
LaCie (storage)
www.lacie.com
Lyson (inks)
www.lyson.com
Macromedia
www.macromedia.com
Minolta
www.minolta.com
Microsoft
www.microsoft.com
NAPP
www.photoshopuser.com
Nikon
www.nikon.com
Olympus
www.olympusamerica.com
Pantone
www.pantone.com
Roxio
www.roxio.com
Ulead
www.ulead.com
Umax
www.umax.com
Wacom
www.wacom.com
Xaos Tools
www.xaostools.com

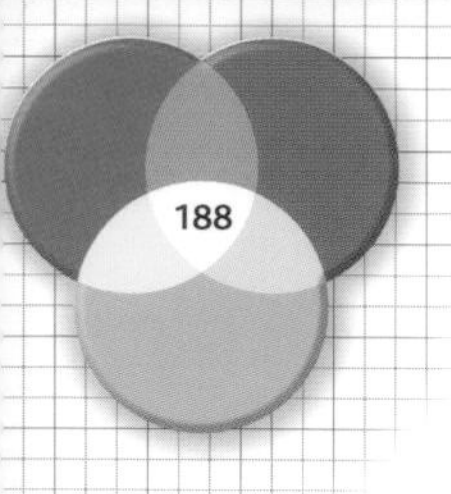

Index

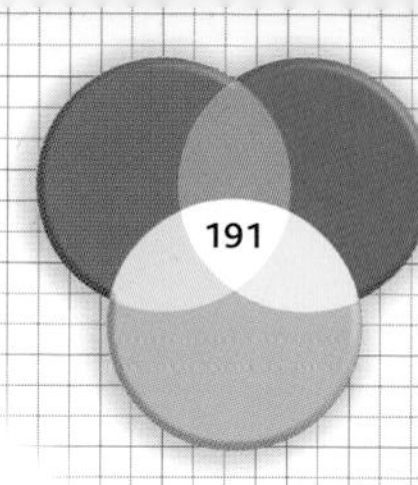

Acknowledgements

The authors would like to thank friends and family who have supported them during the creation of this book, particularly those friends and family members who have posed (often unwillingly) as models in the photos. Thanks also to staff at The Ilex Press for their work in helping to get this book completed.